Professional PHP Web development solutions

University of Hertfordshire

College Lane, Hatfield

Learni

Raj Kumar Dash

Matt Anton

Alison Gianotto

Bryan Waters

Jo Henrik Endrerud

Daniel Solin

Jon Stephens

Wrox Press Ltd. ®

Professional PHP Web Development Solutions

First Printed in November 2002

wrox

Published by Wrox Press Ltd,
Arden House, 1102 Warwick Road, Acocks Green,
Birmingham, B27 6BH, UK
Printed in the United States
ISBN 1-86100-743-4

Trademark Acknowledgements

Wrox has endeavored to provide trademark information about all the companies and products mentioned in this book by the appropriate use of capitals. However, Wrox cannot guarantee the accuracy of this information.

Credits

Authors
Raj Kumar Dash
Matt Anton
Bryan Waters
Alison Gianotto
Jo Henrik Endrerud
Jon Stephens
Daniel Solin

Technical Reviewers
Luis Argerich
Daniel Solin
Jon Stephens
Sascha Schumann
Tony Mobily
Santosh Ramakrishnan
Harish Rawat
Steve Parker
Ken Egervari
Ramesh Mani
Nola Stowe
Deepak Thomas
Sean Cazzell

Author Agent
Safiulla Shakir

Project Manager
Abbas Saifuddin
Rangwala

Managing Editor
Paul Cooper

Commissioning Editor
Dilip Thomas

Technical Editors
Deepa Aswani
Indu Britto
Nilesh Parmar

Production Coordinator
Pippa Wonson

Production and Layout
Santosh Haware
Manjiri Karande

Cover
Dawn Chellingworth

Index
Adrian Axinte

Proof Reader
Victoria Blackburn
Andrew Polshaw
Lee Polshaw

About the Authors
Raj Kumar Dash

Raj Kumar Dash, aka Roo Hoo, is a computer consultant, freelance writer, and delusionally aspiring composer. He lives in Kitchener, Canada, with his kitten and familiar "Aeric Sir Stinkybutt Halfacat, the Lion-hearted Munchkin, Prince of Roo Zoo", as well as all manner of fish (Larry, Curly, and Moe), birds (Nostradamus and Nosferatu), snakes, and lizards, plus not a few ghosts that have taken form as cats, snakes, and flying critters. He thanks his high school math and computer teacher Mr. Hamer, for the encouragement, and his parents for his existence, without which his portion of this book would have taken on some other form in the cosmic scheme of things.

Thanks go to: Dilip Thomas and Safiulla Shakir, both of Wrox Publishing, for their generous assistance on this project; to the technical reviewers that made this book better; and to all the contributors to PHP including developers and other authors for their fine work.

Matt Anton

Matt Anton (LAMP is literally his middle name) is a computer consultant and freelance writer. He leads a quiet life (so he thinks), loves his parents (so they think), and believes in God (so God thinks). He has worked as a co-author on Professional Apache 2.0 and Professional PHP4 XML from Wrox Press. His technology interests include XML, Mac OS X, J2EE technologies, and other web site deployment issues

Bryan Waters

Bryan Waters, a freelance software developer specializing in web-based corporate information systems. He uses PHP, ASP, C++, and Java with database servers such as SQL Server, SQL Anywhere, and MySQL to develop distributed, stand-alone and CD-ROM software for the Medical, Hospitality, and Education industries. He has authored several books on technologies like MFC and OLE 2 and published articles in various trade magazines. He lives and works with his wife, Jann, and his two children, Jarratt and Chloe, in Arizona, U.S.

Acknowledgements -- my wife, who is my inspiration and motivation in all things.

Alison Gianotto

Alison Gianotto (better known in many dubious circles as "snipe") has been a professional geek for 8 years, and has been working with PHP for approximately 4 years. Prior to moving to San Diego to accept the position of technical director at a prominent web development firm, she taught advanced web programming and computer graphics in Brooklyn, NY.

Currently, Alison is kept busy with her web development company and is also the director of a non-profit organization dedicated to tracking and documenting animal abuse crimes. (And we won't even mention the bevy of independent sites she juggles in all her copious free time). You can learn more about her professional exploits at http://www.phpchick.com, or check out her personal website at http://www.snipe.net.

Jo Henrik Endrerud

Jo Henrik Endrerud is a developer currently living in Skien, Norway. He graduated from Buskerud Technical College in 2001 and is employed at eZ systems (http://ez.no/). Jo Henrik is a long time Linux developer, currently working on the Open Source content management system: eZ publish. He has been working on projects ranging from small company websites to multilingual sites with hundreds of thousand of articles, where he has done everything from systems integration to project management.

During his spare time he is usually found at the local airport spending time as a skydive instructor. You can find out more by visiting his personal website; www.johenrik.com (only in Norwegian at the moment).

Daniel Solin

Daniel Solin is a technical writer, reviewer, consultant, and programmer and Linux-enthusiast from Sweden. He has been programming Linux applications and web pages since 1994, and has in this time obtained a broad experience of most technologies used in these areas. When it comes to writing, Daniel has written a book about developing applications using Qt, a C++ GUI library, and he has also been a co-author for several books about Linux. From time to time, he also writes articles about bleeding-edge web development or programming in general. For the last two years, Daniel has been developing various software for one of Europe's largest ISPs.

Jon Stephens

Jon Stephens is American technical writer, reviewer and site developer now living and working in Australia. He works with a number of web technologies, including PHP, JavaScript, MySQL, XML, and ASP (occasionally). He's co-authored 5 previous books on various topics in Web development; this is his third for Wrox Press. Jon was a community leader at the Builder Buzz web development forums for several years, and is now a co-administrator for the new HiveMinds.Info project. When he can be dragged away from the computer, he enjoys nature, the outdoors, and a good book or a bad movie. Jon is married to the Australian designer, Sionwyn Lee.

Acknowledgements -- my parents; Sion; Sion's family and all the other folks who've made me feel welcome Down Under; Jody Kerr and Nick Kairinos in Phoenix; Beatriz in Knoxville; the phpMyAdmin developers; Rasmus Lerdorf for creating PHP and admitting to me, "It all started out as a hack, to get some things done".

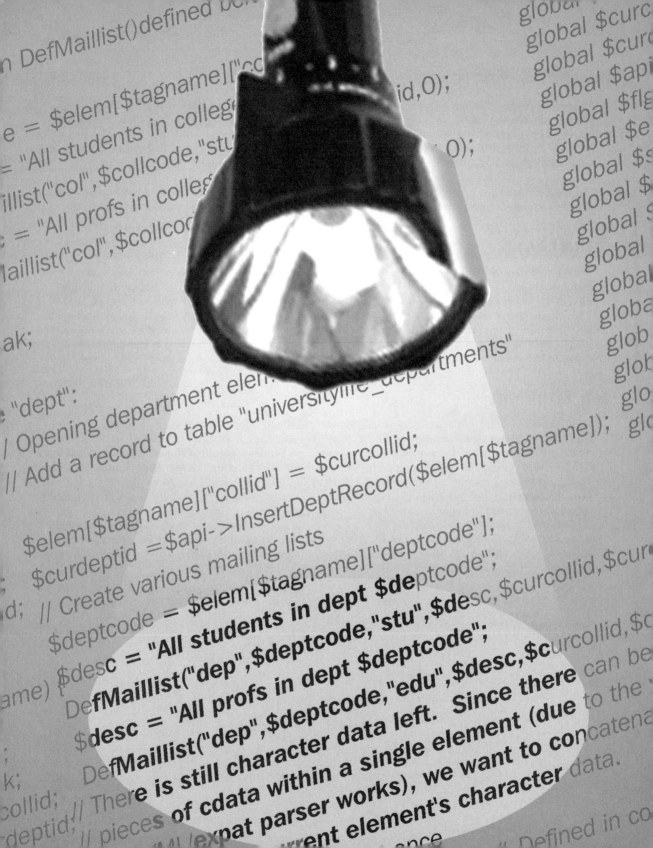

Table of Contents

Table of Contents

Table of Contents

Table of Contents

Table of Contents

Table of Contents

Table of Contents

```
DefMaillist()defined below
e = $elem[$tagname]["co                           id,0);
= "All students in college
list("col",$collcode,"stu                           o);
= "All profs in colleg
aillist("col",$collco

ak;

"dept":
    Opening department elem
/ Add a record to table "universitylife_departments"

$elem[$tagname]["collid"] = $curcollid;
$curdeptid = $api->InsertDeptRecord($elem[$tagname]["deptcode"];
d;  // Create various mailing lists
$deptcode = $elem[$tagname]["deptcode";
me)  $desc = "All students in dept $deptcode";
      DefMaillist("dep",$deptcode,"stu",$desc,$curcollid,$curd
      desc = "All profs in dept $deptcode";
      DefMaillist("dep",$deptcode,"edu",$desc,$curcollid,$cu
ollid;  // There is still character data left.  Since there can be
eptid;  pieces of cdata within a single element (due to the v
          at parser works), we want to concatenat
                    element's character data.
```

global $std
global $curco
global $curc
global $curd
global $api
global $flg
global $el
global $s
global $
global $
global $
global
global
globa
glob
glo
gl

); glo
```
obal $tagname]);  glo
```

1

Introduction

We believe that the true power of PHP lies in its strength to create dynamic web content. Through this book we hope to achieve just that – create a variety of real-world, interactive web sites using PHP4 along with HTML, a DBMS system, and XML or WML wherever applicable.

The slant of this book is 'dive-right-in'. Sometimes you do not necessarily want to read a multitude of chapters just to find out how a handful of functions or techniques work. Hence, those who need to quickly design and develop a web site can learn the fundamentals of web development from this book, as well as the intricacies of using PHP and MySQL while they are at it.

PHP

PHP began as a few scripts created by Rasmus Lerdorf. It was originally called 'Personal Home Page' that later came to be called 'PHP: Hypertext Pre-processor'. Since then, many people have contributed to the software and it has undergone numerous changes with a lot of features added to it. As applications can be developed quickly and with ease, some people doubt the ability of PHP to build industrial-strength web sites. This is not the case, as the owners and developers of over 9,000,000 domains, have found out (according to http://www.php.net/usage.php) at the time of writing.

PHP is now into version 4, with version 5 already being planned. It may have started as a simple set of macros intended for personal use, but it has grown into much more than that with rapid prototyping abilities. Its growing features over the past few versions, including the fact that it works well with web servers and database systems, have made it a serious and substantial tool for web application development. Future versions promise even more.

#### Chapter 1

PHP4

PHP4 has had numerous features added to it. According to http://www.php.net/, the following features are new in PHP4:

❏   Boolean data type (true, false)

❏   `foreach` loop for easier traversal of arrays, associative and otherwise

❏   The 'identical' comparison operator, ══ that checks to see if two values are equal and are of the same data type

❏   Pre-defined associative arrays that contain server and environment variables

❏   Extended API module for integration with web servers (Apache, MS–IIS)

❏   Generalized build process under UNIX

❏   Generic web server interface that also supports multi-threaded web servers

❏   Improved syntax highlighter

❏   Native HTTP session support for easier tracking of user sessions

❏   Output buffering support

❏   More powerful configuration system

❏   Reference counting of variables

❏   Built-in support for Java and XML

❏   Command line interpreter for running PHP on a command line

Why Use PHP?

Let's take a quick look at why PHP deserves its fair share of attention:

❏   PHP is a scripting language that is relatively easy to learn; it combines many of the best features of C and Perl. Its similarity to both languages makes it easy for developers with experience in either language to pick up almost instantly.

❏   PHP has performance advantages over JavaScript, ASP, JSP, and Java Servlets.

❏   A PHP script is compiled by the PHP engine at the web server, and then passed on to the PHP interpreter; that is, it executes the script to produce HTML, XML, WML, or other output, which is then sent to the browser. The result is that the web site visitor only sees the intended markup and content output, and never the PHP script. Because of this server-dependent behavior, PHP is said to be browser-independent.

❏   PHP works well in tandem with other Open Source technologies, such as MySQL and Apache web server. While this is also true for other scripting languages, such as Perl, PHP is much easier to use because it can be embedded within HTML code.

❏   PHP is relatively fast, and it allows developers to quickly prototype powerful and interactive web applications.

❏ PHP can also be configured to run as a web server module, on Apache or on Microsoft Internet Information Server (PHP4 only). This results in even faster performance, as the PHP interpreter stays cached in the server memory and does not have to be loaded for each PHP script requested by a browser. The PHP module is currently more popular than Apache's mod_perl module as per study findings on Apache modules popularity at http://www.securityspace.com/s_survey/data/man.200208/apachemods.html.

Other Technologies

Apart from PHP at its core, our book incorporates other technologies to implement real-world applications. These have been briefly described below.

HTML, JavaScript, and Cascading Style Sheets

Support for HTML is implicit in all web browsers. Also, support for Java Script and Cascading Style Sheets (CSS) is available with most of them. If your browser does not have the required support, please install a Mozilla 1.0 (http://www.mozilla.org/), a higher version of Netscape (http://www.netscape.com/), or Microsoft Internet Explorer (http://www.microsoft.com/) in keeping with the configuration of your machine.

XML and XSLT

At the time of writing, browser support for XML and related technologies varied. Internet Explorer afforded the most complete support for XML features, although Mozilla was purported to have fuller and hidden XML support as well. Please visit the World Wide Web Consortium's web site (http://www.w3.org/) for more details.

WML

WML suffers from the same type of browser support problems as XML, especially due to the variety of wireless devices available for surfing the Internet. The web server hosting a web site must have support for **Wireless Application Protocol (WAP)**, that is, it must have a WAP gateway enabled, or else any WML served to a wireless browser will show unexpected results. For the purpose of this book, we just need a desktop WAP simulator emulator.

PEAR::DB

PHP Extension and Application Repository (PEAR) is a unified API for accessing SQL databases. The PEAR::DB concepts have been used extensively in many case studies in this book for querying MySQL. Although the function names used are by themselves explanatory, it is recommended that you familiarise yourself with the concepts of PEAR::DB.

For more details on PEAR::DB, refer to *Beginning PHP4 Databases* by *Wrox Press (ISBN 1-86100-782-5)*.

Smarty Template Engine

Smarty is a template engine for PHP. One of the unique aspects about Smarty that sets it apart from other templating solutions is that it converts the templates into native PHP scripts upon the first execution. After that, it executes the compiled PHP scripts. Therefore, there is no costly template file parsing for each request.

PHPLib Template Class

The PHPLib template class allows keeping our HTML code completely free of PHP code. The class provides functions, which can fill in the replacement fields with arbitrary strings.

Book Roadmap

This book covers both the basic and advanced concepts of PHP4 required to develop a number of diverse web applications, and the ideas presented here can be translated to a variety of very common real-world web applications.

Here is a roadmap that gives a brief description of each of the 13 case studies in the book and the concepts that have been covered therein:

- ❑ *Chapter 1* includes an introduction to the book and enumerates the software requirements for effective use of the web development concepts in the book. It also discusses the features of PHP as a web development tool.

- ❑ *Chapter 2* is the **Association Directory** case study that focuses on importing existing information in the form of XML markup, to a MySQL database. It extensively makes use of the XML support that PHP offers. The web application allows the people of a fictional University of Life to communicate with each other via an intranet. The architectural concepts covered here include a member directory and an introduction to a messaging system.

- ❑ *Chapter 3* is the **Book of Mankind Project** that describes the cataloging of an online encyclopedia of humankind, whereby visitors can post content. This chapter builds upon the same general architecture as the previous case study, and adds a web forum where people can discuss social issues pertaining to the entire planet. The case study is built using PHP with MySQL with PEAR::DB as the database abstraction layer.

- ❑ *Chapter 4* is a **Shopping Directory** that demonstrates the use of templates to build a site that supports generic HTML browsers, WML support for WAP phones and other mobile devices, such as PalmPilots and handhelds running WindowsCE, or PocketPCs. It builds a store directory that can be used both from HTML and WML browsers.

- ❑ *Chapter 5* is a **Paranormal News Service** for the fictional Mighty GhostHunters, Inc., that allows staff and public to post information about ghost sightings and other paranormal events and experiences. This case study allows users to register themselves with a site and post their experiences. The architectural concept is that of a story server.

- ❑ *Chapter 6* builds a **Web Corpus**, which is a combination of an online dictionary and a thesaurus, with the provision to include words in different languages. The chapter provides a discussion of the techniques used to compile a list of unique words occurring in various types of web content. Other concepts covered include a fuzzy matching facility.

- ❑ *Chapter 7* is a **Mission Control Job Board** that covers the architecture of a 'jobs-available' site with a search facility. It makes use of WML Templates and PHP, with MySQL as the database.

- ❑ *Chapter 8* is a **Classified Ads Board** that covers the planning and development of a classified advertisements board that allows users to post advertisements online.

❑ *Chapter 9* details a **Simple Content Management System** that focuses on how a variety of document structures (that is, content) might be stored and manipulated using a simple database schema. This is accomplished by using XML to define each document. While all documents have the same skeleton set of XML tags, each document type differs in the tags used within the `<body>` element. This content markup is stored as is, in the database. Each document type will require its own application component to parse and manipulate the document body.

❑ *Chapter 10* builds on the previous case study to develop an **Advanced Content Management System**. In particular, the focus is on an XML engine for some of the workflow-related features of a CMS, like enabling user categories, privileges, task lists, messaging, and activity logs. With these features, combined with the application components in the previous case study and an appropriate web interface in any scripting or programming language, we can put together most of the essential ingredients for a complete WCMS.

❑ *Chapter 11* is a **Simple Search Engine** that looks at how to build a search engine that can search through a site with various products. The search should be fast and rank the most exact matches first so that the users can find the information they are looking for, quickly.

❑ *Chapter 12* is a **MyStuff Server** application that allows users to view their personal collections with a wireless device. This is the kind of application that's great for when we are in a store with items on huge discount but cannot remember what we already own.

❑ *Chapter 13* is a **Genealogy Server** where we discuss the planning and programming of a PHP and MySQL-based data repository that can track and search for information about a user's ancestry. It covers the data warehousing and virtual team-authoring architecture that allows anyone to privately record his or her family's genealogical information, for access over the Internet.

❑ *Chapter 14* discusses **Building Portal Sites. It discusses the installation and configuration of PostNuke** – a CMS that provides for the easy implementation of very sophisticated and complicated sites. Like Linux, Apache, PHP, and other major Open Source efforts, PostNuke is one of those Open Source success stories where significant and extremely useful software has been developed by the Internet community.

How to use this Book

This book tries to minimize the details outside of example context. It takes a 'dive-right-in' approach, similar to the way most people learn a human language for the first time.

This book targets experienced PHP Programmers who either have some PHP experience, or the wherewithal to learn rapidly via the case studies. The case study solutions will use PHP concepts in such a manner that programmers can extrapolate techniques for use in their applications. Thus, programmers who intend to write large-scale web applications using PHP and web databases can use this book as a reference and launch point, even finding code samples that are sufficient for their needs.

What You Need to use This Book

The minimum software requirements to run the examples and test the code in this book are listed below:

- ❑ **Operating System**
  You should have installed at least one operating system listed here:

  - ❑ UNIX

  - ❑ Windows (95/98/ME/2000/NT)

  - ❑ Mac OS X

- ❑ **PHP**
  Throughout the book, we have worked exclusively with PHP4 because it has many new features that make PHP scripts faster and more efficient. Hence all code examples and case studies use PHP4 for scripting; all the code samples have been tested on PHP version 4.2 and are verified to be running.

- ❑ **DBMS**
  For all case studies that require the use of a database, we will use the MySQL server. This open source product is free for non-commercial use under the General Public License. Even a commercial license is available for a fraction of the cost of other commercial products.

- ❑ **Browser**
  We can use any of the web browsers: IE5.x or above, Mozilla 1.0, or Netscape 4.x is recommended. A browser that has strong XML support is preferable.

- ❑ **Web Server**
  To test code from this book, or to test any web application, you need a web server on your system. You may use the Apache Server (http://www.apache.org/), Microsoft's PWS (Personal Web Server) http://www.microsoft.com/, or MS-IIS, although Apache is a recommended web server. Instructions for installing these web servers can be obtained at their respective web sites. If you cannot use Apache, or for more serious applications requiring security, you could consider using MS-IIS instead of PWS.

- ❑ **WAP emulator**
  Applications that require the use of WML have been tested on a wireless emulator. These WAP simulators are available as downloads and the web sites where we may get them are http://developer.openwave.com/ and http://www.forum.nokia.com/.

Apart from these software requirements, you also need to be proficient with basic scripting and programming concepts, and possess a basic understanding of HTML, as well as how the HTTP protocol works.

Conventions

To help you get the most from the text and keep track of what's happening, we've used a number of conventions throughout the book.

For instance:

> **These boxes hold important, not-to-be-forgotten information, which is directly relevant to the surrounding text.**

While the background style is used for asides to the current discussion.

As for styles in the text:

- ❏ When we introduce them, we **highlight** important words
- ❏ We show keyboard strokes like this: *Ctrl-K*
- ❏ We show filenames and code within the text like so: `<Location>`

Text on user interfaces and URLs are shown as: Menu

We present code in two different ways:

```
In our code examples, the code foreground style shows new, important, and
    pertinent code,
```

```
while the code background style shows code that's less important in the present
    context or has been seen before.
```

Database Naming Conventions

In most of the chapters in the book, we have followed a naming convention to name tables and columns in the table, like this:

Example	
Database Name	`databasename`
Table Name	`databasename_tablename's'`
Field Name	`tablename_columnname`

The tables are prefixed with the name of the database. This increases the readability of the code and helps us know which table belongs to which database. For example, if an application has two databases, say, `foo` and `bar`, then all the tables in the database `foo`, will be prefixed with `foo_`. So, if we have a table `users`, it is named as `foo_users`. The table names are plural.

Further, columns in a table are prefixed with the table name. Here, we prefix the column name with the singular form of the table name. For example, in the table `foo_users`, all the column names will be prefixed with the singular form of the table name (`user`). So, if the table `users` has a column, of `firstname`, we represent it as `user_firstname`.

Also, we have tried not to use abbreviations in table or field names, but rather whole words.

Customer Support

We always value hearing from our readers, and we want to know what you think about this book – what you liked, what you didn't like, and what you think we can do better next time. You can send us your comments, either by returning the reply card in the back of the book, or by e-mail to feedback@wrox.com. Please be sure to mention the book title in your message.

How to Download the Sample Code

When you visit the Wrox site, http://www.wrox.com/, simply locate the title through our Search facility or by using one of the title lists. Click on Download in the Code column or on Download Code on the book's detail page.

The files that are available for download from our site have been archived using WinZip. When you have saved the attachments to a folder on your hard drive, you need to extract the files using a de-compression program such as WinZip or PKUnzip. When you extract the files, the code is usually extracted into chapter folders. When you start the extraction process, ensure your software (WinZip, PKUnzip, etc.) is set to use folder names.

Errata

We've made every effort to make sure that there are no errors in the text or in the code. However, no one is perfect and mistakes do occur. If you find an error in one of our books, like a spelling mistake or faulty piece of code, we would be very grateful for your feedback. By sending in errata you may save another reader hours of frustration, and of course, you will be helping us provide even higher quality information. Simply e-mail the information to support@wrox.com; your information will be checked and if correct, posted to the errata page for that title, or used in subsequent editions of the book.

To find errata on the web site, go to http://www.wrox.com/, and simply locate the title through our Advanced Search or title list. Click on the Book Errata link, which is below the cover graphic on the book's detail page.

E-Mail Support

If you wish to directly query a problem in the book with an expert who knows the book in detail then e-mail support@wrox.com, with the title of the book and the last four numbers of the ISBN in the subject field of the e-mail. A typical e-mail should include the following:

❑   The **title of the book, last four digits of the ISBN**, and **page number** of the problem in the Subject field.

❑   Your **name, contact information**, and the **problem** in the body of the message.

We won't send you junk mail. We need the details to save your time and ours.

When you send an e-mail message, it will go through the following chain of support:

- ❑ **Customer Support**
  Your message is delivered to our customer support staff who are the first people to read it. They have files on most frequently asked questions and will answer anything general about the book or the web site immediately.

- ❑ **Editorial**
  Deeper queries are forwarded to the technical editor responsible for that book. They have experience with the programming language or particular product, and are able to answer detailed technical questions on the subject.

- ❑ **The Author**
  Finally, in the unlikely event that the editor cannot answer your problem, they will forward the request to the author. We do try to protect the authors from any distractions to their writing; however, we are quite happy to forward specific requests to them. All Wrox authors help with the support on their books. They will e-mail the customer and the editor with their response, and again all readers should benefit.

The Wrox support process can only offer support to issues directly pertinent to the content of our published title. Support for questions that fall outside the scope of normal book support is provided via the community lists of our http://p2p.wrox.com/ forum.

p2p.wrox.com

For author and peer discussion join the P2P mailing lists. Our unique system provides **programmer to programmer**™ contact on mailing lists, forums, and newsgroups, all in addition to our one-to-one e-mail support system. If you post a query to P2P, you can be confident that many Wrox authors and other industry experts on our mailing lists are examining it. At p2p.wrox.com you will find a number of different lists to help you, not only while you read this book, but also as you develop your applications.

To subscribe to a mailing list just follow these steps:

1. Go to http://p2p.wrox.com/

2. Choose the appropriate category from the left menu bar

3. Click on the mailing list you wish to join

4. Follow the instructions to subscribe and fill in your e-mail address and password

5. Reply to the confirmation e-mail you receive

6. Use the subscription manager to join more lists and set your e-mail preferences

Why this System Offers the Best Support

You can choose to join the mailing lists or you can receive them as a weekly digest. If you don't have the time, or facility, to receive the mailing list, then you can search our archives. Junk and spam mails are deleted, and your own e-mail address is protected by the unique Lyris system. Queries about joining or leaving lists, and any other general queries about lists, should be sent to listsupport@wrox.com.

Summary

This book covers both the design and programming techniques for professional web development, using PHP/MySQL concepts and markup languages to develop real-web applications. The ideas and techniques presented in the case studies can be extrapolated to other web architectures to suit the convenience of the reader.

We hope you like this book and enjoy using it, just as much as we enjoyed writing it.

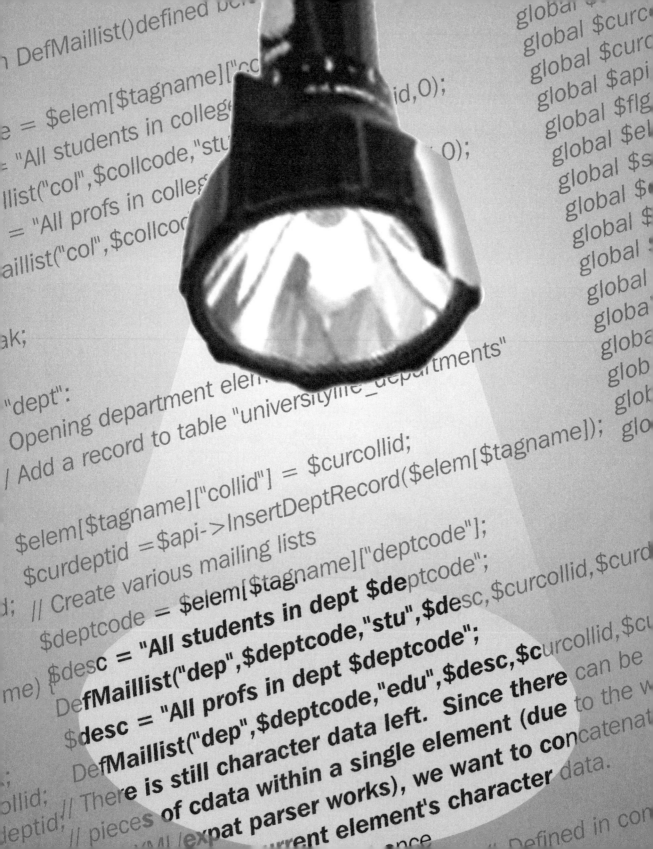

Association Directory

Administrators at the University of Life, in cooperation with student union representatives, want to promote the university's social atmosphere by encouraging contact between students and staff, via an on-campus intranet. The web site will have both a directory listing of staff and students, as well as a simple online messaging system.

These are the steps we'll follow in building the application:

❏ Creating a specification by stating our project objectives clearly

❏ Designing the database to answer the questions like what data is essential to the application, and how is this data best modelled

❏ Managing the data by maintaining and updating all data used in the application

❏ Delivering the content by determining the most effective way to get data from the data store to the site's users

❏ Possible improvements to answer questions like are there better ways to accomplish our objectives than what we're presently using, and what features would enhance the system

This chapter looks at a web application that allows students and professors to communicate with each other regarding course issues.

The messaging system will allow system administrators to contact staff and students, professors to contact the students in their classes or other staff, students to contact each other, and so on.

Contact information for the teaching staff will be limited to on-campus information only, such as building name, office number, phone extension, hours of availability, and so on. Contact information for all other staff (general, system administrators) will initially be left empty. However, they can choose to add their office contact information at their own discretion.

Student contact information will have a privacy flag, to be turned on or off at their discretion, for personal or safety reasons. In other words, contact information for a student may be recorded in the system, which requires the student to turn the privacy flag on.

System administrators do not have to have contact information in the database; in other words, those administering the system are not required to act as participants in it, other than to deal with administrative issues.

Each user, whether staff or student, will be assigned a system account name and password. This account name is what identifies the user online, and will typically consist of the user's first initial and last name or some variation of this in case of duplicate names.

Staff and system administrators will have mailing list creation privileges. System administrators can send bulk messages regarding upcoming events, registration information, facility closures, and the like.

The web application is to be designed in a manner that allows extra features to be added later. This could include web forums or moderated chat rooms based on specific courses, although we'll not discuss any specifics of these here. The application should also track usage to see if the intranet development effort was worthwhile, and whether additional monies should be spent to add more features later.

Application Specification

There are numerous functional requirements for our application, even for one as conceptually simple as this. The University of Life administration has a number of objectives to attain with this application:

❑ The university has existing incompatible computer applications that already store some of the information found in the new application. While this duplication is acceptable, it is desirable that only one application be used to store the master data. In this case, the older applications will continue to be mostly used for data entry. Special modules will be written to export necessary information in an XML format, which will then be imported into the new application. At the end of each semester, the database in the new application will be erased. When the new semester starts, and students have been registered, information is again exported in XML from older applications and re-imported into the new application.

❑ Once information has been imported into the new application's database, the application is ready for use for the semester. Thus another objective of the project is a functioning web application that includes a messaging system with automated mailing lists.

❑ As the University does not have a computer department, the development of the application is up to the student and professor volunteers. While some methods may be more efficient, one objective is to create an opportunity for volunteers to learn PHP programming with MySQL, HTML, and XML. More specifically, volunteers will develop the application over a number of semesters. Since functional needs may change, the project team has decided that the database access code be defined as a set of PHP functions forming an Application Programmer Interface (API). The API functions will be called by any and all interface code, whether it be the XML imported code or the HTML navigation interface.

Space does not permit us to look at the entire application. Therefore we will be focussing on the following aspects:

- ❏ An XML-based markup language for information export from other applications. The information we'll import includes:
    - ❏ An XML list of colleges and departments that are part of the university
    - ❏ An XML list of available courses for the current semester
    - ❏ An XML list of professors, including the courses that they are teaching
    - ❏ An XML list of students, including the courses they are taking
- ❏ The PHP scripts needed to import the XML files
- ❏ The MySQL database schema required for the full application

We'll not look at scripts to produce the exported markup.

As the project is currently in the protoype phase, all other features are ignored for the time being. Since the user interface is not yet complete, we'll use input from text files or the MySQL command line in lieu of actual user input. This is a temporary expedient for developmental purposes only; in the final version of the application, input will be generated via the finished web interface.

User Types

The new web application will be made available from computers across the campus, including the offices of professors and the study rooms of student residences. As such, the application is on a private network. While non-teaching staff and alumni will be welcome to use the system in future versions, the current prototype will focus on supporting features for three types of users:

- ❏ **Web Site System Administrators (member category – adm)**
  System administrators have all possible system privileges including creating, modifying, or removing accounts, creating usage reports and mailing lists, and sending messages to any or all mailing lists or the entire university populace simultaneously. Initially all system administrators will share these privileges, although we might later wish to modify our privilege system so that only one or two key personnel will have the ability to create, modify, or delete administrative accounts.

- ❏ **Teaching staff (member category – prof)**
  Professors have fewer privileges than system administrators. These privileges include the ability to read and send messages, and to maintain mailing lists. While many of the application's mailing lists are automatically created when the XML information is initially imported, professors can create, update, or delete mailing lists, as necessary.

- ❏ **Students (member category – stu)**
  Students have the least privileges on the system. They can read and send messages, and view the class enrollment list for a course that they are registered for.

Since the application, as we present it here, is only in its working prototype stage of development, we'll discuss the minimum that's required to implement the characteristics of these user groups.

Content Types

The web application is currently only intended to contain textual data in the following forms:

- Descriptions of colleges, departments, courses, professors, and students
- Mailbox messages

Later versions of the application may contain a web forum and chat room for each course currently being taught. However, these features are not discussed here.

Importing Existing Information

Here, we'll focus on importing the existing information in the form of XML markup, to a MySQL database. We'll look at all the aspects of this facet of the application in the most logical order.

XML Tagsets for Existing Information

There are three XML tagsets that make up the information being exported from older systems. The sections below discuss these tagsets. Note that we'll refer back to the sample files shown here later in the chapter.

Colleges, Departments, and Available Courses

The University of Life currently has only three colleges and a number of departments within each. They are:

- Health and Spirituality
  - Alternative Medicine and Therapy
  - Spirituality
- Mysticism and Magic
  - Mysticism
  - Magic
- Sciences
  - New Physics
  - Alchemy

Each department offers a number of courses; they are represented in an XML format as below. The necessary information about colleges, departments, and courses can be described in a single XML file (`colleges.xml`), like this:

```
<?xml version="1.0" ?>

<colleges>

  <college collcode="HeSp" collname="Health + Spirituality">
```

```
  <dept deptcode="AlMed" deptname="Alternative Medicine + Therapy">
    <course num="AlMed001" name="Massage Therapy">
      <desc>Course description.</desc>
    </course>
    <course num="AlMed002" name="Qi Gong">
      <desc>Course description.</desc>
    </course>
    <course num="AlMed003" name="Homeopathy + Naturopathy">
      <desc>Course description.</desc>
    </course>
  </dept>

  <dept deptcode="Spir" deptname="Spirituality">
    <course num="Spir001" name="Religions">
      <desc>Course description.</desc>
    </course>
    <course num="Spir002" name="Meditation + Reflection">
      <desc>Course description.</desc>
    </course>
    <course num="Spir003" name="Human Relationships">
      <desc>Course description.</desc>
    </course>
  </dept>
</college>


<college collcode="MyMa" collname="Mysticism + Magic">

  <dept deptcode="Myst" deptname="Mysticism">
    <course num="Myst001" name="Levitation">
      <desc>Course description.</desc>
    </course>
    <course num="Myst002" name="Out-of-Body Experiences">
      <desc>Course description.</desc>
    </course>
  </dept>

  <dept deptcode="Mag" deptname="Magic">
    <course num="Mag001" name="Law of Least Effort">
      <desc>Course description.</desc>
    </course>
    <course num="Mag002" name="How to be Invisible">
      <desc>Course description.</desc>
    </course>
    <course num="Mag003" name="Translocation">
      <desc>Course description.</desc>
    </course>
  </dept>
</college>


<college collcode="Sci" collname="Sciences">
```

```
      <dept deptcode="NwPh" deptname="New Physics">
        <course num="NwPh001" name="Tao of Physics">
          <desc>Course description.</desc>
        </course>
        <course num="NwPh002" name="Acausal Universes">
          <desc>Course description.</desc>
        </course>
        <course num="NwPh003" name="Chaos Theory">
          <desc>Course description.</desc>
        </course>
        <course num="NwPh004" name="Schroedinger's Cat">
          <desc>Course description.</desc>
        </course>
      </dept>

      <dept deptcode="Alch" deptname="Alchemy">
        <course num="Alch001" name="Transmutation">
          <desc>Course description.</desc>
        </course>
        <course num="Alch002" name="Cooking Alchemy">
          <desc>Course description.</desc>
        </course>
       <course num="Alch003" name="Potions">
          <desc>Course description.</desc>
        </course>
      </dept>
    </college>

</colleges>
```

DTD for Colleges, Departments, and Available Courses

In this section we'll discuss the DTD for the XML document above. When using XML to intechange information between applications, it is important to have a way to validate the XML documents to know if they will be processed by the system. If we receive an invalid XML document and try to process it, inconsistencies can creep in or we may get unexpected results.

There're many schema languages in the market to validate XML vocabularies, the most popular options are:

❑   DTDs
❑   XML Schema
❑   Relax NG
❑   Schematron

In this application we'll use DTDs. The other schema languages are more powerful than DTDs and allow us to use data types that provide a better control of the vocabulary. However, DTDs are sufficient for our purposes here and enjoy considerable vendor support too.

The following is a DTD (colleges.dtd) for information about colleges, departments, and available courses:

```
<?xml version="1.0" encoding="UTF-8"?>
```

We start by defining a `<college>` element, which contains one or more `<dept>` elements each of which corresponds to a department:

```
<!ELEMENT college (dept+)>
```

Each `<college>` has two attributes:

- ❑ `collcode` may take one of three values – `HeSp`, `MyMa`, or `Sci` – corresponding to the colleges of Health and Spirituality, Mysticism and Magic, and Science
- ❑ `collname` contains an arbitrary string of character data

```
<!ATTLIST college
    collcode (HeSp | MyMa | Sci) #REQUIRED
    collname CDATA #REQUIRED
>
```

Now we define a `<colleges>` element. The only requirement we make of this element is that it contain one or more `<college>` elements:

```
<!ELEMENT colleges (college+)>
```

Next we define a `<course>` element, corresponding to a course being offered by the University. This element has two attributes – `num` (or course number) and `name`. Each of these attributes contains arbitrary character data.

> *When we say 'arbitrary', we're speaking purely from the DTD's point of view – there may be additional constraints imposed on these values in a database or other application, but for now we're concerned only with the fact that these attributes contain text and not additional tags.*

The `<course>` element also contains one (and only one) `<desc>` element, which corresponds to a course description:

```
<!ELEMENT course (desc)>
  <!ATTLIST course
    num CDATA #REQUIRED
    name CDATA #REQUIRED
  >
```

A `<dept>` element contains one or more `<course>` elements and has two attributes – `deptcode` takes one of the six enumerated values corresponding to the departments listed above, and `deptname` contains character data and corresponds to the name of the department:

```
<!ELEMENT dept (course+)>
  <!ATTLIST dept
    deptcode (AlMed | Alch | Mag | Myst | NwPh | Spir) #REQUIRED
    deptname CDATA #REQUIRED
  >
```

Finally the `<desc>` element corresponds to a course description, and contains PCDATA (that is, mixed tags and text). For now, we don't concern ourselves with going into any greater detail about this element's contents; for instance, in the `colleges.xml` file we only use the string 'Course description.' as a placeholder in each occurrence of `<desc>`:

```
<!ELEMENT desc (#PCDATA)>
```

To make things easier here is a diagrammatic representation of the DTD:

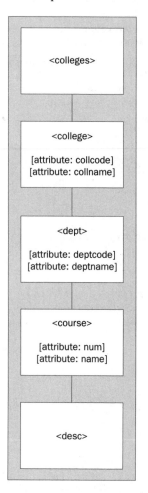

There are a number of free tools that can be used to validate XML documents before importing them to PHP. These include:

- ❑ **Xerces** (http://xml.apache.org/)
  A collection of XML parsers written in C++, Java, and Perl

- ❑ **XMLCookTop** (http://www.xmlcooktop.com/)
  An XML editor and validator for Windows that also handles XSLT and Xpath

- ❑ **IBM's DOMit** (http://www.networking.ibm.com/xml/XmlValidatorForm.html)
  A servlet that validates an XML document online and displays it as a tree
- ❑ **Microsoft's XML Core Services software for Windows**
  (http://msdn.microsoft.com/downloads/default.asp)
  Available via the MSDN Downloads page
- ❑ **Sun's Multi-Schema XML Validator (MSV)**
  (http://wwws.sun.com/software/xml/developers/multischema/)
  An add-on for the Java Development Kit (JDK) that provides validation against DTDs, Relax,
  XML Schema, and other schemata

To indicate that the XML document `colleges.xml` responds to the `college.dtd` DTD, use the following syntax:

```
<?xml version="1.0" encoding="UTF-8"?>

<!DOCTYPE colleges SYSTEM "colleges.dtd">
  <colleges>
    <college collcode="HeSp" collname="Health + Spirituality">
      <dept deptcode="AlMed" deptname="Alternative Medicine + Therapy">
```

Later on in the *PHP Code: Importing Existing Information* section in the chapter, we will look at the PHP script (`add_colleges.php`) that we'll use to import this XML file into the new application's MySQL database.

Teaching Staff

Information about teaching staff is exported from an older application to an XML file. This is the structure of the XML file (`profs.xml`):

```
<?xml version="1.0" ?>

<members>

  <member memcat="edu">
    <univid>UL000001</univid>
    <fname>Basil</fname>
    <lname>Fawlty</lname>
```

We now define the department for this professor by using the department code surrounded by double underscores:

```
<dept>__Spir__</dept>
<cistaff>
  <bldng>Fawlty Towers</bldng>
  <office>301</office>
  <ext>301</ext>
  <hrsavail>1pm-3pm</hrsavail>
</cistaff>
```

Next, we define courses by using the course number surrounded by double underscores:

```
      <teaching>
        <course>__Spir002__</course>
        <course>__Spir003__</course>
        <course>__Myst002__</course>
        <course>__NwPh003__</course>
      </teaching>
    </member>

    <member memcat="edu">
      <univid>UL000002</univid>
      <fname>Manuel</fname>
      <lname>Notfawlty</lname>
      <dept>__Myst__</dept>
      <cistaff>
        <bldng>Paltry Towers</bldng>
        <office>101</office>
        <ext>101</ext>
        <hrsavail>9am-11am</hrsavail>
      </cistaff>
      <teaching>
        <course>__Myst001__</course>
        <course>__NwPh002__</course>
        <course>__AlMed002__</course>
      </teaching>
    </member>

    <member memcat="edu">
      <univid>UL000003</univid>
      <fname>Nos</fname>
      <lname>Feratu</lname>
      <dept>__Myst__</dept>
      <cistaff>
        <bldng>The Castle</bldng>
        <office>202</office>
        <ext>202</ext>
        <hrsavail></hrsavail>
      </cistaff>
      <teaching>
        <course>__Alch003__</course>
        <course>__Mag002__</course>
        <course>__Mag003__</course>
        <course>__Mag001__</course>
      </teaching>
    </member>

  </members>
```

DTD for Teaching Staff

We can use the following DTD (`profs.dtd`) to validate information about the teaching staff:

```
<?xml version="1.0" encoding="UTF-8"?>

<!ELEMENT bldng      (#PCDATA)>
<!ELEMENT cistaff    (bldng, office, ext, hrsavail)>
<!ELEMENT course     (#PCDATA)>
<!ELEMENT dept       (#PCDATA)>
<!ELEMENT ext        (#PCDATA)>
<!ELEMENT fname      (#PCDATA)>
<!ELEMENT hrsavail   (#PCDATA)>
<!ELEMENT lname      (#PCDATA)>
<!ELEMENT member     (univid, fname, lname, dept, cistaff, teaching)>
  <!ATTLIST member
    memcat CDATA #REQUIRED
  >
<!ELEMENT members    (member+)>
<!ELEMENT office     (#PCDATA)>
<!ELEMENT teaching   (course+)>
<!ELEMENT univid     (#PCDATA)>
```

In brief, a single instructor is represented by a `<member>` element that has a single required attribute `memcat` (member category) made up of character data, and which contains six sub-elements. These correspond (in order) to the professor's university instructor ID, first name, last name, department, contact information, and list of courses taught. The first four of these are simply defined as containing PCDATA; the latter two are actually a `<cistaff>` element and a `<teaching>` element, which consists of one or more `<course>` elements.

A `<course>` element is defined in this DTD as containing PCDATA but not further specified.

The `<cistaff>` element (contact info staff) is comprised of four subelements, each of which contains PCDATA (that is tags and/or text) and corresponds (in order) to a professor's building and office, his campus telephone, and hours available. We also define a root element `<members>`, which simply consists of one or more `<member>` elements.

This DTD is a bit more complex than the previous one, so here is a chart showing the elements and their relationships:

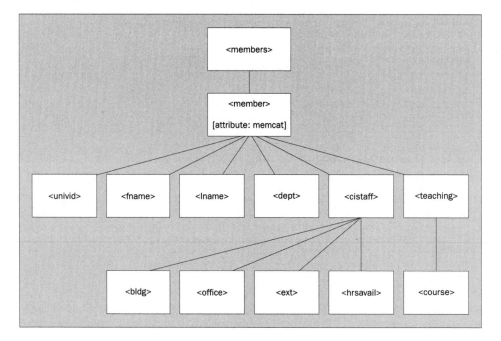

Students

Information about students is similar to that of teaching staff. Here is the students.xml file that stores information about the students:

```xml
<?xml version="1.0" ?>

<members>

  <member memcat="stu">
    <univid>UL100001</univid>
    <fname>golly</fname>
    <lname>gee</lname>
    <dept>__AlMed__</dept>
    <ciother>
      <addr1>123 Stoney Way</addr1>
      <addr2>Apt 5</addr2>
      <city>Somewhere</city>
      <stateprov>Somestate</stateprov>
      <country>USA</country>
      <postcode>12345</postcode>
      <phone></phone>
      <ext></ext>
      <email></email>
    </ciother>
```

```
      <taking>
        <course>__AlMed001__</course>
        <course>__AlMed002__</course>
        <course>__AlMed003__</course>
        <course>__Spir002__</course>
      </taking>
    </member>

    <member memcat="stu">
      <univid>UL100002</univid>
      <fname>mookie</fname>
      <lname>mouse</lname>
      <dept>__Spir__</dept>
      <ciother>
        <addr1>123 Stoney Way</addr1>
        <addr2>Apt 7</addr2>
        <city>Somewhere</city>
        <stateprov>Somestate</stateprov>
        <country>USA</country>
        <postcode>12345</postcode>
        <phone></phone>
        <ext></ext>
        <email></email>
      </ciother>
      <taking>
        <course>__Spir001__</course>
        <course>__Spir002__</course>
        <course>__Spir003__</course>
        <course>__AlMed001__</course>
      </taking>
    </member>

    <member memcat="stu">
      <univid>UL100003</univid>
      <fname>roo</fname>
      <lname>hoo</lname>
      <dept>__Myst__</dept>
      <ciother>
        <addr1>123 Stoney Way</addr1>
        <addr2>Apt 11</addr2>
        <city>Somewhere</city>
        <stateprov>Somestate</stateprov>
        <country>USA</country>
        <postcode>12345</postcode>
        <phone></phone>
        <ext></ext>
        <email></email>
      </ciother>
      <taking>
        <course>__Myst001__</course>
        <course>__Myst002__</course>
        <course>__Mag001__</course>
        <course>__Spir003__</course>
      </taking>
```

```
  </member>

  <member memcat="stu">
    <univid>UL100004</univid>
    <fname>lord</fname>
    <lname>leaftail</lname>
    <dept>__Mag__</dept>
    <ciother>
      <addr1>123 Stoney Way</addr1>
      <addr2>Apt 13</addr2>
      <city>Somewhere</city>
      <stateprov>Somestate</stateprov>
      <country>USA</country>
      <postcode>12345</postcode>
      <phone></phone>
      <ext></ext>
      <email></email>
    </ciother>
    <taking>
      <course>__Mag001__</course>
      <course>__Mag002__</course>
      <course>__Mag003__</course>
      <course>__NwPh002__</course>
    </taking>
  </member>

  <member memcat="stu">
    <univid>UL100005</univid>
    <fname>silly</fname>
    <lname>idol</lname>
    <dept>__NwPh__</dept>
    <ciother>
      <addr1>123 Stoney Way</addr1>
      <addr2>Apt 15</addr2>
      <city>Somewhere</city>
      <stateprov>Somestate</stateprov>
      <country>USA</country>
      <postcode>12345</postcode>
      <phone></phone>
      <ext></ext>
      <email></email>
    </ciother>
    <taking>
      <course>__NwPh001__</course>
      <course>__NwPh002__</course>
      <course>__NwPh003__</course>
      <course>__NwPh004__</course>
    </taking>
  </member>
```

```
<member memcat="stu">
  <univid>UL100006</univid>
  <fname>darth</fname>
  <lname>brooks</lname>
  <dept>__Alch__</dept>
  <ciother>
    <addr1>123 Stoney Way</addr1>
    <addr2>Apt 17</addr2>
    <city>Somewhere</city>
    <stateprov>Somestate</stateprov>
    <country>USA</country>
    <postcode>12345</postcode>
    <phone></phone>
    <ext></ext>
    <email></email>
  </ciother>
  <taking>
    <course>__Alch001__</course>
    <course>__Alch002__</course>
    <course>__Alch003__</course>
    <course>__NwPh004__</course>
  </taking>
</member>

<member memcat="stu">
  <univid>UL100007</univid>
  <fname>elizardbreath</fname>
  <lname>hurley</lname>
  <dept>__Alch__</dept>
  <ciother>
    <addr1>123 Stoney Way</addr1>
    <addr2>Apt 19</addr2>
    <city>Somewhere</city>
    <stateprov>Somestate</stateprov>
    <country>USA</country>
    <postcode>12345</postcode>
    <phone></phone>
    <ext></ext>
    <email></email>
  </ciother>
  <taking>
    <course>__Alch001__</course>
    <course>__Alch002__</course>
    <course>__Alch003__</course>
    <course>__Mag003__</course>
  </taking>
</member>

</members>
```

DTD for students

We can use the `students.dtd` to validate XML documents containing student information:

```
<?xml version="1.0" encoding="UTF-8"?>

<!ELEMENT addr1       (#PCDATA) >
<!ELEMENT addr2       (#PCDATA) >
<!ELEMENT ciother     (addr1, addr2, city, stateprov, country, postcode,
                       phone, ext, email) >
<!ELEMENT city        (#PCDATA) >
<!ELEMENT country     (#PCDATA) >
<!ELEMENT course      (#PCDATA) >
<!ELEMENT dept        (#PCDATA) >
<!ELEMENT email       (#PCDATA) >
<!ELEMENT ext         (#PCDATA) >
<!ELEMENT fname       (#PCDATA) >
<!ELEMENT lname       (#PCDATA) >
<!ELEMENT member      (univid, fname, lname, dept, ciother, taking) >
  <!ATTLIST member
    memcat CDATA #REQUIRED
  >
<!ELEMENT members     (member+) >
<!ELEMENT phone       (#PCDATA) >
<!ELEMENT postcode    (#PCDATA) >
<!ELEMENT stateprov   (#PCDATA) >
<!ELEMENT taking      (course+) >
<!ELEMENT univid      (#PCDATA) >
```

This DTD is similar to `prof.dtd`. The root element is `<members>` and contains one or more `<member>` elements each of which represents a student enrolled in the university. Each `<member>` element has a required `memcat` attribute and contains six sub-elements: `<univid>`, `<fname>`, `<lname>`, `<dept>`, `<ciother>`, and `<taking>`.

The first four of these are defined in the same way as they were in `profs.dtd` – `ciother` (contact information – other) contains more information than the equivalent element of the DTD for professors (`cistaff`). In the order listed, these correspond to the student's address line 1, address line 2, city, state or province, country, postcode, home telephone, campus telephone, and e-mail address. All nine of these elements contain PCDATA. The `<taking>` element is analogous to the `<teaching>` element in `profs.dtd`; both elements consist of one or more course elements each, but where `<teaching>` represented a list of courses being taught by a professor, here `<taking>` represents a list of courses in which the student is enrolled.

If we look at a diagrammatic representation of this DTD, we can see that the element structure it describes is similar to that provided by `profs.dtd`, although this one's a little more complicated since there are more elements relating to contact information for students than for professors:

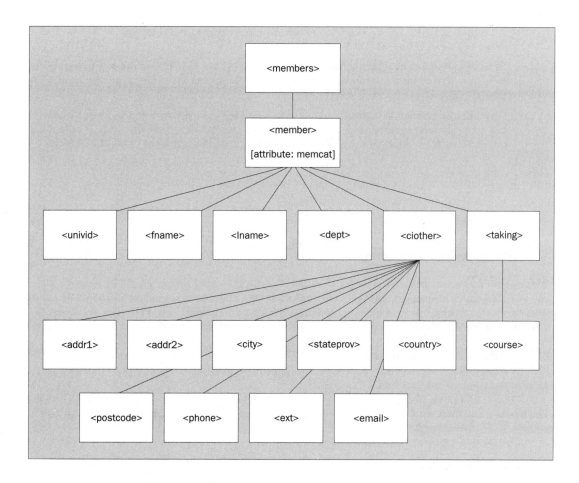

Designing the Database

Although we are not covering all of the features of the finished application, we'll look at the full database schema and then follow up with the PHP code for importing the existing data.

This web application will store information in addition to whatever the university may have stored in other applications. Thus, the following database is not intended to replace any existing information, and there will be some data overlap. While this might not be considered ideal in some respects, there are some valid reasons for doing so in this application:

❑   The flow of data between this application and others that might be in use by the university is one way. This is because data comes into the Association Directory from these other applications, but not the other way round.

❑   As we've already stated, the original data obtained from the university's enrolment and scheduling applications is created at the beginning of each new semester and is not expected to change until the current semester ends.

❑   We're not particularly interested in preserving directory data between semesters, nor is it necessary for us to do so.

❑   By working on a copy of the subset of the university's data, which is of interest to us, we don't have to worry about a mishap with our (non-critical) application affecting mission-critical official University operations or records.

❑   Given the foregoing, it's more economical to recreate the directory's data store at the beginning of each semester and more secure for the University's own datastore. There are instances where redundancy is actually desirable and this would seem to be one of them.

These are the steps we need to take to create and populate the database:

❑   Create database tables
❑   Build table indexes
❑   Create the mailing list for all members (students and professors) of the university by importing the three XML files discussed

We'll cover the first two steps in the sections *Creating Tables* and *Building Indexes* soon. The remaining steps are described under *Algorithms* followed by the *PHP Code: Importing Existing Information* section. Each of these latter two sections describes the remaining steps in either algorithmic form or in PHP, as appropriate. Note that we're discussing only the front-end of the import steps in these two sections.

Following the PHP code, there is a section entitled *UnivLife API Code*, where we'll discuss all the back-end PHP database access code necessary to support both the import steps as well as part of the full web application (member directory and messaging).

The next section discusses the database schema and any possible variations. The resulting tables will exist in a single MySQL database, `universitylife`.

Database Tables

The following tables will be created in the `universitylife` database:

Table Name	Alias	Description
`universitylife_available`	av	Detailed information about each course available in the current semester.
`universitylife_contactinfoother`	cio	Contact information for students.
`universitylife_contactinfostaff`	cis	Contact information for educational staff members.
`universitylife_colleges`	co	List of all colleges in the university.
`universitylife_departments`	de	List of all departments.
`universitylife_mailbox`	mb	All messages, for all members, identified by the sending member's account ID.

Table Name	Alias	Description
universitylife_members	me	Members of the university populace using this web application.
universitylife_messagelistdetails	mld	Stores a record for each member of each mailing list.
		There is a potential overlap in members, due to the fact that either sort of member – professor or student – may be teaching more than one course or enrolled in more than one.
universitylife_messagelistmasters	mlm	Contains the ID and code name for each mailing list.
universitylife_messagecc	mcc	For each message, records the member ID for each recipient. This saves us from having to store the same message text multiple times for multiple recipients.
universitylife_teaching	te	Lists the courses being taught by each professor. The number of records in this table should equal the number of records in the universitylife_available table.
universitylife_taking	ta	Lists courses being taken by all students, in the current semester.

> The only reason for storing course information in this application is so mailing lists can be automatically created. A mailing list is created for each college, department, and course. For each course a student takes, the student is added to the mailing list for that course.

Database Table Specfics

The tables above are listed in alphabetical order. However, they are described below in a more logical order.

Colleges

The universitylife_colleges table represents all colleges on campus. It contains the following columns:

Column Name	Data Type	Description
college_collegeid	INT	Unique integer identifying this record
college_collegecode	CHAR	A short codename for the college, for example, psychphen
college_collegename	CHAR	Full name of college, for example, Psychic Phenomena

Departments

The `universitylife_deptartments` table represents the departments for each college. It contains the following columns:

Column Name	Data Type	Description
department_departmentid	INT	Unique integer identifying this record
department_departmentcode	CHAR	A short codename for this department, for example, `xfiles`
department_departmentname	CHAR	Full name of department, for example, `X-Files`
department_collegeid	INT	Record ID of the college to which this department belongs, that is, a foreign key to the `universitylife_colleges` table

Association Members

The `universitylife_members` table contains the following columns:

Column Name	Data Type	Description
member_accountid	INT	Unique number identifying the account record of this member of the university populace.
member_accountname	CHAR	Unique account name (used for messaging) for this member.
member_universityid	INT	University ID (staff, student).
member_membercategory	CHAR	Member categories are: ❑ adm – admin staff members ❑ edu – teaching staff members ❑ stu – student members Were we to increase the number of membership categories, we might want to consider making this column an enumerated type or an integer that's a key to a 'membertypes' table. However, what we show here will be sufficient for our purposes.
member_privacy	BOOL	Privacy flag (particularly for off-campus students).
member_firstname	CHAR	Member's first name.
member_lastname	CHAR	Member's last name.

Column Name	Data Type	Description
member_status	CHAR	The status of the account can be 'A' – active, 'I' – inactive, or 'B' – blocked.
		Again, if we were to add additional status codes, we might want to make this column an enumerated type or an integer key to a 'statuscodes' table.
member_departmentid	INT	ID of the department that the member belongs to.
		For teaching staff, this is quite straightforward. For students, this represents the department that they are majoring in. However, they are allowed to have courses in other departments.
member_sessionid	CHAR	Session ID for the currently logged in member.

Contact Information – Staff

The universitylife_contactinfostaff table represents contact information for educational staff members. It contains the following columns:

Column Name	Data Type	Description
contactinfostaff_contact infostaffid	INT	Unique integer identifying this record
contactinfostaff_building	CHAR	The name of the building in which this staff member's office is located
contactinfostaff_office	CHAR	The office number of this staff member
contactinfostaff_extension	INT	The campus phone extension number of this staff member
contactinfostaff_hoursavailable	CHAR	Professor's office hours
contactinfostaff_memberid	INT	Account ID of the staff member that this record represents

Contact Information –Other

The `universitylife_contactinfoother` table represents student members. The information in this table is voluntary and is private by default. It has the following columns:

Column Name	Data Type	Description
`contactinfoother_contactinfootherid`	INT	Unique integer identifying this record.
`contactinfoother_address1`	CHAR	Address line 1. This is the first line of the member's current address.
`contactinfoother_address2`	CHAR	Address line 2 (may be left empty).
`contactinfoother_city`	CHAR	This is the city that the member currently lives in.
`contactinfoother_stateprovince`	CHAR	This is the state, province, district, territory, and so on, that the member currently lives in.
`contactinfoother_country`	CHAR	This is the country that the member currently lives in.
`contactinfoother_postcode`	CHAR	Member's postal or zip code.
`contactinfoother_extension`	INT	On-campus student residences often use an extension. Otherwise, this is the student's home telephone number.
`contactinfoother_email`	CHAR	Member's outside e-mail address.
`contactinfoother_memberid`	INT	Account ID of the member that this record represents.

A record for the `universitylife_contactinfoother` table is created for a member only if they enter privacy information. If privacy is turned on, a `universitylife_contactinfoother` record is ignored even if it exists.

Courses Available

The `universitylife_available` table contains the following columns:

Column Name	Data Type	Description
available_courseid	INT	Unique integer identifying a course record.
available_coursenumber	CHAR	Course number as it appears in the university's course calendar. For instance, 'Intro to the Qabbalah' might be course number Myst203 in the course catalog for the College of Mysticism and Magic, and 'Aromatherapy' might be course number AlMed203 under the College of Health & Spirituality. We don't want to depend upon these designations as primary key values as doing so would violate good normalization practices (we can't guarantee that they're completely unique and not dependent in part upon other external values), so we might assign the Qabbalah course a cid value of 234 and the Aromatherapy course a course ID value of 235.
available_name	CHAR	Course name.
available_coursedescription	CHAR	Course description.
available_departmentid	INT	ID of the department that offers this course. Note that a professor from a different department may teach the course.

Courses Being Taught

The universitylife_teaching table contains the following columns:

Column Name	Data Type	Description
teaching_teachingid	INT	Unique ID representing this record.
teaching_courseid	INT	Course ID of the course being taken. This matches the available_courseid column in the universitylife_available table, but this value is not unique in this table, since more than one student could be taking the course. In other words, this acts as a foreign key to the universitylife_available table.
teaching_memberprofessorid	INT	Account ID (that is, member ID) of the professor teaching this course.

Courses Being Taken

The universitylife_taking table contains the following columns. This table in other words is a lookup table between students and courses:

Column Name	Data Type	Description
taking_takeid	INT	Unique ID representing this record
taking_courseid	INT	Course ID of the course being taken. Key to the universitylife_available table
taking_memberid	INT	Account ID of the student taking this course

Mailbox Messages

The universitylife_mailbox table contains the following columns:

Column Name	Data Type	Description
mailbox_messageid	INT	Unique number identifying this message (unique across all messages for all members)
mailbox_datesent	DATE	Date the message was sent and received, since messaging is instant
mailbox_timesent	TIME	Timestamp when the message was sent
mailbox_fromid	INT	The account ID of the member who sent the message
mailbox_subject	CHAR	Subject line text
mailbox_messagetext	TEXT	Text of the message body

Message Recipients

Note that there is no 'to' or 'recipient' column in the universitylife_mailbox table above. Since senders can send to more than one recipient, we create a lookup table between messages and recipients. This is more efficient than duplicating message text in the database.

The universitylife_messagecc table contains the following columns:

Column Name	Data Type	Description
messagecc_ messageccid	INT	Unique ID representing this record.
messagecc_messageid	INT	Non-unique value that matches the messagecc_messageid key in the universitylife_mailbox table. There will be a separate universitylife_messagecc record for each recipient of a given message.
messagecc_tomemberid	INT	The message recipient's member account ID.

Column Name	Data Type	Description
messagecc_status	CHAR	Indicates whether this recipient has read their copy of this message or not. If yes, value is 'R' (read). If not, the value is 'N' (new or not read). If the recipient's copy is deleted, the status is set to 'D'.

Mailing List Master

Each row of the `universitylife_messagelistmasters` table identifies one mailing list, but does not contain information about who is on it. This table contains the following columns:

Column Name	Data Type	Description
messagelistmaster_listid	INT	A unique number identifying this mailing list.
messagelistmaster_listcode	CHAR	A system administrator selected name for this mailing list, for easy reference.
messagelistmaster_listdescription	CHAR	A description of what this mailing list represents.
messagelistmaster_collegeid	INT	ID of the college that created this list.
messagelistmaster_departmentid	INT	ID of the department that created this list.
		The lists belong to colleges or departments.

Mailing List Details

The `universitylife_messagelistdetails` table identifies each member of a particular mailing list. For each member of each mailing list, one record is stored. In other words, this table serves as a lookup between mailing lists and their members and this means that there are not necessarily any unique values in the table other than the `messagelistdetail_listdetailid` column. The table contains the following columns:

Column Name	Data Type	Description
messagelistdetail_listdetailid	INT	Unique ID that represents this record.
messagelistdetail_listid	INT	Identifies which mailing list the member is on.
messagelistdetail_memberid	INT	Identifies which member this record represents.
		Acts as a foreign key to and holds an `acctid` value from the `universitylife_members` table.

The following schematic should help us to visualise the relationships between all the tables in the `universitylife` database:

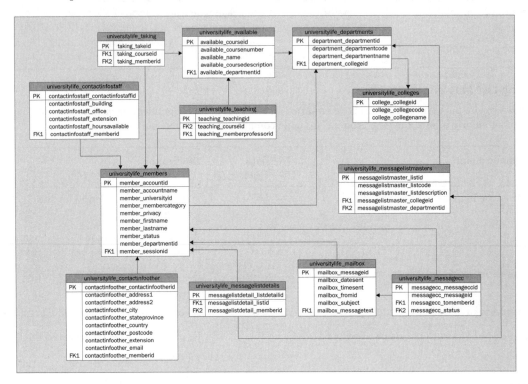

Even though the standard MySQL server doesn't yet support foreign keys as of this writing, we represent foreign key relationships between the above tables. We can enforce foreign keys by using InnoDB tables, which are supported in the **mysql–max** version of the server included in the standard distribution with MySQL 3.23.34a and above. For information about the required syntax for foreign key creation, see the MySQL Manual (http://www.mysql.com/documentation/).

Alternatively, because we shall be using PEAR::DB for database access (as we'll see later on in this chapter), we can create the database using PostgreSQL or another database supporting foreign keys without having to rewrite the PHP database code that we use in this chapter.

PEAR::DB

PHP Extension and Application Repository (PEAR) is a sophisticated set of professionally designed classes. It is a library of reusable PHP objects and code snippets enabling reuse of PHP libraries, distribution of C-based PHP extensions, and encouraging consistent coding practices. Other abstraction layers are available for use in PHP, such as Metabase, eXtremePHP, and ADODB. PEAR::DB is comprised of features available in all of them, is very OO, and is in step with PHP development so should prove to be the most flexible solution in the long run. As one distinct project within PEAR, and indeed the most initially useful part, PEAR::DB is a database abstraction layer coded to comply with the PEAR guidelines.

PEAR classes tend to be elaborate and well conceived, and using them can drastically reduce the time it takes to develop an application. One drawback, however, is that they are not usually the speediest when it comes to code execution. This performance hit from using PEAR is often exaggerated. On most modern equipment, as with tools for caching script binaries and the like, the difference is negligible. Nevertheless, if execution speed is our top priority, then PEAR might not be the best choice. If quality, robustness, and maintainability of code are the top priorities then PEAR is the code base for the job.

For more information refer to Professional PHP4 Databases from Wrox Press (ISBN 1-86100-782-5).

Database User

We begin creating our database by first using the following command:

```
> mysqladmin create universitylife
```

This will have to be modified appropriately if we don't have access to or don't wish to employ the root account on the MySQL installation that we're using.

The tables for this case study can all be placed within a single MySQL database called universitylife. We only need one database user, for example, ADMIN. We'll have to grant privileges to the tables, as well as create the tables. We use the mysql client utility, which comes with MySQL, to grant privileges:

```
mysql> GRANT SELECT, INSERT, UPDATE, DELETE ON universitylife.*
       TO 'ADMIN@localhost' IDENTIFIED BY "ADMIN";
```

Of course, in a real-life deployment, it might be better to use a less obvious password for the ADMIN user and to employ a different user name as well.

Creating Tables

Run the SQL script, crdbs_univlife.sql, on the command line to create the universitylife database and tables as follows:

```
> mysql universitylife < crdbs_univlife.sql
```

The crdbs_univlife.sql file is as follows:

```
#
# FILE: crdbs_univlife.sql
# USE:  create tables for database univlife
#

DROP TABLE IF EXISTS universitylife_colleges;
CREATE TABLE universitylife_colleges(
   college_collegeid   INT UNSIGNED NOT NULL PRIMARY KEY AUTO_INCREMENT,
   college_collegecode VARCHAR(12) NOT NULL,
   college_collegename VARCHAR(30) NOT NULL
);
```

```
DROP TABLE IF EXISTS universitylife_departments;
CREATE TABLE universitylife_departments(
    department_departmentid    INT UNSIGNED NOT NULL PRIMARY KEY
                               AUTO_INCREMENT,
    department_departmentcode VARCHAR(12) NOT NULL,
    department_departmentname VARCHAR(56) NOT NULL,
    department_collegeid       INT UNSIGNED NOT NULL
);

DROP TABLE IF EXISTS universitylife_members;
CREATE TABLE universitylife_members(
    member_accountid      INT UNSIGNED NOT NULL PRIMARY KEY AUTO_INCREMENT,
    member_accountname    VARCHAR (15) NOT NULL,
    member_universityid   VARCHAR(15) NOT NULL,
    member_membercategory VARCHAR(3) NOT NULL,
    member_privacy        BOOL NOT NULL,
    member_firstname      VARCHAR(15) NOT NULL,
    member_lastname       VARCHAR(20) NOT NULL,
    member_status         CHAR(1) NOT NULL,
    member_departmentid   INT UNSIGNED NOT NULL,
    member_sessionid      VARCHAR(15) NOT NULL
);

DROP TABLE IF EXISTS universitylife_contactinfostaff;
CREATE TABLE universitylife_contactinfostaff(
    contactinfostaff_contactinfostaffid INT UNSIGNED NOT NULL PRIMARY KEY
                               AUTO_INCREMENT,
    contactinfostaff_building        VARCHAR(40) NOT NULL,
    contactinfostaff_office          VARCHAR(6) NOT NULL,
    contactinfostaff_extension       SMALLINT UNSIGNED,
    contactinfostaff_hoursavailable  CHAR(64),
    contactinfostaff_memberid        INT UNSIGNED NOT NULL
);

DROP TABLE IF EXISTS universitylife_contactinfoother;
CREATE TABLE universitylife_contactinfoother(
    contactinfoother_contactinfootherid INT UNSIGNED NOT NULL PRIMARY KEY
                               AUTO_INCREMENT,
    contactinfoother_address1        VARCHAR(40),
    contactinfoother_address2        VARCHAR(40),
    contactinfoother_city            VARCHAR(40),
    contactinfoother_stateprovince   VARCHAR(40),
    contactinfoother_country         VARCHAR(60),
    contactinfoother_postcode        VARCHAR(10),
    contactinfoother_extension       SMALLINT UNSIGNED,
    contactinfoother_email           VARCHAR(128),
    contactinfoother_memberid        INT UNSIGNED NOT NULL
);

DROP TABLE IF EXISTS universitylife_available;
CREATE TABLE universitylife_available(
    available_courseid               INT UNSIGNED NOT NULL PRIMARY KEY
                               AUTO_INCREMENT,
```

```
    available_coursenumber        VARCHAR(12) NOT NULL,
    available_name                VARCHAR (32) NOT NULL,
    available_coursedescription   TEXT,
    available_departmentid        INT UNSIGNED NOT NULL
);

DROP TABLE IF EXISTS universitylife_teaching;
CREATE TABLE universitylife_teaching(
    teaching_teachingid           INT UNSIGNED NOT NULL PRIMARY KEY
                                  AUTO_INCREMENT,
    teaching_courseid             INT UNSIGNED NOT NULL,
    teaching_memberprofessorid    INT UNSIGNED NOT NULL
);

DROP TABLE IF EXISTS universitylife_taking;
CREATE TABLE universitylife_taking(
    taking_takeid      INT UNSIGNED NOT NULL PRIMARY KEY AUTO_INCREMENT,
    taking_courseid    INT UNSIGNED NOT NULL,
    taking_memberid    INT UNSIGNED NOT NULL
);

DROP TABLE IF EXISTS universitylife_mailbox;
CREATE TABLE universitylife_mailbox(
    mailbox_messageid    INT UNSIGNED NOT NULL PRIMARY KEY AUTO_INCREMENT,
    mailbox_datesent     DATE NOT NULL,
    mailbox_timesent     TIMESTAMP,
    mailbox_fromid       INT UNSIGNED NOT NULL,
    mailbox_subject      VARCHAR(48) NOT NULL,
    mailbox_messagetext  TEXT
);

DROP TABLE IF EXISTS universitylife_messagecc;
CREATE TABLE universitylife_messagecc(
    messagecc_messageccid  INT UNSIGNED NOT NULL PRIMARY KEY AUTO_INCREMENT,
    messagecc_messageid    INT UNSIGNED NOT NULL,
    messagecc_tomemberid   INT UNSIGNED NOT NULL,
    messagecc_status       CHAR(1) NOT NULL
);

DROP TABLE IF EXISTS universitylife_messagelistmasters;
CREATE TABLE universitylife_messagelistmasters(
    messagelistmaster_listid          INT UNSIGNED NOT NULL PRIMARY KEY
                                      AUTO_INCREMENT,
    messagelistmaster_listcode        VARCHAR(28) NOT NULL,
    messagelistmaster_listdescription VARCHAR(128),
    messagelistmaster_collegeid       INT UNSIGNED NOT NULL,
    messagelistmaster_departmentid    INT UNSIGNED NOT NULL
);

DROP TABLE IF EXISTS universitylife_messagelistdetails;
CREATE TABLE universitylife_messagelistdetails(
    messagelistdetail_listdetailid INT UNSIGNED NOT NULL PRIMARY KEY
                                   AUTO_INCREMENT,
    messagelistdetail_listid       INT UNSIGNED NOT NULL,
    messagelistdetail_memberid     INT UNSIGNED NOT NULL
);
```

Building Indexes

Indexes will be created for most of the columns in the database to speed up common searches. The SQL commands for creating indices are in a file called mkidx_univlife.sql.

Run the following SQL script, mkidx_univlife.sql, on the command line to build the indexes for the universitylife database and tables:

```
> mysql universitylife < mkidx_univlife.sql
```

The mkidx_univlife.sql file is as follows:

```
#
# FILE: mkidx_univlife.sql
# USE:  create indexes for tables in database universitylife
#

# Indexes for table universitylife_colleges
#
CREATE INDEX coll_idxOnCollid        ON universitylife_colleges
                                         (college_collegeid);
CREATE INDEX coll_idxOnCollcode      ON universitylife_colleges
                                         (college_collegecode);
CREATE INDEX coll_idxOnCollname      ON universitylife_colleges
                                         (college_collegename);


# Indexes for table universitylife_departments
#
CREATE INDEX depts_idxOnDeptid       ON universitylife_departments
                                         (department_departmentdeptid);
CREATE INDEX coll_idxOnDeptcode      ON universitylife_deptartments
                                         (department_departmentdeptcode);
CREATE INDEX depts_idxOnDeptname     ON universitylife_deptartments
                                         (department_departmentdeptname);
CREATE INDEX depts_idxOnCollid       ON universitylife_deptartments
                                         (department_departmentcollid);


# Indexes for table universitylife_members
#
CREATE INDEX mems_idxOnAcctid        ON universitylife_members
                                         (member_accountid);
CREATE INDEX mems_idxOnAcctname      ON universitylife_members
                                         (member_accountname);
CREATE INDEX mems_idxOnUnivid        ON universitylife_members
                                         (member_universityid);
CREATE INDEX mems_idxOnMemcat        ON universitylife_members
                                         (member_membercategory);
CREATE INDEX mems_idxOnFname         ON universitylife_members
                                         (member_firstname);
CREATE INDEX mems_idxOnLname         ON universitylife_members
                                         (member_lastname);
CREATE INDEX mems_idxOnDeptid        ON universitylife_members
                                         (member_departmentid);
```

```
# Indexes for table universitylife_contactinfostaff
#
CREATE INDEX cis_idxOnCistaffid        ON universitylife_contactinfostaff
                                          (contactinfostaff_conactinfostaffid);
CREATE INDEX cis_idxOnMemid            on universitylife_contactinfostaff
                                          (contactinfostaff_memberid);

# Indexes for table universitylife_contactinfoother
#
CREATE INDEX cio_idxOnCiotherid        ON universitylife_contactinfoother
                                          (contactinfoother_contactinfootherid);
CREATE INDEX cio_idxOnMemid            ON universitylife_contactinfoother
                                          (contactinfoother_memberid);

# Indexes for table universitylife_available
#
CREATE INDEX avail_idxOnCid            ON universitylife_available
                                          (available_courseid);
CREATE INDEX avail_idxOnNum            ON universitylife_available
                                          (available_coursenumber);
CREATE INDEX avail_idxOnName           ON universitylife_available
                                          (available_name);
CREATE INDEX avail_idxOnDeptid         ON universitylife_available
                                          (available_departmentid);

# Indexes for table universitylife_teaching
#
CREATE INDEX tea_idxOnTeachid          ON universitylife_teaching
                                          (teaching_teachingid);
CREATE INDEX tea_idxOnMemprofid        ON universitylife_teaching
                                          (teaching_memberprofessorid);
CREATE INDEX tea_idxOnCid              ON universitylife_teaching
                                          (teaching_courseid);

# Indexes for table universitylife_taking
#
CREATE INDEX tak_idxOnTakid            ON universitylife_taking
                                          (taking_takeid);
CREATE INDEX tak_idxOnCid              ON universitylife_taking
                                          (taking_courseid);
CREATE INDEX tak_idxOnMemid            ON universitylife_taking
                                          (taking_memberid);

# Indexes for table universitylife_mailbox
#
CREATE INDEX mbox_idxOnMsgid           ON universitylife_mailbox
                                          (mailbox_messageid);
CREATE INDEX mbox_idxOnDatesent        ON universitylife_mailbox
                                          (mailbox_datesent);
CREATE INDEX mbox_idxOnFromid          ON universitylife_mailbox
                                          (mailbox_fromid);
```

```
        CREATE INDEX mbox_idxOnSubject      ON universitylife_mailbox
                                               (mailbox_subject);

        # Indexes for table universitylife_ messagecc
        #
        CREATE INDEX mcc_idxOnMsgccid       ON universitylife_messagecc
                                               (messagecc_messageccid);
        CREATE INDEX mcc_idxOnMsgid         ON universitylife_messagecc
                                               (messagecc_messageid);
        CREATE INDEX mcc_idxOnTomemid       ON universitylife_messagecc
                                               (messagecc_tomemberid);
        CREATE INDEX mcc_idxOnStatus        ON universitylife_messagecc
                                               (messagecc_status);

        # Indexes for table universitylife_messagelistmasters
        #
        CREATE INDEX mlm_idxOnListid        ON universitylife_messagelistmasters
                                               (messagelistmaster_listid);
        CREATE INDEX mlm_idxOnListcode      ON universitylife_messagelistmasters
                                               (messagelistmaster_listcode);
        CREATE INDEX mlm_idxOnListdesc      ON universitylife_messagelistmasters
                                               (messagelistmaster_listdescription);
        CREATE INDEX mlm_idxOnCollid        ON universitylife_messagelistmasters
                                               (messagelistmaster_collegeid);
        CREATE INDEX mlm_idxOnDeptid        ON universitylife_messagelistmasters
                                               (messagelistmaster_departmentid);

        # Indexes for table universitylife_messagelistdetails
        #
        CREATE INDEX mld_idxOnListdetid     ON universitylife_messagelistdetails
                                               (messagelistdetail_listdetailid);
        CREATE INDEX mld_idxOnListid        ON universitylife_messagelistdetails
                                               (messagelistdetail_listid);
        CREATE INDEX mld_idxOnMemid         ON universitylife_messagelistdetails
                                               (messagelistdetail_memberid);
```

Populating the Database

To populate the database, we need to import all of the XML files discussed previously (`colleges.xml`, `profs.xml`, and `students.xml`). After this import has been completed, the application is ready for use by students and professors. Further population of the database will be due to the sending of messages (this is not covered here).

Algorithms

There are a number of options to parse the XML documents and insert the data into the database; we can use SAX, DOM, XSLT, a Pull Parser, or other approaches. In this example, we'll use SAX because the XML documents that we'll be using can grow very large very quickly, and SAX is extremely efficient. Unlike DOM, for example, we aren't required to load the entire XML document into memory before we can begin parsing. For more information on using PHP with XML, see *Professional PHP 4 XML Programming* from *Wrox Press (ISBN 1-86100-721-3)*.

The following three sections describe the general SAX-based algorithms for parsing the three XML files from which we'll import the data necessary to populate the `universitylife` database.

Creating the All Members Mailing List

Before we start the import process, we want to create a mailing list that includes all members (students and professors) that are using the application. To accomplish this, we'll create a new record in the `universitylife_messagelistmasters` table each time a student or professor member is added to the `universitylife_members` table (described below).

Import Colleges, Departments, and Course Information

This step involves several sub-steps. The general algorithm is shown below:

```
1.   Define and declare an XML parser for the general document structure
     implied in colleges.xml.
2.   Define event handlers for a customized parser.
3.   Read colleges.xml.
4.   For each <college> element in this document:
     {
        4.1 Gather college information
        4.2 Generate any implied/missing information
        4.3 Insert a "college" record into the universitylife_colleges
            table
        4.4 Create a mailing list for students of this college:
            -- Insert a "master list" record into the
               universitylife_messagelistmasters table
        4.5 Create a mailing list of professors of this college:
            -- Insert a "master list" record into the
               universitylife_messagelistmasters table
        4.6 For each <dept> element in this college:
            {
            4.6.1 Gather department information
            4.6.2 Generate any implied/missing info
            4.6.3 Insert a 'department' record into the
                  universitylife_deptartments table
            4.6.4 Create a mailing list for students in this department
            4.6.5 Create a mailing list for professors in this department
            4.6.6 For each <course> element in this department:
                  {
                  4.6.6.1 Gather course info
                  4.6.6.2 Generate implied/missing info
                  4.6.6.3 Insert a 'course' record into the
                          universitylife_available table
                  4.6.6.4 Create a mailing list of students enrolled in
                          this course
                  }
            }
     }
```

The names for the mailing lists (`messagelistmaster_listcode` values in the `universitylife_messagelistmasters` table) are generated as follows. Each mailing list name consists of three parts:

- ❏ A three-letter code identifying the list as being specific to a college (`col`), department (`dep`), or course (`crs`), followed by an underscore character.

- ❏ A three-letter code specifying that the list consists of professors (`edu`) or students (`stu`), followed by an underscore character.

- ❏ A short alphabetic or alphanumeric string specific to the college, department, or course to which the list belongs. This value will be one of the following depending upon what sort of list is being created:

  - ❏ The `college_collegecode` value from the corresponding record in the `universitylife_colleges` table

  - ❏ The `department_departmentcode` value from the relevant `universitylife_departments` table

  - ❏ The `available_coursenumber` column value for the corresponding record in the `universitylife_available` table

For example, the name of the mailing list for all students currently taking the course in Qi Gong is `crs_stu_AlMed001`, the mailing list for all professors in the College of Science is named `col_edu_Sci`, and so on. Note that the master mailing list to which all members belong is named `uni_all_mems`.

Import Professor Information

This step involves importing `profs.xml` and creating the necessary database records. The general algorithm for the import is shown below:

```
1.  Define event handlers for a customized parser.
2.  Read in profs.xml.
3.  For each <member> element:
    {
    3.1  Gather "member" information
    3.2  Gather "contact" information (<cistaff> element)
    3.3  Gather "courses teaching" information (<teaching> element)
    3.4  Generate any implied/missing information
    3.5  Insert a "member" record into the universitylife_members table
    3.6  Retrieve the new member ID for use in several steps below.
    3.7  Insert a 'contact information' record into the
         universitylife_contactinfostaff table.
         Use the new member ID as one of the fields, to tie the
         universitylife_members and universitylife_contactinfostaff tables
         together.
    3.8  Add this professor to the mailing list of the department to
         which he or she belongs.
    3.9  Add this professor to the mailing list for the college to which
         he or she belongs. We do this by first looking up the college
         record (in the universitylife_colleges table) for the
         department to which he belongs (as in step 3.8). The college
         code hints at the mailing list name. We search the
         universitylife_messagelistmaster table for the mailing list ID
         and use the ID value to insert a 'detail' record for this
         professor into the universitylife_messagelistdetails table.
```

3.10 Add this professor to 'all-members' mailing list by inserting an appropriate record into the universitylife_messagelistdetails table.

3.11 For each <course> element in the <teaching> parent element:

```
{
    3.11.1 Collect course information.
    3.11.2 Retrieve the corresponding course record from the
           universitylife_available table. Use the course ID and
           professor's member ID to insert a 'teaching course'
           record into the universitylife_teaching table.
}
}
```

Import Student Information

This step involves importing the students.xml file and creating the appropriate database records. The process is very similar to the one for importing professor information. The general algorithm is shown below:

```
1. Define event handlers for a customized parser.
2. Read in students.xml.
3. For each <member> element:
{
    3.1  Gather "member" information.
    3.2  Gather "contact" information (<ciother> element).
    3.3  Gather "courses taking" information (<taking> element).
    3.4  Generate any implied/missing information.
    3.5  Insert a 'member' record into the universitylife_members table.
    3.6  Retrieve the new member ID for use where required below.
    3.7  Insert a "contact information" record into the
    universitylife_contactinfoother table.
    Use the new member ID as one of the fields, to tie the
    universitylife_members and universiytlife_contactinfostaff tables
    together.
    3.8  Add this student to the mailing list of the department they are
         majoring in.
    3.9  Add this student to the mailing list for the college they
         belong to. We do this by first looking up the college record
         (in the universitylife_colleges table) to which the department
         (step 3.8) belongs. We search the
         universitylife_messagelistmasters table for the mailing list ID
         and use this ID value to insert a 'detail' record for this
         student into the universitylife_messagelistdetails table.
    3.10 Add this student to the 'all-members' mailing list by inserting
         an appropriate record into the
         universitylife_messagelistdetails table.
    3.11 For each <course> element in the <taking> parent element:
    {
        3.11.1 Collect course information.
        3.11.2 Retrieve the corresponding course record from the
               universitylife_available table . Use the course ID
               and student's member ID (that is, the account ID) to
               insert a 'taking course' record into the
               universitylife_taking table.
    }
}
```

PHP Code: Importing Existing Information

The following sub-sections cover the necessary front-end PHP code to import the XML files discussed earlier.

All the back-end database access code is covered in a later section called *UnivLife API Code*.

Miscellaneous code such as global variables and class definition code is provided in a section called *Miscellaneous PHP Code*.

> *These code files are available with the code bundle, which can be downloaded from the book's page on the Wrox web site.*

All-Members Mailing List

Before we import the existing data, we want to create a mailing list that will include all members (students and professors) that will use the application in a given semester. The code below shows the front-end PHP code necessary to do this:

```php
<?php

// FILE: cr_allmem_mlist.php
//
include("common.php");

// Main code
$mlinfo["listcode"] = "uni_all_mems";
$mlinfo["listdesc"] = "All members in university";
$mlinfo["collid"]   = 0; # Entire university
$mlinfo["deptid"]   = 0; # No particular department

$api->CreateMailingList($mlinfo); # Defined in "univlifeapi.php"
?>
```

Here is the output of the script on a web browser:

```
mailing list:
array(4) {
  ["listcode"]=>
  string(12) "uni_all_mems"
  ["listdesc"]=>
  string(25) "All members in university"
  ["collid"]=>
  int(0)
  ["deptid"]=>
  int(0)
}

[dbg(mlistm)]: [INSERT INTO universitylife_messagelistmasters (messagelistmaster_listid, messagelistmaster_listcode, messagelistmaster_listdescription, messagelistmaster_collegeid, messagelistmaster_departmentid) VALUES (79,'uni_all_mems','All members in university',0, 0) ]
[dbg(mlistm)]: listid=0
```

The code depends on global variables that are defined in one or more of the include files called from common.php. Since we are developing a prototype application that will presumably be run only in a controlled environment, we are permitting ourselves the luxury of performing only minimal error checking in any of the support code (as we'll see later).

> **When using these scripts from a web browser, include the following lines at the top to prevent the browser from caching the page and doing nothing when one wants to import an XML file:**
>
> ```
> header("Expires: Mon, 26 Jul 1997 05:00:00 GMT");
> header("Last-Modified: ". gmdate("D, d M Y H:i:s") ." GMT");
> header("Cache-Control: no-store, no-cache, must-revalidate");
> header("Cache-Control: post-check=0, pre-check=0", false);
> header("Pragma: no-cache");
> ```
>
> **Alternativley, be sure to clear the browser cache manually after each use.**

Colleges, Departments, and Courses

This step involves parsing an XML file (colleges.xml), followed by inserting appropriate database records. As of PHP 4.0, the Expat XML parser comes as part of the standard PHP source and binary distributions.

The XML/Expat functions in PHP represent an event-driven methodology. We define a customized parser to surround the basic parse functions by defining and declaring user-defined event handler functions. Each time a specific XML event occurs (a start tag, an end tag, character data, entity references, processing instructions, and so on) control is passed to the appropriate event handler function. These event handlers are also known as **callback functions**.

> *Refer to Chapter 5 of Professional PHP4 XML from Wrox Press (ISBN 1-86100-721-3) for more information about the Expat parser and its functions.*

The colleges.xml file has a unique set of tags matching the names of most of the columns in the universitylife_colleges, universitylife_departments, and universitylife_available tables. Each starting and ending tag triggers some action in the XML parser defined in the PHP script add_colleges.php. With all start tags, some global flags are set and a global stack is pushed with the tag name. Depending on the tag name, the start tag may trigger additional actions, which are handled by the switch statement in the StartElementHandler() function. In some cases, the end tag triggers actions, which are handled by the switch statement in the EndElementHandler() function. In all cases, a close tag causes the global flags to be unset and the global stack to be popped.

The table below shows the actions taken upon encountering each type of tag in colleges.xml.

The implicit actions for all start tags are:

❑   set global flags

❑   push the global stack

❑   save tag attributes (if any)

The implicit actions for all end tags are:

- ❏ unset the flags
- ❏ pop the stack

The 'Explicit Actions' column refers to actions taken due to encountering a specific start/end tag:

Event Trigger	Explicit Actions
`<colleges>`	None, as this is the root element.
`<college>`	Collect and extrapolate college information.
	Insert a record into the `universitylife_colleges` table.
	Create a mailing list for all students of the college.
	Create a mailing list for all professors of the college.
`<dept>`	Collect and extrapolate department information.
	Insert a record into the `universitylife_departments` table.
	Create a mailing list for all students of the department.
	Create a mailing list for all professors of the department.
`<course>`	None. The attributes are implicitly saved.
`<desc>`	None. The character data is saved via the `CDataHandler()` function.

Event Trigger	Explicit Actions
`</desc>`	The course description is passed on to the currently open `<course>` element.
`</course>`	Extrapolate information for available courses.
	Insert a record into the `universitylife_available` table.
	Create a mailing list for 'all students of this course'.
`</dept>`	None.
`</colleges>`	None.

The following PHP code imports the `colleges.xml` file into the new application's database, using the event trigger information:

```php
<?php
//
// FILE: add_colleges.php
// USE:  Import colleges.xml and insert the necessary database records
```

Include the common.php file where we create an instance of the API class that will be used to access the database. The common.php file has information about the database, host, user, and password to use, as well as the names of the XML files to import:

```php
include("common.php");
```

Set names of different types of the user-defined event handler (callback) functions:

```php
$handlers["start"]   = "StartElementHandler";
$handlers["end"]     = "EndElementHandler";
$handlers["default"] = "DefaultHandler";
$handlers["cdata"]   = "CDataHandler";
```

Define the handler that is used when a start tag is encountered:

```php
function StartElementHandler($parser, $tagname, $attrs)
{
    global $flg;
    global $elem;
    global $stack;
    global $curcollid;
    global $curdeptid;
    global $api;
```

For all start tags, set a tag flag, and push the tagname onto a stack:

```php
$flg[$tagname] = true;
array_push($stack,$tagname);
```

> **The flags are not used in any of the code. They are only shown for example's sake.**

For all tags having attributes, save the attributes into a data structure:

```php
if (count($attrs)) {
    // Save attributes, if any
    foreach ($attrs as $attrname => $value) {
        $elem[$tagname][$attrname] = $value;
    }
}
```

Now we perform the tagname-specific actions:

```php
switch ($tagname) {
```

For an occurrence of `<college>`, create a record in the `universitylife_colleges` table, and then create two mailing lists. The first list will contain all students in a particular college. The second list will contain all professors in the same college:

```
case "college":
    // Opening college element, <college>

    // Add a record to table "universitylife_colleges"
    $curcollid =$api->InsertCollegeRecord($elem[$tagname]);

    // Create various mailing lists

    // Function DefMaillist()defined below

    $collcode = $elem[$tagname]["collcode"];
    $desc = "All students in college $collcode";
    DefMaillist("col",$collcode,"stu",$desc,$curcollid,0);
    $desc = "All profs in college $collcode";
    DefMaillist("col",$collcode,"edu",$desc,$curcollid,0);

    break;
```

For an occurrence of the `<dept>` tag, create a record in the `universitylife_departments` table, and then create two mailing lists. The first list will contain all students in this department. The second list will contain all the professors in the same department:

```
case "dept":
    // Opening department element, <dept>
    // Add a record to table "universitylife_departments"

    $elem[$tagname]["collid"] = $curcollid;
    $curdeptid =$api->InsertDeptRecord($elem[$tagname]);

    // Create various mailing lists
    $deptcode = $elem[$tagname]["deptcode"];
    $desc = "All students in dept $deptcode";
    DefMaillist("dep",$deptcode,"stu",$desc,$curcollid,$curdeptid);
    $desc = "All profs in dept $deptcode";
    DefMaillist("dep",$deptcode,"edu",$desc,$curcollid,$curdeptid);

    break;

    default:
        break;
    }
} // end function StartElementHandler()
```

Define the data necessary to create a record in the `universitylife_messagelistmasters` table:

```
function DefMaillist($prfx,$collcode,$memcat,$desc,$collid,$deptid)
{
    global $api;

    $mlinfo["listcode"] = $prfx."_".$memcat."_".$collcode; //Ex.,
                            col_stu_HeSp
    $mlinfo["listdesc"] = $desc;
    $mlinfo["collid"]   = $collid;
    $mlinfo["deptid"]   = $deptid;

    $api->CreateMailingList($mlinfo); // Defined in "univlifeapi.php"
}
// end function DefMaillist()
```

Define the handler that is used when an end tag is encountered:

```
function EndElementHandler($parser, $tagname)
{
    global $flg;
    global $elem;
    global $stack;
    global $curcollid;
    global $curdeptid;
    global $api;
```

Do tagname-specific actions first:

```
    switch ($tagname) {
```

If a `</course>` tag is encountered, insert a record into the `universitylife_available` table:

```
    case "course":
        // Closing </course> tag
        // Add a record to table "universitylife_available".
        //By this point, we have already read in the corresponding <desc>
        //element.

        $elem[$tagname]["deptid"] = $curdeptid;
        $api->InsertAvailCourseRecord($elem[$tagname]);
        // Create mailing list for students of this course

        $num = $elem[$tagname]["num"];
        $desc = "All students in course $num";
        DefMaillist("crs",$num,"stu",$desc,$curcollid,$curdeptid);
        break;
```

If a `</desc>` tag is encountered, save information about the course description for the currently open `<course>` element. This information is extracted by the `CDataHandler()` function:

```
    case "desc": // Closing </desc> tag
        // Assign course description to the currently open <course>
        // element
        $elem["course"]["desc"] = $elem["desc"]["__cdata__"];
        break;

    default:
        break;
}
```

For all closing tags that we encounter, pop the tagname stack; set the tag flag to false, and unset the current element's data structure:

```
    array_pop($stack);
    $flg[$tagname] = false;
    unset($elem[$tagname]);

} // end function EndElementHandler
```

Define the event handler function for character data (that is, textual data between two tags). Note that because of the way the XML/Expat functions work, every time a newline character is encountered, a call to the function below is triggered. So we need to check and see if there is some useful CDATA. If there is, we save it to the currently open tag (as indicated by the top of the tagname stack):

```
function CDataHandler($parser, $cdata)
{
    // Save cdata (character data) for the currently open element.
    global $flg;
    global $elem;
    global $stack;

    // Get rid of extraneous newline or tab characters
    $cdata = eregi_replace("[\t\n]+", "", $cdata);

    // Get rid of excess blanks
    $cdata = trim($cdata);
    if (strcmp($cdata,"") != 0)
    {
        // There is still character data left. Since there can be several
        // pieces of cdata within a single element (due to the way that
        // the XML/Expat parser works), we want to concatenate the text in
        //  $cdata to the current element's character data.

        $openelem = $stack[count($stack)-1];
        // We don't want to pop the stack
        $elem[$openelem]["__cdata__"] .= $cdata;
    }
} // end function CDataHandler()
```

Finally, we need to define an event handler function to take care of any remaining types of XML events. In this case, we do not have any tasks to perform, so the function body is empty:

```
function DefaultHandler($parser, $data)
{
    // do nothing
}// end function DefaultHandler()
```

Create an XML parser resource and pass the information back through global variables. We do not want tag names to be 'folded' into uppercase, so we set the case option to zero. After this, we declare all the event handlers we'll want to use for different types of XML events:

```
function DefineXmlParser()
{
    global $handlers;
    global $caseflag; // Set this here
    global $parser;   // Set this here

    $parser = xml_parser_create();
    $caseflag = xml_parser_set_option($parser, XML_OPTION_CASE_FOLDING,
                                      0);
    xml_set_element_handler($parser,$handlers["start"],$handlers["end"]);
    xml_set_character_data_handler($parser, $handlers["cdata"]);
    xml_set_default_handler($parser, $handlers["default"]);
}
// end function DefineXmlParser()
```

The main code initializes some variables, opens a database connection, and then reads the input XML file and parses it. Every time an XML event occurs, as defined in the function above, control is passed to the appropriate event handler function:

```
// Main code
$elem = array();
$stack = array();
DefineXmlParser();

if (!$parser) {
    die("Error defining ML parser resource.<br />\n");
}

// Read in the input file all at once
$markup = GetFile($files["colleges"]); // Defined in common.php

if (!xml_parse($parser, $markup, 1))  { // Single block of XML markup
    $errcode  = xml_get_error_code($parser);
    $errstring = xml_error_string($errcode);
    $linenum  = xml_get_current_line_number($parser);
    die("XML parse error ($errcode): $errstring at line $linenum");
}

xml_parser_free($parser);
?>
```

The above code populates the `universitylife_colleges`, `universitylife_departments`, `universitylife_available`, and `universitylife_messagelistmasters` tables.

Here is a sample of the output of the script on a web browser:

```
college:
array(2) {
  ["collcode"]=>
  string(4) "HeSp"
  ["collname"]=>
  string(21) "Health + Spirituality"
}

mailing list:
array(4) {
  ["listcode"]=>
  string(12) "col_stu_HeSp"
  ["listdesc"]=>
  string(28) "All students in college HeSp"
  ["collid"]=>
  int(4)
  ["deptid"]=>
  int(0)
}

[dbg(mlistm)]: [INSERT INTO universitylife_messagelistmasters (messagelistmaster_listid, messagelistmaster_listcode, messagelistmaster_listdescription, messagelistmaster_collegeid, messagelistmaster_departmentid) VALUES (81,'col_stu_HeSp','All students in college HeSp',4, 0) ]
[dbg(mlistm)]: listid=0
```

Professors

The file `prof.xml` has a set of unique tags matching most of the columns in the `universitylife_members`, `universitylife_cistaff`, and `universitylife_teaching` tables. Like in the case of `colleges.xml`, each start and end tag in `profs.xml` triggers some action.

As before, these triggers are handled by the functions `StartElementHandler()` and `EndElementHandler()`, as appropriate. We have also used entity references to define departments and courses. These entity references serve as triggers that are handled by the `DefaultHandler()` function. As before, character data triggers are handed by the `CDataHandler()` function.

The implicit actions taken upon encountering start or end tags are the same as before. The following table shows the explicit actions taken for various event triggers:

Event Trigger	Explicit Actions
`<members>`	None (root element).
`<member>`	Create a `member` data structure to collect information in, until the closing `</members>` tag is encountered. Save the element's `memcat` attribute.
`<univid>`	None.
`univid cdata`	Extract `cdata` (character data) for the `<univid>` element and save it.
`</univid>`	Pass on `cdata` to the currently open `<member>` element.
`<fname>`	None.
`fname cdata`	Extract `cdata` for the `<fname>` element and save it.
`</fname>`	Pass on `cdata` to the currently open `<member>` element.
`<lname>`	None.
`lname cdata`	Extract `cdata` for the `<lname>` element and save it.
`</lname>`	Pass on `cdata` to the currently open `<member>` element.
`<dept>`	None.
`&deptcode;`	For example, `&NwPh;`. Look up the department code, `department_departmentcode`, in the `universitylife_departments` table, and retrieve the department ID, `department_departmentid`.
`</dept>`	Pass on the department ID to the currently open `<member>` element.
`<cistaff>`	None.
`<bldng>`	None.
`bldng cdata`	Extract `cdata` for the `<bldng>` element and save it.
`</bldng>`	Pass on `cdata` to the currently open `<member>` element.
`<office>`	None.
`office cdata`	Extract `cdata` for the `<lname>` element and save it.
`</office>`	Pass on `cdata` to the currently open `<member>` element.
`<ext>`	None.

Table continued on following page

Event Trigger	Explicit Actions
`ext cdata`	Extract `cdata` for the `<ext>` element and save it.
`</ext>`	Pass on `cdata` to the currently open `<member>` element.
`<hrsavail>`	None.
`hrsavail cdata`	Extract `cdata` for the `<hrsavail>` element and save it.
`</hrsavail>`	Pass on `cdata` to the currently open `<member>` element.
`</cistaff>`	None.
`<teaching>`	None.
`<course>`	None.
`&cnum;`	For example `&NwPh001;`. Look up the course number, `available_coursenumber`, in the `universitylife_available` table, and retrieve the course ID, `available_courseid`, and the owning department ID, `department_departmentid`. The course may belong to one department, but a professor from another department may teach it.
`</course>`	Pass on the course and owning department ID to the currently open `<member>` element.
`</teaching>`	None.
`</member>`	Define the member information, that is, include this professor's department ID.
	Insert a record into the `universitylife_members` table. Retrieve the resulting member id (`memid`) for use in other actions.
	Define the contact information for the staff. Insert a record into the `universitylife_contactinfostaff` table.
	Look up the college ID of the college that this professor is part of.
	Look up the ID of the mailing list for 'all professors of this college'. Add this professor to the mailing list by inserting a record into the `universitylife_messagelistdetails` table.
	Using the department code value retrieved earlier as `$deptcode` from the entity reference '`&deptcode;`', look up the mailing list ID for all professors in this department. Add this professor to the mailing list by inserting a record into the `universitylife_messagelistdetails` table.
	For each `<course>` element saved, create a record in the `universitylife_teaching` table using the course ID and this professor's member ID.
`</members>`	None.

The following PHP code imports the profs.xml file into the new application's database, using the event trigger information shown. Much of the custom parsing code has been either directly borrowed or adapted from add_colleges.php:

```php
<?php
//
// FILE: add_profs.php
// USE:  Import profs.xml and create appropriate database records
//
include("common.php");

$handlers["start"]   = "StartElementHandler";
$handlers["end"]     = "EndElementHandler";
$handlers["default"] = "DefaultHandler";
$handlers["cdata"]   = "CDataHandler";

function StartElementHandler($parser, $tagname, $attrs)
{
    global $flg;
    global $elem;
    global $stack;
    global $member;
    global $courses;
    global $curcollid;
    global $curdeptid;

    // Only one start tag needs to be checked for.

    $flg[$tagname] = true;
    array_push($stack,$tagname);
```

We cannot insert records until the </member> close tag is encountered. So we need to save tag attributes and character data as we encounter it:

```php
    switch ($tagname) {
    case "member": // Opening member element, <member>
        // Initialize a "member" data structure
        $member["memcat"] = $attrs["memcat"];
        break;

    case "teaching": // Opening <teaching> tag
        // Initialize course array for current <member> element
        $courses = array();
        break;
    }
} // end function StartElementHandler()

function EndElementHandler($parser, $tagname)
{
    global $flg;
    global $elem;
    global $stack;
    global $member;
```

```
global $courses;
global $curcollid;
global $curdeptid;
global $api;

// The cases are listed in the expected order of tag occurrence in
// the input XML file.

switch ($tagname) {
case "univid": // Closing </univid> tag
    // Assign university ID to the currently open <member> element
    $member["univid"] = $elem["univid"]["__cdata__"];
    break;

case "fname": // Closing </fname> tag
    // Assign first name to the currently open <member> element
    $member["fname"] = $elem["fname"]["__cdata__"];
    break;

case "lname": // Closing </lname> tag
    // Assign last name to the currently open <member> element
    $member["lname"] = $elem["lname"]["__cdata__"];
    break;

case "dept": // Closing </dept> tag
    // The department is conveyed using a field marker in the form
    // of "__deptcode__" E.g., "__NwPh__".

    // Given the department code stored from the field marker of
    // <dept>, lookup the department ID. Save it to the currently
    // open <member>.
    //
    $deptcode = $elem[$tagname]["__lookup__"];

    // Target table to look in
    $info["tgtTable"] = "universitylife_departments";

    // Target column to retrieve
    $info["tgtCol"]   = "department_departmentid";

    // Criterion column to test
    $info["critCol"]  = "department_departmentcode";

    // Criterion value to test
    $info["critVal"]  = $deptcode;

    // $deptid = $api->get_1fldval($info);
    $deptid = $api->GetSingleFieldValue($info);
    $member["deptcode"] = $deptcode;
    $member["deptid"]   = $deptid;
    break;

case "bldng": // Closing </bldng> tag
    // Assign building name to the currently open <member> element
```

```
        $member["bldng"] = $elem["bldng"]["__cdata__"];
        break;

    case "office": // Closing </office> tag
        // Assign office // to the currently open <member> element
        $member["office"] = $elem["office"]["__cdata__"];
        break;

    case "ext": // Closing </ext> tag
        // Assign phone extension to the currently open <member> element
        $member["ext"] = $elem["ext"]["__cdata__"];
        break;

    case "hrsavail": // Closing </hrsavail> tag
        // Assign "hours available" to the currently open <member> element
        $member["hrsavail"] = $elem["hrsavail"]["__cdata__"];
        break;

    case "course": // Closing </course> tag
        // The course is conveyed using a field marker in the form
        // of "__num__" E.g., "__NwPh003__".
        //
        // Given the course number stored from the field marker of
        // <course>, lookup the course ID and the dept ID. Save it to the
        // global $courses array.

        $num = $elem[$tagname]["__lookup__"];
        $info["tgtTable"] = "universitylife_available";
        // Target table to look in
        $info["tgtCol1"]  = "available_courseid";
        // Target column 1 to retrieve
        $info["tgtCol2"]  = "available_departmentid";
        // Target column 2 to retrieve
        $info["critCol"]  = "available_coursenumber";
        // Criterion column to test
        $info["critVal"]  = $num;         // Criterion value to test

        $aaRes = $api->GetTwoFieldValues($info);
        $cid = $aaRes["available_courseid"]; // Course ID
        $courses["$cid"]["deptid"] = $aaRes["available_departmentid"];
        // Course department ID
        $courses["$cid"]["num"]    = $num;
        break;

    case "member": // Closing </member> tag
        $acctid = $api->InsertMemberRecord($member);
        $member["acctid"] = $acctid;
        $cistaffid = $api->InsertCistaffRecord($member);

        // Add professor member to various mailing lists
        // (see univlifeapi.php)
        $deptcode = $member["deptcode"];
        print "[dbg(&lt;/member&gt;)]: deptcode=[$deptcode]<br>\n";
        $api->AddMemToMlist("uni_all_mems",$acctid);
```

61

```
            $api->AddMemToMlist("dep_edu_".$deptcode,$acctid);
            $listcode = $api->GetCollMlistCodeForDeptcode($deptcode,"edu");
            $api->AddMemToMlist($listcode,$acctid);

            // Add <course> elements to table "teaching"
            foreach ($courses as $scid => $course) {
                $course["cid"]       = $scid;
                $course["memprofid"] = $acctid;
                $api->InsertTeachingRecord($course);
            }
            break;

        default:
            break;
    }

    array_pop($stack);
    $flg[$tagname] = false;
    unset($elem[$tagname]);

} // end function EndElementHandler()

function CDataHandler($parser, $cdata)
{
    // Save cdata (character data) for currently open element.

    global $flg;
    global $elem;
    global $stack;

    // Get rid of extraneous newline or tab characters
    $cdata = eregi_replace("[\t\n]+", "", $cdata);

    // Get rid of excess blanks
    $cdata = trim($cdata);

    if($cdata != "") {
        // There is still character data left.  Since there can be
        // several pieces of cdata within a single element (due to the
        // way that the XML/expat parser works), we want to concatenate
        // the text in $cdata to the current element's character data.

    $openelem = $stack[count($stack)-1];
```

We don't want to pop the stack. If we are inside a <dept> or <course> element, the cdata will be in the form of a field marker (a department code or course number string value surrounded by double underscores). Also, we need to save the string without the underscores. For any other tag, we just have to save the character data:

```
            // Are we in <dept> or <course>?
            if ($openelem == "dept" || $openelem == "course") {
                if (substr($cdata, 0, 2) == "__" && substr($cdata, -2, 2)
                                == "__") {
                    // $cdata contains a field marker of the form "__NwPh__"
```

```php
                        // Save the dept codee (without the start and end
                        // underscores)
                        $elem[$openelem]["__lookup__"] =
                                                 substr($cdata,2,strlen($cdata)-4);
                } else {
                        $elem[$openelem]["__lookup__"] .= $cdata;
                }
        } else {
                        $elem[$openelem]["__cdata__"] .= $cdata;
        }
    }
} // end function CDataHandler()

function DefaultHandler($parser, $data)
{
    // Do nothing
}

function DefineXmlParser()
{
    global $handlers;
    global $caseflag; // Set this here
    global $parser;   // Set this here

    $parser = xml_parser_create();
    $caseflag = xml_parser_set_option($parser, XML_OPTION_CASE_FOLDING, 0);
    xml_set_element_handler($parser,$handlers["start"],$handlers["end"]);
    xml_set_character_data_handler($parser, $handlers["cdata"]);
    xml_set_default_handler($parser, $handlers["default"]);

} // end function DefineXmlParser()

// Main code
$elem = array();
$stack = array();
DefineXmlParser();

if (!$parser) {
    die("Error defining ML parser resource.<br>\n");
}

// Read in the input file all at once
$markup = GetFile($files["profs"]);

if (!xml_parse($parser, $markup, 1))  { // Single block of XML markup
    $errcode   = xml_get_error_code($parser);
    $errstring = xml_error_string($errcode);
    $linenum   = xml_get_current_line_number($parser);
    die("XML parse error ($errcode): $errstring at line $linenum");
}
xml_parser_free($parser);

?>
```

The above code populates the `universitylife_members`, `universitylife_cistaff`, `universitylife_teaching`, and `universitylife_messagelistdetails` tables.

Here is a sample of the output of the script on a web browser:

```
member:
array(11) {
  ["memcat"]=>
  string(3) "edu"
  ["univid"]=>
  string(8) "UL000001"
  ["fname"]=>
  string(5) "Basil"
  ["lname"]=>
  string(6) "Fawlty"
  ["deptcode"]=>
  string(4) "Spir"
  ["deptid"]=>
  string(1) "8"
  ["bldng"]=>
  string(13) "Fawlty Towers"
  ["office"]=>
  string(3) "301"
  ["ext"]=>
  string(3) "301"
  ["hrsavail"]=>
  string(7) "1pm-3pm"
  ["acctid"]=>
  int(11)
}

[dbg(cistaff)]: [INSERT INTO universitylife_contactinfostaff (contactinfostaff_contactinfostaffid, contactinfostaff_building, contactinfostaff_office, contactinfostaff_extension, contactinfostaff_hoursavailable, contactinfostaff_memberid) VALUES (4,'Fawlty Towers', '301', 301, '1pm-3pm', 11) ]
[dbg(</member>)]: deptcode=[Spir]
```

Students

The event triggers for adding students are very similar to those for adding professors. Thus, the PHP code for adding students is very similar to the code for adding professors. However, instead of trying to generalize code that will work for both types of members, let's keep things simple by copying `add_profs.php` to `add_students.php`, and modifying the code as necessary for adding students:

```php
<?php
//
// FILE: add_students.php
// USE:  Import students.xml and create appropriate database records
//
include("common.php");

$handlers["start"]   = "StartElementHandler";
```

```php
function CDataHandler($parser, $cdata)
{
    // Save cdata (character data) for the currently open element.

    global $flg;
    global $elem;
    global $stack;

    // Get rid of the extraneous newline or tab characters
    $cdata = eregi_replace("[\t\n]+", "", $cdata);

    // Get rid of excess blanks
    $cdata = trim($cdata);

    if (strcmp($cdata,"") != 0) {
        // There is still character data left.  Since there can be
        // several pieces of cdata within a single element (due to the
        // way that the XML/Expat parser works), we want to concatenate
        // the text in $cdata to the current element's character data.

    $openelem = $stack[count($stack)-1]; // We don't want to pop the stack

        // Are we in <dept> or <course>?
        if ($openelem == "dept" || $openelem == "course") {
            if (substr($cdata, 0, 2) == "__" && substr($cdata, -2, 2)
                                    == "__") {
                // $cdata contains a field marker of the form "__NwPh__"

                // Save the dept codee (without the start and end
                // underscores)
                $elem[$openelem]["__lookup__"] =
                                    substr($cdata,2,strlen($cdata)-4);
            } else {
                $elem[$openelem]["__lookup__"] .= $cdata;
            }
        } else {
            $elem[$openelem]["__cdata__"] .= $cdata;
        }
    }
} // end function CDataHandler()


function DefaultHandler($parser, $data)
{
    // Do nothing
}

function DefineXmlParser()
{
    global $handlers;
    global $caseflag; // Set this here

    global $parser;   // Set this here

    $parser = xml_parser_create();
    $caseflag = xml_parser_set_option($parser, XML_OPTION_CASE_FOLDING,
                                    0);
    xml_set_element_handler($parser,$handlers["start"],$handlers["end"]);
    xml_set_character_data_handler($parser, $handlers["cdata"]);
```

```
        xml_set_default_handler($parser, $handlers["default"]);
} // end function DefineXmlParser()

// Main code

$elem = array();
$stack = array();
DefineXmlParser();

if (!$parser) {
    die("Error defining ML parser resource.<br>\n");
}

// Read in the input file all at once
$markup = GetFile($files["students"]);
if (!xml_parse($parser, $markup, 1))  { // Single block of XML markup
    $errcode   = xml_get_error_code($parser);
    $errstring = xml_error_string($errcode);
    $linenum   = xml_get_current_line_number($parser);
    die("XML parse error ($errcode): $errstring at line $linenum");
}
xml_parser_free($parser);

?>
```

The code populates the universitylife_members, universitylife_contactinfoother, universitylife_taking, and universitylife_messagelistdetails tables.

This is a sample of the output of the script in a web browser:

Univlife API Code

The PHP code in this section serves two purposes. The first purpose is to support database access needs while importing existing information (discussed above). The second purpose is to support some of the database access needs for the fully functioning University of Life application.

Additional functionality, such as the editing or deleting of database records, is not covered here. We are only covering that portion of the Application Programming Interface (API) that supports the 'import' steps discussed earlier. The API will be implemented as a PHP class and the database access will be done using PEAR::DB, this will allow us to change the DBMS if we want without changing our code. PEAR::DB is a database abstraction mechanism that is almost standarized among PHP applications today.

In this particular case study, using a database abstraction layer is important since the university might decide to migrate their old system to a new system using a relational database system. In this case, we just need to make a minor change or two to our database access code to use the university database instead of the one we've created for this case study (see our discussion of common.php below). The mailing list system should work without additional changes, provided we retain the same table and column names; of course the XML import/export process won't be needed:

```php
<?php
//
// FILE: univlifeapi.php
require_once('DB.php');
```

The constructor will be used to create an internal db object with the PEAR database connection handler; the handler will be used in the API to access the database. The debug member (we can build a SetDebug() method) will be used to turn on/off debug information; APIs shouldn't produce any output or side-effects since that can be very annoying for the calling application. In this example, debug is on by default so we will see the debug output when the script is run:

```php
// A class to access the database for Univ Life.
// You only have to instantiate an object of this class in order to use
// it.
class UnivLifeAPI
{
    var $db;  // The database connection handler;
    var $debug = 1;

    function UnivLifeAPI($host,$user,$pass,$db)
    {
```

If we change to a different RDBMS (say, PostgreSQL or Oracle instead of MySQL), we'll need to make a change here as well, replacing mysql in the data source name ($dsn) with the appropriate database indicator string (for example, pgsql or oci8):

```php
        $dsn = "mysql://$user:$pass@$host/$db";
        $this->db = DB::connect($dsn);
        if (DB::isError($this->db)) {
            die ($this->db->getMessage());
        }
    }
```

If the need should arise, we can produce a more verbose error message than that returned from getMessage() by calling the toString() method instead.

Insert a record into the universitylife_colleges table. All the necessary column information is passed to the function by way of the associative array, $elem:

```
function InsertCollegeRecord($elem)
{
    if($this->debug) {
        print "<pre>\n";
        print "<b>college</b>:\n";
        var_dump($elem);
        print "</pre>\n";
    }
```

Extract the information and build the INSERT query string:

```
$collcode = $elem["collcode"];
$collname = addslashes($elem["collname"]);
$id = $this->db->nextId('collidSeq');
$insquery  = "INSERT INTO universitylife_colleges
                (college_collegeid,college_collegecode,
                 college_collegename)
                VALUES ($id,'$collcode','$collname')";
```

Execute the INSERT query. If it is successful, retrieve and return the resulting record ID:

```
$resultset = $this->db->query($insquery);
if (DB::isError($resultset)) {
    $msg  = "Could not insert record into table
                universitylife_colleges: ";
    $msg .= $resultset->getMessage()."<br>\n";
    die($msg);
}
return($id);
}
```

Note how the PEAR method nextId() was used to obtain an ID for the college_collegeid column. We can then return the id we will use. Of course we have to make sure that all the APIs or methods inserting records into the table are using the sequence to prevent two inserts with the same ID.

Insert a record into the universitylife_departments table. The information that goes into this record is passed via the associative array, $elem:

```
// Using the current <dept> element, insert a record into
// table "universitylife_departments". Add appropriate records for
// mailing lists.
function InsertDeptRecord($elem)
{
    if($this->debug) {
```

```
        print "<pre>\n";
        print "<b>dept</b>:\n";
        var_dump($elem);
        print "</pre>\n";
    }

    $deptcode = addslashes($elem["deptcode"]);
    $deptname = addslashes($elem["deptname"]);
    $collid   = $elem["collid"];
    $id = $this->db->nextId('deptidSeq');
    $insquery  = "INSERT INTO universitylife_departments
                    (department_departmentid,department_departmentcode,
                    department_departmentname,department_collegeid)
                    VALUES ($id,'$deptcode','$deptname',$collid)";

    $resultset = $this->db->query($insquery);
    if (DB::isError($resultset)) {
        $msg  = "Could not insert record into table
                universitylife_departments: ";
        $msg .= $resultset->getMessage()."<br>\n";
        die($msg);
    }
```

For development code, use of the die() function is often sufficient, but for deployment purposes we would need to replace this with something that's more user-friendly.

```
    return($id);
} // end function InsertDeptRecord()
```

Insert a record into the universitylife_available table. As above, the information that goes into this record gets passed to the method handling the INSERT via the associative array, $elem:

```
// Using the current <course> element, insert a record into
// table "universitylife_available". Add appropriate records for
// mailing lists.
function InsertAvailCourseRecord($elem)
{
    if($this->debug) {
        print "<pre>\n";
      print "<b>course</b>:\n";
      var_dump($elem);
        print "</pre>\n";
    }

    $num     = $elem["num"];
    $name    = addslashes($elem["name"]);
    $cdesc   = addslashes($elem["desc"]);
    $deptid  = $elem["deptid"];

    $id = $this->db->nextId('cidSeq');
```

```
        $insquery = "INSERT INTO universitylife_available
                       (available_courseid,available_coursenumber,
                        available_name,available_coursedescription,
                        available_departmentid)
                       VALUES ($id,'$num','$name','$cdesc',$deptid)";
        print "[dbg(courses)]: [$insquery]<br>\n";

        $resultset = $this->db->query($insquery);
        if (DB::isError($resultset)) {
            $msg  = "Could not insert record into table
                    universitylife_available: ";
            $msg .= $resultset->getMessage()."<br>\n";
            die($msg);
        }
        return($id);
    } // end function InsertAvailCourseRecord()
```

Once again we use the associative array $mlinfo to pass the data to the method called to insert a new record into the universitylife_messagelistmasters table:

```
// Insert a record into table "universitylife_messagelistmasters" to
// create a new mailing list.
function CreateMailingList($mlinfo)
{
    $listid = 0;
    if($this->debug) {
        print "<pre>\n";
        print "<b>mailing list</b>:\n";
        var_dump($mlinfo);
        print "</pre>\n";
    }

    $listcode = addslashes($mlinfo["listcode"]);
    $listdesc = addslashes($mlinfo["listdesc"]);
    $collid = $mlinfo["collid"];
    $deptid = $mlinfo["deptid"];
    $id = $this->db->nextId('listidSeq');

    $insquery  = "INSERT INTO universitylife_messagelistmasters
                    (messagelistmaster_listid,
                     messagelistmaster_listcode,
                     messagelistmaster_listdescription,
                     messagelistmaster_collegeid,
                     messagelistmaster_departmentid)
                    VALUES ";
    $insquery .= "($id,'$listcode','$listdesc',$collid, $deptid) ";

    print "[dbg(mlistm)]: [$insquery]<br>\n";
    $id = $this->db->nextId('listidSeq');
    $resultset = $this->db->query($insquery);
    if (DB::isError($resultset)) {
        $msg  = "Could not insert record into table
                universitylife_messagelistmasters: ";
```

```
            $msg .= $resultset->getMessage()."<br>\n";
            die($msg);
        }
        if($this->debug) print "[dbg(mlistm)]: listid=$listid<br>\n";
        return($listid);
    } // end function CreateMailingList
```

Next we write a function that gets the value of a particular column in a given database table, and uses the name of this column to build a WHERE clause for the SQL query string. This function provides a generic way to retrieve a single field, given a single condition:

```
function GetSingleFieldValue($info)
{
    // Given a target table name $table, and one criterion,
    // ('$critCol' = $critVal), get the value of the target
    // column name. We'll make the assumption that only one
    // resultset row will occur.

    $table   = $info["tgtTable"];
    $tgtCol  = $info["tgtCol"];
    $critCol = $info["critCol"];
    $critVal = $info["critVal"];

    $sqlquery  = "SELECT * FROM $table WHERE ";
    if (is_int($critVal)) {
        $sqlquery .= "$critCol = $critVal ";
    } elseif (is_string($critVal)) {
        $sqlquery .= "$critCol = \"$critVal\" ";
    } elseif (is_bool($critVal)) {
        $sqlquery .= "$critCol = \"$critVal\" ";
    } else { // float
        $sqlquery .= "$critCol = $critVal ";
    }

    $results = $this->db->query($sqlquery);

    if (DB::isError($results)) {
        $msg  = "Get single field value->Could perform query:
                $sqlquery: ";
        $msg .= $results->getMessage()."<br>\n";
        die($msg);
    }
    $nrows = $results->numRows();
    if ($nrows == 0) {
        die("No records in table $table (query: $sqlquery)<br>\n");
    }
    // Extract fields
    $aaRow = $results->fetchRow(DB_FETCHMODE_ASSOC);
    $value = $aaRow[$tgtCol];

    return($value);
} // end function GetSingleFieldValue()
```

The next function (`GetTwoFieldValues()`) is similar to the previous one. It provides a generic way to retrieve two fields, given a single condition:

```
function GetTwoFieldValues($info) //$table,$tgtCol,$critCol,$critVal)
{
    // Given a target table name $table, and one criterion,
    // ('$critCol' = $critVal), retrieve 2 field values.
    // We'll make the assumption that only one
    // resultset row will occur.

    $table   = $info["tgtTable"];
    $tgtCol1 = $info["tgtCol1"];
    $tgtCol2 = $info["tgtCol2"];
    $critCol = $info["critCol"];
    $critVal = $info["critVal"];

    $sqlquery  = "SELECT * FROM $table WHERE ";
    if (is_int($critVal)) {
        $sqlquery .= "$critCol = $critVal ";
    } elseif (is_string($critVal)) {
        $sqlquery .= "$critCol = \"$critVal\" ";
    } elseif (is_bool($critVal)) {
        $sqlquery .= "$critCol = \"$critVal\" ";
    } else  { // float
        $sqlquery .= "$critCol = $critVal ";
    }
    $results = $this->db->query($sqlquery);
    if (DB::isError($results)) {
        $msg  = "GetTwoFieldValues->Could not perform query:
                $sqlquery: ";
        $msg .= $results->getMessage()."<br>\n";
        die($msg);
    }
    $nrows = $results->numRows();
    if ($nrows == 0) {
        die("No records in table $table<br>\n");
    }
    // Extract fields
    $aaRow = $results->fetchRow(DB_FETCHMODE_ASSOC);
    $aaRes[$tgtCol1] = $aaRow[$tgtCol1];
    $aaRes[$tgtCol2] = $aaRow[$tgtCol2];
    return($aaRes);
} // end function GetTwoFieldValues()
```

This function defines the record information needed for adding a member (student or professor) to the mailing list named by `$listcode`. The actual insertion into the database happens in the function following this one:

```
function AddMemToMlist($listcode,$acctid)
{
    $info["tgtTable"] =
                   addslashes("universitylife_messagelistmasters");
    $info["tgtCol"]   = "messagelistmaster_listid";
    $info["critCol"]  = addslashes("messagelistmaster_listcode");
```

```
            $info["critVal"]   = $listcode;
            $listid = $this->GetSingleFieldValue($info);
            $detail["listid"] = $listid;
            $detail["memid"]   = $acctid;
            $listdetid = $this->InsertMlistDetailsRecord($detail);
            return($listdetid);
        } // end function AddMemToMlist()
```

Insert a record into the `universitylife_members` table. The information for the student or the professor is passed, as before, via the associative array `$elem`:

```
function InsertMemberRecord($elem)
{
    // Using the current <member> element, insert a record into
    // table "universitylife_members".
    $acctname = addslashes($elem["univid"]);
    // This can be changed to some unique value
    $univid  = $elem["univid"];
    $memcat  = $elem["memcat"];
    $fname   = addslashes($elem["fname"]);
    $lname   = addslashes($elem["lname"]);
    $deptid  = $elem["deptid"];
    $id = $this->db->nextId('acctidSeq');

    $insquery  = "INSERT INTO universitylife_members
                    (member_accountid,member_accountname,
                     member_universityid,member_membercategory,
                     member_privacy,";
    $insquery .= "member_firstname,member_lastname,
                     member_status,member_departmentid) VALUES ";

    $insquery .= "($id,'$acctname', '$univid', '$memcat', 'false'";
    $insquery .= ",'$fname', '$lname', 'I', $deptid)";
    $resultset = $this->db->query($insquery);

    if (DB::isError($resultset)) {
        $msg  = "Could not insert record into table
                    universitylife_members: ";
        $msg .= $resultset->getMessage()."<br>\n";
        die($msg);
    }

    return($id);
} // end function InsertMemberRecord()
```

Again we make use of `$elem`, this time for inserting a record into `universitylife_cistaff`:

```
function InsertCistaffRecord($elem)
{
    // Using the current <member> element, insert a record into
    // table "universitylife_contactinfostaff".

    if($this->debug) {
        print "<pre>\n";
        print "<b>member</b>:\n";
        var_dump($elem);
        print "</pre>\n";
```

```
        }
        $bldng    = addslashes($elem["bldng"]);
        $office   = addslashes($elem["office"]);
        $ext      = addslashes($elem["ext"]);
        $hrsavail = addslashes($elem["hrsavail"]);
        // contactinfostaffid.memberid = members.accountid
        $memid    = $elem["acctid"];

        $id = $this->db->nextId('cistaffidSeq');
        $insquery  = "INSERT INTO universitylife_contactinfostaff
                        (contactinfostaff_contactinfostaffid,
                         contactinfostaff_building,
                         contactinfostaff_office,
                         contactinfostaff_extension,
                         contactinfostaff_hoursavailable,
                         contactinfostaff_memberid)
                         VALUES ";

        $insquery .= " ($id,'$bldng', '$office', ";
        if (!isset($ext) || is_null($ext))
            $insquery .= "null, ";
        else
            $insquery .= "$ext, ";

        $insquery .= "'$hrsavail', $memid) ";

        if($this->debug) print "[dbg(cistaff)]: [$insquery]<br>\n";

        $resultset = $this->db->query($insquery);

        if (DB::isError($resultset)) {
            $msg  = "Could not insert record into table
                        universitylife_contactinfostaff: ";
            $msg .= $resultset->getMessage()."<br>\n";
            die($msg);
        }
        return($id);
    } // end function InsertCistaffRecord()
```

We use the following function for inserting a record into the `universitylife_messagelistdetails` table, which amounts to adding a member (student or professor) to a mailing list. Information is passed via the associative array, `$info`:

```
function InsertMlistDetailsRecord ($info)
{
    // Add a member to a particular mailing list
    if($this->debug) {
        print "<pre>\n";
        print "<b>mlistdetails</b>:\n";
        var_dump($info);
        print "</pre>\n";
    }
```

```
        $listid = $info["listid"];
        $memid  = $info["memid"];
        $id = $this->db->nextId('listdetidSeq');
        $insquery  = "INSERT INTO universitylife_messagelistdetails
                       (messagelistdetail_listdetailid,
                        messagelistdetail_listid,
                        messagelistdetail_memberid) VALUES ";
        $insquery .= "($id,$listid, $memid) ";
        print "[dbg(mlistdetails)]: [$insquery]<br>\n";

        $resultset = $this->db->query($insquery);
        if (DB::isError($resultset)) {
            $msg  = "Could not insert record into table
                     universitylife_messagelistdetails: ";
            $msg .= $resultset->getMessage()."<br>\n";
            die($msg);
        }
        return($id);
    } // end function InsertMlistDetailsRecord()
```

Given a department code and a member category, we want to find the name of a mailing list for the college that the department is in. The $memcat variable will indicate whether the list is for students (stu) or professors (edu):

```
    function GetCollMlistCodeForDeptcode($deptcode,$memcat)
    {
        $sqlquery  = "SELECT co.college_collegecode collcode ";
        $sqlquery .= "FROM universitylife_colleges as co,
                      universitylife_departments as de ";
        $sqlquery .= "WHERE co.college_collegeid =
                      de.department_collegeid ";
        $sqlquery .= "AND de.department_departmentcode = \"$deptcode\" ";

        if($this->debug) print "[dbg(listcode)]: qry=[$sqlquery]<br>\n";
        $results = $this->db->query($sqlquery);
        if (DB::isError($results)) {
            $msg  = "Could not perform $sqlquery: ";
            $msg .= $results->getMessage()."<br>\n";
            die($msg);
        }
        $nrows = $results->numRows();
        if ($nrows == 0) {
            die("No records in table $table<br>\n");
        }
        // Extract fields
        $aaRow = $results->fetchRow(DB_FETCHMODE_ASSOC);
        $collcode = $aaRow["collcode"];
        $listcode = "col_".$memcat."_".$collcode;
        if($this->debug)
            print "[dbg(listcode)]: listcode=[$listcode]<br>\n";
        return($listcode);
    } // end function GetCollMlistCodeForDeptcode()
```

This function inserts a record into the `universitylife_teaching` table, that is, we create a record for a course that a professor is teaching. Information is passed via the `$elem` associative array:

```
function InsertTeachingRecord($elem)
{
    // Insert a record into table "universitylife_teaching" for the
    // current professor
    if($this->debug) {
        print "<pre>\n";
        print "<b>teaching</b>:\n";
        var_dump($elem);
        print "</pre>\n";
    }

    $cid       = $elem["cid"];
    $memprofid = $elem["memprofid"];
    $id = $this->db->nextId('teachidSeq');
    $insquery  = "INSERT universitylife_teaching
                    (teaching_teachid, teaching_courseid,
                     teaching_memberprofessorid) VALUES ";
    $insquery .= "($id,$cid, $memprofid) ";
    if($this->debug) print "[dbg(teaching)]: [$insquery]<br>\n";

    $resultset = $this->db->query($insquery);
    if (DB::isError($resultset)) {
        $msg  = "Could not insert record into table
                    universitylife_teaching: ";
        $msg .= $resultset->getMessage()."<br>\n";
        die($msg);
    }
    return($id);
} // end function InsertTeachingRecord()
```

In much the same way, we insert a contact information record for a student member into the `universitylife_contactinfoother` table:

```
function InsertCiotherRecord($elem)
{
    // Using the current <member> element, insert a record into
    // table "universitylife_contactinfoother".
    if($this->debug) {
        print "<pre>\n";
        print "<b>member</b>:\n";
        var_dump($elem);
        print "</pre>\n";
    }

    $addr1    = addslashes($elem["addr1"]);
    $addr2    = addslashes($elem["addr2"]);
    $city     = addslashes($elem["city"]);
    $stateprov = addslashes($elem["stateprov"]);
    $country  = addslashes($elem["country"]);
    $postcode = addslashes($elem["postcode"]);
    $ext      = addslashes($elem["ext"]);
    $email    = addslashes($elem["email"]);
    $memid    = $elem["acctid"]; // ciother.memid = members.acctid

    $id = $this->db->nextId('ciotheridSeq');
```

```
        $insquery  = "INSERT INTO universitylife_contactinfoother
                        (contactinfoother_contactinfootherid,
                         contactinfoother_address1,
                         contactinfoother_address2, contactinfoother_city,
                         contactinfoother_stateprovince,
                         contactinfoother_country, ";
        $insquery .= "contactinfoother_postcode,
                         contactinfoother_extension,
                         contactinfoother_email,
                         contactinfoother_memberid) VALUES ($id,";
        $insquery .= "'$addr1', '$addr2', '$city', '$stateprov', ";
        $insquery .= "'$country', '$postcode', ";
        if (empty($ext))
            $insquery .= "null, ";
        else
            $insquery .= "$ext, ";
        $insquery .= "'$email', $memid) ";
        if($this->debug) print "[dbg(ciother)]: [$insquery]<br>\n";

        $resultset = $this->db->query($insquery);
        if (DB::isError($resultset)) {
            $msg  = "Could not insert record into table
                        universitylife_contactinfoother: ";
            $msg .= $resultset->getMessage()."<br>\n";
            die($msg);
        }
        return($id);
    } // end function InsertCiotherRecord()
```

The function below inserts a record into the `universitylife_taking` table; in other words, we're recording the fact that a student is taking a particular course:

```
function InsertTakingRecord($elem)
{
    // Insert a record into table "universitylife_taking" for the
    // current student member

    if($this->debug) {
        print "<pre>\n";
        print "<b>taking</b>:\n";
        var_dump($elem);
        print "</pre>\n";
    }
    $cid   = $elem["cid"];
    $memid = $elem["memid"];
    $id = $this->db->nextId('takidSeq');
    $insquery  = "INSERT universitylife_taking
                    (taking_takeid,taking_courseid,taking_memberid)
                    VALUES ";
    $insquery .= "($id,$cid,$memid) ";
    if($this->debug) print "[dbg(taking)]: [$insquery]<br>\n";

    $resultset = $this->db->query($insquery);
    if (DB::isError($resultset)) {
        $msg  = "Could not insert record into table
                    universitylife_taking: ";
        $msg .= $resultset->getMessage()."<br>\n";
```

```
            die($msg);
        }
        return($id);
    } // end function InsertTakingRecord()

} //end class UnivLifeAPI
?>
```

Miscellaneous PHP Code

This section defines the remaining include file used during the import process. Here is the
common.php script:

```
<?php

// FILE: common.php
// USE:  define various non-database access support code for use during
//       both "XML import" and regular UnivLife application use.
//
include_once("univlifeapi.php");
```

In order to use the application with a different database, we just update the values given here for the database
hostname, username, password, and database name.

```
$host = 'localhost';
$user = 'admin';
$pass = 'ADMIN';
$db   = 'universitylife';

$files["colleges"] = "colleges.xml";
$files["profs"]    = "profs.xml";
$files["students"] = "students.xml";


function GetFile($file)
{
    if (file_exists($file)) {
        $aText = file($file);
        $text = join('', $aText);
    }
    return($text);
} // end define function GetFile

$api = new UnivLifeAPI($host,$user,$pass,$db);
?>
```

Improvements

While the focus in this case study was on techniques for importing XML files to a database, there are a
number of improvements that might be made on the database schema.

These suggestions are listed below:

- ❑ Further normalize the database by adding a `universitylife_buildings` table and replacing current references to the `contactinfostaff_building` column with a `buildingid` column.

- ❑ Further normalize the database by adding a `universitylife_membercategories` table and replacing current references to the `member_membercategory` column with a `membercategoryid` column.

- ❑ Enforce foreign key constraints to minimize the possibility that erroneous data could be introduced into the database.

- ❑ Deriving the database schema directly from DTDs or XML files.

Summary

In this case study, we looked at some techniques for importing existing data in XML format into a new database for use by a new application. These included the use of some of PHP XML validation and processing functionality via SAX and Expat.

Working from XML DTDs defining the data sets to be imported into our application, we devised a suitable database design. We then wrote SQL table creation and indexing statements that we could use to create a MySQL database that was ready to receive the data.

Next, we wrote PHP code to parse the actual XML files and to convert the data that these contained into a form suitable for insertion into the database we created. We also made use of the PEAR::DB library from http://pear.php.net/ for our database access code to make our XML importation classes and support code easily portable to other database management systems, such as PostgreSQL, mSQL, SQL Server, or Oracle.

Using the populated database that resulted from our efforts, we can now build the remainder of the Association Directory for the University of Life – an e-mail based communication system with a web user interface, outlined at the beginning of the chapter, quickly and with relative ease using PHP and other standard web technologies.

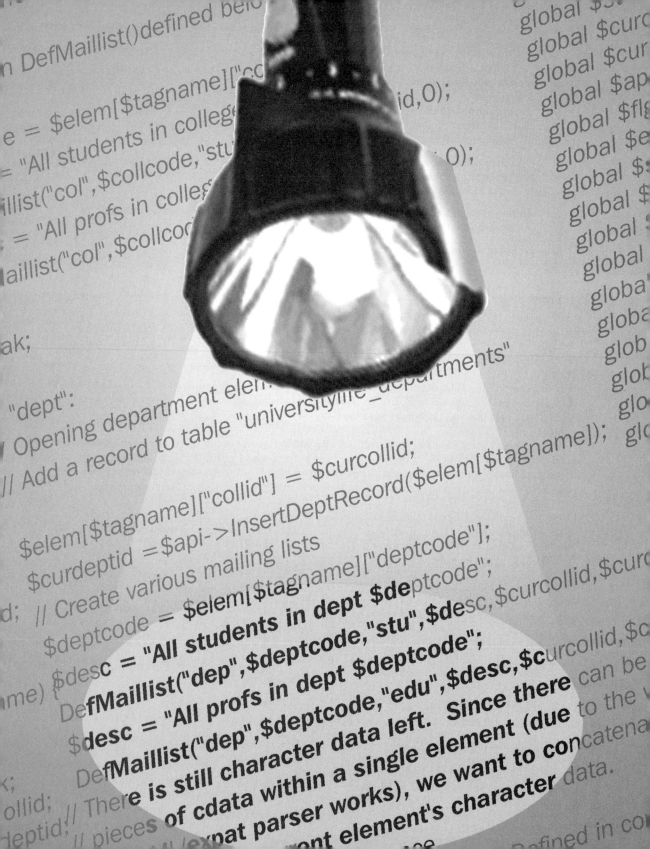

3

Book of Mankind Project

The Book of Mankind Project (BOMP) is a non-profit project that will be an encyclopaedia of humankind. Its concept is inspired by one of the very first Star Trek episodes, where the crew found a 'library' chronicling the history of Earth and other worlds.

The general idea is to set up a web site that catalogues mankind, with stories of individual human beings, as well as whole cultures. BOMP contributors would follow up story submissions with a camera crew, so the web site will feature text, images, streaming video, and audio content. Most, if not all, content would be searchable. The completed site might also have one or more chat rooms and a web forum.

Thus, in the BOMP application:

❑ Members of the public will be invited to tell stories about themselves, their ancestors, or the people of their country. The site will serve as a one-stop source of information about cultures. Homesick travelers could use it to locate organizations of their compatriots (assuming that these groups visit the site to provide contact information).

❑ Shorter articles will be auto-moderated using a 'danger' list of potentially offensive words (stopwords). This list would be continually added to and compiled by a worldwide list of BOMP advisors.

❑ Roving reporters, selected travelers, and recording crews will contribute longer articles and multimedia content. This content should not have to be moderated.

❑ The site will accommodate several different types of access and users. In a project such as this where visitors, as well as the project staff, will be making contributions, it is important to maintain some degree of accountability; therefore, all visitors wishing to contribute ideas or short articles will be required to register in order to do so.

As in the previous case study, we'll follow a series of well-defined steps in planning and building the BOMP application, beginning with a specification of the application's features and objectives.

Application Specification

The scope of this project is enormous and is expected to take quite some time with a full staff, possibly a number of years. For the purposes of this case study, we can only look at a few aspects of the full feature set. To this end, we have also collapsed various staff user types into a single, generic staff type. Since we will focus mostly on the staff end of this application in this chapter, we will also skip user authorization, which is covered in other case studies in this book.

This case study will focus on a subset of the features enumerated above for the purposes of a detailed discussion. Wherever possible, we will provide the PHP code.

User Types

This application has several user types, each with different types of application privileges:

❑ **Staff**
   This is a generic application user type combines the following organization roles:

   ❑ **Admin**
      The admin users handle typical administrative roles for the web application and its components

   ❑ **Reporter**
      The reporters research and write the feature articles

   ❑ **Editor/Moderator**
      The editors or moderators approve content contributed by both the staff and general visitors

   ❑ **Still photographer**
      They make contributions to the site in the form of still images

   ❑ **Videographers**
      They contribute streaming video content to the site.

   ❑ **Recording engineers**
      They are responsible for the recording and handling of audio and visual content

❑ **Public Visitor**
   Anyone who visits the site to browse through it (not detailed in the chapter):

   ❑ **Short article contributor**
      Registered visitors who also contribute

   ❑ **Unregistered visitor**
      This type of user cannot contribute to any thread in the forum (detailed later in the chapter)

Content Types

This is a content-rich web site. The types of content that the full project would contain are:

- **Text**
  The following fall under the category of textual content:

- **Factoids**
  These are tidbits of information contributed by reporters (employees or possibly volunteers). Editors assign the keywords.

- **Short Articles**
  These are contributed by registered visitors and auto-moderated with a list of potentially offensive words. No word in this list should be present in the article; if one or more of them is, the article should be manually reviewed and edited (or even rejected) if and as necessary.

- **Long Articles**
  These are written by reporters and moderated by editors. The keywords assigned by editors.

- **Images**
  These are still images contributed by photographers (like reporters, these could be either employees or volunteers). Editors assign the keywords via the application

- **Video**
  These are streaming video contributed by camera operators (employees or possibly volunteers). Editors assign keywords to them.

- **Audio**
  These are non-commercial music and voice recordings contributed by recordists. Editors assign the keywords.

- **Threads**
  This is a pseudo-forum encouraging visitors to contribute to a story thread.

Features

In the following sections we will focus on the following site features and content:

- Fuzzy Search Engine
- Auto-Moderation
- Shakespeare's Hundredth Monkey Web Forum

Fuzzy Search Engine

A fuzzy search engine is one that finds content on the basis of keywords assigned to a piece of content, rather than searching for words or phrases within the content itself. One advantage of this system is that the content is not limited to text, since we can also assign keywords to images, audio files, video clips, and other media type too. Whenever content is added to the database, an editor examines the content and approves it; part of this approval process includes assigning one or more keywords to the content. For example, a still image of someone walking a dog might have the keywords 'walk', 'dog', 'outdoors', and 'pets' assigned. Keywords are assigned wholly at the discretion of individual editors.

If any keyword is assigned that is not already found in the database, it is added to the `bomp_keywords` table. Then an occurrence entry is made in the `bomp_keyoccurrences` table, which serves as a lookup table for articles by keywords in those articles (we'll discuss these in more detail below). This entry indicates the keyword and the content item to which it was assigned.

The fact that there are several content sources in this application complicates the search process somewhat. However, visitors can perform a fuzzy search on a specific content type, a specific source, or on all sources. We will cover the option for a specific source later in this chapter.

Auto-Moderation of Content

All content contributed to the BOMP web site by members of the general public is subject to moderation. A new entry is not approved until it is moderated for potentially offensive content. What the BOMP staff would like to do is move towards auto-moderation by keeping a list of potentially offensive words contributed by visitors, as well as staff.

When this list is sufficiently large, content will be auto-moderated by rejecting any textual contributions containing five or more instances of potentially offensive terms. Such contributions will have their status field set to `'X'`. Any contributions containing no words from this list will be automatically approved (status = `'A'`). Contributions with between one and five words from the list will continue to be manually moderated.

Later in this chapter we will look at a sample script for auto-moderation.

Shakespeare's Hundredth Monkey Web Forum

The idea behind this feature is twofold. It's said that if a sufficient number of monkeys sat down with typewriters and started typing, they would eventually produce the entire works of William Shakespeare.

The Hundredth Monkey Phenomenon is what might be called urban myth (based on research performed in the middle of the Twentieth Century by some Japanese scientists on various populations of monkeys found on some small islands near Japan) and popularised in the story 'The Hundredth Monkey' by Ken Keyes, Jr (http://newciv.org/worldtrans/pos/monkey.html). It was noted by these scientists that when a young monkey adopted a new behavior, such as washing a sweet potato dropped on a sandy beach, other monkeys in the island's population soon followed suit. This much is well documented. It's also been alleged that, when a critical number of monkeys (say, 100) on one island adopted the new behavior, so did monkey populations on the other islands used in the study, in spite of them being isolated from each other, with no physical means of communication. While this part of the story isn't true, it still makes for a nice metaphor for the spontaneous sharing of ideas across wide distances.

The idea behind introducing the Shakespeare's Hundredth Monkey feature is that one visitor (including staff) can start a new thread and other visitors can add to the content, but the actual number of discussion threads permitted to be active at any given time is limited, and we don't allow successive posts by the same user in any one thread. We don't otherwise place any significant restrictions on these threads, which may be based on topics of any sort, and can be true or fictional in nature.

This 'mini-forum' has a slightly different architecture from the more usual hierarchical tree structure encountered in most web forums:

Here are the rules for the forum:

❑ Only 100 forum threads can be active at any one time. Once a thread has not seen new contributions for 7 consecutive days, its status changes to archive. After a thread has been archived, no new additions may be made to it.

❑ Threads can only be added to, not edited or deleted. Contributions are added in sequence.

❑ A single user can contribute to a thread any number of times, but not in succession. This rule is applied because this feature's purpose is to encourage interaction between visitors, and to maximize the number of participants. Visitors might consider getting around this by registering several accounts. However, since accounts are only approved if a valid e-mail address is supplied during registration, the user would need to have more than one valid e-mail address to bypass this rule.

It is also proposed that an e-mail be sent to the registrant, asking them to confirm their registration; but this sort of user validation is not covered in this chapter.

❑ Users' postings will provide a rich source of human behavioral information, primarily with regard to posting frequencies and patterns. The forum content itself is not of interest for these reporting features.

We'll therefore be looking at rates of adoption of similar posting habits among and between groups of participants in the forum, not unlike the way in which the researchers studied the spread of new behaviors among groups of monkeys.

Designing the Database

Considering the complexity of the web site, much planning and organization is required for the design of the database. The schema of each table has been briefly described in the next section.

Database Tables

The minimum set of tables required to implement the features that we want to focus on for the case study are shown below. It is possible that these tables will suffice to support the features alluded to, but not discussed, in the remainder of this chapter:

Table	Alias	Description
bomp_accounts	ac	Contains user account information for all types of users. The admin staff creates account for the hired staff. Visitors create their own accounts that are auto-approved if all the necessary information is supplied.
bomp_articles	ar	Contains the actual text of long articles (contributed by hired reporters).
bomp_countries	cou	List of countries for which content has been contributed by visitors, reporter, or citizens of a country.

Table continued on following page

Table	Alias	Description
bomp_facts	fa	Contains little tidbits or factoids of information about a particular country. Information is searchable by country name or keyword.
bomp_keyoccurrences	ko	This is a log of all occurrences of a particular keyword. This table is directly linked to the bomp_keywords table and all the content tables (text and media).
bomp_keywords	kw	Keyword entries relating to table content. Each content entry can have one or more keywords associated with it. This allows for fuzzy searching of both textual and non-textual data.
bomp_multimedia	mm	Listing of multimedia files (audio, video, still images).
bomp_monkeys	mo	Contributions by users for various pseudo-forum threads. (See table bomp_threads.)
bomp_shorts	sh	Contains the actual text of short articles contributed by visitors.
bomp_stopwords	sw	List of potentially offensive words contributed by the hired staff and visitors alike. Used to auto-moderate content contributed by registered visitors.
bomp_threads	th	The table that stores the details of each thread initiated in the forum.

Database Table Specifics

All the content tables (text or multimedia) contain a column status. This field can have the following values:

Status	Stands For
U	Unapproved
X	Rejected
C	Check
M	Moderated
A	Approved
R	Archived

```
$handlers["end"]     = "EndElementHandler";
$handlers["default"] = "DefaultHandler";
$handlers["cdata"]   = "CDataHandler";

function StartElementHandler($parser, $tagname, $attrs)
{
    global $flg;
    global $elem;
    global $stack;
    global $member;
    global $courses;
    global $curcollid;
    global $curdeptid;
```

The global variable $api is defined in the support file common.php as an instance of the UnivLifeApi class. This class, whose methods are used for accessing the Association Directory database, is itself defined in the file univelifeapi.php; we'll discuss it below.

Let's continue with the add_students.php script:

```
    global $api;

    // Only one start tag needs to be checked for.

    $flg[$tagname] = true;
    array_push($stack,$tagname);

    switch ($tagname) {
    case "member": // Opening member element, <member>
        // Initialize a "member" data structure
        $member["memcat"] = $attrs["memcat"];
        break;

    case "taking": // Opening <taking> tag
        // Initialize course array for current <member> element
        $courses = array();
        break;

    default:
        break;
    }
} // end function StartElementHandler()

function EndElementHandler($parser, $tagname)
{
    global $flg;
    global $elem;
    global $stack;
    global $member;
    global $courses;
    global $curcollid;
    global $curdeptid;
    global $api;
```

```
// The cases are listed in expected order of tag occurrence in
// the input XML file.

switch ($tagname) {
case "univid": // Closing </univid> tag
    // Assign university ID to the currently open <member> element
    $member["univid"] = $elem["univid"]["__cdata__"];
    break;

case "fname": // Closing </fname> tag
    // Assign first name to the currently open <member> element
    $member["fname"] = $elem["fname"]["__cdata__"];
    break;

case "lname": // Closing </lname> tag
    // Assign last name to the currently open <member> element
    $member["lname"] = $elem["lname"]["__cdata__"];
    break;

case "dept": // Closing </dept> tag
    // The department is conveyed using a field marker in the form
    // of "__deptcode__" E.g., "__NwPh__".
    //
    // Given the department code stored from the field marker of
    // <dept>, // lookup the department ID. Save it to currently open
    // <member>.
    //
    $deptcode = $elem[$tagname]["__lookup__"];

    $info["tgtTable"] = "universitylife_departments";
    // Target table to look in
    $info["tgtCol"]   = "department_departmentid";
    // Target column to retrieve
    $info["critCol"]  = "department_departmentcode";
    // Criterion column to test
    $info["critVal"]  = $deptcode;  // Criterion value to test

    $deptid = $api->GetSingleFieldValue($info);
    $member["deptcode"] = $deptcode;
    $member["deptid"]   = $deptid;
    break;

case "addr1": // Closing </addr1> tag
    // Assign address1 line to the currently open <member> element
    $member["addr1"] = $elem["addr1"]["__cdata__"];
    break;

case "addr2": // Closing </addr2> tag
    // Assign address2 line to the currently open <member> element
    $member["addr2"] = $elem["addr2"]["__cdata__"];
    break;

case "city": // Closing </city> tag
```

```php
        // Assign city to the currently open <member> element
        $member["city"] = $elem["city"]["__cdata__"];
        break;

case "stateprov": // Closing </stateprov> tag
        // Assign state/province to the currently open <member> element
        $member["stateprov"] = $elem["stateprov"]["__cdata__"];
        break;

case "country": // Closing </country> tag
        // Assign country to the currently open <member> element
        $member["country"] = $elem["country"]["__cdata__"];
        break;

case "postcode": // Closing </postcode> tag
        // Assign postal/zip code to the currently open <member> element
        $member["postcode"] = $elem["postcode"]["__cdata__"];
        break;

case "ext": // Closing </ext> tag
        // Assign phone extension to the currently open <member> element
        $member["ext"] = $elem["ext"]["__cdata__"];
        break;

case "email": // Closing </email> tag
        // Assign email to the currently open <member> element
        $member["email"] = $elem["email"]["__cdata__"];
        break;

case "course": // Closing </course> tag
        // The course is conveyed using a field marker in the form
        // of "__num__" E.g., "__NwPh003__".
        //
        // Given the course number stored from the field marker of
        // <course>, lookup the course ID and the dept ID. Save it to the
        // global $courses array.
        //
        $num = $elem[$tagname]["__lookup__"];

        $info["tgtTable"] = "universitylife_available";
                        // Target table to look in
        $info["tgtCol1"]  = "available_courseid";
                        // Target column //1 to retrieve
        $info["tgtCol2"]  = "available_departmentid";
                        // Target column //2 to retrieve
        $info["critCol"]  = "available_coursenumber";
                        // Criterion column to test
        $info["critVal"]  = $num;
                        // Criterion value to test
```

```
            $aaRes = $api->GetTwoFieldValues($info);
            $cid = $aaRes["available_courseid"]; // Course ID
            $courses["$cid"]["deptid"] = $aaRes["available_departmentid"];
                                        // Course department ID

            $courses["$cid"]["num"]    = $num;
            break;

    case "member": // Closing </member> tag
        // Insert records into appropriate tables

        $acctid = $api->InsertMemberRecord($member);
        $member["acctid"] = $acctid;
        $cistaffid = $api->InsertCiotherRecord($member);

        // Add student member to various mailing lists
        // (see univlifeapi.php)
        //
        $deptcode = $member["deptcode"];
        print "[dbg(&lt;/member&gt;)]: deptcode=[$deptcode]<br>\n";

        $api->AddMemToMlist("uni_all_mems",$acctid);
        $api->AddMemToMlist("dep_stu_".$deptcode,$acctid);
        $listcode = $api->GetCollMlistCodeForDeptcode($deptcode,"stu");

        $api->AddMemToMlist($listcode,$acctid);
```

For each <course> element contained by the current <member>, we want to insert a record into the universitylife_taking table. Assuming that the insertion is successful, we'll then want to add the student to the mailing list of all students in this course:

```
        // Add <course> elements to the "universitylife_taking" table
        foreach ($courses as $scid => $course) {
            $course["cid"]    = $scid;
            $course["memid"] = $acctid;
            $api->InsertTakingRecord($course);

            // Add this student to the mailing list of
            // all students taking this course
            //
            $api->AddMemToMlist("crs_stu_".$course["num"],$acctid);
        }
        break;

    default:
        break;
    }

    array_pop($stack);
    $flg[$tagname] = false;
    unset($elem[$tagname]);

} // end function EndElementHandler()
```

There are a number of possible status value sequences that a content entry can take on over time, depending on various conditions. These are described below:

- Manually approved (and moderated) content that is later rejected: U → X
- Manually approved content that is accepted: U → A → R.
  The R occurs if the content entry is archived later. Manual approval includes assigning keywords.
- Content that is auto-moderated and has more than 5 stopwords: U → X
- Content that is auto-moderated and has between 1 and 5 stopwords: U → C.
  If a staff member approves it and assigns keywords: U → C → A.
- Content that is auto-moderated (and manually approved) and has no stopwords: U → M → A.
- For content that is manually moderated and approved (that is, assigned keywords): U → A.

Accounts

This table (bomp_accounts) stores information about all potential users of the application, regardless of whether they are staff or contributes. Staff accounts are created by the admin staff and may contain some empty fields. Those statements that cannot be empty will have a constraint as NOT NULL in SQL:

Column	Data Type	Description
account_accountid	INT	Unique record ID, auto-generated by MySQL.
account_account	CHAR	The username for this account. (Must be unique.)
account_pass	CHAR	The encrypted password for this account.
account_type	CHAR	Account type. Allows for admin and staff accounts to be set up alongside regular registered users: □ adm – admin staff □ edi – editors □ pho – photographers □ rec – recording engineers □ rep – reporters □ usr – regular registered users □ vid – videographers While we only focus on a few of these types in the upcoming code, in the final version of the BOMP application, it might be worthwhile having a user types lookup table to store all of the above types and their descriptions.
account_firstname	CHAR	First name of the user. Typically only requested of non-staff users.
account_lastname	CHAR	Last name of the user. Non-staff users.
account_city	CHAR	City where the user lives. Non-staff users.

Table continued on following page

Column	Data Type	Description
account_stateprov	CHAR	State, province, district, or territory of the user. Non-staff users.
account_ccode	CHAR	Country code identifying the country that the user lives in. Non-staff users.
account_postcode	CHAR	postal/zip code (Optional). Non-staff users.
account_email	CHAR	E-mail address for newsletters and announcements. Non-staff users.
account_status	CHAR	Account status for any type of user: ❑ A (active) – currently logged in. As the logout feature is not enforced, this field may be misleading. ❑ I (inactive) – Not logged in at the moment. ❑ B (blocked) – Temporarily blocked from logging in.

Articles

This table (bomp_articles) stores the content of long articles contributed by hired reporters. Editors assign keywords and store them in the table keywords, under the artic content type:

Column	Data Type	Description
article_articleid	INT	Unique record ID, auto-generated by MySQL
article_title	CHAR	Title for the article
article_content	MEDIUMTEXT(18)	Actual content, up to 262,143 (2^{18}-1) characters
article_whoid	INT	Account ID of contributor (staff)
article_status	CHAR	Status of this content entry

Countries

The entries in this table (bomp_countries) will be entered by editors and may be contributed by both editors and reporters:

Column	Data Type	Description
country_ccode	CHAR	A two or three letter code representing a country. Uses the United Nations authorized two-letter codes for member countries. However, non-UN countries are represented with a 3-letter code starting with an n (non).
country_country	CHAR	Full name of country, as spelt with Latin characters
country_nativename	CHAR	Full name of country as spelt by that country, but in Latin letters. For example, the Japanese call Japan, 'Nippon'.

Facts

This table (`bomp_facts`) stores various facts contributed by staff members:

Column	Data Type	Description
fact_factid	INT	Unique record ID, auto-generated by MySQL
fact_title	CHAR	Title of fact
fact_content	CHAR	Fact entries must be under 256 characters in length
fact_whoid	CHAR	Account ID of contributor (staff only)
fact_status	CHAR	Status of this content entry

Key Occurrences

This table (`bomp_keyoccurrences`) is used to list all occurrences of each keyword in table keywords. A content source code is used to indicate which table (articles or multimedia) the word came from. These keywords can be used to perform a fuzzy search for all types of content:

Column	Data Type	Description
keyoccurrence_koid	INT	Unique ID identifying each record in this table.
keyoccurrence_type	CHAR	Indicates the type of content: ❑ txt: text; ❑ img: still image; ❑ aud: audio; ❑ vid: video. More types can be added later. As an enhanced feature, it might be worthwhile to put these types into a secondary lookup table, if more of them are added.
keyoccurrence_source	CHAR	Indicates the name of the content table containing the item referred to by the keyword.
keyoccurrence_sourceid	INT	Indicates the ID of the record in the table indicated by source that contains the word occurrence or keyword. Only the first occurrence in a document is catalogued.
keyoccurrence_keyid	INT	Foreign key; connects this table to the table keywords `bomp_keywords`.

Keywords

This table (bomp_keywords) contains a list of unique keywords representing various articles/multimedia files. Each of these keywords is assigned to one or more content entries and types (including text, audio, and still images).

Column	Data Type	Description
keyword_kwid	INT	Unique ID for each keyword, auto-generated by MySQL.
keyword_keyword	CHAR	Keyword string.

Multimedia

This table (bomp_multimedia) contains information regarding various multimedia files of type audio, video, and stills:

Column	Data Type	Description
multimedia_recid	INT	A unique integer ID representing a given record.
multimedia_title	CHAR	A short title describing the media file.
multimedia_mfile	CHAR	The name of file (relative to web server document root).
multimedia_type	CHAR	Audio (aud), video (vid), still image (img).
multimedia_subtype	CHAR	Sub-type: ❑ For image files: jpg, gif, and png ❑ For audio files: mp3, ra, wav, and au ❑ For video files: rm, and mpeg
multimedia_status	CHAR	Status of this content entry.
multimedia_whoid	INT	Account ID of contributor (anyone)

Monkeys

This table (bomp_monkeys) contains the text of each contribution of the threads in Shakespeare's Hundredth Monkey web forum:

Column	Data Type	Description
monkey_recid	INT	A unique integer ID representing a given record. This field will also be used as a foreign key in table bomp_threads, to help define the various user-contributed pieces of a thread.
monkey_postdate	DATE	The post date of this contribution. The post date of the first piece of a thread is always the same as the start date of a thread.

Column	Data Type	Description
monkey_contrib	CHAR	The actual text contribution to a specific thread (identified by column monkey_thrid).
monkey_status	CHAR	Status of this content entry.
monkey_thrid	INT	Foreign key identifying the thread this contribution belongs to.
monkey_whoid	INT	Account ID of contributor (anyone).

Shorts

This table (bomp_shorts) contains text of short articles contributed by registered visitors or staff:

Column	Data Type	Description
short_shortid	INT	Unique record ID, auto–generated by MySQL.
short_title	CHAR	Title of short article.
short_content	TEXT	Actual text content of short article. Can have up to 65,535 characters (or approximately 1,000 words).
short_whoid	INT	Account ID of contributor (anyone).
short_status	CHAR	Status of this content entry.

Stopwords

This table (bomp_stopwords) contains a growing list of potentially offensive words. This table's is for future auto-moderation of content supplied by non-staff users:

Column	Data Type	Description
stopword_swid	INT	Unique record ID, auto-generated by MySQL.
stopword_stopword	CHAR	Stopword string.

Threads

This table (bomp_threads)contains crucial information for each forum thread:

Column	Data Type	Description
thread_thrid	INT	A unique integer ID representing a particular thread record.
thread_startdate	DATE	The start date of a thread. This refers to the date on which a user (including staff) starts a new story thread.

Table continued on following page

Column	Data Type	Description
thread_title	CHAR	A title for the thread, supposedly representative of the intended story.
thread_status	CHAR	Indicates whether the thread is open or not: ❑ O – open ❑ C – closed ❑ B – blocked (reserved for future use)
thread_origid	INT	This is the user ID of the user (public or staff) that created the thread.

Relationships Between Tables

The diagram below shows the relationship between the tables in the BOMP database:

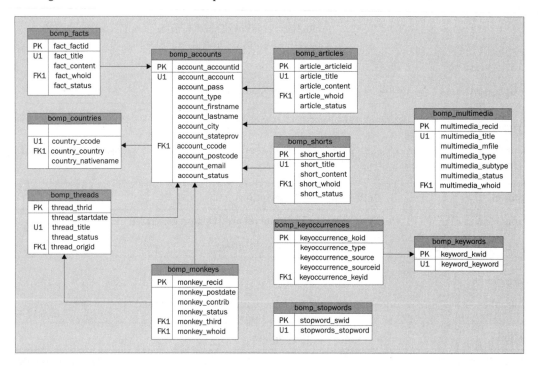

The relationship between tables in the bomp database is fairly complex. Unique keywords are supplied from most of the content tables (bomp_multimedia, bomp_articles, bomp_facts, bomp_shorts, bomp_threads, bomp_monkeys) to the bomp_keywords table. Occurrences of a keyword are logged in the bomp_keyoccurences table.

Database User and Privileges

Let's us first create the database by typing the following command at the shell or command prompt:

```
>mysqladmin create bomp;
```

The tables for this case study can all be placed within a single MySQL database, bomp. Since we are only running test scripts, we only need one database user, say ADMIN. The ADMIN user will need the privileges to create the tables and access them. We use the mysql client utility, to grant these privileges:

```
mysql> GRANT SELECT, INSERT, UPDATE, DELETE ON bomp.*
       TO "ADMIN@localhost" IDENTIFIED BY "ADMIN";
```

Creating the bomp Database

Here is the algorithm for creating and populating the database:

1. Create the database, tables, and build indexes

2. Create user accounts in the bomp_accounts table

3. Add some entries to the bomp_stopwords, bomp_articles, bomp_countries, bomp_facts, bomp_multimedia, and bomp_shorts tables

4. Create a few forum threads and add the initial monkey content entry to each thread; we'll add to this later using a PHP script

These steps are contained within two SQL scripts, which we'll look at in the following two sections.

Table Creation

Then we run the SQL script, crdbs_bomp.sql, on the command line to create the tables:

```
> mysql bomp < crdbs_bomp.sql
```

The following SQL script creates the database:

```sql
# crdbs_bomp.sql
# Create Book of Mankind Project (BOMP) database

DROP TABLE IF EXISTS bomp_accounts;
CREATE TABLE bomp_accounts (
  account_accountid   INT(10) UNSIGNED NOT NULL AUTO_INCREMENT,
  account_account     VARCHAR(12) NOT NULL default '',
  account_pass        VARCHAR(12) NOT NULL default '',
```

```
   account_type        CHAR(3) NOT NULL default '',
   account_firstname   VARCHAR(30) NOT NULL default '',
   account_lastname    VARCHAR(40) NOT NULL default '',
   account_city        VARCHAR(30) default NULL,
   account_stateprov   VARCHAR(30) default NULL,
   account_ccode       CHAR(3) default NULL,
   account_postcode    VARCHAR(10) default NULL,
   account_email       VARCHAR(56) default NULL,
   account_status      VARCHAR(10) NOT NULL default '',
                       PRIMARY KEY (account_accountid),
                       UNIQUE KEY (account_account)
) TYPE=MyISAM;

DROP TABLE IF EXISTS bomp_articles;
CREATE TABLE bomp_articles (
   article_articleid   INT(10) UNSIGNED NOT NULL AUTO_INCREMENT,
   article_title       VARCHAR(56) NOT NULL default '',
   article_content     TEXT NOT NULL,
   article_whoid       INT(10) UNSIGNED NOT NULL default '0',
   article_status      CHAR(1) NOT NULL default '',
                       PRIMARY KEY (article_articleid),
                       UNIQUE KEY (article_title)
) TYPE=MyISAM;

DROP TABLE IF EXISTS bomp_countries;
CREATE TABLE bomp_countries (
   country_ccode       CHAR(3) NOT NULL default '',
   country_country     VARCHAR(56) NOT NULL default '',
   country_nativename  VARCHAR(56) default NULL,
                       UNIQUE KEY (country_ccode),
                       UNIQUE KEY (country_country)
) TYPE=MyISAM;

DROP TABLE IF EXISTS bomp_facts;
CREATE TABLE bomp_facts (
   fact_factid         INT(10) unsigned NOT NULL AUTO_INCREMENT,
   fact_title          VARCHAR(56) NOT NULL default '',
   fact_content        VARCHAR(255) NOT NULL default '',
   fact_whoid          INT(10)  UNSIGNED NOT NULL default '0',
   fact_status         CHAR(1) NOT NULL default '',
                       PRIMARY KEY (fact_factid),
                       UNIQUE KEY (fact_title)
) TYPE=MyISAM;

DROP TABLE IF EXISTS bomp_keyoccurrences;
CREATE TABLE bomp_keyoccurrences (
   keyoccurrence_koid      INT(10) UNSIGNED NOT NULL AUTO_INCREMENT,
   keyoccurrence_type      CHAR(6) default NULL,
   keyoccurrence_source    CHAR(10) NOT NULL default '',
   keyoccurrence_sourceid  INT(10) unsigned NOT NULL default '0',
   keyoccurrence_keyid     INT(10) unsigned NOT NULL default '0',
                           PRIMARY KEY  (keyoccurrence_koid)
) TYPE=MyISAM;
```

```
DROP TABLE IF EXISTS bomp_keywords;
CREATE TABLE bomp_keywords (
  keyword_kwid              INT(10) UNSIGNED NOT NULL AUTO_INCREMENT,
  keyword_keyword           VARCHAR(40) NOT NULL default '',
                            PRIMARY KEY (keyword_kwid),
                            UNIQUE KEY (keyword_keyword)
) TYPE=MyISAM;

DROP TABLE IF EXISTS bomp_multimedia;
CREATE TABLE bomp_multimedia (
  multimedia_recid          INT(10) UNSIGNED NOT NULL AUTO_INCREMENT,
  multimedia_title          VARCHAR(56) NOT NULL default '',
  multimedia_mfile          VARCHAR(255) NOT NULL default '',
  multimedia_type           VARCHAR(6) NOT NULL default '',
  multimedia_subtype        VARCHAR(6) NOT NULL default '',
  multimedia_status         CHAR(1) NOT NULL default '',
  multimedia_whoid          INT(10) unsigned default NULL,
                            PRIMARY KEY  (multimedia_recid),
                            UNIQUE KEY (multimedia_title)
) TYPE=MyISAM;

DROP TABLE IF EXISTS bomp_monkeys;
CREATE TABLE bomp_monkeys (
  monkey_recid              INT(10) UNSIGNED NOT NULL AUTO_INCREMENT,
  monkey_postdate           DATE NOT NULL default '0000-00-00',
  monkey_contrib            VARCHAR(255) NOT NULL default '',
  monkey_status             CHAR(1) NOT NULL default '',
  monkey_thrid              INT(10) unsigned NOT NULL default '0',
  monkey_whoid              INT(10) unsigned NOT NULL default '0',
                            PRIMARY KEY  (monkey_recid)
) TYPE=MyISAM;

DROP TABLE IF EXISTS bomp_shorts;
CREATE TABLE bomp_shorts (
  short_shortid             INT(10) UNSIGNED NOT NULL AUTO_INCREMENT,
  short_title               VARCHAR(56) NOT NULL default '',
  short_content             TEXT NOT NULL,
  short_whoid               INT(10) unsigned NOT NULL default '0',
  short_status              CHAR(1) NOT NULL default '',
                            PRIMARY KEY  (short_shortid),
                            UNIQUE KEY (short_title)
) TYPE=MyISAM;


DROP TABLE IF EXISTS bomp_stopwords;
CREATE TABLE bomp_stopwords (
  stopword_swid             INT(10) UNSIGNED NOT NULL AUTO_INCREMENT,
  stopword_stopword         VARCHAR(40) NOT NULL default '',
                            PRIMARY KEY  (stopword_swid),
                            UNIQUE KEY (stopword_stopword)
) TYPE=MyISAM;

DROP TABLE IF EXISTS bomp_threads;
```

```
CREATE TABLE bomp_threads (
   thread_thrid              INT(10) unsigned NOT NULL auto_increment,
   thread_startdate          DATE NOT NULL default '0000-00-00',
   thread_title              VARCHAR(56) NOT NULL default '',
   thread_status             CHAR(1) NOT NULL default '',
   thread_origid             INT(10) unsigned NOT NULL default '0',
                             PRIMARY KEY (thread_thrid),
                             UNIQUE KEY (thread_title)
) TYPE=MyISAM;
```

Building Indexes

The following SQL code is part of the same file as the code above. It is used to define and create indices for various table columns in the bomp database.

```
> mysql bomp < crdbs_bomp.sql
```

```
# index_bomp.sql
# Create indexes for Book of Mankind Project (BOMP)

# Indexes for table bomp_accounts
CREATE INDEX acct_idxOnAcctid ON bomp_accounts (account_accountid);
CREATE INDEX acct_idxOnLname  ON bomp_accounts (account_lastname);
CREATE INDEX acct_idxOnCity   ON bomp_accounts (account_city);
CREATE INDEX acct_idxOnCcode  ON bomp_accounts (account_ccode);

# Indexes for table bomp_articles
CREATE INDEX art_idxOnWhoid   ON bomp_articles (article_whoid);
CREATE INDEX art_idxOnStatus  ON bomp_articles (article_status);

# Indexes for table bomp_countries
CREATE INDEX cou_idxOnNativename ON bomp_countries (country_nativename);

# Indexes for table bomp_facts
CREATE INDEX fac_idxOnContent ON bomp_facts (fact_content);
CREATE INDEX fac_idxOnWhoid   ON bomp_facts (fact_whoid);
CREATE INDEX fac_idxOnStatus  ON bomp_facts (fact_status);

# Indexes for table bomp_keyoccurrences
CREATE INDEX ko_idxOnType     ON bomp_keyoccurrences (keyoccurrence_type);
CREATE INDEX ko_idxOnSource   ON bomp_keyoccurrences (keyoccurrence_source);
CREATE INDEX ko_idxOnSourceid ON bomp_keyoccurrences
                                        keyoccurrence_sourceid);
CREATE INDEX ko_idxOnKeyid    ON bomp_keyoccurrences (keyoccurrence_keyid);

# Indexes for table bomp_multimedia
CREATE INDEX mm_idxOnTitle    ON bomp_multimedia (multimedia_title);
CREATE INDEX mm_idxOnMfile    ON bomp_multimedia (multimedia_mfile);
CREATE INDEX mm_idxOnType     ON bomp_multimedia (multimedia_type);
CREATE INDEX mm_idxOnSubtype  ON bomp_multimedia (multimedia_subtype);
CREATE INDEX mm_idxOnStatus   ON bomp_multimedia (multimedia_status);
CREATE INDEX mm_idxOnWhoid    ON bomp_multimedia (multimedia_whoid);
```

```
# Indexes for table bomp_monkeys
CREATE INDEX mo_idxOnPdate   ON bomp_monkeys (monkey_postdate);
CREATE INDEX mo_idxOnContrib ON bomp_monkeys (monkey_contrib);
CREATE INDEX mo_idxOnStatus  ON bomp_monkeys (monkey_status);
CREATE INDEX mo_idxOnThrid   ON bomp_monkeys (monkey_thrid);
CREATE INDEX mo_idxOnWhoid   ON bomp_monkeys (monkey_whoid);

# Indexes for table bomp_shorts
CREATE INDEX sh_idxOnWhoid  ON bomp_shorts(short_whoid);
CREATE INDEX sh_idxOnStatus ON bomp_shorts(short_status);
```

Thus, we have created the bomp database, the tables, and its associated indexes.

Populating the Database

Before we can look at some test scripts for the BOMP application, we need to add a representative set of sample data to the database. For test purposes, we will populate the database manually using MySQL's command line monitor, mysql.

The pop_bomp.sql adds sample entries for various tables. Save this file in the MySQL bin directoy and then run it. Run the script at the command prompt to add the entries to the BOMP database, by typing the following command at the shell or command prompt:

```
> mysql bomp < pop_bomp.sql
```

```
# pop_bomp.sql
# Add some countries and country codes

INSERT INTO bomp_countries (country_ccode, country_country,
                            country_nativename) VALUES
  ("ca", "Canada", "Canada"),
  ("us", "United States", "United States"),
  ("mx", "Mexico", "México"),
  ("br", "Brazil", "Brasil"),
  ("en", "England", "England"),
  ("sco", "Scotland", "Scotland"),
  ("ire", "Ireland", "Éire"),
  ("wal", "Wales", "Cymru"),
  ("fr", "France", "France"),
  ("de", "Germany", "Deutschland"),
  ("it", "Italy", "Italia"),
  ("sp", "Spain", "España"),
  ("pt", "Portugal", "Portugal"),
  ("egy", "Egypt", "Egypt"),
  ("za", "Zaire", "Zaïre"),
  ("in", "India", "Bharat"),
  ("pk", "Pakistan", "Pakistan"),
  ("tib", "Tibet", "Tibet"),
```

```
  ("cn", "China", "Zhongguo"),
  ("au", "Australia", "Australia"),
  ("nz", "New Zealand", "New Zealand");


# Create a few user accounts

INSERT INTO bomp_accounts
  (account_account,account_pass,account_type,account_firstname,
   account_lastname,account_email,account_status) VALUES
  ("test1", "test1", "adm", "roo", "hoo", "test1@roozoo.com", "A"),
  ("test2", "test2", "adm", "lord", "leaftail", "test2@roozoo.com", "A"),
  ("test3", "test3", "adm", "golly", "gee", "test3@roozoo.com", "A");


# Add stopwords

INSERT INTO bomp_stopwords (stopword_stopword) VALUES
  ("rooster"), ("meow"), ("bang"), ("crash"), ("boom"), ("unemployed"),
  ("lawyer"), ("accountant"), ("dentist"), ("politician"), ("spicegirl");


# Add articles

INSERT INTO bomp_articles
(article_whoid,article_status,article_title,article_content) VALUES
  (1,"U","<h3>The Cat's Meow</h3>", "<img src=\"aeric.jpg\" /><p>Much
   to the dismay of the IRS, this wee kitten just became the richest animal
   in the world. According to a little known United States tax law, he gets
   to keep all US$126 million that his ticket won in a Powerball-style
   lottery. This law states that any lottery tickets purchased by a pet
   owner for their pet is exempt from lottery taxes. Kitty was quoted as
   saying, &quot;Meow!&quot;.</p>");


# Add facts

INSERT INTO bomp_facts (fact_whoid,fact_status,fact_title,fact_content) VALUES
  (2,"U","Canadian Back Bacon", "If you are what you eat, Canadians are made
   of back bacon and beerm, the breakfast of champion couch potatoes."),
  (3,"U", "Favo(u)rite Canadian Pet, Eh?", "The favo(u)rite pet amongst
   Canadian households is the beaver.");


# Add still images

INSERT INTO bomp_multimedia (multimedia_title, multimedia_mfile,
  multimedia_whoid, multimedia_status, multimedia_type, multimedia_subtype)
  VALUES
  ("Space Alien Found in Canada", "/wrox/webdes/case03/me04.jpg", 1, "U",
   "img", "jpg "),
  ("Cats Claim Companionship Benefits", "/wrox/webdes/case03/aeric2.jpg", 3,
   "U", "img", "jpg");
```

```
# Add short articles

INSERT INTO bomp_shorts (short_whoid,short_status,short_title,short_content)
  VALUES
  (1,"U","<h3>Great Caesar's Ghost!</h3>", "<p>The Warker Hotel + Pub near
  London, England, is home to the ghost of one William Shakespeare.
  Shakespeare's ghost appears every night at exactly 5pm for a pint.</p>"
);


# Create pseudo-forum threads

INSERT INTO bomp_threads
  (thread_origid,thread_startdate,thread_status,thread_title) VALUES
  (3, "2002-5-15", "O", "Six Degrees of Separation"), # thrid = 1
  (1, "2002-5-16", "O", "The Global Village");        # thrid = 2


# Add monkey content

INSERT INTO bomp_monkeys
(monkey_whoid,monkey_thrid,monkey_status,monkey_postdate,monkey_contrib) VALUES
  (3, 1, "U", "2002-5-15", "The concept of 'Six Degrees of Separation' is
  the idea, supposedly provable mathematically, that any two human beings
  are separated in awareness of each other by, at most, six other people in
  a chain of relationships."),
  (1, 2, "U", "2002-5-16", "The invention of the Internet, and its
  subsequent public use, has brought humanity together closer than ever
  before. Despite public web forums spewing all manner of
  &quot;flames&quot;, people are communicating again, via email and web
  forums.");
```

In the next section, we'll discuss the following three steps to ensure content delivery:

❑   Auto–moderate content in a separate script.
     We do it this way since content was added manually. If the content is added via a web
     interface, it will be auto-moderated at that time.

❑   Assign keywords to moderated content.

❑   Add more monkey content to the forum threads.

Content Delivery

Once we have populated the database with content, we can run a few test scripts. As mentioned earlier, the
scope of the full BOMP project is beyond what we can reasonably cover here. Instead, we will focus on the
PHP test scripts required for a minimum feature set.

We need to write scripts for the following web site functions:

- Auto-moderate textual content entry
- Assign keywords
- View web forum thread list
- View a thread
- Fuzzy search on all types of content
- Add content to a thread
- Create a new thread
- Close old threads

For each of these scripts, we will first look at a pseudo-code algorithm, followed by actual PHP code.

Do keep in mind that these are test scripts and not necessarily parts of the final web application; hence certain assumptions may be made. For example, while a user account ID is generally tested for, user validation is assumed and not performed because these are preliminary test scripts. Additional assumptions are specified in each section below as and when necessary.

Auto-Moderate Text Content

The general algorithm for auto-moderating any textual content is as follows:

```
1.Receive text content in a single string. This will be supplied as a
  parameter to the auto-moderation function.

2.Retrieve all stopword entries in the database.

3.Build a regular expression filter with all the stopword table entries
  found. For example,if the list consists of "rooster", "meow", "bang",
  crash"), the filter will be rooster|meow|bang|crash.

4.Using PHP's PCRE (Perl-Compatible Regular Expressions), count the number
  of occurrences of any and all restricted words in the source content.

5.If there are no occurrences of any stopword entries in the source document, the
  status returned is "M" (auto-moderation complete).

6.If there are more than 5 total occurrences of any restricted words, the
  status returned is "X" (content auto-rejected).

7.If there are between 1 and 5 occurrences of any restricted words, the
  status returned is "C" (check content manually).
```

The `common.php` script fits the above algorithm; it should be included in all the PHP scripts that we need to access the database:

```php
<?php

#FILE:common.php

require_once 'DB.php';

$host    = 'localhost';
$user    = 'admin';
$pass    = 'ADMIN';
$dbs     = 'bomp';
$dsn = "mysql://$user:$pass@$host/$dbs";

$db = DB::connect($dsn);
if (DB::isError($db)) {
    die ($db->getMessage());
}
?>
```

Note that we use PEAR to provide a database abstraction layer.

The `automod.php` file auto-moderates the contents of the articles (both long as well as short) and the facts:

```php
<?php

# FILE: automod.php
# USE:  auto-moderate textual content

# A class to moderate textual content

include("common.php");

class AutoMod {
    var $minstop = 5;
    var $debug = 1;
    var $db;

    // PUBLIC METHODS

    function GetMinStop()
    {
        return $this->minstop;
    }

    function SetMinStop($minstop)
    {
        $this->minstop = $minstop;
    }

    // The constructor creates the connection to the database
    function AutoMod($db)
```

```php
{
    $this->db = $db;
}

function AutoModerate($source,$minstop)
{
    // Parse $source for possible occurrences of any stopwords
    // and return an appropriate status code. Use PCRE (Perl-
    // Compatible Regular Expressions).

    $filter = $this->BuildStopwordFilter();
    if (preg_match_all("/\b(?:$filter)\b/is", $source, $matches)) {
        if($this->debug) {
            print "<pre>\n";
            var_dump($matches);
            print "</pre>\n";
        }
        $nstop = $this->CountStopwordOccur($matches);
        if ($nstop > $minstop) {
            // Rejected content due to many stopwords
            $status = "X";
        } else { // between 1 and $minstop occurrences of stopwords
            // Content requires manual check
            $status = "C";
        }
    } else {
        // No stopwords
        $status = "M"; // Acceptably auto-moderated
    }
    return ($status);
} # end function AutoModerate

function PrintStatusMsg($status)
{
    if (strcmp($status,"M")==0) {
        print "The text has been acceptably auto-moderated. ";
        print "Please assign keywords to the text now.<br />";
    } elseif (strcmp($status,"X")==0) {
        print "The text has too many stopwords. It has been
                rejected.<br/>\n";
    } elseif (strcmp($status,"C")==0) {
        print "Text contains a few stopwords. Please check manually.
                <br/>\n";
    }
} # end function PrintStatusMsg

// PRIVATE METHODS

function BuildStopwordFilter()
{
    $sqlquery = "SELECT * FROM bomp_stopwords";
    $results  = $this->db->query($sqlquery);
    if (DB::isError($results)) {
        $msg  = "Could not access table bomp_stopwords in database: ";
```

```
            $msg .= $results->getMessage()."<br>\n";
            die($msg);
        }

    // If there are any stopwords in the table, build a regex filter
    $nrows = $results->numRows();
    if ($nrows == 0) {
        die("No stopwords in table bomp_stopwords<br />\n");
    }
    // Extract all stopwords and append to a filter string
    $aaRow = $results->fetchRow(DB_FETCHMODE_ASSOC);
    $nrows--;
    $filter = $aaRow["stopword_stopword"];
    for ($i=1; $i<=$nrows; $i++) {
        $aaRow   = $results->fetchRow(DB_FETCHMODE_ASSOC);
        $stopword = $aaRow["stopword_stopword"];
        $filter  .= "|$stopword";
    }
    return($filter);
    } # end function BuildStopwordFilter

    function CountStopwordOccur($matches)
    {
        $nstop = 0;
        for ($i=0; $i<count($matches); $i++) {
            for ($j=0; $j<count($matches[$i]); $j++) {
                $nstop++;
            }
        }
        return($nstop);
    } # end function CountStopwordOccur

}

/*
// Main code
$automod = new AutoMod($db);
$text   = "The rooster crowed. Meow, says the cat. Boom bang crash, goes the
unemployed lawyer, while talking to the accountant about the Spicegirl
politicians.";
$status = $automod->AutoModerate($text,$minstop);
$automod->PrintStatusMsg($status);
*/
?>
```

Note that the class constructor receives a $db object, which is created in common.php.

To use another database for BOMP, we will only have to change the values used for the hostname, username, password, and database name in common.php, and the rest of the scripts should work. If we change to a different RDBMS, we'll need to change the database type identifier in the $dsn string as well.

Since we have already created the bomp database (using crdbs_bomp.sql) and populated it (pop_bomp.sql), running the above script will auto-moderate the sample text shown. If we uncomment the call to var_dump() and any debug lines (print "[dbg]: ..."), we'll find that the word "politicians" is not flagged. That's because we added the word "politician", without an "s", to the bomp_stopwords table.

The call to preg_match_all() uses the modifier /is. The i indicates that the regular expression should ignore case. The s indicates that the regular expression works in multi-line mode (that is, it may possibly contain newline characters). However, the reason the function regex() does not match the plurals is because the first parameter to preg_match_all(), that is, the search pattern, specifies \b before and after (?:$filter); the \b metacharacter specifies a **word boundary**, which typically occurs between an alphanumeric character and a whitespace or punctuation character. Surrounding a pattern such as an OR filter (represented by $filter) forces exact matches instead of substrings. Thus, to match plurals of words, they must be explicitly added to the bomp_stopwords table. Alternatively, we could append [s?] to each stopword entry before adding it to the $filter string; in which case our example would match against the patterns like this:

```
rooster[s?]|meow[s?]|bang[s?]|crash[s?]|boom[s?]|unemployed[s?]...
```

to catch the most common English plural forms.

The PHP code above can be used to moderate any textual content provided by the calling routine. This may seem redundant, given that BOMP staff still must assign keywords to each entry manually. However, the purpose of auto-moderation is to reduce the workload by automatically rejecting material that's likely to be offensive. The staff can reduce workload further by reducing the value of the variable $minstop, set at the top of automod.php. Of course, the definition of "offensive" is a relative one, and the staff may later decide to increase the value of $minstop to allow more freedom in the content.

To auto-moderate all current text content entries in the bomp database (from all tables), we need to call the AutoModerate() function, with the text of each entry. Typically, this step would be performed when the content is first being added via an HTML form. However, since we have some content added manually that we need to moderate, we would have to use a SELECT query to produce the necessary text. Then we could display it to the staff member for moderation.

Assign keywords

Assigning keywords to a content entry, be it text or multimedia, is the fundamental step that drives the fuzzy search engine. BOMP staff members, at their discretion, select unapproved content entries and assign keywords to each entry. This is a manner of categorization similar to the way libraries categorize books.

The algorithm for a test script the assign keywords is as follows:

1. Select all content entries (text,media) from one or more tables, for which the entry's status is "U" (unapproved), "C" (check manually), or "M" (successfully auto-moderated).

2. For each entry retrieved, use the title to display a link to a virtual page containing details of the entry. For text, the content will be displayed. For multimedia, an image will be displayed, or video or audio will be played.

3. When a link is selected, the staff user reviews the content and decides upon one or more suitable keywords. These keywords are entered in an HTML text input or textarea, separated by commas and/or spaces.

4. The assigned keywords are parsed. For each assigned keyword, if it does not exist in table keywords, it is first added

5. An occurrence record is added to the bomp_keyoccurrences table. This record keeps track of the source table from which we got the content, the record ID of the content entry in that table, the type of content (text, image, video, audio) and the record ID in the bomp_keywords table of the keyword assigned. Therefore, one record is added to the bomp_keyoccurrences table per assigned keyword.

A sample PHP script implementing the above algorithm is shown below. For brevity, we will only choose content from the bomp_facts table. However, the algorithm is the same regardless of the content source. We use a single script to handle all possible actions associated with the assignment of keywords. The script is intended to illustrate the general principles for handling the assignment of keywords; thus, for clarity, minimal error checking is performed:

```php
<?php

# FILE: assn_kwords.php
# USE:  Assign keywords to already entered content (text,multimedia)

include_once('common.php');
function DisplayFactlist()
{
```

The $db variable is a connection to the bomp database, originally created in common.php; we use the global keyword so that we can access from within the present function.

```php
    global $db;
```

We write a query string, and then execute it using PEAR's query() method.

```php
    $sqlquery = "SELECT fact_factid,fact_title FROM bomp_facts
                 WHERE fact_status IN ('U','C','M')";

    $results  = $db->query($sqlquery);
    if (DB::isError($results)) {
        $msg  = "Could not access bomp_facts table in database bomp: ";
        $msg .= $results->getMessage() . "<br />\n";
        die ($msg);
    }
    $nrows = $results->numRows($results);
    if ($nrows == 0) {
        die("No records in table bomp_facts <br>\n");
    }

    print "<h1>Book of Mankind Project</h1>\n
    <h2>Unassigned Facts</h2>\n"
    <ul>\n";
    for ($i=1; $i<=$nrows; $i++) {
```

For each entry retrieved, we use its title as the text of a link to a page containing the actual content of that entry, that is, the content text, image, video, audio, and so on:

```
        $aaRow   = $results->fetchRow(DB_FETCHMODE_ASSOC);
        $factid = $aaRow["fact_factid"];
        $title  = $aaRow["fact_title"];
        print "<li><a href=\"$PHP_SELF?actn=showcont&source=facts";
        print "&sourceid=$factid\">$title</a></li>\n";
    }
    print "</ul>\n";
} # end function DisplayFactlist()
```

Now that we've displayed a list of links to individual facts entries, we need a way to display the entries themselves. First we write a function to display the linked content, which takes as arguments the name of the table in which the content is found and the id of the record for that content:

```
function ShowContent($source,$sourceid)
{
```

Since the manner in which the content is to be displayed can vary widely with the type, we use a switch... case... construct to determine which display method is to be used. In the case of textual content, we'll print the value being stored in the appropriate column of the table named bomp_source; here, we only implement the case where $source is equal to "facts":

```
    switch($source) {
    case "articles":
        break;
    case "facts":
```

In order to keep our code modular and easy to follow, we'll place the actual display code in a function named DisplayFact(), detailed below:

```
        DisplayFact($sourceid);
        break;
    case "mmedia":
        break;
    case "monkeys":
        break;
    case "shorts":
        break;
    default:
    }
} # end function ShowContent()
```

We pass this function the value for the ID of the facts record for which we wish to display the content as the input parameter $sourceid. When we call DisplayFact(), the function will display both the desired content and an input field for the keyword values that we wish to assign to it:

```
function DisplayFact($sourceid)
{
```

The $db global variable is the same instance of the DB class (that is, a database connection) that we mentioned previously, declared in common.php:

```
global $db;
```

Using PEAR::DB's query() and fetchRow() methods, we obtain the desired data from the bomp_facts table. Since there can be only one record in this table whose fact ID is equal to the value passed as $sourceid we need to call the method just once:

```
$sqlquery = "SELECT fact_title,fact_content FROM bomp_facts WHERE
            fact_factid=$sourceid";

$results  = $db->query($sqlquery);

if (DB::isError($results)) {
    $msg  = "Could not access the bomp_facts table: ";
    $msg .= $results->getMessage()."<br />\n";
    die ($msg);
}
$nrows = $results->numRows($results);
if ($nrows == 0) {
    die("No records in table bomp_facts with the selected fact
        id<br>\n");
}

$aaRow    = $results->fetchRow(DB_FETCHMODE_ASSOC);

$title    = $aaRow["fact_title"];
$content  = $aaRow["fact_content"];
```

Now we can display the content and title data:

```
print "<h1>Book of Mankind Project</h1>\n
      <h2>Unassigned Facts</h2>\n
      <table border=\"0\" bgcolor=\"#CCCCCC\">\n
      <tr>\n<td>[
      <b style=\"color:#FF0000\">$title</b>]<br />\n
      <em>$content</em><br />\n</td>\n</tr>\n</table>\n";
```

Now we display a text field put inputting keywords, using the function defined immediately following this one:

```
    DisplayKeywordInputForm("facts",$sourceid);
} # end function DisplayFact()
```

DisplayKeywordInputForm() does exactly what its name says. It outputs an HTML form containing a text input where keywords to be assigned to the facts record whose title and content are shown can be entered. Also written into the form HTML are two hidden fields containing the $source and $sourceid values which will be needed by the form processor script in order to assign the keywords to the appropriate record in the correct table:

```
function DisplayKeywordInputForm($source,$sourceid)
{
    print "<p>Please enter the keywords you want to assign
           to the content above. If you enter more than one
           keyword, separate them with blanks or commas</p>\n
           <form method=\"GET\" action=\"$PHP_SELF\">\n
           <table border=\"0\">\n<tr>\n<td> </td>\n
           <td><input type=\"text\" name=\"parseterms\" /></td>\n
           <td><input type=\"submit\" value=\"SUBMIT\" /></td>\n
           <td><input type=\"hidden\" name=\"actn\" value=\"parseterms\" />\n
           <input type=\"hidden\" name=\"source\" value=\"$source\" />\n
           <input type=\"hidden\" name=\"sourceid\" value=\"$sourceid\" \
           /></td>\n
           </tr>\n</table>\n</form>\n";
} # end function DisplayKeywordInputForm()
```

When the form is submitted, we'll need to parse out the individual keyword choices and add them to the appropriate tables. `ParseAssignedTerms()` does this for us. Its input parameters are: the name of the source table, the ID for the content record in that table, and a string containing a comma-delimited list of keywords:

```
function ParseAssignedTerms($source,$sourceid,$terms)
{
```

First we replace all commas in the `$terms` string with spaces, strip out any extra spaces, split the resulting string using the space as the delimiter. The resulting array contains the individual keywords as its elements, and is stored as `$aTerms`. Note that we don't do any error checking here to verify that the keyword list passed to `ParseAssignedTerms()` is correctly formatted; of course, we would add such a check in the production version of the site:

```
$terms = preg_replace("/,/s", " ", $terms);
$terms = preg_replace("/\s+/s", " ", $terms);
$aTerms = explode(' ', $terms);
```

Now we can loop through the `$aTerms` array and add new keyword and occurrence records for each of its elements using the two functions – `AddKeyword()` and `AddKeyocc()` – defined below:

```
foreach ($aTerms as $kterm) {
    $kwid=AddKeyword($kterm);
    AddKeyocc("txt",$source,$sourceid,$kwid,$kterm);
}
print "Keywords successfully added<br />\n";

} # end function ParseAssignedTerms()
```

The `AddKeyword()` function takes a single argument, `$keyword`, whose value is the keyword we wish to add to the `bomp_keywords` table. If the keyword doesn't already exist, the function inserts the new keyword into the `bomp_keywords` table:

```
function AddKeyword($keyword)
{
    global $db;
```

First we check to see if the keyword is already present in the table:

```
$sqlquery = "SELECT * FROM bomp_keywords
            WHERE keyword_keyword='$keyword'";
$results  = $db->query($sqlquery);
$results  = $db->query($sqlquery);
if (DB::isError($results)) {
$msg  = "Could not access table bomp_keywords in database bomp: ";
$msg .= $results->getMessage()."<br>\n";
die($msg);
}
$nrows = $results->numRows();
if ($nrows == 0) {
```

If the keyword isn't found (no matching records found), we insert it into keywords:

```
        // The keyword does not exist in table bomp_keywords. Add it.
        $id = $db->nextId('kwid');
        //print("inserted $keyword");
        $insquery = "INSERT bomp_keywords (keyword_kwid,keyword_keyword)
                    VALUES ($id,'$keyword')";
        $insres   = $db->query($insquery);
        if (DB::isError($insres)) {
            die("Could not add keyword '$keyword' to table
                bomp_keywords<br>\n");
        }
        $retquery ="SELECT keyword_kwid from bomp_keywords WHERE
                    keyword_keyword=$keyword";
        $retres   = $db->query($retquery);
        if (DB::isError($retres)) {
            die("The keyword could not be retrieved from bomp_keywords<br>\n");
        }
        $aaRow    = $results->fetchRow(DB_FETCHMODE_ASSOC);
        $kwid = $aaRow["keyword_kwid"];

    } else {
    // Keyword exists (should only be once). Retrieve record id, kwid.
    $aaRow = $retres->fetchRow(DB_FETCHMODE_ASSOC);
    $kwid = $aaRow["keyword_kwid"];
    }
    return($kwid);
} # end function AddKeyword
```

The `AddKeyocc()` function works in a similar fashion – we check to see if there's already a record of this keyword being assigned to the content record in question; if not, we insert a new record into the `bomp_keyoccurrences` table:

```
function AddKeyocc($type,$source,$sourceid,$keyid,$keyword)
{
    global $db;
```

First we write a query to select any record matching this keyword being assigned to this content record:

```
$sqlquery  = "SELECT * FROM bomp_keyoccurrences
              WHERE keyoccurrence_type='$type'
              AND keyoccurrence_source='$source'
              AND keyoccurrence_sourceid='$sourceid'
              AND keyoccurrence_keyid='$keyid'";

$results  = $db->query($sqlquery);
if (DB::isError($results)) {
    $msg  = "Could not access table bomp_keyoccurrences in database
              bomp:<br /> ";
    $msg .= $results->getMessage()."<br>\n";
    die($msg);
}

$nrows = $results->numRows($results);
if ($nrows == 0) {
```

If no matching record is found in bomp_keyoccurrences, we insert one.

```
$insquery ="INSERT INTO bomp_keyoccurrences(keyoccurrence_koid,
              keyoccurrence_type, keyoccurrence_source,
              keyoccurrence_sourceid, keyoccurrence_keyid)
              VALUES ";
$insquery.="('','$type','$source','$sourceid','$keyid')";
$insres   = $db->query($insquery);
if (DB::isError($insres)) {
    $msg  = "Could not add occurrence of $keyword in ";
    $msg .= "$source to keyword occurrences table: ";
    $msg .= $insres->getMessage()."<br>\n";
    die($msg);
} else {
    print "Added occurrence record of $keyword in ";
    print "$source to bomp_keyoccurrences table <br />\n";
}
} else {
```

Otherwise, we inform the user that this keyword has already been assigned to content in question.

```
    $msg  = "Occurrence of $keyword in  $source ";
    $msg .= "already recorded.<br />\n";
}

} # end function AddKeyocc()
```

Now that all the necessary support functions have been defined, we can proceed with the main PHP code for the page. First we check to see if the keyword assignment form has yet been posted.

```
if(!isset($_GET["actn"])) {
```

If not, then we display the facts records needing to have keywords assigned to them:

```
DisplayFactlist();
```

In a complete implementation, we'd display all content needing to have keywords assigned. Since we're only doing so for the facts table, we've commented out the function calls for displaying the other types of content:

```
#DisplayArticles();
#DisplayMmedia();
#DisplayShorts();
#DisplayMonkeys();
} else {
```

If the GET variable actn has, been set, then we know that either a content entry has been selected or that keywords for such an entry have been entered and submitted. Next, we need to determine which of these occurred. First we store the value passed in the GET request for this variable as $actn:

```
$actn = $_GET["actn"];
```

We perform some rudimentary error handling, checking for empty source and sourceid values in the GET request so that subsequent queries based on these won't be likely to fail:

```
if (!isset($_GET["source"])) {
    die("Sorry, no content source table specified.<br />\n");
}
if (!isset($_GET["sourceid"])) {
    die("Sorry, no content source id provided.<br />\n");
}
```

Now we store these two GET variable values as $source and $sourceid:

```
$source = $_GET["source"];
$sourceid = $_GET["sourceid"];
```

The value of $actn should be either showcont or parseterms. If it's the former, we call ShowContent() thereby displaying the list of links for facts records that require keywords to be assigned, as described previously. In the latter case, we check to see if a list of keywords has been entered; if so, we pass these as $parseterms (along with $source and $sourceid) to the function ParseAssignedTerms() which we discussed above:

```
switch ($actn) {
case "showcont": ShowContent($source,$sourceid);
    break;
case "parseterms":
    if (!isset($_GET["parseterms"])) {
        die("Sorry, no keyword terms provided.<br>\n");
    }
    $parseterms = $_GET["parseterms"];
    ParseAssignedTerms($source,$sourceid,$parseterms);
    break;
```

We shouldn't encounter any other values for $actn, but if we do, we provide a default case within our switch block to provide an error message and to exit the script gracefully.

```
    default:
        // Error - we shouldn't ever get here
        die("Sorry. The selected action is not allowed. Try again.<br />\n");
    }
} //  end else {* if(!isset($_GET["actn"]))... *}
?>
```

This is the output of the script:

When running the above script, select the fact about **Canadian Back Bacon** and enter the following string for the keyword terms:

```
canada, pork , ham, bacon, beer, breakfast, lazy
```

The script converts all commas to blanks, and then eliminates extra space. To ensure everything as expected, run the following two SQL queries:

```
SELECT * FROM bomp_keywords;

SELECT * FROM bomp_keyoccurrences
  WHERE keyoccurrence_source='facts' AND keyoccurrence_sourceid=1;
```

Each of these queries should produce 7 records (provided you have not yet added anything else to these tables).

View Web Forum Threads List

The 'Shakespeare's Hundredth Monkey' web forum has, three types of threads, the first two of which are open and closed. Only a thread that is open can have content added to it by a 'monkey' (any user). Threads to which no new content has been added in seven days are closed. They can be viewed but no new postings can be contributed to them. The third type, archive, is reserved for future use. Any code shown below will assume that the third type is in use.

An algorithm for generating a list of available threads is shown below:

1. Retrieve all threads that are not archived.

2. For each thread retrieved, use its title to display a link to a virtual page. This linked page will display the full thread and is discussed in the next section of this chapter.

This is a sample PHP script supporting the above algorithm:

```php
<?php

# FILE: threadlist.php
# USE:  View a list of unarchived Shakespeare's forum threads
```

We start out by assigning the name for the script we'll use to view individual threads; we also include the common.php file, which sets up the database connection using PEAR::DB:

```php
$nextphp = "vw_thread.php";
include_once('common.php');
```

This DisplayThreadList() function displays all unarchived threads.

```php
function DisplayThreadlist()
{
```

As before, $db is a connection object – an instance of PEAR's DB class – whose methods we'll use to access the bomp database.

```php
    global $db;
    global $nextphp;
    global $acctid;
```

We write a query to select all threads whose status is either open or closed and order any results we obtain from most to least recent.

```php
    $sqlquery  = "SELECT thread_thrid, thread_startdate, thread_title FROM
                bomp_threads WHERE thread_status IN ('O', 'C') ORDER BY
                thread_startdate desc";
```

The SQL clause:

```sql
WHERE status IN ('O','C')
```

is just another way of writing:

```sql
WHERE status='O' OR status='C'
```

```
    $results  = $db->query($sqlquery);
    if( DB::isError($results) ) {
        $msg  = "Could not access table bomp_threads: ";
        $msg .= $results->getMessage()."<br>\n";
        die ($msg);
    }
    $nrows = $results->numRows();
    if( $nrows == 0 ) {
        die("No threads in table bomp_threads. Try creating one.<br>\n");
    }
```

If the resultset is non-empty, we write a set of links pointing to the threads using an HTML table to provide some formatting. For each link, the thread title serves as the link text; the link's preceded by the date that the thread was started:

```
    print "<h1>Book of Mankind Project</h1>
            <h2>Shakespeare's Hundredth Monkey Web Forum</h2>\n
            <h3>Threads:</h3>\n
                <table border=\"0\">\n";
    for($i=1; $i<=$nrows; $i++) {
        $aaRow = $results->fetchRow(DB_FETCHMODE_ASSOC);
        $thrid = $aaRow["thrid"];
        $sdate = $aaRow["sdate"];
        $title = $aaRow["title"];
        print "<tr>\n<td>$sdate</td>\n<td> </td>\n<td>
            <a href=\"$nextphp?actn=vwthread&thrid=$thrid&acctid=$acctid\">
            $title</a></td>\n</tr>\n";
    }
    print "</table>\n";
} # end function DisplayThreadlist()
```

Now that we have a means of displaying the thread list, we can call from the main routine in the script, which is quite simple: we merely check to see if there exists a GET variable named $acctid. If there is, we call DisplayThreadList(); if there isn't, we show the user an error message and terminate script execution:

```
if( !isset($_GET["acctid"]) ) {
    // No action specified
    die("No user account id specified.<br />\n");
}
$acctid = $_GET["acctid"];
DisplayThreadlist();

?>
```

The file should look something like the figure below when loaded in the browser. Note that we've supplied `acctid=1` in the querystring:

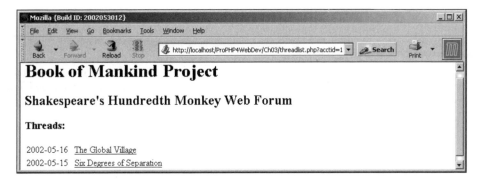

View Selected Thread

Once a thread has been selected, one of the two different virtual pages may be displayed. The first is displayed if the thread is no longer active (that is, it cannot have content added to it). The second is displayed if the thread is still active.

In the algorithm and PHP code below, it is assumed that a thread has been previously selected and that the record ID of the thread is passed to this virtual page in the querystring of the URL request.
The algorithm is as follows:

1. Use URL querystring variable 'thrid' to retrieve the selected thread's record.

2. Retrieve the thread's content from the monkeys table.:

3. Display in chronological order all the content that's been added to the thread since it was created.

4. If the thread is still "open", also display a text area in which the user can add new content to the thread.

Here's the PHP implementation of the algorithm:

```
<!DOCTYPE HTML PUBLIC "-//W3C//DTD HTML 4.01 Transitional//EN"
  "http://www.w3.org/TR/html4/loose.dtd">
<html>
  <head>
  <meta http-equiv="Content-Type" content="text/html; charset=iso-8859-1" />
    <title>Title here!</title>
  </head>
  <body>

  <?php
  # FILE: vw_thread.php
```

```
# USE:  View the contents of a selected web forum thread.

include('common.php');

$script = "vw_thread.php";
$nextphp = "add_monkey.php";
```

After the necessary variable definitions and include() statement (identical to what we've used previously), we define a function that displays the thread and all its content. It takes a single argument, the ID of the thread we want to display:

```
function DisplayThread($thrid)
{
    global $db;
```

We query the database for the thread with the desired ID:

```
$sqlquery = "SELECT thread_title,THREAD_status FROM BOMP_threads
             WHERE thread_thrid='$thrid'";
$results  = $db->query($sqlquery);
if (DB::isError($results)) {
    $msg  = "Could not access bomp_threads table: ";
    $msg .= $results->getMessage()."<br>\n";
    die ($msg);
}
$nrows = $results->numRows($results);
if ($nrows == 0) {
    die("No records in table bomp_threads with the selected thread
        id<br>\n");
}
```

Since a thread record's is guaranteed to be unique, we only need to retrieve one record:

```
$aaRow    = $results->fetchRow(DB_FETCHMODE_ASSOC);

$title    = $aaRow["thread_title"];
$status   = $aaRow["thread_status"];
print "<h1>Book of Mankind Project</h1>\n
       <h2>Shakespeare's Threads</h2>\n
       <table border=\"1\"
       bgcolor=\"#CCCCCC\">\n<tr>\n<td>
       [<b style=\"color:#FF0000\">$title</b>]<br />\n";
```

We display the contributions that have been made to this thread using the DisplayMonkeys() function defined below:

```
DisplayMonkeys($thrid);
print "</td>\n</tr>\n</table>\n";
DisplayMonkeyInputForm($thrid);
} # end function DisplayThread ()
```

The `DisplayMonkeys()` function takes a single parameter, the thread ID, and retrieves and displays all contributions whose thread ID matches that value:

```
function DisplayMonkeys($thrid)
{
```

We retrieve the desired thread contribution records much as we've been doing throughout this chapter, obtaining the posting date, text content, and contributor's ID for each record (`monkey_pdate` and `monkey_contrib` columns from the `bomp_monkeys` table). We also obtain the username by matching the `monkey_whoid` of each record obtained from `bomp_monkeys` against the `account_accountid` column of the `bomp_accounts` table and retrieving the corresponding account value:

```
global $db;

$sqlquery = "SELECT
            m.monkey_postdate,m.monkey_contrib,a.account_account
            FROM bomp_monkeys m LEFT JOIN bomp_accounts a ON
            (m.monkey_whoid=a.account_accountid) WHERE
            m.monkey_thrid='$thrid' ORDER BY monkey_postdate";
$results  = $db->query($sqlquery);
if (DB::isError($results)) {
    $msg  = "Could not access bomp_monkeys table: ";
    $msg .= $results->getMessage()."<br />\n";
    die ($msg);
}
$nrows = $results->numRows();
if ($nrows == 0) {
    die("Error: No contributions to selected thread id=$thrid<br>\n");
}
for ($i=1; $i<=$nrows; $i++) {
    $aaRow = $results->fetchRow(DB_FETCHMODE_ASSOC);
    $pdate   = $aaRow["monkey_postdate"];
    $contrib = $aaRow["monkey_contrib"];
```

If for some reason it doesn't find a matching username in the accounts table, `$acct` is set to the string UNKNOWN USER:

```
    if( !is_null($aaRow["account_account"]) )
        $acct = $aaRow["account_account"];
    else
        $acct = "UNKNOWN USER";
    print "<p>($pdate) [user: $acct]<br />\n<em>$contrib</em></p>\n";
}
} # end function DisplayMonkeys()
```

The following function displays the contribution input form for an open thread:

```
function DisplayMonkeyInputForm($thrid)
{
    global $nextphp;
    global $acctid;

    print "<p> </p>\n
        <p>If you want to add to the above thread, please enter your
```

```
                text below. Only the first 255 characters of your post
                will be saved.<br />
                Please avoid HTML code or special characters.</p>\n
                <form method=\"GET\" action=\"$nextphp\">\n
                <table border=\"0\">\n
                <tr>\n<td> </td>\n
                <td><textarea name=\"newmonkey\" rows=\"7\" cols=\"60\"
                        wrap=\"virtual\"></textarea></td>\n
                <td> </td>\n</tr>\n
                <tr>\n<td> </td>\n
                <td><input type=\"submit\" value=\"ADD\" /></td>\n";
        print "<td><input type=\"hidden\" name=\"actn\" value=\"addmonkey\"
                />\n
                <input type=\"hidden\" name=\"thrid\" value=\"$thrid\" />\n
                <input type=\"hidden\" name=\"acctid\" value=\"$acctid\"
                />\n</td></tr></table></form>\n";
    } # end function DisplayMonkeyInputForm()
```

Now that we've defined all the support functions that we'll use in this script, we can write the body of the script itself. First we perform basic error checking by verifying that the acctid, actn, and acctid variables have been set in the querystring:

```
if (!isset($_GET["acctid"])) {
    die("No user account id specified.<br />\n");
}
$acctid = $_GET["acctid"];

if (!isset($_GET["actn"])) {
    // No action specified
    die("No action specified. Please try again.<br />\n");
}
$actn = $_GET["actn"];
```

Assuming that all three variables have been set in the GET request (in which case we've stored the values of $_GET["acctid"] and $_GET["actn"] in $acctid and $actn, respectively), we write a switch... case... block and test the value of $actn. Even though this variable can take on just one value (vwthread), we do this rather than use an if statement because we may add more capabilities to this script later:

```
switch ($actn) {
case "vwthread":
```

Within the case where $actn is equal to vwthread, we check to see if a thrid value has been sent as part of the GET request, and if so, we call DisplayThread(), passing this value to that function:

```
        if (!isset($_GET["thrid"])) {
            die("Sorry, no thread selected.<br>\n");
        }
        $thrid = $_GET["thrid"];
        DisplayThread($thrid);
        break;
    default:
```

```
        die("Unknown action specified.Please try again.<br />\n");
    }

?>

</body>
</html>
```

Therefore, this code displays a list of the threads that are active, which when clicked upon display the content too.

Contribute to a Thread

If a user adds content to an active thread that they are viewing, three checks need to be performed:

❏   The first check makes sure that the thread is active. Despite that we only display an **Add Content** button for active threads, someone may manually enter the thread ID for a closed thread in the query string of the URL for this page.

❏   The second check ensures that the user making the contribution is not the same as the last one making a contribution to the thread.

❏   The third check ensures that content contains no stopwords (this strictness reduces the workload on staff, so that they do not have to manually moderate forum content).

In both the algorithm and the PHP code, it is assumed that any necessary information is passed in the requested URL's querystring. This includes user ID (**acctid**/$acctid), action to be performed (**actn**/$actn), the thread ID (**thrid**/$thrid), the additional information we are adding to the thread or the 'new monkey' (**newmonkey**/$newmonkey).

As an example this query string may be added to the end of the URL in the address bar of the browser:

?acctid=1&actn=addmonkey&thrid=1&newmonkey='A test addition to the thread'

This content is generally retrieved from an HTML form and will be sent in the querystring. However, such a web form has not been created in this chapter and so for testing purposes this information needs to be passed to the file manually.

Here is the algorithm for managing thread contributions:

```
1.  For the selected thread, retrieve the thread record.

2.  If the result set of the above query has no records, the thread does not
    exist. Display a message to that effect and quit.

3. Otherwise the result set should have one record. If the status is "C",
   then the thread is closed and cannot be contributed to. Display an
   appropriate message and quit. If everything is okay so far, retrieve the
   most recent contribution to the thread.
```

4. If accountid is found equal to whoid, then the user has already posted the most recent contribution to the thread. Display an apology message and quit. Perform auto-moderation on the post, using the algorithm we developed earlier in this chapter for that purpose. If the post fails auto-moderation, we inform the user that the post has been rejected due to potentially offensive content, and exit.

5. If the post has passed all the tests in steps 2, 3, 5 and 6, add the appropriate record to the monkeys table. Display a message indicating success, along with the updated content of the thread.

Here is the PHP script, to suit the above algorithm:

```php
<?php

# FILE: add_monkey.php
# USE:  add a contribution to a specific forum thread

$script = "add_monkey.php";
include_once('common.php');
```

Rather than repeat the auto-moderation code in this script, we've placed it in an include file (automod_incl.php), which contains the same AutoMod class that we saw earlier in this chapter:

```php
include ("automod.php");
```

The AddMonkey() function performs the tests listed in steps 3, 5 and 6 of our algorithm. If the post passes all of these tests, we call another function (AddMonkeyContrib()) that adds a new record to the bomp_monkeys table:

```php
function AddMonkey($thrid,$contrib)
{
        global $acctid;
        global $db;
```

We obtain the thread record using the GetThread() function defined below:

```php
        $aaThread = GetThread($thrid);
```

If the thread's status code is 'C', we inform the user that the thread is closed and terminate the script:

```php
        if( $aaThread["status"] == "C" ) {
            die("Sorry. The selected thread is closed.<br />\n");
        }
```

Otherwise, we obtain the most recent contribution to the thread, and if the contributor's ID matches that of the current user, we inform the user that he cannot make successive posts, and exit:

```
        $aaLastMonkey = GetLastMonkey($thrid);
        if($aaLastMonkey["whoid"] == $acctid) {

            $msg  = "You posted the last contribution to the selected thread.
                    Under the rules of this forum, you cannot post two
                    contributions in succession to the same thread.<br />\n";
            die($msg);
        } else {
```

If the thread's status is open and the last user to post to it wasn't the current user, we perform auto-moderation on the content for the new post using the `AutoModerate()` method of the `AutoMod` class we discussed earlier. If the post passes auto-moderation, we call `AddMonkeyContrib()`, which adds the new post. Otherwise, we inform the user that the post has been rejected, and exit:

```
        $am=new AutoMod($db);
        $status = $am->AutoModerate($contrib,1);
        if($status == "M") {
            AddMonkeyContrib($thrid,$contrib);
        } else {
            die("Content rejected due to potential offensiveness.<br />\n");
        }
    }
} # end function AddMonkey()
```

`GetThread()` returns the row from the `bomp_threads` table whose ID matches the `$thrid` value passed to the function:

```
function GetThread($thrid)
{
    global $db;
    // Retrieve full record
    // Build and execute query
    $sqlquery = "SELECT * FROM bomp_threads WHERE thread_thrid=$thrid";
    $results  = $db->query($sqlquery);
    if (DB::isError($results)) {
        $msg  = "Could not access bomp_threads table: ";
        $msg .= $results->getMessage()."<br />\n";
        die ($msg);
    }
    $nrows = $results->numRows();
    if ($nrows == 0) {
        die("No matching records found in bomp_threads table.<br />\n");
    }
    $aaRow = $results->fetchRow(DB_FETCHMODE_ASSOC);
    return($aaRow);
} # end function GetThread
```

The function `GetLastMonkey()` retrieves the most recent post to a thread, given a thread ID:

```
function GetLastMonkey($thrid)
{

    global $db;

    // Build and execute query
```

```
    $sqlquery  = "SELECT * FROM bomp_monkeys WHERE monkey_thrid=$thrid ";
    $sqlquery .= "ORDER BY monkey_postdate desc limit 0,1";

    $results  = $db->query($sqlquery);
    if (DB::isError($results)) {
        $msg  = "Could not access table bomp_monkeys in database bomp: ";
        $msg .= $results->getMessage()."<br>\n";
        die ($msg);
    }
    $nrows = $results->numRows();
    if ($nrows == 0) {
        die("No records in table bomp_monkeys with the selected thread
            id<br>\n");
    }
    // Retrieve and return the desired record.
    $aaRow = $results->fetchRow(DB_FETCHMODE_ASSOC);
    return($aaRow);
} # end function GetLastMonkey()
```

The following function adds the text in $contrib as the content of a new post to the forum thread having the thread ID $thrid. Once the new record has been inserted, a message indicating success is displayed to the user, along with the updated content of the thread:

```
function AddMonkeyContrib($thrid,$contrib)
{

    global $db;
    global $acctid;

    $today = date("Y-m-d");
    $insquery = "INSERT INTO bomp_monkeys (monkey_recid, monkey_whoid,
                monkey_thrid, monkey_status, monkey_pdate, monkey_contrib)
                VALUES ('',$acctid,$thrid,'M', '$today','$contrib')";

    $insres = $db->query($insquery);
    if (DB::isError($insres)) {
        $msg  = "Could not add post to forum thread: ";
        $msg .= $insres->getMessage() . "<br />\n";
        die($msg);
    } else {
        $recid = $id;
        print "Added new post to thread.<br />\n";
    }
} # end function AddMonkeyContrib()
```

Now we can write the main portion of the script. First we check to make sure that a user account and action have been specified:

```
if(!isset($_GET["acctid"])) {
    die("No user account id specified.<br />\n");
}
```

```
$acctid = $_GET["acctid"];

if(!isset($_GET["actn"])) {
    die("No action specified. Please try again.<br>\n");
}
$actn = $_GET["actn"];
```

As in the previous script, we use a `switch... case...` structure here to facilitate the addition of new functionality to this script at a later date:

```
switch($actn) {
case "addmonkey":
    if(!isset($_GET["thrid"])) {
        die("Sorry, no thread selected.<br />\n");
    }
    if(!isset($_GET["newmonkey"])) {
        die("Sorry, no thread contribution provided.<br />\n");
    }
    $thrid = $_GET["thrid"];
    $newmonkey = $_GET["newmonkey"];
    AddMonkey($thrid,$newmonkey);
    break;
default:
    die("Unknown action specified.Please try again.<br />\n");
}
?>
```

The script above displays a form which accepts content that you want to add to an existing thread, as seen below in the screenshot:

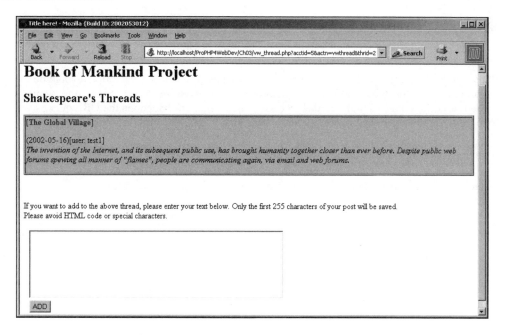

Create New Thread

There is only one rule to be applied when a user requests to add a thread to an active forum:

> *"In keeping with the name of the web forum (Shakespeare's Hundredth Monkey), only 100 active threads are allowed at any time."*

While we can take steps to ensure that a regular user sees the Create New Thread option only if less than 100 threads are active, it's also possible that someone might enter the necessary information by employing some reverse engineering to create a URL with an (in)appropriate querystring and typing it into the browser's address bar.

We provide an algorithm here for managing thread creation that performs an appropriate before creating a new thread:

1. Count the number of open threads; that is, select the threads whose status code is set to "0".

2. If the number of active threads is greater than 99, display an appropriate message to the user and quit.

3. Otherwise, display a form to allow the input of a thread title and the content of the first contribution to the new thread.

4. If the user has submitted information for a new thread, we want to record this. But first we must check the number of open threads again, as someone else could have entered this information via the URL querystring, in the meantime.

5. If there are available threads, add a record to the bomp_threads table, and another to the bomp_monkeys table. Display a message indicating success along with the content of the new thread.

A PHP script supporting the above algorithm is shown below. While it is a test script, it could be called as the result of a Create Thread button from the virtual page represented by threadlist.php, which we discussed earlier. For this example, all the necessary input will be provided via the URL query string. To invoke the script below, in the browser's address bar, enter a URL that ends in something like:

new_thread.php?acctid=2&actn=newthread

Now let's look at the thread creation script, which we've named new_thread.php:

```php
<?php

# FILE: new_thread.php
# USE:  Create new BOMP forum thread.
```

We include the files in which our database access and moderation classes are stored. Next, as we've done before, we define some functions to perform various necessary tasks, which we'll call as needed from the main portion of the script:

```php
include("common.php");
include("automod.php");
```

The first function, `DisplayThreadInputForm()`, generates the input form discussed in step 1 of our algorithm. You'll notice that it's very similar to the `DisplayMonkeyInputForm()` function which we discussed earlier:

```php
function DisplayThreadInputForm()
{
    global $acctid;
    global $script;
    print "<h1>Book of Mankind Project</h1>\n
            <h2>Shakespeare's Threads</h2>\n
            <h3>NEW THREAD:</h3>\n
            <p>Enter the title of your thread in the input box. Enter the
            1st contribution to the thread in the large text area.
            Please avoid HTML code or special characters.</p>\n
            <form method=\"GET\" action=\"$PHP_SELF\">\n
            <table border='0'>\n<tr>\n"
            <td valign=\"top\"><b>Title</b>: </td>\n
            <td> </td>\n
            <td><input type=\"text\" name=\"title\" size=\"56\"></td>\n
            <td> </td>\n</tr>\n
            <tr><td colspan=\"3\"> </td></tr>\n
            <tr>\n
            <td valign=\"top\"><b>Text</b>: </td>\n
            <td> </td>\n
            <td><textarea name=\"newmonkey\" rows=\"7\" cols=\"60\"
                    wrap=\"virtual\"></textarea></td>\n
            <td> </td>\n</tr>\n
            <tr>\n
            <td> </td>\n
            <td> </td>\n
            <td><input type=\"submit\" value=\"Create\"></td>\n
            <td><input type=\"hidden\" name=\"actn\" value=\"addthread\">\n
            <input type=\"hidden\" name=\"acctid\"
                    value=\"$acctid\"></td>\n</tr>\n</table>\n</form>\n";
} # end function DisplayThreadInputForm()
```

After checking that we don't have 100 open threads already, it adds new records:

```php
function AddThread($title,$contrib)
{
    global $db;
      if(CountActiveThreads() > 99) {
        $msg = "Only 100 monkeys allowed active at any one time.
                Please try again later.<br>\n";
        die($msg);
      }
```

129

Before inserting the new thread, we moderate the contribution:

```
    $am=new AutoMod($db);
    $status = $am->AutoModerate($source,1);

    if($status == "M") {
        $thrid = AddThreadInfo($title);
        AddMonkeyContrib($thrid,$contrib);
    } else {
        $msg  = "Content rejected due to potential offensiveness.
                Thread not created.<br />\n";
        die($msg);
    }
}
```

Next we define a function that returns the number of open threads.

```
function CountActiveThreads()
{
    // Count the number of open/active threads and return count.

    global $db;

    $sqlquery  = "SELECT COUNT(*) AS nactive FROM bomp_threads
                    WHERE thread_status = 'O'";

    $results  = $db->query($sqlquery);
    if(DB::isError($results)) {
        $msg  = "Could not access bomp_accounts table: ";
        $msg .= $results->getMessage();
        die ($msg);
    }

    $aaRow = $results->fetchRow(DB_FETCHMODE_ASSOC);
    return $aaRow["nactive"];
} # end function CountActiveThreads()
```

The `AddThreadInfo()` function adds a new thread to the forum if no thread with a duplicate title is found (as determined by the function `IsDuplicateThread()` below):

```
function AddThreadInfo($title)
{
    global $db;
    global $acctid;
    if ( IsDuplicateThread ($title) ) {
        $msg  = "There is already a thread with the title '$title'. <br />\n";
        die($msg);
    }
    $today = date("Y-m-d");
    $insquery = "INSERT INTO bomp_threads
                    (thread_origid, thread_startdate, thread_status,
                    thread_title) VALUES ($acctid,'$today','O', '$title')";
```

```
        $insres   = $db->query($insquery);
        if (DB::isError($insres)) {
            $msg  = "Could not add new thread record: ";
            $msg .= $insres->getMessage()."<br>\n";
            die($msg);
        }
          $thrid = $db->nextId('thread_thrid');
    } # end function AddThreadInfo()
```

This function returns a TRUE or FALSE value depending on whether or not another thread with the same title already exists. IsDuplicateThread() takes a single argument, the desired title text for the new thread:

```
    function IsDuplicateThread($title)
    {
        global $db;
        global $acctid;
```

The value stored in the variable $isdup will be returned to the calling function; its default value is FALSE (that is, no duplicate found):

```
        $isdup = FALSE;
```

Here we query the bomp_threads table to see if there exist any threads with the same title as $title:

```
        $sqlquery .= "SELECT * FROM bomp_threads WHERE thread_title='$title'";

        $results  = $db->query($sqlquery);
        if (DB::isError($results)) {
            $msg  = "Could not access table bomp_threads in database bomp: ";
            $msg .= $results->getMessage()."<br>\n";
            die($msg);
        }
        $nrows = $results->numRows();
```

If any matching records are found, we set $isdup to TRUE:

```
        $isdup = $nrows > 0;
```

Return the value of $isdup to the calling function:

```
        return($isdup);
    }
```

This function is very similar to its namesake in add_monkey.php. The main difference is that here, if we do not succeed in adding the necessary record to the bomp_monkeys table, we must delete the thread record that we just added to the bomp_threads table:

```
function AddMonkeyContrib($thrid,$contrib)
{
    global $db;
    global $acctid;

    $status = "M"; // Auto-moderated, but no keywords assigned yet.

    $today = date("Y-m-d");
    $insquery = "INSERT INTO bomp_monkeys (monkey_whoid, monkey_status,
                 monkey_postdate, monkey_contrib) VALUES
                 ($acctid,'$status','$today', '$contrib')";
    $insres = $db->query($insquery);
    if (DB::isError($insres)) {
        DeleteThread($thrid);
        $msg  = "Could not add monkey contribution to the selected";
        $msg .= "forum thread. Deleted thread record: ";
        $msg .= $insres->getMessage()."<br />\n";
        die($msg);
    }
} # end function AddMonkeyContrib()
```

This function deletes the thread with the given thread ID ($thrid):

```
function DeleteThread($thrid)
{
    global $db;
    global $acctid;

    $delquery = "DELETE FROM bomp_threads WHERE thread_thrid = $thrid";
    $delres   = $db->query($delquery);
    if (DB::isError($delres)) {
        $msg  = "Database problems. Could not access table bomp_threads
                 to ";
        $msg .= "delete thread record: ";
        $msg .= $delres->getMessage()."<br>\n";
        die($msg);
    }
} # end function DeleteThread()
```

Now, in the main body of the script, we first check to see if a user has been specified, that is, if the value of the account ID has ben set in the querystring:

```
if (!isset($_GET["acctid"])) {
    // No action specified
    die("No user account id specified.<br>\n");
}
$acctid = $_GET["acctid"];
```

Next we check to see if a `actn` variable has been set in the GET request, that is, if an action has been specified:

```
if (!isset($_GET["actn"])) {
    // No action specified
    die("No action specified. Please try again.<br>\n");
}
$actn = $_REQUEST["actn"];
```

Depending upon the value set in `$actn` (which we've set equal to `$_GET["actn"]`), we either display the thread input form by calling `DisplayThreadInputForm()` or attempt to add a new thread:

```
switch ($actn) {

case "newthread":
    DisplayThreadInputForm();
    break;
case "addthread":
    if (!isset($_REQUEST["title"])) {
        die("Sorry, no thread title provided.<br>\n");
    }
    if (!isset($_REQUEST["newmonkey"])) {
        die("Sorry, no initial thread contribution provided.<br>\n");
    }
    $title = $_REQUEST["title"];
    $newmonkey = $_REQUEST["newmonkey"];
    AddThread($title,$newmonkey);
    break;
default:
    die("Unknown action specified.Please try again.<br>\n");
}
?>
```

When a user attempts to add a new thread, the following form will be displayed to accept the details, provided less than a hundred threads are active:

Close Old Threads

As indicated earlier, a thread is archived if no one adds content to it in seven days. This check can be done on a nightly basis during system back up. Recall that each thread has a column that records the date of creation of the thread (`thread_startdate`). Each monkey contribution has a column for the posting date (`monkey_postdate`). If the seven-day rule applied to the creation date (that is, a thread is only active for roughly seven days after its last posting), then we can use some of MySQL's date calculation functions to formulate an appropriate query.

Recall that the function `CURDATE()` provides the current date and that the function `TO_DAYS()` converts the operand to a relative number of calendar days. A thread is only deactivated if no one has posted to it for 7 days or more. This means that we have to compare today's date with the date of the most recent contribution to the thread. An algorithm to manage deactivation is given below:

1. Select the most recent posting in each open thread.

2. For each thread retrieved, calculate the number of days since its last posting. Retain only those threads whose most recent posting is more than 6 days old. For each filtered thread in our list we set its status in the table threads to closed (C).

The PHP code for this algorithm is quite easy and is left as an exercise.

Fuzzy Search Engine

Once we have at least a few assigned keywords to the items in table `bomp_facts`, we can use the search feature described in this section on the items in the `bomp_facts` table.

Now that we have some content items in the `bomp_facts` table, we can discuss the fuzzy search engine feature mentioned earlier. A fuzzy search engine differs from a regular search in that we are searching for keywords associated with a content item, possibly including audio files, still images, or streaming video. To make things even more inexact, the keywords assigned to each item added to the database are subject to the judgement of individual BOMP staff members.

For example, say we have a photograph of a man walking a dog in Central Park in New York. There are several possible keywords assignable to the image. However, "New York" is two words, so it cannot be used). If the staff member assigning keywords for this image forget to use 'park', then someone searching for content relating to park will obviously not get this image in the resulting match list. However, if we have a search feature whereby a user can specify a number of keywords, used in an AND or OR condition, this will increase the odds that a user will actually find what he is looking for.

For example, we will describe an algorithm for a fuzzy search of content items from the facts table. Content from any of the other tables can be searched in pretty much the same way, provided keywords have been assigned to the content entries, in the following manner:

1. Display an HTML text input field for entry of keywords to search on. Include a radio button for OR (default) or AND. The logical condition will apply to all keywords supplied. Keywords can be separated with spaces and/or commas, the parsing of which will handled by the PHP code.

2. The user has now submitted a fuzzy search request. All the necessary information will be provided in either POST or GET variables sent by the referring URL.

3. Parse the request. If the OR condition was used for the search:

   If there are any content entries matching at least one of the search terms, display a non-repeating list of content entries (each of which contains at least one of the search terms).

   If there were no entries matching any one or more search terms, display a user-friendly error message, then terminate script execution.

4. If the AND condition was used:

   If any of the requested search terms are not in the keywords table and, display a user-friendly error message, and then quit.

   If all terms are in the keywords table and the AND condition was used for the search, and then produce a non-repeating list of content entries, each of which contains all of the search terms.

A PHP script supporting the above algorithm is shown below. No URL query string parameters are required to activate the first virtual page:

```php
<?php

# FILE: fzsearch_facts.php
# USE: Fuzzy search of facts content using keywords

include('common.php');
```

First we define a function `DisplayFuzzySearchForm()` that generates an HTML form containing a text input for entry of keywords to search against, as well as a pair of radio buttons to allow the user to choose either an AND-style or OR-style search. As we'll see in the main body of the script, displaying this form is the default behavior for this page.

```php
function DisplayFuzzySearchForm($source)
{
    print "<p>Please enter the keywords you want to search for amongst
        entries in table $source. If you enter more than one
        keyword, separate them with blanks or commas</p>\n
        <form method=\"GET\" action=\"$PHP_SELF\">\n
        <table border=\"0\">\n<tr>\n<td> </td>\n
        <td><input type=\"text\" name=\"fzterms\" size=\"60\"></td>\n
        <td><input type=\"radio\" name=\"cond\" value=\"OR\" border=\"0\"
                checked=\"checked\">OR</td>\n
        <td> </td>\n
        <td><input type=\"radio\" name=\"cond\" value=\"AND\"
                border=\"0\">AND</td>\n</tr>\n
        <tr>\n<td> </td>\n
```

```
            <td><input type=\"submit\" value=\"Search\"></td>\n
            <td><input type=\"hidden\" name=\"actn\" value=\"fzsearch\">\n
            <input type=\"hidden\" name=\"source\" value=\"$source\"></td>\n
            </tr>\n</table>\n</form>\n";

    } # end function DisplayFuzzySearchForm
```

When the search form above is submitted, we call the `SearchFacts()` function to conduct the search:

```
function SearchFacts($source,$fzterms,$cond)
{
    print "<h1>Book of Mankind Project</h1>\n";
    print "<h2>Fuzzy Search on Facts</h2>\n";
```

We display the search terms as a comma-delimited list:

```
        $fzterms = preg_replace("/,/s", " ", $fzterms);
        while(ereg(' ',$fzterms)){
            $fzterms = preg_replace("/\s+/s", " ", $fzterms);
        }
        $aTerms = explode(' ', $fzterms);
        print "<b>search terms</b>: (".join(', ',$aTerms).")<br />\n";
        $nterms = count($aTerms);
        $nmiss = 0;
```

For each search term, we call the `FoundKeyword()` function, which returns the ID of the keyword from the `bomp_keywords` table (or zero if the keyword isn't found in keywords):

```
        foreach ($aTerms as $term) {
            if( ($kwid = FoundKeyword($term)) == 0) {
```

If the search term isn't found in keywords, we add it to an array, `$aMiss`, of as-yet unused keywords:

```
            $aMiss[$nmiss] = $term;
            $nmiss++;
        } else
```

Otherwise, we add its ID (`keyword_kwid`) to an associative array `$aaKeywords`, with the search term itself acting as the key (for example, `$aaKeywords["bacon"] = 2;`).

```
        {
            $aaKeywords[$term] = $kwid;
        }
    }
```

If none of the search terms are found in the `bomp_keywords` table, we display an appropriate error message and terminate script execution at that point.

```
        if($nmiss == $nterms) {
            $msg = "None of your search terms have been used
                    as keywords. Please try some different terms.<br />\n";
            die($msg);
        }
```

If a single search term was specified and we've found a match for it in the `bomp_keywords` table, then we search the `bomp_keyoccurrences` table for matches on the search term and content items in the `bomp_facts` table:

```
if (($nmiss==0) && ($nterms==1)) {
    print "Searching for selected term.<br />\n";
    FindDocsOneFact($aaKeywords[$aTerms[0]]);
    die();
}
print "$nterms term(s) using \"$cond\"<br />\n";
```

If all of the search terms are keywords, we conduct a search based on the user's choice of the "AND" or "OR" option, that is, we call one or the other of the functions `FindAllTermsAnd()` or `FindTermsOr()`, both of which are explained below:

```
if($nmiss == 0) {
    print "All search terms are keywords. ";
    if($cond == "AND") {
        print "Searching using \"AND\"<br />\n";
        FindAllTermsAnd("facts",$aaKeywords,$nterms);
    } else {
        print "Searching using 'OR'<br>\n";
        FindTermsOr("facts",$aaKeywords);
    }
    die();
}
```

If the "AND" option was chosen by the user but one or more of the search terms weren't found in the `bomp_keywords` table, then the search has failed:

```
if ( ($nmiss > 0) && ($cond=="AND") ) {
    print "<p>Fuzzy search with 'AND' failed. The following search terms
            are not yet assigned as keywords:</p>\n <ul>\n";
    foreach ($aMiss as $miss) {
        print "<li>$miss</li>-\n";
    }
    print "</ul>\n";
    die();
}
```

If the "OR" search option was selected but some of the search terms aren't keywords, then we search on those that are listed in the `bomp_keywords` table:

```
if ( ($nmiss > 0) && (strcmp($cond,"OR")==0) ) {
    print "<p> The search terms " . join(",",$aMiss) . ") " . "
            are not keywords" . ";" . " searching on available keywords
            using 'OR'.</p>\n";

    FindTermsOr("facts",$aaKeywords);
    die();
}
die("Error in search terms.<br>\n");
} # end function SearchFacts()
```

This is the function called when one search term is used, and it is a keyword:

```
function FindDocsOneFact($termid)
{
    global $db;
    global $script;
```

We query the bomp database, looking for facts that match occurrences of the keyword in the bomp_keyoccurrences table, where the bomp_keyoccurrences record is assigned to bomp_facts:

```
$sqlquery  = "SELECT fa.fact_factid,fa.fact_title
                FROM bomp_facts as fa, bomp_keyoccurrences as ko
                WHERE fa.fact_factid=ko.keyoccurrence_sourceid
                AND ko.keyoccurrence_source='facts'
                AND ko.keyoccurrence_keyid=$termid";

$results  = $db->query($sqlquery);
if (DB::isError($results)) {
    $msg  = "Could not access table bomp_facts in database bomp: ";
    $msg .= $results->getMessage() . "<br />\n";
    die ($msg);
}
$nrows = $results->numRows();
```

If no matching records are found, we inform the user, and exit the script:

```
if ($nrows == 0) {
    $msg  = "No records in table bomp_facts with the
            selected keyword assigned<br />\n";
    die($msg);
}
```

Otherwise, we use the title of each matching entry as the text of a link to the full content of that facts entry:

```
print "<b>Fuzzily-Matched Facts Items</b>\n <ul>\n";
for ($i=1; $i<=$nrows; $i++) {
    $aaRow = $results->fetchRow(DB_FETCHMODE_ASSOC);
    $factid = $aaRow["fact_factid"];
    $title  = $aaRow["fact_title"];
    print "<li><a href=\"$PHP_SELF?actn=vwfact&factid=$factid\">
            $title</a></li>\n";
}
print "</ul>\n";
} # end function FindDocsOneFact()
```

The FoundKeyword() function, as we've already mentioned, returns the ID (keyword_kwid) of a keyword from the bomp_keywords table, or zero, if no match is found:

```
function FoundKeyword($keyword)
{
    global $db;
    $kwid = 0;

    $sqlquery = "SELECT keyword_kwid FROM bomp_keywords
```

```
                          WHERE keyword_keyword='$keyword'";
      $results  = $db->query($sqlquery);
      if (DB::isError($results)) {
          $msg  = "Could not access bomp_keywords table: ";
          $msg .= $results->getMessage() . "<br />\n";
          die($msg);
      }
      $nrows = $results->numRows();
      if ($nrows > 0) {
          $aaRow = $results->fetchRow(DB_FETCHMODE_ASSOC);
          $kwid  = $aaRow["keyword_kwid"];
      }
      return($kwid);
  } # end function FoundKeyword()
```

If the user has specified the search using the "AND" option, then we need to find content items to which all the search terms have been assigned as keywords. FindAllTermsAnd() takes the name of a content table ($source, which we know will be equal to the string 'facts' n this example), an associative array whose elements are the keywords being searched on ($aaKeywords), and the number of search terms ($nterms):

```
function FindAllTermsAnd($source,$aaKeywords,$nterms)
{
```

We use FindTerms() to get the number of unique entries in the bomp_facts table which has been assigned as keywords to each of the search terms and set $nuniq to the number of these entries:

```
$aaUniqEntries = FindTerms($source,$aaKeywords);
$nuniq = count($aaUniqEntries);
$nmiss = 0;
```

Now we check the frequency count for each keyword; if any facts table entry hasn't been matched $nterms times, then we know that one of the search terms wasn't assigned to that entry as a keyword. We keep a running total of the number of these "misses" as $nmiss:

```
foreach ($aaUniqEntries as $sourceid => $freq) {
    if ($freq != $nterms){
        $nmiss++;
    }
}
```

If the number of "misses" and the number of unique entries matching any of the search terms is the same, then no entries matched all of the search terms:

```
if ($nmiss == $nuniq) {
    $msg  = "No documents from table $source
                matched all of the search terms.<br>\n";
    print $msg;
} else {
```

Otherwise, we can print out a list of links to the entries that did match all the search terms. For each of these, the frequency count $freq will be the same as the number of search terms:

```
print "<b>Documents from the $source table containing  one or more
        fuzzy search terms</b>:<br />\n";

foreach($aaUniqEntries as $sourceid => $freq) {
    if(($freq <= $nterms)&&($freq!=0)) {
```

We use switch($source)... case... here even though the only value for $source at the moment is "facts"; in this way, we allow for future expansion of the script to cover fuzzy searches on other content tables in the bomp database:

```
switch($source) {
case "facts":
```

For each link, we use the title of the facts entry in question as the link text:

```
            $aaRow = GetFact($sourceid)
            $title = $aaRow["fact_title"];
            $link  = $script."?actn=vwfact&factid=$sourceid";
            print "<li><a href='$link'>$title</a></li>\n";
            break;

        default:
            $msg  = "Only 'facts' content currently supported ";
            $msg .= "for fuzzy search<br>\n";
            print $msg;
        }
    }
  }
 }
} # end function FindAllTermsAnd()
```

Now for the search on multiple terms using the OR option. FindTermsOr() takes two arguments, the name of the content table ($source) and the same associative array ($aaKeywords) of keywords and keyword_kwid values as above:

```
function FindTermsOr($source,$aaKeywords)
{
```

Once again, we call the FindTerms() function to find any content entries in the bomp_facts table which have been assigned at least one of the keywords in $aaKeywords. This time, we don't have to do any additional testing; we can immediately write a list of links to the content entries using the same method as we did in FindAllTermsAnd():

```
$aaUniqEntries = FindTerms($source,$aaKeywords);

print "<b>Documents from table $source containing one or more ";
print "fuzzy search term<b>:<br />\n";

foreach ($aaUniqEntries as $sourceid => $freq) {
    switch($source) {
```

Again we're only showing code for fuzzy searches on facts content for purposes of this case study, but we can add this capability to other content tables in the bomp database by placing additional case blocks following the first one shown:

```
        case "facts":
            $aaRow = GetFact($sourceid);
            //
            $title = $aaRow["fact_title"];
            $link  = $PHP_SELF . "?actn=vwfact&factid=$sourceid";
            print "<li><a href=\"$link\">$title</a></li><br>\n";
            break;

        default:
            $msg  = "Only \"facts\" content currently supported
                    by fuzzy search<br />\n";
            print $msg;
        } #end switch
    } # end foreach
} # end function FindTermsOr()
```

The function named FindTerms() takes as arguments the name of a content table and an associative array of keyword/keyword ID pairs ($aaKeywords). It returns an associative array whose keys are the same keywords as used in $aaKeywords; the value of each of these keys is the number of times this keyword is referenced in the bomp_keyoccurrences table:

```
function FindTerms($source,$aaKeywords)
{
    // Find any content entries from table $source which have been assigned
    // at least one of the keywords in $aaKeywords.

    global $db;
    global $script;
```

We use the keyword IDs from $aaKeywords to build a query containing all the keyword IDs ORed together. For example, if the search terms were "Canada", "couch" and "bacon" and these three words were the first, third and seventh entries in the keywords table, our query would look like this:

```
SELECT sourceid FROM bomp_keyoccurrences WHERE source='$source'
AND keyid=1 OR keyid=3 OR keyid=7
```

Let's continue with the script:

```
        print "<br />\n";
        $ORCOND = "";   $cnt = 1;
        foreach($aaKeywords as $term => $keyid) {
            if($cnt > 1) $ORCOND .= " OR ";
            $ORCOND .= "keyoccurrence_keyid=$keyid";
            $cnt++;
        }
        $sqlquery  = "SELECT keyoccurrence_sourceid from bomp_keyoccurrences
                    WHERE keyoccurrence_source='$source' AND ";
        $sqlquery .= "($ORCOND)";
        $results  = $db->query($sqlquery);
```

```
    if(DB::isError($results)) {
        $msg  = "Could not access bomp_keyoccurrences table: ";
        $msg .= $results->getMessage()."<br />\n";
        die ($msg);
    }
    $nrows = $results->numRows();
```

If no results were returned by the query, we inform the user:

```
    if($nrows == 0) {
        $msg  = "<p>No content from the $source table found
                relating to any of the fuzzy search terms entered.</p>\n";
        print $msg;
    } else {
```

If any matching records were found, we assemble them into an associative array of unique content items, using the ID of each item as its key. The value of each element is the number of times this ID matched a keyoccurrence_sourceid column value in bomp_keyoccurrences:

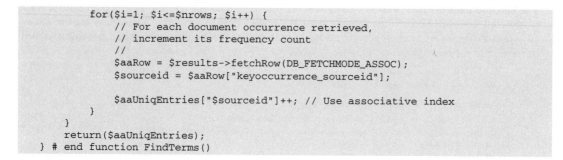

```
        for($i=1; $i<=$nrows; $i++) {
            // For each document occurrence retrieved,
            // increment its frequency count
            //
            $aaRow = $results->fetchRow(DB_FETCHMODE_ASSOC);
            $sourceid = $aaRow["keyoccurrence_sourceid"];

            $aaUniqEntries["$sourceid"]++; // Use associative index
        }
    }
    return($aaUniqEntries);
} # end function FindTerms()
```

The last two support functions for this file, DisplayFact() and GetFact(), are nearly identical to their counterparts in assn_kwords.php and shouldn't require any repeated or additional explanations:

```
function DisplayFact($sourceid)
{
    // Display the fact record
    $aaRow = GetFact($sourceid);
    $title = $aaRow["fact_title"];
    $content  = $aaRow["fact_content"];
    print "<h1>Book of Mankind Project</h1>\n";
    print "<h2>Facts</h2>\n";
    print "<table border='0' bgcolor='#CCCCCC'>\n";
    print "<tr>\n<td>\n";
    print "[<b style=\"color:#FF0000\"><em>$title</em></b>]
            <br />\n<em>$content</em><br />\n";
    print "</td>\n</tr>\n";
    print "</table>\n";

} # end function DisplayFact()

function GetFact($sourceid)
{
```

```
    global $db;

    $sqlquery = "SELECT fact_title,fact_content FROM bomp_facts
                WHERE fact_factid=$sourceid";
    $results  = $db->query($sqlquery);
    if(!$results) {
        $msg  = "Could not access bomp_facts table: ";
        $msg .= $results->getMessage()."<br />\n";
        die ($msg);
    }
    $nrows = $results->numRows();
    if($nrows == 0) {
        die("No records in table bomp_facts with the selected fact
            id<br>\n");
    }
    $aaRow = $results->fetchRow(DB_FETCHMODE_ASSOC);
    return($aaRow);
} # end function DisplayFact()
```

Having defined all of the functions required for our (limited) Fuzzy Search implementation, we can turn our attention to the script's global code.

First we check to see if an action for the script to perform has been specified – that is, if the query string variable $_GET["actn"] has been set by submitting the Search form or following one of the links displayed in the search results. If this variable hasn't been set, then we display the Search form, shown in the figure following the rest of the code listing for this page:

```
if(!isset($_GET["actn"])) {
    DisplayFuzzySearchForm("facts");
} else {
    $actn = $_GET["actn"];
```

Otherwise, we have two possibilities – we either need to run a search (the value of $actn is "fzsearch"), or to display search results ($actn is equal to "vwfact"):

```
    switch($actn) {
    case "fzsearch":
```

If we're handling a search request, then we need to determine what type of content we're searching for – that is, which table we want to query. The name of the relevant table should have been passed as $_GET["source"], but in the event that this variable hasn't been set we'll display the facts search form again:

```
        if(!isset($_GET["source"])) {
            DisplayFuzzySearchForm("facts");
        } else {
```

Otherwise, we use a switch block to determine what we should do next, in response to the value of $_GET["source"]. Currently this isn't very hard, since there's only one value provided for, but as we develop the site further, we'll want to add more cases corresponding to additional content tables to be searched:

```
            $source = $_GET["source"];
            switch($source) {
```

For now we're concerned only with a value of "facts". Within this inner switch, we first verify that search terms and a logical operator were specified in the search request – that is, that $_GET["fzsearch"] or $_GET["cond"] isn't empty. If either one of the values hasn't been set, we display the Search form:

```
case "facts":
    if(!isset($_GET["fzterms"])) {
        print "No search terms specified.<br />\n";
        DisplayFuzzySearchForm();
    } elseif(!isset($_GET["cond"])) {
        print "No 'AND' or 'OR' condition specified.<br>\n";
        DisplayFuzzySearchForm();
    } else {
```

If both values have been set, we can pass them (along with $_GET["source"]) to SearchFacts() and perform the search:

```
        $fzterms = $_GET["fzterms"];
        $cond = $_GET["cond"];
        SearchFacts($source,$fzterms,$cond);
    }
    break;
```

We also provide a default case that prints an error message to take care of any possibility that an invalid table name was passed in the search request. This ends the inner switch block:

```
default:
    print "Cannot search on this type of content.<br />\n";
    break;
//  end switch($source)
```

The other possibility for a requested action is to view the content of a bomp_facts record, for which we require a fact_factid. If one wasn't provided in the search request, we display the Search form:

```
case "vwfact":
    if (!isset($_GET["factid"])) {
        DisplayFuzzySearchForm("facts");
    } else {
```

Otherwise, we call DisplayFact(), and generate the content display for the referenced bomp_facts record:

```
        $factid = $_GET["factid"];
        DisplayFact($factid);
    }
    break;
```

Finally, in the event that some other value was passed for the action string, we display an error message advising the user of the problem:

```
                default:
                    print "Unknown action specified.Please try again.
                        <br />\n";
                }
            }
        }
    }
}
?>
```

The screenshot below shows the Fuzzy search page:

Improvements

We have covered only a selection of likely features that would be included in a complete implementation of the BOMP project site. The items below list some possible improvements that we could make to the application design:

- ❏ Record a log of all transactions by non-staff users. If a user has not requested any site content in 5 –15 minutes, assume that they are logged off and reset their status to inactive.

- ❏ Add a wireless component.

- ❏ Add a **corpus**. A corpus is the list of unique words used in all content posted on the site, regardless of source (except e-mails to the BOMP staff). The concept of a corpus is covered in greater detail in Chapter 6.

- ❏ Add a table of word occurrences. This is a log of all occurrences of a particular word in a text document (tables, articles, facts, monkeys, shorts). This table would be directly linked to the table used to store the word list for the corpus mentioned above, as well as to the textual content tables.

- ❏ Add a regular search engine feature. This feature would use the tables for the corpus and word occurrences.

- ❏ Add a poll so non-staff users could vote for their favorite articles and shorts. Poll scripts are fairly easy to implement and interactive displays of poll results could serve to increase and maintain user interest in the site.

❑ Add tables to support having site sponsors who donate prizes for those non-staff users who contribute short articles that receive the highest numbers of (positive) votes in the poll.

❑ Add a regular web forum feature.

❑ Improve the fuzzy search to allow wildcards for the search terms.

❑ Improve the moderation system by adding anti-'trolling' features such as checking postings for repeated use of arbitrary strings of text and/or strings in excess of a given length without any spaces; by stripping out HTML code and/or excess non-alphanumeric characters, and so on.

❑ Perform additional normalization on the database by creating a table of content table names and essential characteristics to aid in searches and content display; regularize column names; adopt a table type (for example, InnoDB) that supports foreign key constraints and implement these.

Summary

The Book of Mankind Project site is planned in our case study as a 3-tier, multi-client web application that includes a number of sophisticated features, such as a 'fuzzy' search engine, a pseudo-web forum, an article database with auto-moderation and cataloguing of all nearly all the site content. With the exception of our having made use of the PEAR::DB library for database access (this could be replaced with database-specific PHP functions without an inordinate amount of difficulty, if desired), our application requires no tools other than a web server, a MySQL database and a recent standard distribution of PHP4.

All the details for a complete implementation of this project could quite easily fill an entire book, but we were able to examine aspects of all of the critical components mentioned above. We discussed types of users, and the roles and privileges of each type, as well as the different types of content to be made available on the BOMP website. For a project the size of what's contemplated here, a well-ordered data store is essential, and so we discussed at some length the design and creation of a suitable MySQL database; we also provided some sample data for use in the examples making up most of the rest of the chapter.

An essential feature of the site is a keyword-based or "fuzzy" search engine; we examined the process of assigning keywords and provided code implementing this for one subset of the site's content ('short facts' content). Once we're able to associate content with keywords, we can perform searches for content matching those keywords; we implemented a fuzzy search feature for the same subset of content that we assigned keywords. Using what we provided in this chapter as a model, this capability could be extended to cover other types of content offered on the site. We also examined and implemented a proposed feature set for the 'Shakespeare's Hundredth Monkey' mini-forum.

The proposed site is an ambitious project, one that's multicultural and worldwide in scope, and which contains elements of an online magazine, a weblog, a discussion forum, and a searchable text and multimedia repository. It is an excellent example of what can be accomplished using PHP, a database and a few basic queries, along with a healthy exercise of imagination.

```php
n DefMaillist()defined bel

e = $elem[$tagname]["cd
= "All students in college
illist("col",$collcode,"stu         id,0);

c = "All profs in college
aillist("col",$collco                O);

ak;

e "dept":
// Opening department elen
// Add a record to table "universitylife_departments"

$elem[$tagname]["collid"] = $curcollid;
$curdeptid =$api->InsertDeptRecord($elem[$tagname]);
d; // Create various mailing lists
$deptcode = $elem[$tagname]["deptcode"];
name) $desc = $elem[$tagname]["deptcode";
$desc = "All students in dept $deptcode";
DefMaillist("dep",$deptcode,"stu",$desc,$curcollid,$cur
desc = "All profs in dept $deptcode";
DefMaillist("dep",$deptcode,"edu",$desc,$curcollid,$
ame) // There is still character data left. Since there can be
collid; // pieces of cdata within a single element (due to the
deptid;// expat parser works), we want to concatena
k; // /expat parser works), we want to concatena
                     rent element's character data.
```

Store Directory

Due to evolving technology, site designers are forced to be more and more aware of the user agents being used to view their sites. With the rapid proliferation of mobile devices like **WAP** (**Wireless Application Protocol**) phones and handheld computers, there are drastic differences in capability over desktop computers that must be considered in the site presentation. This includes issues that will remind us of the early days of personal computing with black and white displays, low-resolution displays, limited fonts, lack of support for graphics, limited implementations of HTML, and so on. For some of these devices, you must use a completely different presentation language such as **WML** (**Wireless Markup Language**) for WAP phones.

In this case study, we will focus on, and demonstrate, the use of templates to build a site that supports generic HTML browsers, WML support for WAP phones, and other mobile devices such as PalmPilots and handheld devices running WindowsCE or PocketPC.

The web site that we will develop for our case study is a Mobile Retail Store Directory. The purpose is to make it easy to find relevant information using mobile phones and wireless handheld computers. A user will enter a local area code and the site will display a list of retail categories. When the user selects the desired category, the site will display a list of local stores and their phone numbers along with other relevant information, in a device compatible format.

For this case study, we will create with a test site with the name http://www.storewap.com/. The source code used for this site is discussed in this chapter and is available in the code download from http://www.wrox.com/. Please note that the required elements of PHP-Lib are also included with the code download for this chapter.

In addition to MySQL and PHP4, we require a WAP simulator to be able to test the WML scripts in this application.

This is how we'll go about building the application in this chapter:

- ❏ Specifications
- ❏ The User Interface
- ❏ Designing the Application
- ❏ Designing the Database
- ❏ Application Logic
- ❏ HTML Site Templates
- ❏ WAP Site Templates
- ❏ Improvements

Specifications

As an architectural requirement, the entire site will use templates to make the presentation on various devices possible.

The following is a list of specifications for our site. These affect the entire site regardless of display device. Since some features, such as store owner sign-up and adding or modifying store entries, require intensive data entry, we will only provide those features on desktop web browsers. The main specifications are as below:

- ❏ Support various types of handheld devices including WAP, PalmPilot, and small-screen HTML devices. Most devices support some variants of HTML but WAP devices support WML, which requires that our system supports changing the content type.

- ❏ Since cookies are not supported by all devices, the system should allow for the use of cookies if available but not as a requirement.

- ❏ Devices with small screens will require support for pagination of long selection lists.

- ❏ There should be minimal data entry. Handheld devices are notoriously awkward at data entry so the system should do everything possible to accommodate this fact.

- ❏ This application should allow users to obtain a list of stores and store phone numbers for a given location by entering an area code. Stores should be grouped by a category for easy navigation of store lists.

The User Interface

This section will walk you through the main user interface for both a web browser and a WAP phone. Here, we will show you the main screens side by side for both a standard web browser and a WAP-enabled cell phone.

The first page presents the user with the option to select an area code. The web browser templates do this by presenting a list of area codes for all covered areas:

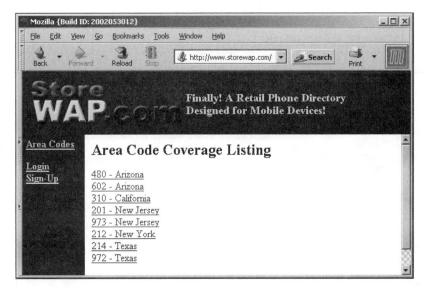

Since this list could get to be quite large on a real implementation of the site, the WAP version of the site presents an area code text entry form to allow quick entry of the desired area code on the phone keypad:

Upon selection or entry of the area code, a list of retail categories is displayed along with a count of the number of stores in that category:

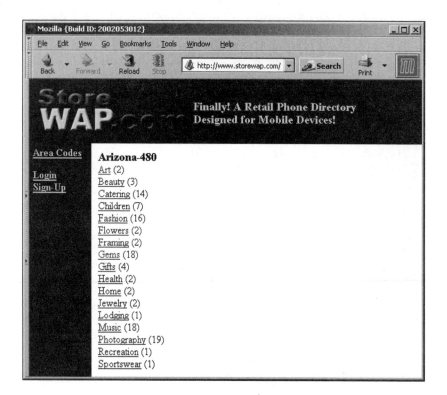

While the web browser implementation of this page displays the entire list of categories, the WAP version of the page lists only nine entries at a time to allow for easy keypad-based selection. Also, the soft button at the bottom of the screen acts as a next and previous function (the display of these options requires the selection of the Menu button in this particular WAP browser.):

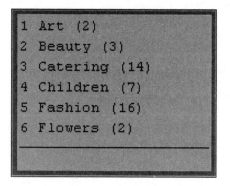

Upon selecting a category, the list of stores for that category is displayed. Notice that the stores are displayed for different area codes. All of the area codes are for a large metropolitan area in the southwest United States and are located in very close physical proximity. Since some larger cities have multiple area codes for a single heavily populated region, associated area codes should be displayed without the user requesting all "local" area codes. The following screenshot demonstrates the site's ability to associate a store with multiple area codes when necessary:

Again, you will notice that the WAP version of the stores display is paged for ease of use. Due to the nature of the template design, this is controlled completely by the template structure of each device:

Finally, upon selection of an individual store, the user is presented with a store detail page containing all available information about the store:

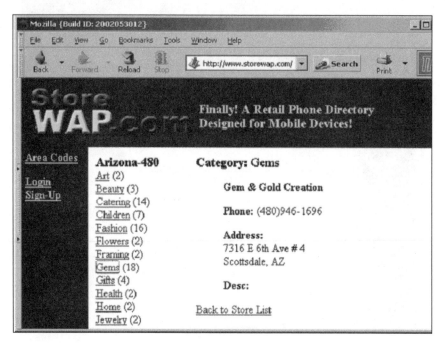

Since the site is primarily designed for access from mobile devices, the store display on a WAP phone offers a couple of good features that are not available on the website:

On the store detail page, for WAP phones that support the **WTAI** (**Wireless Telephone Application Interface**), the WML code adds a Call feature to the first soft button and upon display of the menu, you can also add the entry to your cell phone's phone book.

For the remainder of this chapter, we will discuss the database schema, design, and code architecture for this case study.

Designing the Database

The Store Directory database contains the following tables:

❑ storewap_areacodes
  This table stores details of all supported area codes with in their location

❑ storewap_categories
  This table stores the details of the retail categories for organizing stores

❑ storewap_stores
  This table contains details of the store such as name, phone number, and address

❑ storewap_areajoin
  This is a join table specifying which stores are associated with which area code

❑ storewap_catjoin
  This is a join table specifying which stores belong with which categories

❑ storewap_users
  This table stores the details of the store owners and administrators

Database Tables

In this section, we'll study each database table in detail along with column specifications. We will call our database storewap.

Area Codes

This table (storewap_areacodes) stores a list of all supported telephone area codes. It should be pointed out that the area codes form a natural unique primary key and are used as such in this table:

Column Name	Data Type	Description
areacode_codeno	SMALLINT	Actual area code stored and used as a primary key
areacode_location	VARCHAR	Description of the region covered by the area code, for example, 'Los Angeles Metro Area'

Area Join

It is common for an area to have multiple area codes and this table (storewap_areajoin) allows a store to associate its listing with more than one area code. This is a join table that associates a store using areajoin_storeid with one or more area codes using areajoin_code.

Column Name	Data Type	Description
areajoin_code	SMALLINT	Area code used as a foreign key referring to the storewap_areacodes table
areajoin_storeid	INT	This is used as a foreign key referring to the storewap_stores table

Categories

This table (storewap_categories) stores a list of categories used for grouping stores in a convenient manner, for example, Clothing, Jewellery:

Column Name	Data Type	Description
category_id	INT	A unique integer specifying the category ID
category_name	VARCHAR	Descriptive category name.

Category Join

This is a join table that associates one store with more than one category that it may be listed under. For example, a store owner might want to have an antique bookstore displayed under both Books and Antiques. The structure of the storewap_catjoin table is as follows:

Column Name	Data Type	Description
catjoin_catid	INT	The category ID, used as a foreign key referring to the storewap_categories table
catjoin_storeid	INT	This is used a foreign key referring to the storewap_stores table

Stores

This is the main table used for storing the details of the stores that may be useful for the user. The structure of the storewap_stores table is as follows:

Column Name	Data Type	Description
store_id	INT	A unique ID representing the store
store_name	VARCHAR	The name of the store
store_phone	VARCHAR	The phone number of the store
store_desc	VARCHAR	A short description giving information about the store

Column Name	Data Type	Description
store_address	VARCHAR	The address of the store
store_ownerid	INT	The owner's ID
store_expires	DATE	The date on which this listing expires and beyond which it should not be displayed

Users

This table (storewap_users) would be primarily used to support a back-end administration system, which is beyond the scope of this case study. This table is included in this section because the source code implements a login system that provides easy hooks for the user to implement an administrative system as desired:

Column Name	Data Type	Description
user_id	INT	Unique ID representing a user. This user can be a store owner or an administrator.
user_name	VARCHAR	Name of the user. This field cannot be a NULL. If no value is specified, it defaults to an empty string ('').
user_pass	VARCHAR	Password of the user. This field cannot be NULL. If no value is specified, it defaults to an empty string ('').
user_firstname	VARCHAR	First name of the user
user_lastname	VARCHAR	Last name of the user
user_email	VARCHAR	E-mail address of the user
user_owner	TINYINT	Boolean indicator of whether this user is a store owner. MySQL does not have an explicit Boolean data type; hence we will use a TINYINT for this purpose. This field is used by the administrative interface who may choose to use 1 to indicate TRUE and 0 to indicate FALSE.
user_admin	TINYINT	Boolean indicator of whether this user should have administrative rights. This field is used by the administrative interface, if need be, in the same manner as above.
user_credits	INT	This field can be used to implement a credit-based system for adding stores. The idea is that a user signs up for an account and is given some number of credits to use for adding stores. One credit = one store. When the store owner runs out of credits, he can purchase more credits to add more stores. This field is used by the administrative interface.

The users table has several fields that are used by an administrative interface. The administrative interface is not included in this case study.

157

Database Relationship Diagram

The following figure shows the relationship between the tables in the database:

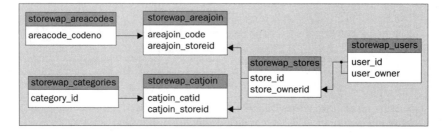

Note that in the diagram above, arrows connecting the related columns show the column relationships and dependencies, with the dependant column being pointed to by the arrow mark.

Creating the Database

We begin by creating our database using the following command:

```
>mysqladmin create storewap
```

The file `storedirectory.sql` contains the SQL code for creating and initializing the database. This file, along with the sample data for the tables, has a default data list that has been omitted due to the length. This can be found in the source code available for downloads from http://www.wrox.com/:

```
#
# Table structure for table storewap_areacodes
#

CREATE TABLE storewap_areacodes(
    areacode_codeno SMALLINT(4) NOT NULL DEFAULT '0',
    areacode_location VARCHAR(50) NOT NULL DEFAULT '',
    PRIMARY KEY  (areacode_codeno),
    KEY location (areacode_location)
) TYPE=MyISAM;

#
# Default Inserts for storewap_areacodes Table omitted.
# Refer to code download file for this information

# Table structure for table storewap_areajoin
#

CREATE TABLE storewap_areajoin(
    areajoin_code SMALLINT(4) NOT NULL DEFAULT '0',
    areajoin_storeid INT(11) NOT NULL DEFAULT '0',
    PRIMARY KEY  (areajoin_code,areajoin_storeid)
) TYPE=MyISAM;
#
```

```
# Table structure for table storewap_catjoin
#

CREATE TABLE storewap_catjoin (
    catjoin_catid INT(11) NOT NULL DEFAULT '0',
    catjoin_storeid INT(11) NOT NULL DEFAULT '0',
    PRIMARY KEY  (catjoin_catid,catjoin_storeid),
    KEY catid (catjoin_catid)
) TYPE=MyISAM;

#
# Table structure for table storewap_categories
#

CREATE TABLE storewap_categories (
    category_id int(11) NOT NULL AUTO_INCREMENT,
    category_name VARCHAR(50) NOT NULL DEFAULT '',
    PRIMARY KEY  (category_id),
    UNIQUE KEY category (category_name),
    KEY category_2 (category_name)
) TYPE=MyISAM;

#
# Table structure for table storewap_store
#

CREATE TABLE storewap_stores (
    store_id INT(11) NOT NULL AUTO_INCREMENT,
    store_name VARCHAR(64) NOT NULL DEFAULT '',
    store_phone VARCHAR(15) NOT NULL DEFAULT '',
    store_desc VARCHAR(255) DEFAULT NULL,
    store_address VARCHAR(255) DEFAULT NULL,
    store_ownerid INT(11) NOT NULL DEFAULT '0',
    store_expires DATE NOT NULL DEFAULT '0000-00-00',
    PRIMARY KEY  (store_id),
    KEY name (store_name,phone),
    KEY ownerid (store_ownerid)
) TYPE=MyISAM;

#
# Table structure for table storewap_user
#

CREATE TABLE storewap_users (
    user_id INT(11) NOT NULL AUTO_INCREMENT,
    user_name VARCHAR(20) NOT NULL DEFAULT '',
    user_pass VARCHAR(20) NOT NULL DEFAULT '',
    user_firstname VARCHAR(50) NOT NULL DEFAULT '',
    user_lastname VARCHAR(50) NOT NULL DEFAULT '',
    user_email VARCHAR(128) NOT NULL DEFAULT '',
    user_owner TINYINT(4) NOT NULL DEFAULT '0',
    user_admin TINYINT(4) NOT NULL DEFAULT '0',
```

```
    user_credits INT(11) NOT NULL DEFAULT '0',
    PRIMARY KEY  (user_id),
    UNIQUE KEY username (user_name),
    KEY username_2 (user_name,user_firstname,user_lastname,user_email)
) TYPE=MyISAM;

INSERT INTO storewap_users VALUES (1, 'admin', 'password', 'Admin', '',
                       'admin@storewap.com', 1, 1, 100);
```

> A table called **db_sequences** is created by the storedirectory.sql commands. This table is inconsequential to the application but is required by the default implementation of the PHP-Lib class **DB_MySQL**. Rather than change the **DB_MySQL** class that is used by this application but is borrowed from PHP-Lib, we added this table. The **CREATE** command for this table is included in the file that is available in the code download.

Create the tables by running the file `storedirectory.sql` at the command prompt as follows:

> **> mysql < storedirectory.sql**

The sample data for the tables can be found in the file `storedirectoryData.sql`. Use the following command to insert the data into the tables:

> **> mysql storewap < storedirectoryData.sql**

Designing the Application

The requirements for the site help determine some of the technology choices that we will make. The first and most obvious is that the site should be template-based to facilitate supporting an arbitrary number of devices. For this, we will use the PHP-Lib template class. For our database, we will use MySQL and the PHP-Lib `db_mysql` class to simplify the database code used to access the database.

The template and the database class are the only two components of PHP-Lib we will use to simplify the installation of the Store Directory. Therefore, we will include both of these classes directly in our code base for our site. If PHP-Lib is already installed on a system and configured in the `php.ini` file using the `auto_prepend_file` option, you will have to remove the `includes` directive for these two classes from each PHP file in our site to avoid name collisions. In either case, the include files are available with the code. Also, for the sake of security, we add a `.php` extension to all files so that access to source code is not accidentally permitted by the web server since the `.inc` extension may not be a parsed MIME type.

Our site will have the following directory structure:

Folder	Description
www/	This directory contains all PHP files for generating web pages for all devices. This is the root directory of the web site.
www/images	This directory contains all images used by the store directory.
www/include	This directory contains the shared code such as the PHP-Lib template and database classes.
templates/	This is the root of the templates directory. It will contain a directory for the templates for the main web site and a template directory for each supported device.
templates/html	Contains the main site templates
templates/wap	Contains all templates for display on WAP devices
templates/palmpilot	Contains all PalmPilot templates
templates/wince	Contains all WindowsCE/PocketPC templates

Common Code and Include Files

Aside from the PHP-Lib template files, we use two other files that contain common code and site configuration settings. These files are kept in the www/include sub directory, or htdocs/include for Apache installations. The contents of this directory are:

File	Description
config.inc.php	Store directory configuration file
db_mysql.inc.php	PHP-Lib DB_MySQL class
template.inc.php	PHP-Lib Template class
utils.inc.php	Device identification and login/session management code.

The config.inc.php file is extremely simple. It contains a global variable called $template_path that is used to specify the path to the template root directory. While this doesn't seem to justify a file by itself, it is an important setting that shouldn't be hard-coded in the site files and it just doesn't fit in the other include files.

Following are the contents of the config.inc.php file:

```php
<?php
    $template_path = "/home/storewap/templates" ;
//If this doesn't work, or for Apache installations, try
//$template_path = "/templates";
?>
```

This setting will have to be changed to an appropriate directory for your particular Apache installation. It is recommend that you create this directory outside of your web site's root directory for security purposes.

Also, the db_mysql.inc.php file contains MySQL server configuration variables that should have been moved into the config.inc.php files but we want to modify the PHP-Lib files as little as possible so the settings remain in the file itself.

The utils.inc.php file contains both device identification code, which we will discuss in the next section, and login management code. The login management code uses PHP sessions, which is a feature of PHP4. This code must be modified before it will work on PHP3 but since the code is isolated, this shouldn't be an overwhelming task. The Session class in PHP-Lib would work nicely as a replacement for PHP4 sessions.

Following is the listing of the utils.inc.php file:

```php
<?php
# util.inc.php
unset($userid) ;
unset($username) ;
unset($firstname) ;
unset($lastname) ;
unset($email) ;
unset($storeowner) ;
unset($admin) ;
unset($credits) ;
unset($loggedin) ;

session_register("userid") ;
session_register("username") ;
session_register("firstname") ;
session_register("lastname") ;
session_register("email") ;
session_register("storeowner") ;
session_register("admin") ;
session_register("credits") ;
session_register("loggedin") ;
```

This code initializes our session variables. Each call to unset() destroys or unsets the variable if it happens to already exist. The calls to session_register() define which variables should be saved as part of the session. If the session doesn't already exist, and it shouldn't at this point, then the first call to session_register() creates a new session.

The unset() functions are used as a safeguard to ensure that the state of the variables that we are registering as part of the session are in a known state the first time the session is created. If you are not careful, this is the sort of thing that can cause major security holes in your PHP code. Consider the case where a user is visiting the site for the first time but instead of using the usual:

http://www.storewap.com/index.php

to address the site, he uses:

http://www.storewap.com/index.php?loggedin=1

If the unset() functions were not used, then the value of $loggedin would be preset to 1 and registered with the session. Depending on the code that follows, this could cause a severe security problem. With the unset() in place, the only values of $loggedin that will ever be associated with the session are generated by the site's code, which is the way it should be:

```php
function IdentifyDevice($user_agent,$accepts)
{
    if( strstr($accepts,"wml") ) define("DEVICE","wap") ;
    elseif( strstr($accepts,"vnd.palm")) define("DEVICE","palm") ;
    elseif( strstr($user_agent,"Windows CE")) define("DEVICE","wince") ;
    else define("DEVICE","html") ;
}

function PrepareDevice($device)
{
    switch($device) {
    case "wap":
        header("Content-type: text/vnd.wap.wml") ;
    break ;
    case "palm":
    case "wince":
    case "html":
    default:
    // since default content-type is nearly always text/html
    // we don't have to do anything here
    }
}

function RequireDevice($device)
{
    if( DEVICE != $device )
    exit("This page not displayable on this device.") ;
}

function RequireUser($require_admin=false)
{
    if(!$loggedin )
    exit("You must be logged in to view this page.") ;
    if($require_admin && !$admin )
    exit("You must be logged in as an administrator to view this
        page.");
}
```

The IdentifyDevice() and PrepareDevice() functions are explained in the next section. The RequireDevice() and RequireUser() functions are simply functions that can be used to indicate that a specific script is only to be used by a valid user or on a specific device.

```php
function LoginUser($luser,$lpass)
{
    global $loggedin,$userid,$username,
    $firstname,$lastname,$email,
    $storeowner,$admin,$credits ;
    $db = new DB_Sql ;
```

```
      if(!$db->connect() ) return false ;
          $db->query("SELECT user_id,user_name,user_pass, user_firstname,
                    user_lastname,user_email,
                    user_owner,user_admin,user_credits FROM storewap_users WHERE
                    user_name='$luser'");

      if($db->next_record() ) {
          list($userid,$username,$pass,$firstname,
                                    $lastname,$email,$storeowner,
          $admin,$credits) = $db->Record ;

          if($pass == $lpass ) {
              $loggedin = true ;
              return true ;
          }
      }
      LogoutUser() ;
      return false ;
  }

function LogoutUser()
{
    global $loggedin,$userid,$username,
    $firstname,$lastname,$email,
    $storeowner,$admin,$credits ;
    $userid = 0 ;
    $username = "" ;
    $firstname = "" ;
    $lastname = "" ;
    $email = "" ;
    $storeowner = 0 ;
    $admin = 0 ;
    $credits = 0 ;
    $loggedin = false ;
    session_destroy() ;
}
?>
```

The function LoginUser() controls the values of the global variables used by the session to indicate a valid user has logged in to the system. After declaring the appropriate variables as global variables, a database object is created. Then, the user name specified in $luser is used to attempt to load a record matching that user from the database. If a record is found matching that user, then the password for the loaded record is compared to the password being validated in $lpass. If the passwords match, then $loggedin is set to true indicating a successful login. Any other path through this function results in a call to LogoutUser(), which resets all the session variables ensuring that no residual data from any part of the login validation code remains.

This is a relatively simple login with an effective user validation system. The benefit of this design is that if you want to integrate this code into a larger site that already has a built-in validation system, you can localize all changes to just this one file and map the key session variables from the user validation system to the ones used in this case study.

It is important to note that if security is a major concern, you should probably not store the database but rather use one of the many methods of encrypting passwords.

Now, let's take a look at the technique used to identify the type of device being used to browse the site.

Browser and Device Identification

To be able to display device and browser specific pages on our site, first we must identify the device being used. This should be a simple thing, but due to the number of different browsers and the myriad versions of each browser, as well as different presentation languages, this is turning into something of a black art. In this section, we will describe the device identification logic used in the Store Directory site.

There are two main HTTP headers that contain information about the user's browser and the desired presentation language. They are the **User-Agent** header and the **Accept** header. Let's look at each of them in turn.

User-Agent Header

The `User-Agent` header contains information about the user's browser and is accessed through the `$HTTP_USER_AGENT` PHP variable.

There is actually a specification for the format of this header and almost all browsers follow this specification. The problem is that different browser manufacturers try to pretend to be other browsers and they outright lie in the `User-Agent` header that is sent to a web site.

For example, some popular browsers send `User-Agent` strings that say that it is a Mozilla browser. Mozilla is the project code-name for the Netscape browser. This was done because web masters built sites that took advantage of features in the Netscape browser, and other browsers wanted to be able to work with these sites, so they also used the same `User-Agent` header. Now it is common to use techniques like sub-string searches through the `User-Agent` header for strings that are known to be common for each particular type of browser.

The current User-Agent specification can be found at http://www.mozilla.org/build/revised-user-agent-strings.html.

For our purposes, we will consider every browser that is a recognized device to be a standard browser. Since we are not exploiting specific features of web browsers, and only those of the device specific browsers, this will work just fine. Following are some of the `User-Agent` strings from the devices we will support with the Store Directory:

Device	User-Agent String
PalmPilot VIIx	Mozilla/2.0 (compatible; Elaine/3.0)
PocketPC	Mozilla/2.0 (compatible; MSIE 3.02; WindowsCE; 240x320)
Nokia 6210 Cell-phone	Nokia6210/1.0 (03.60)

Since nearly all browsers call themselves Mozilla, we obviously need to use some other identifying criteria. For identifying the PalmPilot, we will use the sub-string `"Elaine"` which is evidently the project name for the Palm Wireless Browser. The http://www.PalmOS.com web site recommends checking the `HTTP_USER_AGENT` variable for the sub-string `"Mozilla/2.0"` (compatible with `Elaine/`), but our code will just look for the identifying string `"Elaine"`.

The PocketPC, which is the latest version of the WindowsCE operating system, uses a version of Internet Explorer that identifies the operating system and the size of the display. Since most of the popular PocketPC devices, like the iPaq, use the same size display, we will only use the identifying string WindowCE. In the future, the screen size and development of further devices that support web browsing may require the usage of the screen-size specifier.

For WAP devices however, there is no single way to identify them using the User-Agent string. There are a large number of WAP device manufacturers and several different WAP browsers. We could try to identify them all, but fortunately there is an easier way.

Accept Header

The other HTTP header we mentioned is the Accept header accessed with the PHP variable $HTTP_ACCEPT. This header specifies the data formats that the browser can accept. For example, one of the types that are usually sent by a standard web browser is the text/html type indicating that the browser can support HTML formatted text. Web site designers for standard web sites do not commonly use this header, but since all recent WAP browsers support WML, we check this header for text/vnd.wap.wml. The two major WAP browsers are the Nokia browser and the OpenWave (formerly Phone.com) browser, but for this directory, we will not separate the two since one set of templates can handle both.

> Some of the early WAP browsers only supported a markup language called HDML, but we are not going to discuss it here, as it is obsolete.

The function IdentifyDevice() (listed in the previous section in the file utils.inc.php) is used to set a constant that identifies the device. The code can be used as follows, by passing the appropriate global PHP variables:

```
IdentifyDevice($HTTP_USER_AGENT,$HTTP_ACCEPT) ;
```

After calling this function, the constant DEVICE can be used to change site behavior for a specific device. One more thing that should be mentioned is the need to specify the content type for WAP devices. Since the default Content-type specified by PHP is text/html, the site designer does not normally have to worry about this header, and since WAP devices cannot support HTML, we must set this header when displaying pages in WML. This is done using the following code:

```
header("Content-type: text/vnd.wap.wml") ;
```

This is handled by the function PrepareDevice() contained in the utils.inc.php file. You will see this used often in the site code discussed later.

Now that you understand the underlying code used for device identification, let's start exploring the structure of the Store Directory site.

Application Logic

In this section, we will walk through the core code for the site and explain how key sections of the site work and how they relate to each other. First, let's introduce the files used to create the site. The www/ directory contains the following files:

File	Description
index.php	The main page of the site. It handles the parsing of the main pages of the devices and several of the frames within the main site. This page handles login logic, and basic variable substitution for templates.
areacodes.php	Displays the area codes on web browsers. Due to the length of the list, devices require the area code to be manually entered.
categories.php	Displays the category list for a specified area code on devices and web browsers.
stores.php	Displays the store list for a specified category and area code.
store.php	Displays store information for a specific store.
owner.php	Handles new subscriber sign-up, and editing owner information.
owner_stores.php	Displays store listings belonging to a given storeowner. Allows for adding new stores and allows for the deletion of existing stores.
owner_store.php	Displays store specific information and allows for the modification of this information including associated categories and associated area codes.
users.php	For the use of the Administrator only. Displays all the users in the system and allows for the adding, editing, and deleting of users.
user.php	For the use of the Administrator only. Handles the data-entry for adding and updating a specific user.

There is also an image in the www/images directory called logo.gif. This image is available with the code bundle for this chapter. This is not used on any of the devices, although the templates for any device can reference images if the device supports the display of graphics. In the following sections, we are going to discuss the logic of the main script files that make up the Store Directory and the results they produce on different devices.

While we will not go through every script file that makes up this site, we will cover every major script that introduces a new concept. For example, the categories.php is used to display a list of categories. This script performs a database query and parses the results into a template file, with paging logic allowing the categories to be displayed a handful at a time with full **Next** and **Previous** support to see the next or previous page of categories if appropriate. The file stores.php, owner_stores.php, and users.php all do nearly the same thing with slight differences in the database query being used and the names of the referenced template file.

index.php

The index.php script contains the default display logic for the front page of the web browsers and other devices. We will walk through this script line-by-line because it illustrates concepts used throughout the site. By understanding this file, you can understand the function of the boilerplate logic in the remaining script files. The source code for this script is as follows:

```php
<?php
// include required files

require("include/db_mysql.inc.php");
```

```
require("include/config.inc.php");
require("include/template.inc.php");
require("include/utils.inc.php");
```

We begin with the `require()` statements. These are used for including the four main files discussed earlier in this case study. Next, we need to identify the device and get the device specific information. This is done by calling the two functions `IdentifyDevice()` and `PrepareDevice()`:

```
// determine device to start the system
IdentifyDevice($HTTP_USER_AGENT,$HTTP_ACCEPT) ;
PrepareDevice(DEVICE) ;
```

Note the use of the DEVICE constant that is set by the call to `IdentifyDevice()`. After identifying the device, we have enough information to begin preparing the template. We now create the template object and initialize the path to the templates for the specific browser being used. The convention used for the Store Directory is to name the template directories after the device that they support. The `$template_path` variable, which is defined in `config.inc.php`, is combined with the DEVICE constant to set the path to the templates:

```
// create the template object
$tpl = new Template() ;
$tpl->set_root("$template_path/".DEVICE) ;
```

We then select the template file being used. The code for this might look a bit inefficient and strange, and perhaps it is. However, there is a reason for it. The file `index.php` services more than one template file. For this reason, there is a mechanism to select the template file to be used. The query parameter `$fi` is used for this purpose. As you can see from the following code listing, if `$fi` is not set, it defaults to the value `"main"`. The `switch` statement sets the template file to be used based on the value of `$fi`:

```
if( !isset($fi) ) $fi = "main" ;

switch($fi) {
case "head":
    $tpl->set_file("index","index_head.tpl") ;
break ;

case "left":
    $tpl->set_file("index","index_left.tpl") ;
break ;

case "content":
    $tpl->set_file("index","index_content.tpl") ;
break ;

case "login":
    $tpl->set_file("index","index_login.tpl") ;
break ;

case "blank":
    $tpl->set_file("index","index_blank.tpl") ;
break ;

default:
    $tpl->set_file("index","index.tpl") ;
}
```

You might assume it would be more efficient to code this with something like the following:

```
$tpl->set_file("index","index$fi.tpl") ;
```

The issue with this code is not elegance but security. PHP is extremely versatile in the way variables are declared, and the fact that URL query parameters are automatically parsed and set as global variables allows a user to arbitrarily set variables in your address space. For this reason, we should write PHP code that never trusts a variable that comes from a query parameter directly. Instead of using the value of $fi directly, it is interpreted and if it is not a preset value, then we still default to a known template name.

The line of code above allows the user to set the name of the file directly. Depending on how it is written, the underlying code in the template class could allow a malicious user to arbitrarily request different files to be returned, perhaps even from different directories. Under these circumstances, this is unlikely, but it is still a coding habit that we should adhere to and one that might improve the security of your PHP sites as well.

Next we show the difference in functionality between a standard web browser and a mobile device. Since we don't allow stores to be added or other store owner administrative functions, we don't support the login feature and other related logic from mobile devices:

```
if( DEVICE == "html" ) {
```

The line above states that if the device is just a standard web browser, set different logical sections of the template that should be parsed under different states:

```
$tpl->set_block("index","loggedin_tpl","loggedin") ;
$tpl->set_block("index","loggedout_tpl","loggedout") ;
$tpl->set_block("index","loggingin_tpl","loggingin") ;
```

If there is a user currently logged in to the system, then the loggedin template block will be parsed. If there is not a current user logged in to the system, then parse the loggedout template block. And finally, the loggingin template block is a side effect of wanting to use HTML frames in our main site template. If the user fails an attempt to login, the error message must be propagated to the inner frame of the site, hence the loggingin block, which supports this intermediate state. The adminonly block is only parsed if a user is logged in and that user has administrative rights. Next, we handle the login process as shown below:

```
// handle user login
$loggingin = false ;
$tpl->set_var("loggingin","") ;
if(!$loggedin && isset($luser) && isset($lpass) ) {
    if(!LoginUser($luser,$lpass) ) {
      $loggingin = true ;
      $msg = "<font color=red><b>Invalid username or password.<br>Please
          try again.</b></font><p>" ;
  }
}elseif(isset($logout) && $logout ) {
      LogoutUser() ;
}

$tpl->set_var("msg",$msg) ;
```

```
$tpl->set_var("areacode",$ac) ;
$tpl->set_var("userid",$userid) ;
$tpl->set_var("username",$username) ;
$tpl->set_var("firstname",$firstname) ;
$tpl->set_var("lastname",$lastname) ;
$tpl->set_var("email",$email) ;
$tpl->set_var("admin",$admin) ;
$tpl->set_var("storeowner",$storeowner) ;
$tpl->set_var("credits",$credits) ;

$tpl->set_var("loggedin","") ;
$tpl->set_var("loggedout","") ;
$tpl->set_var("loggingin","") ;
```

The first if statement checks to see if the $loggedin global is false and the variables $luser and $lpass are set. If set, we assume that a login is being attempted. The LoginUser() function checks the database and validates the username and password returning true or false depending on the success of the validation. The $loggedin global is one of the PHP4 session variables that are defined by the initialization code of the utils.inc.php file. If the login fails, then an error message is defined and stored in $msg and a flag is set indicating that mysterious transient state called loggingin. We'll see how that works a little later.

Finally, if a login attempt is not being made, we check the $logout variable, which is an optional query parameter that can be passed to the PHP script to force a logout by a call to the LogoutUser() function, which is also defined in utils.inc.php.

This code parses a different block depending on the current login state. If a user is logged in, then the loggedin block is parsed. If that user is an administrator, then the adminonly block is also parsed. If a user is not $loggingin, a state that only happens after an initial failed login attempt, then we parse the loggedout block, otherwise we must be logging in and we parse that block:

```
if( $loggedin ) {
    $tpl->parse("loggedin","loggedin_tpl") ;
if( $admin ) {
    $tpl->parse("adminonly","adminonly_tpl") ;
}
}elseif( !$loggingin ) {
        $tpl->parse("loggedout","loggedout_tpl") ;
}else{
$tpl->parse("loggingin","loggingin_tpl") ;
}
}
```

The final line of this template, and every other PHP script file in the store directory, is the final call to parse the entire template and send the results to the browser using the following line:

```
$tpl->pparse("output","index") ;
?>
```

Note the call to the pparse() method as opposed to the parse() method used for the template blocks. The pparse() method not only parses but prints the results of the parsed template.

Based on the login logic, the following HTML code inserted in one of the templates can be used to log a user onto the system:

```
<form target="_top" action="/index.php">
Username: <input name="luser" size=15><br>
Password: <input type="password" name="lpass" size=15><br>
<input type="submit" value="Login">
</form>
```

Setting the `target="_top"` just ensures that if the login HTML is embedded in a frame, we don't get our site included in a frame itself, could really confuse a user. Correspondingly, the following HTML would cause the system to log a user out when executed:

```
<a target="_top" href="/index.php?logout=1">Log Me Out</a>
```

areacodes.php

This script provides the logic for displaying the area codes stored in the `storewap_areacodes` table. The key point to understand about this script is that it does not display area codes that do not have associated stores. There is no point in purposely giving a user a navigation link only to find that there is no content.

The `areacodes.php` script uses a single template from the current template directory named `areacodes.tpl`. This script, like the other scripts that display variable length lists of database entries, provides for a basic paging model using the query parameters $s and $p. The parameter $s is the index number of the first entry to display on the page. The parameter $p is the page size or number of entries to display. The paging logic automatically takes into account the number of rows and adjusts all settings accordingly. If $p is set to a negative value, then all rows are automatically displayed.

There are two blocks that are significant for this page: the previous block and the next block. These blocks are used to provide a previous link or a next link if the current page position allows it. As you might expect, the previous block is not parsed if you are at the beginning of the list and the next block is not parsed if you are at the end of the list. Neither block is parsed if the list has no items or you are positioned at the only item in the list.

The following code segment from the `areacodes.php` shows the SQL used for this purpose:

```
// connect to database
$db = new DB_Sql ;
if( !$db->connect() ) return false ;

// setup query
$query = "SELECT ac.areacode_codeno,ac.areacode_location,count(*)
        FROM storewap_stores as s,
        storewap_areacodes as ac,
        storewap_areajoin as aj
        WHERE aj.areajoin_code = ac.areacode_codeno
        AND s.store_id = aj.areajoin_storeid
        GROUP BY ac.areacode_codeno
        ORDER BY ac.areacode_location,ac.areacode_codeno" ;

$db->query($query) ;
$rows = $db->num_rows() ;
```

Since this is only used for standard web browsers and not devices, and the logic is very similar to that used in `categories.php` and `stores.php`, we will not show the entire code listing here.

categories.php

This script lists all categories for a given area code. As with the `areacodes.php` script, only the categories that have stores are listed. It requires the query parameter `ac` to specify the area code to display.

The `categories.php` script uses the template file `categories.tpl`. It also uses the same paging logic as `areacodes.php`, it accepts the same parameters `$s` and `$p` for controlling the paging logic, and uses the same **NEXT** and **PREV** blocks for the next and previous links. Since this is the first major page that shows on all browsers, we will do a walk-through for all the source code for this page.

At the beginning of this script are the `require()` statements for including the four main include files discussed earlier in this case study:

```php
<?php
// include required files
require("include/db_mysql.inc.php") ;
require("include/config.inc.php") ;
require("include/template.inc.php") ;
require("include/utils.inc.php") ;

// determine device to start the system
IdentifyDevice($HTTP_USER_AGENT,$HTTP_ACCEPT) ;
PrepareDevice(DEVICE) ;
```

After initialization, the first significant block of code creates a database object and loads information about the selected area code. The area code is specified by the variable `$ac` which is a query parameter for this page:

```php
// connect to database
$db = new DB_Sql ;
if( !$db->connect() ) exit ;

// get areacode information
$query ="SELECT areacode_location FROM storewap_areacodes WHERE
areacode_codeno=$ac";
$db->query($query) ;
$db->next_record() ;
list($location) = $db->Record ;
```

The variable `$location` is used to store the name of the region that the area code covers. Note that the purpose of this value is for use in the templates but it is not mandatory for the template to display this information. It is provided as an option for HTML coders.

Next, the categories themselves are loaded from the database:

```php
// setup query
$query = "SELECT c.category_id,c.category_name,count(*)
          FROM storewap_categories AS c, storewap_catjoin AS cj, storewap_stores
AS s,
```

```
          storewap_areacodes AS ac, storewap_areajoin AS aj WHERE
          c.category_id = cj.catjoin_catid AND
          s.store_id = cj.catjoin_storeid AND
          aj.areajoin_code = ac.areacode_codeno AND
          s.store_id = aj.areajoin_storeid AND
          ac.areacode_codeno = $ac AND
          s.store_expires >= NOW()
          GROUP BY c.category_id ORDER BY c.category_name" ;
$db->query($query);
$rows = $db->num_rows();
```

The query uses a seemingly confusing multi-table join to group stores for a given area code under categories providing a per-category store count. Translated into English, we provide a list of categories that have stores located in the specified area codes and list the number of stores per category.

For those of you familiar with SQL join syntax, this would be better written as a join, but the MySQL implementation of the standard SQL join syntax is not complete. We certainly couldn't find a way of phrasing the SQL statement in a way that was acceptable to MySQL. For this reason, you will find this old-style multi-table syntax throughout the code for this site. To MySQL's credit, even multi-table joins like this are lightning fast.

Notice that in the query, only stores with expiration dates past the current system date are retrieved in the query. This is a key part of the commerce model for this site. Once a store expires, it is not removed from the database but is listed as expired. This allows the store owner to purchase more credits, add new entries, or renew expired entries.

The next code segment sets up the category template. While this is very similar to the index.php code, there are a couple of key differences worthy of discussion. We'll discuss these differences here:

```
// start parsing template
$tpl = new Template() ;
$tpl->set_root("$template_path/".DEVICE) ;
$tpl->set_file("categories","categories.tpl") ;
$tpl->set_block("categories","catlist_tpl","catlist") ;
$tpl->set_block("categories","next_tpl","next") ;
$tpl->set_block("categories","prev_tpl","prev") ;

// set general template variables
$tpl->set_var("areacode",$ac) ;
$tpl->set_var("location",$location) ;
$tpl->set_var("numcategories",$rows) ;
```

A template object is created and stored in $tpl. The template path is set to the device template directory and the template file is set to the hard-coded categories.tpl filename. Three blocks are then initialized. The first block is the category list defined by the handle catlist_tpl and the template variable name catlist. This is different from other blocks used so far since it is the first repeating block we have discussed. The next_tpl and prev_tpl blocks are used to implement the paging logic. We'll look at how each of these blocks is used in the code a little further in this section.

The block initialization is followed by several set_var() method calls to make the area code, the name of the physical location, and the total number of categories available for the template designer. After the template has been set up, we initialize the variables that relate to the paging logic for the category list:

```
// paging logic
//
// $s = start of list
// $p = page size
//
if( !isset($s) ) $s = 0 ;
if( !isset($p) ) {
    switch(DEVICE) {
    case "wap":
       $p = 9 ;
    break ;

    case "html":
    case "palm":
    case "wince":
    default:
       $p = 10 ;
    break ;
}

// if $p is set to negative value
// then show all items
}elseif( $p <= 0 ) $p = $rows ;
```

The query parameters $s and $p are used for the starting index of the list and the size of the page to be displayed. Notice that the code does not assume that these variables are initialized. Also, the current device is used to set defaults for the page size. While this is strictly not necessary for WAP devices, this improves the usability of the default value to some extent since select lists on WAP devices tend to use the numeric keypad for selection shortcuts, that is, 1 is the first item in the list, 2 is the second and so on up to 9. Also, notice that if $p is set to a negative value, then the page automatically defaults to the entire list. It just so happens that the templates for the desktop web browser automatically display all categories and thereby bypass the paging logic.

Next, the starting index of the next and previous pages are calculated and stored in $nextid and $previd. With some logic we make sure we don't overrun the end or the beginning of the list. These values, along with the starting and ending index for the current page, are passed on to the template using the set_var() method call. If you haven't noticed by now, set_var() is a high traffic method when using templates. The $startno and $endno variables are used as a range specification in the template:

```
// set next and previous id for
// use in template
$previd = $s - $p ;
$nextid = $s + $p ;
if( $previd < 0 ) $previd = 0 ;
if( $nextid >= $rows ) $nextid = $rows - $p ;
if( $nextid < 0 ) $nextid = 0 ;

// set current start and end ids
$startno = $s + 1 ;
$endno = $nextid ;
if( $endno == 0 ) $endno = $rows ;

$tpl->set_var("previd",$previd) ;
$tpl->set_var("nextid",$nextid) ;
$tpl->set_var("startno",$startno) ;
$tpl->set_var("endno",$endno) ;
```

Now, we use the paging variables that we've already calculated to determine whether to parse the next block, the previous block, or both. For the next block, if we are displaying the last item in the list of categories, we simply clear the next block using `set_var()`, otherwise, we call the `parse()` method to include the parsed next block in the template.

We do the same thing for the previous block if the current page does not start at category item with index 0:

```
// if we are not at the end of the list
// then we parse the next block otherwise
// we make the next block go away
if(($s+$p) >= $rows ) {
    $p = $rows - $s ;
    $tpl->set_var("next","") ;

}
else{  // else parse next block to display next link
    $tpl->parse("next","next_tpl") ;
}

// if we are not at the beginning of the list
// then we parse the prev block otherwise
// we make the prev block go away
if($s > 0 )
    $tpl->parse("prev","prev_tpl") ;
else
    $tpl->set_var("prev","") ;
```

Next, we parse the category block. For this, first we use the `seek()` method of the `DB_Sql` class to move to the starting item for this page, as specified by the `$s` variable. This is followed by a loop to parse a page of category entries into the category block. Since the `$p` variable contains the number of items to display, a simple `for` loop will stop us if we hit the end of the page before reaching the end of the category list.

After setting each of the template variables that might be used inside the category block, the call to `parse()` actually does the work of adding an entry to the list of categories. Notice that the call to `parse()` uses a third parameter that we have not used for the next and previous blocks. The third parameter, which we set to `true` (the default value of this parameter is `false`), is used to cause the `parse()` method to append the newly parsed block to the `catlist` template variable, thereby adding a new entry to the list each time it is called in this manner:

```
// now parse the list
$db->seek($s) ;
for($i=0;$i<$p;$i++) {
    if( $db->next_record() ) {
        list($id,$category,$cnt) = $db->Record ;
        $tpl->set_var("catid",$id) ;
        $tpl->set_var("category",$category) ;
        $tpl->set_var("numstores","$cnt") ;
        $tpl->parse("catlist","catlist_tpl",true) ;
    }else break ;
}
```

And finally, we output the entire contents to the web browser:

```
// output the final page
$tpl->pparse("output","categories") ;
?>
```

stores.php

This script functions very much like the `categories.php` script with the exception that it displays stores instead of categories. It takes an area code and a category index as a query parameter, which it uses when forming the database query to select the stores from the database.

Also, there is an extra bit of code that will select the first default category to use if, for some reason, this script is called with only an area code specified. This is relatively easy for a user to do with certain WAP devices. The default category is the first category for that area code that has one or more associated stores. These exceptions aside, the code is nearly identical to `categories.php`. The source for this script is provided with the code downloads.

store.php

This is the final significant script for this case study. A large portion of the beginning of the script should be very familiar to you by now. This script selects a store from the database as specified by the query parameter `$id` and displays it using the `store.tpl` template. The section of code that checks the state of the variable `$id` and performs a database query, if it is not set, is simply accounting for the case where the store ID was not selected properly from the select list on the category screen. The default is the first store in the area code specified by `$ac` with the category specified by `$ci`. Again, this is done as a defense mechanism to avoid problems with certain WAP devices:

```
<?php
// include required files
require("include/db_mysql.inc.php") ;
require("include/config.inc.php") ;
require("include/template.inc.php") ;
require("include/utils.inc.php") ;

// determine device to start the system
IdentifyDevice($HTTP_USER_AGENT,$HTTP_ACCEPT) ;
PrepareDevice(DEVICE) ;

// connect to database
$db = new DB_Sql ;
if( !$db->connect() ) exit ;

// create and initialize the template object
$tpl = new Template() ;
$tpl->set_root("$template_path/".DEVICE) ;
$tpl->set_file("store","store.tpl") ;

// first get category name
$query = "SELECT category_name FROM storewap_categories WHERE category_id=$ci" ;
$db->query($query) ;
$db->next_record() ;
```

```php
list($catname) = $db->Record ;

// now get areacode information
$query = "SELECT LOCATION FROM storewap_areacodes WHERE areacode_codeno=$ac" ;
$db->query($query) ;
$db->next_record() ;
list($location) = $db->Record ;

// if store id was not set correctly
// then get first store from current
// category and current areacode
// this is done for WAP devices that
// allow you to follow a link without
// selecting at least one item from
// a <select> list
if( $id == 0 || $id == "" ) {
    $query = "SELECT s.store_id,s.store_name,s.store_phone FROM
            storewap_catjoin AS cj, storewap_stores AS s, storewap_areacodes AS
ac,
            storewap_areajoin AS aj
            WHERE s.store_id = cj.catjoin_storeid AND
            aj.areajoin_code = ac.areacode_codeno AND
            s.store_id = aj.areajoin_storeid AND
            cj.catjoin_catid = $ci AND
            ac.areacode_codeno = $ac ORDER BY s.name" ;
    $db->query($query) ;
    $db->next_record() ;
    list($id) = $db->Record ;
}

// get store information from database
    $query = "SELECT store_id,store_name,store_phone,store_desc,store_address
            FROM storewap_stores WHERE store_id=$id" ;
    $db->query($query) ;

// set general template variables
$tpl->set_var("categoryname",$catname) ;
$tpl->set_var("location",$location) ;
$tpl->set_var("areacode",$ac) ;
$tpl->set_var("categoryid",$ci) ;

// get store info and set template variables
if( $db->next_record() ) {
    list($id,$name,$phone,$shortdesc,$address) = $db->Record ;
    $tpl->set_var("id",$id) ;
    $tpl->set_var("name",CleanString($name)) ;
    $tpl->set_var("phone",PackPhone($phone)) ;
    $tpl->set_var("address",CleanString($address)) ;
    $tpl->set_var("shortdesc",CleanString($shortdesc)) ;
}else{
$tpl->set_var("id","") ;
$tpl->set_var("name","") ;
$tpl->set_var("phone","") ;
$tpl->set_var("address","") ;
```

```
$tpl->set_var("shortdesc","") ;
}

$tpl->pparse("output","store") ;

function PackPhone($str)
{
    $str = str_replace(" ","",$str) ;
    return trim($str) ;
}

function CleanString($str)
{
    $str = str_replace("&","&amp;",$str) ;
    $str = str_replace("<br>","<br/>",$str) ;
    return trim($str) ;
}

?>
```

The functions PackPhone() and CleanString() are used to improve the display and to avoid special character conflicts especially on WAP devices. The PackPhone() function simply removes spaces from the phone number. This has been done to avoid inconvenient wrapping of telephone numbers on small-screen devices. In practice, this function improves the display of store lists in cell phones quite a bit. Also, stores that use ampersands in the title must be parsed to avoid confusion on certain devices that treat all ampersands as the initial character of an encoded special character. The CleanString() function removes ampersands and replaces them with &.

Also, for displaying multiple line store addresses, the code allows <br/> tags to be embedded and converts these to be XML compliant. This was done for this case study since the data being used contained embedded break tags in the addresses. If desired, you could easily support this same functionality by "cleaning" or translating the input data in the administrative interface before it is stored in the database. Regardless, it is necessary to understand that embedded HTML or other special characters can have a detrimental effect on certain devices and must be considered carefully for each supported device.

HTML Site Templates

This section lists the main templates for the HTML site. The templates should be self-explanatory with all the relevant references to the code in the previous section clearly mentioned. Each template uses blocks and template variables to indicate how and where the corresponding script should act on the template. In cases where the templates do not use a block, the block is placed at the bottom of the template just to move it out of the way, as the template class requires it to exist even if it is not used. This case study is primarily oriented towards mobile devices; however, the HTML templates have been listed in contrast to the WAP templates.

Each template uses a format that is prescribed by the PHP-Lib template class that we are using in this case study. To summarize how this class works, it uses a template file that supports variable substitution and block substitution. Templates are loaded from a file using the following code:

```
$tpl = new Template() ;
$tpl->set_root("/home/mydir/mytemplatedir") ;
$tpl->set_file("index","index.tpl") ;
```

A new `Template` object is created, the path to the templates is set using the `set_root()` method, and the template file to be loaded is set using the `set_file()` method. Variable substitutions are indicated in the template using curly braces as follows:

```
{messages}
```

To actually perform a variable substitution in code, you use the `set_var()` method to set the value of the PHP variable to something interesting:

```
$tpl->set_var("messages",$messages);
```

Block substitution is done in a very similar fashion. Blocks are indicated in the template using the following syntax:

```
<!-- BEGIN storelist_tpl -->
<a href="store.php?&id={id}">
<b>{name}</b>
</a><br>
<!-- END storelist_tpl -->
```

In this sample, you can see that we have defined a block called `storelist_tpl` that contains a link to a store with two variable substitutions for the store name and the store ID. Code that parses this block will look as follows:

```
$tpl = new Template() ;
$tpl->set_root("/home/mydir/mytemplatedir") ;
$tpl->set_file("stores","stores.tpl") ;
$tpl->set_file("stores","stores.tpl") ;
$tpl->set_block("stores","storelist_tpl","storelist") ;

// database recordset was created by code not shown here

while($db->next_record() ) {
    list($id,$name) = $db->Record ;
    $tpl->set_var("id",$id) ;
    $tpl->set_var("name", $name) ;
    $tpl->parse("storelist","storelist_tpl",true) ;
}

// output the final page
$tpl->pparse("output","stores") ;
```

The multiple names being used by the `Template` class for the various parameters can be a little confusing to keep track of, but once you realize that the `Template` class keeps its own internal symbol table for template variables and you are just linking sections of the template to this internal symbol table, it becomes easier to get your mind around.

For more information on this, see the documentation on PHP-Lib at http://phplib.sourceforge.net/ or read the article on PHP-Lib templates at http://www.phpbuilder.com/columns/david20000512.php3.

index.tpl

The template file index.tpl is the primary entry point for the system and how it is constructed determines the rest of the sites structure. It is this template that determines whether the site uses framesets or not, and whether it allows for a user login or not.

The different blocks form part of the logic structure of the site. Different blocks are parsed under different conditions. For example, the loggedin_tpl block is only parsed when a user is logged into the system. Correspondingly, the loggedout_tpl block is only parsed when there is no user logged into the system. For most devices, there will likely be no reason to put code in the loggedin_tpl block since a lot of devices will not support the requirements of PHP sessions such as cookies. That being said, you must still put the empty block in the template, else the template class will denote an error when you try to parse a non-existent block.

The loggingin_tpl block is for the intermediate state where a user is trying to login and enters an incorrect username or password. This allows for an error message to be passed into the system using the {msg} variable to indicate login failure:

```
<frameset rows="100,*" frameborder=0 framespacing=0>
    <frame scrolling=no name="head" src="index.php?fi=head">
    <frameset cols="100,*" frameborder=0 framespacing=0>
    <frame name="left" src="index.php?fi=left">
<!-- BEGIN loggingin_tpl -->
    <frame name="content" src="index.php?fi=login&msg={msg}">
<!-- END loggingin_tpl -->
<!-- BEGIN loggedin_tpl -->
    <frame name="content" src="areacodes.php">
<!-- END loggedin_tpl -->
<!-- BEGIN loggedout_tpl -->
    <frame name="content" src="areacodes.php">
<!-- END loggedout_tpl -->
    </frameset>
</frameset>
```

areacodes.tpl

The areacodes.tpl template is the template that displays a list of area codes. For the main HTML templates, we don't use pagination of long lists of area codes; hence we simply ignore the paging variables by not including them in the code. The WAP templates in the next section will demonstrate how the paging variables are used to implement paging of the area codes and the other data in the system.

The main block in this code is the aclist_tpl block that defines a single area code element. The variables within this block are {areacode} for the area code itself and the {location} variable that is parsed as the description of the location.

Note that we have included the next_tpl and prev_tpl blocks even though they are empty to avoid errors by the Template class. These blocks are used for paging and will be described in the next section:

```
<html>
   <head>
      <title>Store Directory</title>
        <basefont face="arial,verdana">
   </head>
   <body bgcolor=white>

      <table width=350>
         <tr><td>
         <font size=+2><b>Area Code Coverage Listing</b></font><p>

<!-- BEGIN aclist_tpl -->
      <a href="index.php?fi=content&ac={areacode}">{areacode} -
          {location}</a><br>
<!-- END aclist_tpl -->

         <p>
            <!-- BEGIN prev_tpl -->
            <!-- END prev_tpl -->
            <!-- BEGIN next_tpl -->
            <!-- END next_tpl -->
         <br>
         </td></tr>
      </table>
   </center>
   </body>
</html>
```

categories.tpl

The `categories.tpl` template displays a list of store categories. This is the next screen of information displayed after the user selects an area code of interest. For this template, both `{areacode}` and `{location}` are predefined by the selection the user made in the area codes list. The `catlist_tpl` block is parsed for each category in the database and generates a list of links to the stores included in that category.

Notice that the links to `stores.php` contain $s and $p parameter. The $s parameter is the starting index of the store list that, in this case, is hard-coded to 0. The $p parameter is the page length to use when displaying the store list. A value of −1 for this parameter indicates that all stores should be displayed. After installing the system, try changing this value to 10 and see what happens:

```
<html>
   <head>
      <title>Store Directory</title>
      <basefont face="arial,verdana">
   </head>
   <body bgcolor=white>
      <table>
         <tr><td>
            <font size=+1><b>{location}-{areacode}</b></font><br>

         <!-- BEGIN catlist_tpl -->
```

```
            <a target="stores"
                href="stores.php?ci={catid}&ac={areacode}&s=0&p=-
                1">{category}</a> ({numstores})<br>
        <!-- END catlist_tpl -->

    <p>
<!-- BEGIN prev_tpl -->
<!-- END prev_tpl -->
<!-- BEGIN next_tpl -->
<!-- END next_tpl -->
<br>

        </td></tr>
    </table>

    </body>
</html>
```

stores.tpl

The `stores.tpl` template displays a list of stores within a particular category and for a pre-selected area code. By the time this template is parsed, the user has selected both the area code and category. This information is available to the template in the `{categoryname}`, `{categoryid}`, and `{areacode}`. The `storelist_tpl` block is parsed for every store in that category and area code with a link to the store information page generated for each one.

In this template, the `prev_tpl` and `next_tpl` block are parsed if needed. For a more detailed description of the pagination, see the next section on the WAP templates:

```
<html>
    <head>
        <title>Store Directory</title>
        <basefont face="arial,verdana">
    </head>
        <body bgcolor=white>
        <table width=350>
            <tr><td>
                <font size=+1><b>Category:</b> {categoryname}</font><p>

<!-- BEGIN storelist_tpl -->
    <a href="store.php?ac={areacode}&ci={categoryid}
    &id={id}"><b>{name}</b></a><br>    
         {phone}
<p>
    <!-- END storelist_tpl -->

<p>

<!-- BEGIN prev_tpl -->
    <a href="stores.php?ac={areacode}&ci={categoryid}
    &s={previd}">Previous</a>
```

```
      <!-- END prev_tpl -->
      <!-- BEGIN next_tpl -->
        <a href="stores.php?ac={areacode} &ci={categoryid}
           &s={nextid}">Next</a>
      <!-- END next_tpl -->
      <br>
          </td></tr>
       </table>
       </body>
  </html>
```

store.tpl

Finally, the `store.tpl` template file displays the details of the store:

```
<html>
   <head>
      <title>Store Directory</title>
      <basefont face="arial,verdana">
   </head>
   <body bgcolor=white>

      <table width=350>
        <tr><td>
         <font size=+1><b>Category:</b> {categoryname}</font><p>

      <blockquote>
         <b>{name}</b><p>
         <b>Phone:</b> {phone}<p>
         <b>Address:</b><br>
         {address}<p>
         <b>Desc:</b><br>
         {shortdesc}
      </blockquote>
  <p>
      <a href="stores.php?ac={areacode}&ci={categoryid}
              &s={previd}">Back to Store List</a><br>

         </td></tr>
      </table>
   </body>
</html>
```

WAP Site Templates

This section contains the WAP templates used when the site is being viewed with a WAP enabled cell phone. These can be tested on WAP enabled cell phones or using WAP emulators. The best emulators can be downloaded from the following sites:

❏ http://developer.openwave.com/
Sign up for the developer program and download the OpenWave SDK that includes a WAP emulator. This site used to be called Phone.COM. The Phone.com browser is one of the most popular WAP browsers embedded in cell phones, with the big exception of Nokia.

❏ http://www.forum.nokia.com/
Go to this site and click on the **Tools and SDKs** link. At this point the question is not "Where is the emulator?" but "Which one do I download?" This site is loaded with emulators and toolkits for every variation of Nokia phone and platform that they support. It is recommend that you start with the **Nokia Mobile Internet Toolkit** link and download it from there.

index.tpl

If you look at the following template, you will notice that there are no template blocks defined at all. This is because the index.php script only defines the template blocks if the device being used is a standard web browser. As a result, this template is pure WML code designed to allow the WAP user to easily enter an area code for entry into the directory.

Also notice the postfield parameters named s and p. These parameters are use for pagination and define the starting index and the page size for the categories list created by categories.php. In the index template, these values are hard-coded to display the list at the beginning with nine entries per page:

```
<?xml version="1.0"?>
<!DOCTYPE wml PUBLIC "-//WAPFORUM//DTD WML 1.1//EN"
"http://www.wapforum.org/DTD/wml_1.1.xml">
<wml>
    <card id="main" title="StoreWAP">
        <do type="accept" label="Send">
            <go href="/categories.php">
                <postfield name="ac" value="$ac"/>
                <postfield name="s" value="0"/>
                <postfield name="p" value="9"/>
            </go>
        </do>
        <p>
            Enter Local Area Code:
            <input name="ac" format="NNN" maxlength="3" value="" />
        </p>
    </card>
</wml>
```

categories.tpl

This script displays the categories for a given area code. The title displays the start and end range to give the users a visual indicator that they have changed pages when moving forward and backward in the paged category list. This is extremely important since the categories are all number 1-9 regardless of which page you are on. For this template, you will notice that up to four **soft keys** can be set; for the category selection, navigation to the next and previous pages from the category list if appropriate, and to re-enter the area code, if another location is desired.

This template is one of the first to start to take advantage of the pagination logic built into the system. Using the $s and $p parameters for the start of the list and page length respectively, the categories.php script automatically displays the defined subsection of the list starting at $s and continuing for $p entries. If there are entries that occur before or after the requested range then the prev_tpl and next_tpl blocks are parsed. These blocks are omitted if they are not needed. For any given range, if the next or previous blocks are parsed, then the variables, {nextid} and {previd}, are also set to be used as the new value of the s parameter when calling the categories.php script to display the new category range:

```
<?xml version="1.0"?>
<!DOCTYPE wml PUBLIC "-//WAPFORUM//DTD WML 1.1//EN"
"http://www.wapforum.org/DTD/wml_1.1.xml">
<wml>
    <card id="main" title="categories ({startno}-{endno})">
        <do type="accept" label="Display">
            <go href="/stores.php">
                <postfield name="ac" value="{areacode}"/>
                <postfield name="ci" value="$ci"/>
                <postfield name="s" value="0"/>
                <postfield name="p" value="9"/>
            </go>
        </do>
    <!-- BEGIN next_tpl -->
        <do type="accept" label="More">
            <go href="/categories.php">
                <postfield name="ac" value="{areacode}"/>
                <postfield name="s" value="{nextid}"/>
                <postfield name="p" value="9"/>
            </go>
        </do>
    <!-- END next_tpl -->
    <!-- BEGIN prev_tpl -->
        <do type="accept" label="Previous">
            <go href="/categories.php">
                <postfield name="ac" value="{areacode}"/>
                <postfield name="s" value="{previd}"/>
                <postfield name="p" value="9"/>
            </go>
        </do>
    <!-- END prev_tpl -->
        <do type="accept" label="New Area Code">
            <go href="/" />
        </do>
        <p>
            <select name="ci" title="categories" ivalue="0">
    <!-- BEGIN catlist_tpl -->
            <option value="{catid}">{category} ({numstores})</option>
    <!-- END catlist_tpl -->
        </select>
        </p>
    </card>
</wml>
```

stores.tpl

This template uses a structure that is very similar to the categories template with an option to view a store detail page, next and previous stores options, return to the categories list, and re-enter the area code.

The pagination blocks are also set up for the stores template. Notice that the next and previous blocks are responsible for propagating key information when handling paging. In this case, both the {areacode} and {categoryid} must be passed along with the paging parameters:

```
<?xml version="1.0"?>
<!DOCTYPE wml PUBLIC "-//WAPFORUM//DTD WML 1.1//EN"
"http://www.wapforum.org/DTD/wml_1.1.xml">
<wml>
    <card id="main" title="{categoryname} ({startno}-{endno})">
        <do type="accept" label="Display">
            <go href="/store.php">
                <postfield name="ac" value="{areacode}"/>
                <postfield name="ci" value="{categoryid}"/>
                <postfield name="id" value="$storeid"/>
            </go>
        </do>
    <!-- BEGIN next_tpl -->
        <do type="accept" label="More">
            <go href="/stores.php">
                <postfield name="ac" value="{areacode}"/>
                <postfield name="ci" value="{categoryid}"/>
                <postfield name="s" value="{nextid}"/>
                <postfield name="p" value="9"/>
            </go>
        </do>
    <!-- END next_tpl -->
    <!-- BEGIN prev_tpl -->
        <do type="accept" label="Previous">
            <go href="/stores.php">
                <postfield name="ac" value="{areacode}"/>
                <postfield name="ci" value="{categoryid}"/>
                <postfield name="s" value="{previd}"/>
                <postfield name="p" value="9"/>
            </go>
        </do>
    <!-- END prev_tpl -->
        <do type="accept" label="categories">
            <go href="/categories.php">
                <postfield name="ac" value="{areacode}"/>
                <postfield name="s" value="0"/>
                <postfield name="p" value="9"/>
            </go>
        </do>
        <do type="accept" label="New Area Code">
            <go href="/" />
        </do>
        <p>
```

```
        <select name="storeid" title="{categoryname}" ivalue="0">
      <!-- BEGIN storelist_tpl -->
        <option value="{id}">{name} {phone}</option>
      <!-- END storelist_tpl -->
        </select>
      </p>
    </card>
  </wml>
```

store.tpl

This template provides some of the most interesting WML since it actually gets to interact with the user's phone if supported. The first two soft-key options allow the user to either dial the number for the displayed store, or to add the number to the phone book. These options rely on the presence of Wireless Telephony Applicaion Interface (WTAI), which is not available on all phones. WTAI provides a means to create telephony applications using a WTA user-agent. One enhancement to the site would be to add more devices to the `IdentifyDevice()` function described earlier to allow the optional inclusion of these functions depending on whether the device supports the WTAI. For now, all cell phones that have been tested with this code either function properly or simply do nothing:

```
<?xml version="1.0"?>
<!DOCTYPE wml PUBLIC "-//WAPFORUM//DTD WML 1.1//EN"
"http://www.wapforum.org/DTD/wml_1.1.xml">
<wml>
   <card id="main" title="Store Details">
      <do type="accept" label="Call">
         <go href="wtai://wp/mc;+4805551212" />
      </do>
      <do type="accept" label="Add To Phone Book">
         <go href="wtai://wp/ap;+4805551212" />
      </do>
      <do type="accept" label="Stores">
         <go href="/stores.php">
            <postfield name="ac" value="{areacode}"/>
            <postfield name="ci" value="{categoryid}"/>
            <postfield name="s" value="0"/>
            <postfield name="p" value="9"/>
         </go>
      </do>
      <do type="accept" label="categories">
         <go href="/categories.php">
            <postfield name="ac" value="{areacode}"/>
            <postfield name="s" value="0"/>
            <postfield name="p" value="9"/>
         </go>
      </do>
      <do type="accept" label="New Area Code">
        <go href="/" />
      </do>
      <p>
        <b>{name}</b><br/>
          <b>Phone:</b> {phone}<br/>
          <b>Address:</b><br/>
          {address}<br/>
```

```
        <b>Desc:</b><br/>
           {shortdesc}
      </p>
   </card>
</wml>
```

PalmPilot and WindowsCE

The templates for the PalmPilot and WindowsCE devices are nearly identical. They are a simplified version of the standard web browser templates since both devices have fairly good support for HTML with the major limitation being their screen-sizes.

WindowsCE templates are similar. We can use Internet Explorer on a PocketPC that is connected to the Internet and enter the URL for your Store Directory site.

For the PalmPilot, there is one additional step. While the PalmPilot has very good support for HTML, due to the fact that airtime for Palm.NET is billed based on minutes used, the PalmPilot requires a front-end application that initiates the connection to the site and clearly indicates when an action is going to cause a connection to the Internet. These front-end applications are called Web-Clipping Apps or PQA (Palm Query Applications) for short.

A PQA is simply one or more static HTML pages including graphics that are pre-compiled into a front-end application. To build the PQA for this case study, load the following HTML file into the WCABuild application and select the Build PQA option from the file menu:

```html
<html>
   <head>
     <title>StoreWAP</title>
   </head>
  <body>
     StoreWAP.com: Mobile Retail Directory<p>

     <form action="http://www.storewap.com/categories.php">
        <input type="hidden" name="s" value="0">
        <input type="hidden" name="p" value="-1">
           Enter Area Code:
        <input type="text" size="3" name="ac">
        <input type="submit" value="Send">
     </form>
  </body>
</html>
```

You can download the WebClippingBuilder application from the PalmOS.com web site at http://www.palmos.com/dev/tech/webclipping/gettingstarted.html/.

Once you have built the PQA, you will need to install it onto your PalmPilot before you can access the store directory. If you ever launch a live site that uses these techniques, you can upload your PQA to the Palm.NET wireless portal to allow PalmPilot users all over the world to attain access to your site. The code for the templates of PalmPilot and WindowsCE is included with the code bundle.

Improvements

Following are a list of improvements and enhancements that could be added to this site.

- ❏ Administration
    - ❏ Administrator Interface to add, modify, and delete users
    - ❏ Store Owner Interface to add and modify store listings
    - ❏ Support for a credit system that limits the number of listings each store owner can enter into the system
    - ❏ Integration with a payment gateway such as Authorize.net, Paypal, IBill, and other such web sites, to allow for Store Owners to purchase more credits when needed. This is just in case the "we have 5 million customers who pay us nothing" business model doesn't work for you.
- ❏ Security
    - ❏ Encryption of the passwords being stored in the database
- ❏ Major Features
    - ❏ Integration with a travel-mapping site for providing driving directions and other travel related information
    - ❏ Direct integration with cell phones to take advantage of automatic dialing or storing phone numbers

For more information on WML refer to Professional WAP by Wrox Press (ISBN 1-86100-04-4).

Summary

This case study presented the design and structure for a site that can be accessed by three different types of mobile devices. The site facilitates multiple device support by relying on the PHP-Lib template class to separate the site presentation from the logic and code.

This case study demonstrated the following techniques:

- ❏ Creation of a web site using a template architecture (PHP-Lib `Template` class)
- ❏ Selection of templates based on identification of the device being used to browse the site
- ❏ Use of PHP to specify different content types when generating presentation code other than HTML
- ❏ Extensive use of various template techniques such as repeating blocks and option blocks

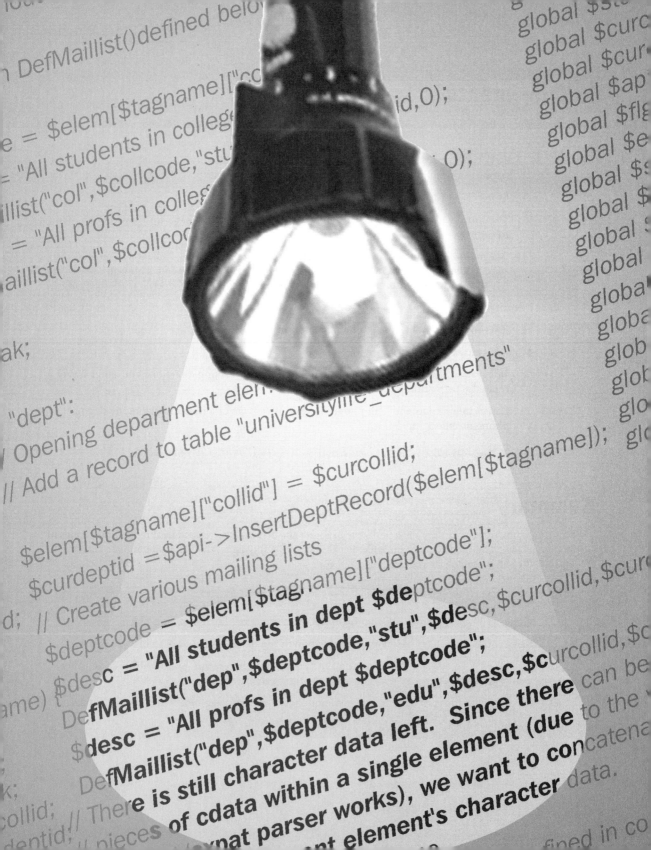

Paranormal News Service

Mighty GhostHunters, Inc. is setting up a web site to track paranormal and supernatural occurrences around the world. The web site will invite registered visitors to log their own paranormal experiences. Staff will select one visitor posting each month and turn it into a feature article for future publication. The user who posted the original experience will be invited to participate in a future ghost hunt, so a registration system is of high importance.

This case study looks at a web application for the fictional Mighty GhostHunters, Inc. that allows their staff and the public to post information about ghost sightings and other paranormal events and experiences.

In the course of this chapter, we will look at:

- ❏ Designing and implementing a user registration system
- ❏ Managing the user, group, permission, and content data
- ❏ Designing the web site

Application Specification

The architecture of the Paranormal News Service application is that of a site with news stories. The scope of the application is fairly large and it is not possible to cover the entire feature set in this chapter. Instead, this chapter will focus more on the user-interface and navigation design; not so much in terms of graphic design, but in terms of the coding and database back-end.

We'll focus on two important aspects in this chapter:

❑ Constructing a generic user registration system to manage users, groups of users, and permissions.

❑ Designing a generic news site (very similar to a weblog) that can then be configured to be used as our Paranormal News Service.

On this site will be articles posted by editors, and submissions suggested by users. An editor approves a submission thus making it an article. The site's home page will show links to the ten most recent articles so users can access and read them.

General Requirements

Here is a list of actions that can be performed on the paranormal site. These can be thought of as permissions in the user registration system:

❑ Register (create an account)

❑ Post article

❑ Edit article

❑ Read article

❑ Remove article

❑ Submit article

❑ View submissions

❑ Edit submission

❑ Approve submission

❑ Remove (reject) submission

Constructing the Generic User Registration System

Our first task will be the construction of a generic user registration system. The characteristics of this system are detailed in this section.

Users have accounts containing login name, password, e-mail, and other personal data. User are grouped together, each group has a name and description. There are four potential types of users. Two of these are public:

❑ General public (Anonymous)

❑ General public registered (Registered)

And two are types used for GhostHunter personnel only:

❑ GhostHunter Editors (Editor)

❑ GhostHunter Admin (Admin)

Permissions are assigned to groups of users and not directly to users because there could be a potentially very large pool of users – it would be impractical to assign permissions to each user individually. If we want to provide a specific user with special permissions, we can always create a group containing only that user and assign permissions to the group. We can also assign a user to more than one group.

Unregistered users (users accessing the site without logging in) are called anonymous users and belong to the Anonymous group, to which all users belong by default. Anonymous users have only very limited access to the system. Registered users (users logged in) belong to the Registered users group

Library for the User Registration System

Here we list the tables that will be used for the generic user registration system.

Users

The users_users table contains information about the users:

Column Name	Data Type	Desctiption
userid	INTEGER	A unique value identifying a user
login	VARCHAR	The login name of the user
password	VARCHAR	The password of the user
realname	VARCHAR	The real name of a user
homepage	VARCHAR	The users homepage, if any
lastlogin	INTEGER	The last time the user logged in
country	VARCHAR	The country to which the user belongs

Groups

The users_groups table contains information about the groups:

Column Name	Data Type	Desctiption
groupName	VARCHAR	The name of the group (Registered or Anonymous)
groupDesc	VARCHAR	The description for the group

Permissions

The users_permissions table contains information about system permissions:

Column Name	Data Type	Description
permName	INTEGER	The name of the group
permDesc	VARCHAR	The permissions for that particular group.

User

The `users_usergroups` table contains information about the group membership:

Column Name	Data Type	Description
userId	VARCHAR	The ID of the user
groupName	VARCHAR	The name of the group the user belongs to

Group

The `users_groupPermissions` table contains information about group permissions:

Column Name	Data Type	Description
groupName	VARCHAR	The name of the group
permName	VARCHAR	The permission for this group

All the tables are prefixed `users_` to allow this set of tables to coexist in the same database (`users`) with another set of tables where the table `groups_` for example may be in use by another application. This is very common in some hosting situations where we may be assigned only one database for all applications:

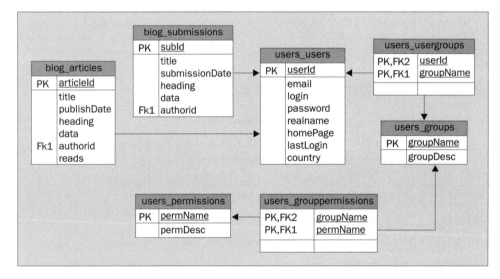

Let's now create the database for the users and the tables:

```
>mysqladmin create users
```

Now create the tables in the users database with the following script:

```sql
# FILE: create_user_tables.sql
# PURPOSE: create tables for Paranormal News Site

CREATE TABLE users_users (
    userId INTEGER(8) NOT NULL AUTO_INCREMENT,
    email VARCHAR(200),
    login VARCHAR(40) NOT NULL,
    password VARCHAR(30) NOT NULL,
    realname VARCHAR(80),
    homePage VARCHAR(200),
    lastLogin INTEGER(14),
    country VARCHAR(80),
    PRIMARY KEY(userId)
);

CREATE TABLE users_groups (
    groupName VARCHAR(30) NOT NULL,
    groupDesc VARCHAR(255),
    PRIMARY KEY(groupName)
);

CREATE TABLE users_usergroups (
    userId INTEGER(8) NOT NULL,
    groupName VARCHAR(30) NOT NULL,
    PRIMARY KEY(userId,groupName)
);

CREATE TABLE users_permissions (
    permName VARCHAR(30) NOT NULL,
    permDesc VARCHAR(250),
    PRIMARY KEY(permName)
);

CREATE TABLE users_groupPermissions (
    groupName VARCHAR(30) NOT NULL,
    permName VARCHAR(30) NOT NULL,
    PRIMARY KEY(groupName, permName)
);
```

Now that we have created the tables, we'll build a library to access the user registration system and to perform tasks like adding users, adding groups, removing users, assigning permissions, and so on. We'll use an instance of the PEAR::DB class to implement the library; the class constructor will receive a connection handler pointing to the database where the user registration system is located.

> **We can use MySQL, PostgreSQL, Oracle, or any other RDBMS without changing the class because the class relies on a PEAR object, which provides a common API to these and other databases.**

195

```php
<?php

//  FILE: userslib.php
//  PURPOSE: class to handle user group functions
//  for Paranormal News Service Site

class UsersLib
{
    var $db;
```

The class constructor receives the database handler object ($db) and assigns it to an object property:

```php
function UsersLib($db)
{
    if(!$db) {
        die("Invalid db object passed to UsersLib constructor");
    }
    $this->db = $db;
}
```

The SqlError() method is called when a query yields a MySQL error:

```php
function SqlError($query, $result)
{
    trigger_error("MYSQL error:  ".$result->getMessage().
                " in query:<br />".$query."<br />", E_USER_WARNING);
    die;
}
```

In a production site, we could replace the body of this method with more sophisticated (and user-friendly) error handling code, but this should provide sufficient information for debugging purposes.

Now let's look at some specific functionality of the user registration system. The UserExists() and GroupExists() methods are used to tell, respectively, if a given login name or group name exists in the database:

```php
function UserExists($user)
{
    $query = "SELECT login FROM users_users WHERE login='$user'";
    $result = $this->db->query($query);
    if(DB::isError($result)) $this->SqlError($query,$result);
    return $result->numRows();
}

function GroupExists($group)
{
    $query = "SELECT groupName FROM users_groups
            WHERE groupName='$group'";
    $result = $this->db->query($query);
    if(DB::isError($result)) $this->SqlError($query,$result);
    return $result->numRows();
}
```

Each of the two preceding functions returns 1 if the user or group exists, and 0 if it doesn't.

`ValidateUser()` indicates if a user is registered under a specified login name and password. If so, the method updates the user's `lastLogin` timestamp with the current time value.

> **We can store encrypted passwords for stronger security, or store a password hash.**

```
function ValidateUser($user,$pass)
    {
        $query = "SELECT login FROM users_users
                WHERE login='$user' AND password='$pass'";
        $result = $this->db->query($query);
        if(DB::isError($result)) $this->SqlError($query,$result);
        if($result->numRows())
        {
            $t = date("U");
            $query = "UPDATE users_users SET lastLogin='$t'
                    WHERE login='$user'";
            $result = $this->db->query($query);
            if(DB::isError($result)) $this->SqlError($query,$result);
            return TRUE;
        }       return FALSE;
    }
```

The `GetUsers()` method can be used to get an array of users from the database. This method accepts the following arguments:

❑ `$offset` is the point at which to start the recordset, use 0 to get a list from the first user (useful for pagination)

❑ `$maxRecords` to specify the maximum number of records to be retrieved from the database

❑ `$sort_mode` to sort the list; the default is `login_desc` and the mode is `fieldName_asc` or `fieldName_desc`

❑ `$find` can be used to enter a string and the method returns a list of users matching the search criteria

This method returns an array containing the users' name, e-mail, last changed page, version, and last Login for each:

```
function GetUsers($offset = 0,$maxRecords = -1,
                $sort_mode = 'login_desc', $find='')
    {
```

For the sort mode, we just replace any underscore characters we find in `$sort_mode` with spaces, and the value is ready to be interpolated into the query:

```
$sort_mode = str_replace("_"," ",$sort_mode);
```

We can impose a `WHERE... LIKE...` search constraint by passing a value for `$find`. If non-empty, the value is used to build the `WHERE` clause, stored as a string in `$mid`. Otherwise `$mid` contains an empty string:

```
if($find)
    $mid=" WHERE login LIKE '%".$find."%'";
else
    $mid='';

$query = "SELECT login, user_email, lastLogin FROM users_users $mid
             ORDER BY $sort_mode LIMIT $offset,$maxRecords";
```

The default value for $maxRecords is −1 (no upper limit). Now we get the number of users with records in the users_users table:

```
$query_cant = "SELECT count(*) FROM users_users";
$result = $this->db->query($query);

if(DB::isError($result)) $this->SqlError($query, $result);

$cant = $this->db->getOne($query_cant);
$ret = Array();
```

Note the use of empty-bracket notation below to auto-increment the array index each time we go through the while loop:

```
while($res = $result->fetchRow(DB_FETCHMODE_ASSOC)) {
    $aux = Array();
    $aux["user"] = $res["login"];
    $user = $aux["user"];
    $aux["email"] = $res["email"];
    $aux["lastLogin"] = $res["lastLogin"];
    $groups = $this->GetUserGroups($user);
    $aux["groups"] = $groups;
    $ret[] = $aux;
}

$retval = Array();
$retval["data"] = $ret;
$retval["cant"] = $cant;

return $retval;
}
```

The data structure returned by this method may appear a bit complex, but can perhaps be more easily understood by looking at it in the form of a diagram:

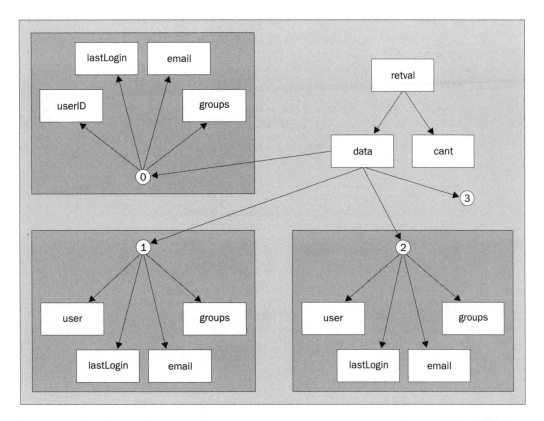

The return value (retval) is an associative array with two elements named data and cant. The second of these is the total number of users in the system (number of records in the users_users table). The first element (data) is an array, each of whose elements is itself an associative array, with elements named user, lastLogin, email, and groups.

We proceed in a similar fashion with groups and permissions. In GetGroups(), the array elements consist of a groupName, groupDesc, and an array of permission names ($perms) returned by GetGroupPermissions(), shown below:

```
function GetGroups($offset = 0,$maxRecords = -1,
                   $sort_mode = 'groupName_desc', $find='')
{
```

Note that we can sort on groupName or groupDesc:

```
$sort_mode = str_replace("_"," ",$sort_mode);

if($find) {
    $mid=" WHERE groupName LIKE '%".$find."%'";
} else {
    $mid='';
```

```
    }
    $query = "SELECT groupName, groupDesc FROM users_groups $mid
    ORDER BY $sort_mode LIMIT $offset,$maxRecords";

    $query_cant = "SELECT count(*) FROM users_groups";

    $result = $this->db->query($query);
    if(DB::isError($result)) $this->SqlError($query, $result);

    $cant = $this->db->getOne($query_cant);
    $ret = Array();

    while($res = $result->fetchRow(DB_FETCHMODE_ASSOC)) {
        $aux = Array();
        $aux["groupName"] = $res["groupName"];
        $aux["groupDesc"] = $res["groupDesc"];
        $perms = $this->GetGroupPermissions($aux["groupName"]);
        $aux["perms"] = $perms;
        $ret[] = $aux;
    }

    $retval = Array();
    $retval["data"] = $ret;
    $retval["cant"] = $cant;

    return $retval;
}
```

GetPermissions() is very similar. The array elements are simpler; each element contains only permName and permDesc:

```
function GetPermissions($offset = 0,$maxRecords = -1,
                        $sort_mode = 'permName_desc', $find='')
{
    $sort_mode = str_replace("_"," ",$sort_mode);
    if($find) {
        $mid=" where groupName like '%".$find."%'";
    } else {
        $mid='';
    }

    $query = "SELECT permName, permDesc FROM users_permissions
            $mid ORDER BY $sort_mode LIMIT $offset,$maxRecords";
    $query_cant = "SELECT count(*) FROM users_permissions";
    $result = $this->db->query($query);
    if(DB::isError($result)) $this->SqlError($query, $result);
    $cant = $this->db->getOne($query_cant);
    $ret = Array();

    while($res = $result->fetchRow(DB_FETCHMODE_ASSOC))
    {
```

As before, $aux is a convenience variable that we use to load up the next element in $ret with the values desired:

```
        $aux = Array();
        $aux["permName"] = $res["permName"];
        $aux["permDesc"] = $res["permDesc"];
        $ret[] = $aux;
    }
```

And it is the array populated in the while loop that is passed back to the calling code:

```
        $retval = Array();
        $retval["data"] = $ret;
        $retval["cant"] = $cant;
        return $retval;
    }
```

In this way, we've been able to include an array of the user groups in the information about users, and an array of permissions in the information about each group.

The RemoveUser() function removes a user from a group – it receives a login name and group name, and removes the user with that login from the specified group. Note that the user's status in other groups isn't affected by this function:

```
function RemoveUserFromGroup($user,$group)
{
    $userid = $this->GetUserId($user);
    $query = "DELETE FROM users_userGroups WHERE userId=$userid
            AND groupName='$group'";
    $result = $this->db->query($query);
    if(DB::isError($result)) $this->SqlError($query, $result);
}
```

The next few functions are self explanatory – GetUserId() returns the user ID when given a login name, RemoveUser() eliminates a user from the database, and RemoveGroup() eliminates a group:

```
function GetUserId($user)
{
    $id = $this->db->getOne("SELECT user_userid FROM users_users
                            WHERE login='$user'");
    if(DB::isError($id)) return false;
    return $id;
}

function RemoveUser($user)
{
    $query = "DELETE FROM users_users WHERE login = '$user'";
    $result =  $this->db->query($query);
    if(DB::isError($result)) $this->SqlError($query,$result);
    return true;
```

```
    }

    function RemoveGroup($group)
    {
        $query = "DELETE FROM users_groups WHERE groupName = '$group'";
        $result = $this->db->query($query);
        if(DB::isError($result)) $this->SqlError($query,$result);
        return true;
    }
```

GetUserGroups() returns an array of groups for a given user:

```
    function GetUserGroups($user)
    {
        $userid = $this->GetUserId($user);

        $query = "SELECT groupName FROM users_userGroups
                WHERE userId='$userid'";

        $result = $this->db->query($query);

        if(DB::isError($result)) $this->SqlError($query,$result);
        $ret = Array();

        while($res = $result->fetchRow(DB_FETCHMODE_ASSOC))
        {
            $ret[] = $res["groupName"];
        }
```

All users are members of the Anonymous group:

```
        $ret[] = "Anonymous";
        return $ret;
    }
```

These methods retrive information from the tables groups and users; they return associative arrays containing all the fields for the users/groups:

```
    function GetUserInfo($user)
    {
        $query = "SELECT * FROM users_users WHERE login='$user'";
        $result = $this->db->query($query);
        if(DB::isError($result)) $this->SqlError($query,$result);

        $res = $result->fetchRow(DB_FETCHMODE_ASSOC);

        $aux = Array();
        foreach ($res as $key => $val) {
            $aux[$key] = $val;
        }
```

```
        $groups = $this->GetUserGroups($user);
        $res["groups"] = $groups;

        return $res;
    }

function GetUseridInfo($user)
{
        $query = "SELECT * FROM users_users WHERE user_userid='$user'";
        $result = $this->db->query($query);
        if(DB::isError($result)) $this->SqlError($query,$result);

        $res = $result->fetchRow(DB_FETCHMODE_ASSOC);

        $aux = Array();
        foreach ($res as $key => $val) {
            $aux[$key] = $val;
        }

        $groups = $this->GetUserGroups($user);
        $res["groups"] = $groups;

        return $res;
    }

function GetGroupInfo($group)
{
        $query = "SELECT * FROM users_groups WHERE groupName='$group'";
        $result = $this->db->query($query);
        if(DB::isError($result)) $this->SqlError($query,$result);

        $res = $result->fetchRow(DB_FETCHMODE_ASSOC);
        $perms = $this->GetGroupPermissions($group);
        $res["perms"] = $perms;

        return $res;
    }
```

Note that GetUserInfo() returns a list of groups to which the user belongs; GetGroupInfo() contains an array, perms, with a list of permissions assigned to that group. We did the same in the GetUsers() and GetGroups() methods.

The next few functions obtain permissions, assign users to groups, assign permissions to groups, and remove permissions from group, or users from groups:

```
function GetGroupPermissions($group)
{
        $query = "SELECT permName FROM users_groupPermissions
                WHERE groupName='$group'";
        $result = $this->db->query($query);

        if(DB::isError($result)) $this->SqlError($query,$result);
```

```php
    $ret = Array();

    while($res = $result->fetchRow(DB_FETCHMODE_ASSOC)) {
        $ret[] = $res["permName"];
    }

    return $ret;
}

function AssignPermissionToGroup($perm,$group)
{
    $query = "REPLACE INTO users_groupPermissions(groupName,permName)
            VALUES('$group','$perm')";

    $result = $this->db->query($query);
    if(DB::isError($result)) $this->SqlError($query,$result);

    return true;
}

function GetUserPermissions($user)
{
    // admin has all the permissions
    $groups = $this->GetUserGroups($user);
    $ret = Array();
    foreach ($groups as $group) {
        $perms = $this->GetGroupPermissions($group);
        foreach ($perms as $perm) {
            $ret[] = $perm;
        }
    }
    return $ret;
}

function UserHasPermission($user,$perm)
{
    // admin has all the permissions
    if($user=='admin') return true;
    // Get user_groups ?
    $groups = GetUserGroups($user);

    foreach ($groups as $group) {
        if(GroupHasPermission($group,$perm)) return true;
    }

    return false;
}

function GroupHasPermission($group,$perm)
{
    $query = "SELECT groupName,permName FROM users_groupPermissions
            WHERE groupName='$group' AND permName='$perm'";
    $result = $this->db->query($query);
    if(DB::isError($result)) $this->SqlError($query,$result);
```

```
                return $result->numRows();
    }

    function RemovePermissionFromGroup($perm,$group)
    {
        $query = "DELETE FROM users_groupPermissions
                    WHERE permName='$perm' AND groupName= '$group'";
        $result = $this->db->query($query);
        if(DB::isError($result)) $this->SqlError($query,$result);

        return true;
    }

    function AssignUserToGroup($user,$group)
    {
        $userid = $this->GetUserId($user);

        $query = "REPLACE INTO users_userGroups(userId,groupName)
                    VALUES($userid,'$group')";
        $result = $this->db->query($query);
        if(DB::isError($result)) $this->SqlError($query,$result);

        return true;
    }
```

The remaining two functions are used to add users and groups. Each of these check to see if the indicated user or group already exists, inserting a new record into the appropriate table if it doesn't:

```
    function AddUser($user,$pass,$email)
    {
        if($this->UserExists($user)) return FALSE;

        $query = "INSERT INTO users_users(login,password,user_email)
                    VALUES('$user','$pass','$email')";

        $result = $this->db->query($query);
        if(DB::isError($result)) $this->SqlError($query,$result);
        $this->AssignUserToGroup($user,'Registered');

        return TRUE;
    }

    function AddGroup($group,$desc)
    {
        if($this->GroupExists($group)) return FALSE;

        $query = "INSERT INTO users_groups(groupName, groupDesc)
                    VALUES('$group','$desc')";
        $result = $this->db->query($query);
        if(DB::isError($result)) $this->SqlError($query,$result);

        return TRUE;
    }
}
    //  end class UsersLib
?>
```

Now that we have a set of methods (saved in the file userslib.php) for accessing the user registration system, let's see the requirements for the paranormal news service.

Insert Permissions into the User Registration System

Let's list the actions that users of one sort or another (registered or unregistered) can take via menu options, links, and HTML forms:

- ❑ Register (create an account)
- ❑ Post Article
- ❑ Edit Article
- ❑ Read Article
- ❑ Remove Article
- ❑ Submit Article
- ❑ View Submissions
- ❑ Edit Submission
- ❑ Approve Submission
- ❑ Remove Submission

The following table shows the relationship between user groups and permissions. X indicates the permission assigned to that group:

PERMITTED ACTIONS: / USER GROUP:	Anonymous	Registered	Editor	Admin
Register	X			X
Post Article			X	X
Read Article	X	X	X	X
Edit Article			X	X
Remove Article			X	X
Submit article		X	X	X
View submissions			X	X
Remove submissions			X	X
Edit submissions			X	X
Approve submissions			X	X
Add users/groups or permissions				X

We can insert the permissions into the user registration system using the following MySQL statements:

```
# FILE: set_permissions.sql
# PURPOSE: set permissions for Paranormal News user groups

### Insert the weblog permissions
INSERT INTO users_permissions(permName,permDesc) VALUES('p_admin','Administrator,
can manage users groups and permissions and all the weblog features');
```

```
INSERT INTO users_permissions(permName,permDesc) VALUES('p_register','Can register
as a new user if not logged');

### Article permissions
INSERT INTO users_permissions(permName,permDesc)
VALUES('p_post_article','Can post an article directly to the weblog');

INSERT INTO users_permissions(permName,permDesc)
VALUES('p_edit_article','Can edit an article');

INSERT INTO users_permissions(permName,permDesc) VALUES('p_read_article','Can read
an article');

INSERT INTO users_permissions(permName,permDesc) VALUES('p_remove_article','Can
remove an article');

### Submissions
INSERT INTO users_permissions(permName,permDesc) VALUES('p_submit_article','Can
submit an article to be approved');

INSERT INTO users_permissions(permName,permDesc)
VALUES('p_approve_submission','Can approve a submission');

INSERT INTO users_permissions(permName,permDesc) VALUES('p_view_submissions','Can
view a list of submissions');

INSERT INTO users_permissions(permName,permDesc) VALUES('p_edit_submission','Can
edit a user submission (any)');

INSERT INTO users_permissions(permName,permDesc) VALUES('p_remove_submission','Can
view a list of submissions');
```

We also create the Anonymous and Registered groups, as well as the admin account that are the user registration system. The Editors group will be created directly using the user registration system administration interface:

```
## Default groups
INSERT INTO users_groups(groupName,groupDesc)
VALUES('Anonymous','Public users not logged');

INSERT INTO users_groups(groupName,groupDesc)
VALUES('Registered','Users logged into the system');

### Administrator account
INSERT INTO users_users(email,login,password,realname)
VALUES ('','admin','admin','System Administrator');
```

In order for unregistered users to register, we should insert these values in the users_groupPermissions table:

```
INSERT INTO users_groupPermissions(groupName,permName)
VALUES('Anonymous','p_register');
```

A Database and Library for the Paranormal Weblog

The next step will be the design of the database (blog) tables used for the paranormal weblog:

We first create the database:

```
> mysqladmin create blog
```

This contains articles and submissions that use the following schema for the tables:

```sql
# FILE: create_blog_tables.sql
# PURPOSE: create tables for Paranormal articles

CREATE TABLE blog_articles (
    articleId INTEGER(8) NOT NULL AUTO_INCREMENT,
    title VARCHAR(80),
    publishDate INTEGER(14),
    heading TEXT,
    data LONGBLOB,
    authorId INTEGER(8),
    reads INTEGER(14),
    PRIMARY KEY(articleId)
);

CREATE TABLE blog_submissions (
    subId INTEGER(8) NOT NULL AUTO_INCREMENT,
    title VARCHAR(80),
    submissionDate INTEGER(14),
    heading TEXT,
    data LONGBLOB,
    authorId INTEGER(8),
    PRIMARY KEY(subId)
);
```

As we created the user registration library, we will also create a Blog library with methods to add, remove, list articles, and submissions.

Here is the code for the Blog class:

```php
<?php

// FILE: bloglib.php
// PURPOSE: creates class to handle article (blog) functions

class Blog
{
    var $db;            // The PEAR::DB object used to access the database

    function Blog($db)
    {
        if(!$db) {
            die("Invalid db object passed to UsersLib constructor");
```

```
        }
        $this->db = $db;
    }

    function IncrementReads($articleId)
    {
        $query = "UPDATE blog_articles SET reads=reads+1
                WHERE articleId=$articleId";
        $result = $this->db->query($query);
        if(DB::isError($result)) $this->SqlError($query,$result);
        return true;
    }
```

GetArticles() and GetSubmissions() are very similar to the GetGroups() and GetPermissions() methods of the UsersLib class. They have the same general input parameters and return similar data structures:

```
    function GetArticles($offset = 0,$maxRecords = -1,
                        $sort_mode = 'publishDate_desc', $find='',
                        $date='')
    {
        $sort_mode = str_replace("_"," ",$sort_mode);
        if($find) {
            $mid=" WHERE title LIKE '%".$find."%' OR heading LIKE
                '%".$find."%' OR data LIKE '%".$find."%' ";
        } else {
            $mid='';
        }
        if($date) {
            if($mid) {
                $mid.=" AND  publishDate<=$date ";
            } else {
                $mid=" WHERE publishDate<=$date ";
            }
        }
        $query = "SELECT * FROM blog_articles $mid
                ORDER BY $sort_mode LIMIT $offset,$maxRecords";
        $query_cant = "SELECT count(*) FROM blog_articles";
        $result = $this->db->query($query);
        if(DB::isError($result)) $this->SqlError($query, $result);
        $cant = $this->db->getOne($query_cant);
        $ret = Array();
        while($res = $result->fetchRow(DB_FETCHMODE_ASSOC)) {
            if(empty($res["data"])) {
                $res["isEmpty"] = 'y';
            } else {
                $res["isEmpty"] = 'n';
            }
            $ret[] = $res;
        }
        $retval = Array();
        $retval["data"] = $ret;
```

```php
        $retval["cant"] = $cant;

        return $retval;
}

function GetArticlesByDate($offset = 0,$maxRecords = -1,
                           $sort_mode = 'publishDate_desc',
                           $find='', $date='')
{
    $sort_mode = str_replace("_"," ",$sort_mode);
    if($find) {
        $mid=" where title like '%".$find."%' or heading like
              '%".$find."%' or data like '%".$find."%' ";
    } else {
        $mid='';
    }
    if($date) {
        $fromDate =
        mktime(0,0,0,date("m",$date),date("d",$date),date("Y",$date));
        $toDate =
        mktime(23,59,59,date("m",$dat),date("d",$date),date("Y",$date));
        if($mid) {
            $mid.=" and  publishDate>=$fromDate and publishDate<=
                  $toDate ";
        } else {
            $mid=" where publishDate>=$fromDate and publishDate<=
                  $toDate ";
        }
    }
    $query = "SELECT * FROM blog_articles $mid order BY
             $sort_mode LIMIT $offset,$maxRecords";

    $query_cant = "SELECT count(*) FROM blog_articles";

    $result = $this->db->query($query);

    if(DB::isError($result)) $this->SqlError($query, $result);
    $cant = $this->db->getOne($query_cant);
    $ret = Array();

    while($res = $result->fetchRow(DB_FETCHMODE_ASSOC)) {
        if(empty($res["data"])) {
            $res["isEmpty"] = 'y';
        } else {
            $res["isEmpty"] = 'n';
        }
        $ret[] = $res;
    }

    $retval = Array();
    $retval["data"] = $ret;
    $retval["cant"] = $cant;
    return $retval;
```

```
    }
    function GetSubmissions($offset = 0,$maxRecords = -1,
                         $sort_mode = 'submissionDate_desc', $find='')
    {
        $sort_mode = str_replace("_"," ",$sort_mode);
        if($find) {
            $mid=" WHERE title LIKE '%".$find."%' OR heading LIKE
            '%".$find."%' OR data LIKE '%".$find."%' ";
        } else {
            $mid='';
        }
        $query = "SELECT * FROM blog_submissions $mid ORDER
                BY $sort_mode LIMIT $offset,$maxRecords";
        $query_cant = "SELECT count(*) FROM blog_submissions";
        $result = $this->db->query($query);
        if(DB::isError($result)) $this->SqlError($query, $result);
        $cant = $this->db->getOne($query_cant);
        $ret = Array();
        while($res = $result->fetchRow(DB_FETCHMODE_ASSOC)) {
            $author_info = GetUserInfo($res["authorId"]);
            $res["author"] = $author_info["login"];
            $ret[] = $res;
        }
        $retval = Array();
        $retval["data"] = $ret;
        $retval["cant"] = $cant;
        return $retval;
    }
```

Each of the following two methods takes the ID of a submission or an article and returns an associative array containing all the information in the corresponding record (from the `blog_submissions` table in the case of `GetSubmissionInfo()`, and from `blog_articles` when using `GetArticleInfo()`):

```
    function GetSubmissionInfo($subId)
    {
        $query = "SELECT * FROM blog_submissions WHERE subId=$subId";
        $result = $this->db->query($query);
        if(DB::isError($result)) $this->SqlError($query, $result);
        if(!$result->numRows()) return false;
        $res = $result->fetchRow(DB_FETCHMODE_ASSOC);
        return $res;
    }

    function GetArticleInfo($articleId)
    {
        $query = "SELECT * FROM blog_articles
                WHERE articleId=$articleId";
        $result = $this->db->query($query);
        if(DB::isError($result)) $this->SqlError($query, $result);
        if(!$result->numRows()) return false;
        $res = $result->fetchRow(DB_FETCHMODE_ASSOC);
        return $res;
    }
```

To approve a submission, we first retrieve all of its `blog_submissions` data by calling `GetSubmissionInfo()`, then insert this data into a new record in `blog_articles` using the `AddArticle()` method detailed below. Finally, we remove the submission's record from the `blog_submissions` table:

```
function ApproveSubmission($subId,$date='')
{
    $sub_info = $this->GetSubmissionInfo($subId);
    if(!$date)
    {
        $date = date("U");
    }
    $this->AddArticle($sub_info["title"],$date,$sub_info["heading"],
                      $sub_info["data"],$sub_info["authorId"]);
    $this->RemoveSubmission($subId);
}
```

We'll use the same error-reporting function (`SqlError()`) that we saw in the `UsersLib` class:

```
function SqlError($query, $result)
{
    trigger_error("MYSQL error:  ".$result->getMessage().
                  " in query:<br/ >".$query."<br />",E_USER_WARNING);
    die;
}
```

Now we just need functions to add, update, and delete submissions and articles:

```
function AddSubmission($title,$heading,$data,$authorId)
{
    $now = date("U");

    $query = "INSERT INTO blog_submissions
                (title,submissionDate,heading,data,authorId)
                VALUES('$title',$now,'$heading',
                                    '$data',$authorId)";

    $result = $this->db->query($query);

    if(DB::isError($result)) $this->SqlError($query,$result);

    return TRUE;
}

function AddArticle($title,$publishDate,$heading,$data,$authorId)
{
    $query = "INSERT INTO blog_articles
                (title,publishDate,heading,data,authorId,reads)
                VALUES ('$title','$publishDate',
                        '$heading','$data',$authorId,0)";
```

```php
        $result = $this->db->query($query);
        if(DB::isError($result)) $this->SqlError($query,$result);
        return TRUE;
    }

    function UpdateSubmission($subId,$title,$heading,$data)
    {
        $query = "UPDATE blog_submissions
                SET title='$title',heading='$heading',data='$data'
                WHERE subId=$subId";
        $result = $this->db->query($query);
        if(DB::isError($result)) $this->SqlError($query,$result);
        return TRUE;
    }

    function UpdateArticle($articleId,$title,
                            $heading,$data,$publishDate='')
    {
        if($publishDate) {
            $mid = " ,publishDate=$publishDate ";
        } else {
            $mid ='';
        }

        $query = "UPDATE blog_articles
                SET title='$title',heading='$heading',data='$data' $mid
                WHERE articleId=$articleId";

        $result = $this->db->query($query);

        if(DB::isError($result)) $this->SqlError($query,$result);

        return TRUE;
    }

    function RemoveArticle($articleId)
    {
        $query = "DELETE FROM blog_articles WHERE articleId=$articleId";
        $result = $this->db->query($query);
        if(DB::isError($result)) $this->SqlError($query, $result);
        return true;
    }

    function RemoveSubmission($subId)
    {
        $query = "DELETE FROM blog_submissions WHERE subId=$subId";
        $result = $this->db->query($query);
        if(DB::isError($result)) $this->SqlError($query, $result);
        return true;
    }
}
?>
```

These three pairs of functions serve as wrappers for the appropriate INSERT, UPDATE and DELETE queries.

Designing the Web Site and Templates

Since we are focusing mostly on the user interface aspect of the GhostHunter application, we will spend some time discussing user-specific menus, virtual page templates, and so on. While we may refer to a number of menus and templates, a select few will be discussed further by showing sample PHP code that implements them.

We'll use Smarty for the paranormal site, which is a PHP template engine available at http://smarty.php.net. Smarty uses templates to separate logic from presentation in a very clear fashion. We will have a quick introduction to Smarty as we move through this section.

We'll use the following directory structure:

In the above figure:

- ❑ blog is the site root directory

- ❑ cache is the cache directory for Smarty

- ❑ Smarty contains the Smarty template engine, all the files and directories that come with Smarty should be put into this directory

- ❑ styles has Cascading Style Sheet (CSS) files used for this project

- ❑ templates is where we'll store our Smarty templates

- ❑ templates_c is where Smarty stores the compiled templates

Note that the entire sourcecode for the case study is available with the code bundle for this chapter from our web site at http://www.wrox.com/.

Introduction to Smarty: The PHP Template Engine

Designing a site with Smarty is easy, for each page we generally create two files, for example, `page.php` and `page.tpl`. We put all the logic code and form processing in the PHP file and create the variables, arrays, and structures that we want displayed. In the template (`.tpl`) file we put all the presentation features, HTML code, tables, and so on using the PHP variables created in the PHP file. Therefore, if we want to change the presentation, we want need to change the code, and if we want to change the code, we won't have to touch the presentation template.

The first thing you have to do is to download Smarty from http://smarty.php.net and then install it. The installation process is straightforward, just unzip the Smarty distribution in a directory accessible from your web application and you are ready to configure and use it.

Configuring Smarty

Configuring Smarty means telling it where to locate the things it needs to work with, such as templates, compiled templates, and the cache. Generally, we use a PHP script that is included in all the application files initializing Smarty. Here is an example of how to configure and initialize it.

First we tell Smarty where the distribution was unzipped to:

```
define('SMARTY_DIR',"Smarty/");
require_once(SMARTY_DIR.'Smarty.class.php');
```

And now we extend the Smarty class by setting up the directory names it needs.

- ❏ `templates/` is the directory used for templates

- ❏ `templates_c/` is the directory that will be used for the compiled templates (Smarty compiles templates automatically)

- ❏ `configs/` is where configuration files are located, if needed (we won't use them in this chapter)

- ❏ `cache_dir/` is where Smarty puts the cached pages

- ❏ `$this->caching = false` sets caching off

```
class SmartyWeblog extends Smarty {
  function SmartyWeblog(){
      $this->teplate_dir = "templates/";
      $this->compile_dir = "templates_c/";
      $this->config_dir = "configs/";
      $this->cache_dir = "cache/";
      $this->caching = false;
  }
}
$smarty = new SmartyWeblog();
```

Now the Smarty object can be used to assign variables and display templates.

Using Smarty (An Example)

This is an example named `hello.php`:

```
include_once("setup.php");  // The file where smarty is initialized
$name = 'Kim'
$smarty->assign('name',$name);
$smarty->display('hello.tpl');
```

Put the `hello.tpl` template in the Smarty's templates directory:

```
<html>
  <body>
    <p>Hello {$name}</p>
  </body>
</html>
```

As you can see, `{$name}` is an instruction that outputs the content of the $name Smarty variable (assigned using the `assign` method in the PHP file)

If you follow this approach you will succeed in separating code from presentation, you can easily render WML instead of HTML for the `hello` example. By changing only the template file, the code is the same.

Smarty has many features for template designers. It provides functions to output variables, modifiers to format variables (text, dates, and so on), and functions to loop arrays (to display tables and listings). Smarty is also extensible; you can add your own functions and modifiers as plugins that are automatically recognized by Smarty.

Having given an introduction to Smarty, let's now get on with the Paranormal News Service application.

Initialization

Our first step connects to the database, creates instances of the `UsersLib` and `Blog` classes, and initalizes Smarty.

The `db_data.php` file contains the information necessary for the database connections:

```php
<?php
// FILE: db_data.php
// PURPOSE: handles database connections for Paranormal News Site
// Database connection for the users system
require_once 'DB.php';

$host_users    = 'localhost';
$user_users    = 'root';
$pass_users    = '';
$dbs_users     = 'users';
$dsn = "mysql://$user_users:$pass_users@$host_users/$dbs_users";
$dbUser = DB::connect($dsn);

if (DB::isError($dbUser)) {
    die ($dbUser->getMessage());
```

```
    }

    // Database connection for the blog system
    $host_blog = 'localhost';
    $user_blog = 'root';
    $pass_blog = '';
    $dbs_blog = 'blog';
    $dsn = "mysql://$user_blog:$pass_blog@$host_blog/$dbs_blog";
    $dbBlog = DB::connect($dsn);

    if (DB::isError($dbBlog)) {
        die ($dbBlog->getMessage());
    }
    ?>
```

Here we've used PEAR::DB to create two database connections – one to the user registration system in the users database, and the other to the blog database for the weblog tables. Note that the user registration system located in a specific database can be accessed/shared from a different system that has the same user database and group/permissions mechanism.

We'll use a setup.php script that must be included in all the application's PHP files; this script will have all the initialization features needed for the site:

```
    <?php

    //   FILE: setup.php
    //   PURPOSE: Paranormal News initialisation file;
    //   calls include files and Smarty template system components

    session_start();
```

First we start a session, and then include the db_data.php script for the database connections and the two class files used:

```
    require_once 'db_data.php';
    require_once 'userslib.php';
    require_once 'bloglib.php';
```

Since we are going to store in the database, articles whose text may include quoted strings or apostrophes, we need to be sure that we don't face potential problems with the magic quotes setting:

```
    // Remove automatic quotes added to POST/GET by PHP
    if (get_magic_quotes_gpc ()) {
        foreach($_REQUEST as $k=>$v) {
            $_REQUEST[$k]=stripslashes($v);
        }
    }
```

> The `magic_quotes_gpc()` function turns on magic quotes (escapes single quotes, double quotes, null, and backslash characters) for, GET, POST, and cookie data, as does `magic_quotes_gpc = On` in the php.ini file. Similarly, `magic_quotes_run time = On` turns on magic quotes for data generated at runtime by MySQL, the `exec()` and `system()` commands, and so on.

If you don't have access to php.ini, you can disable magic quotes in your PHP applications with ini_set("magic_quotes_gpc",0); and ini_set("magic_quotes_runtime",0);. For more information refer to http://www.webmasterstop.com/tutorials/magic-quotes.shtml.

Now let's create the Smarty object that will be used to display templates and provide the Smarty initialization information:

```
// Define and load Smarty components

// Note - if the script is being executed on UNIX make sure
// to change the back slashes (\\) to a forward slash (/)
define('SMARTY_DIR',"Smarty\\");

require_once SMARTY_DIR.'Smarty.class.php';
```

Here we extend the Smarty class as a convenient way to initialize some necessary configuration variables, namely those that tell Smarty where its template, cache, and configuration file directories are, as well as the name of the current application:

```
class SmartyWeblog extends Smarty
{
    function SmartySterling()
    {
        $this->template_dir = "templates/";
        $this->compile_dir = "templates_c/";
        $this->config_dir = "configs/";
        $this->cache_dir = "cache/";
        $this->caching = false;
        $this->assign('app_name','Paranormal');
```

We can uncomment the following two lines to turn on debugging mode and allow Smarty to display debugging messages in a JavaScript popup window:

```
        //$this->debugging = true;
        //$this->debug_tpl = 'debug.tpl';
    }
}
```

Now that we have set Smarty's configuration, we can create the objects to access the Smarty class as well as the two classes we created earlier:

```
$smarty = new SmartyWeblog();
$userlib = new UsersLib($dbUser);
$bloglib = new Blog($dbBlog);
```

Now we determine whether or not we have a logged user and create PHP variables and Smarty variables to hold that information. Here we use Smarty's `assign()` method to make a PHP variable available to Smarty:

```
if(isset($_SESSION["user"])) {
    $user = $_SESSION["user"];
    $userId = $userlib->GetUserId($user);
} else {
    $user = FALSE;
    $userId = '';
}

$smarty->assign('user',$user);
$smarty->assign('userId',$userId);
```

Now we check the user permissions, building up a PHP variable and a Smarty variable for each permission. The variable will have the value `'y'`, if the user has the permission or `'n'` if the user does not.

First we check for the groups and permissions that apply to this user:

```
$allperms = $userlib->GetPermissions();
$allperms = $allperms["data"];

foreach($allperms as $vperm) {
    $perm=$vperm["permName"];
    if($user != 'admin') {
        $smarty->assign("$perm",'n');
        $$perm='n';
    } else {
        $smarty->assign("$perm",'y');
        $$perm='y';
    }
}

if($user != 'admin') {
    $perms = $userlib->GetUserPermissions($user);
    foreach($perms as $perm) {
        $smarty->assign("$perm",'y');
        $$perm='y';
    }
}
?>
```

Further, we can check for permissions in the PHP files using:

```
if ($p_edit_article == 'y') {
}
```

and then for permissions in Smarty templates using:

```
{if $p_edit_article eq 'y'}

{/if}
```

We can also use the comparison operator == in place of eq; however, be careful to set it off with surrounding spaces. Therefore, if you do the following:

```
{if $p_edit_article == 'y'}
```

it will work. If you use the following:

```
{if $p_edit_article=='y'}
```

it also looks like standard PHP code, but will not work. We assume that it will work just as well, but omitting the spaces will cause errors in Smarty.

Now we have all we need in order to start writing templates.

Site Navigation and Layout

First let's see the site layout; we use the same basic layout for all the pages of the Paranormal weblog:

Logo	Title & Menu bar	Login
Left side bar	Application body	

We implement this layout using static HTML and place it into a template file (index.tpl) – this template will provide a layout for all the other templates in our application. Like all our templates, this file will go in the templates directory that we defined in the setup.php file ($this->template_dir = "templates/";):

```
{include file="header.tpl"}
{include file="top_bar.tpl"}

<br />
<table width="100%">
  <tr>
    <td valign="top" width="20%">
      {include file="leftbar.tpl"}
    </td>
    <td width="80%" valign="top">
      {include file=$tbody}
    </td>
  </tr>
</table>

{include file="bot_bar.tpl"}
{include file="footer.tpl"}
```

Note that the template applies the `top_bar.tpl` template, which displays the logo, menu information, and login information. The `leftbar.tpl` template will display the features in the left-hand column of the application. In the main application area, the template includes a file identified by the variable `$tbody`, so we can expect to have a Smarty statement assigning a value to this variable; For example:

```
$smarty->assign('tbody','home.tpl');
$smarty->display('index.tpl');
```

We'll always display `index.tpl` in this fashion, first setting the name of the template used in the body. Using this approach, we can easily change the layout of the whole site by modifying only one template, `index.tpl`.

Now we will look at the rest of the templates. `header.tpl` has the HTML to begin a page:

```
<html>
  <head>
    <link rel="stylesheet" href="styles/main.css" type="text/css" />
    <title>WebLog</title>
  </head>
  <body bgcolor="#FFFFFF">
```

`footer.tpl` has the HTML to close a page:

```
  </body>
</html>
```

`bot_bar.tpl` has the page footer for all pages:

```
<hr/>
<div class="mini">(c) 2002 by Wrox Press Inc.</div>
```

Finally, `top_bar.tpl` contains the logo, menu information, and the login box (or login information if the user is currently logged in). Note how we use permissions in this template to determine which features should or shouldn't be displayed:

```
<table width="100%" border="1" bgcolor="#EEE9E6" cellpadding="0" cellspacing="0">
<tr>
  <td>
  <table width="100%" border="0" bgcolor="#EEE9E6"
   cellpadding="0" cellspacing="0">
<tr>
  <!-- logo linking to home -->
  <td valign="center" align="center" width="11%">
  </td>

  <!-- title and menu buttons -->
  <td width="75%" valign="bottom">
    <table border="0">
    <!-- title -->
```

```
    <tr>
      <td><div class="titlePage">WebLog</div></td>
    </tr>
    <!-- menu bar (generic to all pages) -->
    <tr>
      <td valign="bottom">
      <table border="0">
      <tr>
        <td><div class="button"><a href="index.php"
                class="linkbut">home</a></div></td>
        <td><div class="button"><a href="articles.php"
                class="linkbut">articles</a></div></td>
        {if $p_post_article eq 'y'}
          <td><div class="button"><a href="post.php"
                class="linkbut">post</a></div></td>
        {/if}

        {if $p_submit_article eq 'y'}
          <td><div class="button"><a href="submit.php"
                class="linkbut">submit</a></div></td>
        {/if}

        {if $p_view_submissions eq 'y'}
          <td><div class="button"><a href="submissions.php"
                class="linkbut">submissions</a></div></td>
        {/if}

        {if $p_admin eq 'y'}
          <td><div class="button"><a href="admin.php"
                class="linkbut">admin</a></div></td>
          <td><div class="button"><a href="adminusers.php"
                class="linkbut">admin users</a></div></td>
          <td><div class="button"><a href="admingroups.php"
                class="linkbut">admin groups</a></div></td>
        {/if}
      </tr>
      </table>
      </td>
    </tr>
    </table>
</td>

<!-- Login box -->
<td align="left" valign="bottom">
  <table border="0">
  {if $user}
    <tr><td> </td></tr>
    <tr><td>logged as: {$smarty.session.user}</td></tr>
    <tr><td><a href="logout.php">logout</a></td></tr>
    <tr><td> </td></tr>
  {else}
    <tr>
      <form action="login.php" method="post">
      <td>
```

```
                <table>
                <tr><td>user:</td><td><input type="text" name="user" size="10"
                        /></td></tr>
                <tr><td>pass:</td><td><input type="password" name="pass" size="10"
                        /></td></tr>
                <tr><td><input type="submit" name="login" value="login" /></td>

                {if $p_register eq 'y'}
                  <td valign="bottom">
                  <a class="link" href="register.php">Register</a></td>
                {else}
                  <td> </td>
                {/if}
                </tr>
                </table>
            </td>
            </form>
          </tr>
        {/if}
        </table>
      </td>
    </tr>
    </table>
    </td>
  </tr>
</table>
```

Creating the Home Page

Now let's look at the PHP script of our first page – the home page. In the home page, we'll display the last 5 articles posted on the Paranormal New Service. This page will be called index.php, and the template that will be included in the application area of our layout will be called home.tpl.

Here is the index.php file:

```
<?php
//   FILE:index.php
//   PURPOSE: Paranormal News home page file;


// Initialization
require_once 'setup.php';

// Get articles
$darticles = $bloglib->GetArticles(0,5,'publishDate_desc','',date("U"));
$articles = $darticles["data"];
$smarty->assign('articles',$articles);

// Display the Index Template
$smarty->assign('tbody','home.tpl');
$smarty->display('index.tpl');
?>
```

Note that we use the `bloglib` object to access the Blog library and retrieve the last five articles (5 articles from offset 0, ordered by `publishDate`, descending). We then assign the list of articles (as an array of hashes) to the Smarty `articles` variable. Finally, we assign the value `"home.tpl"` to the `$tbody` variable and display the `index.tpl` template.

Now let's look at what what `home.tpl` does. Smarty's built-in `section()` function takes a minimum of two attributes, a `name` identifying the section, and a `loop` variable over whose range of values the section will iterate. The current value for the loop variable is identified within the section as `$loopVariableName[sectionName]`. Associative arrays created in PHP may be read by using dot notation in Smarty, so the `$articles[arts]title` variable in Smarty refers to a value that was assigned in the PHP script as something like `$articles[indexValue]["title"]` (where `indexValue` is some arbitrary integer):

```
{section name=arts loop=$articles}
        {assign var=article_title value=$articles[arts].title}
        {assign var=article_heading value=$articles[arts].heading}
        {assign var=article_isEmpty value=$articles[arts].isEmpty}
        {assign var=article_reads value=$articles[arts].reads}
        {assign var=article_id value=$articles[arts].articleId}
        {assign var=article_date value=$articles[arts].publishDate}
        {assign var=article_mode value='h'}
        {include file=article.tpl}
    <br />
{/section}
```

In the `home.tpl`, template, the `{section}` Smarty variables is used to loop through the members of the Smarty variable. We then assign values to the `$articles` (`$article_title`, `$srticle_heading`, `$article_isEmpty$articles_reads`, `$articles_id`) and (`$article_date`) variables; we also set the `$article_mode` Variable to `'n'`.

The articles are displayed using various templates hence we use one template, `article.tpl`, to which we delegate all the display functionality.

Here is `article.tpl`:

```
<div class="articletitle">{$article_title}</div>

<div class="articlehead">{$article_heading|replace:"\n":"<br/>"}</div>

{if $article_mode eq 'f' or $article_mode eq 'p'}
<div class="articlebody">{$article_body|replace:"\n":"<br/>"}</div>
{/if}

{if $article_mode eq 'f' or $article_mode eq 'h'}
<div class="articlebar">
  {$article_date|date_format:"%A %d of %B, %Y [%H:%M:%S]"} ({$article_reads}
  reads)

   {if $article_isEmpty eq 'n' and $p_read_article eq 'y'}
    <a class="link" href="read.php?articleId={$article_id}">read more</a>
  {/if}

   {if $p_edit_article eq 'y'}
    <a class="link" href="editarticle.php?articleId={$article_id}">edit</a>
  {/if}
```

```
 {if $p_remove_article eq 'y'}
  <a class="link
     "href="index.php?action=remove&articleId={$article_id}">remove</a>
  {/if}
</div>
{/if}
```

Finally, here's the `leftbar.tpl` file:

```
<table width="80%" cellpadding="0" cellspacing="0" border="1"
       bgcolor="#eeeeff">
  <tr>
    <td class="textbl">
       Search articles
    </td>
  </tr>
  <tr>
    <form action="articles.php" method="get">
      <td>
         <input type="text" name="find" size="20" /><br/>
         <input type="submit" name="search" value="search" />
      </td>
    </form>
  </tr>
</table>

  <br/>

<table width="80%" cellpadding="0" cellspacing="0" border="1"
       bgcolor="#eeeeff">
  <tr><td class="textbl"> Selected Links</td></tr>
  <tr><td>
  <table width="80%" cellpadding="0" cellspacing="0" border="0"
         bgcolor="#eeeeff">
  <tr><td class="text"> link1</td></tr>
  <tr><td class="text"> link2</td></tr>
</table>
    </td>
    </tr>
</table>
```

This template displays the title and heading of an article using the Smarty variables passed as arguments.

Below you can see how the home page looks:

Note that there is a search box and links in the side bar.

Logging In and Logging Out

We use login.php to process a login, and use logout.php to process a logout. Below is login.php:

```php
<?php
//   FILE:login.php
//   PURPOSE: logs a user into the site

// Initialization
require_once 'setup.php';

if(!isset($_REQUEST["login"])) {
    header("location: $HTTP_REFERER");
    die;
}

$isvalid = FALSE;
$isvalid = $userlib->ValidateUser($_REQUEST["user"],$_REQUEST["pass"]);

if($isvalid) {
    session_register("user",$_REQUEST["user"]);
    $user = $_REQUEST["user"];
    $smarty->assign('user',$user);
    header("location: index.php");
    die;
} else {
    $smarty->assign('msg',tra("Invalid username or password"));
    $smarty->display('error.tpl');
}
?>
```

The application checks if the user has been validated and, if so, it assigns the user session variable to hold the user login name, this will be used in `setup.php` to get the user ID and Smarty variables.

Given below is the screenshot of the administrator login screen. In this screenshot, the top bar shows links to all possible features:

Here is the `logout.php` script:

```php
<?php
//   FILE: logout.php
//   PURPOSE: Logs a user out;

// Initialization
require_once 'setup.php';

session_unregister("user");
session_destroy();

unset($user);
header("location: index.php");
die;
?>
```

The logout process just eliminates the user variable from the session. This might be a good time to remember that we must take care whenever we use PHP's `header()` function that no output has yet been sent to the browser; even a single linefeed character occurring in the file before the initial `<?php` PHP code delimiter can break scripts employing `header()`.

If we use the logout link, we'll be logged out of the application. We also, have a login box and a link to the register feature when we are logged out. The menu bar has links only to home or articles since we didn't assign anonymous users permissions to do anything but see articles.

Posting Articles

Our next steps will involve much of the same process as we did for the earlier scripts. Let's now see post.php and post.tpl – the scripts used to post a new article to the weblog.

This is post.php:

```php
<?php
//  FILE: post.php
//  PURPOSE:Post a new article;

require_once 'setup.php';
```

Now we check if the user has permission to post an article; if not, we display the error.tpl template that shows an error message. error.tpl just displays an error message using text from $msg:

```php
// Permission: p_post_article
if($p_post_article != 'y') {
    $smarty->assign('msg',tra("You dont have permission to use this
                        feature"));
    $smarty->display('error.tpl');
    die;
}
```

If we are previewing a post, then we assign Smarty variables with the information that we are reviewing (passed as POST data to this script):

```php
$preview='n';
$smarty->assign('preview_title','');
$smarty->assign('preview_heading','');
$smarty->assign('preview_data','');
if(isset($_REQUEST["preview"])) {
  $preview='y';
  $smarty->assign('preview_title',$_REQUEST["title"]);
  $smarty->assign('preview_heading',$_REQUEST["heading"]);
  $smarty->assign('preview_data',$_REQUEST["data"]);
}
$smarty->assign('preview',$preview);
```

If we are posting an article, we call the AddArticle() method of the Blog class to add a new article to the database:

```php
if(isset($_REQUEST["post"])) {

    $bloglib->AddArticle
    (addslashes($_REQUEST["title"]),date("U"),
     addslashes($_REQUEST["heading"]), addslashes($_REQUEST["data"]),
     $userlib->GetUserId($user));
}
```

Finally, we set the `tbody` variable to `post.tpl` and display the `index.tpl` file:

```
// Display the Index Template
$smarty->assign('tbody','post.tpl');
$smarty->display('index.tpl');
?>
```

This is the `post.tpl` template file:

```
<h2>Post a new article</h2>

{if $preview eq 'y'}
  <h3>Preview</h3>
  <table width="100%"><tr><td>
  {assign var=article_title value=$preview_title}
  {assign var=article_heading value=$preview_heading}
  {assign var=article_body value=$preview_data}
  {assign var=article_isEmpty value='n'}
  {assign var=article_mode value='p'}
  {include file=article.tpl}
  </td></tr></table>
{/if}

<form action="post.php" method="post">
<table>
  <tr><td>Title</td><td><input size="80" type="text" name="title"
    maxlength="250" value="{$preview_title}" /></td></tr>
  <tr><td>Heading</td><td><textarea cols="80" rows="5"
    name="heading">{$preview_heading}</textarea></td></tr>
  <tr><td>Data</td><td><textarea cols="80" rows="10"
    name="data">{$preview_data}</textarea></td></tr>
  <tr><td> </td><td><input type="submit" name="post"
    value="post" /><input type="submit" name="preview" value="preview" />
  </td></tr>
</table>
</form>
```

Note the use of Smarty variables set in `post.php` to display a preview of the article. Here a form is included to post new articles, and this is the form that we process in `post.php`.

Here is the post screen of the application:

Note that only registered users or GhostHunt staff can post articles. So, in order to test this, you have to login appropriately to post an article.

If we type an example article and click the preview button, the page looks like this:

Finally, once we are satisfied with the article appearance in the preview, we can click post to insert the article in the database.

Note that we used the same `article.tpl` template that we use in the home page, so we can see the previewed article exactly as it will be displayed in the home page.

The Next Steps

This listing describes the functionality of the remaining screens for the Paranormal weblog application; we can code them based on the home page and the post screen:

Files	Description
`submit.php`, and `submit.tpl`	Very similar to `post.php` and `post.tpl` but instead of posting an article they submit an article.
`editarticle.php`, and `editarticle.tpl`	Screens to edit existing articles.
`editsubmission.php`, and `editsubmission.tpl`	Almost the same as `editarticle.php` and `editarticle.tpl`, but used to edit existing submissions, editors frequently need to edit a submission before approving it.
`submissions.php`, and `submissions.tpl`	A screen showing a list of submissions with links to edit, remove or approve a submission.
`articles.php`, and `articles.tpl`	A list of articles with links to edit them, or remove them.
`read.php`, and `read.tpl`	Used to display a full article

Note that we did not cover the screens for the user registration system; we can either create them from scratch, or we can just insert or update information for the user registration system from the MySQL command line.

For reference, we will now show some of the screens.

> The code for the chapter is available in the code bundle that can be downloaded from http://www.wrox.com/. It includes all the features described here and it can be used as an example of using Smarty to design and create web sites and applications.

Here is the screenshot of the Submit an article page:

This is the web page listing the articles submitted:

Here is the listing of articles that anonymous users can read:

Here is the screen where the user can edit the article:

Here is the Edit submission page:

Here is the Admin users page where new users can be added:

Here is the Admin groups page where new groups of administrators can be added:

Finally, here is the Assign permissions to groups page where permissions can be assigned to different groups:

Possible Improvements

There are several ways in which we could improve the design and implementation of our Paranormal News Server. Here are two of them:

❏ Normalize the database. Our database schema could be improved to something like what is shown in the following diagram, in which all tables have distinct primary and foreign keys. In addition, we've changed the naming system to be a little more consistent and to avoid potentially confusing table names, such as `users_user_groupPermissions`:

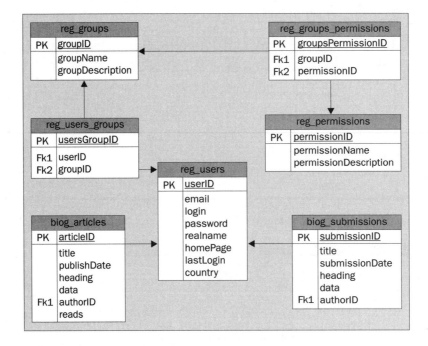

We might also consider dropping one of the two `blog_*` tables and using a `status` column to determine when a submission's been granted full article status.

❏ We wrote two very generic "class libraries" (`UsersLib` and `Blog`) to encapsulate all the functionality required for our user-groups permissions system and the content submissions. Both of these classes are rather monolithic. For example, the `UsersLib` class could sensibly be broken up into `User`, `Group` and `Permission` classes, each with its own properties, and methods. The `Blog` class could also be replaced with one or more new classes that model article submissions more realistically – for instance, we could have an `Article` class whose `approve()` method (and possibly a `reject()` method as well) updates the value of a `status` property appropriately.

Summary

In this chapter we looked at some techniques for creating applications using class libraries and the Smarty template engine. We learned how to build a user registration system class to manage users, groups, and permissions. We then built a small library to manage a weblog with submissions and articles. We then looked at how to build sites or web applications using the Smarty template engine for PHP.

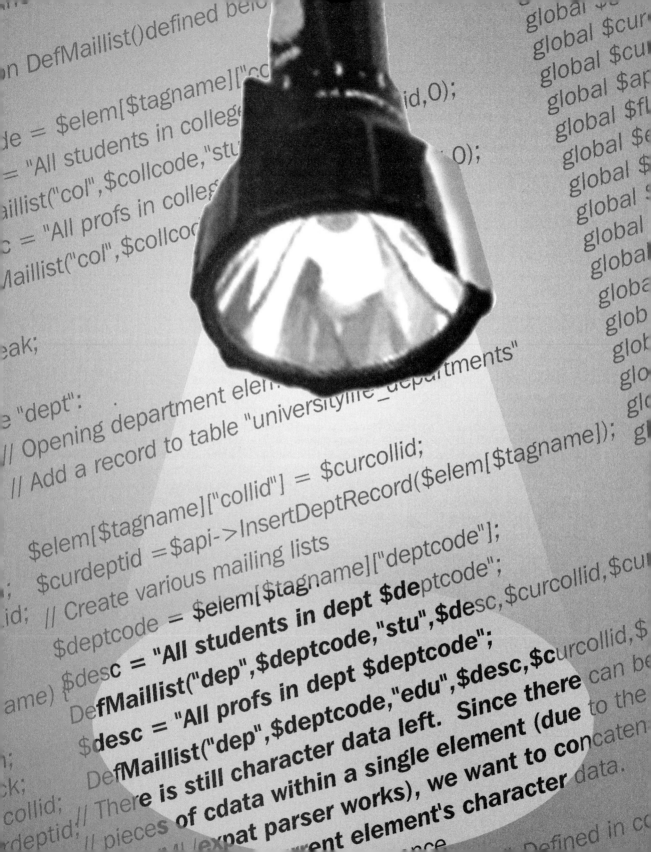

Web Corpus

A corpus is a language-specific subset or body of words. For example, the Brown Corpus, originally published in 1964 by the Department of Linguistics, Brown University, Providence, Rhode Island, USA, is essentially a list of words used in American English. There are now several other English and non-English individual corpora as well (see http://khnt.hit.uib.no/icame/manuals and http://ling.kgw.tu-berlin.de/corpus/art.htm). All corpora are compiled using a number of sampling techniques, including manual input based on popular literature and newspapers, review of audio recordings, computer scan of print materials, and so on.

While discussing a corpus might seem a linguistic exercise, a fair number of more recent corpus have been compiled for use with computers, for various purposes. First and foremost, the purpose of compiling a corpus is to study word usage and trends. For example, **COLT** (Bergen **C**orpus **of** **L**ondon **T**eenage Language, http://khnt.hit.uib.no/icame/manuals/colt.pdf, colt.doc) is a compilation of words used by British teenagers. Recompiling this corpus every few years shows general trends in slang.

Compiling teenage English corpora in various countries and comparing them over time also helps to illustrate the process and progress of word migration. Anecdotal evidence suggests that, during the 1970s and '80s, United States slang took three to five years to make it into general usage in Canada. Since the early 1990s, with the Internet and dozens of American TV channels available through cable and satellite dishes, American slang seems to make it into the Canadian dialect far sooner than before. The same appears true of Canadian speech migrating to the United States, as a number of Canadian TV channels are now broadcast on cable and satellite in the US.

Apart from being a basis for linguistic studies, corpora are also the fundamental building blocks of many Internet search engines. If you set up a robot or web spider to sample at least three or four pages each from 10,000 web sites and then index unique words and their occurrences within documents, you now have a web corpus. This corpus is the building block for a search engine for at least those 10,000 web sites.

What constitutes a word in a web corpus is largely determined by context. Is "ek2000" a word? Some web spiders are designed to consider any alphanumeric sequence of characters as a word (including underscores), other crawlers only record and index purely alphabetic strings. Contractions such as "won't" or "we've"could be recorded as a single word or as "won", "t", "we", and "ve"; the latter choice makes no sense, but that is the way some crawlers build their corpus. With the HTML tags within a web page, should tag names and attributes like "a", "href", "html", "head", "img", "src", and so on, be considered words?

The answer is determined by the purpose we have for compiling the web corpus.

We'll follow the same general outline in this chapter as we've done with regard to the case studies previously examined in this book. First, we'll specify the goals to be met by the finished application. Next, we'll determine our data storage, access, and processing needs. After this, we'll decide how we are to present the results of this to the user. Finally, we'll take a look at some of the uses to which a corpus might be put, and add some suggestions for ways in which you might improve or refine the very basic application that we provide here.

Specification

This case study looks at how to compile a web corpus. The only distinction between a regular corpus and a web corpus is the source of the raw text used to compile the word list. All content used to compile a web corpus comes from the Internet, either as the result of surfing one or more web sites, or through any text content added by visitors and staff to a specific site.

Depending on the purpose for which the web corpus is being compiled, the regular expressions used to parse the input text might define a particular word as a string having alphanumeric characters, as well as the underscore character. If reserved words that are part of HTML or JavaScript, are not desirable as part of the corpus, they can be filtered out.

Depending on the method of access, PHP, ASP, and JSP pages should not be an issue, as the web server generally serves them as HTML (possibly JavaScript). If such script files are accessed directly from a native file system, it may be necessary to strip out such code before parsing for the corpus. The choice to do so or not depends on the nature of our access to the site or sites from which we're obtaining content and the purpose for the corpus. Programming code as such isn't very interesting in a purely linguistic sense, as we're usually concerned with words that people use when communicating with other people, not with machines. For this reason, we'll most likely want to strip out any markup and programming code we may encounter.

For the examples in this chapter, a "word" is defined as a sequence of alphanumeric and underscore characters only, delimited by word boundaries, which are typically understood to be whitespace or punctuation characters.

User Types

Since we are not discussing a stand-alone application here, we will look at only two types of potential users:

❑   General (public) users

❑   Administrators

Features

We will look at a couple of features:

- ❑ Find occurrences of a word in one or more documents
- ❑ Find occurrences of "word1 AND word2" or "word1 OR word2"

Actions

The only user action required here is that of adding a content entry. The steps for handling these actions are:

- ❑ Parse content entry for unique words
- ❑ For each unique word
    - ❑ Add word entry to table `corpus` (if it doesn't already exist)
    - ❑ Add an occurrence record to table `wordocc`

Designing the Database

Before designing the database, we should determine what kinds of information and reporting are required. We'll want to be able to obtain the following sorts of information from our application:

- ❑ Occurrences of a given word
- ❑ An alphabetical list of words from the corpus
- ❑ List of words from the corpus according to frequency
- ❑ List of the ten most commonly used words

Database Schema

The schema for this project is relatively simple. There are just three database tables that we need to provide the minimum of necessary support for the features/actions and reporting that we've discussed so far:

Table	Description
`webcorpus_entries`	Contains textual content entries, possibly with HTML and code
`webcorpus_words`	The list of unique words compiled
`webcorpus_occurrences`	Occurrences of each word in the corpus

Database Tables

Now let's examine the specifics of each table.

Entries

This table (webcorpus_entries) contains the text entries from which the corpus is compiled:

Column	Data Type	Description
entry_id	int	Unique record ID, auto-generated by MySQL.
entry_content	char	The actual content entry. Depending on functional needs, this might be a single line from a source file, or the entire file. This will be decided by the size of the column in the SQL script that creates the table.

This table might not be used for some corpus applications. If, for example, the content used for corpus compilation is from web pages, there may be no desire to store the content. Some search engines store part of the content, others store the URL.

Words

This table contains a list of the unique words encountered in all entries of the webcorpus_entries table. As the number of entries in the table increases, the fewer new words are likely to be added. Consider, however that some English and non-English corpora individually contain anywhere from 65,000,000 to over 100,000,000 words. Some corpora projects have a goal to compile 365 million words.

The average English-speaking North American adult with a college education was once said to have a vocabulary of about 100,000 words. This figure is pre-Internet era. Now, consider whether words in HTML and other programming code are to be used as part of the corpus. An educated guess suggests that it will take the processing of many content entries before the decreasing exponential pattern becomes apparent.

Given below is the schema of the webcorpus_words table:

Column	Data Type	Description
word_id	int	Unique record ID, auto-generated by MySQL.
word_text	char	Unique word text

Occurrences

This table has a number of possible schemas. If the entries table is used to store content, then one schema for the webcorpus_occurrences table is as follows:

Column	Data Type	Description
occurrence_id	int	Unique record ID, auto-generated by MySQL
entry_id	int	Record ID of the content entry in the entries table
word_id	int	Points to the record in the word table that represents the occurring word

If the content source is a set of web pages, then the webcorpus_entry table may or may not be used to store all or part of each page. If content is not stored, then the schema for the webcorpus_occurrence table might be as follows:

Column	Data Type	Description
occurrence_id	int	Unique record ID, auto-generated by MySQL
occurrence_url	char	URL where the word indicated by word_id occurs once or more
word_id	int	Points to the record in the words table that represents the occurring word

We have used this latter scheme in the following example. There are a number of other possible variations. The choice again depends on the purpose of the web corpus. Note that, if it is desirable to store multiple occurrences of a word in a single document (content entry or web page), then line numbers of the input must be recorded as well.

Relationships Between Tables

The diagram below shows the relationship between the tables in the webcorpus database.

As we can see here, the webcorpus_occurrences table acts as a look-up table between the words and the content in which they're found.

Creating the Database

First of all, create a database by typing the following command at the command prompt:

```
>mysqladmin create webcorpus
```

The tables for this case study can all be placed within a single MySQL database, webcorpus. Since we are only running test scripts, we only need one database user, for example, ADMIN. We will have to grant privileges to the tables, as well as create the tables. Use the following statement from the mysql client utility's command line to grant the necessary privileges to the ADMIN database user account:

```
mysql> GRANT SELECT, INSERT, UPDATE, DELETE ON webcorpus.* TO
'ADMIN@localhost' IDENTIFIED BY 'ADMIN';
```

Creating Tables

To create the webcorpus database tables, run the following SQL script, webcorpus_tables.sql, on the command line as follows:

```
> mysql webcorpus < webcorpus_tables.sql
```

The following SQL code snippets all belong to the file webcorpus_tables.sql, which creates the webcorpus database.

Depending on what kind of content is being stored in the entries table, the entry_content column's datatype might be defined as CHAR, VARCHAR, or one of the TEXT sub-types. We'll use LONGTEXT for now:

```
#
# FILE: webcorpus_tables.sql
#
CREATE TABLE webcorpus_entries (
   entry_id int(11) NOT NULL AUTO_INCREMENT PRIMARY KEY,
   entry_content longtext NOT NULL
);
```

The remaining two tables are defined and created as shown here. Note that we use the alternative form for the webcorpus_occurrences table, rather than the version shown in the diagram above, since all of our content is to be obtained from files on the web.

```
CREATE TABLE webcorpus_words (
   word_id int(11) NOT NULL AUTO_INCREMENT PRIMARY KEY,
   word_text varchar(50) NOT NULL default '',
   UNIQUE KEY word_text (word_text)
);

CREATE TABLE webcorpus_occurrences (
   occurrence_id int(11) NOT NULL AUTO_INCREMENT PRIMARY KEY,
   occurrence_url varchar(255) NOT NULL default '',
   word_id int(11) NOT NULL default '0'
);
```

As we've already discussed, we can always change the schema of the webcorpus_occurrences table whenever there's a need to do so for a specific application.

Building Indexes

Given the columns that we have defined above, we want indexes on most of those that aren't indexed already. The code is in a file called `webcorpus_indices.sql`. Create the indexes by typing the following at the command prompt:

```
> mysql < webcorpus_indices.sql
```

```
//
// FILE: webcorpus_indices.sql
//

USE webcorpus;

CREATE INDEX word_idxOnWordText    ON wordcorpus_word(word_text);
CREATE INDEX occ_idxOnUrl     ON webcorpus_occurrences(occurrence_url);
CREATE INDEX occ_idxOnWordId  ON webcorpus_occurrences( word_id);
```

Now let's look at how to populate our `webcorpus` database, as well as some useful SQL queries for retrieving stored information.

Populating the Database

We will look at two ways of compiling a corpus and populating the associated database:

❑   Unique words in web content supplied by site visitors

❑   Unique words in web content retrieved by surfing a single site

Unique Words: Visitor-Supplied Content

The following PHP code (`uniqwords_file.php`) can be used to parse a content file for unique words:

First we define counter variables for the number of words and the number of unique words we find, initializing both to zero:

```php
<?php
//
// FILE: uniqwords_file.php
//
$nwords = 0;
$nuniq  = 0;
```

Note that in order to run this script successfully, you'll need to supply a filename for the value of `$file`:

```php
$file = "__your_input_filename_here__";
```

If the file exists, we open it, and if for some reason we can't open it, we display an error message and terminate the script:

```
if (file_exists($file)) {

    $fp = fopen($file,"r");
    if (!$fp) {
       die("Cannot open file '$file' for reading<br />\n");
    }
    else
    {
```

Assuming that the file was opened successfully, we now read through it line-by-line. The value passed into the fgets() function call isn't set in stone. 1,024 characters per line should be more than enough under most circumstances. You can however change this value as you see fit, so long as you don't make it so small that you start cutting lines short.

```
while( !feof($fp) )
{
    $line = fgets($fp,1024);
```

Next, we trim any leading and trailing whitespace and newline characters from each non empty line.

```
if($line)
{
    trim($line);
```

Then we use the preg_match_all() function to obtain an array of matches ($matches) in each line to a given regular expression pattern – each of these matches counts as one word. We supply three of these patterns, with two of them commented out. To make use of a different pattern, merely comment out the line that's currently being employed, and uncomment the one containing the regular expression you wish to use.

The first of these patterns is quite simple, matching any group of characters (upper or lowercase letters, digits, and underscores) delimited by word boundaries:

```
// if(preg_match_all("/\b\w+\b/", $line, $matches) )
```

The second regular expression pattern excludes digits and underscores, and adds the apostrophe character:

```
// if(preg_match_all("/\b['a-zA-Z]+\b/", $line, $matches) )
```

The pattern in the line below may appear a bit more complex. Ignoring the word boundaries, we have (?:'|\w)+. The presence of the ?: means that the sub-pattern preceding the alternation operator (|) does not match by itself, but only in combination with the following sub-pattern. We could also write this as ('?\w+)+. In either case, we match an optional apostrophe followed by at least one word character, so that we don't match isolated apostrophes.

```
if(preg_match_all("/\b(?:'|\w)+\b/", $line, $matches) )
{
```

Note that $matches is actually a nested array. That is, each element in $matches is itself an array. Exactly what's contained in each of these arrays and sub-arrays and how they're all ordered depends upon the value of an optional fourth argument to preg_match_all(). The default value is PREG_PATTERN_ORDER, which means that the first element in $matches is an array containing all the matches found in $line for the complete regular expression pattern.

The second element is an array of all matches to the first parenthesized sub-expression in that pattern; $matches[2] contains all matches to the second sub-expression, and so on. (For additional options, see http://www.php.net/manual/en/function.preg-match-all.php.) We're not interested in any matches on portions of words, only those on complete word. We are therefore only concerned with the first element of $matches:

Now we iterate through the $words. Each word is used as a key in the hash $aaFreq, and the value associated with that key is incremented each time the word is encountered in the $words array. (If you'd like to see each word as it's found, just uncomment the print statement.)

```
        $words = $matches[0];
        $total = count($words);
        for($i=0; $i<$total; $i++)
        {
                // print "\$words[$i]: " . $words[$i] . "<br />\n";
                $aaFreq[strtolower($words[$i])]++;
        }
    } // end if( preg_match_all(...) )
  } // end if( $line )
} // end while( !eof($fp) )
```

The result is that we have a list of unique words (that is, the keys in $aaFreq) and the number of times each word occurs in the original source file (the values associated with each of the keys). Now we close the file, sort the $aaFreq hash by key, and output the keys and values in order:

```
fclose($fp);

ksort($aaFreq);
foreach ($aaFreq as $word => $cnt)
    print " $word occurred $cnt times<br />\n";
$nuniq = count($aaFreq);
```

Finally, we output the total number of words and the number of unique words found in the document. Alternatively an error message is output if the file isn't found:

```
    print "Total number of word occurrences: $total\n";
    print "Total number of unique words: $nuniq\n";
  } // end if( !file_exists($file) )
}
else
{
    print "Sorry, file '$file' does not exist<br />\n";
}
?>
```

The unique words in a database yet haven't been stored. We can do so by taking each key or word in the associative array $aaFreq and adding it to the webcorpus_words table. First, we check to see if the word is already listed in that table:

```
$connection = mysql_connect("localhost", "ADMIN", "ADMIN")
  or die("Error: could not connect to localhost as ADMIN.");

mysql_select_db("webcorpus", $connection)
  or die("Error: could not select webcorpus database on localhost.");
foreach($aaFreq as $keyword)
{
$sqlquery = "SELECT word_id FROM webcorpus_words
             WHERE word_text ='$keyword'";
$result = mysql_query($sqlquery);
$row = mysql_fetch_row($result);
$result = mysql_result($sqlquery);
}
```

The $keyword variable contains the current word being checked. If the word does not already exist in the table, the $result variable will be NULL. In that case, we add it to the webcorpus_words table and retrieve the new record ID (word_id column) as $word_id:

```
if( !is_null($result) )
{
   $insquery = "INSERT INTO webcorpus_words (word_text)
                VALUES ('$keyword')";
   $results  = mysql_query($insquery);
   $nrows    = mysql_affected_rows($results);
   $corpus_wordid  = mysql_insert_id();
}
```

Now we check the webcorpus_occurrences table to determine if an occurrence record for this word and this document already exist. Despite the fact that the sample PHP code in the uniqwords_file.php, shown earlier, takes its content from a file, let's assume that the content will be stored in the webcorpus_entries table with the record ID $entry_id. Now we can determine whether or not a corresponding webcorpus_occurrence record exists:

```
$sqlquery = "SELECT entry_id,word_id FROM webcorpus_occurrences
             WHERE entry_id='$entry_id' AND word_id='$word_id'";
$result = mysql_result($query,0)
  or die("Database query failed.");
```

If a record does not already exist for word_id and entry_id, we display a warning and do not add a record to occurrences. Otherwise, we add a new record as follows:

```
if( is_null($result) )
{
   $insquery  = "INSERT INTO webcorpus_occurrences (entry_id,word_id)
                 VALUES ('$contid','$wordid')";
   $result = mysql_query($insquery)
     or die("Unable to add new occurrence record.");
}
```

The next time we try to import new words into the corpus, those that we've just added will be included in the word list to be checked against.

Unique Words: Single-Site Surfing

Now we look at PHP code that starts at a web site's home page and traverses all local pages, parsing out unique words:

The following four variables are, in order:

❑ The number of (all) links found on the target site

❑ The number of unique links found

❑ The total number of words found on the site

❑ The number of unique links on the target site

All four of these are initialized to zero:

```php
<?php
#
# FILE: uniqwords_web.php
#
$nlinks = 0; // Non-unique count of href links over all pages on site
$nuniq  = 0; // Unique count of href links over all pages
             // (with query string vars being distinct)
$nwords = 0; // Non-unique count of words
$nuniqw = 0; // Unique count of words
```

Next, $root is defined as the site root URL, and $link as the URL of the page we're currently examining. We use http://www.wrox.com/ for our example, but of course this is entirely arbitrary and can be changed to whatever you like. Since both of these variables have the same initial value, we can set them in a single statement:

```php
$root = "http://www.wrox.com";
$link = "http://www.wrox.com"; // Starting web page
```

Now we define a regular expression pattern that we'll use to obtain the href attributes of all the links in a given page:

```php
$filter = '<a href=\\"([^"]+?)"[^>]*?>';
```

The last task we need to perform at initialization, is declare an array (or "stack") of URLs found in each page ($linkstack), which initially contains a single element ($-link), and a variable ($stackitems) that tells us how many links remain to be followed. To start with there's just one link to be "explored":

```php
$linkstack = array($link);
$nstackitems = 1;
```

We can now start the main loop for this page, in which we'll look for links in the current page, follow all of the unique ones, and add new words to our corpus found in each linked page. As mentioned already, we'll be limiting ourselves to http:// URLs on the same site as our starting point. Additionally, we've added a condition to the while loop to limit ourselves to the first 100 links found, although this constraint can easily be removed.

```
while ( ($nstackitems > 0) && ($nlinks < 101) )
{
    // Pop the stack
    // Add link to hash $aVisited
    // Visit the page and extract links
```

To start with, we shift the first link from $-linkstack and decrement $-stackitems:

```
$link = array_shift($linkstack);
$nstackitems--;
$aFreq[$link]++;
```

Then we obtain the content of the page whose URL is $link, and store this as $html:

```
$html = implode('', file($link));
```

We then check to see if there are any links in the HTML of this page:

```
if (preg_match_all("/$filter/is", $html, $matches))
{
    $i = 1;
    for ($j=0; $j<count($matches[$i]); $j++)
    {
        $link = strtolower(trim($matches[$i][$j]));
```

Next we perform a series of tests on each URL to determine whether or not we wish to add it to the list of those to be followed; we'll set a Boolean variable $ignore accordingly (this will be 0 if we want to follow the link). First we need to know if the link is absolute or not – that is, whether or not it begins with a protocol identifier of the form *xxxx:* (for example, http:, ftp:, gopher:, javascript:, etc.).

If it is an absolute link, then we need to know whether it's for an HTTP or some other kind of resource. If it's HTTP the URL begins with http then we check to see whether or not the link points to a page residing on the same domain we started. If it's internal to the site we're examining, then $ignore gets set to 0; in all other cases in which the link is absolute, this variable is assigned a value of 1:

```
if (ereg("^mailto:",$link,$arr))
{
    $ignore = 1;
}
elseif (ereg("^file:",$link,$arr))
{
    $ignore = 1;
}
elseif (ereg("^ftp:",$link,$arr))
{
    $ignore = 1;
```

```
      }
      elseif (ereg("javascript:",$link,$arr))
      {
        $ignore = 1;
      }
      else
      {
        $ignore = 1;
        if (ereg("^http:",$link,$arr))
        {
          // Ignore any http: links that are outside wrox
          if (ereg($root,$link,$arr))
          {
            // This is a wrox link
            $ignore = 0; // We want this link
          }
        }
        else
        {
          if (ereg("^/",$link,$arr))
          {
            // This is a relative with a starting slash
            $link = $root.$link; // Preface with root domain
          }
```

Next we handle relative links by converting them to their absolute equivalents. If the first character of the URL is a slash character or word character, we do this by prefixing the $root string to the link, inserting a slash character in between them if one is not already present. If the first character is neither a slash nor a word character, then the URL is probably malformed and we will therefore ignore it:

```
          else
          {
            // This is a relative without a starting slash, '/'
            $link = $root.'/'.$link; // Preface with root domain + slash
          }
          $ignore = 0; // This is relative link, which we want
        }
      }
```

Now we're ready to obtain words from the linked page. First we increment the count for all links found, and then increment the frequency count of the $aaLinkFreq element, whose key, is the URL we've obtained as $link. This is the same method we've employed before. We should note that PHP requires us to initialize neither $aaFreq nor the values of any of its elements:

```
      if (!$ignore)
      {
        // Now record the link if it hasn't already been recorded
        $nlinks++;
        print "match($nlinks): '$link'<BR>\n";
        $aaFreq[$link]++;
```

If we've not previously encountered this link, we add it to the $linkstack array (recall that array_push() returns the number of elements in the array after any new elements have been added):

```
                if ($aaFreq[$link] == 1)
                {
                    // This link has not been previously encountered
                    // Push the link onto a stack
                    $nstackitems = array_push($linkstack, $link);
                }
```

Now we can parse the content of the linked file. Since we're interested in strings containing only word characters, we strip out any HTML tags, and then use the same algorithm as before to obtain words and the frequency with which they occur. It continues doing this for each link and linked page until it either exhausts all links internal to the site or examines 100 URLs, whichever happens first:

```
                // Now parse the current HTML page for "words"
                // "words" are allowed to have [_a-zA-Z0-9]
                //
                if (preg_match_all("/\b\w+\b/", $html, $words) )
                {
                    for ($i=0; $i<count($words); $i++)
                    {
                        for ($j=0; $j<count($words[$i]); $j++)
                        {
                            // Store info about the word
                            $word = strtolower($words[$i][$j]);
                            #print "\$words[$i][$j]: '$word'<BR>\n";
                            $aaWordFreq[$word]++;
                            $nwords++;
                        } # end for $j
                    } # end for #i
                }
            }
        } # for $j
    } # if preg_match_all
} # end while
```

Next we sort the link frequency and word frequency hashes, and output a list of each along with the number of times the link or word occurred:

```
#ksort($aaFreq); // Sort hash by keys ## Uncomment if you want
foreach ($aaFreq as $link => $cnt)
{
  print "[$cnt] $link<br>\n";
  $nuniq++;
}
print "<br><br>\n";

ksort($aaWordFreq); // Sort hash by keys
foreach ($aaWordFreq as $word => $cnt)
{
  print "[$cnt] $word<br>\n";
  $nuniqw++;
}
```

Finally, we output the total number of links found, the number of unique links, the total number of words, and the number of unique words:

```
print "Total # of link occurrences: $nlinks\n";
print "Total # of unique links: $nuniq\n";

print "Total # of word occurrences: $nwords\n";
print "Total # of unique words: $nuniqw\n";

?>
```

To record each unique word of each web page in the webcorpus_words table, the following INSERT query must be run:

```
INSERT INTO webcorpus_words VALUES (NULL,'$word');
```

The query above must occur inside the nested for loop that follows the pattern match for words (indicated by the comment in the source listing). The insert is performed only if the word does not already exist in the words table. This is a bit of a performance hit because each and every word in the document, unique or not, must be checked for every occurrence, in every web page visited. There is no real way around this, as each word's occurrence must be recorded immediately after this check. However, provided there is an index for the word_id column in the occurence_words table, the search for an existing word will be relatively quick.

To facilitate the above INSERT, we first query the database to check if the word already exists. The check is done as follows:

```
SELECT webcorpus_wordid FROM corpus
WHERE word = '$word';
```

In the SELECT query above, $word is a PHP variable. If the SELECT query produces a record (No more than one should exist), then the corresponding word_id value is used in the second INSERT (discussed below).

If the SELECT query produces nothing, then this word is inserted and the new record ID value is retrieved and used for the second INSERT statement.

The occurrence of the current word in the same nested loop, now has to be recorded for the web page. Since we are not recording more than one occurrence of a word in a web page, we first need to check that that the word has not already occurred. We do this with the following query:

```
SELECT COUNT(*) FROM webcorpus_occurrences
WHERE word_id = '$wordid'
AND occurrence_url = '$link';
```

If the word has not already occurred in the current web page ($link), then we can insert it into the occurrences table:

```
INSERT INTO webcorpus_occurrences
VALUES (NULL, '$link', '$wordid');
```

If it is important to record every occurrence of a word in a web page, there are a number of adjustments needed in the PHP code presented earlier. The first change is that each page has to be processed line-by-line. Next, word occurrences have to be recorded as each line is processed. It may also be desirable to store the line number, along with the page name, which requires another column (for example, the addition of `occurrence_line`) to the `occurrences` table.

Common Queries

Here we are going to look at SQL queries that might typically be used for general users (via a web interface) and `admin` users (via the MySQL command line monitor or a web interface). All queries available to a general user are also available to `admin` users.

User Queries

The following queries apply to general users of a web corpus-based application feature (such as a search engine). We are focusing here on the necessary SQL query to support a feature, not the PHP code or PHP MySQL functions necessary to support the feature.

Finding Word Occurrences

Assume that content entries are stored in the `entries` table, and that the `occurrences` table contains a record ID pointing to the content entry. The schema for the table `webcorpus_occurrences` given earlier needs to be modified so that instead of containing the `occurrence_url` column, it would have an `entry_id` pointing to `entries`:

```
SELECT e.entry_id FROM webcorpus_entries e
LEFT JOIN webcorpus_occurrences o
USING (entry_id)
LEFT JOIN webcorpus_words w
USING (word_id)
WHERE w.word_text='__word__';
```

The field marker __word__ is replaced with the actual word being searched for in the above query. The result set contains the IDs of records in `occurrences` for which the content contains at least one occurrence of the desired word. The record IDs can be used to create a list of hyperlinks to each document / entry.

This list would be infinitely more readable if each content entry had a title. In the situation where content is coming from various sources, however titles may not always be available, or not necessarily be unique. One alternative, if the content is from a web page, is to use the source URL as the title. Alternatively a small number of characters from the start of the content string can be used.

Find Documents Containing "word1 OR word2"

To find documents / entries containing either or both of two words, two steps need to be performed. The first step finds all documents containing either word:

```
SELECT con.content_contid entryid, cor.corpus_word term FROM content as con,
       corpus as cor, wordocc as wo
WHERE con.content_contid = wo.wordocc_contid
AND cor.corpus_wordid = wo.wordocc_wordid
AND cor.word IN ("__word1__", "__word2__");
SELECT e.entry_id AS entryid,o.word_id AS term
FROM entries e
LEFT JOIN occurrences o
USING (entry_id)
LEFT JOIN words w
USING (word_id)
WHERE w.word_text IN ('__word1__','__word2__');
```

The WHERE clause can be expanded to include any number of search terms. If the words being searched are "PHP" and "Perl" the query above might produce a result set that looks like this:

entryid	term
1	PHP
1	Perl
2	PHP
2	Perl
3	Perl
4	PHP

This means that content entry number 1 contains both search words, as does entry number 2. Entry number 3 contains only "Perl" and entry number 4 contains only "PHP", so there are a total of six rows in the result set, but only four unique content entries.

The second step takes the above result set and collapses it into a unique list of entries / documents using an associative array to produce this list. The ID of the content entry record (or the title / or source URL) will serve as the key. Each time the same ID is encountered, we increase the frequency count by one. The following snippet of PHP code assumes that we are working with a $results variable that holds the result set of a mysql_query() command, using the SQL query shown previously:

```
// ...

while( $aaRow   = mysql_fetch_array($results) )
{
    $entryid = $aaRow["entryid"];
    $term    = $aaRow["term"];
    $aaUniqEntries["$entryid"]++;
}
```

The reason that we surround the $entryid variable in double quotes is that we want don't want to have to deal with the inevitable gaps in array indexes if we use numeric values. If the document IDs are 3, 54, and 367, for example, then using numeric indexes [3], [54], and [367] leaves a big gap in item indexes, and causes array management difficulties. If we instead use ["3"], ["54"], and ["367"], PHP handles this as an associative array.

We now have an associative array variable called $aaUniqEntries. The indexes / keys are the record IDs of the documents containing one or more search terms. The actual number of terms matched is given by the value of each key. Since we specified an OR condition between each search term, we do not care how many terms were matched. However, because of the way that the SQL query was constructed, we will never have keys in $aaUniqEntries with a value of zero. We can now generate a list of links to each document.

Find Documents Containing "word1 AND word2"

This feature uses exactly the same query as given in the last section. We also produce the associative array $aaUniqEntries, as above. The difference is that we now care about the value of each key in the array. We only want to list the documents for which the value of a key in $aaUniqEntries is the same as the number of search terms specified.

```
...
foreach($aaUniqEntries as $entryid => $nmatches)
{
  if ($nmatches == $nsearchterms)
  {
    // display an appropriate link to this entry
  }
}
...
```

Admin Queries

Now, we'll look at a few queries that would typically be performed in the context of application administration.

List Unique Words in Alphabetical Order (Dictionary)

```
SELECT corpus_word FROM corpus
ORDER BY corpus_word;
```

List Unique Words based on Frequencies

We want to produce a frequency count of word occurrences, along with each word. Let's start by getting a frequency count of each word, using corpus_word_id:

```
SELECT COUNT(*) AS noccur, word_id FROM words
GROUP BY word_id
ORDER BY word_id;  // Change this to 'ORDER BY noccur DESC' for a list
                   // of most frequent to least frequent words by ID.
```

Since we want to see the actual word associated with each frequency count, and not that word's record ID, modify the above query as follows:

```
SELECT COUNT(*) AS noccur, w.word_text AS word
FROM words w
LEFT JOIN occurrences o
USING (word_id)
GROUP BY word
ORDER BY word;  // Change this to 'ORDER BY noccur DESC' for a list of
                // most frequent to least frequent words.
```

Top Ten Words by Frequency of Occurrence

This is the same as the previous query, with one minor modification:

```
SELECT count(*) noccur, w.word_text AS word
FROM webcorpus_words w
LEFT JOIN webcorpus_occurrences o
USING (word_id)
GROUP BY word
ORDER BY noccur DESC
LIMIT 10;
```

Uses of a Corpus

There are a number of uses to which we can put a web corpus. These include text and keyword (or **fuzzy**) searches, linguistic comparisons or trends analyses, content or applicability ratings, as a basis for a site indexing system. For most of these uses, we want real words (no numbers or underscores).

Search Engine

The most common use for a web corpus is for a search engine. Examples of searching for one or more words were given in the SQL form earlier.

Fuzzy Searching

Fuzzy searching is similar to regular searching, except that keywords, or subjects, are assigned to each piece of content. Similar to the corpus, a unique list is stored of all keywords assigned to all content in a database. This might include multimedia content, such as still images or audio files neither of which have text associated with them. A fuzzy search enhances a regular search by displaying links to content that have keywords matching the search terms. For example, a document about Benjamin Franklin may never mention the words "famous" or "American". However, if these are assigned as keywords for this document, then a search on "famous" will result in a link to (or the full display of) the document in question.

Comparisons of Two or More Languages

If we compile separate corpora for each of two languages for which there is web site content on the Internet, the corpora might be used to compare the languages to see if either language is creeping into the other, due to the global nature of the Internet. This would be even more effective when done as part of a study extending over several years time.

One challenge to this occurs in cases where the languages being compared make use of different alphabets or other writing systems; another lies in the fact that different languages have differing sound schemes. Both transliteration and the taking into account of phonetic and other differences would be required. For example, what's known as an "elevator" in North American English a "lift" in the United Kingdom or Australia is erubator in Japanese, which uses Latin characters (known as *Rom ji*) for rendering foreign words and names. However, for most purposes, Japanese uses syllabic characters or ideographs.

For each alphabet, there exists multiple schemes for rendering words from that language using the Latin character set. Dialects also need to be taken into account: French as written or spoken in Québec is significantly different from that spoken in Paris; Chinese is even more challenging in this regard. While the ideograms used for Chinese writing are more or less universal, their pronunciation can vary widely between different spoken dialects, many of which are not mutually intelligible.

Applications can be devised to link word pairs together. For each pair, one word would be expected to occur exclusively in one web corpus, and the other word in the other language's web corpus. This linking can be used to study the frequency of occurrence of certain concepts over several languages.

Language Trends

Trends within a single language can also be studied over time. While it is unlikely that anyone regularly speaks Elizabethan English, for example, there is source text available for this time period and others at Project Gutenberg (http://www.promo.net/pg).

General Site Content Rating

Content available on a single web site (or even a single e-text) can be rated in a variety of ways. For example, if you have a list of terms relating to a particular subject or knowledge area, to varying degrees, you can check a corpus for a frequency count of each term. This frequency count can then be multiplied by a weighting factor representing the term's applicability or relative importance. The weighted frequencies could then be added up to a figure representing a rating for that site. The higher the rating, the more applicable or useful the site is likely to be to those with an interest in that subject.

List of Unique Domain Names

Only the most efficient search engines offer a feature whereby you can type in part of the name of a web domain and get back a list of matches, which are longer than the content entered. For example, a search on "dream" might bring back combinations such as "http://www.dream.com/", "http://www.dreams.com/", or "http://www.dreamtheater.com".

Conceptually, this feature is relatively simple to support. In actuality, there are few ways to solve this problem:

- ❏ Start a database whereby domain name owners manually submit their domain name, possibly with a brief title representing the site. This is similar to what Yahoo does, however there are no categories attached.

- ❏ Scan your web corpus for a list of words containing the string for which we are searching for. Use this to in turn generate a list of possible domain names. Use the latter list to query InterNIC (Note that InterNIC limits the number of successive requests allowed from the same IP address; queries would have to be run in batches.)

- ❏ Surf every single web page on the Internet, all several million of them, and compile a unique list of domain names. This would indeed be a major undertaking.

Given the options, it becomes fairly obvious why this feature is generally unavailable on most search engines.

A New Way to Index Web Pages

Given that a corpus represents a unique list of words occurring in one or more bodies of text, it can be used to represent a search engine index for a web site. Unfortunately, each index-generating software package has its own proprietary way of representing the index and corpus. There are number of ways that indexing might be standardized. A couple of methods are discussed below.

Digital Dewey System

Use a coding system similar to the "Dewey Decimal System" used by some libraries to catalog books. This "Digital Dewey" system would only index concepts relating to site content, not the site content itself. So if you were looking for a site exclusively about "extreme sports", this sort of feature would be very handy and might save you from having to surf hundreds of useless links where the word "extreme" and the word "sports" occur on a page, but not together.

Despite what some engines suggest, their exact-phrase searching does not always work properly. Yahoo has tried to do this but has not fully succeeded.

Web Corpus Markup Language

Devise is an XML application for Web Corpus Markup Language (WCML) that indexes a corpus for a single web site. This might also combine the Digital Dewey categorization for the web site as a whole. A committee such as W3C (World Wide Web Consortium, http://www.w3.org/) might oversee the standards for such an XML application. Alternatively a separate committee consisting of industry participants might oversee it, and submit their updates to the W3C.

To use WCML effectively, a search engine site would not send out a web spider / robot / agent to index other sites. Instead, each organization that wants their index to be publicly available would index their own site using a WCML SDK. The index would reside in a particular URL location (for example, index.wcml) on the organization's web site. This location would be recorded in an XML synopsis document that is submitted to the search engine site. The search engine would then retrieve a copy of the index instead of bombarding the organization's web site with URL requests.

There have been many attempts at improving website searches, but few, if any, of these have involved devising a single standard that all interested parties could employ. A system such as WCML would have at least two possible benefits. For organizations, one advantage might be that WCML-based indexing would provide them with better control over how and when indexing is performed on their web pages. For users, the results could be more complete, reliable, and relevant when using search engines.

Improvements

The database provided earlier, stores the text content used to compile the web corpus. Currently, only single word searching (or multi-word with AND or OR) is supported. To support full-text searching of phrases requires indexing the content column in the content table.

Programmatically, a more elegant and maintainable solution might be to write a recursive function to perform the task of following links and processing the content of the linked pages. Depending upon environmental factors, however, this might prove to be more resource-intensive than the method we've used in this chapter.

We've assumed in this case study that any linked file we access contains HTML or text. One potential problem that this assumption fails to anticipate arises in the case where a link points to some other kind of resource, such as an image or Acrobat PDF file. There are two different methods for determining this; neither of these solutions is bulletproof. Nonetheless, this is a possibility that may need to be provided for. One of the possible solutions is to check the file extension (perhaps using something like `$arr = explode(".",$link); $ext = $arr[count($arr)-1];`) and ignore all files whose extensions aren't typical of HTML, or common server-generated pages. The other is to use the `mime_content_type()` function. Unfortunately, this function is available only if we're using PHP compiled from the CVS tree (when the most recent official release was PHP 4.2.3).

Summary

This chapter has provided a discussion of the techniques used to compile a web corpus, or list of unique words occurring in various types of web content. This includes web pages on one or more sites, or text content added by visitors to a site. One of the most common applications for a web corpus is a search engine. While we do not provide PHP code here for a search engine, we do provide the basic SQL queries necessary to implement a search feature, using one or more search words and possibly AND or OR condition. We also suggested some ways in which a web corpus could be used for various linguistic studies, as well as some problems that we would encounter when trying to work with content in multiple languages. Finally, we looked at how we could improve on what's been accomplished in this chapter from both a programmatic and application or database design perspective.

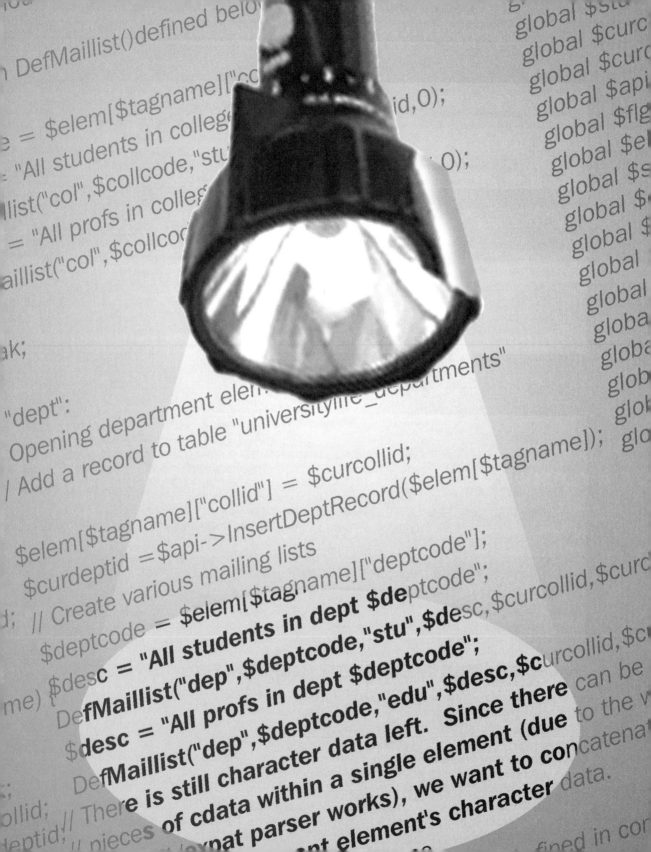

Mission Control Wireless Job Board

This case study focuses on a job board with a wireless component or user interface. The application components include both wired (HTML) and wireless (WML) pages.

These are the steps we will follow to build this application:

- ❏ Specifications
- ❏ Designing the Web Site and Templates
- ❏ Designing the Database
- ❏ Managing the Data
- ❏ Delivering the Content

Apart from PHP and MySQL, we will use the Smarty Template engine to segregate the code from the presentation, details on which have been included in the chapter.

Specifications

To develop this application, we will use a fictional profile of a company that might commission a web site such as this one. This is only done to have a guideline to incorporate as many features as possible for enhanced functionality in this application.

I-Spy Inc. is a fictional, but busy, espionage company with international clients, both dangerous and mundane. They have agents working in the field on a frequent basis and found it necessary to be able to hand out assignments remotely. To optimise the use of agents, they will be kept busy and have a minimum of downtime while flying back and forth from home base.

Under I-Spy's new Mission Control Job Board, clients provide instructions for new missions. Missions are allotted on a first come, first served basis. The agents pick missions they feel qualified for and apply. Clients view the profiles of agents that apply for each mission. Clients can assign more than one agent to the same mission. When clients make their selection(s) via the application, each agent automatically receives a text message on their wireless device. The agents then use their wireless device to phone the mission's client contact for full mission details. If the device supports it, the application will even dial the number.

To reduce the wait time for an agent, clients send a response, positive or negative, to all agents that applied for a mission. This way, an agent can apply for other assignments fairly quickly instead of wondering if they have been assigned. This ensures minimum downtime while waiting, which is particularly important since the agents only work on one mission at a time.

In addition to the wireless features, agents can also use a regular HTML browser for certain activities. Clients only use an HTML browser, as do admin users, except for testing purposes.

While clients can view an agent's profile, they cannot see all the fields, for example, clients only see a special agent code instead of an agent's name. Similarly, agents do not see all of the client information. This anonymity is a matter of company policy.

Due to the limitations of WAP browsers, and scope limitations in this chapter, we will focus only on the wireless features that agents need to work with when in the field. Other features may be referred to, with relevant SQL query code provided on occasions. However, no PHP code is covered for these extra features.

The technologies we cover here are PHP, MySQL, and WML. Within the context of the wireless agent features covered here, there is no absolute necessity for WMLScript.

User Types

The full version of this application has three user types:

❑ **Admin**
Admin users have full privileges. However, they typically have no interest in viewing mission details.

❑ **Agent**
Agent users have partial privileges. They can view missions and their profiles. They cannot view client information.

❑ **Client**
Client users have partial privileges. They can add, edit, view, or remove mission postings, view agent profiles (but not names or phone numbers), and view and select applicants. Note that admin staff must change any other client information, for I-Spy accounting purposes.

Content Types

The full version of this application deals with text content and possibly images showing agent disguises. However, for the purpose of this case study we are dealing only with text content.

Features

Some of the features described here are necessary for our discussion but are not initiated by agents. The focus of this case study is on the WML; hence all administration of the system will be done manually through the MySQL command line prompt. Items with an asterix (*) after them are done manually:

- ❑   Create user accounts (agent and client contact) – Admin user *

- ❑   Create agent records – Admin user *

- ❑   Create client records – Admin user *

- ❑   Create client contact records – Admin user *

- ❑   Add missions – Client user *

- ❑   Agent login – wireless – Agent user

- ❑   Agent logout – wireless – Agent user

- ❑   Agent change account password – wireless – Agent user

- ❑   View a list of open missions – wireless – Agent user

- ❑   View the details of a mission –wireless – Agent user

- ❑   Apply to a mission –wireless – Agent user

- ❑   View a list of missions applied to – wireless – Agent user

The features above are the basic set needed to cover all of the wireless features for agents in this application.

Component Hierarchy

The Mission Control Job Board web application has both wired and wireless software components. The diagram below illustrates the application's component hierarchy:

Designing the Web Site and Templates

We will focus only on the agent-specific features in this case study; the screenshots and menus shown below pertain only to the wireless pages.

Site Navigation

Once an agent successfully logs in to the Mission Control Job Board application, there is a standard menu that appears on every page. The menu can be represented as shown below:

Missions
Applications
Change Pswd
Logout

In addition to these standard features in the menu, additional features are available on certain pages in the form of WML hyperlinks. All of these features are discussed below.

Agent Screens

WAP browsers display WML pages differently, depending on the wireless device in use. The screenshots below are taken using the UP browser, with the generic configuration. The corresponding WML templates are described later in this chapter, in the *Delivering the Content* section.

Login

The first screenshot shows the initial login page:

There are a variety of errors that might occur, including incomplete login information, erroneous login information, or even MySQL errors. One of the criteria for valid login is that the user be of type admin or agent.

Welcome

Once an agent successfully logs in, they will see the screenshot on the left. The main menu is split into two parts accessible by two soft buttons, Missions and Menu. Missions will show a list of available missions. Menu, displays three options. These options are discussed in the following sections.

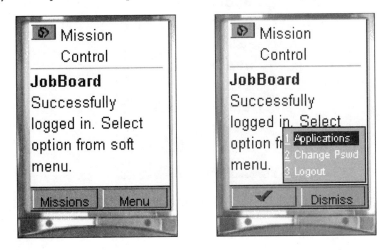

List of Missions

If an agent selects the Missions soft key, the following screenshot will appear. If there are more missions than can be displayed on one screen, you can scroll down to see more items:

Mission Details

To see the details of a particular mission, select a mission from the list and either press Send, or use the Mission soft key. For most missions in this application, the details will take up two or more screens. To see additional information, use the scroll buttons on your WAP device:

Notice that nowhere in the details does the client's name or that of the contact person appear. It is I-Spy policy to be as discreet as possible. After the details of the selected mission are displayed, a WML hyperlink is provided for agents to apply (on as is) the mission.

Apply to Mission

If an agent selects the Apply to this mission link from the Mission details page, the following page is displayed. If the application is successful (that is, the mission is open and still requires agents), then the screenshot below appears:

List of Mission Applications

If an agent picks the Applications option from the main menu, a list of any mission applications that they may have made is displayed, provided the mission status is either Open(O) or Active(A). If a mission has been Closed(C), the application is not displayed. Some sample screenshots are shown below:

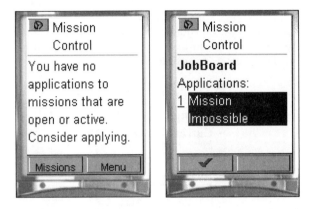

The screenshot on the left indicates that the agent making the request has no active applications, or possibly has never applied to a mission. The screenshot on the right shows a list of mission applications for the current agent. Additional applications, if any, may be accessed by scrolling down. Selecting application and pressing Send, or using the soft key AppDetail, generates an Application Detail page.

Application Details

From the list on the Applications page, if an agent selects an item, the details of the application are displayed. The user interface of this is similar to the one shown in the mission details section. Selecting the Cancel this application link attempts to cancel the job application for this mission for the current user.

Cancel Application

An agent can cancel an application provided that the mission is still open, they have not already been accepted or rejected, and a few more criteria, which are discussed on in the chapter later. Some sample screenshots are shown below, showing the messages before and after a successful cancellation:

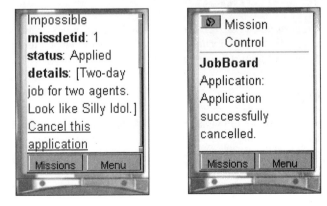

Note that if you try to cancel the mission when it has been closed, you often generate a number of error messages. The alternative to generating all these error screens is to generate the Cancel this application link (see *Application Details* section above) only when the mission is still Open and the agent's application status is still Applied. However, the reason for using this method is to show the handling of various error conditions using PHP.

Change Password

The Change Password page starts with a request for the agent to enter their current password. Once it has been entered and sent, the next part of the form is displayed, asking for the desired new password. After that, the agent is requested to re-enter the new password:

There are a number of errors that can occur when an agent tries to change their password. These are mostly errors in data entry, as well as database errors. If the agent's password is successfully changed, the message "Password for account <accountname> was successfully changed" is displayed.

Logout

The logout page uses the same WML template as the login error page. After a successful logout, the user is presented with the login page again.

Designing the Database

There are a number of reports that an admin user may want to generate regarding agents, clients, missions, and applications. However, since we are focusing only on the wireless agent interface, we will show a select set of SQL queries necessary to support basic admin features and reporting.

Database Tables

The database tables necessary for the full version of the Job Board application are listed below. Note that we will be using only a subset of these tables for the wireless agent features being covered in this chapter. The remaining tables are listed so they can be used for further improvements:

Table	Alias	Description
jobboard_accounts	ac	Information about user accounts for the various components of the application. admin, agent, and client accounts are all included.
jobboard_agents	ag	General information about agents. Each record in this table is linked to one record in the table jobboard_accounts.
jobboard_disguises	di	Filenames of images showing agent disguises. Each disguise for an agent requires a separate record in this table.
jobboard_languages	la	A list of all languages spoken by all agents at I-Spy collectively. Each language has a corresponding code assigned to it.
jobboard_langdet	ld	A list of all the languages spoken by each agent. One record is used for each language spoken by one agent.
jobboard_clients	cl	General information about clients.
jobboard_clicontacts	cc	Client contact information. One record in the jobboard_clients table can be linked to one or more contact records in this table.
jobboard_missions	mi	Information about jobs / missions. One record is used for each mission from a client. The records in this table are linked to the jobboard_clicontacts table. One client contact can post one or more missions in this table.
jobboard_missiondets	md	Information about each agent application for a mission, and the status of the application. One record in the jobboard_missions table can have several agent application records in this table.

Now, we'll discuss each of the tables listed above in more detail. Specifically, we'll list the various column names and their data types for each table.

Accounts

This table (jobboard_accounts) contains information about all types of user accounts:

Column	Data Type	Description
account_acctid	INT	Unique record ID, auto-generated by MySQL.
account_acct	CHAR	The account name for this user.
account_pass	CHAR	The password for this account.
account_type	CHAR	Account type –adm (administrator), cli (client), agn (agent).
account_status	CHAR	For registered users, this column indicates whether the user, including admin, is currently logged in (A - Active), not logged in (I -Inactive), or Blocked (B).

Table continued on following page

Column	Data Type	Description
account_logdatetime	CHAR	We'll store the date / time of the most recent login as a character string. This string is used to encrypt the account name and use the result to generate the session ID.
account_sessid	CHAR	While a user is logged in, this field stores a value to indicate that the user is legitimately logged in. It is a form of user authentication.

Agents

This table (jobboard_agents) contains information about agents. Only a subset of the columns here are accessible to clients, and only if a particular agent applies to a mission.

Column	Data Type	Description
agent_agentid	INT	Unique record ID, auto-generated by MySQL.
agent_fname	CHAR	The first name of the agent.
agent_lname	CHAR	The last name of this agent.
agent_agcode	CHAR	Agent code name (for viewing by clients).
agent_cell	CHAR	Agent's cell phone number. Either this field or pager must be filled in. This is enforced in the PHP code.
agent_pager	CHAR	Agent's pager number.
agent_sex	CHAR	Agent's sex.
agent_age	INT	Agent's actual age.
agent_agerange	CHAR	Agent's visible age range, that is, the age range that they can pass for in disguise.
agent_height	FLOAT	Agent's actual height in inches.
agent_weight	FLOAT	Agent's actual weight in pounds.
agent_yrsexp	FLOAT	Years of experience in this business.
agent_phystyp	CHAR	Agent's physical type. One of the physical type categories that all human beings fall into. For example, skinny or plump and other such descriptives.
agent_agdesc	CHAR	Contains information about the agent's skills, abilities, and experience, beyond what is indicated in the above fields.

Column	Data Type	Description
agent_status	CHAR	Indicates the working status of an agent. ❑ A – Assigned (Active) Currently assigned to a mission ❑ U – Unassigned (Inactive) Currently unassigned ❑ V – On vacation Source code in this chapter does not currently allow this value to be set and this feature is only listed as an improvement ❑ I – Illness Code in this chapter does not currently allow this value to be set and this feature is only listed as an improvement
agent_acctid	CHAR	The corresponding account ID for this agent.

Disguises

This table (jobboard_disguises) contains image filenames showing various disguises for specific agents:

Column	Data Type	Description
disguise_disguid	INT	Unique record ID, auto-generated by MySQL
disguise_imgfile	CHAR	The name of the image file, relative to the document root of the web server, containing a disguise image of the agent indicated by the agent_agentid field
disguise_agentid	INT	The agent ID from the jobboard_agents table of the agent that this disguise refers to

Languages

This table (jobboard_languages) lists all the languages spoken by agents, not all the languages spoken in the world. It will be up to an administrator to add new language entries as needed.

Column	Data Type	Description
language_langid	INT	Language ID. Unique record ID, auto-generated by MySQL.
language_langcode	CHAR	A short code that identifies the language, for example, en_us (English, United States).
language_language	CHAR	The full name of the language, in English. For example, what English speakers refer to as German, Germans call Deutsche.

Langdet

This table (jobboard_langdet) represents a list of all of the languages spoken by each agent. One record is used for each language spoken by a specific agent.

Column	Data Type	Description
langdet_langdetid	INT	Language detail ID. Unique record ID, auto-generated by MySQL.
langdet_langid	INT	This ID represents a record in jobboard_languages table. This is the language spoken by the agent indicated by agent_agentid.
langdet_agentid	INT	This is the ID in the jobboard_agents table that indicates which agent speaks the language represented by language_langid.

Clients

This table (jobboard_clients) contains information about clients. None of this information is accessible to agents.

Column	Data Type	Description
client_clientid	INT	Unique record ID, auto-generated by MySQL.
client_clientname	INTr	The name of the client, usually a business.
client_city	CHAR	The city where the client is located (usually the billing location).
client_state	CHAR	The state, province, district, or territory where the client is located. For simplicity, we are not normalizing this field, this is left as an exercise for the reader.
client_country	CHAR	The country where the client is located. Not normalized, see client_state.
client_postcode	CHAR	The zip code or postal code of the client.
client_status	CHAR	Indicates the status of the client: A –Approved, B – Blocked.

Clicontacts

This table (jobboard_clicontacts) contains information about each client contact. A client can have more than one contact who posts missions. This information is not available to agents.

Column	Data Type	Description
clicontact_contid	INT	Unique record ID, auto-generated by MySQL
clicontact_fname	CHAR	The first name of the client contact
clicontact_lname	CHAR	The last name of the client contact
clicontact_phone	CHAR	A phone number for the contact
clicontact_email	CHAR	An e-mail address for the contact
clicontact_clientid	INT	The ID of the client for whom this contact works
clicontact_acctid	INT	Corresponding user account ID for this client contact

Missions

This table (jobboard_missions) contains a listing of all missions posted by client contacts:

Column	Data Type	Description
mission_missid	INT	Unique record ID, auto-generated by MySQL.
mission_misscode	CHAR	A short title or code for the mission. This code is used in the List of missions feature, as well as other places.
mission_missdet	CHAR	The relevant details of the mission. Further details are given directly to the agent(s) actually assigned to the mission.
mission_naneeded	INT	The total number of agents needed for the mission.
mission_nassigned	INT	The number of agents assigned so far. When the positions are all filled, the status of the mission is changed to Active (A).
mission_status	CHAR	O – Open; A – Active and fully assigned; C –Closed.
mission_contid	INT	The ID of the client contact who posted this mission.

Missiondets

This table (jobboard_missiondets) contains a list of all applications by agents to any and all missions:

Column	Data Type	Description
missiondet_missdetid	INT	Unique record ID, auto-generated by MySQL
missiondet_missid	INT	The ID of the mission being applied to
missiondet_agentid	INT	The ID of the agent applying for the mission

Table continued on following page

Column	Data Type	Description
missiondet_status	CHAR	The status of the job application. The codes used to denote this status are:

    ❏ AP
An agent has applied for the position. This also implies that the mission is still open.

    ❏ AS
An agent has been assigned to the position. The mission status must be Open when an agent is assigned. Once assigned, this application status remains the same regardless of mission status.

    ❏ NA
The agent applied but was Not Accepted, for various reasons, including positions being assigned to other agent(s). Once rejected, this application status remains the same regardless of mission status.

    ❏ AC
Agent Cancelled. The agent applied but cancelled their application manually. The mission status can only be Open for a manual cancellation to take place. Once cancelled, this application status remains the same regardless of mission status.

Relationships Between Tables

The diagram below shows the relationship between tables. The arrow points to a table where the primary key of the source table (on the circle end of the arrow) is used as a foreign key. For example, the jobboard_clients table has a primary key client_clientid. This key is used in the jobboard_clicontacts table as a foreign key and hence there is a line from jobboard_clients to jobboard_clicontacts:

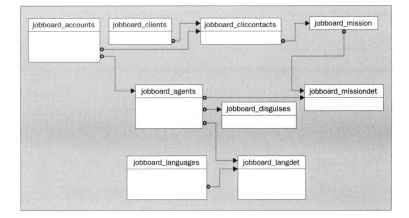

Note that the relationship between jobboard_accounts, and jobboard_clients and jobboard_agents is not entirely accurate, since the jobboard_accounts table also contains admin staff accounts. There are no tables containing administrator staff information shown here.

Database User

Let's first create the database. Type the following command at the line prompt:

```
> mysqladmin create jobboard
```

The tables for this case study can all be placed within a single MySQL database: jobboard. We will only run test scripts, so we need only one database user, for example ADMIN. We will have to grant privileges to the tables, as well as create the tables. Use the mysql client utility, which comes with MySQL, as shown in the following command line to grant privileges:

```
mysql> GRANT SELECT, INSERT, UPDATE, DELETE ON jobboard.* TO
'ADMIN@localhost' IDENTIFIED BY "ADMIN";
```

Creating Tables

Run the following SQL script, crdbs_jobboard.sql, on the mysql command line prompt to create the tables in the jobboard database:

```
> mysql jobboard < create_tables_jobboard.sql
```

The following listing shows the code found in the `crdbs_jobboard.sql` file:

```sql
//
// FILE: crdbs_jobboard.sql
// USE:  Create I-Spy Wireless Job Board database
//

    CREATE TABLE jobboard_accounts(
        account_acctid     INT UNSIGNED NOT NULL AUTO_INCREMENT PRIMARY KEY,
        account_acct       VARCHAR(12) NOT NULL,
        account_pass       VARCHAR(12) NOT NULL,
        account_type       CHAR(3) NOT NULL,
        account_status     CHAR(1) NOT NULL,
        account_logdatetime CHAR(20),  // Always the same length
        account_sessid     VARCHAR(128) NOT NULL
    );

    CREATE TABLE jobboard_agents(
        agent_agentid  INT UNSIGNED NOT NULL AUTO_INCREMENT PRIMARY KEY,
        agent_fname    VARCHAR(30) NOT NULL,
        agent_lname    VARCHAR(40) NOT NULL,
        agent_agcode   VARCHAR(12) NOT NULL,
        agent_cell     VARCHAR(15),
        agent_pager    VARCHAR(15),
        agent_sex      CHAR(1) NOT NULL,
        agent_age      TINYINT UNSIGNED,
        agent_agerange CHAR(7) NOT NULL,
        agent_height   FLOAT UNSIGNED,      // In inches (in)
        agent_weight   FLOAT UNSIGNED,      // In pounds (lb)
        agent_yrsexp   TINYINT UNSIGNED,
        agent_phystyp  VARCHAR(12),
        agent_agdesc   text,
        agent_status   CHAR(1) NOT NULL,  // Available for assignment: A;
                                          // unavailable: U

        agent_acctid   INT UNSIGNED NOT NULL
        );

    CREATE TABLE jobboard_disguises(
        disguise_disguid  INT UNSIGNED NOT NULL AUTO_INCREMENT PRIMARY KEY,
        disguise_imgfile  VARCHAR(255) NOT NULL,
        disguise_agentid  INT UNSIGNED NOT NULL
    );

    CREATE TABLE jobboard_languages(
        language_langid    INT UNSIGNED NOT NULL AUTO_INCREMENT PRIMARY KEY,
        language_langcode CHAR(5) NOT NULL,
        language_language VARCHAR(25) NOT NULL
    );

    CREATE TABLE jobboard_langdet(
        langdet_langdetid INT UNSIGNED NOT NULL AUTO_INCREMENT PRIMARY KEY,
        langdet_langid    INT UNSIGNED NOT NULL,
        langdet_agentid   INT UNSIGNED NOT NULL
```

```
    );

    CREATE TABLE jobboard_clients(
        client_clientid   INT UNSIGNED NOT NULL AUTO_INCREMENT PRIMARY KEY,
        client_clientname VARCHAR(60) NOT NULL,
        client_city       VARCHAR(40) NOT NULL,
        client_state      VARCHAR(60) NOT NULL,
        client_country    VARCHAR(60) NOT NULL,
        client_postcode   VARCHAR(12),
        client_status     VARCHAR(12)   // Reserved
    );

    CREATE TABLE jobboard_clicontacts(
        clicontact_contid   INT UNSIGNED NOT NULL AUTO_INCREMENT PRIMARY KEY,
        clicontact_fname    VARCHAR(30) NOT NULL,
        clicontact_lname    VARCHAR(40) NOT NULL,
        clicontact_phone    VARCHAR(15) NOT NULL,
        clicontact_email    VARCHAR(128),
        clicontact_clientid INT UNSIGNED NOT NULL,
        clicontact_acctid   INT UNSIGNED NOT NULL
    );

    CREATE TABLE jobboard_missions(
        mission_missid    INT UNSIGNED NOT NULL AUTO_INCREMENT PRIMARY KEY,
        mission_misscode  VARCHAR(20) NOT NULL,
        mission_missdet   VARCHAR(255),
        mission_naneeded  TINYINT UNSIGNED NOT NULL,
        mission_nassigned TINYINT UNSIGNED NOT NULL,
        mission_status    CHAR(1) NOT NULL,
        mission_contid    INT UNSIGNED NOT NULL
    );

    CREATE TABLE jobboard_missiondets(
        missiondet_missdetid INT UNSIGNED NOT NULL AUTO_INCREMENT PRIMARY
                                                                       KEY,
        missiondet_missid    INT UNSIGNED NOT NULL,
        missiondet_agentid   INT UNSIGNED NOT NULL,
        missiondet_status    CHAR(2) NOT NULL
    );
```

Building Indexes

Indexes are not necessary for the test scripts given in this chapter. Having said that, feel free to build indexes on fields that are likely to be queried very often, particularly the primary key for each database table.

Managing the Data

This section covers populating the database tables, as well as SQL queries that are necessary for supporting some of the features covered here.

Populating the Database

We are not covering all the user interface features, hence we will populate the database with sample data manually. We use the MySQL command line client `mysql` to add sample data. The minimum data needed to cover the wireless agent features in the application is given in the following sections:

- ❑ Create two to three user accounts
- ❑ Add two to three clients. Add one to two client contacts per client.
- ❑ Add three to seven missions requiring one to three agents apiece
- ❑ Add agent records
- ❑ Add applications for each user
- ❑ Add application acceptances / rejections

Create Agent User Accounts

Start by creating user accounts for a few agents using the `job_add_accts.sql` file:

```
>mysql jobboard < job_add_accts.sql
```

The contents of which are shown below:

```
//
// FILE: job_add_accts.sql
// USE:  Add agent user accounts
//
  INSERT INTO jobboard_accounts
  (account_acct, account_pass, account_type, account_status, account_sessid)
  VALUES
  ("roohoo","roo","agn","I",""),
  ("golly","gee","agn","I",""),
  ("mookie","moo","agn","I","");
```

Add Clients and Contacts

Now let's add a few records to these three tables:

- ❑ jobboard_clients
- ❑ jobboard_accounts
- ❑ jobboard_clicontacts

```
>mysql jobboard < job_add_clients.sql
```

The `job_add_clients.sql` file contains the following:

```
//
// FILE: job_add_clients.sql
// USE:  Add clients, contacts, and user accounts for contacts
//
    INSERT INTO jobboard_clients
    (client_clientname, client_city, client_state, client_country)
    VALUES
    ("Client1", "Atlanta", "Georgia", "USA"),
    ("Client2", "El Cerrito", "California", "USA"),
    ("Client3", "Bloomington", "Indiana", "USA");

// Create 1 contact per client.
// First create user account for each contact.
//
    INSERT INTO jobboard_accounts (account_acct, account_pass, account_type,
    account_status, account_sessid)
    VALUES
    ("contact11","p11","cli","I",""),   // Client 1, contact 1
    ("contact21","p21","cli","I",""),   // Client 2, contact 1
    ("contact31","p31","cli","I","");   // Client 3, contact 1

//
// Now create clicontact records
//
    INSERT INTO jobboard_clicontacts (clicontact_fname, clicontact_lname,
    clicontact_phone, clicontact_clientid, clicontact_acctid)
    VALUES
    ("Silly", "Idol", "111-555-1212", 1, 4),          // Client 1, contact 1
    ("Liza", "Hurley", "222-555-1212", 2, 5),         // Client 2, contact 1
    ("Darth", "Brooks", "333-555-1212", 3, 6);        // Client 3, contact 1
```

Add missions Records

Once clients, contacts, and user accounts for contacts have been created, missions can be posted:

```
>mysql jobboard < job_add_misns.sql
```

```
//
// FILE: job_add_misns.sql
// USE:  Add client missions
//
// Add 1-4 open missions per client
//
    INSERT INTO jobboard_missions
    (mission_misscode, mission_naneeded, mission_nassigned, mission_status,
     mission_contid, mission_missdet) VALUES
    ("Boldly Go", 1, 0, "O", 1,
     "One-day job for a single agent, any disguise."),
    ("Mission Impossible", 2, 0, "O", 1,
     "Two-day job for two agents. Look like Silly Idol."),
    ("Industrial Espionage", 1, 0, "O", 2,
```

```
        "Infiltrate music and film inudstry."),
    ("Ind. Esp. Pt 2", 1, 0, "O", 2,
    "Darth Brooks lookalike needed."),
    ("Ind. Esp. Pt 3", 2, 0, "O", 2,
    "Details to be revealed."),
    ("Serve and Protect", 1, 0, "O", 2,
    "Serve and protect Jennifer Love-Pitt."),
    ("That Was Never 5 Min", 3, 0, "O", 3,
    "Ministry of Silly Arguments requires debating agent.");
```

Add agent Records

Before we can have agents applying to missions, we need to add agent records. For the sake of this example, we are only adding the fields in the jobboard_agents table that have been marked NOT NULL. agent records must be tied to the corresponding jobboard_accounts record using the account_acctid field:

```
>mysql jobboard < job_add_agents.sql
```

```
//
// FILE: job_add_agents.sql
// USE:  Add agent records to table 'jobboard_agents'
//

INSERT INTO jobboard_agents (agent_fname, agent_lname, agent_agcode, agent_sex,
agent_agerange, agent_status, agent_acctid)
VALUES ("roo",    "hoo",   "001", "M", "28-60", "A", 1),
       ("golly", "gee",    "006", "F", "1-3",   "A", 2),
       ("mookie", "mouse", "009", "M", "2-4",   "A", 3);
```

Add Applications to Missions

This step can be performed using the sample interface code given later in the chapter.

Add Application Acceptances / Rejections

Once we have used the interface code to apply for missions for one or more agents, we will come back to this step and simulate the acceptance or rejection of the applications. Changing the status field of various application records (jobboard_missiondets table) will do this. An example is given below (run this inside of the mysql monitor):

```
mysql> UPDATE jobboard_missiondets SET missiondet_status="AC" WHERE
missiondet_missdetid=1;
```

The example above is only useful if one or more agents using the wireless interface have added applications. Now we can go back to the interface and view Applications for each agent and see if they are accepted or rejected.

Delivering the Content

As indicated earlier, the PHP and WML code presented here focuses only on the wireless features for agents. Now that we have defined all the functionality, we can look at the code necessary for this application. Space limitations prohibit us from showing the entire application code, so we will only look at a few select markup templates, most of the code, and some of the PHP scripts. The code presented here is available in the code download for this book at http://www.wrox.com.

We'll be using templates in this application to separate code from presentation, for which we'll use a template engine. In this case study, we'll be using Smarty (see http://smarty.php.net), a very powerful template engine for PHP.

For a quick introduction to the Smarty Template Engine refer to Chapter 5 of this book.

Script and Template Listing

The following table lists all WML page templates and PHP scripts required to support the wireless features for agents:

Script/Template File	Description
login.tpl	This template shows a login form and is called from login.php. It is the form displayed as the first screenshot of the application.
loginerr.tpl	Template used to display an error message and the login form. It is used to process login errors, namely an invalid username or password. This template is also called from login.php.
error.tpl	A generic error template. It displays an error message set in the calling PHP script.
general.tpl	General template used for logged in users; it allows the user to show missions or display a menu with options. This template is also used as the base template for all the screens of the application. It has a content section where some WML content set by the PHP script can be displayed.
chgpswd.tpl	The template used to display the change password form. It is called from chgpswd.php.
login.php	Script used to process logins and display the login form. After a successful login, it displays main.tpl, after an unsuccessful login it displays loginerr.tpl, if no login is submitted it displays login.tpl.
logout.php	Script used to logout a user. It unsets the session variables and displays login.tpl.
chgpswd.php	The script used to change a user password; it uses the change password template (chgpswd.tpl). It also processes the change password submissions, and displays the main menu after a password is changed.
missions.php	The script used to collect all the missions and set the content variable that will then be displayed in general.tpl, showing the list of available missions.

Table continued on following page

Script/Template File	Description
missiondet.php	Script used to collect information about a specific mission that will then be displayed in general.tpl.
apps.php	Used to view a list of all open applications to missions.
apply.php	Script used to process the application to a mission.
applydet.php	Script used to collect application details that will then be displayed in the general.tpl template.
cancel.php	Script used to cancel a mission application.
setup.php	Generic script where the Smarty template engine is initialized and the general application startup is performed.
misc.php	Another generic script with some functions that will be used from the other scripts.

PHP and WML Code

In this section, we'll discuss the PHP and WML scripts used for this application.

setup.php

The setup.php script is used to initialize the Smarty template engine, the database connection, and other application initialization code:

```php
<?php
session_start();
// Load application library files here
include("misc.php");

// Define and load Smarty components

define('SMARTY_DIR',"Smarty/");
require_once(SMARTY_DIR.'Smarty.class.php');

function insert_header()
{
    echo header("Content-type: text/vnd.wap.wml");
    echo header("Cache-Control: no-cache, must-revalidate");
    echo header("Pragma: no-cache");
    echo ("<?xml version='1.0'?>");
}

// Connection to the MySQL database
mysql_connect('localhost','root');
if (!mysql_select_db('jobboard'))
{
    $smarty->
    assign('errmsg',"Cannot access database $dbs:".mysql_error()."<br/>\n");
    $smarty->display('loginerr.tpl');
```

```
        die;
    }

class Smarty_Jobboard extends Smarty {
    function Smarty_Jobboard(){
        $this->teplate_dir = "templates/";
        $this->compile_dir = "templates_c/";
        $this->config_dir = "configs/";
        $this->cache_dir = "cache/";
        $this->caching = false;
        $this->assign('app_name','Jobboard');
    }
}
$smarty = new Smarty_Jobboard();
?>
```

misc.php

The misc.php script contains functions that will be used by other PHP scripts. The functions are self-explanatory. Here is the code for this file:

```
<?php
// FILE: misc.php
// USE:  various validation functions
//

function IsValidLogin($acct,$pass)
{
$errmsg = "";
    $sqlquery   = "SELECT account_acctid FROM jobboard_accounts WHERE
                   account_acct='$acct' AND account_pass='$pass' AND
                   account_type in ('agn','adm')";

    $results    = mysql_query($sqlquery);
    if (!$results) return false;
    if(mysql_num_rows($results)!=1) return false;
    $res = mysql_fetch_array($results);
    return $res["account_acctid"];
} // end function IsValidLogin

function GetAggentIdOnAcctid($acctid)
{
    // Get the agentid for this user, from table "jobboard_agents"
    $sqlquery   = "SELECT agent_agentid FROM jobboard_agents ";
    $sqlquery  .= "WHERE agent_acctid=$acctid ";

    $results    = mysql_query($sqlquery);
    if (!$results){
        return false;
```

```
    }
    // Query succeeded; retrieve agentid
    $aaRow = mysql_fetch_array($results);
    $agentid = $aaRow["agent_agentid"];
    return($agentid);
} // end function GetAggentIdOnAcctid

function CancelApplication($agentid,$missdetid)
{
    $updquery  = "UPDATE jobboard_missiondets SET missiondet_status='AC' ";
    $updquery .= "WHERE missiondet_missdetid=$missdetid AND
                 missiondet_agentid=$agentid ";

    $updres   = mysql_query($updquery);
    if (!$updres) return false;
    return true;
} // end function CancelApplication

?>
```

login.php

Now, we'll go through the PHP scripts for specific parts of our application. Let's start with the `login.php` script. This is the script that will be called when an agent accesses the application; agents will bookmark a URL in the form http://hostname/login.php/ to access the Job Board WAP application from their cell phones. The PHP code processes the login form if submitted or displays the `login.tpl` template. When processing a login form, the PHP code can display `main.tpl` if the login was successful or `loginerr.tpl` if there was an error. The following is the code for `login.php`:

```
<?php
//
// FILE: login.php
// USE:  Display login form
//       process the login and show error page or main menu
//
include("setup.php");

// If we are processing a login then verify the information
if(isset($_REQUEST["acct"]) && isset($_REQUEST["pass"])) {
    if(! ($acctid = IsValidLogin($_REQUEST["acct"],$_REQUEST["pass"]))) {
        $smarty->assign('errmsg','invalid username or password');
        $smarty->display('loginerr.tpl');
        die;
    }
// Since the login was successful set the acctid and acct session variables

    $acct = $_REQUEST["acct"];
    session_register("acct");
    session_register("acctid");
    $smarty->assign('acct',$acct);
    $smarty->assign('acctid',$acctid);
    $smarty->display('main.tpl');
}
$smarty->display('login.tpl');
?>
```

The template file used for accepting the login information is `login.tpl`. The `login.tpl` file is as shown below:

```
{insert name=header}
<!DOCTYPE wml PUBLIC "-//WAPFORUM//DTD WML 1.1//EN"
                     "http://www.wapforum.org/DTD/wml_1.1.xml">
<wml>
  <card id="login" title="Mission Control" newcontext="true">
    <p>
      <b>Agent JobBoard</b><br/>
         Please log in.<br/>
      <b>Username</b>:
         <input name="acct" title="Username" type="text"/>
      <b>Password</b>:
         <input name="pass" title="Password" type="password"/>
      <do type="accept" label="Submit">
        <go method="get"
           href="login.php?acct=$(acct:esc)&amp;pass=$(pass:esc)"/>
      </do>
    </p>
  </card>
</wml>
```

Note the `{insert name=header}` instruction at the beginning of the template, this will call the `insert_header()` function defined at `setup.php`, the function sends the WAP/WML headers needed for WAP devices. This is a naming convention used in Smarty; `{insert name=foo}` calls the `insert_foo()` function. The output of the `{insert}` section is not cached by Smarty so `{insert}` is cache-safe.

When we access the application, this is what `login.php` displays:

If there's an error when logging in, `loginerr.tpl` is displayed. This template is almost equal to `login.tpl` but it also displays an error message notifying the user of an invalid login attempt. The `loginerr.tpl` file code is:

```
{insert name=header}
<!DOCTYPE wml PUBLIC "-//WAPFORUM//DTD WML 1.1//EN"
                     "http://www.wapforum.org/DTD/wml_1.1.xml">
<wml>
<!-- Use when a login error has occurred, or when logging out -->
  <card id="login" title="Mission Control" newcontext="true">
    <p>
      <b>{$errmsg}</b>
      <b>Account name</b>:
        <input name="acct" title="Username" type="text"/>
      <b>Password</b>:
        <input name="pass" title="Password" type="password"/>
      <do type="accept" label="Submit">
        <go method="get"
          href="login.php?acct=$(acct:esc)&amp;pass=$(pass:esc)"/>
      </do>
    </p>
  </card>
</wml>
```

Now let's login to the application using User: roohoo and Password: roo. We will be redirected to the main menu, with the main.tpl template. The template is WML code mixed with Smarty directives to insert Smarty variables. We use the $acct and $acctid variables for the account information of the user:

```
{insert name=header}
<!DOCTYPE wml PUBLIC "-//WAPFORUM//DTD WML 1.1//EN"
                     "http://www.wapforum.org/DTD/wml_1.1.xml">
<wml>
<!-- Main menu and main page after successful login -->
  <template>
    <do type="prev"><noop/></do>
    <do type="accept" label="Missions">
      <go href="missions.php" method="get">
        <postfield name="acct" value="{$acct}"/>
        <postfield name="acctid" value="{$acctid}"/>
      </go>
    </do>
    <do type="accept" label="Applications">
      <go href="apps.php" method="get">
        <postfield name="acct" value="{$acct}"/>
        <postfield name="acctid" value="{$acctid}"/>
      </go>
    </do>
    <do type="accept" label="Change Pswd">
      <go href="chgpswd.php" method="get">
      <postfield name="acct" value="{$acct}"/>
      <postfield name="acctid" value="{$acctid}"/>
      </go>
    </do>
    <do type="accept" label="Logout">
      <go href="logout.php" method="get">
        <postfield name="acct" value="{$acct}"/>
        <postfield name="acctid" value="{$acctid}"/>
```

```
      </go>
    </do>
  </template>
  <card id="login" title="Mission Control">
    <p>
      <b>JobBoard</b>
      Successfully logged in.
      Select option from soft menu.<br/>
    </p>
  </card>
  </wml>
```

The main menu displayed in a WAP browser is as below:

Now let's examine the options. We have two options in the main application menu: Missions and Menu. The Missions button takes us to the list of available missions. This is a screenshot of the list of available missions:

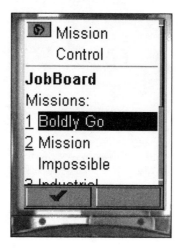

missions.php

The missions.php script is used to generate the list of available missions:

```php
<?php
//
// FILE: missions.php
// USE:  View a list of all open missions
//
include_once("setup.php");

if (!isset($_SESSION["acct"])) {
  $smarty->assign('errmsg', "You are not logged in<br/>\n");
  $smarty->display('loginerr.tpl');
  die;
}

$acct = $_SESSION["acct"];
$acctid = $_SESSION["acctid"];

// Now generate data needed to display all open missions
$sqlquery  = "SELECT mission_missid, mission_misscode FROM jobboard_missions
              WHERE mission_status IN ('O', 'A') ";
              // Open or Active
$sqlquery .= "AND (mission_naneeded - mission_nassigned) > 0 ";
// If agents still needed
$results   = mysql_query($sqlquery);
if (!$results) {
    $smarty->assign('errmsg','invalid username or password');
    $smarty->display('error.tpl');
  die;
}

if(! mysql_num_rows($results)) {
    $smarty->assign('content','<p>There are currently no available missions.
                  Consider taking a vacation.</p>');
    $smarty->display('general.tpl');
  die;
}

$content.= "<p>\n";
$content.= "<b>JobBoard</b>\n";
$content.= "Missions:\n";
$content.= "<select name=\"missid\">\n";
while( $aaRow = mysql_fetch_array($results)) {
      $missid = $aaRow["mission_missid"];
      $misscode = $aaRow["mission_misscode"];
      $content.= "<option value=\"$missid\">$misscode</option>\n";
}
$content.= "</select>\n";
$content.= "</p>\n";
$content.= "<do type=\"accept\" label=\"Mission\">\n";
$content.= "  <go href=\"missiondet.php\">\n";
$content.= "    <postfield name=\"acct\" value=\"$acct\"/>\n";
```

```
$content.= "    <postfield name=\"acctid\" value=\"$acctid\"/>\n";
$content.= "    <postfield name=\"missid\" value=\"\$(missid:n)\"/>\n";
$content.= "  </go>\n";
$content.= "</do>\n";
$smarty->assign('content',$content);
$smarty->display('general.tpl');
?>
```

The following template is called `general.tpl`. This is similar to `main.tpl` but has a content section where we can display information:

```
{insert name=header}
<?xml version='1.0'?>
<!DOCTYPE wml PUBLIC "-//WAPFORUM//DTD WML 1.1//EN"
                    "http://www.wapforum.org/DTD/wml_1.1.xml">
<wml>
<!-- General page after successful login -->
  <template>
    <do type="prev"><noop/></do>
    <do type="accept" label="Missions">
      <go href="missions.php" method="get">
        <postfield name="acct" value="{$acct}"/>
        <postfield name="acctid" value="{$acctid}"/>
      </go>
    </do>
    <do type="accept" label="Applications">
      <go href="apps.php" method="get">
        <postfield name="acct" value="{$acct}"/>
        <postfield name="acctid" value="{$acctid}"/>
      </go>
    </do>
    <do type="accept" label="Change Pswd">
      <go href="chgpswd.php" method="get">
        <postfield name="acct" value="{$acct}"/>
        <postfield name="acctid" value="{$acctid}"/>
      </go>
    </do>
    <do type="accept" label="Logout">
      <go href="logout.php" method="get">
        <postfield name="acct" value="{$acct}"/>
        <postfield name="acctid" value="{$acctid}"/>
      </go>
    </do>
  </template>
<card id="login" title="Mission Control">
{$content}
</card>
</wml>
```

If we select a mission, we'll see the mission details and a link to apply to the mission. The following is a screenshot of mission detail:

The `missiondet.php` script is used to generate mission details:

```php
<?php
//
// FILE: missiondet.php
// USE:  View the details of the selected mission
//

include_once('setup.php');

if (!isset($_SESSION["acct"])) {
  $smarty->assign('errmsg', "You are not logged in");
  $smarty->display('loginerr.tpl');
  die;
}

$acct = $_SESSION["acct"];
$acctid = $_SESSION["acctid"];

if (!isset($_REQUEST["missid"])) {
  $smarty->assign('errmsg', "No mission indicated");
  $smarty->display('error.tpl');
  die;
}

// Get information about the mission

$sqlquery  = "SELECT * from jobboard_missions ";
$sqlquery .= "WHERE mission_status in ('O', 'A')";
              // Open or Active
$sqlquery .= "AND (mission_naneeded - mission_nassigned) > 0 ";
              //If agents still needed
$sqlquery .= "AND mission_missid=$missid "; // Only selected mission
```

```php
$results    = mysql_query($sqlquery);

if (!$results)  {
  $smarty->assign('errmsg','invalid username or password');
  $smarty->display('error.tpl');
  die;
}

if(! mysql_num_rows($results) )
{
  $smarty->assign('content','<p>Either the selected mission does not exist
                        or it does not require more agents.</p>');
  $smarty->display('general.tpl');
  die;
}

// Mission identified, get data
$aaRow = mysql_fetch_array($results);
$missid    = $aaRow["mission_missid"];
$misscode  = $aaRow["mission_misscode"];
$missdet   = $aaRow["mission_missdet"];
$naneeded  = $aaRow["mission_naneeded"];
$nassigned = $aaRow["mission_nassigned"];

$itemmarkup .= "<p>\n";
$itemmarkup .= "<b>JobBoard</b><br />\n";
$itemmarkup .= "Mission <b>$misscode</b><br />\n";
$itemmarkup .= "<b>missid</b>: $missid<br />\n";
$itemmarkup .= "<b>#needed</b>: $naneeded<br />\n";
$itemmarkup .= "<b>#assigned</b>: $nassigned<br />\n";
$itemmarkup .= "<b>Details</b>: [$missdet]<br />\n";
$itemmarkup .= "<anchor>\nApply to this mission\n";
$itemmarkup .= "  <go href=\"apply.php\">\n";
$itemmarkup .= "    <postfield name=\"acct\" value=\"$acct\"/>\n";
$itemmarkup .= "    <postfield name=\"acctid\" value=\"$acctid\"/>\n";
$itemmarkup .= "    <postfield name=\"sessid\" value=\"$sessid\"/>\n";
$itemmarkup .= "    <postfield name=\"missid\" value=\"\$(missid:n)\"/>\n";
$itemmarkup .= "  </go>\n";
$itemmarkup .= "</anchor>\n";
$itemmarkup .= "</p>\n";

$smarty->assign('content',$itemmarkup);
$smarty->display('general.tpl');

?>
```

apply.php

When we click on the Apply To Mission link the apply.php script is executed. The code for the script is as follows:

```php
<?php
//
// FILE: apply.php
// USE:  Attempts to create an "job application" for the
//       selected mission, by the current agent.
//
```

```php
include_once("setup.php");

if (!isset($_SESSION["acct"])) {
  $smarty->assign('errmsg', "You are not logged in<br/>\n");
  $smarty->display('loginerr.tpl');
  die;
}

$acct = $_SESSION["acct"];
$acctid = $_SESSION["acctid"];

/*
  Verify that an application to a selected mission can take place
  Rules:
    1. Mission status must be Open ("O")
    2. Mission must have unfilled positions (naneeded-nassigned > 0)
*/

// Retrieve $agentid
$agentid = GetAggentIdOnAcctid($acctid); # Defined in misc.php

if(!$agentid) {
  $smarty->assign('errmsg','couldnt identify you as an agent');
  $smarty->display('error.tpl');
  die;
}

// We only need to update table "missiondet"
$insquery .= "INSERT INTO jobboard_missiondets (missiondet_missid,
              missiondet_agentid, status) VALUES ";
$insquery .= "($missid,$agentid,'AP') "; // AP=Applied
$insres = mysql_query($insquery);
if (!$insres)   {
  $smarty->assign('errmsg','database error:'.mysql_error().' when trying to
                        apply for the mission try again later');
  $smarty->display('error.tpl');
  die;
}

// Mission application accepted
$pgcont  = "<p>Application accepted. Check ";
$pgcont .= "'Applications' list later to determine ";
$pgcont .= "acceptance.</p>";

$smarty->assign('content',$pgcont);
$smarty->display('general.tpl');
?>
```

The screenshot below shows the page that displays the acceptance of the application from an agent who has applied:

This set of operations can be performed to apply to different missions also.

If the Menu button is pressed, there is an option called Applications where we can see a list of applications made by the agent, as shown:

apps.php

The script used to generate the list is apps.php, which is given below:

```php
<?php
//
// FILE: apps.php
// USE:  View a list of all open applications to missions
//
include_once("setup.php");

if (!isset($_SESSION["acct"])) {
  $smarty->assign('errmsg', "You are not logged in<br/>\n");
```

```
    $smarty->display('loginerr.tpl');
    die;
}
$acct = $_SESSION["acct"];
$acctid = $_SESSION["acctid"];

 // Display a list of any mission applications made by this agent,
// provided the mission has not been closed or blocked.
//
// To do this, we need to perform a quadruple-join on 4 tables.
//
$sqlquery = "SELECT mi.mission_misscode, md.missiondet_missdetid";
$sqlquery .= "FROM jobboard_missions as mi, jobboard_missiondets as md,";
$sqlquery .= "jobboard_accounts as ac, jobboard_agents as ag ";
$sqlquery .= "WHERE mi.mission_missid = md.missiondet_missid ";
$sqlquery .= "AND md.missiondet_agentid = ag.agent_agentid ";
$sqlquery .= "AND ag.agent_acctid = ac.account_acctid ";
$sqlquery .= "AND mi.mission_status in ('O','A') ";
$sqlquery .= "AND ac.account_acctid = $acctid ";

$results = mysql_query($sqlquery);
if (!$results) {
  $smarty->assign('errmsg','Database error trying to get applications try
                            again later');
  $smarty->display('error.tpl');
  die;
}

if(!mysql_num_rows($results)) {
  $smarty->assign('content','<p>You have no applications to missions that
                              are open or active. Consider applying.</p>');
  $smarty->display('general.tpl');
  die;
}

// Retrieve applications
$pgcont = "";
$pgcont .= "<p>\n";
$pgcont .= "<b>JobBoard</b><br/>\n";
$pgcont .= "Applications:<br/>\n";
$pgcont .= "<select name=\"missdetid\">\n";


while($aaRow = mysql_fetch_array($results)) {
      $missdetid = $aaRow["missiondet_missdetid"];
      $misscode  = $aaRow["mission_misscode"];
      $pgcont .= "<option value=\"$missdetid\">$misscode</option>\n";
}
$pgcont .= "</select>\n";
$pgcont .= "</p>\n";
$pgcont .= "<do type=\"accept\" label=\"AppDetail\">\n";
$pgcont .= "  <go href=\"appdet.php\">\n";
$pgcont .= "    <postfield name=\"acct\" value=\"$acct\"/>\n";
$pgcont .= "    <postfield name=\"acctid\" value=\"$acctid\"/>\n";
```

```
$pgcont .= "      <postfield name=\"sessid\" value=\"$sessid\"/>\n";
$pgcont .= "      <postfield name=\"missdetid\"
                  value=\"\$(missdetid:n)\"/>\n";
$pgcont .= "  </go>\n";
$pgcont .= "</do>\n";

$smarty->assign('content',$pgcont);
$smarty->display('general.tpl');
?>
```

appdet.php

We can view the details for an application by selecting it; the script that does this is called `appdet.php`. The following screenshot shows the application details:

This is the code for `appdet.php`:

```
<?php
//
// FILE: appdet.php
// USE:  View the details of the selected mission application
//
include_once("setup.php");

if (!isset($_SESSION["acct"])) {
    $smarty->assign('errmsg', "You are not logged in<br/>\n");
    $smarty->display('loginerr.tpl');
    die;
}

$acct = $_SESSION["acct"];
$acctid = $_SESSION["acctid"];

// Display the details of the selected mission application.
```

```
$pgcont= "";
$sqlquery= "SELECT mi.mission_misscode, md. missiondet_missdetid, ";
$sqlquery.= "md.missiondet_status, mi.mission_missdet ";
$sqlquery.= "FROM jobboard_missions AS mi, jobboard_missiondets AS md, ";
$sqlquery.= "jobboard_accounts AS ac, jobboard_agents AS ag ";
$sqlquery.= "WHERE mi.mission_missid = md.missid ";
$sqlquery.= "AND md.missiondet_agentid = ag.agent_agentid ";
$sqlquery.= "AND ag.agent_acctid  = ac.account_acctid ";
$sqlquery.= "AND mi.mission_status IN ('O','A') ";
$sqlquery.= "AND ac.account_acctid = $acctid ";

$results   = mysql_query($sqlquery);
if (!$results) {
  $smarty->assign('errmsg','Database error trying to get application
                           details try again later');
  $smarty->display('error.tpl');
  die;
}

if(! mysql_num_rows($results)) {
  $smarty->assign('errmsg','Could get information for the application try
                           again later');
  $smarty->display('error.tpl');
  die;
}

// Mission exists. Assume just one item.
$aaRow = mysql_fetch_array($results);
$misscode  = $aaRow["mission_misscode"];
$missdetid = $aaRow["missiondet_missdetid"];
$mdstatus  = $aaRow["missiondet_mdstatus"];
$missdet   = $aaRow["mission_missdet"];
switch ($mdstatus) {
  case "AC": // Agent cancelled application manually
    $statcode = "Cancelled";
  break;

  case "AP": // Applied for position.
    $statcode = "Applied";
  break;

  case "AS": // Assigned to position.
    $statcode = "Assigned";
  break;

  case "NA": // Not accepted to position.
    $statcode = "Rejected";
  break;

  default:
    $statcode = "Unknown";
}
```

```
$pgcont .= "<p>\n";
$pgcont .= "<em>Applic'n Detail</em><br/>\n";
$pgcont .= "<b>misscode</b>: $misscode<br/>\n";
$pgcont .= "<b>missdetid</b>: $missdetid<br/>\n";
$pgcont .= "<b>status</b>: $statcode<br/>\n";
$pgcont .= "<b>details</b>: [$missdet]<br/>\n";
$pgcont .= "<anchor>\nCancel this application\n";
$pgcont .= "  <go href=\"cancel.php\">\n";
$pgcont .= "    <postfield name=\"acct\" value=\"$acct\"/>\n";
$pgcont .= "    <postfield name=\"acctid\" value=\"$acctid\"/>\n";
$pgcont .= "    <postfield name=\"sessid\" value=\"$sessid\"/>\n";
$pgcont .= "    <postfield name=\"missdetid\" value=\"$missdetid\"/>\n";
$pgcont .= "  </go>\n";
$pgcont .= "</anchor>\n";
$pgcont .= "</p>\n";

$smarty->assign('content',$pgcont);
$smarty->display('general.tpl');

?>
```

cancel.php

We can cancel an application by using the Cancel the Application link, which calls cancel.php:

```php
<?php
//
// FILE: cancel.php
// USE:  Cancel the selected mission application
//
include_once("setup.php");

if (!isset($_SESSION["acct"])) {
  $smarty->assign('errmsg', "You are not logged in<br/>\n");
  $smarty->display('loginerr.tpl');
  die;
}

$acct = $_SESSION["acct"];
$acctid = $_SESSION["acctid"];
```

To cancel an application, the following criteria should be met:

❑   The mission status must be Open ("O")

❑   The agent must not have been assigned to the mission (missiondet.status!="AS")

❑   The agent must not have already cancelled the application (missiondet.status!="CA")

❑   The agent must not have been rejected (missiondet.status!="NA")

❑   The application in question ($missdetid) must have been made by the current agent / user

This amounts to: `missiondet_status = "AP"`. As we want to display an appropriate message, we will not check this status in the SQL query. We will defer the check to the relevant PHP code:

```
$sqlquery   = "SELECT mi.mission_misscode, md.missiondet_missdetid, ";
$sqlquery .= "        md.missiondet_status, ag.agent_agentid ";
$sqlquery .= "FROM jobboard_missions AS mi, jobboard_missiondets AS md, ";
$sqlquery .= "        jobboard_accounts AS ac, jobboard_agents AS ag ";
$sqlquery .= "WHERE mi.mission_missid = md.missiondet_missid ";
$sqlquery .= "AND md.missiondet_agentid = ag.agent_agentid ";
$sqlquery .= "AND ag.agent_acctid  = ac.account_acctid ";
$sqlquery .= "AND mi.mission_status = 'O'";
$sqlquery .= "AND ac.account_acctid = $acctid ";

$results    = mysql_query($sqlquery);
if (!$results) {
    $smarty->assign('errmsg','Database error trying to get application
                            details try again later');
    $smarty->display('error.tpl');
    die;
}

if (! mysql_num_rows($results)) {
    $smarty->assign('errmsg','Could get information for the application try
                            again later');
    $smarty->display('error.tpl');
    die;
}

// There is an application that matches. Now consider the criteria
// discussed above.
$pgcont = "";
$pgcont .= "<p>\n";
$pgcont .= "<b>JobBoard</b><br/>\n";
$pgcont .= "Application:<br/>\n";

$aaRow = mysql_fetch_array($results);
$missdetid = $aaRow["missiondet_missdetid"];
$misscode  = $aaRow["mission_misscode"];
$mdstatus  = $aaRow["missiondet_mdstatus"];
$agentid   = $aaRow["agent_agentid"];

switch ($mdstatus) {
  case "AC": // Agent cancelled application manually
    $pgcont .="Error: Application previously cancelled.<br/>\n";
  break;
  case "AP": // Applied for position.
    // We can cancel the application.
    if(!CancelApplication($agentid,$missdetid)) {
      $smarty->assign('errmsg','Error when trying to cancel application');
      $smarty->display('error.tpl');
      die;
    }
    $pgcont .= "Application successfully cancelled.<br/>\n";
```

```
  break;
  case "AS": // Assigned to position.
    $pgcont .="Error: Already assigned to this mission.<br/>\n";
  break;
  case "NA": // Not accepted to position.
    $pgcont .="Error: You were not accepted to this mission.<br/>\n";
  break;
  default:
    $pgcont .="Error: Unknown application status. ";
    $pgcont .= "Cannot cancel.<br/>\n";
}
$pgcont .= "</p>\n";

$smarty->assign('content',$pgcont);
$smarty->display('general.tpl');
?>
```

The other options are Logout and Change Password.

chgpswd.php

If we select Change Password, this is the form that is displayed:

The script chgpswd.php has the following code:

```
<?php
//
// FILE: chgpswd.php
// USE:  Display PDA change password form
//
include_once("setup.php");

if (!isset($_SESSION["acct"])) {
  $smarty->assign('errmsg', "You are not logged in<br/>\n");
```

```php
    $smarty->display('loginerr.tpl');
    die;
}
$acct = $_SESSION["acct"];
$acctid = $_SESSION["acctid"];

// Check if we have to perform a password change operation here
// Check to see if a user correctly changed their password
if(isset($_REQUEST["pass"]) && isset($_REQUEST["npass1"]) &&
isset($_REQUEST["npass2"])) {
    if( $npass1 != $npass2 ) {
        $smarty->assign('errmsg','The new password and the repeated value are
                                different');
        $smarty->display('error.tpl');
        die;
    }
    $sqlquery = "SELECT account_pass FROM jobboard_accounts WHERE
                account_acctid=$acctid ";
    $results = mysql_query($sqlquery);
    if(!$results || !mysql_num_rows($results)) {
        $smarty->assign('errmsg','Canot get account information');
        $smarty->display('error.tpl');
        die;
    }
    $aaRow = mysql_fetch_array($results);
    $act_pass = $aaRow["account_pass"];
    if($act_pass != $_REQUEST["pass"]) {
        $smarty->assign('errmsg','Invalid old password');
      $smarty->display('error.tpl');
      die;
    }
    // All input checks out. Change password and save to database
    $updquery  = "UPDATE jobboard_accounts SET account_pass='$npass1' ";
    $updquery .= "WHERE account_acctid=$acctid ";
    $updres    = mysql_query($updquery);
    if(!$updres) {
        $smarty->assign('errmsg','Cannot change password');
        $smarty->display('error.tpl');
        die;
    }
    $pgcont  = "<p>Password for account $acct was ";
    $pgcont .= "successfully changed</p>";
    $smarty->assign('content',$pgcont);
    $smarty->display('general.tpl');

}

$smarty->display('chgpswd.tpl');

?>
```

The template used to display the **Change Password** form is `chgpswd.tpl`, as shown below:

```
<?xml version='1.0'?>
<!DOCTYPE wml PUBLIC "-//WAPFORUM//DTD WML 1.1//EN"
                     "http://www.wapforum.org/DTD/wml_1.1.xml">
<wml>
  <card id="chgpwsd" title="Mission Control" newcontext="true">
    <p>
      <b>Change Password</b><br/>
      <b>Current Pswd</b>:
        <input name="pass" title="Password" type="password"/><br/>
      <b>New Pswd</b>:
        <input name="npass1" title="Password" type="password"/><br/>
      <b>Repeat New</b>:
        <input name="npass2" title="Password" type="password"/><br/>
      <do type="accept" label="SubmitChg">
        <go href="chgpswd.php" method="get">
          <postfield name="acct"   value="{$acct}"/>
          <postfield name="acctid" value="{$acctid}"/>
          <postfield name="pass"   value="$(pass:e)"/>
          <postfield name="npass1" value="$(npass1:e)"/>
          <postfield name="npass2" value="$(npass2:e)"/>
        </go>
      </do>
    </p>
  </card>
</wml>
```

logout.php

Finally, this is the code for `logout.php`:

```php
<?php
//
// FILE: logout.php
// USE:  Log user out of system
//
include_once("setup.php");

if (!isset($_SESSION["acct"])) {
    $smarty->assign('errmsg', "You are not logged in<br/>\n");
    $smarty->display('loginerr.tpl');
    die;
}

$acct = $_SESSION["acct"];
$acctid = $_SESSION["acctid"];

// Display the login page with a "logout" message, and
// unset all the session information.
$pgcontent = "";
session_unregister("acct");
session_unregister("acctid");

$smarty->display("login.tpl");

?>
```

Improvements

The focus in this case study was on using of WML. However, there are a number of things that could be done to improve the applicaton. Here are two:

❑ We performed the administration tasks manually by using the MySQL command line prompt. The full version can implement this feature for both WAP as well as browser based interfaces.

❑ The current implementation dealt only with the text content. We could also have images to show agent disguises.

Summary

This chapter gives an example of the wireless features of a 3-tier, multi-client web application resembling a job board. While the case study focuses on the needs of a fictional spy agency that wants to publish mission information from clients, the techniques provided here can be extrapolated for a regular job board as well.

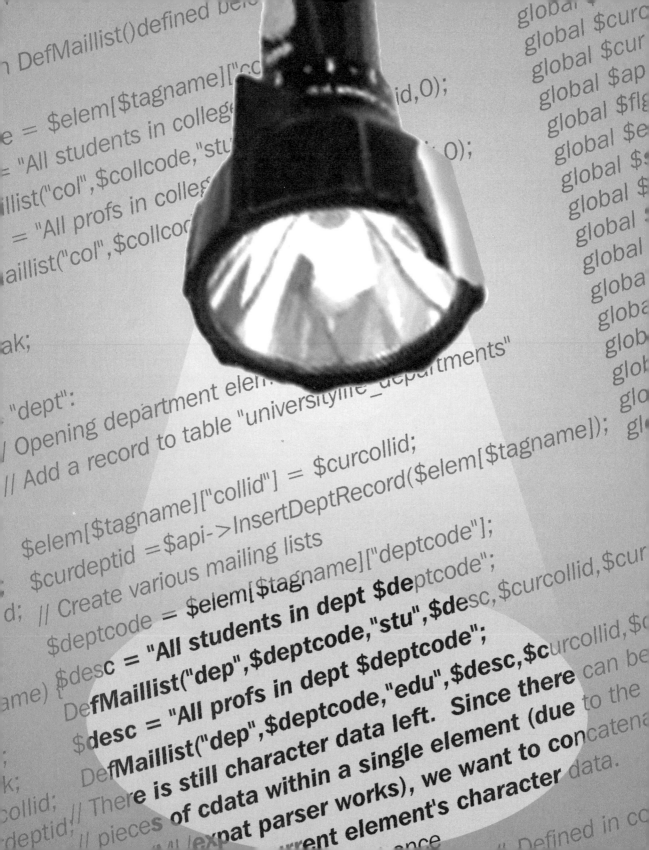

Classified Ads Board

This chapter goes through the planning and development of an online classified advertisements board. An online classifieds board is generally set up with specific categories for users to place ads within. Depending on the type of site that the classifieds appear on, those categories may be fairly broad to allow the listing of many different types of items. On the other hand, a site that has a very specific target audience might limit their classifieds board to categories that are most relevant to their subject matter.

It's important to carefully develop the specifications of our application before we start coding. Here's the format that this case study will follow to achieve our ends:

❑ Specifications

❑ Designing the Database

❑ Designing the Web Site and Templates

❑ Delivering the Content

❑ Improvements

Specifications

The primary function of the site is to allow users to post ads onto the board. We will also add a few more features, to increase the functionality of this site, including:

❑ Classifieds are listed by category

❑ Multi-level category listings

❑   Ads may appear in an unlimited number of categories.

❑   All users may view classified ads.

❑   Users must be logged in to post, edit, or delete ads. Users will only see the buttons they have permissions to use, so if they are not logged in, they will not see any edit buttons. Users can only edit their own posts.

❑   Users should be able to sort their results by ad name and price.

A Sample Site

An auto mechanic's web site is using a classified board to allow their members to sell used cars. The web site has a category structure that deals with a vehicle's make and model, as illustrated below:

Category: Cars
Ford
Honda
Plymouth
Mitsubishi
Category: Motorcycles
Suzuki
Yamaha
Ducati

As we can see, the categories consist of parent categories (Cars, Motorcycles), and child categories (Ford, Honda). This allows the users to quickly and easily locate what they are looking for, through a logical process of selecting a category, and then selecting the sub-category that best represents what they are looking for. In this way, the category structure is not unlike the kind we find on web site directory like http://www.yahoo.com/.

To get some idea of what the users' experience will be like as they use this program, the following flow chart allows us to walk through the process step by step:

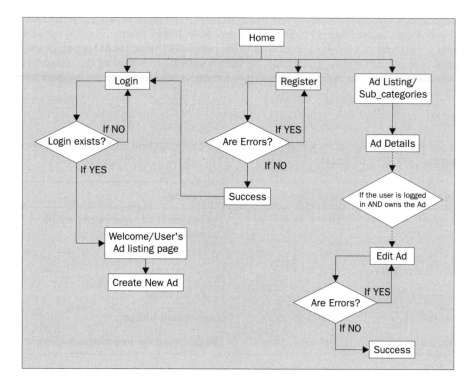

Designing the Database

Let's first look at the tables we need to set up a fully functional database that satisfies all our criteria. We will call our database `adboard`:

Table Name	Description
adboard_users	Holds the user data
adboard_categories	Holds the category data, including category parent, which will allow us to determine where each category belongs
adboard_ad_details	Holds the actual classified ad information
adboard_ad_category_join	Holds the information that will tell the program what categories each ad should be listed in

Now, let's look at the schema for each of these tables. Keep in mind that even without expanding the actual feature set, we could easily add more fields to these tables if we wanted to add further information. For example, in our `adboard_users` table, we could easily add fields to hold more information about our users, such as their web site URL, e-mail address, phone number, and so on. To achieve our ends, we will be using MySQL as our database server.

All ad categories are contained within the `adboard_categories` table. When a new member signs up, their information gets inserted into the `adboard_users` table. If they create a new ad, the ad details will be inserted into the `adboard_ad_details` table, and the categories that ad should appear in will be inserted into the `adboard_ad_category_join` table. By using a separate table to store the category information for each ad, we can easily have the ad appear in multiple categories, while keeping the database normalized at the same time.

Users

This table will store the details of each registered user. The `user_id` field is automatically generated using MySQL's `AUTO_INCREMENT` feature:

Field Name	Data Type	Description
user_id	INT(11)	The automatically generated user ID Constraints: NOT NULL AUTO_INCREMENT
user_firstname	VARCHAR(25)	User's first name
user_lastname	VARCHAR (25)	User's last name
user_email	VARCHAR (50)	User's e-mail address
user_password	VARCHAR (20)	The password the member uses to log in

The password provided by the user could have been stored using the `PASSWORD()` function of MySQL, but for simplicity of design, this has been left out.

Categories

This table lists the details of each category and their specifics:

Field Name	Data Type	Description
category_id	INT(11)	The automatically generated category ID Constraints: NOT NULL AUTO_INCREMENT
category_name	VARCHAR (35)	The category name
category_parentid	INT(11)	ID of the parent category. This is used to define the category heirarchy. (The default value of 0 specifies that the category is a top-level category.) Constraint: DEFAULT '0'

Details

As evident, this table stores the details of each ad:

Field Name	Data Type	Description
ad_detail_id	INT (11)	The automatically generated ad detail ID Constraints: NOT NULL AUTO_INCREMENT
ad_detail_title	VARCHAR (64)	Title of the ad
ad_detail_body	TEXT	The actual ad text
ad_detail_price	DECIMAL (15,2)	The price of the item being sold Constraint: UNSIGNED
ad_detail_img_url	VARCHAR (255)	External URL of image file
ad_detail_addedon	DATETIME	Date the ad was added
ad_detail_userid	INT (11)	The ID from the adboard_users table of the person who created the ad

Category Join

This table is instrumental in storing information about ads that may be listed in multiple categories, by storing the ID of the ad, and category it belongs in. For each category an ad belongs in, there will be a corresponding record in this table – so an ad that is listed in four different categories will have four entries in this table.

Field Name	Data Type	Description
category_join_id	INT(11)	The automatically generated unique ID Constraint: NOT NULL AUTO_INCREMENT
category_join_ad_id	INT(11)	ID of the ad
category_join_cat_id	INT(11)	ID of the category Constraint: DEFAULT '0'

Creating the Database

Having looked at the schema of the tables, we will go on to create the database now. First we create the database, then the tables, and finally we populate the tables with the data in the following code snippets.

To create the adboard database, run the following at the command prompt:

```
>mysqladmin create adboard
```

The following SQL code creates the tables in the adboard database. Save this code in a file called crtbs_adboard.sql in the MySQL bin/ directory and then run this file by typing the following command at the MySQL prompt:

```
>mysql adboard < crtbs_adboard.sql
```

```
#
# File Name: crtbs_adboard.sql
# Table structure for table `adboard_ad_category_join`
#
USE adboard;
CREATE TABLE adboard_ad_category_join (
  category_join_id INT(11) NOT NULL AUTO_INCREMENT,
  category_join_ad_id INT(11) NOT NULL DEFAULT '0',
  category_join_cat_id INT(11) NOT NULL DEFAULT '0',
  PRIMARY KEY(category_join_id)
) TYPE=MyISAM;
# --------------------------------------------------------
#
# Table structure for table `adboard_ad_details`
#
CREATE TABLE adboard_ad_details (
  ad_detail_id INT(11) NOT NULL AUTO_INCREMENT,
  ad_detail_title VARCHAR(64) NOT NULL DEFAULT '0',
  ad_detail_body TEXT,
  ad_detail_price DECIMAL(15,2) NOT NULL DEFAULT '0',
  ad_detail_img_url VARCHAR(255) DEFAULT NULL,
  ad_detail_addedon DATETIME DEFAULT NULL,
  ad_detail_userid INT(11) NOT NULL DEFAULT '0',
  PRIMARY KEY  (ad_detail_id)
) TYPE=MyISAM;
# --------------------------------------------------------
#
# Table structure for table `adboard_categories`
#
CREATE TABLE adboard_categories (
  category_id INT(11) NOT NULL AUTO_INCREMENT,
  category_name VARCHAR(35) DEFAULT NULL,
  category_parentid INT(11) DEFAULT NULL,
  KEY id2 (category_id)
) TYPE=MyISAM;
# --------------------------------------------------------
#
# Table structure for table `adboard_users`
#
CREATE TABLE adboard_users (
  user_id int(11) NOT NULL AUTO_INCREMENT,
  user_firstname VARCHAR(25) DEFAULT NULL,
  user_lastname VARCHAR(25) DEFAULT NULL,
  user_email VARCHAR(50) DEFAULT NULL,
  user_password VARCHAR(12) DEFAULT NULL,
  KEY id1 (user_id)
) TYPE=MyISAM;
```

As this is only a case study, we will not go into the details of a web-based administration panel, and the category structures will need to be inserted into the database manually. Some sample data has been provided to get started with. It should be noted that the category ID numbers do not need to be manually entered, as the AUTO_INCREMENT feature of MySQL will take care of generating them for us.

This command helps us populate our database:

```
>mysql adboard < pop_adboard.sql
```

and the contents of the file are shown below:

```
#
#File Name: pop_adboard.sql
#Function: Populating the tables of the database
#
#Inserting some categories
USE adboard;
INSERT INTO adboard_categories (category_id, category_name, category_parentid)
VALUES (1,'Cat Licenses','0');
INSERT INTO adboard_categories (category_id, category_name, category_parentid)
VALUES (2,'Cheese Shops','0');
INSERT INTO adboard_categories (category_id, category_name, category_parentid)
VALUES (3,'Crunchy Frogs','0');
INSERT INTO adboard_categories (category_id, category_name, category_parentid)
VALUES (4,'Lumberjacks','0');
INSERT INTO adboard_categories (category_id, category_name, category_parentid)
VALUES (13,'Small Red Parrots',10);
INSERT INTO adboard_categories (category_id, category_name, category_parentid)
VALUES (6,'Tracts of Land','0');
INSERT INTO adboard_categories (category_id, category_name, category_parentid)
VALUES (7,'Wooden Badgers','0');
INSERT INTO adboard_categories (category_id, category_name, category_parentid)
VALUES (8,'Very Small Rocks','0');
INSERT INTO adboard_categories (category_id, category_name, category_parentid)
VALUES (9,'Parrots','0');
INSERT INTO adboard_categories (category_id, category_name, category_parentid)
VALUES (10,'Red Parrots',9);
INSERT INTO adboard_categories (category_id, category_name, category_parentid)
VALUES (11,'Blue Parrots',9);
INSERT INTO adboard_categories (category_id, category_name, category_parentid)
VALUES (12,'Green Parrots',9);
INSERT INTO adboard_categories (category_id, category_name, category_parentid)
VALUES (14,'Med. Red Parrots',10);

# insert a user
INSERT INTO adboard_users (user_id, user_firstname, user_lastname, user_email,
user_password) VALUES (1,'Alison','Gianotto','snipe@snipe.net','wr0xrul3s');

# Add a classified ad to start with
INSERT INTO adboard_ad_details
(ad_detail_id, ad_detail_title, ad_detail_body, ad_detail_price, ad_detail_img_url,
ad_detail_addedon, ad_detail_userid)
VALUES
(1,'Thor\'s Parrot','Restless and self-centered, this bird is best suited to
someone with lots of patience. One of the more ill-tempered choices out there,
Thor\'s Parrots are high-maintance. \r<br/>\r<br/>I\'m sure it could be a
rewarding experience for the right person and he really is very loyal, but I just
don\'t have the time to deal with such a moody
beast!','10.00','http://www.snipe.net/snipe/photos/pics/358.jpg','2002-05-04
04:16:01',1);
```

As we can see from our sample data, the top-level categories have a `category_parentid` of 0, and the categories that appear underneath them have their `category_parentid` set to the ID of the category that they appear under. Now that our database is all set up, let's get to some actual coding.

Designing the Web Site and Templates

We will plan the site in advance to make sure there won't be any glitches later, after which we can start slinging some code.

To help us keep the presentation separate from the programming code, we'll use the Smarty template engine.

> *The Smarty template engine is discussed briefly in Chapter 5. If you are unfamiliar with Smarty, we recommend you go through it before we proceed with this chapter.*

> **The following code should work whether `register_globals` is turned on or off in the `php.ini` file. It will not work with a version of PHP that is lower than 4.1, because it utilizes the superglobal syntax ($_POST, $_GET, $_REQUEST, and $_SESSION) that was added in 4.1.**

This case study uses a number of template and PHP files that are outlined in this table:

File Name	Purpose
`index.php`	This file displays the categories/sub_categories, and a listing of ads with the selected category. Templates used: `adlisting.tpl`, `categories.tpl`
`login.php`	Displays the login box when not logged in, and a list of the user's ads when logged in. Templates used: `login.tpl`
`logout.php`	Logs the user out, and provides a login box for the user to log back in with. Templates used: `login.tpl`
`session.php`	Creates the login session information and verifies the login information.
`setup.php`	Initiates the Smarty class files and contains variables used elsewhere in the program.
`header.php`	The header layout file for the program. This file contains some logic to determine what to output to the `header.tpl` file. Templates used: `header.tpl`
`view.php`	Displays ad details. Templates used: `view.tpl`
`register.php`	Registration form. Templates used: `register_form.tpl`, `reg_field_error.tpl`, `reg_email_error.tpl`, `reg_success.tpl`

File Name	Purpose
`ad_form.php`	File that handles adding, editing, and deleting of ads. Templates used: `ad_success.tpl`, `delete_success.tpl`, `perm_error.tpl`, `view.tpl`
`functions.php`	The file which contains the main functions for the system.
`header.tpl`	Template for the title bar category navgation and side navigation of the layout.
`footer.tpl`	Template for the bottom of the program pages.
`categories.tpl`	The template file that prints the classified ad categories and sub-categories.
`adlisting.tpl`	Template that prints the list of articles within a selected category.
`view.tpl`	Template file that displays the selected classified ad details.
`register_form.tpl`	Template that displays the form, and also displays error messages if the form submission was not complete.
`reg_email_err.tpl`	Error message displayed if the e-mail address already exists in the database.
`reg_field_error.tpl`	Error message displayed if there were missing/incorrect fields.
`ad_form.tpl`	Template containing the **Ad a Classified Ad** form – also displays errors if the required fields are missing/incomplete.
`ad_success.tpl`	Template containing the success message displayed upon successful completion of inserting a new ad.
`edit_success.tpl`	Template containing the success message displayed upon successful completion of editing an ad.
`delete_success.tpl`	Template containing the success message displayed upon successful deletion of an ad.
`general_error.tpl`	Template containing generic error page letting the user know that something went wrong.
`perm_error.tpl`	Template containing the error message notifying the user that they do not have access to the page they are trying to reach (for example, if they are trying to create an ad while not logged in).

The focus of this section is not so much on how good the site looks, but on how easy to use it is. Hence, we need to plan the interface to make the web site as user friendly as possible.

Using just HTML and **CSS (Cascading Style Sheets)**, we can easily create a good layout for the application.

The following page is the home page for the site:

We now have a good idea of what the main layout of the site is going to be; left-sided navigation with most of the dynamic areas in the central frame of the page.

Since this classified board supports multiple categories and sub-categories, users will be able to jump up to any previous level, no matter where they are in a category without needing to use the BACK button on their browser. For example:

Home > Category 1 > Subcategory 1

Before we plan our ad-listing page, we need to remind ourselves of one thing. Lists can get long and tedious to scroll through, so we will build in page numbering. The results will then be broken up across several pages if the content extends over one page.

There are only a handful of modifications we need to make, and most of them are in the navigation area, which will be broken up into separate files. When the user is logged in, the navigation bar changes to display a **Create New Ad** button, as well as a **LogOut** button. The **Register** link will not appear, as the user is already registered.

The user can register by clicking on the **Register** button on the navigation bar, which leads to the page shown below:

During the registration process, the form goes through a series of server-side data validations to ensure that the data provided by the user is relevant and complete.

We could also add client-side validations using JavaScript if we wish, but given a choice server-side should always be picked. Client-side validation relies on the user's browser, and can easily be by-passed by disabling JavaScript in their browser preferences.

The screenshot below shows the registration error page, which is the same as the registration form page with error messages below the fields that have errors:

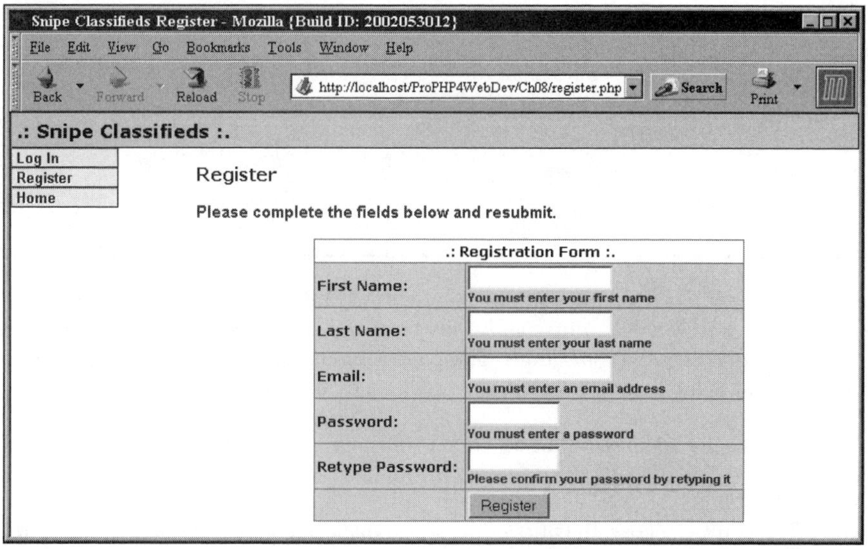

The login screen is displayed when the user clicks on the Log In link on the navigation bar:

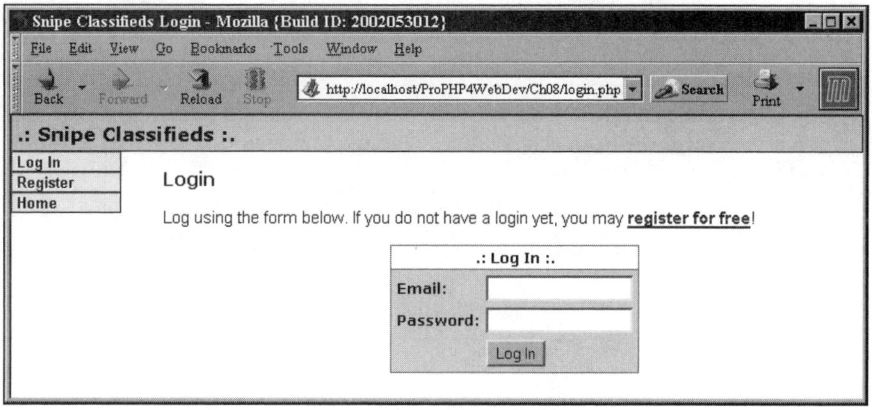

After the user attempts to log in, the script will check the database for a correct match. If it does not find one, the login form will be re-displayed with an error message.

The login confirmation page is presented to the user as the result of a successful login attempt. This page lists the ads the user has previously entered, enabling quick access to them. Now the user may add, delete, or modify the ads:

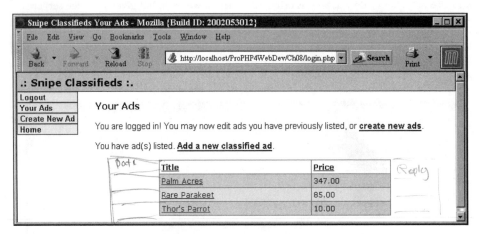

If the user decides to edit an ad, the edit link on the View Ad Details page must be clicked. On the Edit page, the user will see a screen that prints out the edit form and allows them to change any of the fields, including modifying the category associations. This page is similar to the Create New Ad page with all the details already present in the fields. These may be modified by the user.

If they choose to delete the ad, they will be asked to confirm this before the ad gets deleted, as the action cannot be undone.

When the user clicks on a category, the titles of the ads in that category are displayed. This screenshot appears when the user is logged in and clicks on any of the ad titles:

Remember that the loggedin and not loggedin rules apply for the entire system; so all pages need to have their navigation bars modified accordingly.

If the user is logged in and is the one who created the ad, there will also be an option to edit or delete the ad.

Finally, the form that the link **Create New Ad** leads to, where we can enter information about the ad that we want to post, is shown below:

Looks good so far, so now we will start planning how this site will work.

The Look and Feel

The look and feel should be built into a common HTML file, so we can have uniformity in the appearance of the web site. As we have already established that we'll be using the Smarty template engine, this should be easy enough to do. We'll also be using CSS to control some of the layout details such as fonts, table background colors, and so on.

setup.php

First we'll first address the file that initiates Smarty. We need to change the path names to reflect the location of our Smarty installation, and the database login information to match our database access.

Additionally, we need to ensure that our template files are placed in the directory specified in the `$this->template` setting. We incorporate all of this information in the following file called `setup.php`:

```php
<?php
// file setup.php - the file that initializes the Smarty templates

define('SMARTY_DIR', "/Smarty/");
require_once(SMARTY_DIR."Smarty.class.php");

class Smarty_Classified extends Smarty {
    function Smarty_Classified()
    {
        $this->template_dir = "/smarty/templates";
        $this->compile_dir = "/smarty/lib/templates_c";
        $this->config_dir = "/smarty/lib/configs";
        $this->cache_dir = "/smarty/lib/cache";
        $this->caching = "0";
    }
}

$smarty = new Smarty_Classified();


// Connection to the MySQL database
mysql_connect('localhost','uname','upwd');
if (!mysql_select_db('adboard'))
{
    $smarty->
    assign('errmsg',"Cannot access database:".mysql_error()."<br />\n");
    $smarty->display('header.tpl');
    $smarty->display('loginerr.tpl');
    $smarty->display('footer.tpl');
    die;
}
```

To make things easier, we'll include a variable we'll address later, which specifies the number of ads that should be listed on each page:

```php
// Variable that determines how many ad listings should be displayed per page
$user_view_limit = "10";

// END of setup.php
?>
```

style.css

Our header and footer files refer to the CSS file for formatting. Here's what our CSS file, named `style.css`, looks like:

```
/* file: style.css */

/* SIDE BUTTON LINKS */
a.sidenav:Link {
color: //000000;
text-decoration: none;
white-space:nowrap;
}

a.sidenav:Visited {
color: //2E2E2E;
text-decoration: none;
white-space:nowrap;
}
. . .
```

The entire stylesheet has not been included for restrictions of space. However, it is available with the code download at the web site for this book, http://www.wrox.com/.

header.tpl and footer.tpl

Now we can create our header and footer template files. Smarty allows us to place variable information inside our template files using curly braces. So, in a template file if we wanted to echo the value of `$foo`, we would simply write `{$foo}`.

Although the purpose of templaing systems such as Smarty is to remove the functionality from the presentation, Smarty uses its own basic scripting syntax that will allow us to apply simple logic in our template files. An example of this would be:

```
{if $page_title ne ""}
    {$page_title}
{/if}
```

All this code does is evaluate whether the value of `$page_title` is equal to " " or not, with "ne" meaning "not equal to" in Smarty syntax.

With this out of the way, let's take a look at our `header.tpl` file:

```
<html>
  <head>
    <title>Snipe Classifieds
    {if $page_title ne  ""}
        {$page_title}
    {/if}
    </title>
  <link rel="stylesheet" href="style.css" type="text/css" />
  </head>
  <body>
    <table border="0" cellspacing="0" cellpadding="0" width="100%">
      <tr>
        <td class="titlebar" colspan="2">
        <!-- start title bar content -->
        <span class="titletxt">.: Snipe Classifieds :.</span>
        <!-- end title bar content -->
        </td>
      </tr>
      <!-- begin topnav -->
      <tr>
        <td valign="top">
          <table border="0" cellspacing="0" cellpadding="0" width="100"
                class="darkbg">
          {if $logged_in eq  "1"}
            <tr>
              <td class="sidenavbar">
              <a href="logout.php?cat_id={$cat_id}" class="sidenav">
                Logout </a>
              </td>
            </tr>
            <tr>
              <td class="sidenavbar">
                <a href="login.php?cat_id={$cat_id}" class="sidenav">
                   Your Ads </a>
              </td>
            </tr>
            <tr>
              <td class="sidenavbar">
                <a href="ad_form.php" class="sidenav">
                   Create New Ad </a>
              </td>
            </tr>
            {else}
            <tr>
              <td class="sidenavbar">
                <a href="login.php?cat_id={$cat_id}" class="sidenav">
                   Log In </a>
```

```
                    </td>
                  </tr>
                  <tr>
                    <td class="sidenavbar">
                      <a href="register.php" class="sidenav">  Register </a>
                    </td>
                  </tr>
                  {/if}
                  <tr>
                    <td class="sidenavbar">
                      <a href="index.php" class="sidenav"> Home </a>
                    </td>
                  </tr>
                </table>
              </td>
              <td>
              <table border="0" cellspacing="0" cellpadding="0" width="100%">
                <tr>
                  <td class="navbar">{$show_trail}</td>
                </tr>
                <tr>
                  <td class="body">
                  {if $page_title ne  ""}
                      <h3>{$page_title}</h3>
                  {/if}
```

We've used the Smarty {if $foo ne ""} logic here to display the title of the page. The $page_title variable will be set in each of our subsequent main script pages. We'll also evaluate the $logged_in variable, which is set to 1 only if the user is logged in. This process is handled by our session.php file, which we will come to in due course.

By evaluating whether or not the user is logged in, we can correctly display the relevant side navigation bar. For example, if the user is logged in, we don't want the Log In or Register buttons to appear in the navigation, as that would be confusing to the user. On the other hand, we do want to display a link for the user to logout, view their ads, and create a new ad.

Additionally, there is a {$show_trail} variable in the header template. This is going to be used for the category trail shown in the screenshots. Next up is the footer.tpl file:

```
          </td>
        </tr>
      </table>
    </td>
  </tr>
  <!-- end topnav -->
  </table>
  </body>
</html>
```

As we can see, all this file does is close the table and the other HTML tags that were opened in header.tpl.

header.php

We'll need a `header.php` file in addition to the `header.tpl` file, to call the `header.tpl` file. This file is elemental in creating the top category navigtion trail at the top of the screen:

```php
<?php
    // show the header template file
    $smarty->display('header.tpl');

?>
```

Now let's put them all together; for this we create a file named `index-test.php`:

```php
<?php
//file: index-test.php

// include the Smarty setup file
include_once("setup.php");
include_once("header.php");

?>

<p>This is a test!</p>

<?php
// load the footer template
$smarty->display('footer.tpl');
?>
```

When we access `index-test.php`, we should see the whole page in its proper layout, with the words "This is a test !" in the main white part of the page.

general_error.tpl

Before we go any further, we need to create the `general_error.tpl` file. This file is used by most of the other files in this program to let the user know that an error has occured. When the database runs into problems and cannot complete the task, this template gets pulled in:

```html
<!-- begin generic error message - general_error.tpl -->

<p class="errortxt">An error has occurred. Please contact the web site
administrator.</p>

<!-- end generic error message - general_error.tpl -->
```

Delivering the Content

The program needs to know whether or not the user is logged in so it can determine whether or not to allow a new ad to be posted, or existing ads be edited. This authenticating piece of code will act as a "wrapper" for the rest of the pages in the system, when the user is logged in. So we will put all the code that determines whether or not the user is logged in, (or whether or not the login information they have provided is valid), into a separate file and include it in all the pages of the program.

session.php

In the login form, we'll pass a variable called $action through a hidden form tag. The $action variable will be set to logging_in if the user is attempting to submit login information. Because we need to accomplish two different things depending on what the user is trying to do, we'll build the SQL query accordingly. If they are trying to login, we need to check their submitted information within the database. If they have already logged in, we just need to verify that they are authentic users. This is important because we need to ensure that they cannot add, edit, or delete ads unless they have access.

Our session will contain two session variables – $logged_in and $login_id. The $logged_in variable is used to help determine the side navigation (as seen in header.tpl) and ensure that the user is allowed to create a new ad. The $login_id session variable is used to make sure users cannot edit or delete any ads that they did not create.

Let's look at the session.php file:

```php
<?php
// file: session.php

// If the user is NOT logging out
if (!isset($logout)) {

    // The user is trying to log in, or has already logged in
    if (($_POST['action']=="logging_in") || (isset($_SESSION['logged_in']))) {
        // if they are logged in
        if ($_SESSION['logged_in']==1) {
            $sql = "SELECT user_id FROM adboard_users WHERE ";
            $sql .="user_id ='".$_SESSION['login_id']."'";

            // if they are submitting login information to try to login
        } elseif ((!empty($_POST['login_email']))&&
                            (!empty($_POST['login_password']))) {
            $sql = "SELECT user_id FROM adboard_users WHERE ";
            $sql .="user_email ='".$_POST['login_email'];
            $sql .="'AND user_password='".$_POST['login_password']."'";
            // If they are submit an empty form, unset the login status
            // Also set a login failed flag, and a useful message -
            // the message will be printed out in the login form
        } else {

            unset($_SESSION['login']);
            unset($_SESSION['logged_in']);
            $login_failed=1;
            $login_error_msg = "You must enter a username and password ";
            $login_error_msg .=" to log in.";


        }
```

```php
            // if a sql query has been created (above) - query the database
        if (!empty($sql)) {
            if ($get_user = mysql_query($sql)) {
                $valid_user = mysql_num_rows($get_user);
                // If the user is valid, set the session information
                if ($valid_user==1) {
                    list($login_id) = mysql_fetch_row($get_user);
                    $_SESSION['login_id'] = $login_id;
                    $_SESSION['logged_in'] = 1;

                    $smarty->assign('logged_in',$_SESSION['logged_in']);
                    $smarty->assign('this_user_id', $_SESSION['login_id']);

                    // if the login failed, let the user know
                } else {
                    $login_failed=1;
                    unset($_SESSION['login']);
                    unset($_SESSION['logged_in']);
                    $login_error_msg = "That username and/or password does not
                                        exist in our database.";
                }
            }
        }

    // If the user is logging out, unset the session variables
    } elseif (isset($logout)) {
        unset($_SESSION['login_id']);
        unset($_SESSION['logged_in']);
        $login_error_msg = "You have successfully logged out.";
}

// END session.php

?>
```

login.tpl

Now that we have our session code set up, let's create the login. We'll start by creating the template file that the `login.php` page will use to display the form and results:

```
<!-- Begin login.tpl -->

<p>Log using the form below. If you do not have a login yet, you may <b><a
href="register.php">register for free</a></b>!</p>
<center>
<table cellspacing="0" cellpadding="0" border="0" width="200" class="ltrtablebg">
  <tr>
    <td class="ltrtablebg">
      <table cellspacing="1" cellpadding="2" border="0" width="200"
             class="ltrtablebg">
        <tr><td class="whheading" align="center">.: Log In :.</td></tr>
        <tr>
          <td class="result-line">
            <form method="post" action="login.php">
            <center>
              <table cellspacing="0" cellpadding="3" border="0">
                <tr>
                  <td class="result-line"><b>Email:</b></td>
                  <td class="result-line"><input type="text" name="login_email">
                  </td>
                </tr>
                <tr>
                  <td class="result-line"><b>Password:</b></td>
                  <td class="result-line">
                    <input type="password" name="login_password">
                  </td>
                </tr>
                <tr>
                  <td class="result-line"> </td>
                  <td class="result-line">
                    <input type="submit" value="Log In">
                    <input type="hidden" name="action" value="logging_in">
                    <input type="hidden" name="cat_id" value="{$cat_id}">
                  </td>
                </tr>
              </table>
            </center>
            </form>
          </td>
        </tr>
      </table>
    </td>
  </tr>
</table>
</center>

<!-- End login.tpl -->
```

In this login form, we will pass several variables:

- ❑ `$login_email`
  The user's submitted e-mail address.

- ❑ `$login_password`
  The user's password.

- ❑ `$action`
  The hidden field that lets `session.php` know that the user is logging in.

- ❑ `$cat_id`
  The ID of the category that the user accessed the login page from. This is used to take the user to the same category navigation at the top of the screen from before clicking on the login link.

login.php

Next we create `login.php`, which is the actual script that will call `login.tpl`. Notice that we include the `setup.php` file at the very top of the file:

```php
<?php
include_once("setup.php");
include_once("session.php");

// If the user is not logged in, assign the  "Login" page title
if ((empty($_SESSION['logged_in'])) || $login_error_msg==1) {
    $print_page_title = "Login";
// If they ARE logged in, this page will display their ad listings, so
// title the page appropriately
} else {
    $print_page_title = "Your Ads";
}

// assign the $page_title variable to the Smarty template
$smarty->assign('page_title',$print_page_title);

// if a category ID was passed, assign it to the Smarty template
if (!empty($_REQUEST['cat_id'])){
    $smarty->assign('cat_id',$_REQUEST['cat_id']);
}

// Include the header.php file
include_once("header.php");


// If the login failed, assign the error message created by session.php to the
// Smarty template so that the user knows what they did wrong. Also tell
// Smarty to load up the login form again, to let them try again
if ((empty($_SESSION['logged_in'])) || $login_error_msg==1) {
    if ($login_failed=1) {
        $smarty->assign('print_msg', $login_error_msg);
        $smarty->display('loginerr.tpl');
        // load the login template
```

```
        $smarty->display('login.tpl');
    }

}
// load the footer template
$smarty->display('footer.tpl');
?>
```

loginerr.tpl

Finally, we create the `loginerr.tpl` template, which simply displays the error that `session.php` came up with during the authentication attempt:

```
<!-- begin loginerr.tpl -->
<p class="errortxt">{$print_msg}</p>
<!-- end loginerr.tpl -->
```

We should be able to test this page by loading `login.php` and using the sample login that we inserted into the database.

functions.php

The login page will list the user's ads. We'll keep most of the main functions in a separate file so that they can be shared across all of the script pages. The file we'll store our functions in is called `functions.php`.

We're going to allow the user to sort the results by title or price. Hence, we will have to incorporate this logic in the function that gets the list of categories, `GetCategories()`.

We start off by coding the `PageNumbers()` function that breaks up the results across pages if the ad count goes beyond a certain fixed limit. We'll need this function for the page that displays the ad listings.

We'll pass two arguments to this function:

- ❑ `$totalrows`
  The total number of results, without breaking them down by page

- ❑ `$print_query`
  The text string that should be added to the links to carry variable values across multiple pages

Notice that we globalize the `$user_limit_view` variable we set in `setup.php`. We also need to make sure that the `$smarty` variable is globalized so that the function has access to the Smarty classes:

```
<?php
// File: functions.php


function PageNumbers($totalrows, $print_query)
{
    global $user_view_limit;
    global $smarty;
```

```php
    /* if there is no page number passed, assign $page the value of 1 */
    if ((empty($_REQUEST['page'])) || ($_REQUEST['page'] <= 0)){
        $page = 1;
    } else {
        $page =  $_REQUEST['page'];
    }

    $page_num_links .="<div class=\"numtext\" align=\"right\"><b>Pages:</b> ";

    /* PREV LINK: print a Prev link, if the page number is not 1 */
    if($page != 1) {
        $pageprev = $page - 1;
        $page_num_links .="<a href=\"".$_SERVER['PHP_SELF'].$print_query.
                        "page=".$pageprev."\"> &lt;Prev</a> ";
    }

    /* get the total number of pages that are needed */
    $numofpages = $totalrows/$user_view_limit;

    /* loop through the page numbers and print them out */
    for($i= 0; $i < $numofpages; $i++) {
    /* if the page number in the loop is not the same as the page we're
on, make it a link */
        $real_page = $i + 1;
        if ($real_page!=$page){
            $page_num_links .=" <a href=\"".$_SERVER['PHP_SELF'].$print_query."
                page= ".$real_page."\" class=\"numlinks\">".$real_page."</a> ";

            /* otherwise, if the loop page number is the same as the page
            we're on, do not make it a link, but rather just print it out */
        } else {
            $page_num_links .="<b>".$real_page."</b>";
        }
    }

    /* NEXT LINK - If the totalrows - $user_view_limit * $page is > 0
     (meaning there is a remainder), print the Next button. */
    if(($totalrows-($user_view_limit*$page)) > 0){
        $pagenext = $page + 1;
        $page_num_links .=" <a href=\"".$_SERVER['PHP_SELF'].$print_query.
                            "page=".$pagenext."\">Next &gt;</a> ";
    }
    $page_num_links .="</div>";

    // assign the page numbering to a Smarty variable so we can use it in the
    // template
    $smarty->assign('page_num_links', $page_num_links);

    return $page_num_links;
}
```

The GetAdsInCat() function gets the ID, title, and price of the ads within any specified category. Notice that we once again globalize the $user_limit_view variable we set in setup.php. As this listing may need to be broken up across several pags depending on the number that match the criteria in the database, we need to fix the number of ads that should be listed on each page.

To this function, we'll pass two arguments:

❑ $current_cat_id
    The ID of the current category, so the function knows which ads to display.

❑ $action
    This is used to determine whether or not the function should query the database for all the ads
    in a category, or ads belonging to the user. If the $action variable is set to memberlist, it
    implies that the function should display the ads that belong to the user.

In this function, we need to build two queries. One gets the actual data to be displayed, and the other does a count
of the matches. This is used to determine whether or not the PageNumbers() function needs to be called:

```php
/* GET THE LIST OF ADS WITHIN THE CURRENT CATEGORY */
function GetAdsInCat($current_cat_id, $action)
{
    global $user_view_limit;
    global $smarty;

    /* if there is no page // passed, assign $page the value of 1 */
    if ((empty($_REQUEST['page'])) || ($_REQUEST['page'] <= 0)){
        $page = 1;
    } else {
        $page = $_REQUEST['page'];
    }

    // if there is no category ID given assign it a value of 0
    if (empty($current_cat_id)) {
        $current_cat_id = 0;
    }

    // set some defaults and make some decisions about the column ordering
    // we'll set the sql order to order by title, asc if no sorting
    //  values are passed
    if (!isset($_REQUEST['orderby'])) {
        $orderby = "title";
    } else {
        $orderby = $_REQUEST['orderby'];
    }

    if (!isset($_REQUEST['order'])) {
        $order = "asc";
    } else {
        $order = $_REQUEST['order'];
    }

    // Sets up the "flag" that will show the user what column they are
    // sorting by
    if ($_REQUEST['orderby'] == "title"){
        $title_flag= "*";
        $price_flag= "";
    }
    if ($_REQUEST['orderby'] == "price"){
```

```
    $title_flag= "";
    $price_flag= "*";
}


// Now let's switch the sort order so the next time they click on the
// column header, it swiches to sort the opposite way
if ($_REQUEST['order']=="asc") {
    $new_order="desc";
} elseif ($_REQUEST['order']=="desc") {
    $new_order="asc";
} else {
    $new_order="asc";
}


/* $print_query is used by the function  to build the hyperlink on the
"Next/Prev" links - it allows us to retain the category number
and sort order across multiple pages, and for each new sort done
by the user */

// print query is used for the table headers
$print_query ="?cat_id=".$current_cat_id."&order=".$new_order."&";

// print_num_query is used for the page numbering
$print_num_query ="?cat_id=".$current_cat_id;
$print_num_query .="&order=".$order."&orderby=".$orderby."&";

// now assign those to the smarty variables so that we can use them in
// our templates
$smarty->assign('print_string',$print_query);
$smarty->assign('price_flag',$price_flag);
$smarty->assign('title_flag',$title_flag);


/* this code figures out the limit for the sql statement that actually
gets that page's item data */
$limitvalue = $page*$user_view_limit-($user_view_limit);

// if this function is being called from login.php, build the query
// that gets the logged in users' ads
if ($action=="memberlist") {

    /* query for the data using the limits from $limitvalue (if needed)  */
    $sql ="SELECT ad_detail_id,ad_detail_title,ad_detail_price FROM
          ad_ details";
    $sql .= " WHERE ad_detail_userid=" . $_SESSION['login_id'];
    $sql .= " order by $orderby $order LIMIT $limitvalue, $user_view_limit  ";

    /* get the total number of matching results */
    $sqlcount ="SELECT count(*) FROM adboard_ad_details WHERE
                ad_detail_userid=$".
    $_SESSION['login_id'];
```

```php
    // Otherwise, if this function is not being called with memberlist as
    // the argument, get the results that match the category ID
} else {
    $sql ="SELECT a.ad_detail_id, a.ad_detail_title, a.ad_detail_price FROM
            adboard_ad_details AS a, ";
    $sql .="adboard_ad_category_join AS j WHERE j.category_join_cat_id =
            $current_cat_id ";
    $sql .= "and a.ad_detail_id=j.category_join_ad_id order by $orderby ";
    $sql .= "$order LIMIT $limitvalue, $user_view_limit";
    $sqlcount ="SELECT count(*) FROM ad_details a,
                adboard_ad_category_join j ";
    $sqlcount .="WHERE j.category_join_cat_id=$current_cat_id ";
    $sqlcount .="and a.ad_detail_id=j.category_join_ad_id";
}

// assign the total number query results a variable name
$sql_countresult = mysql_query($sqlcount);
list($totalrows) = mysql_fetch_row($sql_countresult);

$res = mysql_query($sql);
$num_ads = mysql_num_rows($res);

// if there are no matching ads in the category, and the category isn't
// the top level, print out a useful message
if ($num_ads < 1){
    if ($current_cat_id!=0){
        $ads_msg = "No ads in ". get_cat_name($current_cat_id). ". ";
    }
}

// if there are matching ads, print out the number of matches
if ($num_ads > 0){
    if ($action=="memberlist") {
        $ads_msg = "You have $totalrows ad(s) listed. ";
    } else {
    $ads_msg = "There are $totalrows ad(s) listed in this category. ";
}

// put the results into an array
$ad_results = array();
$i=0;
while ($r=mysql_fetch_array($res)) {
        $tmp = array(
            'ad_id' => $r['ad_detail_id'],
            'ad_title'=> $r['ad_detail_title'],
            'ad_price'=> $r['ad_detail_price']
        );
        $ad_results[$i++] = $tmp;
}

// if the total number of results is greater than the number of
// results allowed per page, call the page numbering function
if ($totalrows > $user_view_limit) {
    PageNumbers($totalrows, $print_num_query);
}
}
```

```
    // If the user is logged in, print a link to add a new ad
    if ($_SESSION['logged_in']==1) {
        $ads_msg .= "<b><a href=\"ad_form.php\">Add a ";
        $ads_msg .="new classified ad</a></b>.";
    // If they are not logged in, let them know they can login or
    // register
    } else {
        $ads_msg .= "<b><a href=\"login.php\">Login</a></b> or ";
        $ads_msg .="<b><a href=\"register.php\">register</a></b> to ";
        $ads_msg .="create new ads.";
    }

    // Now assign the $ads_msg to the Smarty template
    $smarty->assign('ads_msg',$ads_msg);

    // and return the results array
    return $ad_results;
}
?>
```

adlisting.tpl

Now we need to create the template file that contains Smarty variables that are used to display the HTML table with the data – called `adlisting.tpl`. These Smarty vriable names should look familiar – they are the variables we assigned values to using `$smarty->assign("foo", $bar)` in the functions above.

Using the Smarty scripting, we'll set up a loop to have alternate row colors:

- ❑   `{section name=ads loop=$ad_results}` – assigns a name to the loop
- ❑   `{if $smarty.section.ads.iteration is odd}` – allows the template to alternate between the row colors.

Notice how we have to refer to Smarty variables differently when we're in a loop; instead of just writing `{$ad_title}`, we have to specify `{$ad_results[ads].ad_title}`. To break that down, `$ad_results` is the name of the variable we are extracting the information from, ads is the name we assigned the section, and `$ad_title` is the Smarty variable we use:

```
<!—begin adlisting.tpl -->

<p>{$ads_msg}</p>
{if count($ad_results) gt 0}
    <center>
    <table cellpadding=3 cellspacing=1 border=0 width=400 class="ltrtablebg">
      {if $page_num_links ne ""}
      <td class="numtext" colspan="2">{$page_num_links}</td>
      {/if}
      <tr>
        <td class="whheading">
        <a href="index.php{$print_string}orderby=ad_detail_title">
        {$title_flag}Title{$title_flag}</a></td>
        <td class="whheading">
```

```
            <a href="index.php{$print_string}orderby=ad_detail_price">
            {$price_flag}Price{$price_flag}</a>
          </td>
        </tr>
        {section name=ads loop=$ad_results}
        <tr>
          <td{if $smarty.section.ads.iteration is odd} class="result-line" {else}
           class="result-line-alt" {/if}>
            <a href="view.php?ad_id={$ad_results[ads].ad_id}&cat_id={$ad_cat_id}">
            {$ad_results[ads].ad_title}</a></td>
          <td{if $smarty.section.ads.iteration is odd} class="result-line"{else}
          class="result-line-alt" {/if}>
          {$ad_results[ads].ad_price}</td>
        </tr>
        {/section}
        {if $page_num_links ne ""}
          <td class="numtext" colspan="2">{$page_num_links}</td>
        {/if}
      </table>
      </center>
      {/if}

<!-- end adlisting.tpl -->
```

Now let's return to our login.php page. Since we have two of our core functions in place, we can add the functionality of being able to list the user's ads on the page. We need to add the include() for functions.php and then also add in the function call to get the ads for the user:

```php
<?php
include_once("setup.php");
include_once("session.php");
include_once("functions.php");
if ((empty($_SESSION['logged_in'])) || $login_error_msg==1) {
    $print_page_title = "Login";
} else {
    $print_page_title = "Your Ads";
}
$smarty->assign('page_title',$print_page_title);

if (!empty($_REQUEST['cat_id'])){
    $smarty->assign('cat_id',$_REQUEST['cat_id']);
}
include_once("header.php");


if ((empty($_SESSION['logged_in'])) || $login_error_msg==1) {
    if ($login_failed=1) {
        $smarty->assign('print_msg', $login_error_msg);
        $smarty->display('loginerr.tpl');
        // load the login template
        $smarty->display('login.tpl');
    }

// Now add in the function call to GetAdsInCat() to display the users ads
} else {

    $ad_results = GetAdsInCat($_GET['cat_id'], "memberlist");
```

```
        // pass the results to the template
        $smarty->display('logintxt.tpl');
        $smarty->assign('ad_results', $ad_results);


        // load the ad listing template
        $smarty->display('adlisting.tpl');

}
// load the footer template
$smarty->display('footer.tpl');
?>
```

Now if we reload the login.php page, we'll be able to see a listing of all the ads assigned to the test user who has logged in.

logout.php

The users have a way to login now, but no way to logout, so we'll address that issue next. Fortunately, most of the real work in this has been handled already by session.php. All we need to do is create a page that sets the $logout variable, and lets users know when they have logged out. For this we will need to create just one new file – logout.php the file that sets the $logout variable and calls the templates. This script calls for the loginerr.tpl and login.tpl templates; which we created when we built the login system.

The key code in this file is the $logout=1 line at the very top of the page, which tells session.php that the user has logged out, and unsets the session variables:

```
<?php
// file: logout.php

$logout=1;
include_once("setup.php");
include_once("session.php");
include_once("functions.php");
$print_page_title = "Log Out";
$smarty->assign('page_title',$print_page_title);
include_once("header.php");

$smarty->assign('print_msg', $login_error_msg);

// print the $login_err_msg created by session.php, and then display
// the login box
$smarty->display('loginerr.tpl');
$smarty->display('login.tpl');

// load the footer template
$smarty->display('footer.tpl');
?>
```

register.php

Now, let's create the registration page so that new users can register to post ads. The PHP file will be named `register.php`, and will use the following template files:

- ❏ `register_form.tpl` – the template form
- ❏ `reg_email_error.tpl` – error message explaining that the e-mail address already exists in the database
- ❏ `general_error.tpl` – generic error if an error occurs in the database query (already created)
- ❏ `reg_success.tpl` – the success page
- ❏ `login.tpl` – the login box (already created)

We'll get the error templates out of the way first, as they are just static template files. Starting first with the error alerting the user that the e-mail address already exists in the database – `reg_email_error.tpl`:

```
<!-- begin reg_email_error.tpl-->
<p class="errortxt">Sorry - it appears as though a user with that e-mail address
is already registered.</p>

<!-- end reg_email_error.tpl -->
```

And now we create `reg_field_error.tpl` to let the user of a forgotten required field, or if information was entered incorrectly:

```
<!-- begin reg_field_error.tpl-->
<p class="errortxt">Please complete the fields below and resubmit.</p>

<!-- end reg_field_error.tpl-->
```

Both of these error templates will be used in conjunction with `register_form.tpl`, so that the user doesn't reach a dead-end with an error and use the **BACK** button. Instead the user will see the error message, and then have the opportunity to edit the form entry.

We still have to create `reg_success.tpl`, that lets the users know that they've successfully registered and may now begin posting ads:

```
<!-- begin reg_success.tpl -->
<p>Success!  Your account has been successfully created!  You may now sign in and
begin creating ads!</p>

<!-- end reg_success.tpl -->
```

This will be used in conjunction with `login.tpl` to deliver the success message.

The next step is to create the registration form template itself. Once again, we'll use Smarty scripting, but it should be fairly simple:

```
<!-- begin register_form.tpl -->
<center>
<form method="post" action="register.php">
<table cellspacing="0" cellpadding="0" border="0" width="400" class="ltrtablebg">
  <tr>
    <td class="ltrtablebg">
      <table cellspacing="1" cellpadding="2" border="0" width="400"
             class="ltrtablebg">
        <tr>
          <td class="whheading" align="center" colspan="2">:Registration Form</td>
        </tr>
        <tr>
          <td class="result-line"><b>First Name:</b></td>
          <td class="result-line">
            <input type="text" name="reg_firstname" maxlength="25" value="
            {if $reg_firstname ne  ""}{$reg_firstname}{/if}"><br>
            {if $firstname_err ne  ""}
            <span class="formerror">{$firstname_err}</span>{/if}
          </td>
        </tr>
        <tr>
          <td class="result-line"><b>Last Name:</b></td>
          <td class="result-line">
          <input type="text" name="reg_lastname" maxlength="25" value="
          {if $reg_lastname ne  ""}{$reg_lastname}{/if}"><br>
          {if $lastname_err ne  ""}<span class="formerror">{$lastname_err}</span>
          {/if}
          </td>
        </tr>
        <tr>
          <td class="result-line"><b>Email:</b></td>
          <td class="result-line">
            <input type="text" name="reg_email" maxlength="50" value="{if
            $reg_email ne  ""}{$reg_email}{/if}"><br>
            {if $email_err ne  ""}<span class="formerror">{$email_err}</span>
            {/if}</td>
        </tr>
        <tr>
          <td class="result-line"><b>Password:</b></td>
          <td class="result-line">
            <input type="password" name="reg_password" size="12" maxlength="12"
                   value=""><br>
          {if $password_err ne  ""}
          <span class="formerror">{$password_err}</span> {/if}
          {if $match_password_err ne  ""}<br>
          <span class="formerror">{$match_password_err}</span>{/if}
          </td>
        </tr>
        <tr>
```

```
            <td class="result-line"><b>Retype Password:</b></td>
            <td class="result-line">
            <input type="password" name="reg_confirm_password" size="12"
                   maxlength="12" value=""><br>
            {if $confirm_password_err ne  ""}
            <span class="formerror">{$confirm_password_err}</span>{/if}
            {if $match_password_err ne  ""}<br>
            <span class="formerror">{$match_password_err}</span>{/if}
            </td>
        </tr>
        <tr>
            <td class="result-line"> </td>
            <td class="result-line">
               <input type="hidden" name="register_user" value="1">
               <input type="submit" value="Register"></td>
        </tr>
      </table>
    </td>
  </tr>
</table>
</center></form>

<!-- end register_form.tpl -->
```

A vast majority of this file is plain HTML, however we can easily see what we're doing with the few pieces of Smarty scripting as well. Each of the required fields has a bit of code that looks like this, underneath them:

```
{if $firstname_err ne  ""}<span class="formerror">{$firstname_err}</span>{/if}
```

These $foo_err variables are set by the register.php form when there is a problem with the field entry. The variables contain useful error messages that let the user know exactly what went wrong.

Note the hidden form field at the bottom of the form: register_user. We assign a value of 1 to this variable, which will help register.php determine whether the form is being submitted, or accessed, for the first time.

The other bit of Smarty code simply echoes the field values back to the user, with the values filled in the first time round. If we didn't do this, the user would have to fill in the whole form all over again just because of small mistakes.

```
<input type="text"
       name="reg_firstname"
       maxlength="25"
       value="{if $reg_firstname ne ""}{$reg_firstname}{/if}">
```

The templates are all in order now, so we can create the PHP file: register.php. Notice how the file begins with including all the necessary files.

Our error check in this file will validate the data, and return a respective error if the field does not meet its requirements. The validation sequence checks if the user entered all the fields, if they were entered correctly, if the format of the e-mail ID was correct, and if the two passwords matched.

This error-checking process is more time-consuming than just doing a catch-all error check, that tells the user that they did something wrong. But it's well worth the investment of time, and effort for the increased flexibility:

```php
<?php // file: register.php

include_once("setup.php");
include_once("session.php");
include_once("functions.php");

// give the page a title
$print_page_title = "Register";
// assign that title to the template
$smarty->assign('page_title',$print_page_title);

// and now include the header
include_once("header.php");


// If register_user is equal to 1, we know that the user is
// submitting this page in an attempt to register
if ($_POST['register_user']==1) {

    // Begin the error checking
    // Did the user enter a first name?
    if (trim($_POST['reg_firstname'])=="") {
        $firstname_err="You must enter your first name ";
        $smarty->assign('firstname_err', $firstname_err);
        $are_errors=1;
    }

    // Did the user enter a last name?
    if (trim($_POST['reg_lastname'])=="") {
        $lastname_err="You must enter your last name";
        $smarty->assign('lastname_err', $lastname_err);
        $are_errors=1;
    }

    // Did the user enter an email address
    if (trim($_POST['reg_email'])=="") {
        $email_err="You must enter an email address";
        $smarty->assign('email_err', $email_err);
        $are_errors=1;
    // If an email address was entered, does it look syntactically correct?
    } else {
        if (!eregi("^[_a-z0-9-]+(\.[_a-z0-9-]+)*@[a-z0-9-]+(\.[a-z0-9-]+)*(\.[a-z]{2,3})$", $_POST['reg_email'])) {
            $email_err="Invalid email address";
            $smarty->assign('email_err', $email_err);
            $are_errors=1;
        }

    }

    // Did they enter a password?
```

```
if (trim($_POST['reg_password'])=="") {
    $password_err="You must enter a password";
    $smarty->assign('password_err', $password_err);
    $are_errors=1;
}
// Did they confirm the password?
if (trim($_POST['reg_confirm_password'])=="") {
    $confirm_password_err="Please confirm your password by retyping it";
    $smarty->assign('confirm_password_err', $confirm_password_err);
    $are_errors=1;
}
// Do the password and the confirmation match?
if (trim($_POST['reg_password'])!=trim($_POST['reg_confirm_password'])) {
    $match_password_err="Your password and password confirmation entries do
                         not match";
    $smarty->assign('match_password_err', $match_password_err);
    $are_errors=1;
}


// If there are no errors and the user is submitting the form, check
// to make sure their email address doesn't already exist

if (($are_errors!=1) && ($_POST['register_user']==1)) {
    $reg_email = $_POST['reg_email'];

// query the database for the email address
    $sql ="SELECT user_email FROM adboard_users WHERE user_email='$reg_email'";
    if ($is_dup = mysql_query($sql)) {
        $num_matches = mysql_num_rows($is_dup);

        // if there are no matches, insert the data
        if ($num_matches < 1 ) {
            $reg_firstname = addslashes($_POST['reg_firstname']);
            $reg_lastname = addslashes($_POST['reg_lastname']);
            $reg_password = $_POST['reg_password'];

            $sql ="INSERT into adboard_users(user_firstname, user_lastname, ";
            $sql .= "user_email, user_password) values ('$reg_firstname', ";
            $sql .= " '$reg_lastname', '$reg_email', ";
            $sql .= " '$reg_password')";
            // If the query went through okay, display the
            // reg_success.tpl template, and offer them a
            // login box with login.tpl
            if ($insert_user_data = mysql_query($sql)) {
                $smarty->display('reg_success.tpl');
                $smarty->display('login.tpl');
                // Otherwise, print out an error message
            } else {
                $smarty->display('general_error.tpl');

            }
            // If the email address already exists, print out the form
            // again with the values pre-filled in, and let them know
```

```
                        // that the email address exists in the database by calling
                        // the reg_smail_err.tpl
                } else {
                    $smarty->assign('reg_firstname',
                             stripslashes($_POST['reg_firstname']  ));
                    $smarty->assign('reg_lastname',
                             stripslashes($_POST['reg_lastname']));
                    $smarty->display('reg_email_error.tpl');
                    $smarty->display('register_form.tpl');
                }

            }

            // If there were errors in the submission, print out the form again
            // with the fields pre-filled in, and let the user know they missed
            // something with the reg_field_err.tpl

            } else {
             $smarty->assign('reg_firstname', stripslashes($_POST['reg_firstname']));
             $smarty->assign('reg_lastname', stripslashes($_POST['reg_lastname']));
             $smarty->assign('reg_email', stripslashes($_POST['reg_email']));

             $smarty->display('reg_field_error.tpl');
             $smarty->display('register_form.tpl');
        }
        // If they are accessing the form for the first time, just print out the
        // form template
    } else {

        $smarty->display('register_form.tpl');
    }

// load the footer template
$smarty->display('footer.tpl');
?>
```

We should be able to register new users using this form.

Additional Function : GetCategories( )

Now we have enough groundwork laid to put together the category hierarchy display so that the users can traverse through the categories and sub-categories. For this, we go back to the functions.php file to add a function that grabs all of the category names and IDs. The GetCategories() function accepts only one argument, $current_cat_id:

```
// append to file" functions.php

/* GET THE LIST OF CATEGORIES */
function GetCategories($current_cat_id)
{
    // if we're in the top level (home), set the parent category to zero
    if (empty($current_cat_id)) {
        $current_cat_id = 0;
    }

    // query the database for the ID and name of all
```

```
    // the "child" categories of the category ID being passed as
    // an argument
    $sql = "SELECT category_id, category_name FROM adboard_categories WHERE ";
    $sql .= "parent_id=$current_cat_id order by category_name asc";
    $res = mysql_query($sql);

    // Now we have to loop through the results and put them in an array
    // so that we can return them and do something useful with them
    $cat_results = array();
    $i=0;
    while ($r=mysql_fetch_array($res)) {
        $tmp = array(
        'cat_id' => $r['category_id'],
        'cat_name'=> $r['category_name']
        );
        $cat_results[$i++] = $tmp;
    }

    return $cat_results;
}
// End of GetCategories function
```

Our main category and ad display occurs on the same page, and fortunately we have already created the ad listing function and template. To make the page that will display all of the category and ad information, we have to create only two new files.

categories.tpl

The first file is `categories.tpl`, which is the Smarty template file that will do the actual displaying:

```
<!-- begin categories.tpl -->

{if count($cat_results) gt 0}
<center>
<table cellpadding="0" cellspacing="0" border="0">

{section name=catlistings loop=$cat_results}

  <tr>
    <td class="categories" nowrap="nowrap">
    <nobr><li>
    <a href="index.php?cat_id={$cat_results[catlistings].cat_id}">
    {$cat_results[catlistings].cat_name}</a></nobr>
    </td>
  </tr>
<td nowrap="nowrap">   </td>

{/section}
</table>
</center>
<br /><br/>
{/if}

<!-- end categories.tpl -->
```

Once again we've used some of the Smarty scripting code. However with a closer look, we'll see that it's quite simple.

First, we make sure there are categories to be returned, with the following line of code:

```
{if count($cat_results) gt 0}
```

This simply stands for "If the number of values in the $cat_result array is greaten than 0:", perform the following action. Put simply, the categories.tpl template takes care of the display of categories on the home page.

For more details on the Smarty scripting functions, see http://smarty.php.net/.

index.php

The following file is called index.php; this is the file that calls the GetCategories() and GetAdsInCat() functions. This file is also the home page of the application:

```php
<?php
include_once("setup.php");
include_once("session.php");
include_once("functions.php");
include_once("header.php");

// get the categories for the current category ID
$cat_results = GetCategories($_GET['cat_id']);

// pass the results to the template
$smarty->assign('cat_results', $cat_results);

// load the category template
$smarty->display('categories.tpl');

// Now get the ad listing for the current category ID
$ad_results = GetAdsInCat($_GET['cat_id'], "");

// pass the results to the template
$smarty->assign('ad_results', $ad_results);
$smarty->assign('ad_cat_id', $_GET['cat_id']);

// load the category template
$smarty->display('adlisting.tpl');

// load the footer template
$smarty->display('footer.tpl');
?>
```

We should now be able to load the index.php page, and see a listing of the sample categories we inserted into the database at the beginning of the chapter. If we click on any of the categories, it will lead to a page that contains the "child" categories for that category, as well as the ad listings in it. In turn, if we click on the child category, we will see all of the child categories and ads for that category, and so on.

Additional Function : GetCrumbs( )

The "breadcrumb trail" category navigation that appears at the top of the page, allows the user to backtrack through several parent categories, and gives them a clear picture of the category heirarchy. For example, if the user started at the homepage and then selected the Parrots category, they would have seen all of the ads and sub-categories for the Parrots category. If they knew they were in the market for a red parrot, they would have narrowed down their search by selecting the Red Parrots sub-category, where the child categories and ads for Red Parrots will be displayed. In this example, the breadcrumb trail category navigation along the top of the screen would look like this:

Home >> Parrots > Red Parrots > Small Red Parrots

With this kind of navigation, the user can quickly and easily back out of any category they were in, without having to use their browser's BACK button.

Next, we will create a function called GetCrumbs(), which will recursively cycle through the category relationships to generate this breadcrumb trail. The GetCrumbs() function takes one argument, the current category ID. We need to go back to the functions.php file and add this function there:

```php
// append to file: functions.php

/* GENERATE BREADCRUMB TRAIL */
function GetCrumbs($this_cat_id)
{
    // this forces the function to remember the array from previous iterations
    static $make_print_trail;

    if (!isset($this_cat_id)) {
        // if we are already "home", set the category ID to 0
        $this_cat_id ="0";
    }

    // if we're not on the homepage, go ahead and query
    if ((isset($this_cat_id)) && ($this_cat_id!=0)) {

        $sql = "SELECT category_parentid, category_name FROM adboard_categories
            WHERE category_id = '$this_cat_id'";
        if ($show_crumb_trail = mysql_query($sql))
            $num_crumbs = mysql_num_rows($show_crumb_trail);

        // our category is apparently valid
        if ($num_crumbs > 0) {
            list($cat_parent, $cat_name) =
                mysql_fetch_row($show_crumb_trail);
            // create the $make_print_trail array, which will store the
            // ID and the category name
            $make_print_trail[$this_cat_id] = $cat_name;

            // Now call the function again, to recurse through the chain
            // until there are no more categories left
            GetCrumbs($cat_parent);

        }
    }
    // and return the result array
    return $make_print_trail;
}
```

Now we have to go back to header.php and set up the code that will call this function to create the breadcrumb trail:

```php
<?php
// file: header.php

// If the category ID isn't empty, assign the category ID to the Smarty
// template and  start the breadcrumb function
if (!empty($_REQUEST['cat_id'])) {
    $smarty->assign('cat_id', $_REQUEST['cat_id']);
    $get_trail =    GetCrumbs($_REQUEST['cat_id']);

    // Since the trail always has to start  with "Home", set that first
    $trail = "<a href=\"index.php\">Home</a> &gt;&gt; ";
}

// If the $get_trail array has values continue wih the trail
if (count($get_trail) > 0){
    // Because the array works from the current category backwards
    // we must reverse the array to get the categories to show up in
    // the right order in the nav. We want to make sure we set the second
    // function argument to TRUE, so that the categories will
    // retain their correct ID numbers.
    $get_trail = array_reverse($get_trail, TRUE);
    // Now loop through the array and build the $trail string
    foreach ($get_trail  as $key => $value) {
            // If the ID value in the array equals the category we're
            // currently in, and he user is not viewing an ad,
            // no not make the current category name a link
            if (($_REQUEST['cat_id']==$key) && (empty($_REQUEST['ad_id']))) {
                    $trail .="$value";

                // But if the arry key oes not match the current category
                // ID and/or the user is viewing an ad, mke the category
                // name a link so they can get back easily
            } else {
                    $trail .="<a href=\"index.php?cat_id=$key\">$value</a> &gt; ";

            }

    }

}

// Now assign the $trail to the template
$smarty->assign('show_trail', $trail);

// show the header template file
$smarty->display('header.tpl');

?>
```

Additional Function: ModifyDateTime( )

Now when we reload the `index.php` page of our program, and travel through a few of the categories and sub-categories, we can see the breadcrumb trail.

Now it's time to create the files that let the user view the ad details: `view.php` and `view.tpl`. Before doing anything else, we need to add three functions to the `functions.php` file.

The first one is a quickie – `ModifyDateTime()`, used solely to convert the value of the datetime field in the database into something more user friendly:

```
// append to file: functions.php

/* PUT DATES INTO "HUMAN" FORMAT */
function ModifyDateTime($date)
{
    $break = explode(" ", $date);
    $datebreak = explode("-", $break[0]);
    $time = explode(":", $break[1]);
    $datetime = date("F j, Y - g:i A",
    mktime($time[0],$time[1],$time[2],$datebreak[1],$datebreak[2],$datebreak[0]));
    return $datetime;
}
```

Additional Function: GetCatSelectList( )

Next we add the function that will get the category select list. Although we don't need this to view the ads, we will be reusing some of these functions in the edit screens.

This function accepts two arguments: `$current_cat_id`, which is the category ID to be queried on, and `$count`, which is a counter used by the function to create an array that will store the results.

We'll notice that there is a variable called `$indent_flag` used here as well. The purpose of this variable is to incrementally indent the sub-category names in the category listing, as shown below:

```
// append to file: functions.php

/* GET THE DROP DOWN LIST OF CATEGORIES */
function GetCatSelectList($current_cat_id, $count)
{
    // make the resulting array static, so that the function remembers the
    // results of the previous iterations
```

```
    static $option_results;

    // if there is no category ID set, set $current_cat_id to 0
    if (!isset($current_cat_id)) {
        $current_cat_id =0;
    }

    // $count is used for building the array
    $count = $count+1;

    // Query the database
    $sql = "SELECT category_id, category_name FROM adboard_categories WHERE
            category_parentid = '$current_cat_id' order by category_name asc";
    $get_options = mysql_query($sql);
    $num_options = mysql_num_rows($get_options);

    // our category is apparently valid
    if ($num_options > 0) {
        while (list($cat_id, $cat_name) = mysql_fetch_row($get_options)) {
            // if the current category is not 0, build an indent flag to
            // show the user that the category is a subcategry
            if ($current_cat_id!=0) {
                $indent_flag = "  ";

                // Loop through the count to see how many indents
                // to assign to the name
                for ($x=2; $x<=$count; $x++) {
                    $indent_flag .= "--&gt; ";
                }
            }
            $cat_name = $indent_flag.$cat_name;

            // Add the result to the array
            $option_results[$cat_id] = $cat_name;

            // And now do it all over again, to recurse through
            // the categories
            GetCatSelectList($cat_id, $count );
        }   // endwhile
    } // endif
    return $option_results;
}
```

Additional Function: GetAdDetail( )

The GetAdDetail() function accepts two arguments: the current ad ID and the current category ID. Again, as a reminder, we need to make the $smarty variable global in both of these functions:

```
// append to file: functions.php

/* GET AD DETAILS */
function GetAdDetail($current_ad_id, $current_cat_id)
{
    global $smarty;

    $login_id = $_SESSION['login_id'];
```

```
// If there was no ad ID specified, throw back an error
if (!isset($current_ad_id)) {
    echo "<p class=\"errortxt\">Sorry - no ad was specified.</p>";

} else {
    // Otherwise query the database to get the ad
    $sql = "SELECT ad_detail_id, ad_detail_title, ad_detail_body,
            ad_detail_price, ad_detail_image_url, ad_detail_addedon, ";
    $sql .="ad_detail_userid FROM adboard_ad_details WHERE
            ad_detail_id=$current_ad_id";

    $get_details = mysql_query($sql);
    $is_valid_ad = mysql_num_rows($get_details);
    list($ad_id, $ad_title,  $ad_body, $ad_price, $ad_image_url,
        $ad_added_on, $ad_member_id) = mysql_fetch_row($get_details);

    // use the ModifyDateTime() function to
    // convert the dateinto something presentable
    $ad_pretty_date = ModifyDateTime($ad_added_on);

    // assign the result variable to the smarty template
    $smarty->assign('ad_is_valid', $is_valid_ad);
    $smarty->assign('ad_id', $ad_id);
    $smarty->assign('ad_title', $ad_title);
    $smarty->assign('ad_body', nl2br($ad_body));
    $smarty->assign('ad_price', $ad_price);
    $smarty->assign('ad_image_url', $ad_image_url);
    $smarty->assign('ad_added_on', $ad_pretty_date);
    $smarty->assign('ad_member_id', $ad_member_id);

    if (!empty($current_cat_id)) {
        $current_cat_name = get_cat_name($current_cat_id);
        $smarty->assign('ad_cat_name', $current_cat_name);
        $smarty->assign('ad_cat_id', $current_cat_id);
    }
    // Now we have to query the database to get the
    // information on the person who posted the ad
    // and assign their information to the smarty templates
    $sql = "SELECT user_firstname, user_lastname, user_email FROM ";
    $sql .="adboard_users WHERE user_id=$ad_member_id";
    if ($get_member_info = mysql_query($sql)) {
        $valid_member = mysql_num_rows($get_member_info);
        if ($valid_member > 0 ) {
            list($member_firstname, $member_lastname,
                $member_email) = mysql_fetch_row($get_member_info);
            $smarty->assign('member_firstname', $member_firstname);
            $smarty->assign('member_lastname',$member_lastname);
            $smarty->assign('member_email', $member_email);
        }
    }

    // And now we get the categories associated with this ad
    // This is not directly needed for view.php, but
    // we will be using this function again later in the edit
    // ad screens
```

```
        $sql = "SELECT category_join_cat_id FROM adboard_ad_category_join WHERE ";
        $sql .="category_join_ad_id='$current_ad_id'";
        if ($get_cat_info = mysql_query($sql)) {
            $cats_selected = mysql_num_rows($get_cat_info);
            // if there are categories returned, put them into
            // an array so we can work with them later
            if ($cats_selected > 0 ) {
                $x=0;
                while(list($ad_category_id) = mysql_fetch_row($get_cat_info)) {
                    $categories[$x]=$ad_category_id;
                    $x++;
                }
            }
        }
        // call the get_selectlist function to generate a
        // listbox of the categories. (This will be used
        // when editing the ad)
        $get_options = GetCatSelectList(0, 0);
        if (count($get_options) > 0){
            foreach ($get_options as $key => $value) {
                    $options .="<option value=\"$key\"";
                    for($count = 0; $count < count($categories); $count++) {
                        // if the array key is the
                        // same as the selected category
                        // ID, mark it as selected in the
                        // listbox
                        if ($categories[$count] == $key) {
                            $options .="selected=\"selected\"";
                        }
                    }
                    $options .=">$value</option>\n";
            } // end foreach

        } // end if count(get_options)

        // assign the listbox options to a Smarty variable
        $smarty->assign('options', $options);

    }
    // return that the ad ID is valid
    return $is_valid_ad;
}
```

view.tpl

With that done, we just have to create the view.php and view.tpl files. We'll start with view.tpl, the ad details display template. Remember that we want to display edit and delete options if the user is logged in and is the creator of the ad. We'll put the ad ID number into a hidden form field so that the edit or delete screens know what ad to modify. The Smarty variables used here are the ones we assigned in the GetAdDetail() function in the functions.php file.

Notice that we include Smarty scripting to check if the user has the right to edit or delete the current ad. If they do not, the buttons will not be displayed. If the member ID in the ad records matches the user's login ID, the buttons will be displayed. The hidden form fields will come into play in the ad_form.php file to help the script determine what action to take.

```
<!-- begin view.tpl -->
<center>
<form method="post" action="ad_form.php">
<input type="hidden" name="ad_id" value="{$ad_id}">
<table cellspacing="1" cellpadding="3" border="0" width="500" class="ltrtablebg">
  <tr>
    <td class="whheading" align="center" colspan="2">
    .: Details for <i>{$ad_title}</i> :.
    </td>
  </tr>
  {if $ad_body ne  ""}
  <tr><td class="result-line" colspan="2">{$ad_body}</td></tr>
  {/if}
  <tr>
    <td class="result-line"><b>Price:</b></td>
    <td class="result-line">{$ad_price}</td>
  </tr>
  <tr>
    <td class="result-line"><b>Added:</b></td>
    <td class="result-line">{$ad_added_on}</td>
  </tr>
  {if $ad_image_url ne  ""}
  <tr>
    <td class="result-line"><b>Image:</b></td>
    <td class="result-line">
    <a href="{$ad_image_url}" target=\"_new\">{$ad_image_url}</a>
    </td>
  </tr>
  {/if}
  <tr>
    <td class="result-line"><b>Contact:</b></td>
    <td class="result-line">
      <a href="mailto:{$member_email}">{$member_firstname}
      {$member_lastname}</a>
    </td>
  </tr>
  {if $ad_cat_id ne  ""}
  <tr>
    <td  class="whheading" align="center" colspan="2"><b>
    <a href="index.php?cat_id={$ad_cat_id}" class="titletxt">
    &lt;&lt;All ads in {$ad_cat_name}</a></b>
    </td>
  </tr>
  {/if}

  {if $ad_member_id eq  $this_user_id}
  <tr>
    <td class="result-line" colspan="2" align="right">
    <input type="submit" name="do_what" value="delete">
    <input type="submit" name="do_what" value="edit">
    </td>
  </tr>
  {/if}
</table>
</form>
</center>
<!-- end view.tpl -->
```

We don't want to show the user the details for an ad that has been deleted, in which case we display an error using the error template called id_error.tpl. This error message will be called upon if the ID of the ad the user is trying to view does not occur in the database.

```
<!-- begin generic error message - id_error.tpl -->

<p class="errortxt">That ID is invalid.</p>

<!-- end generic error message - id_error.tpl -->
```

view.php

Now we can create the view.php file:

```php
<?php
// file: view.php
include_once("setup.php");
include_once("session.php");
include_once("functions.php");

// give the page a nice title and assign it to Smarty
$print_page_title = "View Ad Details";
$smarty->assign('page_title',$print_page_title);

// include the header
include_once("header.php");

// call our GetAdDetail function to  return the information about the
// ad record
$ad_details = GetAdDetail($_REQUEST['ad_id'], $_REQUEST['cat_id']);

// if the record is valid, assign the results to the Smarty template
// call up the view.tpl template
if ($ad_details > 0 ) {
    $smarty->assign('ad_details', $ad_details);
    $smarty->display('view.tpl');

// if it is not valid, display the id_error.tpl message
} else {
    $smarty->display('id_error.tpl');
}

// show the footer template
$smarty->display('footer.tpl');
?>
```

We should now be able to browse through the categories and view ads in the program, with the handy breadcrumb trail along the top to help us navigate.

ad_form.php

All of our add, edit, and delete actions will be handled through one main script, `ad_form.php`. Notice that the `view.tpl` form uses this file as the form action. Before we create `ad_form.php` though, we should set up the template pages it will use. We'll get the message templates out of the way first:

`edit_success.tpl`:

```
<!-- begin edit_success.tpl -->
<p>Your ad has been successfully updated!</p>
<!-- end edit_success.tpl -->
```

`ad_success.tpl`:

```
<!-- begin ad_success.tpl -->
<p>Success!  Your ad has been successfully entered. You may <b><a
href="view.php?ad_id={$new_ad_id}">review the ad you just posted</a></b>, or <b><a
href="ad_form.php">add another classified ad</a></b> now.</p>

<!-- end ad_success.tpl -->
```

`delete_confirm.tpl`:

```
<!-- begin delete_confirm.tpl -->
<p class="errortxt">Are you SURE you wish to delete this ad? This action cannot be
undone.</p>
<table><tr><td><form method="post" action="ad_form.php"><input
name="confirm_delete" type="submit" value="Yes"> <input name="confirm_delete"
type="submit" value="No"><input type="hidden" name="ad_id" value="{$ad_id}"><input
type="hidden" name="cat_id" value="{$cat_id}"></form></td></tr></table>
<!-- end delete_confirm.tpl -->
```

`delete_success.tpl`:

```
<!-- begin delete_success.tpl -->
<h3>Success!</h3>
<p>Your ad has been deleted. You may now <b><a href="login.php">go back to your
ads listing</a></b>, or <b><a href="ad_form.php">create a new ad</a></b>.<p>

<!-- end delete_success.tpl -->
```

`perm_error.tpl`:

```
<!-- begin perm_error.tpl -->

<p class="errortxt">You are trying to access an area which requires that you are
logged in, or that your login does not allow you to access.</p>

<!-- end perm_error.tpl -->
```

Regarding the ad form template, as the error messages are brief and fairly standard, we'll be assign them to a variable called `$insert_err_msg` when there's a problem with the user's submission. We have the Smarty scripting to determine whether an error message was set by the `ad_form.php` error check. We also use a series of `{if}` statements towards the end of the form to determine what variables need to be re-displayed as hidden fields.

ad_form.tpl

This is the template that displays all the HTML controls that accept feedback from the user:

```
<!-- begin ad_form.tpl -->
{if $insert_err_msg ne    ""}
<p>{$insert_err_msg}</p>
{/if}
<center>
<form method="post" action="ad_form.php">
<table cellspacing="0" cellpadding="0" border="0" width="400" class="ltrtablebg">
  <tr>
    <td class="ltrtablebg">
      <table cellspacing="1" cellpadding="2" border="0" width="400"
        class="ltrtablebg">
        <tr>
          <td class="whheading" align="center" colspan="2">
          .: {if $ad_id ne    ""}Edit {else}Create New{/if} Classified Ad :.
          </td>
        </tr>
        <tr>
          <td class="result-line"><b>Title of Ad:</b></td>
          <td class="result-line">
            <input type="text" name="ad_title" maxlength="64" value="{if $ad_title
            ne    ""}{$ad_title}{/if}">
            <br>
            {if $title_err ne    ""}
            <span class="formerror">{$title_err}</span>
            {/if}
          </td>    .
        </tr>
        <tr>
          <td class="result-line"><b>Categories:</b></td>
          <td class="result-line">
            <SELECT size="10" name="categories[]" multiple>
            {$options}
            </SELECT><br />
            <span class="formsmnote">
            Hold down the ctrl key and click to select more than one
            category</span><br>
            {if $cat_err ne    ""}
            <span class="formerror">{$cat_err}</span>{/if}
          </td>
        </tr>
        <tr>
          <td class="result-line"><b>Price:</b></td>
          <td class="result-line">
          $<input type="text" name="ad_price" size="12" maxlength="12" value="
          {if $ad_price ne    ""}{$ad_price}{/if}"><br />
```

```
          <span class="formsmnote">No commas, please </span><br>
          {if $price_err ne  ""}
          <span class="formerror">{$price_err}</span>{/if}
        </td>
      </tr>
      <tr>
        <td class="result-line">Ad Body:</td>
        <td class="result-line">
        <textarea name="ad_body" rows="6" cols="30" wrap="vitrual">
        {if $ad_body ne  ""}{$ad_body}{/if}</textarea><br />
        <s pan class="formsmnote">Note: HTML is NOT allowed.</span>
        </td>
      </tr>
      <tr>
        <td class="result-line">Image URL:</td><td class="result-line">
        <input type="text" name="ad_image_url" maxlength="255" value="
        {if $ad_image_url ne  ""} {$ad_image_url}{/if}"><br />
        <span class="formsmnote">Example:
        http://www.snipe.net/images/image.gif</span><br>
        {if $img_err ne  ""}<span class="formerror">{$img_err}</span>{/if}
        </td>
      </tr>
      <tr>
        <td class="result-line"> </td><td class="result-line">
          <input type="hidden" name="cat_id" value="{$cat_id}">
          {if $ad_id ne  ""}
          <input type="hidden" name="do_what" value="save_edits">
          <input type="hidden" name="ad_id" value="{$ad_id}">
          {else}
          <input type="hidden" name="do_what" value="new">
          {/if}
          <input type="submit" value="save">
        </td>
      </tr>
    </table>
  </td>
  </tr>
</table>
</center>
</form>

<!-- end ad_form.tpl -->
```

Next file up is ad_form.php, which takes care of all the ground work for the edit, add, and delete functionality.

Notice the htmlspecialchars() function around the $ad_title and $ad_body. This will convert any HTML the user submits into its HTML equivalent. For example, <b> would become <b>. This is often a good idea when accepting and displaying user-entered data, to prevent any malicious users from coding in images or META redirects:

```php
<?php
//file: ad_form.php
include_once("setup.php");
include_once("session.php");
include_once("functions.php");
include_once("header.php");
```

```php
// Since all of these functions require the user to be logged in,
// lets make sure they are
if ($_SESSION['logged_in']==1) {
    $smarty->assign('cat_id', $_REQUEST['cat_id']);

    // If the user is editing an ad, get the ad details to print out to the
    // form template
    if (($_POST['do_what']=="edit") && ($_POST['ad_id'])) {
        GetAdDetail($_POST['ad_id'], "");

    } else {
        // Otherwise, if they are adding a new ad, assign the posted
        // set the $categories variable as the posted category form information
        // This comes in when the user iscreating a new ad and missed
        // another field. The selected categories must be preserved, and
        // this is the part that does just that
        if (!isset($categories)){
            $categories  = ($_POST['categories']);
        }

        // get the category select list
        $get_options =    GetCatSelectList(0, 0);

        // if categories are returned, cycle through them to create the option
        // list and see what is selected
        if (count($get_options) > 0){
            foreach ($get_options  as $key => $value) {
                    $options .="<option value=\"$key\"";
                    for($count = 0; $count < count($categories);$count++) {
                        if ($categories[$count] == "$key") {
                            $options .=" selected=\"selected\"";
                    }
            }
            $options .=">$value</option>\n";
        }
    }
    // assign the option list to the Smarty template
    $smarty->assign('options', $options);
}


// if they are CREATING an ad or SAVING edits
// begin error-checking
if (($_POST['do_what']=="new") || ($_POST['do_what']=="save_edits")){

    // if its an edit, make sure we keep the ad ID
    if (!empty($_POST['ad_id'])) {
        $smarty->assign('ad_id', $_POST['ad_id']);
    }

    // Assign the postd information to the Smarty templates, since
    // we will have to print them back out in the form if the user
    // made a mistake
```

```php
        $smarty->assign('ad_title', $_POST['ad_title']);
        $smarty->assign('ad_price', $_POST['ad_price']);
        $smarty->assign('ad_image_url', $_POST['ad_image_url']);
        $smarty->assign('ad_body', $_POST['ad_body']);

        // Did they enter an ad title?
        if (trim($_POST['ad_title'])=="") {
            $title_err="You must enter a title for your ad";
            $smarty->assign('title_err', $title_err);
            $are_errors=1;
        }

        // did they select at last one category?
        if ($_POST['categories']=="") {
            $cat_err="You must select at least one category";
            $smarty->assign('cat_err', $cat_err);
            $are_errors=1;
        }

        Did they enter a price?
        if ($_POST['ad_price']=="") {
            $price_err="You must enter a price";
            $smarty->assign('price_err', $price_err);
            $are_errors=1;
            // lets make sure the price entered is actually a number
        } elseif (!is_numeric($_POST['ad_price'])) {
                $price_err="You must enter a valid number for price";
                $smarty->assign('price_err', $price_err);
                $are_errors=1;
        }

        // If they entered an ad image url, make sure it looks correct
        if ($_POST['ad_image_url']!="") {
            // make sure the url is formatted correctly
            $good_url = strpos($_POST['ad_image_url'], "http://");
            if ($good_url === false) {
                $img_err="Your image url is not valid";
                $smarty->assign('img_err', $img_err);
                $are_errors=1;
            }
        }


} // End the error-checking if statement

// If there are no errors, and the user is submitting a new ad, go ahead and
// insert the data
if (($are_errors!=1) && ($_POST['do_what']=="new")) {

    $smarty->assign('options', $options);

    // escape any quotes or apostrophe's out of the data
    $ad_title = addslashes($_POST['ad_title']);
    $ad_body = addslashes(htmlspecialchars($_POST['ad_body']));
```

```php
$ad_price = $_POST['ad_price'];
$ad_image_url = $_POST['ad_image_url'];

$sql = "INSERT into adboard_ad_details (ad_detail_title, ad_detail_body, ";
$sql .="ad_detail_price, ad_detail_img_url, ad_detail_addedon, ";
$sql .="ad_detail_userid) values ('$ad_title', '$ad_body', ";
$sql .="'$ad_price', '$ad_image_url', NOW(), $login_id)";
if ($insert_ad_data = mysql_query($sql)) {
    $new_ad_id = mysql_insert_id();

    // add the proper category associations to the ad_category_join
    // database table
    for($count = 0; $count < sizeof($categories); $count++) {
        $sql = "INSERT into adboard_ad_category_join (category_join_ad_id, ";
        $sql .="category_join_cat_id) values ";
        $sql .="($new_ad_id,$categories[$count])";
        // if the query passes, set the $db_error flag to 0
        if ($insert_join_data = mysql_query($sql)) {
            $db_error = 0;
        }
    }

    // if the query went through, assign the new ad id to the Smarty
    // template, and display the success screen
    if ($db_error==0) {
        $smarty->assign('new_ad_id', $new_ad_id);
        $smarty->display('ad_success.tpl');
        // If the query broke, display the generic error message
    } else {
        $smarty->display('general_error.tpl');
    }

}

// if there are no errors, and the user is saving the ad
} elseif (($are_errors!=1) && ($_POST['do_what']=="save_edits")) {

    // escape the data
    $ad_title = addslashes(htmlspecialchars($_POST['ad_title']));
    $ad_body = addslashes(htmlspecialchars($_POST['ad_body']));
    $ad_price = $_POST['ad_price'];
    $ad_image_url = $_POST['ad_image_url'];
    $categories = $_POST['categories'];

    // update the ad_details table
    $sql = "UPDATE adboard_ad_details SET ad_detail_title='$ad_title',
            ad_detail_body='$ad_body', ad_detail_price='$ad_price',
            ad_detail_img_url='$ad_image_url' WHERE
            ad_detail_id=".$_POST['ad_id'];

    // and update the category associations. You must first delete the
    // previous associations
    if ($update_ad_data = mysql_query($sql)) {
        $sql = "DELETE FROM adboard_ad_category_join WHERE
```

```
                    category_join_ad_id=".$_POST['ad_id'];
            $delete_join_data = mysql_query($sql);

            // loop through the selected categories to insert them into the
            // ad_cat_join table
            for($count = 0; $count < sizeof($categories); $count++) {
                $sql = "INSERT into adboard_ad_category_join (category_join_ad_id,
                        category_join_cat_id) values ";
                $sql .= "(".$_POST['ad_id'].", $categories[$count])";
                $add_join_data = mysql_query($sql);
            }

        // Get the new ad details and display the edit_success.tpl template as
        // well as the updated ad information
        $ad_details = GetAdDetail($_POST['ad_id'], "");
        $smarty->display('edit_success.tpl');
        $smarty->assign('ad_details', $ad_details);
        $smarty->display('view.tpl');
    }


// If the user clicks on the delete button
} elseif ($_POST['do_what']=="delete") {

            // assign the ad ID and category ID to the Smarty template
            // and display the delete confirmation template
            $smarty->assign('ad_id', $_POST['ad_id']);
            $smarty->assign('cat_id', $_POST['cat_id']);
            $smarty->display('delete_confirm.tpl');

// if the user has clicked "yes" to confirm the delete
} elseif ($_POST['confirm_delete']=="Yes") {

    // delete the ad from the ad_details table
    $sql = "DELETE FROM adboard_ad_details WHERE
            ad_detail_id=".$_POST['ad_id'];
    if ($delete_ad_data = mysql_query($sql)) {

        // and also delete the categry associations in the
        // ad_cat_join table
        $sql = "DELETE FROM adboard_ad_category_join WHERE ";
        $sql .="category_join_ad_id=". $_POST['ad_id'];
        $delete_join_data = mysql_query($sql);
        // If the deletion went through, display the
        // delete_success.tpl template
        if ($delete_join_data = mysql_query($sql)) {
            $smarty->display('delete_success.tpl');
            // Otherwise if something broke the query, print
            // the error template
        } else {
            $smarty->display('general_error.tpl');
        }
```

```
        }

            // If the user selects "no" from the delete confirmation page
            // redisplay the view.tpl template
        } elseif ($_POST['confirm_delete']=="No"){
            $ad_details = GetAdDetail($_POST['ad_id'], "");
            $smarty->assign('ad_details', $ad_details);
            $smarty->display('view.tpl');
        } else {

            // If there was a problem found in error checking,
            // display a message instructing the user to correct the form
            if ($are_errors==1) {
                $insert_err_msg = "Please complete the fields below ";
                $insert_err_msg .="and resubmit. ";
                $smarty->assign('insert_err_msg', $insert_err_msg);

                // If it's a new ad being created, print out some instructional
                // text
            } else {
                $insert_msg = "Fill in the form below to create a new ad.";
                $smarty->assign('insert_msg', $insert_msg);

            }

            // get the categories that were selected and print the listbox
            $get_options =    GetCatSelectList($_REQUEST['cat_id'], 0);
            $smarty->assign('options', $options);

            // load the form template
            $smarty->display('ad_form.tpl');

        }

    } else {

        // if the user does not have permission to edit this page, display an error
        $smarty->display('perm_error.tpl');
    }

    // load the footer template
    $smarty->display('footer.tpl');
    ?>
```

And that's it! Our classified ads board is fully functional now!

Improvements

The core functionality of the program has all been built, now there are some peripheral enhancements we can include, specifically a welcome to the side navigation bar, highlighting the side navigation element that the user is currently in, and so on. For this, we can add a few more functions and call them from the header.php and sidenav.php files.

A detailed description of these enhancements is available at our web site. You can also download the code for these features from our downloads available for this book at http://www.wrox.com/.

As we've probably already realized, no software program is ever really done, and this one is no exception. In case you want to take this project further, here's some food for thought:

- ❏ Auto-expiration of ads after a certain amount of time
- ❏ Ability for users to "renew" ads to prevent expiry
- ❏ Holding queue for ads that await administrator approval
- ❏ Web-based administration panel for category editing
- ❏ Ability to send messages directly to the classified ad owner from the program
- ❏ E-mail confirmation function for registration
- ❏ Database abstraction using PHPLib
- ❏ Edit feature for member profiles
- ❏ Template integration to allow full control over layout
- ❏ Image upload feature
- ❏ A category watch, where users could mark certain categories as "watched", and would receive an e-mail whenever new posts were added to it
- ❏ Ability to rate users (similar to http://www.ebay.com)
- ❏ Hook into with PayPal or other payment gateway

Summary

In this case study, we went through the feature development, user interface planning, database planning, and code development phases of building a web-based classified ads system. We learned that recursive functions could be used effectively and, illustrated how a little forethought can make for a good programming experience.

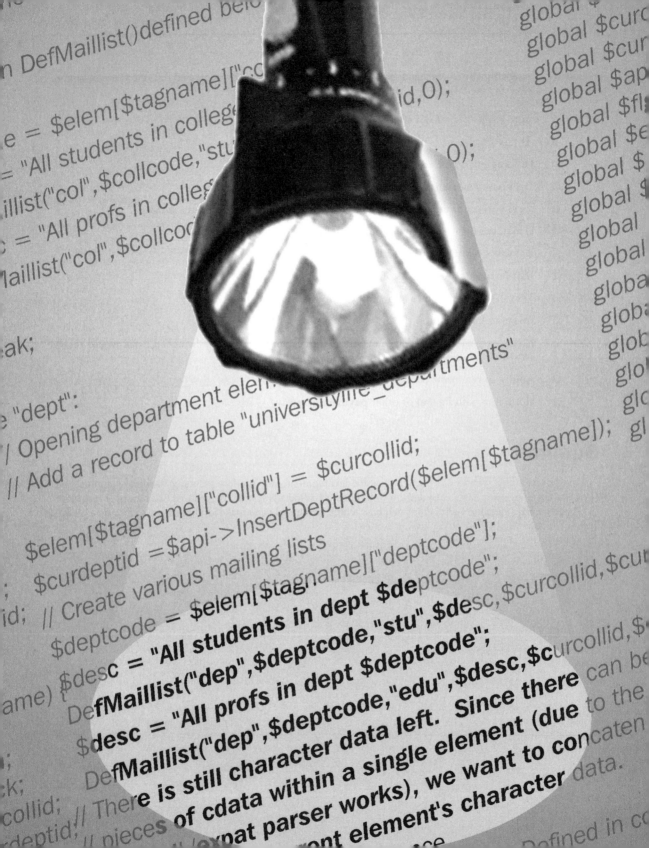

A Simple Content Management System

This case study explores a very basic **Content Management System (CMS)** designed for internal use by a team of technically capable contributors. For those who are looking for a CMS that can be used by by administrators and non-technical contributors, it would be advisable to go through this case study first and then proceed to Chapter 10, which deals with an an advanced Content Management System (CMS).

In the course of this chapter we will look at:

- **Specifications**
  To begin with, we need to define the features of the CMS.

- **Designing the Data**
  The CMS will be based on a MySQL database. This section describes how the tables in this database are structured.

- **Managing the Data**
  We need some PHP code that manages the data in the database.

- **Possible Enhancements**
  The most obvious enhancements to the core application are presented at the end of the chapter.

This chapter discusses a very simple CMS in which the content of a document takes on several forms while using a single database. This is accomplished by using XML to define each document.

While all documents have the same skeleton set of XML tags, each document type differs in the tags used within the <body> element. This content markup is actually stored as is in the database. Each document type will require its own application component to parse and manipulate the document body.

Specifications

The types of documents that may be stored via this application are limitless, provided that they all follow the same XML skeleton (discussed in the next section). This necessitates the use of an XML authoring tool, whether manual or automated, like XML Spy (see http://www.xmlspy.com/) or oXygen (see http://www.oxygenxml.com/). The examples in this chapter provide a sample of what can be stored. However, because XML is used, the average application user requires some technical skills. Alternatively, a more user-friendly Graphical User Interface (GUI) can be wrapped around this application engine, but that is beyond the scope of this case study.

Note that the source documents do not necessarily represent web pages although they can. In fact, we could store HTML, WML, CML, SVG, or any other document in the database as well. In the case of WML, however, the <?xml ...?> **Processing Instruction** (**PI**) does not get stored. It would have to be added by the application component that manipulates WML documents. The same goes for XML documents. The XML PI gets stripped off.

This chapter does not cover XSLT stylesheets. However, they can be used in various application components that manipulate the stored documents. Such stylesheets could be used to export document content in various formats including HTML, WML, RTF, PDF, and so on.

The list below highlights some of the functional specifications and features that can be a part of the application (not all of these items are covered in this chapter):

❑ **Private System**
Technically skilled users could use this system. There is no login feature in the present application, but this could be added later.

❑ **Variety of document content**

- ❑ Web pages
- ❑ Wireless web pages
- ❑ General XML documents
- ❑ Articles
- ❑ Product manuals (print and online versions)
- ❑ Indexes
- ❑ Bibilography
- ❑ Research notes
- ❑ Non-fiction books
- ❑ General lists

- ❑ Company records
- ❑ Recipes
- ❑ Letters
- ❑ Poems
- ❑ Short stories
- ❑ Fiction/novels
- ❑ **Variety of export facilities**
  - ❑ Text
  - ❑ XML
  - ❑ WML
  - ❑ HTML
  - ❑ RTF
  - ❑ PDF

As an application for storing a wide variety of XML-based document structures, export facilities are limited to pre-defined formats based on content type and subtype. The only facility for changing the appearance of finished documents is XSLT, which we do not discuss here.

On the surface, this application appears to be an awkward alternative to a word processing package. However, for users who want to store a wide range of documents in XML format, this is an ideal, albeit simplified, application. The advantage is that we now have an abstract model of a document to which we can add interfaces. Using these we can generically search for information regardless of the type of the stored document.

To aid in building a generic search engine, we can go a step further by building a document **corpus**. A corpus is a unique-word list used in the sampling of documents. By temporarily stripping off XML tags for each document, we can add any new unique words, which we encounter, to a web corpus.

> *A web corpus is the necessary set of database tables and their contents that represent the list of unique words and pointers to their occurrences in documents*

For a simple web corpus, we simply log one occurrence of a word in a document. For example, if the word 'science' occurs one or more times in three different imported documents, we would catalog one occurrence in each document by creating three **occurrence** records. Each record would contain a reference to the actual word, as well as a reference to the document where it occurs.

> *Refer to Chapter 6 for more information about a web corpus and on how to build a search engine based on a web corpus.*

A different type of search engine could be designed by parsing an imported document's body markup, recording tag, and attribute names. This would allow users to search for all documents containing a specific tag name or even all tags that have a particular attribute. This is particularly useful if we are designing parsing components for this application on a need-to basis and have recurring tag names that must have the same attributes.

For example, if we are storing company documents that are mostly about employees, some document types might have an `<employee>` tag with the following attributes:

```
<employee lname="mouse" empid="1234567890"/>
```

Storing occurrences of a tag name and its attribute names in a database gives us the ability to query for specific documents based on the inclusion of this tag and its attributes. In the case of the `<employee>` tag, we can query for a list of documents in which this tag occurs either with or without the attributes. This makes it easy to pinpoint markup errors, for instance in legacy documents that have been converted into XML through brute force methods. The type of search engine mentioned here is briefly touched upon towards the end of this chapter.

> **All content blocks are supplied using custom XML tagsets defined by the end user. Documents can be defined in an incomplete manner (provided they are still well-formed XML) and updated later (the application code for update is not covered here). The code that is covered in the rest of this chapter is the basic import code required to catalog each document. Numerous interfaces can be built over the top of the database that results from running the import code.**

Several examples for different types of content are detailed after a discussion of the general structure required. As usual, we will use PEAR::DB for communicating with the MySQL database on which this whole application relies. By using PEAR::DB, we also makes it easy to change database server if that ever gets interesting.

Because we are only covering a batch mode document import component, there are no particular web page needs.

General Structure of XML Documents

The following listing shows the general tree structure of a content document for the simple CMS application:

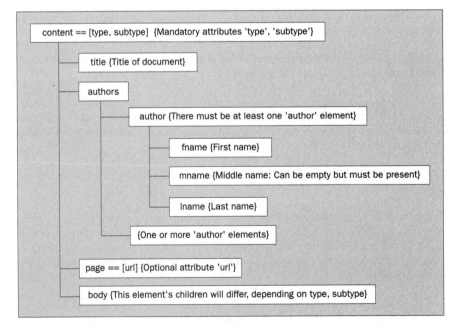

Here is the DTD for the above:

```
<!DOCTYPE CONTENT[
  <!ELEMENT CONTENT (TITLE,AUTHORS,PAGE,BODY)>
      <!ATTLIST CONTENT TYPE CDATA #REQUIRED>
      <!ATTLIST CONTENT SUBTYPE CDATA #REQUIRED>
  <!ELEMENT TITLE (#PCDATA)>
  <!ELEMENT AUTHORS (FNAME,MNAME,LNAME)>
  <!ELEMENT FNAME (#PCDATA)>
  <!ELEMENT MNAME (#PCDATA)>
  <!ELEMENT LNAME (#PCDATA)>
  <!ELEMENT PAGE (#PCDATA)>
      <!ATTLIST PAGE URL CDATA #IMPLIED>
  <!ELEMENT BODY (#PCDATA)>

  ]>
```

All documents imported into this simple CMS database must follow this skeleton structure; the documents will differ only in the <body> element's subtree structure. The equivalent XML template looks like this:

```
<content type="__type__" subtype="__subtype__">
  <title>__title__</title>
  <authors>
    <author>
      <fname>__firstname__</fname>
      <mname>__middlename__</mname>
      <lname>__lastname__</lname>
    </author>
  </authors>
  <page url="__url__"/> <!-- Attribute 'url' is optional -->
  <body>
  __body_of_content__
  </body>
</content>
```

Values for attributes and tags are shown as field markers, in bold. For example, the value of type is indicated by the marker __type__. When a document is added to the database, only the above tags will be parsed. Everything in the <body> element will be stored as a block of XML-like markup. The XML PI that starts every XML file will be stripped off.

The resulting <body> block will be parsed later by an application component that knows how to process the particular document type/subtype. That component is not talked about here though.

Such components are not dicussed in this chapter.

Example 1: Non-fiction Book (Beginning Stages)

This example represents a non-fiction book. The following XML listing (nonfic01.xml) is broken up into sections in order to explain the tags:

```
<?xml version="1.0" ?>
```

Each document must start with the root element `<content>` and include two attributes – `type` and `subtype` (`subtype` can be a blank string). The resulting combination of attribute values will determine the structure of the sub-document within the `<body>...</body>` tag block.

```
<content type="nonfiction" subtype="book">
```

The combination of `type`, `subtype`, and the `title` must be unique. In other words, for a given type/subtype combination, all relevant documents must have a unique title:

```
<title>Web Development Methodologies</title>
```

Note, however, that titles can be repeated in a different type/subtype combination.

Each document may have one or more contributors. For each author, use one `<author>...</author>` block. This block defines two authors:

```
<authors>
  <author>
    <fname>mary</fname>
    <mname>elizabeth</mname>
    <lname>smith</lname>
  </author>
  <author>
    <fname>john</fname>
    <mname>q</mname>
    <lname>doe</lname>
  </author>
</authors>
```

Additional authors can be added later.

If we use an automated batch method for updates, we might use code similar to the following:

```
<?selectdoc type="nonfiction" subtype="book"
            title="Web Development Methodologies" ?>
<?addauthor ?>

<author>
  <fname>bernard</fname>
  <mname/>
  <lname>rubble</lname>
</author>
```

The XML PI `<?selectdoc...?>` would be interpreted as a request to retrieve a particular document; the three attributes – `type`, `subtype`, and `title` – would jointly form a unique key. Once the document has been selected, the XML PI `<?addauthor ?>` would be interpreted as a request to add an `<author>...</author>` block to the `<authors>...</authors>` block of the document.

The document's URL is defined next:

```
<page url="test.doc"/>
  <body>
```

Some documents will either not have a URL associated with them, or the URL may be presently undefined. When no URL is defined, use the empty form, `<page/>`.

To update the URL (either to define it or to change it), we might use the following code in batch mode:

```
<?selectdoc type="nonfiction" subtype="book"
          title="Pro PHP Web Site Solutions" ?>
<?changeurl pageurl="__newurl__" ?>
```

Finally, the `<body>` element is where the actual document structure is defined. Each unique combination of content type and subtype will likely have a different XML tagset. Further, each combination will need to have a custom XML parser built for it to allow manipulation of documents:

In this example, we are defining a non-fiction book. In particular, we are defining a subset of the information in the book that we are reading. For the first chapter, we are only defining the title, chapter number, and style (the style attribute defines a font) attributes. For now, we shall leave out the content in the chapter:

```
<chap num="1" title="Introduction" style="chapter title"/>
```

In the listing above, `"chapter title"` represents the font used for chapter titles, not the actual text that constitutes the title. For the second chapter, we shall define the chapter number, title, and style. We are also defining sections in the chapter (and their level, title, and style). However, we are not defining any chapter or section textual content. Notice that the sections are not numbered. Instead, we only define a level. For example, a level 1 section is equivalent to the font style `Heading 1`. A level 2 section is equivalent to a `Heading 2`, and is a sub-section of a level 1 section, and so on.

While the level attribute (`lev`) is not strictly necessary, it actually makes the parsing of the markup much easier.

The last of ten design goals in the XML specification (http://www.w3.org/TR/2000/REC-xml-20001006) states that, "Terseness of XML markup is of minimal importance". Keeping this in mind, the markup below adds explicit information that can be retrieved easily, to reduce docoument-parsing time:

```
<chap num="2" title="PHP Overview" style="chapter title">
  <sec lev="1" title="Introduction" style="Heading 1"/>
  <sec lev="1" title="PHP File Extensions" style="Heading 1"/>
  <sec lev="1" title="Comments" style="Heading 1"/>
  <sec lev="1" title="Identifiers + Variables" style="Heading 1"/>
  <sec lev="1" title="Variable Scope" style="Heading 1"/>
```

The above `<sec>` elements use the 'empty' form of tag, since no child elements are defined. The next section contains three level 2 sections, so we cannot use the 'empty' tag form for the parent element's open tag:

```
<sec lev="1" title="Data Types + Casting" style="Heading 1">
  <sec lev="2" title="Miscellaneous Type-Related Functions"
       style="Heading 2"/>
  <sec lev="2" title="Converting Data Types" style="Heading 2">
    <sec lev="3" title="Casting Data Types" style="Heading 3"/>
  </sec>
  <sec lev="2" title="Arithmetic on Strings" style="Heading 2"/>
</sec>
```

The remainder of the <body> block simply shows a few more examples of section definition:

```
<sec lev="1" title="Expressions" style="Heading 1">
  <sec lev="2" title="Constants" style="Heading 2">
    <sec lev="3" title="User-defined Constants" style="Heading 3"/>
  </sec>
  <sec lev="2" title="Operators" style="Heading 2">
    <sec lev="3" title="String Operators" style="Heading 3"/>
    <sec lev="3" title="Arithmetic Operators" style="Heading 3"/>
    <sec lev="3" title="Comparison Operators" style="Heading 3"/>
    <sec lev="3" title="Logical Operators" style="Heading 3"/>
    <sec lev="3" title="Reference Operators" style="Heading 3"/>
    <sec lev="3" title="Bitwise Operators" style="Heading 3"/>
    <sec lev="3" title="Assignment Operators" style="Heading 3"/>
    <sec lev="3" title="Miscellaneous Operators"
             style="Heading 3"/>
  </sec>
  <sec lev="2" title="Operator Precedences" style="Heading 2"/>
</sec>

<sec lev="1" title="Statements" style="Heading 1">
  <sec lev="2" title="Assignments" style="Heading 2"/>
  <sec lev="2" title="Input/Output" style="Heading 2">
    <sec lev="3" title="Output" style="Heading 3">
      <sec lev="4" title="echo" style="Heading 4"/>
      <sec lev="4" title="print()" style="Heading 4"/>
      <sec lev="4" title="printf()" style="Heading 4"/>
      <sec lev="4" title="sprintf()" style="Heading 4"/>
    </sec>
    <sec lev="3" title="Output" style="Heading 3"/>
  </sec>
</sec>

      </chap>
    </body>
  </content>
```

Example 2: Online Manual

This example (onlineman01.xml) sets up a placeholder document for an online manual:

```
<?xml version="1.0" ?>
<content type="nonfiction" subtype="onlinemanual">
  <title>Guide to the TOOLS Language - Online Edition</title>
  <authors>
    <author>
      <fname>mookie</fname>
```

```
        <mname/>
        <lname>mouse</lname>
      </author>
    </authors>
    <page/>
    <body>
    </body>
  </content>
```

Currently, there is no content in the `<body>`...`</body>` block. Content might be added later in batch mode as follows:

```
<?selectdoc type="nonfiction" subtype="onlinemanual" title="Guide to the TOOLS
Language - Online Edition" ?>

<?definebody ?>

<body>
  <toolsmanual>
    <functions>
      <function>
        <name>print()</name>
        <params>
          <param><i>stringexpr</i></param>
        </params>
      <function>
    </functions>
  </toolsmanual>
</body>
```

The application component that parses the above would select the appropriate document from the database and then add the segment of markup code. The component would have to have some scheme for adding functions to the online manual. One possibility, of course, is adding functions in alphabetical order.

Example 3: Geek Poetry

This example (`geekpoetry01.xml`) defines an arbitrary document of the type 'geek poetry':

```
<?xml version="1.0" ?>
<content type="poetry" subtype="geek">
  <title>ODE TO PHP</title>

  <authors>
    <author>
      <fname>golly</fname>
      <mname/>
      <lname>gee</lname>
    </author>
  </authors>

  <page/>
```

371

```
<body>

    <stanza>
      <line>$str = "How do I love PHP?</line>
      <line>Let me count the ways.</line>
    </stanza>

    <stanza>
      <line>I love thy dynamic typing,</line>
      <line>With options galore.</line>
      <line>Strongly typed languages</line>
      <line>Are such a bore.</line>
    </stanza>

    <stanza>
      <line>My data type mistakes</line>
      <line>Are my own to make</line>
      <line>That's an option</line>
      <line>That I choose to take.</line>
    </stanza>

    <stanza>
      <line>I love thy ease of use,</line>
      <line>And focus on the web.</line>
      <line>I love that I can weave</line>
      <line>Web apps quickly - thanks, Zeev.</line>
    </stanza>

    <stanza>
      <line>I love you PHP</line>
      <line>Because you're so simple.</line>
      <line>Changing you too much too soon</line>
      <line>Would cause such a ripple.</line>
    </stanza>

    <stanza>
      <line>I love you PHP</line>
      <line>And so does the "web"</line>
      <line>Seven million domains</line>
      <line>Just can't be wrong!</line>
      <line>";</line>
      <line>print $str;</line>
    </stanza>

  </body>
</content>
```

Example 4: Recipes

This example (recipes01.xml) defines a document that will contain one or more recipes. This sample document shows one recipe:

```xml
<?xml version="1.0" ?>
<content type="nonfiction" subtype="recipes">
  <title>Guide to Spicy Cooking - Online Edition</title>

  <authors>
    <author>
      <fname>mookie</fname>
      <mname/>
      <lname>mouse</lname>
    </author>
  </authors>

  <page/>

  <body>
    <recipes>
      <recipe title="Savoury Curry Minced Lamb" categ="">

        <ingredients>
          <item num="1">
            <ingred>Olive oil</ingred>
            <quantity units="tbsp">2</quantity>
            <notes></notes>
          </item>

          <item num="2">
            <ingred>Curry powder</ingred>
            <quantity units="tbsp">2-3</quantity>
            <notes></notes>
          </item>

          <item num="3">
            <ingred>Haldi (turmeric)</ingred>
            <quantity units="tbsp">2</quantity>
            <notes></notes>
          </item>

          <item num="4">
            <ingred>Ginger powder</ingred>
            <quantity units="tbsp">1</quantity>
            <notes></notes>
          </item>

          <item num="5">
            <ingred>Ground lamb, thawed</ingred>
            <quantity units="oz">16</quantity>
            <notes>(or subst. beef, chicken or turkey)</notes>
          </item>

          <item num="6">
            <ingred>Mushrooms, sliced</ingred>
            <quantity units="">3 med</quantity>
            <notes></notes>
          </item>
```

```
        <item num="7">
          <ingred>Large calamata olives, quartered</ingred>
          <quantity units="">4-6</quantity>
          <notes>optional</notes>
        </item>

        <item num="8">
          <ingred>Scallions (green onion)</ingred>
          <quantity units="">5-6</quantity>
          <notes>sliced - white portion only</notes>
        </item>

        <item num="9">
          <ingred>Tomato sauce</ingred>
          <quantity units="cups">1/2</quantity>
          <notes>Dilute with 1/2 cup water or substitute with
                 1 cup of tomato or vegetable juice.</notes>
        </item>

        <item num="10">
          <ingred>Cooked rice</ingred>
          <quantity units="cups">4</quantity>
          <notes>or one cup per person</notes>
        </item>

    </ingredients>

    <instructions>
      <step num="1">Heat olive oil in skillet at med-high (8)
                    heat.</step>

      <step num="2">Add dry spices (curry powder, turmeric, ginger
                    powder) and roast for less than 30 seconds. Keep
                    an eye out, as these spices will burn fairly
                    quickly.</step>

      <step num="3">Add thawed or fresh ground meat and break up with
                    spatula or chopsticks.</step>

      <step num="4">When meat has nearly browned, add sliced
                    mushrooms. Toss with a spatula.</step>

      <step num="5">If desired, add quartered olives now.</step>

      <step num="6">Add tomato sauce and water, or tomato juice or
                    vegetable juice. Simmer for 10 minutes.</step>

      <step num="7">Remove from stove; add sliced scallions.</step>

    </instructions>

    <serving>
      <suggestion>
```

```
        Serve on steamed rice, with slices of mango or watermelon.
        </suggestion>
        <serves>Serves 4-6 as a main dish, 8-10 as an appetizer.
        </serves>
      </serving>

    </recipe>
   </recipes>
  </body>
</content>
```

More recipes can be added later using something like the following:

```
<?selectdoc type="nonfiction" subtype="recipes" title="Guide to Spicy Cooking -
Online Edition" ?>
<recipe title="Peace and Harmony">
...
</recipe>
```

The application component that handles recipes would have some scheme for adding `<recipe>...</recipe>` blocks to the current document, for example, alphabetically by title or by category of the dish, if such information is included in each recipe. However, at this point, we could order the output in any way we want.

Example 5: Fiction – Short Story Fragment

This example (shortstory01.xml) shows a fragment of a short story:

```
<?xml version="1.0" ?>
<content type="fiction" subtype="short">
  <title>The Great Lake</title>

  <authors>
    <author>
      <fname>aeric</fname>
      <mname>sir stinkybutt</mname>
      <lname>halfacat</lname>
    </author>
  </authors>
  <page url="/stories/fiction/short/thegreatlake.html"/>

  <body>
    <p>The small rowboat rocked violently from the wake of the large
       speedboat that passed. Brent waved with one hand, the other still
       holding his fishing rod. Joe harumpphed. \"Damn idiots. No
       respect for others.\"</p>

    <p>\"What now, Dad?\" Brent asked.</p>

    <p>\"Did you see how close they came, son?\" Joe responded. \"They were
       too close by at least 15 feet.\"</p>

    <p>\"Yeah, I guess you're right,\" Brent agreed. \"But what can we do
```

```
            about it?\"</p>

    <p>\"Do? We can't do nothing, boy. If the harbor patrol wasn't so damn
        busy making sure the lake was full of water, they'd be paying
        attention to stuff like this. But we can't do nothing. Not one
        thing.\" A distant look came into Joe's eyes.</p>

    <p>\"Dad?! What are you up to now?\" Brent asked. \"I know that look,
        Dad. You're thinking of some form of revenge.\"</p>

    <p>\"Nothing that shouldn't be done, son. Did you happen to catch the
        name on that boat? Never mind, I got it. Give me that pen over
there...\" Just then, Joe's fishing line gave a mighty tug. \"Whoa. I
        think I caught a big one!\" Joe reeled in his line as fast as he
        could, fighting the tugging, only to discover that he'd bagged an
        old tire. \"Just what the hell would a car tire be doing in the
        middle of the lake? I never understand people. It's bad enough
        that they pollute. But some seem to go to great lengths to do
        so.\"</p>

    <?timechange ?>

    <p>Joe and Brent made their way in to shore. Brent jumped out and
        tied up the boat to their small berth, then helped his father to
        unload the gear. \"Wait a minute, son. I want to talk to the harbor
        patrol.\"</p>

    <p>Brent stood with the gear while Joe made his way down the docks to
        the little boathouse office that the harbor patrol maintained. Joe
        had a way with people, despite his general crotchety composure,
        which made people laugh and agree to more things than they might
        normally do. In the distance, he could see the on-duty
        harbormaster <?check term?> laughing away with his father.
        Whatever Joe had said, the harbormaster had given him a salute and
        re-entered the boathouse.</p>

    <p>\"I know you're up to something, Dad,\" Brent said when his father
        returned.\"</p>
  </body>
</content>
```

Note that this is not necessarily the best way to represent the content of a short story. To allow for later update in batch mode, the appropriate `<? processinginstruction ?>` PIs would have to be defined. However, such instructions would need a means to reference paragraphs for adding, editing, or deleting. One possibility is to change the tagset slightly. For example, we could number the paragraphs by adding a num attribute to each start `<p>` tag. This would provide the short story application component a means of numbering paragraphs. Then we could insert several paragraphs, after the first one above, as follows:

```
<?selectdoc type="fiction" subtype="short" title="The Great Lake" ?>
<?insertpara after="1" ?>
<p num="1.1">...</p>
<p num="1.2">...</p>
<p num="1.3">...</p>
<p num="1.4">...</p>
```

This is simply one possible method. The database is a very simple and open starting point for building a variety of content management systems using XML.

Example 6: Resume

This example (resume01.xml) defines the XML skeleton for a resume:

```xml
<?xml version="1.0" ?>
<content type="nonfiction" subtype="resume">
  <title>RESUME: Bam Bam Rubble</title>

  <authors>
    <author>
      <fname>bam</fname>
      <mname>bam</mname>
      <lname>rubble</lname>
    </author>
  </authors>

  <page/>

  <body>

    <dateofbirth>
      <year>20000 AD</year>
      <month>May</month>
      <day>29</day>
    </dateofbirth>

    <education>
      <school>kindergartrock</school>
      <training>
        <program>
        </program>
      </training>
    </education>

    <experience>
    </experience>

    <hobbies>
      <hobby>Breaking rocks</hobby>
    </hobbies>

    <references>
      <reference>Frederick Flintstone</reference>
      <reference>Mr. Slate</reference>
    </references>

  </body>
</content>
```

A set of PIs will have to be defined for manipulating a resume document. The instruction targets (names) are abitrary, but necessary functionality includes the update of most of the tags used above.

The above examples mainly show the starting points of various types of documents. The document types that can be stored are limitless, provided they are marked up in XML.

Each type of document, after import, requires an application component that allows for batch or live update of documents. Each component must be coded around the implicit needs of the tagset used for the document type. Each component, out of necessity, must have some form of XML parsing code. A parser could be defined using the PHP XML/Expat functions or from scratch. Each parser would have to know how to interpret PIs and then manipulate the stored document as necessary. This could be done through XQuery (XML Query).

Unfortunately, at the time of writing, PHP does not support this XML technology. One alternative is to write the necessary code from scratch. Another alternative is to send the relevant XML markup and the processing request to some other scripting/programming language that does support XQuery. Alternatively, one can use XPath. PHP has some functions for using XPath in the DOM XML module. (This would have to be done through system calls, as PHP's pipe/socket functions are still in an experimental stage.)

The bulk of the PHP code in this case study focuses only on the import of XML documents. Additional application components for manipulating the content require more space than we have here for discussion.

The types of users for this application would be technically-skilled contributors. However, given the right interface, less technical contributors might also use the database to store and update content.
All content stored in the database will be either plain text or XML-like markup.

Designing the Database

The database required for storing a wide variety of XML documents is relatively simple.

Every document stored by this application contains certain common information:

- ❑ Content Type
- ❑ Content Subtype
- ❑ Title
- ❑ Author(s)
  - ❑ First name
  - ❑ Middle name, if any
  - ❑ Last name
- ❑ Virtual URL associated with the document, if any
- ❑ Body of the document (XML-like markup)

Any differences in the document structure are retained in an XML markup form.

Database simplecms

The above information can be represented in two tables, for a non-normalized database:

Table Name	Alias	Description
`simplecms_contents`	`co`	This table stores meta-information about each document, as well as the actual content in pseudo-XML form
`simplecms_authors`	`au`	This table stores information about the author of each document

To normalize the database, we need two lookup tables:

Table Name	Alias	Description
`simplecms_doctypes`	`dt`	This table stores combinations of type and subtype. It could also store an XML DTD, which could be used to validate an imported XML document claiming to be of a certain type and subtype. *This is left as an exercise for the reader.*
`simplecms_authordocs`	`ad`	This table stores reference information about author(s) who contributed to a particular document.

Database Table Specifics

The database tables discussed above are described in more detail in the sections below.

Doctypes

The `simplecms_doctypes` lookup table stores a list of document type/subtype combinations:

Column Name	Data Type	Description
`doctype_typeid`	`INT`	Unique integer, generated by MySQL that identifies this type/subtype combination.
`doctype_type`	`CHAR`	Type of document, for instance, 'nonfiction', 'fiction', 'poetry'. If we knew what document types we were planning to store in the database, we could make an `ENUM` of this column. This would increase performance quite a bit.

Column Name	Data Type	Description
doctype_subtype	CHAR	Subtype of document, for instance, short, onlinemanual, geek, book. As for previous column, we could make an ENUM of this if we had a predefined number of subtypes. Note that type and subtype values are rather arbitrary. What matters is that for each unique combination of type and subtype, a different tagset should be used within the <body>...</body>. Adding a DTD column to this table could enforce the correct document structure. This column, for a particular type/subtype combination would store an appropriate XML DTD. This is left as an exercise for the reader.

If type/subtype combinations are known beforehand, the simplecms_doctypes table can be pre-populated before document import. Otherwise, a record is inserted each time a combination that is not stored in the database is encountered.

We could further normalize the table by adding two separate lookup tables – one each of type and subtype information. However, this is unnecessary and complicates the queries.

Authors

The simplecms_authors lookup table stores information about document authors. This table could very well be expanded at a later stage. If the table gets expanded, this must also be reflected in the XML markup.

Column Name	Data Type	Description
author_authorid	INT	Unique integer generated by MySQL that identifies this author
author_firstname	CHAR	First name of this author
author_middlename	CHAR	Middle name of this author, if any
author_lastname	CHAR	Last name of this author

As with the simplecms_doctypes table, the table can be pre-populated if some or all potential authors are known beforehand. Otherwise authors are added once to this table as they are encountered.

Contents

The simplecms_contents table stores most of the information extracted from each imported XML document. One record is used for each document. The author information is stored in the simplecms_authors table:

Column Name	Data Type	Description
content_contentid	INT	A unique integer, generated by MySQL that identifies this record.
content_title	CHAR	Title of the document. This field can be empty.
content_pageurl	CHAR	A URL associated with this document. This field can be empty.
content_body	CHAR	The XML content extracted from between the `<body>...</body>` block, that is, the `<block>` and `</block>` tags are not included. This field can be empty.
content_typeid	INT	This is a foreign key that points to the appropriate record in the simplecms_doctypes table, and thus indirectly identifies the type/subtype of this document.

Authordocs

The simplecms_authordocs table stores reference information indicating which authors contributed to a particular document. For each document, one record is added to this table for each author:

Column Name	Data Type	Description
authordoc_id	INT	A unique integer, generated by MySQL that identifies this record.
authordocs_authorid	INT	This is a foreign key that points to the appropriate record in the simplecms_authors table, and thus indirectly identifies an author of the document pointed to by authordocs_contentid.
authordocs_contentid	INT	This is a foreign key that identifies the document for which the author pointed to by authordetail_authorid is a contributor for. This column points to the appropriate record in the simplecms_contents table.

Relationships Between Tables

The diagram below shows the relationship between the tables in the simplecms database:

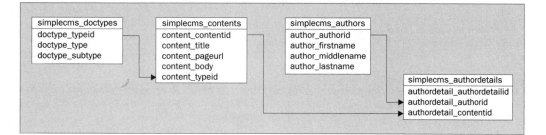

Database User

First create a MySQL database for this application:

```
> mysqladmin create simplecms
```

The tables for this case study can all be placed within a single MySQL database, simplecms. We only need one database user, say ADMIN. We will have to grant privileges to the tables, as well as create the tables. Once the database is created, we use the mysql client utility, which comes with MySQL, in the following command line to grant privileges:

```
mysql> GRANT SELECT, INSERT, UPDATE, DELETE ON simplecms.*
       TO 'ADMIN@localhost' IDENTIFIED BY "ADMIN";
```

Creating Tables

Run the following SQL script, crdbs_simplecms.sql, on the command line to create the simplecms database and tables:

```
> mysql simplecms < crdbs_simplecms.sql
```

```
# FILE: crdbs_simplecms.sql
# USE:  create tables for database simplecms

CREATE TABLE simplecms_doctypes (
    doctype_typeid  INT unsigned NOT NULL PRIMARY KEY AUTO_INCREMENT,
    doctype_type    VARCHAR(28) NOT NULL,
    doctype_subtype VARCHAR(28) NOT NULL
);

CREATE TABLE simplecms_authors (
    author_authorid    INT UNSIGNED NOT NULL PRIMARY KEY AUTO_INCREMENT,
    author_firstname   VARCHAR(40) NOT NULL,
    author_middlename  VARCHAR(40),
    author_lastname    VARCHAR(40) NOT NULL
);

CREATE TABLE simplecms_contents (
    content_contentid  INT UNSIGNED NOT NULL PRIMARY KEY AUTO_INCREMENT,
    content_title   VARCHAR(128) NOT NULL,
    content_pageurl VARCHAR(255),
    content_body    MEDIUMTEXT NOT NULL,
    content_typeid  INT UNSIGNED NOT NULL
);

CREATE TABLE simplecms_authordocs (
    authordocs_authordid INT UNSIGNED NOT NULL PRIMARY KEY AUTO_INCREMENT,
    authordocs_authorid    INT UNSIGNED NOT NULL,
    authordocs_contentid   INT UNSIGNED NOT NULL
);
```

Building Indexes

Indexes will be created for most columns in the database, to speed up common searches. The SQL commands for creating indexes are in a file called mkidx_simplecms.sql.

Run the following SQL script, mkidx_simplecms.sql, on the command line to build the indexes for the simplecms database and tables. Note that MySQL creates indexes automatically on primary keys, so creating indexes on the ID-columns of our tables may seem a little redundant. However, they are included in the listing below for clarity reasons:

```
> mysql simplecms < mkidx_simplecms.sql
```

```
# FILE: mkidx_simplecms.sql
# USE:  create indexes for tables in database simplecms

# Indexes for table simplecms_doctypes
#
CREATE INDEX dt_idxOnTypeid    ON simplecms_doctypes(doctype_typeid);
CREATE INDEX dt_idxOnType      ON simplecms_doctypes(doctype_type);
CREATE INDEX dt_idxOnSubtype   ON simplecms_doctypes(doctype_subtype);

# Indexes for table authors
#
CREATE INDEX au_idxOnAuthid    ON simplecms_authors(author_authorid);
CREATE INDEX au_idxOnFname     ON simplecms_authors(author_firstname);
CREATE INDEX au_idxOnMname     ON simplecms_authors(author_middlename);
CREATE INDEX au_idxOnLname     ON simplecms_authors(author_lastname);

# Indexes for table simplecms_contents
# (No index for column 'body', because of MySQL indexing limitations for
#  type 'text' and its variations)
#
CREATE INDEX co_idxOnContid    ON simplecms_contents(content_contentid);
CREATE INDEX co_idxOnTitle     ON simplecms_contents(content_title);
CREATE INDEX co_idxOnPageurl   ON simplecms_contents(content_pageurl);
CREATE INDEX co_idxOnTypeid    ON simplecms_contents(content_typeid);

# Indexes for table authordetails
#
CREATE INDEX ad_idxOnAuthdetid
            ON simplecms_authordetails(authordetail_authordetailid);
CREATE INDEX ad_idxOnAuthid
            ON simplecms_authordetails(authordetail_authorid);
CREATE INDEX ad_idxOnContid
            ON simplecms_authordetails(authordetail_contentid);
```

Managing the Data

Let's now take a look at the import component of the simple CMS application. It is this component that we are focusing on in the following sections.

Populating the Database

To initially populate the database, we need to import some of the XML-based documents discussed in the previous examples. These are the steps we need to take to populate the database:

1. Create database tables

2. Build table indexes

3. Import documents

   a. Import `nonfic01.xml`

   b. Import `onlineman01.xml`

   c. Import `geekpoetry01.xml`

   d. Import `recipes01.xml`

   e. Import `shortstory01.xml`

   f. Import `resume01.xml`

Refer to the sections *Creating Tables* and *Building Indexes* to perform steps 1 and 2. Next we will look into step 3.

Importing Documents

A single script that scans for the basic tagset and creates a database record can perform all of the import sub-steps in step 3. A point to be made clear here is that we are not using the PHP XML/Expat functions to parse the documents. The reason we do not is because we only want to parse a part of each document's tag blocks. We want to keep each `<body>...</body>` block intact. Since we cannot do this easily with the PHP XML functions, it is best that we write a relatively simple script that uses Perl-Compatible Regular Expressions (PCRE).

Algorithm

The following pseudo-code presents a general algorithm for importing the sample XML files:

```
1.0 Create a list of XML document files to be imported
2.0 Build the regexp filters for each 'common' tag pair with XPath
3.0 For each document to be imported
    {
        3.1  Read in the entire XML file
        3.2  Apply the regex filter to extract the 'type' and 'subtype'
             attributes
        3.3  If the combination exists in the 'simplecms_doctypes' table
             {
                 3.3.1 Retrieve the 'doctype_typeid' from the
                       ' simplecms_doctypes' table
             }
        3.4  else
             {
```

```
                  3.4.1 Insert the record into the 'simplecms_doctypes' table
                  3.4.2 Retrieve the new 'doctype_typeid'
            }
      3.5  Apply the regex filter to extract the document title
      3.6  For each author
            {
                  3.6.1 Apply the regex filter to extract the author info (one or
                        more)
                  3.6.2 If the author exists in the 'simplecms_authors' table
                        {
                              3.6.2.1 Retrieve the 'author_authorid' from the
                                      'simplecms_authors' table
                        }
                  3.6.3 else
                        {
                              3.6.3.1 Insert the record into the
                                      'simplecms_authors' table
                              3.6.3.2 Retrieve the new 'author_authorid'
                        }
            }
      3.7  Apply the regex to extract the page URL, if any
      3.8  Apply the regex to extract the contents of "<body>...</body>"
           block
           (without start/end 'body' tags)
      3.9  Insert the document information as a record into the
           'simplcms_contents' table
      3.10 For each author of this document
            {
                  3.10.1 Insert the author and the document details as a record
                         into the 'simplecms_authordetails' table
            }
      }
```

This is only a generic guideline. The actual PHP code may differ slightly in structure.

PHP Code

The following code loosely follows the above algorithm to import any of the XML document files described early. Document information is stored in the `simplecms` database, described earlier. Note that the debugging code has been left out of the following listing. If one finds problems while importing the XML files, it might indicate that the document does not have well-formed XML markup. Let's first define some global constants for later database access:

```php
<?php

// FILE: importxmldocs.php
// USE: Import a content document and store it in the simplecms database
// Define information for database connection
$host = "localhost";       // MySQL server
$user = "admin";           // Username
$dbs  = "simplecms";       // Database name
$pass = "";                // Password
```

Next import the PEAR::DB class:

```
require_once 'DB.php';
```

The following class that will be used to import XML documents and define data members:

```
class ImportXMLDocument
{
    var $filename;      // Document to parse
    var $db;
    var $type;          // Document type
    var $subtype;       // Document subtype
    var $title;         // Document title
    var $authors;       // Array of author information
    var $pageurl;       // The URL, if any, associated with this document
    var $body;          // The XML-like markup of the <body>...</body>
                        // block
    var $doc;           // The parsed representation of the XML document
```

The constructor will receive information about the database to use and connect to the database using PEAR::DB, and $this->db will keep the connection to the database that will be used in this class:

```
    function ImportXMLDocument($host,$user,$pass,$dbs)
    {
        $dsn = "mysql://$user:$pass@$host/$dbs";
        $this->db = DB::connect($dsn);
        if (DB::isError($db)) {
            die ($this->db->getMessage());
        }
    }
}
```

To parse the XML documents and extract content information we'll use XPath; the XPath `eval()` functions are part of the DOM XML extension in PHP. We'll need PHP 4.0.4 or later compiled with the DOM extension enabled in order to use this code.

> *XPath is a widely-used language to query XML documents. For more information on XPath and the DOM extension refer to Chapter 6 and 7 in Professional PHP4 XML from Wrox Press (ISBN 1-861007-21-3).*

First we define a function to get an array of strings when an XPath expression is executed. The function can be used to get the value of attribute nodes (`//foo/@some`) or text node (`//some/text()`). Note that for PHP versions prior to 4.0.4, the array returned by `xpath_eval()` looks a little different:

```
    function XpathGetTextNodes($doc,$expr)
    {
        $data = Array();
        $xpath=$doc->xpath_init();
        $ctx = $doc->xpath_new_context();
        $result=$ctx->xpath_eval($expr);
        $nodes=$result->nodeset;
        foreach($nodes as $a_node) {
            if($a_node->node_type() == XML_ATTRIBUTE_NODE) {
```

```
            $value = $a_node->value;
        } elseif ($a_node->node_type() == XML_TEXT_NODE) {
            $value = $a_node->content;
        }
        $data[] = $value;
    }
    return $data;
}
```

The next function returns an XML fragment for the element selected by an XPath expression; it will be used to get an XML fragment for all the authors in an XML document:

```
function XpathGetXmlNodes($doc,$expr)
{
    $xpath=$doc->xpath_init();
    $ctx = $doc->xpath_new_context();
    $result=$ctx->xpath_eval($expr);
    $nodes=$result->nodeset;
    $data = Array();
    foreach($nodes as $a_node) {
        $data[] = $a_node->dump_node($a_node);
    }
    return $data;
}
```

With these functions in mind, we can write the `ParseDocument()` function that will parse an XML document and store the information in the object's data members so we can then store the information in the database. The function will receive the name of the filename to parse. The first part parses the XML document using the DOM extension, and if there is an error we exit:

```
function ParseDocument($filename)
{
    $this->filename = $filename;
    // We parse the XML document here
    $this->doc = xmldocfile($this->filename);
    if(!$this->doc) {
        die("XML parser error the document cannot be found or it is
            not well-formed");
```

Now we can use the `XpathGetTextNodes()` function defined earlier to get the content type, the XPath expression that will return the content of the `type` attribute in the `<content>` element is `/content/@type`. Here is the code:

```
        $aux = $this->XpathGetTextNodes($this->doc,"/content/@type");
        $this->type = $aux[0];
```

The same type of code is needed for the `subtype`, `pageurl`, and `title`:

```
$aux  = $this->XpathGetTextNodes($this->doc,"/content/@subtype");
$this->subtype = $aux[0];

$aux = $this->XpathGetTextNodes($this->doc,
                                "/content/title/text()");
$this->title = $aux[0];

$aux = $this->XpathGetTextNodes($this->doc,"/content/page/@url");
$this->pageurl = $aux[0];
```

Now we will get all the XML fragments for each author in the `authors` element:

```
$authors = $this->XpathGetXmlNodes ($this->doc,
                                "/content/authors/author");
$this->authors = Array();
```

And for each author fragment, we parse the `fname`, `mname`, and `lname` using the same approach we used for the title of the page:

```
foreach($authors as $author) {
    $author_xml = xmldoc($author);
    if(!$author_xml) {
        die("Author portion is not well formed!");
    }
    $aux = $this->XpathGetTextNodes($author_xml,
                                    "/author/fname/text()");
    $aut["fname"] = $aux[0];
    $aux = $this->XpathGetTextNodes($author_xml,
                                    "/author/mname/text()");
    $aut["mname"] = $aux[0];
    $aux = $this->XpathGetTextNodes($author_xml,
                                    "/author/lname/text()");
    $aut["lname"] = $aux[0];
    $this->authors[] = $aut;
}
```

Finally we get the XML content for the `<body>` element:

```
$aux = $this->XpathGetXmlNodes($this->doc,"/content/body");
$this->body = $aux[0];
} // end of ParseDocument() method
```

Now let's define a member function to save all the collected information for the current document to the `simplecms` database:

```
function AddToDbs()
{
    // Add the collected information about the current document to
    // the 'simplecms' database.

    // Lookup type/subtype combination in table 'simplecms_doctypes'
    $typeid = $this->LookupTypes();
```

```
        // Insert an appropriate record into table 'simplecms_contents'
        $contid = $this->InsertContentRecord($typeid);

        for ($i=0; $i < count($this->authors); $i++)
        {
            // Lookup author in table 'simplecms_authors'. Add author to
            // table if they are not already in it.
            $authid = $this->LookupAuthor($this->authors[$i]);

            // Insert author details record into table
            // 'simplecms_authordetails'
            $this->LookupAuthorDetail($authid, $contid);
        }
    } // end of AddToDbs() method
```

The following member function has two related purposes. The first purpose is to check if the current document's type and subtype combination already exist in the database (table `simplecms_doctypes`). If so, the record ID (column `doctype_typeid`) for this combination is returned. If the combination does not exist, it is added to the database and the new record's `typeid` value is returned:

```
function LookupTypes()
{
    // Determine if the current document type/subtype combination
    // exists in the 'simplecms_doctypes' table. If so, just retrieve
    // the 'doctype_typeid' field.
    // If not, insert a record into the table and retrieve the new
    // doctype_typeid

    $typeid = 0;

    $type    = $this->type;
    $subtype = $this->subtype;
```

Build the query string to determine if the current `type`/`subtype` combination exists in the database:

```
    sqlquery  = "SELECT * FROM simplecms_doctypes ";
    $sqlquery .= "WHERE doctype_type = '$type'
                    AND doctype_subtype = '$subtype' ";
    #print "[dbg(lookupTypes)]: qry=[$sqlquery]<br>\n";

    $results = $this->db->query($sqlquery);
    if (DB::isError($results))
    {
        $msg  = "Could not query table simplecms_doctypes: ";
        $msg .= $results->getMessage()."<br>\n";
        die($msg);
    }
    $nrows = $results->numRows();
```

If the combination exists then get the value of the column `doctype_typeid` for this combination:

```
if ($nrows != 0) {
    // This combination exists (assume one resultset row).
    // Retrieve field 'doctype_typeid'
    $aaRow = $results->fetchRow(DB_FETCHMODE_ASSOC);
    $typeid = $aaRow["doctype_typeid"];
    #print "dbg[doctype]: combo exists ($typeid)<br>\n";
}
```

If the combination does not exist then build an `INSERT` query string and add a record:

```
else {
    // This combination does not exist. Insert record.
    $insquery = "INSERT INTO simplecms_doctypes
                    (doctype_type,doctype_subtype) VALUES ";
    $insquery.= "('$type', '$subtype') ";
    #print "[dbg]: qry=($insquery)<br>\n";

    $insres = $this->db->query($insquery);
    if (DB::isError($insres)) {
        // Problems accessing database.
        $errmsg = "MySQL Error: Cannot access table
                    simplecms_doctypes in ";
        $errmsg .= "database $dbs: ".
        $results->getMessage()."<br>\n ";
        die($errmsg);
    } else {
        // Check how many rows were "affected" by the insert
        $naff = $this->db->AffectedRows();
        if ($naff != 1) {
            // Problems accessing database.
            $errmsg = "Problems with database. ";
            $errmsg .= "Doctype record not inserted.<br>\n";
            die($errmsg);
        }
```

Now a new `type/subtype` combination record has been added to the database. Next we retrieve the value of the `doctype_typeid` column:

```
        else {
            // Doctype record inserted
            $typeid = $this->db->getOne("SELECT doctype_typeid
                            FROM simplecms_doctypes
                            WHERE doctype_type='$type'
                            AND doctype_subtype='$subtype'");
            #print "dbg[simplecms_doctypes]: created new
                    ($typeid)<br>\n";
        }
    }
}
return($typeid);
} // end of LookupTypes() method
```

The following member function checks to see if the current document has already been added to the database. If it hasn't been added, a new record is added to the `simplecms_contents` table:

```
function InsertContentRecord($typeid)
{
    // Insert an appropriate record into 'simplecms_contents'. However,
    // there is a rule that for a given document type/subtype
    // combination, only one use of a particular title is allowed.
    // We need to check for duplicate titles first.
```

Here we copy some of the class properties to local variables:

```
$title   = $this->title;
$pageurl = $this->pageurl;
$body    = addslashes($this->body);
```

Build a query string to determine if this document has already been recorded. The criteria for this check is that for a given `type`/`subtype` combination, there must be only one document with a particular title. However, there is no comparison of document content:

```
$sqlquery  = "SELECT content_contentid FROM simplecms_contents ";
$sqlquery .= "WHERE content_typeid = '$typeid' ";
$sqlquery .= "AND content_title = '$title' ";

#print "[dbg(lookup title)]: qry=[$sqlquery]<br>\n";

$results = $this->db->query($sqlquery);
if (DB::isError($results)) {
    $msg  = "Could not query table content: ";
    $msg .= $results->getMessage()."<br>\n";
    die($msg);
}
$nrows = $results->numRows();
```

If the content record exists, get the value of the record ID and return it to the calling code:

```
if ($nrows != 0) {
    // This content record exists (assume one resultset row).
    // Retrieve field 'content_contentid'

    $aaRow = $results->fetchRow(DB_FETCHMODE_ASSOC);
    $contid = $aaRow["content_contentid"];
    print "dbg[content]: content record exists ($contid)<br>\n";
}
```

If no document with this title and document type exists in the database, add a new record:

```
else {
    // This content record does not exist. Insert record.
    $insquery ="INSERT INTO simplecms_contents
                (content_typeid,content_title,
                 content_pageurl,content_body) VALUES ";
    $insquery.="($typeid, '$title', '$pageurl', '$body') ";
    print "[dbg]: qry=($insquery)<br>\n";
```

```
            $insres = $this->db->query($insquery);

            if (DB::isError($insres)) {
                // Problems accessing database.
                $errmsg  = "MySQL Error:Cannot access table content in ";
                $errmsg .= "database $dbs: ".$this->db->getMessage().
                          "<br>\n ";
                die($errmsg);
            } else {
                // Check how many rows were "affected" by the insert
                $naff = $this->db->affectedRows();
                if ($naff != 1) {
                    // Problems accessing database.
                    $errmsg  = "Problems with database. ";
                    $errmsg .= "Content record not inserted.<br>\n";
                    die($errmsg);
                }
```

Once the record is inserted, retrieve the ID of the new record:

```
            else {
                // Content record inserted
                $contid = $this->db->getOne("SELECT content_contentid
                                    FROM simplecms_content
                                    WHERE content_title='$title'
                                    AND content_pageurl='$pageurl'
                                    AND content_body='$body'");
                print "dbg[content]: created new ($contid)<br>\n";
            }
        }
    }
    return($contid);
} // end of InsertContentRecord() method
```

The following member function checks to see if an author already exists in the simplecms_authors table. If the author exists, the appropriate record ID is returned, else they are added to the database and the ID of the new record is returned:

```
function LookupAuthor($author)
{
    // Check whether this author is already in table
        'simplecms_authors'.
    // If it is, retrieve the 'author_authorid' field.
    // Otherwise add the author and retrieve the new
        'author_authorid' field.

    // Uncomment the following code to get the author printed out.
    #print "<pre>\n";
    #print "[dbg(lookup)]: author\n";
    #var_dump($author);
    #print "</pre>\n";
```

```
$fname = $author["fname"];
$mname = $author["mname"];
$lname = $author["lname"];

$sqlquery  = "SELECT author_authorid FROM simplecms_authors ";
$sqlquery .= "WHERE author_firstname = '$fname' ";
$sqlquery .= "AND author_middlename = '$mname' ";
$sqlquery .= "AND author_lastname = '$lname' ";

#print "[dbg(lookupAuthor)]: qry=[$sqlquery]<br>\n";

$results = $this->db->query($sqlquery);
if (DB::isError($results)) {
    $msg  = "Could not query table simplecms_authors: ";
    $msg .= $results->getMessage()."<br>\n";
    die($msg);
}
$nrows = $results->numRows();
if ($nrows != 0) {
    // This combination exists (assume one resultset row).
    // Retrieve field 'author_authorid'

    $aaRow = $results->fetchRow(DB_FETCHMODE_ASSOC);
    $authid = $aaRow["author_authorid"];
    print "dbg[simplecms_authors]: author exists
            ($authid)<br>\n";
}

else {
    // This author does not exist. Insert record.
    $insquery = "INSERT INTO simplecms_authors
                (author_firstname, author_middlename,
                 author_lastname)  VALUES ";
    $insquery.= "('$fname', '$mname', '$lname') ";
    print "[dbg]: qry=($insquery)<br>\n";

    $insres = $this->db->query($insquery);
    if (DB::isError($insres)) {
        // Problems accessing database.
        $errmsg  = "MySQL Error: Cannot access table
                    simplecms_authors in ";
        $errmsg .= "database $dbs: ".
                    $insres->getMessage()."<br>\n ";
        die($errmsg);
    } else {
        // Check how many rows were "affected" by the insert
        $naff = $this->db->affectedRows();
        if ($naff != 1) {
            // Problems accessing database.
            $errmsg  = "Problems with database. ";
            $errmsg .= "Author record not inserted.<br>\n";
            die($errmsg);
```

```
                } else {
                    // Author record inserted
                    $authid = $this->db->getOne("SELECT author_authorid
                                        FROM simplecms_authors
                                        WHERE author_firstname='$fname'
                                        AND author_middlename='$mname'
                                        AND author_lastname ='$lname'");
                    print "dbg[author]: created new ($authid)<br>\n";
                }
            }
        }
        return($authid);
    } // end of LookupAuthor() method
```

The following member function checks to see whether the author details for a particular document have been added. Author details simply refer to a particular author's record ID from the simplecms_authors table. For example, if an author's record ID (author_authorid) in the simplecms_authors table is 5, and the record ID (authordetail_contentid), of the document in question is 17, then we are checking to see if the simplecms_authordetails table has a record with these two values. If there is a record, then the author details for this document have already been added, else we need to add a new record:

```
function LookupAuthorDetail($authid, $contid)
{
    // Check to see whether this author's contribution to the
    // indicated document has already been recorded. If so, retrieve
    // the 'authordetail_authordetailid' field. Otherwise, insert an
    // 'author detail' record and retrieve the new 'authordetailid'.

    $authdetid = 0;

    $sqlquery  = "SELECT authordetail_authordetailid
                    FROM simplecms_authordetails ";
    $sqlquery .= "WHERE authordetail_authorid = $authid ";
    $sqlquery .= "AND authordetail_contentid = $contid ";

    print "[dbg(lookupAuthDet)]: qry=[$sqlquery]<br>\n";

    $results = $this->db->query($sqlquery);
    if (DB::isError($results)) {
        $msg  = "Could not query table simplecms_authordetails: ";
        $msg .= $results->getMessage()."<br>\n";
        die($msg);
    }
    $nrows = $results->numRows();

    if ($nrows != 0) {
        // This author detail record exists
        // (assume one resultset row).
        // Retrieve field 'authordetail_authordetailid'

        $aaRow = $results->fetchRow(DB_FETCHMODE_ASSOC);
        $authdetid = $aaRow["authordetail_authordetailid"];
        print "dbg[simplecms_authordetails]: author detail record
```

```
                            exists $authdetid)<br>\n";
        } else {
            // This author detail record does not exist. Insert record.
            $insquery = "INSERT INTO simplecms_authordetails
                            (authordetail_authorid, authordetail_contentid)
                            VALUES ";
            $insquery.= "($authid, $contid) ";
            print "[dbg]: qry=($insquery)<br>\n";

            $insres = $this->db->query($insquery);
            if (DB::isError($insres)) {
                // Problems accessing database.
                $errmsg  = "MySQL Error: Cannot access table
                                simplecms_authordetails in ";
                $errmsg .= "database $dbs: ".
                                $insres->getMessage()."<br>\n ";
                die($errmsg);
            } else {
                // Check how many rows were "affected" by the insert
                $naff = $this->db->affectedRows();
                if ($naff != 1) {
                    // Problems accessing database.
                    $errmsg  = "Problems with database. ";
                    $errmsg .= "Author detail record not
                                    inserted.<br>\n";
                    die($errmsg);
                } else {
                    // Author detail record inserted
                    $authdetid = $this->db->getOne("SELECT
                                    authordetail_authordetailid
                                    FROM simplecms_authordetails
                                    WHERE authordetail_authorid='$authid'
                                    AND authordetail_contentid='$contid'");
                    print "dbg[authordet]: created new
                                ($authdetid)<br>\n";

                }
            }
        }
        return($authdetid);
    } # end of LookupAuthorDetail() method

} # end of ImportXMLDocument class
```

The main code can be written to parse one or many XML documents. This is an example of how to parse one document:

```
$d1 = new ImportXMLDocument($host,$user,$pass,$dbs);
$d1->ParseDocument("C:\Program Files\Apache Group\Apache2\htdocs\
                ProPHPSiteDesign\Ch09\\resume01.xml");
$d1->AddToDbs();
?>
```

Of course we can define a list of documents and parse all of them, if necessary, in a loop.

This is the output of the `importxmldocs.php` script on the browser:

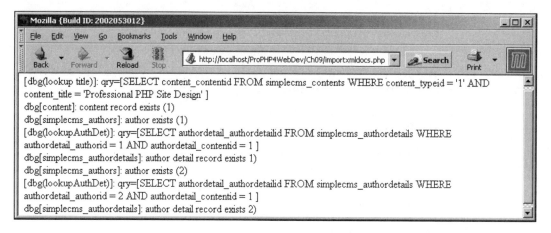

Delivering the Content

As stated earlier in this chapter, the focus of the case study is the addition of tags to and import of the document content. How the stored content is used depends on the needs of the end user. How the content of a particular document is manipulated and delivered depends on the `type`/`subtype` combination (that is, depends on the inherent tagset and document structure for a particular document type).

Since there are virtually unlimited types of XML document structures that can be stored in the `simplecms` database, we cannot get into a detailed discussion of writing application components for the manipulation and delivery of the content of each. However, we will look at algorithms for some example components.

List all Documents

A report that is very likely to be used frequently is a list of documents that are currently in the database. The algorithm below lists all documents ordered by `type`, `subtype`, and then `title`. Depending on functional requirements, the output might be plain text, XML, or some other format:

1. Retrieve all documents in the database by selecting from the content-table, and join it together with the doctypes-table using the typeid-key.

2. Process retrieved data and output list of documents by type, subtype, and title.

List Documents of a Specific Type and Subtype

What might be more useful is a list of document titles for a specific type and/or subtype. The algorithm below shows the necessary steps. Once again, the output might be plain text, XML, or some other format:

```
1.Specify document type

2.Specify document subtype

3.Retrieve all relevant documents by selecting from the content-table, defining a
  specific type and subtype, and grouping by both type and subtype.

4.Process retrieved data and output list of documents by type, subtype, and title.
```

Note the way in which the end user will convey the necessary information (type, subtype) depends on the functional requirements. The information might be conveyed via an HTML form or in batch mode as:

```
<?listdocs_by_type type="fiction" ?>
```

or:

```
<?listdocs_by_subtype subtype="resume" ?>
```

or:

```
<?listdocs_by_doctype type="nonfiction" subtype="book" ?>
```

We would then have to write an application component that could interpret these XML PIs.

Display Table of Contents for Non-Fiction Book

Finally, we give the algorithm, for one example, of how an application-parsing component would behave. If we want to see the Table of Contents for a non-fiction book document, we might use the following algorithm:

```
1. Specify document type

2. Specify document subtype

3. Specify document title

4. Retrieve document content by selecting from the content-table, and define
   a specific type, a specific subtype, and a specific title.

5. Parse the retrieved XML content:

   5.1 Create a 'doctree' object
   5.2 For each chapter tag, <chap>, encountered
       {
           5.2.1 Create a 'chap' object and add it to the doctree
           5.2.2 Extract the 'num', 'title', and 'style' attributes of the
                 <chap> tag and save them in the chap object.
```

```
        5.2.3 For each section tag, <sec>, encountered
            {
                5.2.3.1 Create an 'sec' object and it to the currently
                        open chap or parent sec object.
                5.2.3.2 Extract lev, title, style attributes from the
                        <sec> tag and save them to the sec object.
                5.2.3.3 For each paragraph tag (not shown in example) or
                        other sectional document content
                    {
                        Ignore the content
                    }
            }
        }

    6. Output the TOC in the desired format.
```

We now have a document tree in the form of a complex object data structure. Depending on functional needs, there are many ways in which the table of contents can be displayed.

Tagname Search Engine

Earlier we have discussed two types of search engines that might be built for retrieving the content. The second type discussed was the **tag name** search engine. Given a specific tag name and optional attribute names, a list of documents could be produced which contain the specified tag in the body. This is a useful search engine, particularly if we are developing application components to parse different document types.

To implement such an engine, we would need to record the occurrences of each and every tag and all the attribute names that occur in each imported XML document's body (that is, between the <body> and </body> tags). Since this step would be best performed during import, we have two choices for implementation:

❑   Toss out the custom parser defined earlier for the common tags (that is, <content>, <title>, <authors>, <author>, <fname>, and so on) and replace it with code built around PHP's XML/Expat functions

❑   Add some new code that uses the XML/Expat functions to just parse the document body markup

Whichever choice we make, recording tags and attribute occurrences is relatively simple. We need one database table to store a list of unique tag names. A second table would store attribute names and a pointer to the tag name they belong to. A third table would record occurrences of tags. Such a scheme would also implicitly define where the attributes occur. This allows an end user to search for documents containing tags that have a specific attribute name.

The tables we can use are simplecms_taglist, simplecms_attributes, and simplecms_tagoccurrences, shown in the relationship diagram below. Note that the simplecms_content table is repeated here (with just the ID columns) to show the relationship with the previously discussed database tables:

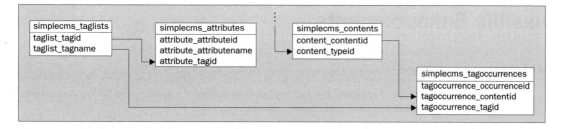

Here is the general algorithm for populating the three new tables:

```
For each tag encountered in the current document's body
{
    Check to see if the current tag has already been recorded in the tag
    list. If it has not, add it:
    If the tagname is already in the "taglist" table {
        Retrieve the record id, tagid
    } else {
        Add the tagname to table "taglist"
        Retrieve id, tagid, of new record
    }
```

Now we can store even a single occurrence of a particular tagname and its attributes. Keep in mind that some tags may have optional attributes. Even though the tag occurs several times, the attributes used may be in different combinations. The code snippet below stores multiple occurrences, even of the same combination in a single document, as it is easy to do, and provides the user a quick method of determining how many times a particular tag occurred in a document:

```
// Store an "occurrence" record for this tag in the current document:

Add a record to table "tagocc" containing the id of the current
document, contentid, and the current tag, tagid.
```

Now we store attribute names for the current tag. Since we are storing multiple occurrences of a tag within the current document, we will want to know which attributes were used in each occurrence. So we simply add a record to the `attribs` table for each attribute used with the current tag:

```
Add a record to table "attribs" (use tagid from above)
```

Note that more complex queries can be performed than what we have discussed above. For example, a feature that allows recording the occurrences of tag and attribute names allows searching for tag names or attribute names based on the document type. This can be used to enforce certain tagging requirements for specific document types.

Possible Enhancements

A couple of suggestions for the application in this case study are suggested below:

❑ Ensure database integrity; if the author detail records (the `simplecms_authordetails` table) for a particular document are not successfully added then there should be a provision to delete the appropriate record from table content

❑ Build a web corpus and set up a regular search engine

❑ Add a web interface to the import application, particularly for manipulating common information for each document

❑ Add an application parsing component for each document type/subtype combination

Summary

This case study looks at a relatively simple method of storing textual content with different document structures. Content is marked up in a custom XML tagset that follows the same general structure and can thus be stored in a single database. XML parsers are then defined for each combination of content type and subtype and are tied to the application's features.

While XML's predecessor SGML was used mostly for technical documentation and XML is often used for representing structured data, there are still numerous advantages to marking up various types of textual documents in XML. Note, however, that although we are not converting the body of each document into appropriate database records (beyond the basic tags common to each type of document), the application could work very well for a production web site, maintaining a database from which you could draw content.

For those who are interested in a CMS for web pages, with multiple contributors both technical and non-technical contributors, please consult Chapter 10.

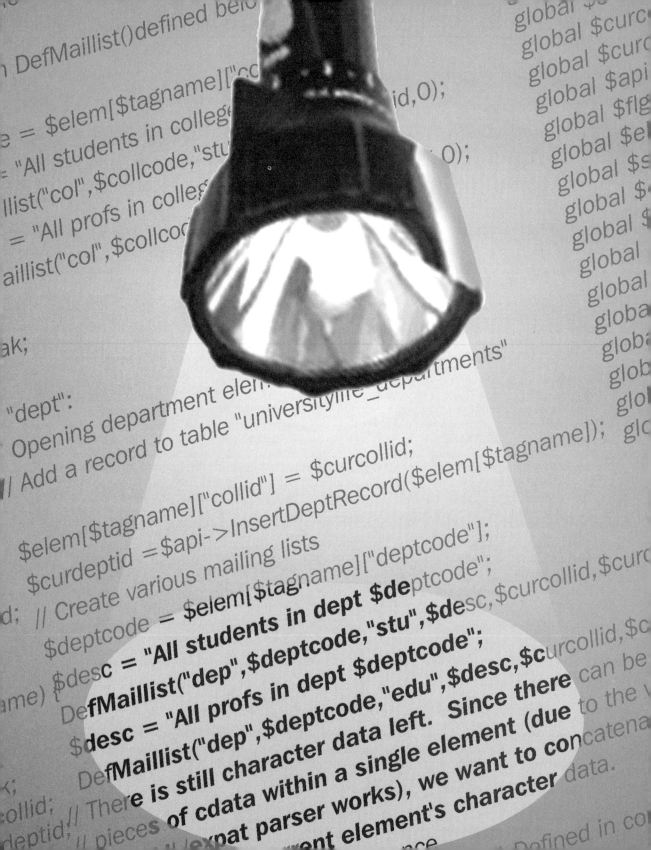

10

Advanced Content Management System

In the last chapter we discussed a basic Content Management System (CMS) designed for internal use by a team of technically capable contributors. This case study explores an advanced Content Management System (CMS), which users of varying technical skills can design and use. Thus, this application is supplemental to the information in the previous case study.

In the course of this chapter, we will look at:

❑ **Specifications**
Of course, we first need to decide what the application should be able to do, and how it generally should be designed.

❑ **Designing the Database**
We need a well-defined database structure to handle the content of this application.

❑ **Managing the Data**
In this application, all data is handled as XML. We therefore need to define XML structures and PIs to manage the data.

❑ **Delivering the Content**
We also need to define PHP classes and functions to retrieve data from the CMS.

In this chapter, we focus on some of the workflow aspects of an advanced CMS (Content Management System). While the last case study, 'A Simple Content Management System', focused on how a variety of document structures (that is, content) might be stored and manipulated using a simple database schema, this case study looks at user categories, privileges, task lists, messaging, and activity logs. The techniques discussed in both of these case studies, if combined, would result in an application resembling an essentially complete CMS.

Specification

A case study on all the facets of an advanced CMS could fill an entire book. Since space does not permit us such an in-depth study we will focus on the following aspects:

- ❏ User types and privileges
- ❏ Task lists
    - ❏ Assignment of a task
    - ❏ Acceptance of an assigned task
    - ❏ Rejection of an assigned task
    - ❏ Viewing the task list
- ❏ File check-in/check-out
- ❏ Team messaging
- ❏ Action usage logs
- ❏ Activity reports that have user-specific access.

Here we are focussing on a CMS 'engine' that requires XML-compatible input to carry out the requested action. This means that requests are in the form of XML processing instructions (PIs):

```
<?adduser ?>
```

The data supplied to the application with the XML PI must be in XML-compatible markup:

```
<user>
  <acct>mookie</acct>
  <pass>mouse</mouse>
  ...
</user>
```

Here, the XML PI makes a request to add a user, and the `<user>...</user>` block supplies the necessary information for creating the user. In the *Accessing the CMS Engine* section later on in the chapter, we will discuss the various XML PIs needed to access the CMS engine that we are focusing on in this case study.

Assumptions

Any full WCMS built around the 'engine' that we are focusing on in this case study would most likely be used on an internal server that has been separated from outside access by a firewall. Thus security is not as rigorous as it would otherwise be. The expectation is that no employee will sabotage the database.

User Types

Many different types of users, with varying levels of technical skills, could use a WCMS based on the features that we are focusing on. Some common user types (categories) are listed below:

❑ Administrators

❑ Technical users (developers, technical webmaster)

❑ Content authors

❑ Editors

❑ Content reviewers

❑ Graphic designers

❑ Business webmaster

❑ Channel managers

❑ Site producer

Content Type and Features

For the purposes of this case study, we are focusing on plain text and markup content. Markup content can be in HTML, XML, or WML.

> **Refer to Chapter 9 for a discussion about storing XML content in a database.**

While the implied content in this case study can be stored on an internal server, the content can also be intended for different channels:

❑ Intranet

❑ Departmental intranet

❑ Extranet/VPN

❑ Public Internet

However, due to space limitations, we shall discuss storing content on an internal server.

Designing the Database

The `advancedcms` database in this case study is far more complex than the one discussed in the last chapter. In the following sections, we shall describe the information that needs to be captured.

Database Information

The data that we are focusing on in this case study is shown in the list below:

❑ User accounts

❑ User account categories

❑ User privileges

- ❑ Task lists
- ❑ Task categories
- ❑ Task assignment details
- ❑ Virtual pages and native files
- ❑ Files/pages checked out
- ❑ Team messages
- ❑ Application actions
- ❑ Action usage log

Database Tables

The above information can be represented in the following tables, in normalized form:

Table Name	Alias	Description
advancedcms_usercategories	uc	Stores a list of possible user categories. Each user will belong to one category.
advancedcms_users	usr	Stores a list of user accounts, with a pointer to table advancedcms_usercategories.
advancedcms_userprivileges	up	Specifies all possible privileges that any user might have.
advancedcms_privilegedetails	pd	For each privilege that a specific user has been assigned, there is one privilege detail record.
advancedcms_pages	pg	Contains the list of virtual pages stored in the CMS. *Note that we shall not discuss the storage of content in this chapter, since we wrote already deal with it in chapter 9.*
advancedcms_taskcategories	tc	Contains a list of all possible task categories.
advancedcms_tasklist	tl	Contains a list of all tasks ever assigned, from and to all users.

Table Name	Alias	Description
advancedcms_taskdetails	td	Indicates whether a specific assigned task was accepted or rejected by indicating who actually ended up with the task. For example, if user 12 assigned task 3 to user 15, but user 15 rejected the assignment, then the record in table advancedcms_taskdetails would be (taskdetail_whoid, taskdetail_taskid) = (12,3), not (15,3). The associated record in the advancedcms_tasklist table will indicate the task acceptance status. There may be a string of assignments/ reassignments, so we need the advancedcms_taskdetails table to indicate only who ended up with the assignment.
advancedcms_checkinandout	co	Each time the file for a virtual page gets checked out, a record is added to the advancedcms_checkinandout table. When the file is checked back in, the appropriate record is updated. Since this table tracks check-out and check-in dates, a file change log can be generated.
advancedcms_messages	msg	Stores all messages sent by one user to another user. Some messages are sent by the CMS application under the user name 'system'. *Not that we do not discuss message deletion here.*
advancedcms_actions	act	This is a list of all possible actions that a user can take, based on their user privileges.
advancedcms_usagelog	ul	Whenever a user makes some request for action, the action is logged here. This table is used for activity reporting.

Relationships Between Tables

The diagram below shows the relationship between the tables in the advancedcms database:

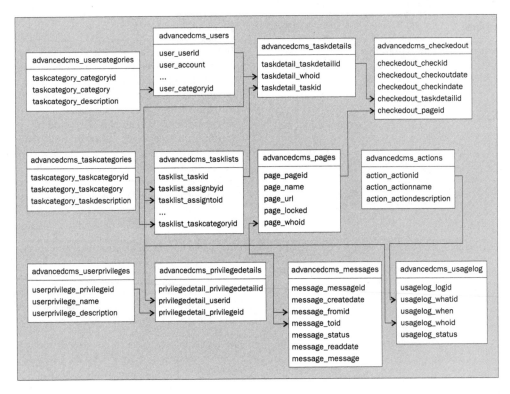

Note that not all columns of every table are shown.

Database Table Specfics

Let's now discuss the database tables in more detail.

User Categories

The `advancedcms_usercategories` table stores a list of all possible user categories like administrator, developer, reviewer, editor, channel manager, and so on:

Column Name	Data Type	Description
usercategory_categoryid	INT	Unique record ID generated by MySQL to represent this user category record. Note that if one intends to build an application that is easily adopted to another database server, it is best to use the to use the functions for generating unique IDs in the database abstraction layer instead of the server's internal function. Both PHP-LIB and PEAR::DB come with this feature.
usercategory_category	CHAR	User category label
usercategory_description	CHAR	Description of user category [Optional]

Users

The `advancedcms_users` table stores all the user account information for the CMS application:

Column Name	Data Type	Description
user_userid	INT	Unique record ID generated by MySQL to represent this user account record. As mentioned before, it is best to use the database abstraction layer generate IDs.
user_account	CHAR	Name of user account, for login, messaging, tasking, and activity tracking purposes.
user_password	CHAR	The password for this user account.
user_status	CHAR	This column indicates whether the user is currently logged in (A – active), not logged in (I – inactive), or blocked (B). The flaw is that we cannot enforce the use of the logout feature, so this field can be misleading if not maintained correctly. Therefore, make sure a user gets logged out automatically after a certain time of inactivity.
user_logdatetime	DATETIME	We'll store the date/time of the most recent login as a character string. This string is used to encrypt the account name, with the result used to produce the session ID.
user_sessid	CHAR	While a user is logged in, this field stores a value to indicate that the user is legitimately logged in. That is, it's a form of user authentication.
user_categoryid	INT	A pointer to the user category for this user (refer to the `advancedcms_usercategories` table).

User Privileges

The `advancedcms_userprivileges` table stores all possible privileges that a user can have:

Column Name	Data Type	Description
userprivilege_privilegeid	INT	Unique record ID generated by MySQL to represent this privilege record
userprivilege_name	CHAR	Short name or code for a particular privilege
userprivilege_description	CHAR	Description of the privilege (typically used by a system administrator user)

This does not necessarily mean that all users in the same user category will have the same privileges, but they might. Typically, being in a particular user category implies certain basic privileges. On top of that, some users may require additional privileges.

Privilege Details

The `advancedcms_privilegedetails` table stores a list of the actual privileges assigned to each user:

Column Name	Data Type	Description
`privilegedetail_privilegedetailid`	INT	Unique record ID generated by MySQL to represent this privilege detail record. Your database abstraction layer could also generate this column.
`privilegedetail_userid`	INT	This is a foreign key (table `advancedcms_users`) that indicates which user a privilege is being assigned to.
`privilegedetail_privilegeid`	INT	This is a foreign key (table `advancedcms_userprivilege s`) that indicates which privilege is being assigned.

For each privilege that the user has, including the basic privileges determined by the user category, one record is added to this table.

Pages

The `advancedcms_pages` table stores a list of all the virtual pages in the system:

Column Name	Data Type	Description
`page_pageid`	INT	Unique record ID generated by MySQL to represent this virtual page record. Your database abstraction layer could also generate this column.
`page_name`	CHAR	This is the name or title for the page.
`page_url`	CHAR	If the CMS stores virtual page content in native files, then this is a URL (relative to the web server document root) for the native file.
		If the CMS stores page content in the database, then this URL might represent the file name for a static snapshot of the page, or the URL query string value which requests the page via a PHP script.
`page_locked`	CHAR	This indicates whether the native file is currently locked.
		For file systems that do not support explicit locking, the value in this column is useful for mimicking a locking mechanism.

Column Name	Data Type	Description
page_whoid	INT	This indicates which user has the file locked, in case another user needs it.
		Further, as an improvement feature, we can store the date of the most recent lock. If another user wants the file, they will be more inclined to ask the 'lock' user if they have had the file for a long time. Experience shows that users tend to be more reluctant to ask if they don't know how long the other user has had a file.

Task Categories

The advancedcms_taskcategories table stores the list of possible categories that a task can be in:

Column Name	Data Type	Description
taskcategory_taskcategoryid	INT	Unique record ID generated by MySQL to represent this 'task category' record. Your database abstraction layer could also generate this column.
taskcategory_taskcategory	CHAR	This is a short name or label for a task category
taskcategory_taskdescription	CHAR	This is a description of a task category; it is typically used by system administrator users

Tasklists

The advancedcms_tasklists table stores all tasks assigned to the users:

Column Name	Data Type	Description
tasklist_taskid	INT	Unique record ID generated by MySQL to represent this task record. Your database abstraction layer could also generate this column.
tasklist_taskname	CHAR	This is a short name or label for the task.
tasklist_taskdescription	TEXT	This is a description of the task to be performed.
tasklist_assigndate	DATE	This is the date that the task was first assigned be the assignee (tasklist_assignnbyid). Keep in mind that a task might be assigned to the user who rejects the assignment or passes on the assignment to someone else.
tasklist_duedate	DATE	The date the task is to be completed.

Table continued on following page

Column Name	Data Type	Description
tasklist_acceptdate	DATE	The date the task was accepted. Note that a task may be assigned to several users before someone accepts it.
tasklist_completedate	DATE	The date that the task was completed.
tasklist_rvwdate	DATE	Some tasks require that files/pages be updated, and then the results reviewed by other teammates. This column indicates the date that all reviews are complete.
tasklist_approvedate	DATE	This is the date that either the task assignor or a channel manager approves the completed task (including the reviews).
tasklist_status	ENUM('opn', 'rej', 'aa', 'cmp', 'cnc')	The status of the task: assigned but not yet accepted (opn), currently rejected (rej), assigned and active (aa), completed (cmp), cancelled (cnc).
tasklist_workflowid	INT	This is a pointer to a table of workflow rules.
tasklist_assignbyid	INT	This is the account ID of the assignor (the user who assigned the task).
tasklist_assigntoid	INT	This is the account ID of the assignee (the user who has currently been assigned to the task). If the assignee rejects the task, the assignors might either complete the task themselves or assign it to another user. Once a user accepts the task (including the assignor), a task detail record is created (see the advancedcms_taskdetails table).
tasklist_taskcategoryid	INT	This is a pointer to the advancedcms_taskcategories table, and identifies this task's category.

Taskdetails

The advancedcms_taskdetails table stores details of an assigned task that has been accepted. Until an assigned task is accepted, no record is added to this table for that task. Note that advancedcms_checkinandout could hold multiple references to a certain record in this table.

Column Name	Data Type	Description
taskdetail_taskdetailid	INT	Unique record ID generated by MySQL to represent this task detail record. Your database abstraction layer could also generate this column.
taskdetail_whoid	INT	This indicates which user accepted an assigned task. Note that a task might be assigned several times before someone accepts it.
taskdetail_taskid	INT	This indicates the accepted task (see the advancedcms_tasklist table).

Checkinandout

The advancedcms_checkinandout table keeps a list of files checked (including historical information):

Column Name	Data Type	Description
checkinandout_checkid	INT	Unique record ID generated by MySQL to represent this 'file checked out' record. Your database abstraction layer could also generate this column.
checkinandout_checkoutdate	INT	This is the date that the file was checked out.
checkinandout_checkindate	DATE	This is the date that the file was checked back in.
checkinandout_taskdetailid	INT	This is the task detail ID with which the file checkout is associated. There may be more than one record in this table with the same checkinandout_taskdetailid value.
checkinandout_pageid	INT	This is a pointer to the native file or virtual page that is checked out. (See the advancedcms_pages table).

Messages

The advancedcms_messages table stores all the messages sent to the users of this application:

Column Name	Data Type	Description
message_messageid	INT	Unique record ID generated by MySQL to represent this message record.
message_createdate	DATE	This is the date that the message was created.
message_message	CHAR	This is the body of the message. Messages are expected to be relatively short (255 characters). Longer instructions should be passed between team mates through other means.

Table continued on following page

Column Name	Data Type	Description
message_status	ENUM('new', 'read', 'deleted')	This is the status of the message (new, read, or deleted).
message_readdate	DATE	This is the date that the message was read. The value could be used for automated maintenance. For example, 120 days or more after a message has been read, it might deleted by a batch process.
message_fromid	INT	This is the ID of the user account that the message was sent from. System messages use ID 0.
message_toid	INT	This is the ID of the user account that the message was sent to.

Actions

The advancedcms_actions table stores a list of all possible actions that any user can take, provided that they have the appropriate privileges:

Column Name	Data Type	Description
action_actionid	INT	Unique record ID generated by MySQL to represent this action record
action_actionname	CHAR	This is a short name or code for this action
action_actiondescription	CHAR	This is a description of the action

Usagelog

The advancedcms_usagelog table records all actions taken by all the users:

Column Name	Data Type	Description
usagelog_logid	INT	Unique record ID generated by MySQL to represent this 'usage log' record
usagelog_actwhen	DATETIME	This is the date and time that the action was taken
usagelog_status	CHAR	This is the status (success, failure, other) of the action
usagelog_whatid	INT	This is a pointer to the advancedcms_actions table and indicates which action was taken
usagelog_whoid	INT	This is a pointer to the advancedcms_users table and indicates the user that took the action

This table is used to generate activity reports.

Database User

The tables for this case study can all be placed within a single MySQL database, `advancedcms`. Let us first create the database:

```
>mysqladmin create advancedcms
```

We only need one database user, say ADMIN. We will have to grant privileges to the tables, as well as create the tables. The `mysql` client utility that comes with MySQL, can be used to grant privileges:

```
mysql> GRANT SELECT, INSERT, UPDATE, DELETE ON advancedcms.* TO
       'ADMIN@localhost' IDENTIFIED BY "ADMIN";
```

Creating Tables

Run the following SQL script, `crdbs_advcms.sql`, on the command line to create the `advancedcms` database and tables:

```
> mysql advancedcms < crdbs_advancedcms.sql
```

```
# FILE: crdbs_advancedcms.sql
# USE:  Create tables for database 'advancedcms'
#
CREATE TABLE advancedcms_usercategories(
   usercategory_categoryid          INT UNSIGNED NOT NULL PRIMARY KEY
                                    AUTO_INCREMENT,
   usercategory_category            CHAR(6) NOT NULL,
   usercategory_description         VARCHAR(255)
);

CREATE TABLE advancedcms_users(
   user_userid                      INT UNSIGNED NOT NULL PRIMARY KEY
                                    AUTO_INCREMENT,
   user_account                     VARCHAR(12) NOT NULL,
   user_password                    VARCHAR(12) NOT NULL,
   user_status                      CHAR(1) NOT NULL,
   user_categoryid                  INT UNSIGNED NOT NULL,
   user_logdatetime                 DATETIME,
   user_sessionid                   VARCHAR(128) NOT NULL
);

CREATE TABLE advancedcms_userprivileges(
   userprivilege_privilegeid        INT UNSIGNED NOT NULL PRIMARY KEY
                                    AUTO_INCREMENT,
   userprivilege_name               VARCHAR(56) NOT NULL,
   userprivilege_description        VARCHAR(255)
);
```

```
CREATE TABLE advancedcms_privilegedetails(
    privilegedetail_privilegedetailid   INT UNSIGNED NOT NULL PRIMARY KEY
                                        AUTO_INCREMENT,
    privilegedetail_userid              INT UNSIGNED NOT NULL,
    privilegedetail_privlegeid          INT UNSIGNED NOT NULL
);

CREATE TABLE advancedcms_pages(
    page_pageid                         INT UNSIGNED NOT NULL PRIMARY KEY
                                        AUTO_INCREMENT,
    page_name                           VARCHAR (255),
    page_url                            VARCHAR (255),
    page_locked                         CHAR(1), # Y (yes), N (no)
    page_whoid                          INT UNSIGNED
);

CREATE TABLE advancedcms_taskcategories(
    taskcategory_taskcategoryid         INT UNSIGNED NOT NULL PRIMARY KEY
                                        AUTO_INCREMENT,
    taskcategory_taskcategory           VARCHAR(28) NOT NULL,
    taskcategory_taskdescription        VARCHAR(255)
);

CREATE TABLE advancedcms_tasklists(
    tasklist_taskid                     INT UNSIGNED NOT NULL PRIMARY KEY
                                        AUTO_INCREMENT,
    tasklist_taskname                   VARCHAR(128),
    tasklist_taskdescription            TEXT NOT NULL,
    tasklist_assigndate                 DATE,
    tasklist_duedate                    DATE,
    tasklist_acceptdate                 DATE,
    tasklist_completedate               DATE,
    tasklist_reviewdate                 DATE,
    tasklist_approvedate                DATE,
    tasklist_status                     ENUM('opn', 'rej', 'aa', 'cmp',
                                        'cnc' ),
    tasklist_workflowid                 INT UNSIGNED,
    tasklist_assignedbyid               INT UNSIGNED NOT NULL,
    tasklist_assignedtoid               INT UNSIGNED NOT NULL,
    tasklist_taskcategoryid             INT UNSIGNED NOT NULL
);

CREATE TABLE advancedcms_taskdetails (
    taskdetail_taskdetailid             INT UNSIGNED NOT NULL PRIMARY KEY
                                        AUTO_INCREMENT,
    taskdetail_whoid                    INT UNSIGNED NOT NULL,
    taskdetail_taskid                   INT UNSIGNED NOT NULL
);

CREATE TABLE advancedcms_checkinandout(
    checkinandout_checkid               INT UNSIGNED NOT NULL PRIMARY KEY
                                        AUTO_INCREMENT,
    checkinandout_checkoutdate          DATE,
```

```
        checkinandout_checkindate          DATE,
        checkinandout_taskdetailid         INT UNSIGNED NOT NULL,
        checkinandout_pageid               INT UNSIGNED NOT NULL
);

CREATE TABLE advancedcms_messages(
    message_messagei                       INT UNSIGNED NOT NULL PRIMARY KEY
                                           AUTO_INCREMENT,
    message_createdate                     DATE NOT NULL,
    message_message                        VARCHAR(255) NOT NULL,
    message_status                         ENUM( 'new', 'read', 'deleted' ),
    message_readdate                       DATE,
    message_fromid                         INT UNSIGNED NOT NULL,
    message_toid                           INT UNSIGNED NOT NULL
);

CREATE TABLE advancedcms_actions(
    action_actionid                        INT UNSIGNED NOT NULL PRIMARY KEY
                                           AUTO_INCREMENT,
    action_actionname                      VARCHAR(56) NOT NULL,
    action_actiondescription               VARCHAR(255)
);

CREATE TABLE advancedcms_usagelogs
(
    usagelog_logid                         INT UNSIGNED NOT NULL PRIMARY KEY
                                           AUTO_INCREMENT,
    usagelog_actwhen                       DATETIME NOT NULL,
    usagelog_status                        CHAR(3),
    usagelog_whatid                        INT UNSIGNED NOT NULL,
    usagelog_whoid                         INT UNSIGNED NOT NULL
);
```

Building Indexes

Indexes will be created for most columns in the database, in order to speed up common searches. The SQL commands for creating indices can be place in an SQL file, say mkidx_advancedcms.sql.

Run the following mkidx_advancedcms.sql SQL script, on the command line, to build the indexes for the advancedcms database and tables:

```
> mysql advancedcms < mkidx_advancedcms.sql
```

Here is the sample of the script:

```
# FILE: mkidx_advancedcms.sql
# USE:  create indexes for tables in database advancedcms
# create indexes for table advancedcms_usercategories
#
CREATE INDEX uc_idxOn_catid        ON
            advancedcms_usercategories(usercategory_categoryid);
CREATE INDEX uc_idxOn_cat          ON
            advancedcms_usercategories(usercategory_category);
```

```
# create indexes for table advancedcms_users
#
CREATE INDEX usr_idxOn_userid      ON advancedcms_users(user_userid);
CREATE INDEX usr_idxOn_acct        ON advancedcms_users(user_account );
CREATE INDEX usr_idxOn_status      ON advancedcms_users(user_status);
CREATE INDEX usr_idxOn_catid       ON advancedcms_users(user_categoryid);
CREATE INDEX usr_idxOn_logdatetime ON
                                      advancedcms_users(user_logdatetime);
CREATE INDEX usr_idxOn_sessid      ON advancedcms_users(user_sessionid);
    .
    .
    .
# create indexes for table advancedcms_usagelogs
#
CREATE INDEX ul_idxOn_logid   ON advancedcms_usagelogs(usagelog_logid);
CREATE INDEX ul_idxOn_actwhen ON advancedcms_usagelogs(usagelog_actwhen);
CREATE INDEX ul_idxOn_status  ON advancedcms_usagelogs(usagelog_status );
CREATE INDEX ul_idxOn_whatid  ON advancedcms_usagelogs(usagelog_whatid);
CREATE INDEX ul_idxOn_whoid   ON advancedcms_usagelogs(usagelog_whoid);
```

Note that SQL script for the indexes is available with the book's code that can be downloaded from Wrox web site.

Managing the Data

We now take a look at how the CMS workflow data is handled in this application.

Populating the Database

There are three steps to pouplating the database:

1. Create database tables

2. Build table indexes

3. Request engine actions to populate the database

Refer to the sections *Creating Tables* and *Building Indexes* to perform steps 1 and 2. Step 3 above is discussed in the context of the engine code.

Delivering the Content

In this case study, we are focussing on a back end engine for an advanced CMS application. We have left out any discussion of a web interface, as defining an engine leaves room for many possibilities for an interface.

Accessing the CMS Engine

The following sections show some of the basic XML PIs required to ask the CMS engine to perform common actions. The XML format of the necessary input data is also shown, wherever necessary.

Add User Category

To add a user category, use this XML PI:

```
<?addusercat ?>
```

To supply the necessary data to create the new user category, use the following markup:

```
<user>
  <cat>adm</cat>
  <descr>Administrative user.</descr>
</user>
```

Add User

To add a user, use this XML PI:

```
<?adduser ?>
```

To supply the necessary data to create the new user, use the following markup:

```
<user>
  <acct>mookie</acct>
  <pass>mouse</pass>
  <cat>adm</cat>
</user>
```

If the value `usercat.catid` is known, we use the following markup instead of `<cat>..</cat>`:

```
<catid>1</catid>
```

However, the assumption is that any interface that we wrap around this engine should supply the ID information whenever possible.

If an error occurs while trying to create the user, some XML markup, will be returned:

```
<error request="adduser">
  <errormsg>...</errormsg>
</error>
```

The content of the `<errormsg>` element will be in the form of an XML CDATA section. This element would be generated in case there are any special characters that are illegal in XML.

Add a Task Category

To add a task category, use the following XML PI:

```
<?addtaskcat ?>
```

To supply the necessary data, use the following markup:

```
<taskcat>
  <tcat>edit page</tcat>
  <tdescr>General edit of a virtual page or native file</tdescr>
</taskcat>
```

Assign Task

To assign a task, use the following XML PI:

```
<?assigntask ?>
```

To supply the necessary data, use the following markup:

```
<task>
  <taskname>edit home page</taskname>
  <taskdescr>Please add the company logo to the home page.</taskdescr>
  <assndate>...</assndate>
  <duedate>...</duedate>
  <assnbyid>13</assnbyid>
  <assntoid>15</asstoid>
  <tcatid>...</tcatid>
</task>
```

If the value of any of the ID fields above is unknown, the equivalent name field can be specified, like this:

```
<assnbyacct>mookie</assnbyacct>
<assntoacct>golly</assntoacct>
<tcat>edit page</tcat>
```

If an error occurs while trying to create the user, the following XML markup will be returned:

```
<error request="assigntask">
  <errormsg>...</errormsg>
</error>
```

Reject Task

To reject a task, we use the following XML PI:

```
<?rejecttask taskid="5" ?>
```

The `taskid` field will automatically imply which task is being rejected, who assigned the task, and who the task is currently assigned to. The appropriate engine component should take care of the rest of the request. That is, the database is updated to reflect the task rejection.

Reassign Task

A task that has been rejected can be reassigned to another user in two ways.

❑ The first way to reassign a task is to specify the task ID and the user ID to assign the task to:

```
<?reassigntask taskid="5" userid="15" ?>
```

❑ If the user ID is unknown, use the user account name:

```
<?reassigntask taskid="5" acct="golly" ?>
```

Also, the user doing the reassignment can either be the originator or the rejector. It does not matter who is reassigning the task (the originator or the current assignee). The task assignor remains the first user to assign the task to another user.

Accept Task

A task may go through several reassignments before a user accepts it. To accept a task, use the following PI:

```
<?accepttask taskid="5" ?>
```

This PI not only causes the advancedcms_tasklist table to be updated to reflect the task acceptance, a new record is added to the advancedcms_taskdetails table. The new record represents which user accepted which task. While this information might be deduced from just the task list record, the task detail record makes things easier.

List All Outstanding Tasks

To get a list of all outstanding tasks for all users, use the following PI:

```
<?listalloutstandingtasks ?>
```

As a CMS is typically a collaborative system, any user should be able to see the outstanding tasks for any other user. To specify a particular user, we can use either of the following PIs:

```
<?listalloutstandingtasks userid="15" ?>
```

```
<?listalloutstandingtasks acct="golly" ?>
```

List Tasks by Keyword

To get a list of all tasks (outstanding or otherwise) by using a keyword (or phrase), we use either of the following PIs:

```
<?listtasksbykeyword taskname="home page" ?>
```

```
<?listtasksbykeyword taskdescr="home page" ?>
```

List Unaccepted Tasks

To get a list of unaccepted tasks, we use the following PI:

```
<?listunacceptedtasks ?>
```

Additional ways to generate a list of tasks can be created by defining the criteria, writing PHP and MySQL code, and tying the code to an appropriate XML PI.

List Task Details

To list the details of a task (that is, all column values from the task record in the `advancedcms_tasklist` table), use the following PI:

```
<?listtaskdetail taskid="5" ?>
```

Check Out Page

To check out a virtual page or a native file, depending on how we set up our CMS, we can use any of the following PIs:

```
<?checkoutpage userid="15" pageid="23" taskid="10" ?>

<?checkoutpage acct="golly" pageid="23" taskid="10" ?>

<?checkoutpage pageid="23" tdetid="7" ?>
```

Notice that in the first two PIs, we used a `tasklist_taskid` attribute. This value points to the appropriate record in the `advancedcms_tasklists` table. Alternately, we can specify a task detail ID. This points to the appropriate record in the `advancedcms_taskdetails` table, which in turn points to the `tasklist` record (which identifies the task assignee).

In addition to the above methods of checking out a file, the `pageid` attribute can be replaced by either a 'name' or 'url' attribute (see the `advancedcms_pages` table). Which method we choose to code for depends on the needs of our CMS interface.

Check In Page

When a page has been updated at the request of a task assignment, it needs to be checked back in. There are a few ways to do this. A few examples are shown below. Once again, which methods we choose to code for depends on the needs of our CMS interface:

```
<?checkinpage chid="3"?>

<?checkinpage pageid="23"?>

<?checkinpage name="..." ?>

<?checkinpage url="..." ?>
```

Send Message

To send a message, we need both an XML PI to make the request and some XML-like markup to provide message details. There are two ways to provide the necessary information:

With from/to user ids:

```
<?sendmsg ?>
<message>
  <fromid>13</fromid>
  <toid>15</toid>
  <msg>I've assigned a task to you.</msg>
</message>
```

❑   With from/to user account names:

```
<?sendmsg ?>
<message>
  <fromacct>mookie</fromacct>
  <toacct>golly</toacct>
  <msg>I've assigned a task to you.</msg>
</message>
```

Send System Message

At times, the system needs to send one or more users a message. The format is the same as above. However, a `fromid` of 0 is used:

```
<?sendmsg ?>
<message>
  <fromid>0</fromid>
  <toid>15</toid>
  <msg>Please delete your old messages by Friday.</msg>
</message>
```

Activity Reports

Each time a user requests an action; it is logged to the `advancedcms_usagelogs` table. A record from the `advancedcms_actions` table supplies the necessary action information. This allows for system administrators to produce activity reports. There are a number of different activity reports that can be produced.

Next we will look at two examples on how to produce these reports. In both of these examples, data is supplied as part of the XML PI rather than as XML markup. XML PIs can by definition receive data in this way. Also, each request directly corresponds to an SQL SELECT query that must be implemented in class code. There is no checking of data required, as was the case in the examples above (the same is true for the *General Reports* examples that follow).

Monthly Activity for One User

To produce a list of activities for a given user in a given month, we might use the following XML PI:

```
<?monthlyuseractivity userid="15" month="2002-06" ?>
```

If the user ID is unknown, an alternate PI is:

```
<?monthlyuseractivity acct="golly" month="2002-06" ?>
```

In either case, the XML PI will require code that compares the month value against the dates of records in the `advancedcms_usagelogs` table.

Most Popular Activity for a Given Month

To determine the most popular activity for all users in a given month, we might use the following XML PI:

```
<?monthlypopularactivity month="2002-06" ?>
```

General Reports

In addition to various activity reports, there are a number of other reports that system administrators may want to generate for various management personnel. Let's look at a few examples.

Total Number of Tasks Assigned in a Given Month

To determine the total number of tasks assigned in a given month by all users, we can use the following XML PI:

```
<?monthlynumtasksassigned month="2002-06" ?>
```

Due to the way the database and the application engine has been designed, if a task has been rejected by one user but accepted by a second user, it counts as only one task. If this was not the case, counting tasks could generate a completely irrelevant number.

Total Number of Unaccepted Tasks

To determine the total number of unaccepted tasks assigned in a particular month, we can use the following XML PI:

```
<?numtasksunaccepted month="2002-06" ?>
```

Total Number of Outstanding Tasks

To determine the total number of outstanding tasks assigned in any month, we can use the following XML PI:

```
<?numoutstandingtasks ?>
```

Note that 'outstanding' only means that the task has not yet been completed. It has nothing to do with the due date for the task.

Total Number of Overdue Tasks

To determine the total number of overdue tasks assigned in any month, we can use the following XML PI:

```
<?numoverduetasks ?>
```

PHP Code

The majority of the code for the engine follows the same general algorithm:

```
1. Parse XML PI
2. Parse any XML-like markup, if applicable
3. Query database for relevant records, if applicable
4. Insert new records, if applicable
5. Generate output or error messages in XML-like markup
```

Instead of providing PHP code for the entire set of 'request' examples given above, we will present code for a few examples that should cover most of the variations. Since the CMS request engine has been designed in a modular form, additional code can easily be added for interpreting other XML PIs and relevant data.

The code presented here gives us enough information to make adding additional parsing code relatively easy. In most cases, to add code for handling an additional XML PI, all we would have to do is to simply cut and paste the code from an existing class that performs similar data checks and actions and then tweak the code to reflect the needs of the new PI.

Basic Parser

A basic XML parser is used to parse any CMS engine requests. When an XML PI is encountered in the input, a 'CMS request' object is created. This object will contain the following information:

name of request	For example, "adduser" from <?adduser ?>
input information	For example, accountname, password, and so on, in parsed form
handler function name	For example, function CmsEngineAdduser()

The CMS request object will then create an appropriate 'request information' object that depends on the request. Each different request (XML PI) will cause a different object to be created. However, member function names will be the same. At the same time, an appropriate 'request handler' function name will be set by the basic parser, depending on the name of the request. When all the information has been collected for the request, the handler function will be called to take care of the request.

> **While the engine is expected to be used in a batch mode, it can also be tested in a web browser.**

The PHP code for the basic parser is detailed below. Following the basic parser are several sections, each of which shows the class code and handler function for some of the engine requests discussed earlier. Assume for the time being that the data for a CMS engine request is supplied via the `acmsrequest.xml` file. We can change this if we build our own interface around this engine.

Note that the code in both `acmsengine.php` and `classes.php` have commented debugging statements; these lines can be uncommented to get a better look at how the code works.

Below we'll present the `acmsengine.php` script. It starts out by including some files we need:

```php
<?php
#
# FILE: acmsengine.php
# USE:  Define engine code for the "Advanced CMS" application
require_once 'DB.php';
include_once("classes.php");
```

These global variables define the name of the handlers. Note that these are actual PHP function-names:

```php
### Global variables ##################

// include the sample XML file
$file     = "acmsrequest.xml";

$activereq = false;

$handlers["start"]   = "StartElement";
$handlers["end"]     = "EndElement";
$handlers["pi"]      = "PIHandler";
$handlers["cdata"]   = "CDataHandler";
```

Next, we set all information needed for connecting to the database:

```php
### Database connection code ##################

$host = "localhost";        # MySQL server
$user = "admin";            # Username
$pass = "";                 # Password
$dbs  = "advancedcms";      # Database name
$dbc  = null;               # MySQL connection resource (set elsewhere)
```

The `OpenDatabaseConnection()` function uses the variables set above to establish a database connection:

```php
function OpenDatabaseConnection($host,$user,$pass,$dbs)
{
    // Establish a database connection and save the resource link in
    // a global variable.

    $dsn = "mysql://$user:$pass@$host/$dbs";
    $db = DB::connect($dsn);
    if (DB::isError($db)) {
        die ($this->db->getMessage());
    }

    return $db;
} # end function OpenDatabaseConnection()
```

We also need a function to handle the XML PI:

```
### Parser code ###############################

function PIHandler($parser, $target, $data)
{
    global $aaCMSClasses;
    global $oReq;
    global $activereq;
    global $dbc;
```

If there is a an existing request, complete that one before proceeding:

```
    // Complete any existing request first
    if ($activereq) {
        $oReq->SaveToDbs($dbc);
        $activereq = false;
    }
```

Below, we print out the requested XML PI, generate the PHP code to be executed, and make sure it gets executed by passing it to the eval() function:

```
    print "[dbg(xmlpi)]: [$target]<br>\n";
    $cmd = "\$oReq = new ".$aaCMSClasses[$target]."(\$dbc);";
    #print "[dbg(PI)]: $cmd<br>\n";
    eval($cmd);
```

Also, we need to tell the application that there is an active request:

```
    $activereq = true;
} # end function PIHandler()
```

The following two functions will act as the start and end element handlers:

```
function StartElement($parser, $tagname, $attrs)
{
    global $oReq;

    #print "[dbg(start)]: tag=$tagname<br>\n";

    if ($tagname != "requests") {
        $oReq->PushStack($tagname);
        if (count($attrs)) {
            $oReq->SaveTag($tagname,$attrs);
        }
    }
} # end function StartElement()

function EndElement($parser, $tagname)
{
    global $oReq;

    if ($tagname != "requests") {
        $oReq->PopStack($tagname);
    }
} # end function EndElement()
```

The following function, CDataHandler(), will take care of character data:

```
function CDataHandler($parser, $cdata)
{
    global $oReq;

    // Eliminate extraneous newline character
    $cdata=eregi_replace("\n+","",$cdata);

    // Get rid of excess blanks
    $cdata = trim($cdata);

    if (strcmp($cdata,"") != 0) {
        #print "[dbg(cdata)]: [$cdata]<br>\n";

        $oReq->SaveCData($cdata);
    }
} # end function CDataHandler()
```

Now, when we have all our functions and variables set up, we can start the actual XML parsing. Of course, we first need to connect to the database:

```
### Main code    ###############################
$dbc = OpenDatabaseConnection($host,$user,$pass,$dbs);
```

Create a new XML parser:

```
$parser = xml_parser_create();
```

We also need to tell PHP about the handler-function that we have defined:

```
xml_parser_set_option($parser, XML_OPTION_CASE_FOLDING, 0);
xml_set_element_handler($parser,$handlers["start"],$handlers["end"]);
xml_set_processing_instruction_handler($parser, "PIHandler");
xml_set_character_data_handler($parser, $handlers["cdata"]);
```

With a very simple trick, we open the file to be parsed, and make sure it's valid, at the same time:

```
if (!($fp = @fopen($file, "r"))) {
    die("Could not open XML file $file for input<br>\n");
}
```

Opening the file was successful, so we start reading from it to parse the data:

```
// Read in the input file all at once
while ($markup = fread($fp, 4096)) {

    if (!xml_parse($parser, $markup, feof($fp))) {
        $errcode   = xml_get_error_code($parser);
        $errstring = xml_error_string($errcode);
```

```
        $linenum   = xml_get_current_line_number($parser);

        die("XML parse error ($errcode): $errstring at line $linenum");
    }
}
```

Finally, we free up the XML parser and save the object:

```
xml_parser_free($parser);

// Save current object, if we have reached the end of the request file
$oReq->SaveToDbs($dbc);

?>
```

Class and General Database Lookup Code

For every XML PI that we need to handle, we will define a class. However, each of these classes will be derived from the base class, RequestInfo. All class code and related global variables are in a file called classes.php, which is included in the main acmsengine.php script. The classes.php script will be split over this section and the 'request' sections that follow.

> *Note that a stub code has been provided for all the XML PI handlers; however, only the constructor function for same of the classes has been provided. Filling in the necessary code for these in complete classes is left as an exercise for the reader.*

We begin by defining the names of our classes in an array. The reason for this is simple - if we decide to change the name of a class, we only need to modify the code at one place:

```
<?php

// FILE: classes.php
// USE:  Define class + database lookup code for Advanced CMS application

$aaCMSClasses = array();
$aaCMSClasses["addusercat"]            = "addUserCat";
$aaCMSClasses["adduser"]               = "addUser";
$aaCMSClasses["addtaskcat"]            = "addTaskCat";
$aaCMSClasses["assigntask"]            = "assignTask";
$aaCMSClasses["rejecttask"]            = "rejectTask";
$aaCMSClasses["reassigntask"]          = "reassignTask";
$aaCMSClasses["accepttask"]            = "acceptTask";
$aaCMSClasses["listalloutstandingtasks"] = "outstandingTasks";
$aaCMSClasses["listtasksbykeyword"]    = "tasksByKeyword";
$aaCMSClasses["listunacceptedtasks"]   = "unacceptedTasks";
$aaCMSClasses["listtaskdetail"]        = "taskDetail";
$aaCMSClasses["checkoutpage"]          = "checkoutPage";
$aaCMSClasses["checkinpage"]           = "checkinPage";
$aaCMSClasses["sendmsg"]               = "sendMsg";
```

Next we define a function called LookupCatidByCat(). As the name implies, this function can be used to get a category ID for a specific category name:

```
### General dbs code ############################

function LookupCatidByCat($db,$cat)
{
    // Determine if the specified user category
    // is already in table "advancedcms_usercategories"

    $catid = 0;
    $sqlquery  = "SELECT usercategory_categoryid
                    FROM advancedcms_usercategories ";
    $sqlquery .= "WHERE usercategory_category = '$cat' ";

    #print "[dbg(LookupCatidByCat)]: qry=[$sqlquery]<br>\n";

    $results = $db->query($sqlquery);

    if (DB::isError($results)) {
        $msg  = "Could not query table advancedcms_usercategories: ";
        $msg .= $results->getMessage()."<br>\n";
        die($msg);
    }
    $nrows = $results->numRows();
    if ($nrows != 0) {
        // This user category exists (assume one resultset row).
        // Retrieve field 'usercategory_categoryid'

        $aaRow = $results->fetchRow(DB_FETCHMODE_ASSOC);
        $catid = $aaRow["usercategory_categoryid"];
    }
    return($catid);

} # end function LookupCatidByCat
```

The function `LookupUseridByAcct()` takes an account name as argument, and, if the name exists in the database, the ID for that specific user account is returned:

```
function LookupUseridByAcct($db,$acct)
{
    // Determine if the specified user account name
    // is already in table "advancedcms_users"

    $userid = 0;

    $sqlquery  = "SELECT user_userid FROM advancedcms_users ";
    $sqlquery .= "WHERE user_account = '$acct' ";

    #print "[dbg(LookupUseridByAcct)]: qry=[$sqlquery]<br>\n";

    $results = $db->query($sqlquery);
    if (DB::isError($results)) {
        $msg  = "Could not query table advancedcms_users: ";
        $msg .= $results->getMessage()."<br>\n";
        die($msg);
```

```
        }

    $nrows = $results->numRows();
    if ($nrows != 0) {
        // This user exists (assume one resultset row).
        // Retrieve field 'user_userid'

        $aaRow = $results->fetchRow(DB_FETCHMODE_ASSOC);
        $userid = $aaRow["user_userid"];
    }

    return($userid);

} # end function LookupUseridByAcct
```

The next function, `LookupTcatidByTcat()`, returns the ID for a given category name if that category exists. If it does not exist, this function will just return '0':

```
function LookupTcatidByTcat($db,$tcat)
{
    // Determine if the specified task category
    // is already in table "advancedcms_taskcategories"

    $tcatid = 0;

    $sqlquery  = "SELECT taskcategory_taskcategoryid
                    FROM advancedcms_taskcategories ";
    $sqlquery .= "WHERE taskcategory_taskcategory = '$tcat' ";

    #print "[dbg(LookupTcatidByTcat)]: qry=[$sqlquery]<br>\n";

    $results = $db->query($sqlquery);
    if (DB::isError($results)) {
        $msg  = "Could not query table advancedcms_taskcategories: ";
        $msg .= $results->getMessage()."<br>\n";
        die($msg);
    }

    $nrows = $results->numRows();
    if ($nrows != 0) {
        // This task category exists (assume one resultset row).
        // Retrieve field 'taskcategory_taskcategoryid'

        $aaRow = $results->fetchRow(DB_FETCHMODE_ASSOC);
        $tcatid = $aaRow["taskcategory_taskcategoryid"];
    }

    return($tcatid);

} # end function LookupTcatidByTcat
```

Below you see the `RequestInfo` class. It is used as the base-class for the following classes to extend them with functionality to push and pop data from them:

```
### Class code #################################

class RequestInfo
{
    var $stack;
    var $dbc;

    function RequestInfo($dbc)
    {
        $this->stack = array();
        $this->dbc = $dbc;
    }

    function PushStack($tagname)
    {
        array_push($this->stack,$tagname);
    }

    function PopStack()
    {
        array_pop($this->stack);
    }
} # end class RequestInfo
```

Add User Category

This request involves the insertion of a new user category record into the `advancedcms_usercategories` table. Since we do not want duplicate category codes, we will need to check for this first before inserting a record. Either way, we return the appropriate category ID value:

```
class AddUserCat extends RequestInfo
{
    /*
    <?addusercat ?>
    <user>
      <cat>adm</cat>
      <descr>Administrative user.</descr>
    </user>
    */

    # Define variables to match columns in table
    # "advancedcms_usercategories". We only define
    # those columns which will be in the SQL INSERT statement.
    #
    var $cat;
    var $descr;
```

Below is the simple constructor for `AddUserCat()`. It simply creates a new array by calling the constructor of its base-class, `RequestInfo`:

```
    function AddUserCat($dbc)
    {
        $this->RequestInfo($dbc);

        #print "[dbg]: AddUserCat() object created<br>\n";
    }
```

```
function SaveTag($tagname,$attrs)
{
 # None of the tags for this request have any attributes. However, we
 # define this function anyway, because we want a generic interface
 # for all "request" classes.
}
```

If you pass some character data to SaveCData(), the data gets saved:

```
function SaveCData($cdata)
{
    $openelem = $this->stack[count($this->stack)-1];

    #print "[dbg(SaveCData)]: [$openelem]<br>\n";

    if ($openelem == "cat") {
        $this->cat = $cdata;

            #print "[dbg(SaveCData)]: cat=[$cdata]<br>\n";
    } elseif ($openelem == "descr") {
        $this->descr = $cdata;

        #print "[dbg(SaveCData)]: descr=[$cdata]<br>\n";
    }
}
```

To save the user category to the database, you simply call SaveToDbs():

```
function SaveToDbs()
{
// Insert a "usercat" record, if the category does not already exist.

    $cat = $this-> cat;
    $descr = $this-> descr;

    $catid = LookupCatidByCat($this->dbc, $cat);
    if ($catid != 0) {
        print "dbg[advancedcms_usercategories]:
                user category '$cat' exists ($catid)<br>\n";
    } else {
        // This user category does not exist. Insert a record
        $insquery = "INSERT INTO advancedcms_usercategories
                    (usercategory_category,usercategory_description)
                    VALUES ";
        $insquery.= "('$cat', '$descr') ";

        print "[dbg]: qry=($insquery)<br>\n";

        $insres = $this->dbc->query($insquery);
        if (DB::isError($insres)) {
            // Problems accessing database.
```

```
                    $errmsg  = "MySQL Error: Cannot access table
                               advancedcms_usercategories in ";
                    $errmsg .= "database ".$insres->getMessage()."<br>\n ";
                    die($errmsg);
                } else {
                    // Check how many rows were "affected" by the insert
                    $naff = $this->dbc->affectedRows();
                    if ($naff != 1) {
                        // Problems accessing database.
                        $errmsg  = "Problems with database. ";
                        $errmsg .= "User category record not
                                    inserted.<br>\n";
                        die($errmsg);
                    } else {
                        // User category record inserted
                        $catid = $this->dbc->getOne("SELECT
                                    max(usercategory_categoryid)
                                    FROM advancedcms_usercategories
                                    WHERE usercategory_category='$cat'
                                    AND usercategory_description='$descr'");

                        print "dbg[advancedcms_usercategories]: created new
                                ($catid)<br>\n";
                    }
                }
            }
        return($catid);
    } # end function SaveToDbs
} # end class AddUserCat
```

Add User

This request involves the insertion of a new user record into the `advancedcms_users` table. Since we do not want duplicate user records, we will need to check for this first before inserting a record. Either way, we return the appropriate user ID value:

```
class AddUser extends RequestInfo
{
    /*
    <?adduser ?>
    <user>
      <acct>mookie</acct>
      <pass>mouse</mouse>
      <cat>adm</cat>
    </user>
    */

    /*
    <?adduser ?>
    <user>
      <acct>mookie</acct>
      <pass>mouse</mouse>
      <catid>1</catid>
```

```
</user>
*/

# Define variables to match columns in table "advancedcms_users".
# We only define
# those columns which will be in the SQL INSERT statement.
#
var $userid;
var $acct;
var $pass;
var $status;
var $catid;
```

Just like for `AddUserCat`, the constructor for `AddUser` first calls `RequestInfo()` to create a new array. However, here we also set the status for the user to 'I' (inactive):

```
function AddUser($dbc)
{
    $this->RequestInfo($dbc);
    $this->status = "I";
    #print "[dbg]: AddUser() object created<br>\n";
```

If any of the tags for this request had any attributes, we would use this function to save them:

```
function SaveTag($tagname,$attrs)
{
    # None of the tags for this request have any attributes.
}
```

`SaveCData()` saves character data belonging to this user:

```
function SaveCData($cdata)
{
    $openelem = $this->stack[count($this->stack)-1];
    #print "[dbg(SaveCData)]: $openelem=[$cdata]<br>\n";;

switch($openelem) {
        case "acct": // Set user account name
                $this->acct = $cdata;
        break;

        case "pass": // Set user account password
                $this->pass = $cdata;
        break;

        case "catid": // Set user category ID
                $this->catid = $cdata;
         break;

    case "cat":
        // Determine and set user category ID from user category
```

```
                    $catid = LookupCatidByCat($this->dbc,$cdata);
                    if ($catid == 0) {
                        // This user category does not exist
                        $errmsg = "User category '$cdata' does not exist ";
                        $errmsg .= "in table
                                    advancedcms_usercategories.<br>\n";
                        die($errmsg);
                    } else {
                        $this->catid = $catid;
                    }
                    break;

            default:
                default: // Invalid/unknown tag
                $errmsg = "Invalid or unknown tag '$openelem' ";
                $errmsg .= "in 'add user' request<br>\n";
                die($errmsg);
            }
        }
```

Also, we need a `SaveToDbs()` method for creating a record for this user in the database:

```
function SaveToDbs()
{
    // Insert a "advancedcms_users" record, if the user does not
    // already exist.

    $acct   = $this->acct;
    $pass   = $this->pass;
    $status = $this->status;
    $catid  = $this->catid;

    $userid = LookupUseridByAcct($this->dbc, $acct);
    if ($userid != 0) {
        print "dbg[advancedcms_users]: user '$acct' exists
                ($userid)<br>\n";
    } else {
        // This user does not exist. Insert a record.
        $insquery = "INSERT INTO advancedcms_users
                        (user_account,user_password,user_status,
                         user_categoryid) VALUES ";
        $insquery.= "('".addslashes($acct)."', '$pass', '$status',
                    $catid) ";
        print "[dbg]: qry=($insquery)<br>\n";

        $insres = $this->dbc->query($insquery);
        if (DB::isError($insres)) {
            // Problems accessing database.
            $errmsg = "MySQL Error: Cannot access table
                        advancedcms_users in ";
            $errmsg .= "database ".$insres->getMessage()."<br>\n ";
            die($errmsg);
        } else {
```

```
                    // Check how many rows were "affected" by the insert
                    $naff = $this->dbc->affectedRows();
                    if ($naff != 1) {
                        // Problems accessing database.
                        $errmsg  = "Problems with database. ";
                        $errmsg .= "User record not inserted.<br>\n";
                        die($errmsg);
                    } else {
                        // User record inserted
                        $userid = $this->dbc->getOne("SELECT max(user_userid)
                                        FROM advancedcms_users
                                        WHERE user_account ='$acct'
                                        AND user_password ='$pass'");
                        print "dbg[advancedcms_users]: created new
                                ($userid)<br>\n";
                    }
                }
            }
            return ($userid);
        } # end function saveToDbs
} # end class AddUser
```

Add a Task Category

This request involves the insertion of a new task category record into the
advancedcms_taskcategories table, provided the category does not already exist. Either the existing
or a new 'task category id' record ID is returned:

```
class AddTaskCat extends RequestInfo
{
    /*
    <?addtaskcat ?>
    <taskcat>
      <tcat>edit page</tcat>
      <tdescr>General edit of a virtual page or native file</tdescr>
    </taskcat>
    */

    # Define variables to match columns in table
    # "advancedcms_taskcategories". We only define
    # those columns which will be in the SQL INSERT statement.
    #
    var $tcat;
    var $tdescr;
```

As usual, the constructor only passes the work on to RequestInfo():

```
    function AddTaskCat($dbc)
    {
        $this->RequestInfo($dbc);
        #print "[dbg]: AddTaskCat() object created<br>\n";
    }
```

This class won't handle any tags with attribute, so we don't need any logic in `SaveTag()`:

```
function SaveTag($tagname,$attrs)
{
    # None of the tags for this request have any attributes.
    # However, we define this function anyway, because we want a
    # generic interface for all "request" classes.
}
```

A `SaveCData()` method for saving character data for this task category:

```
function SaveCData($cdata)
{
    $openelem = $this->stack[count($this->stack)-1];

    #print "[dbg(SaveCData)]: [$openelem]<br>\n";

    if ($openelem == "tcat") {
        $this->tcat = $cdata;
        #print "[dbg(SaveCData)]: tcat =[$cdata]<br>\n";
    } elseif ($openelem == "tdescr") {
        $this->tdescr = $cdata;
        #print "[dbg(SaveCData)]: tdescr =[$cdata]<br>\n";
    }
}
```

When all data is there, it's time create a new record in `taskcat` for this task category:

```
function SaveToDbs()
{
    # Insert a "taskcat" record, if the task
    #category does not already exist.

    $tcat = $this->tcat;
    $tdescr = $this->tdescr;

    $tcatid = LookupTcatidByTcat($this->dbc, $tcat);
    if ($tcatid != 0) {
        print "dbg[advancedcms_taskcategories]:
                task category '$tcat' exists ($tcatid)<br>\n";
    } else {
        // This task category does not exist. Insert a record
        $insquery = "INSERT INTO advancedcms_taskcategories
                    (taskcategory_taskcategory,
                     taskcategory_taskdescription) VALUES ";
        $insquery.= "('$tcat', '$tdescr') ";

        #print "[dbg]: qry=($insquery)<br>\n";

        $insres = $this->dbc->query($insquery);
        if (DB::isError($insres)) {
```

```
                        // Problems accessing database.
                        $errmsg = "MySQL Error: Cannot access table
                                    advancedcms_taskcategories in ";
                        $errmsg .= "database ".$insres->getMessage()."<br>\n ";
                        die($errmsg);
                } else {
                        // Check how many rows were "affected" by the insert
                        $naff = $this->dbc->affectedRows();
                        if ($naff != 1) {
                            // Problems accessing database.
                            $errmsg = "Problems with database. ";
                            $errmsg .= "Task category record not
                                        inserted.<br>\n";
                            die($errmsg);
                        } else {
                            // Task category record inserted
                            $tcatid = $this->dbc->getOne("SELECT
                                    max(taskcategory_taskcategoryid)
                                    FROM advancedcms_taskcategories
                                    WHERE taskcategory_taskcategory ='$tcat'
                                    AND taskcategory_taskdescription ='$tdescr'");
                            print "dbg[advancedcms_taskcategories]: created new
                                    ($tcatid)<br>\n";
                        }
                }
        }
        return($tcatid);
    } # end function SaveToDbs
} # end class AddTaskCat
```

Assign Task

This request involves the insertion of a new 'task' record into the `advancedcms_tasklists` table. While we do not want duplicate tasks stored, it is difficult to find a criterion for determining duplication. This would involve comparing the task name (duplication allowed) as well as the actual task description. This is not a reasonable thing to have to do for each task. So we will not check for duplication; instead we will leave it up to users to remove or ignore duplicate tasks.

```
class AssignTask extends RequestInfo
{
    /*
    <?assigntask ?>
    <task>
      <taskname>edit home page</taskname>
      <taskdescr>
       Please add the company logo to the home page.
      </taskdescr>
      <assndate>2002/07/01</assndate>
      <duedate>2002/07/05</duedate>
      <assnbyid>13</assnbyid>
      <assntoid>15</asstoid>
      <tcatid>1</tcatid>
    </task>
```

```
        */

        /*
        <?assigntask ?>
        <task>
          <taskname>edit home page</taskname>
          <taskdescr>Please add the company logo to the home page.</taskdescr>
          <assndate>2002/07/01</assndate>
          <duedate>2002/07/05</duedate>
          <assnbyacct>mookie</assnbyacct>
          <assntoacct>golly</assntoacct>
          <tcat>edit page</tcat>
        </task>
        */

        # Define variables to match columns in table "advancedcms_users". We only
define
        # those columns which will be in the SQL INSERT statement.
        #
        var $taskname;
        var $taskdescr;
        var $assndate;
        var $duedate;
        var $assnbyid;
        var $assntoid;
        var $tcatid;
```

The constructor asks `RequstInfo()` to create a new array:

```
function AssignTask($dbc)
{
    $this->RequestInfo($dbc);
}
```

No attributes for the tags for this request either:

```
function SaveTag($tagname,$attrs)
{
    # None of the tags for this request have any attributes.
}
```

Tasks also have character data that needs to be saved:

```
function SaveCData($cdata)
{
    $openelem = $this->stack[count($this->stack)-1];

    #print "[dbg(SaveCData)]: $openelem=[$cdata]<br>\n";

    switch($openelem) {
```

```
        case "taskname": // Set task name
            $this->taskname = $cdata;
        break;

        case "taskdescr": // Set task descr
            $this->taskdescr = $cdata;
        break;

        case "assndate": // Set "task assigned" date
            $this->assndate = $cdata;
        break;

        case "duedate": // Set "task due" date
            $this->duedate = $cdata;
        break;

        case "assnbyid": // Set assignor's user ID
            $this->assnbyid = $cdata;
        break;

        case "assnbyacct": // Determine and set assignor's user ID
            $this->assnbyid = LookupUseridByAcct($this->dbc, $cdata);
        break;

        case "assntoid": // Set assignee's user ID
            $this->assntoid = $cdata;
        break;

        case "assntoacct": // Determine and set assignee's user ID
            $this->assntoid = LookupUseridByAcct($this->dbc, $cdata);
        break;

        case "tcatid": // Set task category ID
            $this->tcatid = $cdata;
        break;

        case "tcat":
            // Determine and set task category ID from task category
            $tcatid = LookupTcatidByTcat($this->dbc, $cdata);
            if ($tcatid == 0) {
                // This task category does not exist
                $errmsg  = "Task category '$cdata' does not exist ";
                $errmsg .= "in table advancedcms_taskcategories.<br>\n";
                die($errmsg);
            } else {
                $this->tcatid = $tcatid;
            }
        break;

        default: // Invalid/unknown tag
            $errmsg  = "Invalid or unknown tag '$openelem' ";
            $errmsg .= "in 'assign task' request<br>\n";
            die($errmsg);
        }
    } # end function SaveCData
```

In this `SaveToDbs()`, we don't check if a task with this name already exist. This is simply because we want to have the possibility of multiple tasks with the same name in the database:

```
function SaveToDbs()
{
    // Insert a "task" record.
    // We are not checking if the task already exists.

    $taskname  = $this->taskname;
    $taskdescr = $this->taskdescr;
    $assndate  = $this->assndate;
    $duedate   = $this->duedate;
    $assnbyid  = $this->assnbyid;
    $assntoid  = $this->assntoid;
    $tcatid    = $this->tcatid;

    $insquery  = "INSERT INTO advancedcms_tasklists
                    (tasklist_taskname,tasklist_taskdescription,
                     tasklist_assigndate,";
    $insquery .= "tasklist_duedate,tasklist_assignedbyid,
                    tasklist_assignedtoid, tasklist_taskcategoryid)
                    VALUES ";
    $insquery .= "('$taskname', '$taskdescr', '$assndate', ";
    $insquery .= "'$duedate', $assnbyid, $assntoid, $tcatid) ";
    print "[dbg]: qry=($insquery)<br>\n";

    $insres = $this->dbc->query($insquery);
    if (!$insres) {
        // Problems accessing database.
        $errmsg  = "MySQL Error: Cannot access table
                    advancedcms_tasklists in ";
        $errmsg .= "database $dbs: ".$insres->getMessage()."<br>\n ";
        die($errmsg);
    } else {
        // Check how many rows were "affected" by the insert
        $naff = $this->dbc->affectedRows();
        if ($naff != 1) {
            // Problems accessing database.
            $errmsg  = "Problems with database. ";
            $errmsg .= "Tasklist record not inserted.<br>\n";
            die($errmsg);
        } else {
            // Tasklist record inserted
            $taskid = $this->dbc->getOne("SELECT max(tasklist_taskid)
                        FROM advancedcms_tasklists WHERE
                        tasklist_taskname ='$taskname' AND
                        tasklist_taskdescription ='$taskdescr'");
            print "dbg[advancedcms_tasklists]: created new
                                            ($taskid)<br>\n";

        }
    }
    return($taskid);
} # end function SaveToDbs
} # end class AssignTask
```

Reject Task

This request involves looking up an existing task list record and updating its status to 'rejected' by the current 'assignee'. We show only the class constructor here, so this class won't do any good without implementing some logic/member functions to it. These functions would, however, look much like the ones shown in previous classes:

```
class RejectTask extends RequestInfo
{
    /*
    <?rejecttask taskid="5" ?>
    */

    function RejectTask($dbc)
    {
        $this->RequestInfo($dbc);
    }
} # end class RejectTask
```

Reassign Task

This request involves looking up an existing task list record and updating its status to 'assigned' but not accepted; by whoever is reassigning the task. Only the class constructor is shown here:

```
class ReassignTask extends RequestInfo
{
    /*
    <?reassigntask taskid="5" userid="15" ?>
    */

    /*
    <?reassigntask taskid="5" acct="golly" ?>
    */

    function ReassignTask($dbc)
    {
        $this->RequestInfo($dbc);
    }
} # end class ReassignTask
```

Accept Task

This request involves looking up an existing task list record and updating its status to 'accepted' by whoever is accepting the task. Only the class constructor is shown here:

```
class AcceptTask extends RequestInfo
{
    /*
    <?accepttask taskid="5" ?>
    */

    function AcceptTask($dbc)
    {
        $this->RequestInfo($dbc);
    }
} # end class AcceptTask
```

Send Message

This request involves inserting a new message record. As with the classes we've looked at earlier, SendMsg has a simple constructor that uses the logic from RequestInfo(), a SaveTag() method for getting possible tag attributes, a SaveCData() fom saving character data, and a SaveToDbs() method for adding the data to the database. There will not be a check for a duplicate message:

```
class SendMsg extends RequestInfo
{
    /*
    <?sendmsg ?>
    <message>
      <fromid>13</fromid>
      <toid>15</toid>
      <msg>I've assigned a task to you.</msg>
    </message>
    */

    /*
    <?sendmsg ?>
    <message>
      <fromacct>mookie</fromacct>
      <toacct>golly</toacct>
      <msg>I've assigned a task to you.</msg>
    </message>
    */

    # Define variables to match columns in table "advancedcms_users".
    # We only define those columns which will be in the SQL INSERT
    # statement.

    var $crdate;
    var $msg;
    var $status;
    var $fromid;
    var $toid;

    function SendMsg($dbc)
    {
        $this->RequestInfo($dbc);
        $this->status = "nw"; # New message
    }

    function SaveTag($tagname, $attrs)
    {
        # None of the tags for this request have any attributes.
    }

    function SaveCData($cdata)
    {
        $openelem = $this->stack[count($this->stack)-1];
        #print "[dbg(SaveCData)]: $openelem=[$cdata]<br>\n";

        switch($openelem) {
```

```php
        case "crdate": // Set "message creation" date
            $this->crdate = $cdata;
        break;

        case "msg": // Set message content
            $this->msg = $cdata;
        break;

        case "fromid": // Set sender's user ID
            $this->fromid = $cdata;
        break;

        case "fromacct": // Determine and set sender's user ID
            $this->fromid = LookupUseridByAcct($this->dbc, $cdata);
        break;

        case "toid": // Set receiver's user ID
            $this->toid = $cdata;
        break;

        case "toacct": // Determine and set receiver's user ID
            $this->toid = LookupUseridByAcct($this->dbc, $cdata);
        break;

        default: // Invalid/unknown tag
            $errmsg  = "Invalid or unknown tag '$openelem' ";
            $errmsg .= "in 'send message' request<br>\n";
            die($errmsg);
    }
} # end function SaveCData

function SaveToDbs()
{

    // Insert a "message" record.
    // We are not checking if the message already exists.

    $crdate  = $this->crdate;
    $msg     = $this->msg;
    $status  = $this->status;
    $fromid  = $this->fromid;
    $toid    = $this->toid;

    $insquery  = "INSERT INTO advancedcms_messages
                    (message_createdate,
                    message_message,message_status,
                    message_fromid,message_toid) ";
    $insquery .= "VALUES ";
    $insquery .= "('$crdate', '$msg', '$status', $fromid, $toid) ";
    print "[dbg]: qry=($insquery)<br>\n";

    $insres = $this->dbc->query($insquery);
    if (DB::isError($insres)) {
```

445

```
                        // Problems accessing database.
            $errmsg  = "MySQL Error: Cannot access table
                        advancedcms_messages in ";
            $errmsg .= "database ".$insres->getMessage()."<br>\n ";
            die($errmsg);
        } else {
            // Check how many rows were "affected" by the insert
            $naff = $this->dbc->affectedRows();
            if ($naff != 1) {
                // Problems accessing database.
                $errmsg  = "Problems with database. ";
                $errmsg .= "Message record not inserted.<br>\n";
                die($errmsg);
            } else {
                // Message record inserted
                $msgid = $this->dbc->getOne("SELECT
                                max(message_messageid)
                                FROM advancedcms_messages
                                WHERE message_createdate ='$crdate'
                                AND message_message ='$msg'");
                print "dbg[advancedcms_messages]: created new
                        ($msgid)<br>\n";
            }
        }
        return($msgid);
    } # end function SaveToDbs
} # end class SendMsg
```

List all Outstanding Tasks

This request involves looking up all tasks that have been assigned and. Only the class constructor is shown here:

```
class OutstandingTasks extends RequestInfo
{
    /*
    <?listalloutstandingtasks ?>
    <?listalloutstandingtasks userid ="15" ?>
    <?listalloutstandingtasks acct="golly" ?>
    */

    function OutstandingTasks($dbc)
    {
        $this->RequestInfo($dbc);
    }
} # end class OutstandingTasks
```

List Unaccepted Tasks

This request involves looking up all tasks whose name or description contains the specified keyword. Only the class constructor is shown here:

```
class UnacceptedTasks extends RequestInfo
{
    /*
    <?listunacceptedtasks ?>
    */

    function UnacceptedTasks($dbc)
    {
        $this->RequestInfo($dbc);
    }
} # end function UnacceptedTasks
```

List Tasks by Keyword

This request involves looking up all tasks whose name or description contains the specified keyword. Only the class constructor is shown here:

```
class TasksByKeyword extends RequestInfo
{
    /*
    <?listtasksbykeyword taskname="home page" ?>
    <?listtasksbykeyword taskdescr="home page" ?>
    */

    function TasksByKeyword($dbc)
    {
        $this->RequestInfo($dbc);
    }
} # end class TasksByKeyword
```

List Task Details

This request involves looking up a particular task record and retrieving all information about. Only the class constructor is shown here:

```
class TaskDetail extends RequestInfo
{
    /*
    <?listtaskdetail taskid="5" ?>
    */

    function TaskDetail($dbc)
    {
        $this->RequestInfo($dbc);
    }
} # end class TaskDetail
```

Check Out Page

This request involves inserting a new 'page check out' record in the `advancedcms_checkinandout` table, and tying the record with the associated task. Only the class constructor is shown here:

```
class CheckoutPage extends RequestInfo
{
    /*
    <?checkoutpage userid ="15" pageid="23" taskid="10" ?>
    <?checkoutpage acct="golly" pageid="23" taskid="10" ?>
    <?checkoutpage pageid="23" tdetid="7" ?>
    */

    function CheckoutPage($dbc)
    {
        $this->RequestInfo($dbc);
    }
} # end class CheckoutPage
```

Check In Page

This request involves looking up an existing 'page check out' record and updating the 'check in date' to reflect when the page got checked back in. Only the class constructor is shown here:

```
class CheckinPage extends RequestInfo
{
    /*
    <?checkinpage chid="3"?>
    <?checkinpage pageid="23"?>
    <?checkinpage name="..." ?>
    <?checkinpage url="..." ?>
    */

    function CheckinPage($dbc)
    {
        $this->RequestInfo($dbc);
    }
} # end class CheckinPage
?>
```

Other Engine Requests

Any other engine requests that one might want to code for should be handled using the same methods we have discussed so far. Here are the steps:

1. Devise a unique XML PI. For example:

    ```
    <?rejecttask taskid="5" ?>
    ```

2. Add an entry to the array $aaCMSClasses that uses the name/target of the XML PI as the index, and the name of the associated class to call when the XML PI is encountered in input. Also include parentheses in the string value to define what argument should be sent to the function. If the XML PI has parameters, then reflect that in the array entry. For example:

    ```
    $aaCMSClasses["rejecttask"] = "rejectTask($data)";
    ```

3. Now define a class for the PI, which extends the `RequestInfo` base class. Include the class constructor. If the parameters are being passed from the XML PI, then reflect this in the constructor function. For example:

```
class RejectTask extends RequestInfo
{
    function rejectTask($dbc,$xmlpidata)
    {
        $this->requestInfo($dbc);

        // Now parse out the parameters of the XML PI and
        // save the values to the appropriate member
        // properties.
    }
} # end class RejectTask
```

4. Now define member properties that correspond to columns in the database table. We may not need to define properties for all columns. For examples, to reject a task, we would be mainly dealing with the columns `tasklist_taskid` and `tasklist_status`. The `tasklist_assigntoid` column will imply who the task is currently assigned to.

The assumption is that only the person to whom the task is assigned will be rejecting it. We can change the parameters passed in with the XML PI to perform a check on the rejector. For example:

```
class RejectTask extends RequestInfo
{
    var $taskid;
    var $status;
    ...
} # end class RejectTask
```

5. If the XML PI requires additional XML markup to provide data, devise an appropriate tagset. Try to use tagnames that correspond to the associated database columns.

6. Define the remaining class functions `SaveTag()`, `SaveCData()`, and `SaveToDbs()`:

- ❏   The `SaveTag()` member function is used to save any attributes that a tag might have.
- ❏   The `SaveCData()` function is used to save the text between a start and close tag. In this function, define a switch/case construct that handles all input tags for the current XML PI, including any allowable tag variations. (For instance, `user_account` instead of `userid`). Handling tag variations often amounts to doing a lookup and retrieving the desired value. For example, if the input uses `user_account` instead of `user_userid`, we will need to do a lookup of the desired userid in the `advancecms_users` table using the supplied acct value.
- ❏   The `SaveToDbs()` function is used typically used to either insert a new record to one or more database tables, or to update one or more existing records. In some cases, we may need to verify that a duplicate record is not being added.

7. Now we can add the necessary request to the `acmsrequest.xml` file and test the new code.

Sample Input File

Here is a sample `acmsrequest.xml` file that we can run the above code on. Here we do not need to have the initial `<?xml ?>` PI. Also notice that when we have more than one engine request to be performed, you should use the root element, `<requests>`:

```
<requests>

<?addusercat ?>
<usercat>
  <cat>adm</cat>
  <descr>Administrative user.</descr>
</usercat>

<?addusercat ?>
<usercat>
  <cat>dev</cat>
  <descr>General developer.</descr>
</usercat>

<?addusercat ?>
<usercat>
  <cat>edi</cat>
  <descr>Editor.</descr>
</usercat>

<?addusercat ?>
<usercat>
  <cat>rvw</cat>
  <descr>General reviewer.</descr>
</usercat>

<?adduser ?>
<user>
  <acct>mookie</acct>
  <pass>mouse</pass>
  <cat>adm</cat>
</user>

<?adduser ?>
<user>
  <acct>golly</acct>
  <pass>gee</pass>
  <catid>2</catid>
</user>

<?addtaskcat ?>
<taskcat>
  <tcat>edit page</tcat>
  <tdescr>General edit of a virtual page or native file</tdescr>
</taskcat>

<?assigntask ?>
<assntoacct>golly</assntoacct>
  <tcat>edit page</tcat>
</task>

<?sendmsg ?>
<message>
```

```
    <crdate>2002/07/01</crdate>
    <fromacct>mookie</fromacct>
    <toacct>golly</toacct>
    <msg>I assigned a task to you.</msg>
  </message>

</requests>
```

And here is the output:

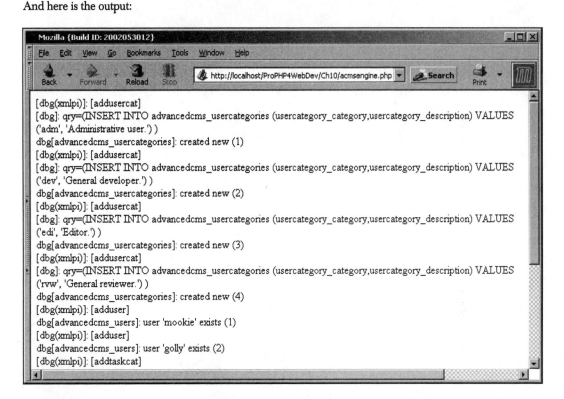

Summary

This case study focuses on some of the more advanced peripheral aspects of a CMS. In particular, the focus is on an XML engine for some of the workflow-related features of a CMS. With these features, combined with the content storage functionality that was discussed in the previous case study, and an appropriate web interface in any scripting or programming language, we can put together most of the essential ingredients for a complete CMS.

```
n DefMaillist()defined belo
e = $elem[$tagname]["co
= "All students in college                              id,0);
llist("col",$collcode,"stu                              O);
= "All profs in colleg
aillist("col",$collcod

ak;

"dept":
        Opening department elem
/ Add a record to table "universitylife_departments"

$elem[$tagname]["collid"] = $curcollid;
        $curdeptid =$api->InsertDeptRecord($elem[$tagname]);
d;  // Create various mailing lists
        $deptcode = $elem[$tagname]["deptcode"];
me)  $desc = $elem[$tagname]["deptcode";
        DefMaillist("dep",$deptcode,"stu",$desc,$curcollid,$curc
        $desc = "All profs in dept $deptcode";
        DefMaillist("dep",$deptcode,"edu",$desc,$curcollid,$c
ollid;  // There is still character data left.  Since there can be
eptid;// pieces of cdata within a single element (due to the w
deptid;  // expat parser works), we want to concatena
                         rent element's character data.
```

global $
global $cur
global $cur
global $cur
global $api
global $flg
global $e'
global $s
global $
global $
global $
global
global
globa
globa
glob
glol
glo
glo

"All students in dept $deptcode";
"All profs in dept $deptcode";

Simple Search Engine

A search engine is vital for the efficient usage of a site, and especially if the site holds a large number of articles or products. Users of the site should be able to find the information they are looking for. One big problem is that if we search for a very common word, we might get a list of hundreds of matches. Usually, the users don't bother to check more than the first ten to twenty occurrences. Thus, it becomes very important to get the most relevant matches at the top of the list.

In this case study, we will look at how to develop a search engine. The search should be fast and rank the most exact matches first so that the user will find the necessary information as fast as possible.

We will look into creating a product catalog with a search engine. The search engine should be fast and it should return the most relevant products for the search. However, because of space limitations, we shall not look at adding any functionality that lets the end user actually purchase any products here; this will only be a product catalog.

In the course of this chapter we will look into:

- ❑ **Application Specification** – we need to decide what the application should be able to do, and generally how it should be designed.

- ❑ **Designing the Web site** – the application will be used in a browser, so we need to define a working web presentation for it.

- ❑ **Design of the Search Engine** – the application is intended to build a search facility so that readers can easily find the product that they are looking for.

❏ **Database Design** – we need a well-defined database structure to handle the content of this application.

❏ **Delivering the Content** – we need some basic functions for delivering raw data from the database to the client.

❏ **Improvements** – the most obvious enhancements to the core application are presented at the end of the chapter.

Application Specification

For our search application, there are two kinds of users: one is the general surfer (the end user of our application), and the other is an administrator. The end user is the person who uses our custom search application or utility to search for products that are hosted on our site. The administrator manages the products being displayed in the product catalog.

The first thing we should do is to analyze the requirements for our application. We should find out everything the system should be able to do. By doing this at the beginning, we are less likely to run into unforeseen problems later in the development. Let's list the requirements for each of the users of our site.

End User

Here, we identify all the actions a user wishes to do when he visits our site. Once the user accesses the site, he should be able to:

❏ Browse a list of the products in the catalog

❏ Search the product catalog

❏ Get the most relevant matches first

❏ Search fast, even with a large number of products in the catalog

❏ Search for products in several categories at once

❏ Search for products in one specific category

❏ View products in one field of interest

❏ View detailed information about a product

If we look at all the actions a user is performing when he visits our site, it would be like this:

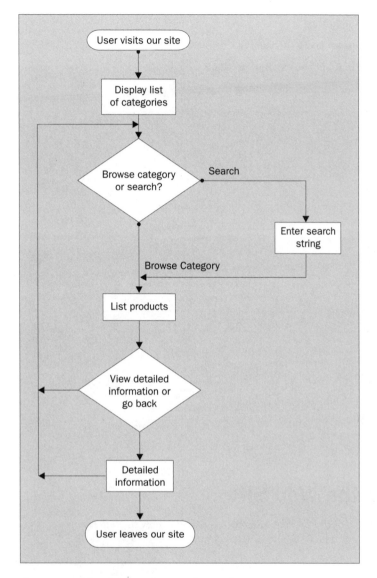

Note that the user does not need to log in to browse the catalog.

Administrator

The administrators have extended access to the product catalog and so have more requirements. They should be able to:

- ❑ Log in to access the administrator pages
- ❑ Add categories
- ❑ Edit categories

❑ Remove categories

❑ Add new products to the catalog

❑ Edit details about the existing products

❑ Delete products from the catalog

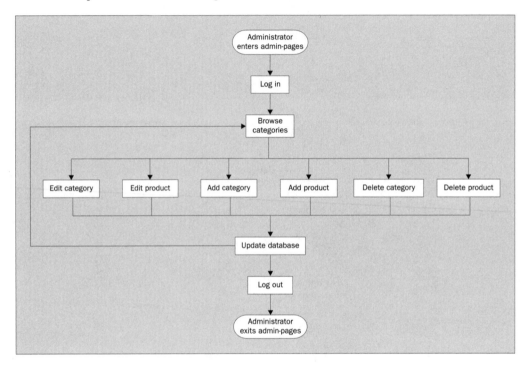

Designing the Web Site

Now that we have analyzed the requirements, let's look at how the different parts of our site should interact, and what kind of information the site should present.

Products

We'll make a simple product catalog where we store computer products from computer software to ISDN-cards. Since we wish to present all these different types of products on the same web site using the same database, we need a good system for categorizing. Also, we need the fields in the database to be usable for all of this information.

Our database will include the following information about the products that we display:

❑ **Product Number**
A unique number used to identify each product in the database. The manufacturer of the product usually sets the product number.

❑ **Product Title**
The name of the product. For example, the title of a product can be something like 'Microsoft Windows 98 CD-ROM' or 'D-Link DSS 16 Switch'.

❑ **Manufacturer**
The name of the company producing the product.

❑ **Description**
A large description field. It allows the administrator to add appropriate information about the product, which is given to them by the content management team, or the manufacturers who wish to add a description of their product.

❑ **Price**
The price of the product.

❑ **Category**
We should also assign every product to a category. Some catalogs would need to categorize products in several categories, but we will not go into that in this example. We will discuss categories in the next section.

This is the information we shall present to the user about each product. Further, the information will be presented in two ways:

❑ **List form**
This format will be used when a user is browsing the contents of a category. The list will hold some information about each product. The user can then click on one of the products and get detailed information about each product. In our application, we'll look into keeping the product title as a link that leads to detailed information of the products.

❑ **Detailed form**
This format will display all the information about one product. When a user selects one product from the list, he will be taken to the page that displays all the details about the product.

Categories

Every product should be placed into a particular category. This will make it easier for the users to navigate through the different products in our catalog. Every category should be able to have an infinite number of sub-categories and each category should be able to store an infinite number of products.

We don't need much information about the categories:

❑ **Category Name**
A short name to describe our category, for instance, 'CPU', 'Software', and so on.

❑ **Parent Category**
This is used to identify the parent category of the current category, giving us the possibility of having as many categories with as many sub-categories as necessary. For instance, if we have a category named 'Network' and this category contained one new category called 'Network cards' then 'Network' would be the parent category of 'Network Cards'.

Design of the Search Engine

There are many ways to search through a database. The most common way to do this is by using the `LIKE` option in an SQL command. If we wish to search through the product titles for titles containing the word 'CD-ROM', we could do it like this:

```
SELECT * FROM productcatalog_products WHERE product_title LIKE '%CD-ROM%';
```

This would search through `productcatalog_products` table and return every product that has the word 'CD-ROM' somewhere in its title. The `%` symbol is used as a wildcard to let the title have text both in the front and back of the search string. However, this is not an efficient way of searching. This kind of search is quite slow, especially if we have a large number of entries in the table where we are performing the search.

There is one definite advantage to this method. It allows the user to search for small parts of a word, thereby increasing the chances of a user finding what he is searching for. However, for performance reasons, this type of search should be employed only on small web sites.

In order for the search engine to be fast, we have to avoid using the `LIKE` option. To make a really fast search, we should have a word list where all the words on our site are indexed. This will make a huge table, and searching will be very fast. We also update the information in this table when we add or edit new products. By doing this, the biggest job for our database will be done each time the administrator is making changes, not each time a user searches the site. Because we read from the database much more often than write to it, we will have a much more efficient database.

To always return the most relevant matches first, we need some kind of functionality to set the ranking of each word for each product.

Scaling the Word List

Let's say we have a product as shown in the table below:

Product Number	Product Title	Manufacturer	Description	Price	Category
24526-BC5642-3490	Super Ethernet HUB	Network Inc.	This is a very good HUB. It has four ports and let's you connect computers easily to make your own private network in your office or at home.	$100	1

We have to decide how much of this information we should let the user search for. In our example, we let the user search for everything except the product number, price, and category.

Now we need some kind of scaling to be able to rank this product. If a user searches for HUB, this should be a good match since it has the word in the title. If the user however searches for office, it's not that likely that this is the product he was looking for. The best way to solve this is if we let words in the **Product Title** column rank higher than words in the **Description** column. The same goes to words in the **Manufacturer** column.

We also need to check the frequency of the word. If the word is typed two places in the description, the word should rank higher than if the word is only typed once.

The ratio of the frequency of the search word to the length of the text should be considered. For instance, if a product has a description of 20 words and one occurrence of the search word, this should rank higher than a product with 500 words and one occurrence of the search word. For this, we should create a word list where we list every word used, and link this list against the product catalog with the ranking for the word in each product. Then we let words in the title count three times and the words in the manufacturer field count twice as much as the words in the description.

Database Design

We need four tables for this design. They are:

- ❑ productcatalog_products
- ❑ productcatalog_categories
- ❑ productcatalog_wordlists
- ❑ productcatalog_wordlistlinks

All these tables are stored in a database called productcatalog.

Products

The productcatalog_products table contains all the information that we need to store about the different products:

Column Name	Description
product_id	A unique identification for this record in the database
product_number	The product number of the product
product_title	The title of the product
product_manufacturer	The company producing the product
product_price	The price for the product
product_category	The category assigned to the product
product_description	The description of the product

Categories

The `productcatalog_categories` table stores the information about the categories of the system:

Column Name	Description
Category_id	A unique identification for this record in the database
Category_name	The name of this category
Category_parent	The parent of this category

Wordlists

The `productcatalog_wordlists` table contains a list of every word used in the product catalog:

Column Name	Description
wordlilst_id	A unique identification for this record in the database
wordlist_word	One word used in the catalog

Wordlistlinks

The `productcatalog_wordlistlinks` table is a link between the `productcatalog_products` and `productcatalog_wordlists` tables. In this table we specify what product each word belongs to and the frequency of this word in the product:

Column Name	Description
wordlistlink_id	A unique identification for this record in the database
wordlistlink_wordid	The ID of the word from the `productcatalog_wordlists` table
wordlistlink_productid	The ID of the product from the `productcatalog_products` table
wordlistlink_frequency	A constant describing how often the word is used in the product

Let's look at how these tables work together:

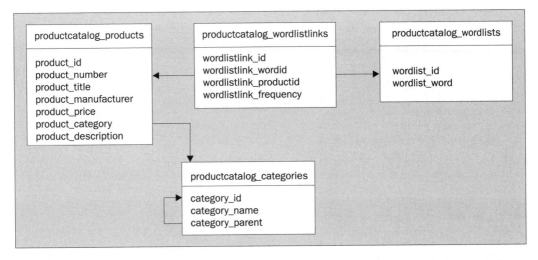

Each product has its own record in the `productcatalog_products` table. The ID of the category is found in the `product_category` field and stores what category the product is placed in. Each category has its own record in the `productcatalog_categories` table and we store the ID of that record to represent the parent category. The `productcatalog_wordlists` table contains every word used, each as one record. The `productcatalog_wordlistlinks` table stores the relation between the product and the word. Each record in this table contains the ID of the word and the ID of the product that contains the word.

Creating the Tables

In this case study, we use MySQL as our database server, but this can easily be changed to another database, if desirable.

First let's create the database:

```
> mysqladmin create ProductCatalog;
```

To create the tables, we use the following command at the command line prompt:

```
> mysql ProductCatalog < crdbs_productcatalog.sql
```

The `crdbs_productcatalog.sql` file is as follows:

```
# FILE: crdbs_productcatalog.sql
USE:   Create the ProductCatalog database

# CREATE TABLE productcatalog_products (
    product_id              INT(11) NOT NULL AUTO_INCREMENT,
    product_number          VARCHAR(30),
    product_title           VARCHAR(100),
```

```
        product_manufacturer   VARCHAR(100),
        product_description    TEXT,
        product_price          FLOAT(10,2),
        product_category       INT(11) DEFAULT 0 NOT NULL,
        PRIMARY KEY (product_id)
);

CREATE TABLE productcatalog_categories (
        category_id            INT(11) NOT NULL AUTO_INCREMENT,
        category_name          VARCHAR(30),
        category_parent        INT(11) DEFAULT 0 NOT NULL,
        PRIMARY KEY (category_id)
);

CREATE TABLE productcatalog_wordlists (
        wordlist_id            INT(11) NOT NULL AUTO_INCREMENT,
        wordlist_word          VARCHAR(50) NOT NULL,
        PRIMARY KEY (wordlist_id)
);

CREATE TABLE productcatalog_wordlistlinks (
        wordlistlink_id        INT(11) NOT NULL AUTO_INCREMENT,
        wordlistlink_wordid    INT(11) NOT NULL,
        wordlilstlink_productid INT(11) NOT NULL,
        wordlistlink_frequency  FLOAT(1,5),
        PRIMARY KEY (wordlistlink_id)
);
```

Setting Indexes

When we are using a relational database, we should always set all foreign keys as indexes. This all are much faster searching when we are searching several tables at once.

We should set indexes on product_category in the productcatalog_products table, category_parent in the productcatalog_categories table, and wordlistlink_wordid and wordlistlink_productid in productcatalog_wordlistlinks table:

> **mysql productcatalog < cridxs_productcatalog.sql**

Here is the SQL file to set the indexes:

```
# FILE: cridxs_productcatalog.sql
# USE:  Create indexes productcatalog database

CREATE INDEX category_index ON productcatalog_products(product_category);
CREATE INDEX parent_index   ON productcatalog_categories(category_parent);
CREATE INDEX word_index     ON productcatalog_wordlists(wordlist_id);
CREATE INDEX product_index ON productcatalog_wordlistlinks(wordlistlink_id);
```

User and Password

MySQL requires a user and a password for establishing a connection. The MySQL connection can be local to the same machine where the PHP script is running or over a network to a different server. The username and password must be known by the PHP script to be able to connect to the database. Let's set a username and password for our database so that the product catalog can use it:

```
mysql> GRANT ALL PRIVILEGES ON productcatalog.*
       TO myuser@localhost IDENTIFIED BY 'mypassword';
```

This gives `myuser` the privileges to use the `productcatalog` database by entering the password `mypassword` and connecting from the same server where MySQL is running. This means that the PHP script must be run on the same server as MySQL.

Delivering the Content

We are going to deliver our catlog content by using a partly object-oriented (OO) approach, and creating two classes to control our products and categories:

❑ Category

❑ Product

Let's look at the details of these different classes.

The Category Class

`Category` is the class that we use to represent one category in the catalog. The objects will connect to the database and fetch all relevant information about the category that they are representing.

Variables

We have a few values from the database that we need to store in some variables. The variables we need are:

❑ `categoryID` – the unique ID of this category

❑ `categoryName` – the name of this category

❑ `parentCategory` – the ID of the parent category of this category. These values will be 0 if the category has no parent

PHP doesn't have the possibility to set private variables like many other OO languages, but we should avoid changing the variables in an object directly. Instead, this should be done using methods. Let's discuss the various methods for this class.

Methods

The methods for the `Category` class are as follows:

- ❏ `Category()` – the constructor of the class, which fetches the information from the database or creates a new category
- ❏ `GetAllCategories()` – returns all the categories in the catalog
- ❏ `GetCategories()` – returns all the sub-categories
- ❏ `GetCategoryID()` – returns the ID of the category
- ❏ `GetCategoryName()` – returns the name of the category
- ❏ `SetCategoryName()` – sets the name of the category
- ❏ `GetParentCategory()` – returns the parent directory as a `Category` object
- ❏ `SetParentCategory()` – sets the parent category of the category
- ❏ `GetProducts()` – returns all products associated to the current category
- ❏ `Store()` – this method stores the information about the category to the database
- ❏ `Delete()` – this method deletes the current category and all the sub-categories

These are very basic methods; most of them only set and get information about the category. Let's discuss the pseudo code some of the more important methods for this class.

Category()

The constructor should be able to fetch data from the database about the current category, and let the object start as an empty category if we wish to create a new one:

```
function Category($id = false)
{
 if no argument
        set ID to 0
 else
 get record from database where id equals argument
    set id variable
    set category name variable
    set parent category variable
 end if
 }
```

If we don't send any arguments to the constructor, then we assume that we should create a new, empty category and set the ID to 0. If we get an argument, we fetch the category with this ID from the database and set all the variables in the object.

Store()

When we store the category, we have to check if we should save the category as a new record in the database, or if we should update an old record:

```
function Store()
{
    if ID is 0
        insert new record into table
        ID = new ID
    else
        update old record in table
    end if
}
```

As defined in the constructor, the ID of the category is set to 0 if it is a new category, therefore, we should store the category as a new record and update our ID. If the category has an ID, we update the old record in the table.

GetCategories()

This method should return every sub-category in the current category. It should execute a query and get all categories with the current category ID as parent categories. By doing this, we are getting every sub-category for this category:

```
function GetCategories()
{
    if ID > 0
        categories = select every category with ID as parent
        foreach category in categories
            append category object to return_array
        end foreach
        return return_array
    else
        return empty array
    end if
}
```

GetAllCategories()

This method should return all categories with sub-categories. The method will be used to get all the categories when we are making a list where the user can select categories for the search or the category for products in the administrator interface. The list that this method returns, should be created such that we can easily see which categories are the sub-categories of other categories. This functionality is needed if we wish to create 'drop-downs' or lists of all categories where the user can see the hierarchy of the category tree.

The function `GetAllCategories()` will be done recursively. The method will check one level in the hierarchical category tree and then execute itself for the next level:

```
function GetAllCategories($parent=0, $indents=0)
{
    get all categories with current parent from database
    foreach category in current level
        append category name with indenting to return_array
        append id to return_array
        list = GetAllCategories(category id, indents + 1)
        append list to return_array
    }
    return return_array
}
```

The Product Class

The `Product` class will contain information about each product in the catalog. We will create one object for each product we wish to show. This class should get the information about the current product from the database and return the information needed if other classes or functions need it. The class should also store the information to the database when necessary and create and update the word list for this product.

Let's look at this class now.

Variables

We would need variables for each value stored in the database. The variables are as follows:

❑   `productID` – the unique ID of this product

❑   `productNumber` – the product number of this product

❑   `productTitle` – a string containing the title of the product

❑   `productManufacturer` – a string containing the manufacturer of the product

❑   `productDescription` – a string containing the description of the product

❑   `productPrice` – the price of this product

❑   `productCategory` – a category object representing the category of the product

Methods

The following are the methods needed to set the variables.

❑   `Product()` – the constructor of the class which connects to the database and gets the necessary information

❑   `GetProductID()` – should return the ID of our product

❑   `GetProductNumber()` – returns the product number of the product

❑   `SetProductNumber()` – sets the product number of the product

❑   `GetProductTitle()` – returns the title of the current product

❑   `SetProductTitle()` – sets the title of the current product

❑   `GetManufacturer()` – returns the current manufacturer of the product

❑   `SetManufacturer()` – sets the current manufacturer of the product

❑   `GetProductDescription()` – returns the description of the product

❑   `SetProductDescription()` – sets the description of the product

❑   `GetPrice()` – returns the price of the product

❑   `SetPrice()` – sets the current price of the product

❑   `GetCategory()` – this method returns a category object representing the category of the product

❑   `SetCategory()` – sets the current category of the product

❑   `Store()` – stores the current information to the database

❑   `CreateWordList()` – creates or updates the word list for this product

❑   `Search()` – searches through the word list for products

❑   `Delete()` – deletes all information about this product from the database

In these methods, we set or get information about the product. The three methods we need to look at in more detail are: `CreateWordList()`, `Search()`, and `Delete()`.

CreateWordList()

This is an important method for the entire case study. The method creates a searchable word list of the relevant text found in the product information. It should create or update all the words with a frequency that is equal to the number of times it appears in the word array.

Let's look at some pseudo-code of what this method does:

```
function CreateWordList()
{
    remove all word links for this product in the database

    wordlist = description of product
    wordlist .= manufacturer + manufacturer
    wordlist .= title + title + title

    wordlist = lowercase( wordlist )
    remove special characters from wordlist

    word_array = array of wordlist

    total_word_count = words in wordlist

    group and count each word into word_array

    foreach unique word in word_array
        if word doesn't exists in wordlist table
            insert word into wordlist table
        end if
            frequency = number of times this word exists in the
                        word_array / total_word_count

        insert word link with frequency into wordlistlinks table
    end foreach
}
```

Now let's look at this step by step. We start off by removing every word link in the `productcatalog_wordlistlinks` table for this product, because we should update the word list information if we have been changing the content of the product. Next, we create our word list. As said earlier, we want to rank words that are in the title and manufacturer higher than the words in the description. That's why we let the `productcatalog_wordlist` table contain the description once, the manufacturer twice, and the title three times. For the product in the earlier example, the word list would contain:

```
This is a very good HUB. It has four ports and let's you connect computers easily
to make your own private network in your office or at home. Network Inc. Network
Inc. Super Ethernet HUB Super Ethernet HUB Super Ethernet HUB
```

If we wish to let the title rank even more, we could add the title to the word list more times. The developer should adjust this to best match his needs when he is developing the site.

The next thing we doing is to remove all special characters like periods, commas, and so on. This is to avoid these characters appear in our word list. We should also remove double spaces and HTML special characters, and turn the whole string into lowercase. The case of the words doesn't matter for the users that search our site. That's why we store every word in lowercase in the database. For instance, 'Network' and 'network' should return the same matches if a user searches for either of these. Therefore, the word list will now contain:

```
this is a very good hub it has four ports and lets you connect computers easily to
make your own private network in your office or at home network inc network inc
super ethernet hub super ethernet hub super ethernet hub
```

We should now split this string into an array. Each word should be stored as a value. To do this, we split the string with space as the pattern and store this in our word_array. To be able to calculate the frequency of each word, we have to count how many words we have in the word_array. In this example, the total word count is 41.

The next thing we need to do is to group and count each word in the word list. This is because we need to know how often each word is used in the product information. PHP has a function for this called array_count_values() (only in PHP 4.0.0 and later). This function returns an associative array containing each word as the key and how often the word occurred in the array as the value. In this example we would get the following array:

```
Array
(
    [this] => 1
    [is] => 1
    [a] => 1
    [very] => 1
    [good] => 1
    [hub] => 4
    [it] => 1
    [has] => 1
    [four] => 1
    [ports] => 1
    [and] => 1
    [lets] => 1
    [you] => 1
    [easy] => 1
    [connect] => 1
    [computers] => 1
    [to] => 1
    [make] => 1
    [your] => 2
    [own] => 1
    [private] => 1
    [network] => 3
```

```
            [in] => 1
            [office] => 1
            [or] => 1
            [at] => 1
            [home] => 1
            [inc] => 2
            [super] => 3
            [ethernet] => 3
    )
```

Next, we have to go through a loop and check each of these words. First, we check if the word exists in the word list. If it does, we get the ID of the word, and if it doesn't, we insert it as a new record. Then we need to check the frequency for the current word. Since the word this exists once in the word list, the frequency for this word is 1/41 (about 0.024). The word hub exists four times, and the frequency is 4/41 (about 0.097). This value is inserted into the database for each word, and we are finished.

When we are done, the contents of the table will be updated accordingly. Now when we perform a search for a word, we sort the results in the descending order of frequency. By doing this, we will get the most relevant matches first since these have the highest frequency of the searched word. If the user is searching for more than one word, we add up the frequencies for each product and search by this.

As you may see, this causes a lot of database queries. The method is very slow but we have to remember that this is a task that is done very rarely. This is only done when an administrator is adding products to the database or editing products that already exist.

Search()

This method does the actual searching – it searches through the word list to find the best matches. If the user searches for more than one word, the word list should be checked for every word he searches for and the frequency for all matching words for each product should be added up. By doing this, the frequency for the words for each product gets added and we will get the matches sorted by the total frequency for each product. This search is a logical OR search which means that it only matches products that have one of the words, but because of the ranking, the products with more of the words will rank higher than the products with fewer of the words.

Let's look at some pseudo-code of how we should solve this:

```
function Search($search_string, $categories = false)
{
    remove special characters from search_string
    search_array = split search_string based on spaces

    if categories
        build query with categories
    else
        build query without categories
    end if

    execute query;

    foreach every result in query
        append product object for result to return_array
    end foreach

    return return_array
}
```

The function takes two arguments – the search string and an array of each category we wish to search through. The function will return an array of product objects, each representing one product that matches the search. If no categories are sent as an argument, all the categories will be searched.

Delete()

One important thing to remember is to delete the affected records from the `productcatalog_wordlistlinks` table when we delete a product. The search will also return previously deleted products if we don't do this. Let's look at how this method should be implemented:

```
function Delete()
{
    id = current product ID

    delete from products where product_id equals id
    delete from wordlistlinks where wordlistlink_productid equals id
}
```

Now, none of the deleted products will show up in a search.

Designing the Framework

In addition to the classes discussed, we need something to make sure it all works together. The different scripts we need are:

❑   List of categories and products

❑   Form for the search engine and list of matches from the search

❑   Detailed page for the products

❑   Admin page for listing the categories and products

❑   Admin page for adding and editing the categories

❑   Admin page for adding and editing the products

Our site will have the following directory structure:

Folder	Options
Chapter11/	This folder will contain the general PHP scripts required for the application.
Chapter11/templates	This folder will contain the templates for the PHP scripts. This includes the class template.inc, and other templates that we create.
Chapter11/admin	This will contain the admin PHP scripts.

Each script has one important task to do on our site. The admin scripts for editing will be used twice, both to present the form where the administrator fills in information and to store the information in the database. We will use an `action` variable to know which of these jobs the script should do. Let's look at how these scripts work in further detail.

Category and Product List

This is the script that produces the list a all sub-categories and products in the current category. The script takes the ID of the current category as a parameter. It will then make a list of all sub-categories for the current category. Finally, the script will get all products from the current category and list them.

If users click on one of the categories, they will be taken to a list for that category. So, if the users click on a product, they will see detailed information about that product.

Let's look at some pseudo-code for this script:

```
if ID not provided
    ID = 0
end if

category = category object for ID

categories = sub-categories for category
products = products for category

print category title

foreach category in categories
    print category link
end foreach

foreach product in products
    print product link
end foreach
```

The classes carry out most of the functionality of this script. At the start, we check to see if we have an ID supplied in the URL. If not, we set the ID to 0 to show the contents of the root category.

Searching

This script, if executed without parameters, shows a search form where the user can enter search words and, optionally, select categories to search in. If we have variables from the search form, we execute the search and display the results:

```
create search box
category_array = all categories
create list with all categories

if contents in search_text
    results = Product::search

    foreach product in results
        print product link
    end foreach

end if
```

We start off by checking `search_text`. `search_text` is the variable containing the search words that the user enters in the form. We present the search form and, if the `search_text` isn't empty, we make a search based on this variable and display the results in a list at the bottom.

Product Details

The user requests this script when he clicks a product in any of the lists. These lists are either in the category list or in the search results. The script will be requested with the ID of the product as a parameter:

```
if ID is empty
    print error message
else
    product = product object with current id
    category = category of product

    print product title
    print category name
    print product number
    print manufacturer
    print product description
    print price
end if
```

We should always print error messages if no ID variable is supplied. This happens usually if the user starts to mess around with the URL and tries to directly access pages on our site by typing the URL instead of clicking on links.

Admin Page for Listing Categories and Products

The admin page for the listing of categories and products should look very much like the user page. The only differences are:

❑   The administrator has to log in to access this page

❑   The administrator has the possibility to choose either a category or a product for editing

Let's look at the pseudo code:

```
if user has logged in
    if not ID provided
        ID = 0
    end if

    category = category object for ID

    categories = sub-categories for category
    products = products for category

    print category title
    foreach category in categories
        print category link
        print category edit link
```

```
        end foreach

    foreach product in products
        print product link
        print product edit link
    end foreach
else
    print login screen
end if
```

Admin Page for Adding and Editing Categories

We have to make a form for the user to fill in when he wishes to add a new category or edit an old one. The form we present to the user is the same, but when we edit an already existing category, the form should be filled in with the old values.

The ID of the edited category has to be stored somewhere in the form so that we'll know which category we were editing when we store the changes. We store this as a hidden value in the form:

```
if user has logged in
    if store == true
        if ID == 0
            category = empty category object
            set values of category to values provided by user
            save category
        else
            category = category object for ID
            set values of category to values provided by user
            save category
        end if
    else
        if ID is provided
            category = category object for ID
            print form with preset values
            hidden ID value = ID
        else
            print form with empty values
            hidden ID value = 0
        end if
    end if
else
    print login screen
end if
```

As always, in the admin section, we start by checking if the administrator has logged in. If the administrator has logged in, we check if the `store` variable is set. This variable should tell us if we should present the form for editing categories, or if we should store variables to the database.

If this variable is set, we should store the data to the database and check if this is a new category that we should update. If we should create a new category, then the hidden ID field is 0. If we should update an already existing category, the hidden ID field should hold the ID of this category.

If the `store` variable is not set, we should show the category form for the administrator. We will check for an ID variable here as well. If this is set, we show the category form with the values of the category defined by the ID variable, if not, we show an empty category form.

Admin Page for Adding and Editing Products

The page for editing the products should work like the page for editing the categories. We should present the same form both for editing and adding, but if we are editing, all the values should be filled in. As for categories, we need to store the ID for the edited product in a hidden field. We also need a variable to tell us if we should present the form or save the new values to the database:

```
if user has logged in
    if store == true
        if ID == 0
            product = empty product object
            set values of product to values provided by user
            save product
        else
            product = product object for ID
            set values of product to values provided by user
            save product
        end if
    else
        if ID is provided
            product = product object for ID
            print form with preset values
            hidden ID value = ID
        else
            print form with empty values
            hidden ID value = 0
        end if
    end if
else
    print login screen
end if
```

Classes

Some of the issues in this case study are also been tackled in other chapters in the book. Therefore, we will only show the parts of the code that are relevant for the search and the framework for the end user. Both the classes will be presented with full source code because it is the classes that store the products, search for products, and create the word list.

The admin pages are quite similar to the other examples in this book; therefore, we shall not list them here. However, these PHP scripts will be part of the code download for the book from the Wrox web site at http://www.wrox.com/.

Category.class.php

Here is the PHP script for the Category class:

```php
<?php

# FILE: Category.class.php

class Category
{
    var $categoryID;
    var $categoryName;
    var $parentCategory;

    function Category($id = false)
    {
        if ($id) {
            $result = mysql_query("SELECT * FROM productcatalog_categories
                                WHERE category_id='$id'");
            $row = mysql_fetch_array($result);

            $this->categoryID = $id;
            $this->categoryName = $row["category_name"];
            $this->parentCategory = $row["category_parent"];
        } else {
            $this->categoryID = 0;
        }
    }

    function GetCategoryID()
    {
        return $this->categoryID;
    }

    function GetCategoryName()
    {
        return $this->categoryName;
    }

    function SetCategoryName($value)
    {
        $this->categoryName = $value;
    }

    function GetCategoryParent()
    {
        return new Category($this->parentCategory);
    }

    function SetCategoryParent($value)
    {
        if (get_class($value) == "Category") {
            $this->parentCategory = $value->GetCategoryID();
        } else {
```

```
            $this->parentCategory = $value;
        }
    }

    function Store()
    {
        if ($this->GetCategoryID() == 0) {
            mysql_query("INSERT INTO productcatalog_categories
                        (category_name, category_parent) VALUES
                        ('$this->categoryName', '$this->parentCategory')");
            $this->CategoryID = mysql_insert_id();
        } else {
            mysql_query("UPDATE productcatalog_categories SET
                        category_name= '$this->categoryName',
                        category_parent='$this->parentCategory'
                        WHERE category_id='$this->categoryID'");
        }
    }

    function Delete()
    {
        if ($this->categoryID > 0) {
            $product_list = $this->Products();
            foreach ($product_list as $product) {
                $product->delete();
            }

            $category_list = $this->GetCategories();
            foreach ($category_list as $category) {
                $category->delete();
            }

            mysql_query("DELETE FROM productcatalog_categories WHERE
                        category_id='$this->categoryID'");
        }
    }

    function Products()
    {
        $return_array = array();
        if ($this->categoryID > 0) {

        $product_list = mysql_query("SELECT * FROM productcatalog_products
                                    WHERE
                                    product_category='$this->categoryID'
                                    ORDER BY product_title");

        while ($row = mysql_fetch_array($product_list)) {
                $return_array[] = new Product($row["product_id"]);
            }
        }
        return $return_array;
    }
```

```php
    function GetCategories()
    {
        $return_array = array();
        if ($this->categoryID > 0) {
        $category_list = mysql_query("SELECT * FROM
                                productcatalog_categories WHERE
                                category_parent='$this->categoryID'
                                ORDER BY category_name");
        while ($row = mysql_fetch_array($category_list)) {
                $return_array[] = new Category($row["category_id"]);
            }
        }
        return $return_array;
    }

    function GetAllCategories($parent = 0, $indents = 0)
    {
        $return_array = array();
        $category_list = mysql_query("SELECT * FROM
                                productcatalog_categories WHERE
                                category_parent='$parent'
                                ORDER BY category_name");
        while ($row = mysql_fetch_array($category_list)) {

            $return_array[] = array($row["category_id"],
                                str_repeat("  ", $indents) .
                                        $row["category_name"]);
            foreach
             (Category::GetAllCategories($row["category_id"], $indents + 1)
                                                    as $category) {
                $return_array[] = $category;
            }
        }
        return $return_array;
    }
}
?>
```

Product.class.php

Here is the PHP script for the Product class:

```php
<?php

# FILE: Product.class.php

class Product
{
    var $productID;
    var $productNumber;
    var $productTitle;
    var $productManufacturer;
```

```php
    var $productDescription;
    var $productPrice;
    var $productCategory;

    function Product($id = false)
    {
        if ($id) {
            $result = mysql_query("SELECT * FROM productcatalog_products
                                WHERE product_id='$id'");
            $row = mysql_fetch_array($result);
            $this->productID = $id;
            $this->productNumber = $row["product_number"];
            $this->productTitle = $row["product_title"];
            $this->productManufacturer = $row["product_manufacturer"];
            $this->productDescription = $row["product_description"];
            $this->productPrice = $row["product_price"];
            $this->productCategory = $row["product_category"];
        } else {
            $this->productID = 0;
        }
    }

    function GetProductID()
    {
            return $this->productID;
    }

    function GetProductNumber()
    {
        return $this->productNumber;
    }

    function SetProductNumber($value)
    {
        $this->productNumber = $value;
    }

    function GetProductTitle()
    {
        return $this->productTitle;
    }

    function SetProductTitle($value)
    {
        $this->productTitle = $value;
    }

    function GetProductManufacturer()
    {
        return $this->productManufacturer;
    }

    function SetProductManufacturer($value)
    {
```

```php
        $this->productManufacturer = $value;
}

function GetProductDescription()
{
    return $this->productDescription;
}

function SetProductDescription($value)
{
    $this->productDescription = $value;
}

function GetPrice()
{
    return $this->productPrice;
}

function SetPrice($value)
{
    $this->productPrice = $value;
}

function GetProductCategory()
{
    return new Category($this->productCategory);
}

function SetProductCategory($value)
{
    if (get_class($value) == "Category") {
        $this->ProductCategory = $value->GetCategoryID();
    } else {
        $this->ProductCategory = $value;
    }
}

function Store()
{

    if ($this->GetProductID() == 0) {
        mysql_query("INSERT INTO productcatalog_products
                    (product_number, product_title,
                     product_manufacturer, product_description,
                     product_price, product_category) VALUES
                    ('$this->productNumber', '$this->productTitle',
                     '$this->productManufacturer',
                     '$this->productDescription', '$this->productPrice',
                     '$this->productCategory')");
        $this->ProductID = mysql_insert_id();
    } else {
        mysql_query("UPDATE productcatalog_products SET
                    product_number='$this->productNumber',
                    product_title='$this->productTitle',
```

```
                        product_manufacturer='$this->productManufacturer',
                        product_description='$this->productDescription',
                        product_price='$this->productPrice',
                        product_category='$this->productCategory' WHERE
                        product_id=$this->productID");
        }
        $this->CreateWordList();
    }

    function Delete()
    {
        if ($this->GetProductID() == 0) {
            mysql_query("DELETE FROM productcatalog_products WHERE
                        product_id='$this->productID'");
            mysql_query("DELETE FROM productcatalog_wordlistlinks WHERE
                        wordlistlink_id='$this->productID'");
        }
    }

    function CreateWordList()
    {
        mysql_query("DELETE FROM productcatalog_wordlistlinks
                    WHERE wordlistlink_id='$this->ProductID'");
        $wordlist = $this->ProductDescription . " ";
        $wordlist .= str_repeat($this->productManufacturer . " ", 2);

        $wordlist .= str_repeat($this->productTitle . " ", 3);
        $wordlist = strtolower($wordlist);
        $wordlist = str_replace ("\n", "", $wordlist );
        $wordlist = str_replace ("\r", "", $wordlist );
        $wordlist = str_replace ("(", " ", $wordlist );
        $wordlist = str_replace (")", " ", $wordlist );
        $wordlist = str_replace (",", " ", $wordlist );
        $wordlist = str_replace (".", " ", $wordlist );
        $wordlist = str_replace ("/", " ", $wordlist );
        $wordlist = str_replace ("-", " ", $wordlist );
        $wordlist = str_replace ("_", " ", $wordlist );
        $wordlist = str_replace ("\"", " ", $wordlist );
        $wordlist = str_replace ("'", " ", $wordlist );
        $wordlist = str_replace (":", " ", $wordlist );
        $wordlist = str_replace ("?", " ", $wordlist );
        $wordlist = str_replace ("!", " ", $wordlist );
        $wordlist = str_replace ("\"", " ", $wordlist );
        $wordlist = str_replace ("|", " ", $wordlist );
        $wordlist = preg_replace("(&.+?;)", " ", $wordlist );
        $wordlist = preg_replace("(\s+)", " ", $wordlist );

        $word_array =& split(" ", $wordlist);
        $total_word_count = count($word_array);

        $grouped_word_array = array_count_values($word_array);

        reset($grouped_word_array);
        while ($single_word_array =each($grouped_word_array)) {
```

```
        $result = mysql_query("SELECT * FROM productcataolg_wordlists
                        WHERE
                        wordlist_word='" . $single_word_array[0] .
                        "'");
    if (mysql_num_rows($result) == 0) {
        mysql_query("INSERT INTO productcataolg_wordlists
                    (wordlist_word) VALUES
                    ('$single_word_array[0]')");
        $wordId = mysql_insert_id();
        } else {
        $row = mysql_fetch_array($result);
        $wordId = $row["wordlist_id"];
    }

    $frequency = $single_word_array[1] / $total_word_count;

    mysql_query("INSERT INTO productcataolg_wordlistlink
                (wordlistlink_id, wordlistlink_productid,
                 wordlistlink_frequency) VALUES
                ($wordlistlink_id, $this->productID, $frequency)");
    }
}

function Search( $search_string, $categories = -1)
{
    if (is_numeric($categories) && $categories > -1)
        $categories = array($categories);

    $search_string = strtolower($search_string);
    $search_string = str_replace ("\n", "", $search_string );
    $search_string = str_replace ("\r", "", $search_string );
    $search_string = str_replace ("(", " ", $search_string );
    $search_string = str_replace (")", " ", $search_string );
    $search_string = str_replace (",", " ", $search_string );
    $search_string = str_replace (".", " ", $search_string );
    $search_string = str_replace ("/", " ", $search_string );
    $search_string = str_replace ("-", " ", $search_string );
    $search_string = str_replace ("_", " ", $search_string );
    $search_string = str_replace ("\"", " ", $search_string );
    $search_string = str_replace ("'", " ", $search_string );
    $search_string = str_replace (":", " ", $search_string );
    $search_string = str_replace ("?", " ", $search_string );
    $search_string = str_replace ("!", " ", $search_string );
    $search_string = str_replace ("\"", " ", $search_string );
    $search_string = str_replace ("|", " ", $search_string );

    $search_array = split( " ", $search_string);
    $word_string = "(";
    for ($counter = 0; $counter < count($search_array); $counter++) {
        $word_string .= "WL.wordlist_word = '$search_array[$counter]'";
        if ($counter == count($search_array) - 1) {
            $word_string .= ")";
        } else {
            $word_string .= " OR ";
```

```
                }
        }

        if ($categories != -1) {
            $category_string = "(";
            for ($counter = 0; $counter < count($categories); $counter++) {
                $category_string .= "P.product_category =
                $categories[$counter]";
                if ($counter == count($search_array) - 1) {
                    $category_string .= ")";
                } else {
                    $category_string .= " OR ";
                }
            }

            $query = "SELECT WLL.wordlistlink_productid AS ID,
                    SUM(WLL.wordlistlink_frequency) as
                    Frequency FROM productcatalog_wordlists as WL,
                    productcatalog_wordlistlinks as WLL,
                    productcatalog_products as P WHERE
                    WLL.wordlistlink_wordid = WL.wordlist_id AND
                    P.ID = WLL.wordlistlink_productid AND
                    $word_string AND $category_string
                    GROUP BY WLL.wordlistlink_productid
                    ORDER BY WLL.wordlistlink_frequency DESC";
        } else {
            $query = "SELECT WLL.wordlistlink_productid AS ID,
                    SUM(WLL.wordlistlink_frequency) as
                    Frequency FROM productcatalog_wordlists as WL,
                    productcatalog_wordlistlinks as WLL
                    WHERE WLL.wordlistlink_wordid = WL.wordlist_id AND
                    $word_string GROUP BY WLL.wordlistlink_productid
                    ORDER BY WLL.wordlistlink_frequency DESC";
        }

        $result = mysql_query($query);
        $result_array = array();

        while ($row = mysql_fetch_array($result)) {
            $result_array[] = new Product($row["productID"]);
        }

        return $result_array;
    }
}
?>
```

Templates and PHP Scripts

We have to solve the HTML design based on templates. By using templates, we are separating the business logic code from the presentation. All the HTML files will be stored in separate files and the design can be altered without needing any knowledge of PHP development. Let's make the templates we need for this case.

The template file looks very much like a normal HTML file. The one major difference is that it has no actual data to present to the user, instead it has fields where we would like the data to be placed. Instead of collecting data from the database and printing it out with `print()` or `echo()`, we place the data into fields in the template.

Templates are not a standard PHP feature and therefore, we need a library that can handle this. There are several templates and they all have their strengths and weaknesses. In this chapter we use the template class included in 'PHP Base Library'. We only need the `template.inc` so we can either install this library in the default way or just copy this file to the PHP directory.

Category and Product list

This list should include every sub-category and product in the current category. We do this by using blocks in our template, and if some categories don't have sub-categories or products, we remove that block:

```html
<html>
  <head>
    <title>Product catalog</title>
  </head>
<body>
    <h1>Product catalog</h1>
    <h2>{category_name}</h2>

    <!-- BEGIN category_list_tpl -->
    Categories:<br>
    <!-- BEGIN category_item_tpl -->
      <a href="productlist.php?ID={sub_category_id}">
             {sub_category_name}</a><br>
    <!-- END category_item_tpl -->
    <br>
    <!-- END category_list_tpl -->
     <hr>
     <!-- BEGIN product_list_tpl -->
    Products:<br>
    <!-- BEGIN product_item_tpl -->
    <a href="productdetails.php?ID={product_id}">{product_name}</a><br>
    <!-- END product_item_tpl -->
    <br>
    <!-- END product_list_tpl -->
  </body>
</html>
```

We save this file as `productlist.tpl`. Here is the `productlist.php` script:

```php
<?php

FILE: productlist.php

mysql_connect("localhost", "myuser", "mypassword");
mysql_select_db("productcatalog");

include_once("./templates/template.inc");
include_once("product.class.php");
```

```php
include_once("category.class.php");

$template = new Template(".");

$template->set_file("list_tpl", "./templates/productlist.tpl");

$template->set_block("list_tpl", "category_list_tpl", "category_list");

$template->set_block("category_list_tpl", "category_item_tpl",
                     "category_item");

$template->set_block("list_tpl", "product_list_tpl", "product_list");

$template->set_block("product_list_tpl", "product_item_tpl",
                     "product_item");

if (!isset($ID)) {
    $ID = 0;
}

$category = new Category($ID);

$categories = $category->GetCategories();
$products = $category->Products();

$template->set_var("category_name", $category->GetCategoryName());

foreach ($categories as $category_item) {
        $template->set_var("sub_category_id",
        $category_item->GetCategoryID());
        $template->set_var("sub_category_name",
        $category_item->GetCategoryName());
        $template->parse("category_item", "category_item_tpl", true);
}

$template->parse("category_list", "category_list_tpl");

foreach ($products as $product) {
    $template->set_var("product_id", $product->GetProductID());
    $template->set_var("product_name", $product->GetProductTitle());
    $template->parse("product_item", "product_item_tpl", true);
}

$template->parse("product_list", "product_list_tpl");
$template->pparse("output", "list_tpl");

?>
```

Which will produce a page similar to the following:

Searching

The search template can be used to view the search form at the top, and a list of matches if the search gave any results:

```html
<html>
  <head>
      <title>Search in the product catalog</title>
  </head>
  <body>
    <h1>Search</h1>
    <form action="search.php" method="post">
    <b>Search string:</b><br>
     <input type="text" value="{search_string}"
          name="search_string"><br><br>
      <b>Search categories:</b><br>
       <select multiple name="search_categories">
          <option value="-1" selected>All categories
          <!-- BEGIN category_item_tpl -->
          <option value="{category_id}">{category_name}
          <!-- END category_item_tpl -->
      ,</select>
    <input type="submit">

    </form>
      <!-- BEGIN search_results_tpl -->
      <hr>
        Search results: {search_count}<br>
```

```
              <!-- BEGIN result_element_tpl -->
              <a href="productdetails.php?ID={product_id}">{product_name}</a><br>
              <!-- END result_element_tpl -->
          <hr>
        <!-- END search_results_tpl -->
      </body>
    </html>
```

This file is stored as search.tpl. The following is the PHP script search.php:

```php
<?php

# FILE: Search.php

mysql_connect("localhost", "myuser", "mypassword");
mysql_select_db("productcatalog");

include_once("./templates/template.inc");
include_once("product.class.php");
include_once("category.class.php");

$template = new Template(".");

$template->set_file("search_tpl", "./templates/search.tpl");

$template->set_block("search_tpl", "category_item_tpl", "category_item");

$template->set_block("search_tpl", "search_results_tpl", "search_results");

$template->set_block("search_results_tpl", "result_element_tpl",
                     "result_element");

$categories = Category::GetAllCategories();
foreach ($categories as $category) {
    $template->set_var("category_id", $category[0]);
    $template->set_var("category_name", $category[1]);
    $template->parse("category_item", "category_item_tpl", true);
}

if (isset($search_string)) {
    $results = Product::search($search_string, $search_categories);
    $template->set_var("search_count", count($results));
    foreach ($results as $result) {
        $template->set_var("product_id", $result->GetProductID());
        $template->set_var("product_name", $result->GetProductTitle());
        $template->parse("result_element", "result_element_tpl", true);
    }
    $template->parse("search_results", "search_results_tpl");
} else {
    $template->set_var("search_results", "");
}

$template->pparse("output", "search_tpl");

?>
```

The search page looks like this:

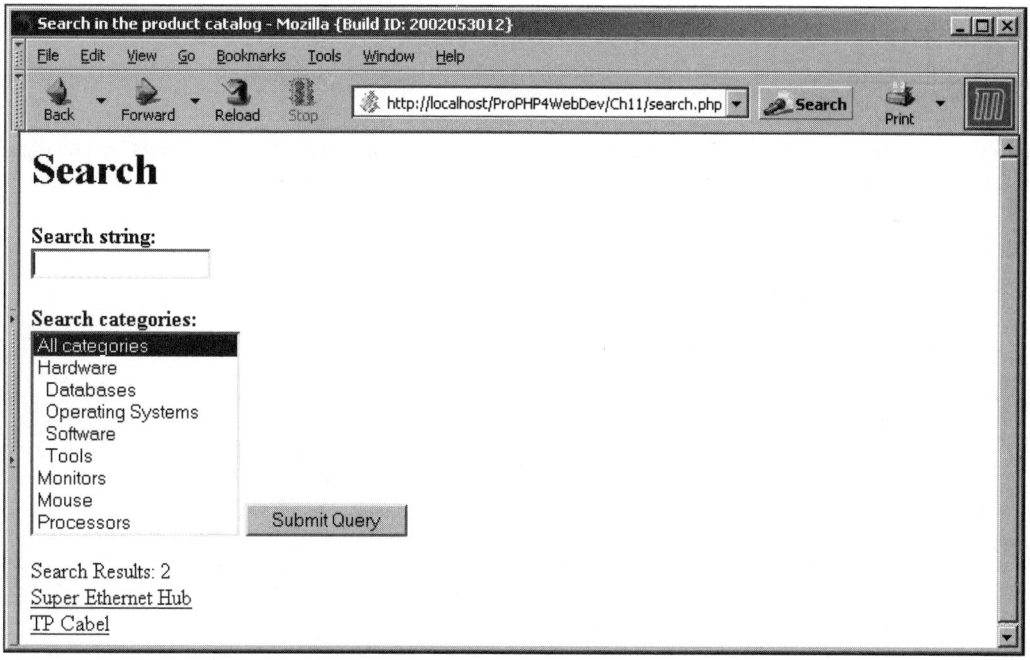

This screenshot shows the search screen after a search has been done, so it shows the search form and a list of matching products.

Product Details

When a user clicks on a product in one of the lists, he or she will be presented with more detailed information about that product. The template for this looks like:

```html
<html>
  <head>
    <title>Details</title>
  </head>
  <body>
    <h1>{product_name}</h1>

      <a href="productlist.php?ID={category_id}">{category_name}</a><br>

      <b>Product number:</b><br>
      {product_no}<br><br>

      <b>Manufacturer:</b><br>
      {manufacturer}<br><br>

      <b>Description:</b><br>
      {description}<br><br>
```

```
    <b>Price:</b><br>
    {price} $<br><br>
  </body>
</html>
```

This file is stored as `productdetails.tpl` and displays the information about a product by placing data in the template fields. Here is the corresponding PHP script:

```php
<?php

# FILE: productdetails.php

mysql_connect("localhost", "", "");
mysql_select_db("productcatalog");

include_once("./templates/template.inc");
include_once("product.class.php");
include_once("category.class.php");

$template = new Template(".");

$template->set_file("product_details_tpl",
                    "./templates/productdetails.tpl");

if (!isset($ID)) {
    print("No product requested");
} else {
    $product = new Product($ID);
    $category = $product->GetProductCategory();

    $template->set_var("product_name", $product->GetProductTitle());
    $template->set_var("category_id", $category->GetProductID());
    $template->set_var("category_name", $category->GetCategoryName());
    $template->set_var("product_no", $product->GetProductNumber());
    $template->set_var("manufacturer", $product->GetProductManufacturer());
    $template->set_var("description", $product->GetProductDescription());
    $template->set_var("price", $product->GetPrice());
}

$template->pparse("output", "product_details_tpl");

?>
```

If the `$ID` variable is empty, the user is not requesting any information about any products and we show the **No product requested** message. If `$ID` has a value, we create an object of the product with this ID and show all information about the product.

In this case the output looks like this:

Admin Page for Listing Categories and Products

For easier maintenance, we place all the admin pages in a separate `admin` directory on the server. Also, we prefix all admin files with `admin_`:

```html
<html>
  <head>
    <title>Edit product catalog</title>
  </head>
  <body>
    <h1>Product catalog</h1>
    <h2>{current_category_name}</h2>


    <!-- BEGIN category_list_tpl -->
    Categories:<br>

    <!-- BEGIN category_item_tpl -->
    <a href="admin_categorylist.php?ID={category_id}">
            {category_name}</a> 
    <a href="admin_categoryedit.php?ID={category_id}">
            Edit category</a><br>
    <!-- END category_item_tpl -->

    <a href="admin_categoryedit.php">New category</a>
    <br>
    <!-- END category_list_tpl -->


    <hr>
```

```
<!-- BEGIN product_list_tpl -->

Products:<br>

<!-- BEGIN product_item_tpl -->
<a href="admin_productedit.php?ID={product_id}">
    {product_name}</a><br>
 <!-- END product_item_tpl -->

 <a href="admin_productedit.php">New product</a>
 <br>
 <!-- END product_list_tpl -->


  </body>
</html>
```

The admin page for listing all categories and products looks very much like the user page. The only differences are that we have added links for editing each category, adding a new category, editing the products, and adding new products.

We save this file in the `admin` directory as `admin_categorylist.tpl`.

Admin Page for Adding and Editing Categories

We are using the same template for adding and editing categories. To do this, we need to be able to set or remove the values in the form whenever we want.

```
<html>
  <head>
    <title>Category edit</title>
  </head>

  <body>

  <h1>Category edit</h1>
    <form action="admin_categoryedit.php?store=true" method="post">

      <b>Category name:</b><br>
      <input type="text"
             value="{category_name_value}"
             name="categoryName"><br><br>

        <b>Parent category:</b><br>
        <select name="parentCategory">
        <!-- BEGIN category_item_tpl -->
          <option value="{category_id}" {selected}>{category_name}</option>
        <!-- END category_item_tpl -->

        </select><br><br>
      <input type="hidden" name="ID" value="{categoryID}">
      <input type="submit" value="OK">
    </form>

  </body>
</html>
```

The selected template variable is used if we should automatically set one of the categories as selected. This is usually needed when we are editing old categories. We set {selected} to selected for that category and to " " for all the other categories.

This file is saved as admin_categoryedit.tpl in the admin directory.

Admin Page for Adding and Editing Products

As for the category edit page, we are using the same template both for adding and editing products:

```html
<html>
  <head>
    <title>Product edit</title>
  </head>

  <body>

    <h1>Product edit</h1>

    <form action="admin_productedit.php?store=true" method="post">

      <b>Product title:</b><br>
      <input type="text" name="productTitle"
             value="{product_title}"><br><br>

      <b>Product number:</b><br>
        <input type="text" name="productNo" value="{product_number}"><br><br>

      <b>Manufacturer:</b><br>
        <input type="text" name="manufacturer" value="{manufacturer}"><br><br>

      <b>Price:</b><br>
        <input type="text" name="price" value="{price}"><br><br>

      <b>Description:</b><br>
      <textarea name="description">{description}</textarea>

      <b>Category:</b><br>
        <select name="productCategory">
      <!-- BEGIN category_item_tpl -->
      <option value="{category_id}" {selected}>{category_name}</option>
      <!-- END category_item_tpl -->

    </select><br><br>
      <input type="hidden" name="ID" value="{productID}">
      <input type="submit" value="OK">
      </form>

  </body>
</html>
```

491

This file is stored as `admin_productedit.tpl` in the `admin` directory.

Improving the Search

This search is very general. There are several things that can be done to improve it for our use. Next let's discuss some point of how the search facility can be improved.

Difficult Search Words

Sometimes the user doesn't always spell the search words correctly and he might not get what he was looking for. If we are developing a store on the Internet, we can loose a lot of customers due to this. A solution can be to store several variations of difficult words in the database. If we have a record store, the user might not know if he or she should search for 'R.E.M.', 'REM', or 'R E M'. Therefore, we can add all these variations to our word list. This will ensure that the user will more often find what they are looking for, and we will sell more records.

If we wish to make this even more advanced, we can use several functions to allow 'fuzzy searches'. We can add a new field in the database and store constants like 'levenshtein', 'soundex', or 'metaphone' – these are constants describing how the word sounds. The search can then use this to search words with a similar content. More information about these functions can be found in the PHP documentation at http://www.php.net/docs.php.

Wildcards

As we said in the beginning of the chapter, queries using `LIKE` to search with wildcards are very slow, but sometimes it would be very nice for the user to be able to search for only parts of the word. The fastest way to do this is by letting the user specify a wildcard that causes the search engine to use a `LIKE` search for that word only. Usually if the user searches for network hub we would check:

```
WHERE Word='network' AND Word='hub'
```

If the user on the other hand searches for net* hub we could use a `LIKE` search for net and an ordinary search for hub:

```
WHERE Word LIKE 'net%' AND Word='hub'
```

This will be a bit slower, but only slower when the user requests a partial search.

Paginating results

For large catalog we can often get hundreds or maybe thousands of matching results. It would be a lot better to divide this over several pages so the user only gets the first 10 interesting matches. This can be done with an offset variable and the `LIMIT` command. At the end of the SQL command we add:

```
LIMIT 10, $Offset
```

This would only give us `10` results starting from `$Offset`. At the bottom of the page we can place links to allow the user to get the next 10 results by linking to itself and increasing the offset by 10.

Sorting results

It is often convenient for the user to be able to sort the search results by one of the variables. Adding another variable to the search page in the same way as when we paginate the results can do this. The `$Sort` variable contains the name of the field in the database we wish to sort by. We can add this to the query:

```
ORDER BY $Sort
```

References

The eZ publish project has an interesting article on creating a search engine. It can be found at http://developer.ez.no/.

Summary

In this chapter, we've looked at how to create a search engine. We've done this by creating a product catalog where we store the details of products and the categories they belong to. All words about the products have been placed in an index table to make the search as efficient as possible. One of the most important things about creating an efficient search engine is to make sure as much information as possible is computed when we create new information in the database, and not when the end user is requesting information.

Several of these techniques can always be improved, but the most important thing that we hoped to achieve in this case study was to detail the basics on how efficient searching is done. Now we can explore the possibilities and find customized solutions.

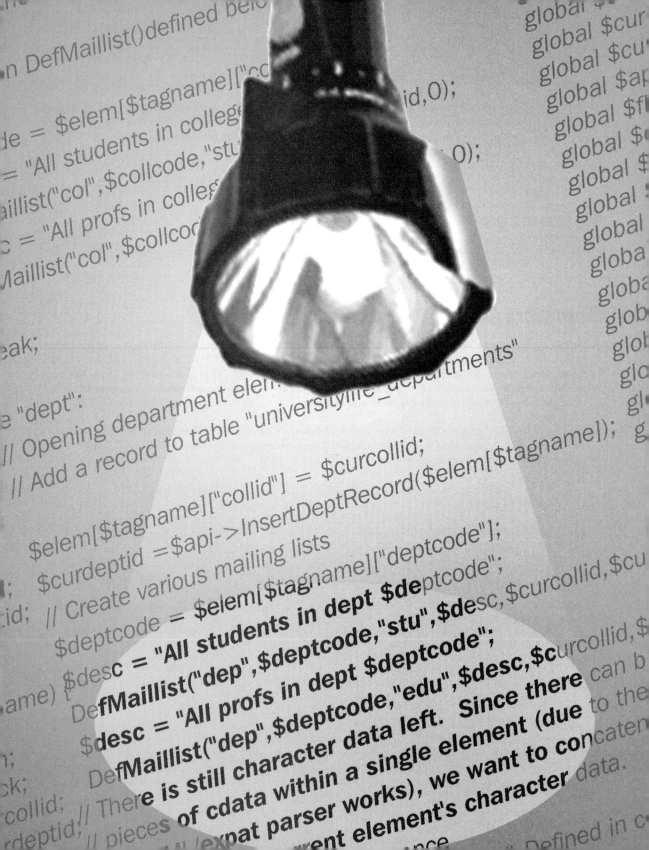

12

Wireless MyStuff Server

Ever get tired of forgetting what is in your personal collection, be it CDs, DVDs, tapes, books, comics, or magazines? Have you ever gone shopping and bought something, find that you already had it when you got home? This data warehousing application tries to solve that problem with a web application that allows users to view their personal collections with a wireless device.

These are the steps we will go through:

❑ **Application Specification**
Define the general features, user types, and hierarchy of the application.

❑ **Designing the Database**
A MySQL database will be used as the back-end for the application. Here we define the architecture of this database.

❑ **Managing the Data**
In this section, we will populate the database with some example content, and look at a few examples of SQL queries for working with the data.

❑ **Delivering the Content**
We need to define PHP scripts that retrieve content from the database, and Smarty-templates that present the content to the end-user. Since we're concentrating on the wireless feature of the application here, the Smarty templates will present the content as WML.

Introduction

This case study focuses on a multi-database public data warehouse application with features available to wireless devices.

Users register an account using their PCs and a regular browser. They can define their collections (up to 10 collections at one time) and view, add, edit, and delete entries too. Also, they can delete old collections, thereby freeing up space for a new collection (collection ID's are not reused). Each collection resides in its own table, which the user can partially define.

The entire set of user menu options is available via a normal (HTML) browser. Due to the limitations of wireless browsers, they can be used only for viewing the collections and deleting the items; no editing options are available.

Application Specification

While a complete system would have administrator and user panels (for wired and wireless features, as necessary), space limitations only permit us to focus on a subset of features for the general wireless user. Out of necessity to support the wireless features, we will need to refer to some of the non-wireless features, including those used by the administrator. For these features, we will mimic them by using the MySQL command line monitor, mysql, to access or update the necessary database tables.

While this application is relatively simple in concept, much of the concepts discussed in Chapter 7 apply here. In fact much of the PHP code and WML templates are borrowed from that case study. Therefore, refer to Chapter 7 for any code implied here but not provided. The same applies to any user screens implied but not shown here.

User Types

This application has two user types:

❑ **Admin**
Admin users have full privileges via MySQL's command line monitor (mysql) and a wired (regular) web browser interface (not discussed here). However, aside from testing, an admin user is unlikely to use the collection features.

❑ **Users**
Regular users have access to a smaller set of features than admin users. Also, they have a wired and a wireless component.

Content Types

The content type is limited to short items of text strings. Each user will partially define their content meaning, for example, one user might use the application to store CD information, while another might store books. The trick to implementing this application is to design a database schema and the supporting code for the most generalized definition of a collection.

Content and Features

There are a number of types of text content that are relevant to specific features. Here is a listing of the features and their related content:

- ❑ Create user accounts – normally, this would be done by each user through registration in the non-wireless component. Here, we mimic the feature manually using the MySQL command line monitor.

- ❑ Create user collection records (for regular users) – the feature is mimicked with mysql.

- ❑ Create collection items records (for regular users) – the feature is mimicked with mysql.

- ❑ User login (for wireless users).

- ❑ User logout (for wireless users).

- ❑ Change account password for user (for wireless users) .

- ❑ View list of collections for the current user (for wireless users).

- ❑ Pick a collection and view the list of items (for wireless users).

- ❑ Pick an item and view the item's details (for wireless users).

These features are the basic set we need to cover all of the wireless user features. We will not present PHP code for implementing all of these features, some are only mentioned and are not included in the code listings.

Component Hierarchy

The MyStuff web application has both wired and wireless software components. The diagram below illustrates the application's component hierarchy:

Site Navigation

Once a regular user successfully logs in to the MyStuff server application, there is a standard menu that appears on every page. Here is a schematic representation of the menu:

Collections
Change Pswd
Logout

This is a very simple menu with only three items (to which more options can be added later). In addition to these menu features, additional features are available on certain pages in the form of WML hyperlinks. Some of these features are discussed later.

Designing the Database

In the following sections we shall describe the information that needs to be captured in the `mystuff` database.

Reports

There are a number of reports that an admin user may want to generate regarding users, collection quantities, item quantities, and so on. Because we are only focusing on the wireless user interface, we will only show a select set of SQL queries necessary to support some basic administration features and reporting.

> The code download for this chapter includes a file titled `Common Queries`. This file includes some common queries that can be used by the PHP code to retrieve data for specific Admin or User features. Keep in mind that these are not necessarily complete SQL queries but are query templates that can serve as a reference. The PHP code that uses them may need to replace fields in the template before it can be run.

Database Tables

These are the steps we need to take to create and populate the database:

1. Create tables
2. Build indexes
3. Populate the database:
   - ❑ Create two – three user accounts
   - ❑ Define zero – three collections per account
   - ❑ Create zero – six items per collection

We'll cover the first two steps in the *Creating Tables* and *Building Indexes* sections. Step 3 shall be discussed in the context of the engine code.

These are the database tables necessary for the full version of the `MyStuff` server application:

Table	Alias	Description
mystuff_accounts	ac	User and admin account information.
mystuff_collections	co	General information about each collection, for all users.
mystuff_collmetadets	cmd	The table schema information for each user's collections.
mystuff_coll_*_*	coll	This group of tables contains all of the item information. Each collection has its own table. The name of each table is defined by a combination of the user ID and the collection ID (unique for each user, not across all users).

We will use these tables for the sample PHP code provided later. Now, let's discuss the database tables in more detail.

Accounts

The `mystuff_accounts` table contains information about regular and admin users. Note that for privacy reasons, the address information is not stored. Also, any other contact info is purely optional:

Column	Data Type	Description
account_acctid	INT	Unique record ID auto-generated by MySQL.
account_acct	CHAR	The account name for the user.
account_pass	CHAR	The password for the account.
account_type	CHAR	Account type. Allows for admin accounts to be set up.
account_fname	CHAR	The first name of the user.
account_lname	CHAR	The last name of the user.
account_stateprov	CHAR	State, province, district, or territory that the user lives in.
account_country	CHAR	Country the user lives in.
account_email	CHAR	An e-mail address for newsletters or announcements. This is only stored if the user has indicated that they want to receive such e-mail.

Table continued on following page

Column	Data Type	Description
account_status	ENUM('U','A', 'I','B')	For unregistered users, this column is set to 'U' (unapproved).
		For registered users, this column indicates whether the user, including Admin, is currently logged in ('A' – active), not logged in ('I' – inactive), or blocked ('B'). The flaw here is that using the Logout feature is not enforced, so this field can be misleading.
		For users denied registration approval, this column is set to 'D' (denied).
account_ncoll	INT	Number of collections stored on the mystuff server.
account_lastcollid	INT	ID of the last collection defined by the user. Note that since users are allowed to delete old collections and define new ones (maximum 10 collections simultaneously), this value may not be the same as the ncoll column. This ID is unique per user but not to the entire database.
		A collection is uniquely identified by combining this ID and account_acctid as a paired primary key. It is used to name the collections table for this user and the collection.
account_logdatetime	CHAR	We'll store the date/time of the most recent login as a character string. This string is used to encrypt the account name, with the result used to produce the session ID.
account_sessid	CHAR	While a user is logged in, this field stores a value to indicate that the user is legitimately logged in, that is, it's a form of user authentication.
account_lastactn	DATETIME	The date and time of the last action taken by the user. This field is used to determine whether a user may have implicitly logged off. For example, if 15 minutes have passed since the last time the user did anything on the system, it is likely that they have logged off. The session ID is then reset to zero, and the user status is set to inactive ('I').
		Note that this field is not used in the PHP code given later in the chapter. It's simply here to make an implementation of an automatic logout feature easier, and give you an idea of how it could be done.

Collections

The `mystuff_collections` table contains the information necessary for defining a collection:

Column	Data Type	Description
collection_collid	INT	Non-unique record ID, paired with the foreign key `account_acctid` to create a unique primary key.
collection_acctid	INT	Account ID of the user to whom the collection belongs.
collection_collname	CHAR	Full name of the collection. It is used in collection lists on the regular (non-wireless) interface.
collection_collcode	CHAR	A short name for the collection. It is used in a collection list on the wireless interface.
collection_nitems	INT	The number of items in the collection so far.
collection_itemtype	CHAR	A user-defined value that is used to indicate what is in the collection (for example, CDs, comics, magazines, paper clips).
collection_tblnmsfx	CHAR	Suffix of the collection table name defined for this collection.

Coll_*_*

This table contains the item records for a particular collection:

Column	Data Type	Description
coll_*_*_itemid	INT	Unique record ID, auto-generated by MySQL.
coll_*_*_itemname	CHAR	The name of the collection item, for example, 'Ekova – Space Lullabies and Other Fantasmagore'.
coll_*_*_itemcode	CHAR	A short name for the item, for example, 'Ekova – Space Lullabies'.
coll_*_*_itemdesc	CHAR	Additional, optional information about the item, for example, 'Label: Six Degrees Records'.
coll_*_*_detid	INT	The record ID of the corresponding record in the `mystuff_collmetadets` table.

The collection is identified by the suffix of the table name. For example, if a user's account ID is 11, the items in their second collection are identified by the `coll_11_2` table. At present, this table has a predetermined set of fields. However, in the full version of this application, it would have fields defined by the user.

Notice that without the extra fields defined by the users (not covered here), the table will still be normalized, technically speaking, but the user will have to enter redundant information.

Collmetadets

The `mystuff_collmetadets` table contains the table schema details for defining an item table for each collection. The reason for putting this information in a table is so that future improvements to the application may allow users to add their own fields. The additional information can be stored in this table and used to dynamically generate the item table for a particular collection. While such a feature complicates queries to the `mystuff_coll_*_*` tables, it adds flexibility to the application:

Column	Data Type	Description
collmetadet_detid	INT	Unique record ID, auto-generated by MySQL
collmetadet_fldname	CHAR	The name of a particular item table field
collmetadet_fldtype	CHAR	The field type (CHAR, INT, FLOAT, and so on)
collmetadet_fldmaxsize	INT	The maximum size for values of this field
collmetadet_flddecl	CHAR	Actual MySQL field declaration (with flags but without a comma at the end of the string), for example, `publisher CHAR (20) NOT NULL`
collmetadet_collid	INT	The ID of the related record in the `collections` table
collmetadet_acctid	INT	The account ID of the user who owns this collection

Note that we do not use this table in the sample PHP code provided later in this chapter, as we are not implementing the feature that allows users to add their own columns to the 'collection item' tables (`mystuff_coll_*_*`).

Relationships Between Tables

The diagram below shows the relationship between the tables in the `mystuff` database.

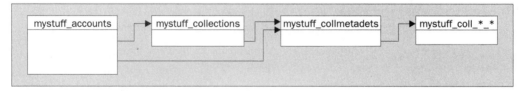

Database User

First let's create a database to hold the tables for this application:

```
> mysqladmin create mystuff
```

The tables for this case study can all be placed within a single MySQL database, `mystuff`. Since we are only running test scripts, we only need one database user, for example, `ADMIN`. We will have to grant privileges to the tables, as well as create the tables.

We are using the `mysql` client utility, which comes with MySQL, to grant privileges, as shown:

```
mysql> GRANT SELECT, INSERT, UPDATE, DELETE ON mystuff.*
       TO 'ADMIN@localhost' IDENTIFIED BY "ADMIN";
```

Creating Tables

Run the following SQL script, `crdbs_mystuff.sql`, on the command line to create the `mystuff` database and tables:

```
>mysql mystuff < crdbs_mystuff.sql
```

The following SQL code creates the `mystuff` database:

```
// FILE: crdbs_mystuff.sql
// USE:  Create MyStuff Server database

CREATE TABLE mystuff_accounts
(
   account_acctid      INT UNSIGNED NOT NULL AUTO_INCREMENT PRIMARY KEY,
   account_acct        VARCHAR(12) NOT NULL,
   account_pass        VARCHAR (12) NOT NULL,
   account_type        CHAR (3) NOT NULL,
   account_fname       VARCHAR (30) NOT NULL,
   account_lname       VARCHAR (40) NOT NULL,
   account_addr1       VARCHAR (40),
   account_addr2       VARCHAR (20),
   account_city        VARCHAR (30),
   account_stateprov   VARCHAR (30),
   account_country     VARCHAR (40),
   account_postcode    CHAR(10),
   account_email       VARCHAR (56),
   account_status      ENUM('U','A','I','B') NOT NULL,
   account_ncoll       SMALLINT UNSIGNED NOT NULL,
   account_lastcollid  SMALLINT UNSIGNED NOT NULL,
   account_logdatetime CHAR(20),                      // Always the same
   account_sessid      VARCHAR (128) NOT NULL,
   account_lastactn    DATETIME
);

CREATE TABLE mystuff_collections
(
   collection_collid    SMALLINT UNSIGNED NOT NULL,
   collection_acctid    INT UNSIGNED NOT NULL,        // Foreign key
   collection_collname  VARCHAR(40) NOT NULL,
   collection_collcode  VARCHAR(16) NOT NULL,
   collection_nitems    SMALLINT NOT NULL,
   collection_itemtype  VARCHAR(12),
   collection_tblnmsfx  VARCHAR(11) NOT NULL,
   PRIMARY KEY (collection_collid,account_acctid)     // Joint primary key
);

CREATE TABLE mystuff_collmetadets
```

```
(
   collmetadet_detid       INT UNSIGNED NOT NULL AUTO_INCREMENT PRIMARY KEY,
   collmetadet_fldname     VARCHAR(12) NOT NULL,
   collmetadet_fldtype     VARCHAR(12) NOT NULL,
   collmetadet_fldmaxsize  TINYINT UNSIGNED NOT NULL,
   collmetadet_flddecl     VARCHAR(50) NOT NULL,
   collmetadet_collid      SMALLINT UNSIGNED NOT NULL,
   collmetadet_acctid      INT UNSIGNED NOT NULL
);
```

Notice that we do not initially create any coll_*_* item tables. These are created only when a user defines a new collection (with the '*' replaced by real strings, of course). For the present time, each table has a fixed number of columns, so the collmetadets table is presently redundant. The current schema for the item tables is as follows:

```
CREATE TABLE mystuff_coll_*_*
(
   coll_*_*_itemid    INT UNSIGNED NOT NULL AUTO_INCREMENT PRIMARY KEY,
   coll_*_*_itemname  VARCHAR(128) NOT NULL,
   coll_*_*_itemcode  VARCHAR(32) NOT NULL,
   coll_*_*_itemdesc  VARCHAR(255),
   coll_*_*_detid     INT UNSIGNED NOT NULL
)
```

Building Indexes

Indexes are not necessary for the test scripts given later in this chapter. That said, feel free to build indexes on fields that are likely to be queried often, but keep in mind that MySQL creates indexes automatically on the primary key for each database table.

Populating the Database

Before we can test the PHP scripts and WML pages discussed later, we need some sample data in the database tables. Since we are only focusing on the features available to general users via the wireless interface, we need to populate the database manually using the MySQL command line monitor.

Create User Accounts

First we create three user accounts:

```
// FILE: mss_add_accts.sql
// USE:  Create sample user accounts

INSERT INTO mystuff_accounts
   (account_acct, account_pass, account_type, account_fname, account_lname,
    account_status, account_ncoll, account_lastcollid, account_sessid)
VALUES
   ("roohoo","roo","reg","roo",    "hoo",  "I",  0,  0,        ""),
   ("golly", "gee","reg","golly", "gee",  "I",  0,  0,        ""),
   ("mookie","moo","reg","mookie","mouse","I",  0,  0,        "");
```

Define the Collections for each Account

Keeping in mind that we are performing this step manually, we will have to know how many items we are adding to each collection. We will also need to know which user has what account ID (account_acctid):

```
// FILE: mss_add_collns.sql
// USE:  Define collections

INSERT INTO mystuff_collections
   (collection_collid, collection_acctid, collection_collname,
    collection_collcode, collection_nitems, collection_tblnmsfx)
VALUES
   (1,      2,       "Music: CD",          "Music:CD", 7,     "2_1"),
   (2,      2,       "Music: Vinyl",       "Music:LP", 4,     "2_2"),
   (3,      2,       "Film: DVD",          "Film:DVD", 3,     "2_3"),
   (1,      3,       "Books: Non-fiction", "Books:Non",0,     "3_1"),
   (2,      3,       "Books: Fiction",     "Books:Fic",6,     "3_2");
```

Create Some Items for the Collections

Now we can add items to the collections defined above. Note that before we can do so, we will need to create the individual item tables for each collection. We defined a total of five collections for two users, so we need to create five item tables. After that, we can insert the records.

```
// FILE: mss_add_items.sql

// Create individual collection "item" tables

// Item table for coll #1 of acctid #2
CREATE TABLE mystuff_coll_2_1
(
  coll_2_1_itemid   INT UNSIGNED NOT NULL AUTO_INCREMENT PRIMARY KEY,
  coll_2_1_itemname VARCHAR(128) NOT NULL,
  coll_2_1_itemcode VARCHAR(32) NOT NULL,
  coll_2_1_itemdesc VARCHAR(255),
  coll_2_1_detid    INT UNSIGNED NOT NULL
);

// Item table for coll #2 of acctid #2
CREATE TABLE mystuff_coll_2_2
(
  coll_2_2_itemid   INT UNSIGNED NOT NULL AUTO_INCREMENT PRIMARY KEY,
  coll_2_2_itemname VARCHAR(128) NOT NULL,
  coll_2_2_itemcode VARCHAR(32) NOT NULL,
  coll_2_2_itemdesc VARCHAR(255),
  coll_2_2_detid    INT UNSIGNED NOT NULL
);

// Item table for coll #3 of acctid #2
CREATE TABLE mystuff_coll_2_3
```

```
(
  coll_2_3_itemid    INT UNSIGNED NOT NULL AUTO_INCREMENT PRIMARY KEY,
  coll_2_3_itemname VARCHAR(128) NOT NULL,
  coll_2_3_itemcode VARCHAR(32) NOT NULL,
  coll_2_3_itemdesc VARCHAR(255),
  coll_2_3_detid     INT UNSIGNED NOT NULL
);

// Item table for coll #1 of acctid #3
CREATE TABLE mystuff_coll_3_1
(
  coll_3_1_itemid    INT UNSIGNED NOT NULL AUTO_INCREMENT PRIMARY KEY,
  coll_3_1_itemname VARCHAR(128) NOT NULL,
  coll_3_1_itemcode VARCHAR(32) NOT NULL,
  coll_3_1_itemdesc VARCHAR(255),
  coll_3_1_detid     INT UNSIGNED NOT NULL
);

// Item table for coll #2 of acctid #3
CREATE TABLE mystuff_coll_3_2
(
  coll_3_2_itemid    INT UNSIGNED NOT NULL AUTO_INCREMENT PRIMARY KEY,
  coll_3_2_itemname VARCHAR(128) NOT NULL,
  coll_3_2_itemcode VARCHAR(32) NOT NULL,
  coll_3_2_itemdesc VARCHAR(255),
  coll_3_2_detid     INT UNSIGNED NOT NULL
);
```

Now we can insert records into the item tables:

```
// Insert records into collection 'item' tables

// Insert items for coll #1 of acctid #2: "Music:CD"
//
INSERT INTO mystuff_coll_2_1
  (coll_2_1_itemname, coll_2_1_itemcode, coll_2_1_detid)
VALUES
  ("Moby - Ambient", "Moby - Ambient", 0),
  ("Ekova - Space Lullabies and Other Fantasmagore",
   "Ekova - Space Lullabies", 0),
  ("Euphoria - Beautiful My Child", "Euphoria - Beautiful", 0),
  ("Banco de Gaia - The Magical Sounds of",
   "Banco de Gaia - Magical Sounds", 0),
  ("Delerium - Semantic Spaces", "Delerium - Semantic Spaces", 0),
  ("Leftfield - Leftism", "Leftfield - Leftism", 0),
  ("Ekova - Soft Breeze and Tsunami Breaks", "Ekova - Soft Breeze", 0);

// Insert items for coll #2 of acctid #2: "Music:LP"
//
INSERT INTO mystuff_coll_2_2
  (coll_2_2_itemname, coll_2_2_itemcode, coll_2_2_detid)
VALUES
  ("Leftfield - Rhythm and Stealth", "Leftfield - Rhythm and Stealth", 0),
```

```
    ("Delerium - Silence", "Delerium - Silence", 0),
    ("Emerson, Lake and Palmer - Works Volume 1", "ELP - Works Vol 1", 0),
    ("Tangerine Dream - Dream Sequences", "Tangerine Dream -Dream Sequences",
    0);

// Insert items for coll #3 of acctid #2: "Film:DVD"
//
INSERT INTO mystuff_coll_2_3
    (coll_2_3_itemname, coll_2_3_itemcode, coll_2_3_itemdesc, coll_2_3_detid)
VALUES
    ("Rear Window", "Rear Window", "Director - Alfred Hitchcock", 0),
    ("East of Eden", "East of Eden",
    "Director - Elia Kazan. Based on novel. Actors - James Dean", 0),
    ("Shadow Magic", "Shadow Magic", "Director - Ann Hu", 0);

// Insert items for coll #1 of acctid #3: "Book:Non"
//
// (No records to insert, since we defined this collection
//  as currently having no items.)

// Insert items for coll #2 of acctid #3: "Book:Fic"
//
INSERT INTO mystuff_coll_3_2
    (coll_3_2_itemname, coll_3_2_itemcode, coll_3_2_detid)
VALUES
    ("Tom Robbins - Another Roadside Attraction",
    "Robbins - Roadside Attraction", 0),
    ("Tom Robbins - Jitterbug Perfume", "Robbins - Jitterbug Perfume", 0),
    ("Tom Robbins - Still Life With Woodpecker", "Robbins - Woodpecker", 0),
    ("Tom Robbins - Even Cowgirls Get the Blues", "Robbins - Cowgirls", 0),
    ("Tom Robbins - Skinny Legs and All", "Robbins - Skinny Legs", 0),
    ("Tom Robbins - Half Asleep in Frogs Pajamas",
    "Robbins - Frogs Pajamas", 0);
```

Note that we do not insert any records for the mystuff_coll_3_1 table, since earlier in mss_add_colln.sql we defined the collection as having no items.

Also we set the detid column to zero in every item insertion. Because we are adding an item manually via mysql, we are not linking this field with its associated table schema in the mystuff_collmetadets table. We set the value to zero to avoid the issue of the field being non-null.

Finally, all five coll_*_* tables are exactly the same. This seems wholly redundant, and it is. As we are focusing on a select set of features in this chapter for the sake of the example, we have limited the fields in each of these collection item tables to a standard set. In the full-blown version of this application, users would be able to define a few extra fields. Since the fields can vary widely, there is a separate table for each set of collection items. Thus, the redundant tables are shown here so that we can discuss how to manage separate tables from within the PHP script.

Delivering the Content

As indicated earlier, the PHP and WML code presented here focuses only on the wireless features for general users. Now that we have defined all the functionality and the necessary SQL queries for each wireless feature, we can look at the code necessary for this application. Space limitations prohibit us from showing the code for the entire application, so we are going to look at a few select markup templates, most of the pseudo-code, and some PHP scripts.

> **The code presented here is available for download from the book's page on the Wrox web site (http://www.wrox.com).**

We'll use Smarty as our template engine. The templates will render the appropriate WML code and the PHP scripts will generate the Smarty variables that will be displayed in the templates. The whole process is very similar to the one used in Chapter 7.

Script and Template Listing

The following table lists all the WML page templates and PHP scripts required to support the features we are focusing on. SQL script names were provided earlier:

Script/Template File	Description
login.tpl	This form is displayed as the first screen of the application, and shows a login form called from login.php. This is the general template used for login error pages and the logout page.
loginerr.tpl	This is the template used to display an error message on the login form. It is used to process login errors, typically invalid usernames or passwords. This template is also called from login.php.
main.tpl	The template used for the welcome page (after a successful login).
collns.tpl	This is the general template used for all pages after login, except errors and the initial welcome page.
login.php	The initial script that gives a regular or admin user access to the wireless component.
vwall_colln.php	The interface to the view all collections for this user feature.
view.php	The interface to the view all items in this collection feature.
item.php	The interface to the view item details feature.
logout.php	The interface to the logout feature.

Script/Template File	Description
`setup.php`	This script serves two purposes. The first purpose is to define the WML templates to use for various virtual pages. The second purpose is to check the incoming URL query string and extract any and all name/value pairs. All of the interface scripts listed include this script.
`misc.php`	This script performs some miscellaneous database accesses. It is included in all of the interface scripts listed.

WML Templates

This section provides a listing of some of the WML templates in use to support the wireless features.

The template for the change password feature is not detailed here; it can be easily adapted from the corresponding template from Chapter 7 (`chgpswd.tpl`).

login.tpl

```
{insert name=header}
<!DOCTYPE wml PUBLIC "-//WAPFORUM//DTD WML 1.1//EN"
                      "http://www.wapforum.org/DTD/wml_1.1.xml">
<wml>
```

On entry into the following card, use a `newcontext`, that is, unset any WML card/deck variables:

```
<card ID="login" title="MyStuff Server" newcontext="true">
  <p>
    <b>Welcome to MyStuff Server</b>. Please log in.<br/>
    <b>Account name</b>:
    <input name="acct" title="Accountname" type="text"/>
    <b>Password</b>:
    <input name="pass" title="Password" type="password"/>
    <do type="accept" label="Submit">
      <go method="get"
          href="login.php?acct=$(acct:esc)&amp;pass=$(pass:esc)"/>
    </do>
  </p>
</card>
</wml>
```

loginerr.tpl

```
{insert name=header}
<?xml version='1.0'?>
<!DOCTYPE wml PUBLIC "-//WAPFORUM//DTD WML 1.1//EN"
                      "http://www.wapforum.org/DTD/wml_1.1.xml">
<wml>
<!-- Use when a login error has occurred -->
<card ID="login" title="MyStuff Server" newcontext="true">
```

```
  <p>
    <b>{$errmsg}</b><br/>
    <b>Account name</b>:
    <input name="acct" title="Accountname" type="text"/>
    <b>Password</b>:
    <input name="pass" title="Password" type="password"/>
    <do type="accept" label="Submit">
      <go method="get"
           href="login.php?acct=$(acct:esc)&amp;pass=$(pass:esc)"/>
    </do>
  </p>
</card>
</wml>
```

main.tpl

```
{insert name=header}
<?xml version='1.0'?>
<!DOCTYPE wml PUBLIC "-//WAPFORUM//DTD WML 1.1//EN"
                      "http://www.wapforum.org/DTD/wml_1.1.xml">
<wml>
<!-- Main menu + main page after successful login -->
<template>
  <do type="prev"><noop/></do>
  <do type="accept" label="Collections">
    <go href="vwall_colln.php" method="get">
      <postfield name="acct" value="{$acct}"/>
      <postfield name="acctid" value="{$acctid}"/>
    </go>
  </do>
  <do type="accept" label="ChgPasswd">
    <go href="chgpswd.php" method="get">
      <postfield name="acct" value="{$acct}"/>
      <postfield name="acctid" value="{$acctid}"/>
    </go>
  </do>
  <do type="accept" label="Logout">
    <go href="logout.php" method="get">
      <postfield name="acct" value="{$acct}"/>
      <postfield name="acctid" value="{$acctid}"/>
    </go>
  </do>
</template>
<card id="login" title="MyStuff Server">
  <p>
    <b>Welcome to MyStuff Server</b>.
    Successfully logged in.<br/>
    Please select an option from the soft menu<br/>
  </p>
</card>
</wml>
```

collns.tpl

```
<?xml version='1.0'?>
<!DOCTYPE wml PUBLIC "-//WAPFORUM//DTD WML 1.1//EN"
                     "http://www.wapforum.org/DTD/wml_1.1.xml">
<wml>
<!-- List of collections page after successful login -->
<template>
  <do type="accept" label="Collections">
    <go href="vwall_colln.php" method="get">
      <postfield name="acct" value="{$acct}"/>
      <postfield name="acctid" value="{$acctid}"/>
    </go>
  </do>
  <do type="accept" label="ChgPasswd">
    <go href="chgpswd.php" method="get">
      <postfield name="acct" value="{$acct}"/>
      <postfield name="acctid" value="{$acctid}"/>
    </go>
  </do>
  <do type="accept" label="Logout">
    <go href="logout.php" method="get">
      <postfield name="acct" value="{$acct}"/>
      <postfield name="acctid" value="{$acctid}"/>
    </go>
  </do>
</template>
<card id="login" title="MyStuff Server">
{$collnlist}
</card>
</wml>
```

PHP Code

This section provides listings for PHP scripts to support most of the wireless user features being discussed here.

Again, the code for the change password feature is not given, as it can be easily adapted from the corresponding code in Chapter 7 (chgpswd.php). In fact, much of the code here has been directly borrowed, or adapted, from code in the Wireless Job Board case study. It is recommended that one follows the comments for the PHP code in that case study before looking at the code here.

> All code shown here is for test purposes only. User validation and session management is being performed in a manner similar to that of PHP4's new session functions, but without the use of cookies. Many WAP devices do not support cookies. Neither method is secure without the use of server security such as SSL (Secure Sockets Layer). However, secure programming is outside the scope of this book and therefore, is not detailed in this study.

Tips on Coding WAPplications

Writing WAPplications (WAP applications) can be quite frustrating when of debugging the errors. If one has the luxury to do so, it is good to test all the middle tier and database code without WML templates first. If not, and the code generates errors that are not XML-compliant, it may be hard to track down the problem source when delivering the WML content.

Once the bugs are worked out, we can develop the navigation framework for the WML content using function stubs. Function stubs are PHP functions that have been declared but either have no code, or the very minimal amount necessary to deliver a blank WML page, possibly with a navigation message indicating where we are. When the framework is functioning correctly, the back-end code should be integrated into the navigation framework one feature at a time.

Keep in mind that we cannot just print a debug message when an error occurs, like we can with HTML applications. Any text that we want displayed in a WAP browser must be wrapped with valid WML markup. Thus, integrating and debugging one feature at a time ensures that we successfully pursue a series of milestones. On the other hand, if one tries to integrate all the back-end code into the navigation framework simultaneously, we might encounter one seemingly endless error after another. Experience shows that this is the least efficient way to code applications.

Space limitations do not allow us to show a number of code iterations here. The code below, while not part of a finished product that one would publish on a web site, is complete enough to show the WAP and PHP coding principles being focused on in this case study.

User Screens

WAP browsers display WML pages differently, depending on the wireless device in use. The screens shown below are snapshots of the UP browser using version 6.1 (http://developer.phone.com/download/index.html), with the generic configuration. Note that we are only showing screens pertaining to the user collections.

> **Refer to the case study in Chapter 7 for information on the change password and logout screens. The screens in that case study are very similar to those used here.**

setup.php

The setup.php script is used to initialize the Smarty template engine, the database connection, and other application initialization code:

> *For an introduction to the Smarty template engine, refer to the section titled Introduction to Smarty: The PHP template engine, in Chapter 7.*

```php
<?php
session_start();
// Load application library files here
include_once("misc.php");

// Define and load Smarty components
define('SMARTY_DIR',"Smarty/");
```

```
require_once(SMARTY_DIR.'Smarty.class.php');

function insert_header()
{
 echo header("Content-type: text/vnd.wap.wml");
 echo header("Cache-Control: no-cache, must-revalidate");
 echo header("Pragma: no-cache");
 echo ("<?xml version='1.0'?>");
}

// Connection to the MySQL database
mysql_connect('localhost','root', '');
if (!mysql_select_db('mystuff'))
{
 $smarty->assign('errmsg',"Cannot access database $dbs:
".mysql_error()."<br/>\n");
 $smarty->display('loginerr.tpl');
 die;
}

class Smarty_Mystuff extends Smarty {
  function Smarty_Mystuff() {
    $this->teplate_dir = "templates/";
    $this->compile_dir = "templates_c/";
    $this->config_dir = "configs/";
    $this->cache_dir = "cache/";
    $this->caching = false;
    $this->assign('app_name','Mystuff');
    //$this->debugging = true;
    //$this->debug_tpl = 'debug.tpl';
  }
}

$smarty = new Smarty_Mystuff();

?>
```

misc.php

This script defines a few miscellaneous database access functions, mostly for validating user login and user sessions.

```
<?php
# FILE: misc.php
#
#

function IsValidLogin($acct,$pass)
{
  $errmsg = "";
  $sqlquery  = "SELECT account_acctid FROM mystuff_accounts
               WHERE account_acct='$acct' AND account_pass='$pass'";
  $results   = mysql_query($sqlquery);
```

```
    if (!$results) return false;
    if(mysql_num_rows($results)!=1) return false;
    $res = mysql_fetch_array($results);
    return $res["account_acctid"];
} end function IsValidLogin

function UserOwnsColln($acctid, $tblnmsfx)
{

    // Does the user represented by $acctid own the collection
    // represented by $tblnmsfx?
    $errmsg = "";
    $sqlquery  = "SELECT collection_collid,collection_collcode
                  FROM mystuff_collections ";
    $sqlquery .= "where collection_acctid=$acctid and
collection_tblnmsfx='$tblnmsfx' ";
    $results = mysql_query($sqlquery);
    if (!$results)
    {
      $errmsg .= "<p>MySQL Error: Could not access table collections ";
      $errmsg .= "in database $dbs.</p>";
      $owns = -1;
    }
    else
    {
      $nrows = mysql_num_rows($results);
      if ($nrows == 0)
      {
        // Either user acctid is incorrect or they do not own the collection
        $errmsg .= "<p>You are not the owner of this collection.</p>";
        $owns = 0;
      }
      else
      {
        // This user owns this collection
        $aaRow = mysql_fetch_array($results); # Assume one resultset row
        $collid = $aaRow["collection_collid"];
        $collcode = $aaRow["collection_collcode"];
        $owns = 1;
      }
    }
    $aaRes["err"]      = $errmsg;
    $aaRes["owns"]     = $owns;
    $aaRes["collid"]   = $collid;
    $aaRes["collcode"] = $collcode;
    return($aaRes);
} end function UserOwnsColln

?>
```

login.php

This is the initial script used to access the wireless portion of the `mystuff` server application. When the script is run, a login screen is displayed:

```php
<?php
  FILE: login.php
  USE:  Display PDA login form
        process the login and show error page or main menu

include("setup.php");

// If we are processing a login then verify the information
if(isset($_REQUEST["acct"]) && isset($_REQUEST["pass"])) {
  if(! ($acctid = IsValidLogin($_REQUEST["acct"],$_REQUEST["pass"]))) {
    $smarty->assign('errmsg','invalid username or password');
    $smarty->display('loginerr.tpl');
    die;
  }
  // Since the login was successful set the acctid and acct session variables
  $acct = $_REQUEST["acct"];
  session_register("acct");
  session_register("acctid");
  $smarty->assign('acct',$acct);
  $smarty->assign('acctid',$acctid);
  $smarty->display('main.tpl');
}
$smarty->display('login.tpl');
?>
```

This is the first screen that appears when the application is started:

Each wireless device will display the screen in its own manner.

Once a user successfully logs in, this will be the next screen they see:

Depending on the WAP browser we are using, the main menu will be split into two parts, as it is with the UP browser. In this case, at the bottom left of the first screen, there is a soft button called Collections – this is the first option in the main menu. The second soft button, called Menu, links to a list of the remaining menu options.

vwall_colln.php

This script is the interface for the view all collections for this user feature. Users can only view their own collections.

```php
<?php
#
# FILE: vwall_colln.php
# USE:  View a list of all collections that a user has
#

include ("setup.php");

/*If (!isset($HTTP_SESSION_VARS["acct"])) {
    echo "the acct variable ". $acct. "<br>";
    $smarty->assign('errmsg', "You are not logged in<br/>\n");
    $smarty->display('loginerr.tpl');
    die;
} */

//$acct = $_SESSION["acct"];
//$acctid = $_SESSION["acctid"];
//echo "the acct variable ". $acct. "<br>";
//echo "the acctid variable ". $acctid. "<br>";
$collnlist = "";
//echo $acctid;
$sqlquery   = "SELECT
                collection_collid,collection_collcode,collection_tblnmsfx
                FROM mystuff_collections WHERE collection_acctid=$acctid ";
//echo $sqlquery;
$results   = mysql_query($sqlquery);
```

```php
if (!$results)
{
    echo "hi";

    $errmsg .= "<p>MySQL Error: Could not access table collections ";
    $errmsg .= "in database $dbs.</p>";
    $collnlist = $errmsg;
    $smarty->assign('collnlist',$collnlist);
    $smarty->display('collns.tpl');
    die;
}

$nrows = mysql_num_rows($results);
if ($nrows == 0)
{
    $errmsg .= "<p>You have no collections! Please add some in the ";
    $errmsg .= "non-wireless version of MyStuff Server.</p>";
    $collnlist = $errmsg;
    $smarty->assign('collnlist',$collnlist);
    $smarty->display('collns.tpl');
    die;
}

$collnlist = "";
$collnlist .= "<p>\n";
$collnlist .= "<b>MyStuff Server</b><br/>\n";
$collnlist .= "Collections:<br/>\n";
$collnlist .= "<select name=\"tblnmsfx\">\n";

for ($i=1; $i<=$nrows; $i++)
{
  $aaRow = mysql_fetch_array($results);

  // Field collid is non-unique in table collections but unique
  // to acctid. Field collcode is used instead of collname for
  // PDA version of MyStuff Server app.
  //
  $collid = $aaRow["collid"];
  $collcode = $aaRow["collcode"];
  $tblnmsfx = $aaRow["tblnmsfx"];
  $collnlist .= "<option value=\"$tblnmsfx\">$collcode</option>\n";
}   end for
$collnlist .= "</select>\n";
$collnlist .= "</p>\n";
$collnlist .= "<do type=\"accept\" label=\"Collection\">\n";
$collnlist .= "  <go href=\"view.php\">\n";
$collnlist .= "    <postfield name=\"acct\" value=\"$acct\"/>\n";
$collnlist .= "    <postfield name=\"acctid\" value=\"$acctid\"/>\n";
$collnlist .= "    <postfield name=\"sessid\" value=\"$sessid\"/>\n";
$collnlist .= "    <postfield name=\"tblnmsfx\" value=\"\$(tblnmsfx:n)\"/>\n";
$collnlist .= "  </go>\n";
$collnlist .= "</do>\n";

$smarty->assign('collnlist',$collnlist);
$smarty->display('collns.tpl');

?>
```

517

If the user has no collections, this screen appears:

If a collection has been inserted into the database, then a screen like this is shown:

view.php

This script is the interface for the view items in this collection feature:

```php
<?php

   FILE: view.php
   USE:  View a list of all the items in a selected user collection


include ("setup.php");

/*if (!isset($_SESSION["acct"])) {
    $smarty->assign('errmsg', "You are not logged in<br/>\n");
```

```
    $smarty->display('loginerr.tpl');
    die;
}

$acct   = $_SESSION["acct"];
$acctid = $_SESSION["acctid"];
*/
// Display all the items in the collection represented
// by acctid and collid.
$itemlist = "";

// Verify that this user owns this collection
$aaRes = UserOwnsColln($aactid,$tblnmsfx);
$owns  = $aaRes["owns"];
if (!$owns)
{
    // Either a database error or user does not own collection
    $itemlist = $aaRes["err"];
    $smarty->assign('collnlist',$itemlist);
    $smarty->display('collns.tpl');
    die;
}

$collcode = $aaRes["collcode"];
$collid   = $aaRes["collid"];

$sqlquery = "SELECT coll_*_*_itemid,coll_*_*_itemcode FROM coll_$tblnmsfx ";
$results  = mysql_query($sqlquery);
if (!$results)
{
    $errmsg .= "<p>MySQL Error: Could not access table coll_$tblnmsfx ";
    $errmsg .= "in database $dbs.</p>";
    $itemlist = $errmsg;
   $smarty->assign('collnlist',$itemlist);
    $smarty->display('collns.tpl');
    die;
}

$nrows = mysql_num_rows($results);
if ($nrows == 0)
{
    $errmsg .= "<p>You have no items in the collection. Please add   ";
    $errmsg .= "some either in the wireless version (short-form) or ";
    $errmsg .= "in the non-wireless version of MyStuff Server.</p>";
    $itemlist = $errmsg;
    $smarty->assign('collnlist',$itemlist);
    $smarty->display('main.tpl');
    die;
}

$itemlist = "";
$itemlist .= "<p>\n";
$itemlist .= "<b>MyStuff Server</b><br/>\n";
$itemlist .= "Items in collection <b>$collcode</b>:<br/>\n";
```

```
$itemlist .= "";
$itemlist .= "<select name=\"itemid\">\n";

for ($i=1; $i<=$nrows; $i++)
{
  $aaRow = mysql_fetch_array($results);
  $itemid = $aaRow["itemid"];
  $itemcode = $aaRow["itemcode"];
  $itemlist .= "<option value=\"$itemid\">$itemcode</option>\n";
} # end for
$itemlist .= "</select>\n";
$itemlist .= "</p>\n";
$itemlist .= "<do type=\"accept\" label=\"Item\">\n";
$itemlist .= "  <go href=\"item.php\">\n";
$itemlist .= "    <postfield name=\"acct\" value=\"$acct\"/>\n";
$itemlist .= "    <postfield name=\"acctid\" value=\"$acctid\"/>\n";
$itemlist .= "    <postfield name=\"itemid\" value=\"\$(itemid:n)\"/>\n";
$itemlist .= "    <postfield name=\"tblnmsfx\" value=\"$tblnmsfx\"/>\n";
$itemlist .= "  </go>\n";
$itemlist .= "</do>\n";
// We are re-using the same template as for the "collection list" page.
//
$smarty->assign('collnlist',$itemlist);
$smarty->display('collns.tpl');

?>
```

When this script is accessed in the application, the browser displays the items in the user's CD collection:

item.php

This script is the interface for the view item details feature:

```
<?php
#
# FILE: item.php
# USE:  View the details of the selected item
#
```

```php
include ("setup.php");

/*if (!isset($_SESSION["acct"])) {
  $smarty->assign('errmsg', "You are not logged in<br/>\n");
  $smarty->display('loginerr.tpl');
  die;
}

$acct = $_SESSION["acct"];
$acctid = $_SESSION["acctid"];
 */
$itemmarkup = "";

// Verify that this user owns this collection
$aaRes = UserOwnsColln($acctid, $tblnmsfx);
$owns = $aaRes["owns"];
if (!$owns)
{
  // Either a database error or user does not own collection
  $itemlist = $aaRes["err"];
  $smarty->assign('collnlist',$itemlist);
  $smarty->display('collns.tpl');
  die;
}

// User owns this collection. Retrieve list of items.
$collcode = $aaRes["collcode"];
$collid   = $aaRes["collid"];

$sqlquery  = "SELECT * FROM coll_$tblnmsfx ";
$sqlquery .= "where itemid=$itemid ";
$results   = mysql_query($sqlquery);
if (!$results)
{
  $errmsg .= "<p>MySQL Error: Could not access table coll_$tblnmsfx ";
  $errmsg .= "in database $dbs.</p>";
  $itemmarkup = $errmsg;
  $smarty->assign('collnlist',$itemmarkup);
  $smarty->display('collns.tpl');
  die;
}

$nrows = mysql_num_rows($results);
if ($nrows == 0)
{
  $errmsg .= "<p>The selected item does not exist in collection ";
  $errmsg .= "$collcode.</p>";
  $itemmarkup = $errmsg;
  $smarty->assign('collnlist',$itemmarkup);
  $smarty->display('main.tpl');
  die;
}

// Item exists. Assume just one item.
$itemmarkup = "";
$itemmarkup .= "<p>\n";
$itemmarkup .= "<b>MyStuff Server</b><br/>\n";
$itemmarkup .= "Collection <b>$collcode</b><br/>\n";

$aaRow = mysql_fetch_array($results);
```

```
$itemid = $aaRow["itemid"];
$itemcode = $aaRow["itemcode"];
$itemname = $aaRow["itemname"];
$itemdesc = $aaRow["itemdesc"];
$itemmarkup .= "<b>itemid</b>: $itemid<br/>\n";
$itemmarkup .= "<b>itemcode</b>: $itemcode<br/>\n";
$itemmarkup .= "<b>itemname</b>: $itemname<br/>\n";
$itemmarkup .= "<b>itemdesc</b>: $itemdesc<br/>\n";
$itemmarkup .= "</p>\n";

/*
        $itemmarkup .= "<do type=\"accept\" label=\"Item\">\n";
        $itemmarkup .= "  <go href=\"view.php\">\n";
        $itemmarkup .= "    <postfield name=\"acct\" value=\"$acct\"/>\n";
        $itemmarkup .= "    <postfield name=\"acctid\" value=\"$acctid\"/>\n";
        $itemmarkup .= "    <postfield name=\"itemid\" value=\"$itemid\"/>\n";
        $itemmarkup .= "    <postfield name=\"tblnmsfx\" value=\"$tblnmsfx\"/>\n";
        $itemmarkup .= "  </go>\n";
        $itemmarkup .= "</do>\n";
*/

$smarty->assign('collnlist',$itemmarkup);
$smarty->display('collns.tpl');

?>
```

When this script is accessed in the application, the browser displays the items in the CD collection named Moby – Ambient:

Note that in this sample screenshot, no text is displayed for the itemdesc field, since none was entered for this item.

logout.php

This script is the interface for the logout feature:

```php
<?php
#
# FILE: logout.php
# USE:  Log user out of system
#
include_once("setup.php");

/*if (!isset($_SESSION["acct"])) {
  $smarty->assign('errmsg', "You are not logged in<br/>\n");
  $smarty->display('loginerr.tpl');
  die;
}

$acct = $_SESSION["acct"];
$acctid = $_SESSION["acctid"];
*/
// Display the login page with a "logout" message, and
// unset all the session information.
$pgcontent = "";
session_unregister("acct");
session_unregister("acctid");

$smarty->display("login.tpl");

?>
```

After viewing the items, the user can logout by using the Logout option found by pressing the Menu button:

Improvements

Here are some feature improvements that could be made to the application in its full version:

❑   Add a `countries` table with pre-defined entries, like the country code and country name. This can be used for information on who is using the system.

❑   Allow for item categories within the collections. For example, instead of having to enter 'Ekova – Space Lullabies' and 'Ekova – Tsunami Breaks', a user can define one level 1 category (artists) entry – 'Ekova', and two level 2 items – 'Space Lullabies & Other Stories' and 'Tsunami Breaks & Soft Breeze'. This complicates the navigation of the application, as well as the SQL queries required however, it reduces redundancy of information and is more user-friendly than the present situation.

❑   Allow items in a collection to be deleted from the wireless version.

❑   Allow items to be added to a collection from the wireless version. In this case, only a subset of the necessary fields would have to be entered from the wireless device. Later, the user would have to use a regular HTML browser to edit each item and add additional information.

❑   If the number of collections grows to a few hundred, the database can get quite hard to oversee with one table for each collection. A solution, at that point, would be to convert all collection tables into one table, with a column ID for each row, defining which collection that specific row belonged to.

Summary

This chapter gives a complete example of a three-tier, multi-client, wireless web application. The basic model here is that of private information for multiple users. In this case study, there is one database but one or more tables per user. Each user can enter information about their personal collections of items (CDs, DVDs, books, magazines, comics, sports cards, and so on). The collection item tables do not exist until a user defines a collection, and it is the discussion of techniques to manage this feature for wireless devices that has been the intent of this case study.

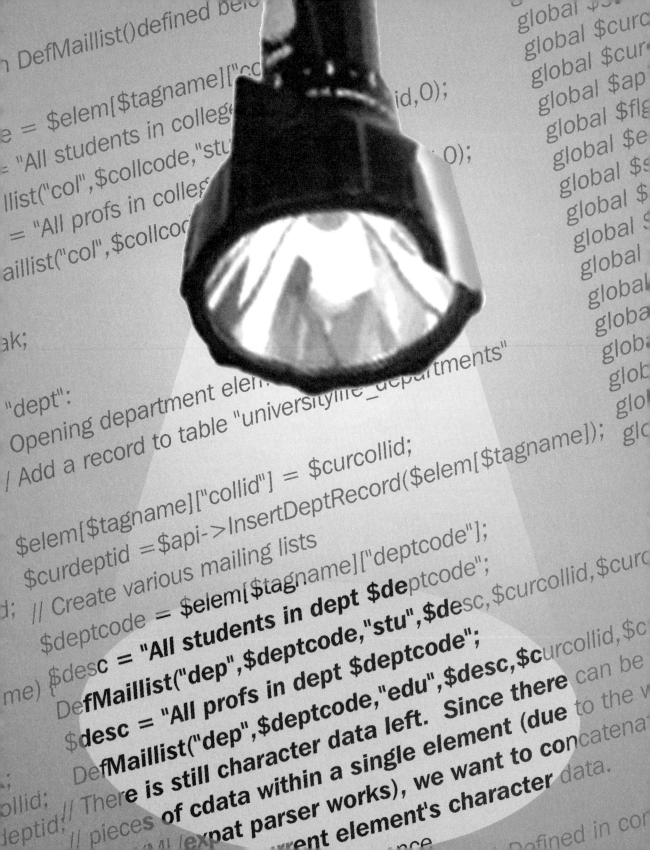

```php
n DefMaillist()defined bel...
e = $elem[$tagname]["...
= "All students in colleg...
llist("col",$collcode,"stu...    id,0);
= "All profs in colleg...
aillist("col",$collco...    0);
ak;

                                          global $cur
                                        global $cur
                                      global $cur
                                    global $ap
                                  global $flg
                                global $e
"dept":                        global $s
Opening department elem...    global $
/ Add a record to table "universitylife_departments"    global

$elem[$tagname]["collid"] = $curcollid;
$curdeptid = $api->InsertDeptRecord($elem[$tagname]);
$deptcode = $elem[$tagname]["deptcode"];
d;  // Create various mailing lists

me) $desc = "All students in dept $deptcode";
DefMaillist("dep",$deptcode,"stu",$desc,$curcollid,$cur
$desc = "All profs in dept $deptcode";
DefMaillist("dep",$deptcode,"edu",$desc,$curcollid,$c
ollid; // There is still character data left. Since there can be
deptid; // pieces of cdata within a single element (due to the w
// XML expat parser works), we want to concatenat
current element's character data.
Defined in co...
```

13

Genealogy Server

In this chapter, we discuss the planning and programming of a PHP and MySQL-based genealogy server. By a genealogy server, we mean a data repository that can track and search for information about a user's ancestry – their children, parents, grandparents, and so on. Examples of this concept can be seen at http://www.ancestry.com/ and http://www.genealogy.com/.

Due to complexities in families caused by multiple marriages, this type of software can get extremely complicated, depending on how far the programmer decides to take it. In this case study, we'll look at the following:

❑ **Data Requirements**
We will model a basic family relationship using a simple MySQL database, which we'll also employ to keep track of users with write access to the database.

❑ **Designing the Database**
We'll design the database schema to be used for the application.

❑ **Designing the Application**
We will design and implement a simple yet serviceable user interface employing HTML, CSS, and SSI. We don't want our data to become "tainted" or our database compromised by unauthorized parties, possibly using SQL injection techniques, We'll address these issues by testing INSERT and UPDATE queries before they're allowed to act on the database, and by requiring user authentication. Also, we'll examine the problems that can arise due to the vagaries of human language (names especially) and offer some techniques for obtaining inexact as well as exact matches.

"To-may-toh", "To-mah-toh"

Unlike the case with most languages, written English is not phonetic. The same word may be spelled in one of several different ways, and the same letter or combination of letters can be pronounced differently – or even be silent altogether. One extreme example of this dichotomy is suggested in the writings of G.B. Shaw, with the "word" **ghoti**. This, as it is suggested, should be pronounced like the word "fish", with *gh* as in cough, *o* as in women, and *ti* as in motion.

As poor as phonetic representation may be in written English for common nouns, verbs, adjectives, and so on, at least there are standard spellings and pronunciations for these, which can be obtained from the dictionary. However, when we turn our attention to proper or personal names, we very quickly find ourselves in a phonetic free-for-all. This is especially true in the United States (and to some extent Canada and Australia), where, historically, immigrants have often arrived speaking no English, bearing names that contained sounds unfamiliar to English speakers, and that in some cases didn't even have a standard representation in the Latin alphabet (should we render as Kuznetzov, Kusnitsoff, Kuznietsov, or...?).

In addition, there's the possibility that family names may change in spelling or pronunciation over time – not to mention the tendency of users to misunderstand, misspell, or mistype information. Given all these hurdles, how can we hope to match up modern names with their earlier or possible variant forms? PHP provides three functions that can help. Chief among these is soundex(), which we'll use to perform a phonetic search, so that names sounding similar to a target name, as well as exact matches, will be retrieved.

Soundex has been around for some time now – since the late nineteenth century. First used in the 1880 census, Soundex is a phonetic indexing system that turns sounds into alphanumeric codes using mathematical equations. This allows us to bridge the gap between words that sound the same but are spelled differently, such as Smith and Smyth.

Very often, even after sounding it out, the name is wrongly spelled – Gianotto turns into Gianetti, Giordano, Giasnotto, you name it. Soundex is not in and of itself an ultimate solution, but we'll see how it can prove extremely useful in helping us to connect our users with their ancestors.

Another, similar function is metaphone(), which tries to reduce words to their consonant sounds as these are actually pronounced. This can be helpful when we try to match up names such as Cline and Klein, which produce different Soundex values (C450 and K450), but the same metaphone value (KLN).

Finally, we have the levenshtein() function, which takes two strings as arguments, and calculates the minimum number of characters that must be changed in the first string in order for it to match the second. This number is sometimes referred to as the **Levenshtein distance** between two strings. We've included a sample file (phonetic.php) with the code bundle for this chapter, which illustrates the use of and output from all three of these functions.

Here's a screenshot of the script executed on a browser:

We'll use only soundex() in our code for the genealogy site, but you should experiment with the other two functions as well. For more about the use of soundex(), metaphone(), and levenshtein(), see the PHP Manual.

Specifications

The most important part of any programming project is its planning. We'll develop an overview of the objectives for our site and a flow plan to guide us in meeting our goals in a systematic fashion. Let's start off with identifying the problems we're likely to encounter, and for which we'll need to devise solutions to develop an effective and useful site.

Planning

Flow plans help us work out the logic to be applied before we get to the programming phase. They also allow us to begin thinking about possible glitches we may run into. Flow plans force us to put ourselves in the user's shoes and walk through the site and imagine what they will experience, where they might need help, and where they may end up making errors.

Here is an example:

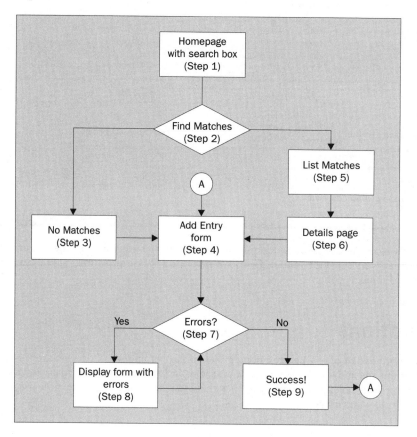

Let's walk through the flow diagram:

1. The user will be able to perform a search with the last name, first name, gender, birth city, and birth year to locate a record – using only the last name will suffice, but we can narrow the search with the additional information. Notice that we do not allow the user to add a new entry until they have searched the database to make sure it doesn't already exist.

As with any database application, we want to minimize redundancy. Because of the way the entries relate to each other in this program, this is especially important. We attempt to compare submitted entries with existing data to see if they match, but that isn't fool-proof, as slight variations in the entered data could return no match.

2. Using the submitted search criteria, the script will query the database and look for both exact and similar matches from the database.

3. If the record the user is looking for is not found in the database, they can search again or add a new record.

4. This is the stage where the user can add a new record.

5. If the search is successful, a list of matches linked to the full details page is displayed. We offer the user the opportunity to add a record in the event that the actual person the user was looking for doesn't come back as one of the results.

6. On the details page, the user can add a child or sibling to an entry, or a mother or father if any of these details that aren't listed. This will allow many different users to share the information that they have about a particular person recorded in the database.

7. If the user chooses to add a new record, or any information, to an existing record, the data will be checked for errors and duplicate records. The User will also be required to authenticate themselves so that we know who's entered which records into the database.

8. If the data is erroneous, the form will be re-displayed with the fields filled out and error flags shown next to those fields that are in error. This will be repeated until the user submits the form with no errors, in which case it will display the Success page.

9. After entering one record, they may choose to add additional family connections to it. This facilitates the addition of data relating to members of family units, rather than to individuals in isolation.

The User Interface

Users may view six distinctly different screens:

❑ Index page

❑ No matches page

❑ List of Matches page

❑ Record Details page

❑ Add Record Form: the display form with errors page will be identical, with errors shown

❑ Add Record 'Success' page

The user is forced to search before adding an entry, so we don't have to worry about any navigational elements. We've added a search box in the top header space, so that user can perform a quick search on anything if they are on another page of the site. We add a little explanatory text and search boxes and we're good to go. The first screen the user will encounter:

Now the user may search again or add a new record, so a navigation link is added at the top. The results are displayed in a table with the exact matches in bold. We should take into consideration that limiting the results to a certain number per page is a good practice, since the list of results could get quite long:

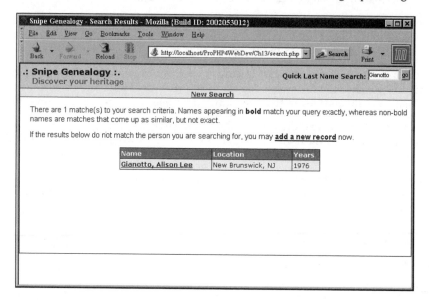

If there are no current matches, a link to search again or add a record, along with a message explaining that there weren't any matches found is offered:

![Snipe Genealogy - Search Results window showing no matches message]

The record details page displays all the details for the selected record, and gives the user the option to add a sibling or a child in the event that this information is missing. Additionally, if there are no parent records listed, or if we want to give the user the ability to add a half-sibling to the parent(s), we may do that too.

The parts of the page that are used to add records to the database will be dynamically generated depending on which link the user clicked to get there. For example, if they clicked on **Add Mother** in the details page, we will not ask them for the gender in the new record, since we know that it must be **Female**. The page used to Add Records looks like this:

If the user forgets to fill in the required fields, or enters data that doesn't comply with the format or content criteria, we re-display the form out with the field's pre-populated, and flag the erroneous fields:

The following confirmation page informs the user that the record was added successfully, and allows them to extend the branch of the family tree they have created:

We now have a fairly detailed set of HTML pages that are designed with the user in mind.

Designing The Database

The database that stores the records for our site will be named `genealogy`. Let us first create the database:

```
>mysqladmin create genealogy
```

We will name the MySQL table that holds the data about each person `genealogy_records`.

Records

This table stores the data on each and every person in the `genealogy` database. Notice that each record has a `record_maternal_id` and `record_paternal_id` column. These are the two fields that tie siblings and children together. Thus, if two records have identical maternal and paternal IDs, we know that they represent siblings. We can also determine that two individuals are half-siblings if they share only a `record_maternal_id` or a `record_paternal_id`:

Field Name	Data Type	Description
Record_id	INT(11)	Unique ID associated with each person
Record_firstname	VARCHAR(60)	The person's first name
Record_middlename	VARCHAR(60)	The person's middle name
Record_lastname	VARCHAR(60)	The person's last name
Record_maiden_surname	VARCHAR(60)	The person's surname (last name) that she was born with – this will help in dealing with maiden names, or name changes due to marriage
Record_gender	CHAR(1)	The person's gender (M or F)
Record_birthyear	INT(4)	The person's year of birth
Record_deathyear	INT(4)	The person's year of death (if applicable)
Record_birthcity	VARCHAR(60)	The person's city of birth
Record_birthstate	CHAR(5)	The person's state or province of birth. For the U. S. and Canada, we use the standard two-letter postal abbreviations; however, other countries may use longer abbreviations, so we've allowed for up to five letters.

Table continued on following page

Field Name	Data Type	Description
Record_birthcountry	CHAR(2)	The person's country of birth – here we'll use the standard two-letter country codes (for example, us for the U.S., ca for Canada, de for Germany, fr for France, and so on) as per ISO 3166 (see http://www.iso.ch/iso/en/prods-services/iso3166ma/index.html for a complete listing)
Record_maternal_id	INT(11)	The unique ID of the person's mother, if available in the database
Record_paternal_id	INT(11)	The unique ID of the person's father, if available in the database
Record_created	DATETIME	The date on which the person's record was added to the database
Record_created_by_user_id	INT(11)	The ID of the user who created this record (foreign key to genealogy_users table)

> In a more evolved version of this application, we would create a separate lookup table containing information about spouses and dates of marriages in order to accommodate multiple marriages.

Users

This table (genealogy_users) stores the information about the registered users:

Field Name	Data Type	Description
user_id	INT(11)	Unique identifier for each user
user_acct_name	VARCHAR(25)	Unique user name
user_password	VARCHAR(16)	Password for this user
user_email	VARCHAR(50)	User's email address

We include a minimal amount of user information here, as we will perform just very basic authentication in this example: we'll verify only that a record is being added or updated by a valid user. We won't go into creating or administering users here – for an example of a more complete user and user-privilege management system, see Chapter 5.

Creating Tables

Let's now create the tables in the genealogy database. Run the following command on the command prompt:

```
>mysql genealogy < crtbl_gen.sql
```

Of course, you may use a database administration tool such as MySqlGUI or phpMyAdmin to create the genealogy database and run the table creation and population script, if you so desire.

```sql
# Table structure for table 'records'
# crtbl_gen.sql

CREATE TABLE genealogy_records(
    record_id int(11) NOT NULL AUTO_INCREMENT,
    record_firstname varchar(60) DEFAULT NULL,
    record_middlename varchar(60) DEFAULT NULL,
    record_lastname varchar(60) DEFAULT NULL,
    record_maiden_surname varchar(60) DEFAULT NULL,
    record_gender char(1) DEFAULT NULL,
    record_birthyear int(4) DEFAULT NULL,
    record_deathyear int(4) DEFAULT NULL,
    record_birthcity varchar(60) DEFAULT NULL,
    record_birthstate varchar(60) DEFAULT NULL,
    record_birthcountry varchar(60) DEFAULT NULL,
    record_maternal_id int(11) DEFAULT NULL,
    record_paternal_id int(11) DEFAULT NULL,
    record_created datetime NOT NULL DEFAULT '0000-00-00 00:00:00',
    record_created_by_user_id int (11) NOT NULL DEFAULT 0,
    PRIMARY KEY  (record_id),
    UNIQUE KEY id (record_id)
  );

# Table structure for table 'genealogy_users'

CREATE TABLE genealogy_users(
    user_id INT(11) NOT NULL AUTO_INCREMENT,
    user_name VARCHAR(25) NOT NULL,
    user_password VARCHAR(16),
    user_email VARCHAR(50) NOT NULL,
    PRIMARY KEY (user_id),
    UNIQUE KEY id (user_id),
    UNIQUE KEY (user_password),
    UNIQUE KEY (user_email)
);
```

We'll add some sample information to get started (this is also part of the file above). First we create a user:

```sql
INSERT INTO genealogy_users VALUES
('', 'alison', 'fishsticks', 'alison@my.email');
```

Then we add some sample records:

```
INSERT INTO genealogy_records VALUES
('','Alison','Lee','Gianotto','Marchuk','f',1976,'','New
Brunswick','NJ','US',3,4,'2002-08-01 06:19:12',1);

INSERT INTO genealogy_records VALUES
('','Shanen','Lee','Aranmor','Marchuk','f','1972','','New
Brunswick','NJ','US',3,4,'2002-08-02 07:27:17',1);

INSERT INTO genealogy_records VALUES
('','Deborah','Lee','Gingrich','Frezza','f',1951,'','Raritan','NJ','US','','','200
2-08-03 07:51:32',1);
INSERT INTO genealogy_records VALUES
('','Kenneth','Lee',' Marchuk ','','m',1954,'','','VT','US',6,8, '2002-08-03
07:41:29',1);
```

We now have our database built and ready to go.

Designing the Application

We'll manage the look and feel of this system by using included layout files. For a more complex implementation of this site, we might consider using a full-blown template system such as Smarty, or FastTemplates, but a few SSI's will suffice for our needs here.

We will create a series of layout files that we will be included in our program – a header, a footer, and a navigation bar file. This will split out all of the HTML code, which forms the application's layout, into separate files that can be re-used.

This process is in fact quite simple. We build the HTML templates first, check them with the HTML and CSS validators available at http://www.w3c.org/, and then proceed to split them up in the places where it seems logical to do so. Once we have the layout files done, we move on to the files that interact with the database.

File Breakdown

Our layout files will consist of the following:

File name	Description
style.css	The Cascading Style Sheet for the program
header.php	The HTML layout code to appear the before the page content
footer.php	The HTML layout code to appear after the page content
topnav.php	The top navigation bar menu

The content pages, which will include the layout files, are:

File name	Description
index.php	The search form
search.php	The search results
details.php	The record details page
add.php	The add record form

In addition to these, we have some files that help us efficiently organize and accomplish tasks we have to do more than once. These files are the ones that wind up doing most of the work:

File name	Description
functions.php	The common functions in this application will be included in this file
dropdown.functions.php	The common drop-down function code
config.php	The database connection code
session.php	The code for the session that remembers what search term was last used

The header.php controls the layout of the top part of the page and the topnav.php file dynamically generates the top navigation, depending on the page the user is on. The index.php section is where the main content page output will appear. Finally, footer.php contains the static HTML that closes the remaining HTML tags of the page.

To further understand how we're breaking the visual layout down, see the diagram below:

It will be helpful to determine which files are being called inside of others. The following diagram illustrates the general relationship the files in the program have with each other. We won't be working through these files in the order that they are shown below; it is just to understand the interaction between the files:

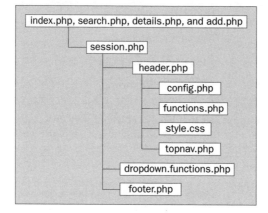

It should also be noted that we are going to use two images in this application. Neither of them are needed for the program to work, they simply enhance the site's user friendliness:

❑   `spacer.gif`
A one pixel by one pixel transparent gif file used for the sole purpose of forcing browsers to maintain the correct height and width (for both the older browsers that do not like to cooperate with CSS, and the more recent browsers). This image is used in `header.php`.

❑   `error-alert-sm.gif`
A small warning icon to help users visually recognize that they have made an error. This image is used in `add.php`, and could easily be substituted for a text-based flag.

style.css

Since we want to control the appearance of many repetitive elements, we'll use a single CSS file and link to it from all of our pages. This style sheet will control all of the style properties such as table cell colors, font sizes, font colors, and so on, throughout our entire program. You can find more information on using CSS here: http://www.w3c.org/Style/CSS/.

We create the style sheet as follows, and name it `style.css`:

```
/* file: style.css*/

/*"BUTTON" LINK EFFECTS ON RECORD DETAIL PAGE */
a.detailadd:link {
color: #000000;
text-decoration: none;
background-color: #D2D2D2;
border: 2px;
```

```
border-style: outset;
font-family: Arial, Helvetica, sans-serif;
font-size: 8pt
}

a.detailadd:visited {
color: #2E2E2E;
text-decoration: none;
background-color: #D2D2D2;
border: 2px;
border-style: outset;
font-family: Arial, Helvetica, sans-serif;
font-size: 8pt
}
  . . .
```

The complete style sheet has not been given here, this file is available with the code bundle of this case study. You may change the attributes in this style sheet to suit your own preferences.

Next, we'll get to the main HTML pages.

header.php

First we create the header.php file:

```
<!-- begin file: header.php -->
<link rel="stylesheet" href="style.css" type="text/css" />
</head>
<body>
  <table border="0" cellspacing="1" cellpadding="0" width="100%" class="darkbg">
  <tr>
    <td class="titlebar">
        <!-- begin title bar content -->
        <table border="0" cellspacing="0" cellpadding="4" width="100%">
          <tr>
            <td nowrap="nowrap">
              <span class="titletxt">.: Snipe Genealogy :.</span><br />
              <span class="tagline">
                        Discover your heritage
                </span>
            </td>
            <td align="right" nowrap="nowrap">
              <form method="get" action="search.php">
              <span class="searchtxt">Quick Last Name Search:</span>
                <input type="text" name="lname"/>
              </form>
            </td>
            </tr>
          </table>
          <!-- end title bar content -->
        </td>
      </tr>
      <?php
      // include the navigation that goes along the top horizontal bar
      include ("topnav.php");
       ?>
```

```
    <tr>
      <td class="body">
        <table border="0" cellspacing="0" cellpadding="0" width="100%">
          <tr>
          <td width="10" class="body">
          <img src="spacer.gif" width="20" height="300"
               border="0" alt="?"/>
      </td>
        <td valign="top" class="body">
```

Notice how the `header.php` file starts mid-way through the standard HTML `<head>` sequence. The beginning of that sequence will be contained in the individual content files. This allows us to include page-specific JavaScript code or META tag information for search engine optimization.

This entire file contains only HTML code, with the exception of a PHP `include()` statement for the top horizontal navigation file.

topnav.php

Now we will create our top navigation file (`topnav.php`):

```
<!-- begin topnav -->
<tr>
  <td class="navbar" align="center">
  <?php
  if( $nav_section!="") {
      ?>
      <a href="index.php">New Search</a>
      <?php
  }
  if( $nav_section=="detail") {
      ?>: <a href="add.php">Add Unrelated Record</a>
      <?php
  }
  else {
      ?> 
      <?php
  }
  ?>
  </td>
</tr>
<!-- end topnav -->
```

You can see that we're using a variable named `$nav_section` in this file. This variable is declared in the content pages where we want to include the top navigation. The `topnav.php` file evaluates the value of the `$nav_section` variable every time the header loads. If it finds that we have not set the `$nav_section` variable, it displays a link to the home page. If the `$nav_section` variable is set to `detail`, it will display a link to add information to the database. If it finds anything else, it simply inserts a space. This is done to ensure that the layout of the page remains visually consistent; it will be very confusing if the navigation bar appears and disappears throughout the script.

footer.php

We now create the footer file, `footer.php`:

```
        <p> </p>
        </td>
      </tr>
    </table>
    </td>
  </tr>
</table>

</body>
</html>
```

This file simply closes the HTML tags that were started in `header.php`.

index.php

Our layout files are now complete. Next we will create the home page, called `index.php`. The home page will contain the main search form that allows users to search the database:

```
<!DOCTYPE html PUBLIC "-//W3C//DTD XHTML 1.0 Transitional//EN"
"http://www.w3.org/TR/xhtml1/DTD/xhtml1-transitional.dtd">
<html xmlns="http://www.w3.org/1999/xhtml" xml:lang="en" lang="en">
<head>
  <title>Snipe Genealogy</title>
  <?php
  // include our header file
  include ("header.php");
  ?>
  <!-- Add some instructional text -->
  <h3>Welcome</h3>
  <p>Using the form below, please enter your search information.
  Only the <b>last name is required</b>, and if you are unsure how
  to spell the entire last name, you may enter just the first few
  letters.
  </p>
  <form method="post" action="search.php">
    <table align="center">
      <tr>
        <td class="formtxt"><b>*Last Name:</b></td>
        <td class="formtxt"><input type="text" name="lname" /><td>
      </tr>

      <tr>
        <td class="formtxt">First Name</td>
        <td class="formtxt"><input type="text" name="fname" /><td>
      </tr>

      <tr>
        <td class="formtxt">Gender:</td>
```

```
            <td class="formtxt" align="left">
              <select name="gender">
                <option value="">??Select Gender ??</option>
                <option value="m">Male</option>
                <option value="f">Female</option>
              </select>
            </td>
      </tr>

    <tr>
      <td class="formtxt">Birth City:</td>
      <td class="formtxt"><input type="text" name="city" /><td>
    </tr>

    <tr>
      <td class="formtxt">Birth Year:</td>
      <td class="formtxt" align="left">
      <input type="text" name="birthyear" size="4" maxlength="4" /> 
      <span class="formnote">(yyyy)</span>
        </td>
    </tr>

    <tr>
    <td> </td>
    <td class="formtxt"><input type="submit" value="Begin Search" /><td>
    </tr>
  </table>
</form>
<?php
// include the footer
include ("footer.php");
?>
```

Once all of these files are completed, we can access index.php from a browser, and see the layout of the document.

config.php

Now we will create a file that helps us interact with the database, named config.php. This file is included in the header.php file, and gets loaded every time a content page is loaded. This makes the file an ideal place for us to add any important code that is required in every page.

Let's start with the database connection code:

```php
<?php
// file: config.php

/* DATABASE CONNECTION CODE */

if( !mysql_connect("localhost", "myuser", "mypassword"))
    die('FATAL ERROR: Cannot connect to MySQL server');
if( !mysql_select_db("genealogy"))
    die('FATAL ERROR: Cannot select MySQL database');
```

Be sure to replace the database hostname, username, password, and database name above with the variables that will connect to your MySQL database.

We will declare some variables here that will be used on every page. Using an external configuration file of this sort is helpful when we have variables that are not necessarily used on every page, but might need to be changed later on; in such a case we can do so without having to search through hundred of lines of code. An example of this is the variable $user_view_limit, which specifies how many database results should be displayed per page:

```
/* DECLARE SOME USEFUL VARIABLES */

// Generic error message
$cfg_sql_errortxt =  "<p class=\"errortxt\">A database error has occurred.<br/>";
$cfg_sql_errortxt .=  "</p>\n<p><b>Query:</b> <br />$sql</p>\n<p><br/>";
$cfg_sql_errortxt .=  "<b>MySQL Error:</b>";

// How many records to display per page
$user_view_limit = "5";

// The number of years the search should allow to return matches
$byear_cushion = "10";

/* END CONFIGURATION SETTINGS */
```

Lastly, we need to include some important security code that will ensure that the user cannot manipulate the content of the site with malicious query strings in the URL of our pages. We determine what security code needs to be included by first establishing the variable names that will tell the scripts what the user is trying to do. This segment checks that the value of $page in the search page to determine which records to return when there is more than one page of results:

```
/* BEGIN SECURITY CODE */
/* if there is no page # passed or if the page # passed is not a positive number
 assign $page the value of 1 */

if( (empty($_REQUEST['page'])) || ($_REQUEST['page'] <= 0)){
    $page = 1;
}
else {
    $page = $_REQUEST['page'];
}
```

Security precautions are most important when the user tries to access or add records, especially when we have not allowed them to do so. To handle that, let's look at the main variables used to make decisions in our scripts.

❏   id
    Stores the ID to get individual details of each record.

❏   addwho
    Stores a value that tells the script whom we are adding, that is the relation with the primary entry (for instance, we could be adding a maternal record, adding a child, and so on). The value of addwho is important to the way the database reacts. We will ensure that if the user changes the value of addwho by inserting a new value in their URL, they won't be allowed to continue. The addwho variable can only take one of the following values: child, sibling, mom, or dad.

❏   addto
    Used to store the ID of the record that we're affecting through addwho. When this variable is used in a query string, we need to make sure it is a valid record ID to an existing database entry. This will also help us avoid running into disconnected relationships between name records. We'll use a variable named $is_valid to show whether or not all of the security checks have been successfully cleared:

```
// determine if the values for addto are correct, or if the user
// hacked the query string
   if( (!empty($_REQUEST['addto'])) && (!empty($_REQUEST['addwho']))) {
      if(($_REQUEST['addwho']=="child") || ($_REQUEST['addwho']=="sibling")
         || ($_REQUEST['addwho']=="mom")
            || ($_REQUEST['addwho']=="dad")) {
               $addto = $_REQUEST['addto'];
               // If everything looks okay, continue with the query
               $sql = "SELECT record_firstname, record_middlename,
               record_lastname, record_maiden_surname, record_gender,
               record_birthyear, record_deathyear, record_birthcity,
               record_birthstate,record_birthcountry,record_maternal_id,
               record_paternal_id, record_created FROM genealogy_records
               WHERE record_id='$addto'";
      }
         else {
         // otherwise set the valid flag to 0
         $is_valid =0;
         }

         // if the user is looking at a details page, check to make sure it's a
         //valid ID
   }
   elseif( ((empty($_REQUEST['addto']))&&(empty($_REQUEST['addwho'])))&&
               (!empty($_REQUEST['id']))) {
               $recid = $_REQUEST['id'];
               // build the sql query
         $sql = "SELECT record_firstname, record_middlename,
                  record_lastname, record_maiden_surname,
                  record_gender, record_birthyear, record_deathyear,
                  record_birthcity, record_birthstate,
                  record_birthcountry, record_maternal_id,
                  record_paternal_id, record_created FROM genealogy_records
                  WHERE record_id='$recid'";

   }
   // if one of the two "if" statements above created a query string (which will
```

```
              // only happen if they passed the security checks), query the db

    if( !empty($sql)) {
        $get_personal = mysql_query($sql);
        $id_exists = mysql_num_rows($get_personal);
        if( $id_exists > 0) {
          list($name_firstname, $name_middlename, $name_lastname,
            $name_given_surname, $name_gender,  $name_birth_year,
            $name_death_year, $name_birth_city,  $name_birth_state,
            $name_birth_country, $name_maternal_id,  $name_paternal_id,
            $name_record_created) = mysql_fetch_row($get_personal);
            // if we have a match, set the is_valid flag to 1
            $is_valid =1;
        }
          // If no variable values are passed, set the flag to 1
    }
    else
    if( (empty($_REQUEST['addto'])) && (empty($_REQUEST['addwho'])) &&
          (empty($_REQUEST['id']))) {
        $is_valid =1;
    }

    ?>
```

Finally open header.php once again, and add an include() for config.php to the very top of the file so that what was previously:

```
<link rel="stylesheet" href="style.css" type="text/css" />
</head>
```

Will now be:

```
<link rel="stylesheet" href="style.css" type="text/css" />
<?php
// include the configuration file
include ("config.php");
?>
</head>
```

And every page that loads the header.php file will also load the config.php file.

session.php

Next, we'll create a file that remembers the **Last Name** the user searched on last. This will allow us to display it in the search box that appears at the top of every page for the same session. This functionality isn't essential to the program, but makes for a more user-friendly experience. Name this file session.php:

```php
<?php
// file: session.php
// if no search has been requested, just start the session
if( empty($_REQUEST['lname'])) {
    session_start();
}// otherwise register the search term in the session
elseif( !empty($_REQUEST['lname'])) {
        session_start();
        $_SESSION['search_lastname'] = $_REQUEST['lname'];
}
?>
```

We need to make sure that this file is included in the first line of every content page, so we add the following code just above the doctype declaration, on the very first line of the index.php file:

```php
<?php include ("session.php"); ?>
```

functions.php

Before we move on to coding the search page, we create the file that contains some of our commonly used functions, which we will name functions.php.

Although this file contains only two functions, it's a good idea to keep them in a separate file so that the functions are easier to edit, and also more functions may be easily added later to implement additional features.

For now, we will just include the function that breaks the results up into multiple pages, but we will come back to this file later to add more to it. The PageNums() function takes three arguments:

❑ $totalrows: total number of matches in the database

❑ $print_query: additional query string fields and values so that the search criteria is not lost from page to page

❑ $page_name: name of the file for which we'll create the page number links

Create a new file called functions.php:

```php
<?php
// file: functions.php
// PageNums function
//

function PageNums($totalrows, $print_query, $page_name)
{
    global $user_view_limit;
    global $limitvalue;
    global $page;

    echo "<div class=\"numtext\" align=\"right\"><b>Pages:</b> ";
```

```
    // PREV LINK: print a Prev link, if the page number is not 1
    if($page != 1) {
      $pageprev = $page - 1;
      echo "<ahref=\"".$page_name.$print_query."page=".$pageprev."\">
            &lt;Prev
            </a> ";
    }

    // Get the total number of pages that are needed
    $numofpages = $totalrows/$user_view_limit;
    // loop through the page numbers and print them out
    for($i= 0; $i < $numofpages; $i++) {
        // if the page number in the loop is not the same as the
        // page we're on, make it a link
        $real_page = $i + 1;
          if( $real_page!=$page){
            echo "<a href=\"".$page_name.$print_query."page=".$real_page."\"
                  class=\"numlinks\">".$real_page."</a> ";
        // otherwise, if the loop page number is the
        // same as the page we're on, do not make it
        // a link, but rather just print it out
        }
         else {
         echo "<b>".$real_page."</b>";
        }
    }
    // NEXT LINK -


    //If the totalrows - $user_view_limit * $page is > 0 (meaning
    // there is a remainder), print the Next button.
    if(($totalrows-($user_view_limit*$page)) > 0){
      $pagenext = $page + 1;
      echo " <a href=\"".$page_name.$print_query."page=".$pagenext."\">
            Next &gt;</a> ";
    }
    echo "</div>";
}
/* END PageNums function */
```

Now we must include the `functions.php` file within the `header.php` file. Open `header.php`, and add an include just below the `include()` to the `config.php` file, so what was previously:

```
<link rel="stylesheet" href="style.css" type="text/css" />
<?php
// include the configuration file
include ("config.php");
?>
</head>
```

Will now be:

```
<link rel="stylesheet" href="style.css" type="text/css" />
<?php
// include the configuration file
include ("config.php");
include ("functions.php");
?>
</head>
```

Now we're ready to move on to the search results page.

search.php

The search results page will display the matches to the user's submitted criteria. It will build a tabular listing of results that will indicate the exact matches, and the similar matches. Considering the fact that there will be many matches returned if the user is searching with only the last name, we should limit the number of results per page. This is where the variable $user_view_limit – which we declared in config.php – comes into play. Create a new file called search.php:

```
<?php include ("session.php"); ?>
<!DOCTYPE html PUBLIC "-//W3C//DTD XHTML 1.0 Transitional//EN"
"http://www.w3.org/TR/xhtml1/DTD/xhtml1-transitional.dtd">

<html xmlns="http://www.w3.org/1999/xhtml" xml:lang="en" lang="en">
  <head>
  <title>Snipe Genealogy  - Search Results</title>
    <?

  // set the $nav_section value to search, so that the topnav.php file will

  // return the New Search page
  $nav_section = "search";

  // include the header.php file
  include ("header.php");

  // This determines the value the search query will use for the LIMIT statement
  // used to display the correct results per page
  $limitvalue = $page * $user_view_limit - ($user_view_limit);

  // make sure there is a name entered to search on - otherwise show an error
  if( (!isset($_REQUEST['lname'])) || ($_REQUEST['lname']=="") ) {
    echo "<p class="errortxt">
          Sorry - you must enter at least a last name to search on. Please try
          your <a href="index.php">search again</a>.</p>";

  // if there is a name given to search on, then proceed
  }
  else {
      // print_query is used to generate the links to each page number
      // to make sure the search criteria is not lost
      $print_query ="?lname=".$_REQUEST['lname']."&";
```

When a script needs to break up search results across several pages, we execute two queries – one to find out how many total records there are, and another that actually gets the data using the limit specified in $user_view_limit from our config.php file.

This next segment actually builds the query. It may look a little confusing at first, but really all we're doing is dynamically building the query statements depending on what the user entered for their search criteria. We're also breaking the first part of the SQL query into its own variable, so we can reuse the second part for the query that checks for the total number of records that match. The two parts are explained below:

❑ $start_sql
The first part of the query string that actually searches for results.

❑ $build_sql
The query string that is determined by what the user submitted as the search criteria. This is used by both queries.

```
$start_sql = "SELECT record_id, record_firstname, record_middlename,
              record_lastname, record_maiden_surname, "record_gender,
              record_birthcity, record_birthstate,
              record_birthcountry, record_birthyear, record_deathyear
              FROM genealogy_records WHERE ";

// Since last name is required, we can assume that $lname is given
$build_sql ="(((soundex(record_lastname) = ";
$build_sql .="soundex('".addslashes($_REQUEST['lname'])."')) OR";
$build_sql .="(record_lastname LIKE '%".addslashes($_REQUEST['lname'])."%'))";
$build_sql .="OR ((soundex(record_maiden_surname)=";
$build_sql .="soundex('".addslashes($_REQUEST['lname'])."')) ";
$build_sql .= "OR (record_maiden_surname
$build_sql .= "LIKE '%".addslashes($_REQUEST['lname'])."%'))) ";
```

Now we add the optional search fields into the query:

```
if( $_REQUEST['fname']!="") {
    $build_sql .="AND ((soundex(record_firstname) = ";
    $build_sql .= "soundex('".addslashes($_REQUEST['fname'])."')) ";
    $build_sql .= "OR (record_firstname LIKE "'";
    $build_sql .= ".addslashes($_REQUEST['fname'])."%')) ";
    $print_query .= "fname=".urlencode($_REQUEST['fname'])."&";
}
if( $_REQUEST['city']!="") {
    $build_sql .="AND ((soundex(record_birthcity) = ";
    $build_sql .="soundex('".addslashes($_REQUEST['city'])."')) ";
    $build_sql .= "OR (record_birthcity LIKE '".$_REQUEST['city']."%')) ";
    $print_query .= "city=".urlencode($_REQUEST['city'])."&";
}
if( $_REQUEST['birthyear'] > 0) {
    $low_year = ($_REQUEST['birthyear'] - $byear_cushion);
    $high_year = ($byear_cushion + $_REQUEST['birthyear']);
    $build_sql .="AND ((record_birthyear < $high_year) AND ";
    $build_sql .= "(record_birthyear > $low_year)) ";
    $print_query .= "birth_year=".$_REQUEST['birthyear']."&";
```

```
    }
    if( $_REQUEST['gender']!="") {
        $build_sql .="AND (record_gender = '".$_REQUEST['gender']."')  ";
        $print_query .= "gender=".$_REQUEST['gender']."&";
    }
```

We sew the queries together by concatenating $start_sql and $build_sql:

```
    $sql = $start_sql . $build_sql
    $sql.="ORDER BY record_lastname ASC LIMIT  $limitvalue, $user_view_limit ";
    $sqlcount = "select count(*) FROM genealogy_records WHERE ".$build_sql;
```

As our query strings are complete, we can query the database:

```
    // get the total numbers
    $sql_countresult = mysql_query($sqlcount);
    list($totalrows) = mysql_fetch_row($sql_countresult);


    // get the actual record information
    if( $getmatches = mysql_query($sql)) {
        $num_matches = mysql_num_rows($getmatches);

        // if we have results, let the user know
        if( $num_matches > 0) {
          echo "<p>There are $totalrows matche(s) to your search criteria. ";

          // and if those results exceed the per page limit, let them know
          // how many appear per page
          if( $user_view_limit  < $totalrows) {
            echo "Results are shown $user_view_limit per page. ";
          }

          echo "Names appearing in <b>bold</b> match your query exactly, ";
          echo "whereas non-bold names are matches that come up as similar, ";
          echo "but not exact.</p>\n\n<p>If the results below do not
                match the ";
          echo "person you are searching for, you may ";
          echo "<b><a href=\"add.php\">add a new record</a></b>  now.</p>";
          echo "\n\n<!-- begin database results -->\n\n<center>\n";
          echo "<table cellspacing=\"0\" cellpadding=\"0\" border=\"0\"
                class=\"ltrtablebg\">\n":
          echo "<tr>\n<td class=\"ltrtablebg\">\n\n";"

          // if the number of results exceeds the per page limit,
          // call the function that creates the page numbers
          if( $user_view_limit  < $totalrows) {
              PageNums($totalrows,$print_query, $_SERVER['PHP_SELF']);
          }
          echo "<table cellspacing=\"1\" cellpadding=\"2\" border=\"0\"
              width=\"400\" class=\"darkbg\">\n
                  <tr>
                      <td class=\"resultheader\">Name</td>
                      <td class=\"resultheader\">Location</td>\n
                      <td class=\"resultheader\">Years</td>\n
```

```
                    </tr>\n\n";

          // cycle through the results
          while (list($name_id, $name_firstname, $name_middlename,
                  $name_lastname, $name_given_surname, $name_gender,
                  $name_birth_city,  $name_birth_state, $name_birth_country,
                  $name_birth_year, $name_death_year) =
                  mysql_fetch_row($getmatches)) {

              // make it look nice if there is no birth year given
              if( $name_birth_year < 1) {
                $name_birth_year = "N/A";
              }
```

We want to see whether the result is exact, or just similar, so we compare the values that were submitted against the results that were returned. This is a long `if` statement, but don't panic, when you break it down you can see that we are simply checking to see if the results are equal.

If it finds a match, it changes the style of the display. The $result_class and $result_txt_class variables are assigned the values of the respective CSS elements to modify the appearance of the result rows; for example, the exact matches are displayed with a different cell background color and the text is made bold:

```
    if( (((strtolower($_REQUEST['lname'])) == (strtolower($name_lastname)))
         || ((strtolower($_REQUEST['lname']))==(strtolower($name_given_surname))))
        && (($_REQUEST['fname']=="")
         || ((strtolower($_REQUEST['fname']))==(strtolower($name_firstname))))
        && (($_REQUEST['city']=="")
         || ((strtolower($_REQUEST['city']))==(strtolower($name_birth_city))))
        && (($_REQUEST['birthyear']=="")
         || ((strtolower($_REQUEST['birthyear']))==(strtolower($name_birth_year))))
        && (($_REQUEST['gender']=="")
         || ((strtolower($_REQUEST['gender']))==(strtolower($name_gender))))) {
          $result_class="exactresults";
          $result_txt_class="exacttxt";
      }
    else {
        $result_class="results";
        $result_txt_class="resulttxt";
      }
```

Now we display the table rows with the appropriate styles applied:

```
          echo "<tr><td class=\"$result_class\" nowrap=\"nowrap\"><span
              class=\"$result_txt_class\">
              <a href=\"details.php?id=$name_id\">
              $name_lastname, $name_firstname $name_middlename
              </a></span></td>";
          echo "<td class=\"$result_class\" nowrap=\"nowrap\">";
          // improve the display by not printing any commas between
          // city and state if both values are not present
          if( !empty($name_birth_city)) {
              echo "$name_birth_city, ";
```

```
        }
        if( !empty($name_birth_state)) {
            echo "$name_birth_state";
        }
        echo " </td>";
        echo "<td class=\"$result_class\" nowrap=\"nowrap\">$name_birth_year";

        // Modify the display by printing a death year only if
        // the current record has one
        if( (isset($name_death_year)) &&($name_death_year!=0)) {
            echo "-$name_death_year";
        }
        echo "</td>\n</tr>\n";

        // end the "while" loop
    }
    // add the page numbering code if needed and close off the table
    echo "\n\n<!-- end database output -->\n\n</table>";
    if( $user_view_limit < $totalrows) {
        PageNums($totalrows, $print_query, $_SERVER['PHP_SELF']);
    }
    echo "</td>\n</tr>\n</table>\n\n";
```

If there are no results, we let the user know and prompt them to add a record or search again:

```
}
else {
    echo "<p class=\"errortxt\">Sorry, there were no matches for the criteria
        &quot;".$_REQUEST['lname']."&quot;. Please go back and try your
        <a href=\"index.php\">search again</a> or <a href=\"add.php\">add a
        new record</a>.</p>";
}
```

If the query failed, we use our generic error text variable from config.php and echo the error message:

```
}
else {
        echo $cfg_sql_errortxt;
        echo mysql_error();
    }
}

// include the page footer
include ("footer.php"); ?>
```

At this point, we should be able to view our index.php page in a web browser, and have a fully functional search ready to go.

Getting the Family Tree

In order to continue on to the details.php page, we have to go back to the functions.php file and add one more function. This function gets the family tree and displays it on the page in a logical sequence. We will be using a recursive function to achieve this. This will cause it to traverse the family line until it hits the last known record connected to the current ID being searched for from the details.php page.

Although the actual order of the functions within the functions.php file doesn't really matter, it's a good idea to organize your functions in a way that will make them easy to locate. In this case, we'll list them alphabetically, so this new function will go at the top of the file, above the PageNums() function.

The GetRelatives() function takes three arguments:

❑ $relative_id: ID of the person we will find parents for

❑ $mindent_count: maternal indent flag that allows the " |-- name" tree effect

❑ $pindent_count: paternal indent flag that allows the " |-- name" tree effect

Add the following function in functions.php:

```php
function GetRelatives($relative_id, $mindent_count, $pindent_count)
{
    $pindent_count .="       ";
    $mindent_count .="       ";

    // query the database for the parents
    $sql = "SELECT record_firstname, record_middlename, record_lastname,
            record_birthyear, record_deathyear, record_maternal_id,
            record_paternal_id  FROM genealogy_records WHERE
            record_id='$relative_id'";
    $get_relative = mysql_query($sql);

    // get the results
    list($relative_firstname, $relative_middlename, $relative_lastname,
    $relative_birth_year, $relative_death_year, $relative_maternal_id,
    $relative_paternal_id) = mysql_fetch_row($get_relative);

    // print out the parent name
    echo "<a href=\"details.php?id=$relative_id\">$relative_firstname
            $relative_middlename $relative_lastname</a>\n";

    // if there is a birth year and death year given, print them out
    if( $relative_birth_year!=0) {
        echo "($relative_birth_year";
        if( (isset($relative_death_year)) &&($relative_death_year!=0)) {
            echo "-$relative_death_year";
        }
        echo ")";
    }

    if( $relative_maternal_id!=0) {
```

```
        echo "<br /><span class=\"formnote\">$mindent_count|</span>--";
        GetRelatives($relative_maternal_id, $mindent_count, $pindent_count);
    }

    // if the parent we just got has a parent ID listed, call the function
    // call the function again to get their parents, this time passing the new
    // information as the arguments

    if( $relative_paternal_id!=0) {
        echo "<br /><span class=\"formnote\">$pindent_count|</span>--";
        GetRelatives($relative_paternal_id, $mindent_count, $pindent_count);
    }

} // end of function
```

details.php

Now that we have a function that allows us to trace the roots of a selected record ID, let's tackle the page that displays the retrieved details next. We call it details.php:

```
<?php include ("session.php"); ?>
<!DOCTYPE html PUBLIC "-//W3C//DTD XHTML 1.0 Transitional//EN"
"http://www.w3.org/TR/xhtml1/DTD/xhtml1-transitional.dtd">

<html xmlns="http://www.w3.org/1999/xhtml" xml:lang="en" lang="en">
  <head>
    <title>Snipe Genealogy - Details</title>
    <?php
    $nav_section = "detail";

    // include the page header
    include ("header.php");

    // make sure the ID number passed is valid
    if( $is_valid==1) {
?>

  <h3>Details for
  <?php echo "$name_firstname $name_middlename $name_lastname";?></h3>
  <table>
    <?php
      // if a given surname value exists, print it out
      if( ($name_lastname!= "$name_given_surname") &&
          (!empty($name_given_surname))) {
        echo "<tr>\n
                <td class=\"formtxt\" align=\"right\">
                <b>Given Surname:</b></td>
                <td class=\"formtxt\">$name_given_surname</td>\n
              </tr>\n";
      }
        // make the gender display look nicer
      if( $name_gender=="m") {
        $print_gender = "Male";
```

```php
        }
      elseif( $name_gender=="f") {
           $print_gender = "Female";
      }
    echo "<tr>\n<td class=\"formtxt\" align=\"right\"><b>Gender:</b></td>";
    echo "<td class=\"formtxt\">$print_gender</td>\n</tr>\n";
       // make the display look pretty depending on what location information
       // is listed for the record

    if( $name_birth_country || $name_birth_state || $name_birth_city) {

        echo "<tr>\n <td class=\"formtxt\" align=\"right\">
                <b>Birthplace:</b></td><td class=\"formtxt\">";
          if( !empty( $name_birth_city)){
            echo "$name_birth_city, ";
      }

      if( !empty( $name_birth_state)){
          echo "$name_birth_state";
      }

    if( !empty($name_birth_country)){
          echo " ($name_birth_country)";
    }
      echo " </td>\n</tr>\n";
    }
    if( $name_birth_year!=0) {
      echo "<tr>\n
                <td class=\"formtxt\" align=\"right\">
                <b>Born:</b></td>
                <td class=\"formtxt\">$name_birth_year</td>\n
            </tr>\n";
    }

    if( $name_death_year!=0) {
      echo "<tr>\n
                <td class=\"formtxt\" align=\"right\"><b>Died:</b></td>
                <td class=\"formtxt\">$name_death_year</td>\n
            </tr>\n";
    }
```

Here we will display the family lineage tree from the mother's side of the family. If there is a maternal_id given with the record, we call the GetRelatives() function from the functions.php file. We will also give the user the opportunity to add a maternal half-sister or half-brother, that is, a sibling with the same mother but different father:

```php
    echo "<tr>\n
            <td class=\"formtxt\" align=\"right\"><b>Mother:</b></td>
            <td class=\"formtxt\">";
        // if there is a maternal ID given
    if( $name_maternal_id!=0) {
      echo GetRelatives($name_maternal_id,"","");
      echo "<br /><br />";
      // add maternal half-sibling link
      echo "<a href=\"add.php?addwho=child&addto=".$name_maternal_id."\"
```

```
                class=\"detailadd\"> + Add Maternal Half-Sibling  + </a>";
// otherwise if the record has no maternal ID, print a link to
//     allow the user to add a record for the mother
      }
       else {
         echo "<a href=\"add.php?addwho=mom&addto=".$_REQUEST['id']."\"
                   class=\"detailadd\"> + Add Mother + </a>";
      }
      echo "</td>\n</tr>\n";
```

Now we do the same thing for the father's side using the `paternal_id`:

```
      echo "<tr>\n
                <td class=\"formtxt\" align=\"right\"><b>Father:</b></td>
                <td class=\"formtxt\">";
      if( $name_paternal_id!=0) {
          echo GetRelatives($name_paternal_id,"","");
          echo "<br /><br />
                   <a href=\"add.php?addwho=child&addto=".$name_paternal_id."\"
                    class=\"detailadd\">
                     + Add Paternal Half-Sibling  + 
                    </a>";
      }
         else {
         echo "<a href=\"add.php?addwho=dad&addto=".$_REQUEST['id']."\"
                   class=\"detailadd\">
                     + Add Father + 
                    </a>";
      }
      echo "</td>\n</tr>\n";
```

Getting The Children

To find out if the entity we're looking at has any children, we must query the database looking for any records that have the record ID listed as a parent ID:

```
      echo "<tr>\n
                <td class=\"formtxt\" align=\"right\"><b>Children:</b></td>
                <td class=\"formtxt\">";
      $sql = "SELECT record_id, record_firstname,  record_middlename,
             record_lastname, record_birthyear, record_deathyear FROM
             genealogy_records WHERE record_maternal_id='".$_REQUEST['id']."'
             OR record_paternal_id='".$_REQUEST['id']."' ORDER BY
             record_birthyear DESC ";
      $get_kids = mysql_query($sql);
      $num_kids = mysql_num_rows($get_kids);

      // if there are children in the db
      if( $num_kids > 0) {
          while (list($kids_id, $kids_firstname, $kids_middlename,
                    $kids_lastname, $kids_birth_year, $kids_death_year) =

                 mysql_fetch_row($get_kids)) {
              echo "<a href=\"details.php?id=$kids_id\">
```

```
                            $kids_firstname $kids_middlename $kids_lastname</a>";

                // once again make the display look nice depending on
                // birth and death years given
                    if( $kids_birth_year!=0) {
                        echo " ($kids_birth_year";
                        if( (isset($kids_death_year)) && ($kids_death_year!=0)) {
                            echo "-$kids_death_year";
                        }
                        echo ")";
                    }
                    echo "<br />";
                }
                // otherwise if there are no children, print (none)
        }
            else {
                echo "(none)";
        }
```

We will also allow them to add a child to the record, so we'll display a link to the add page, passing `addwho` as `child` and `addto` as the record's ID number:

```
            // give the user the choice to add a child to the record.
            echo "<br /><a href=\"add.php?addwho=child&addto=".$_REQUEST['id']."\"
                    class=\"detailadd\">
                 + Add Child + </a></td>\n</tr>\n";
```

Getting Siblings

Checking for siblings gets a little more complicated since we not only find siblings that share identical mothers and fathers, but we also include half-siblings. Once again, we build the query dynamically depending on whether or not the record we're looking at has values listed for the `record_maternal_id` and `record_paternal_id` columns. Again, the entities with no records of parents in the database have their parent ID set to zero, but zero cannot be searched with, as that would result in returning every record that has a zero for any of their parent IDs. Here's how we go about this task:

```
    echo "<tr>\n
            <td class=\"formtxt\" align=\"right\"><b>Siblings:</b></td>
            <td class=\"formtxt\">";
    // If either parents are specified, we begin building the query
    // Make sure not to allow the current record ID as a result, otherwise
    // the current person will show up as their own sibling.

    if( ($name_maternal_id!=0) || ($name_paternal_id!=0)){
        $sql = "select record_id, record_firstname, record_middlename,
                record_lastname, record_birthyear, record_deathyear,
                record_maternal_id, record_paternal_id FROM genealogy_records
                WHERE record_id!='".$_REQUEST['id']."' ";

        // if BOTH parents are specified, search both individually as a
        // parental record in the database
    if( ($name_maternal_id!=0) && ($name_paternal_id!=0)){
```

```
                $sql .="AND (record_maternal_id='".$name_maternal_id."' ";
                $sql .="OR record_paternal_id='".$name_paternal_id."') ";
    }
    else {
      // if there is a maternal_id but no paternal_id,
     // search for a match on the maternal_id

       if( ($name_maternal_id!=0) && ($name_paternal_id==0)){
                $sql .="AND record_maternal_id='".$name_maternal_id."' ";
        }
     // if there is a paternal_id but no maternal_id,
     // search for a match on the paternal_id
       if( ($name_maternal_id==0) && ($name_paternal_id!=0)){
                $sql .="AND record_paternal_id='".$name_paternal_id."' ";
          }
        }

        $sql .="order by record_birthyear desc ";

        // execute the query
        $get_siblings = mysql_query($sql);
        $num_siblings = mysql_num_rows($get_siblings);
        // if there are siblings, list them
        if( $num_siblings > 0) {
```

Now we need to look at the results and determine whether they are full or half-siblings:

```
        while (list($siblings_id, $siblings_firstname,
                $siblings_middlename, $siblings_lastname,
                siblings_birth_year, $siblings_death_year,
                $siblings_maternal_id, $siblings_paternal_id) =
                mysql_fetch_row($get_siblings)) {

            // echo their name
            echo "<a href=\"details.php?id=$siblings_id\">
                    $siblings_firstname." ". $siblings_middlename." ".
                    $siblings_lastname</a>";

            // if the siblings have different maternal or paternal ids,
            // flag them as half siblings
            if( ($siblings_maternal_id!=$name_maternal_id)
            || ($siblings_paternal_id!=$name_paternal_id)) {
              echo "*";
              $are_half_sibs = 1;
            }

            // Once again, display the birth and death years
                if( $siblings_birth_year!=0) {
              echo " ($siblings_birth_year";
            if( (isset($siblings_death_year))
                && ($siblings_death_year!=0)) {
                echo "-$siblings_death_year";
```

```php
                    }
                      echo ")";
                    }
                    echo "<br />";
                } // endwhile

                // otherwise if there are no siblings found, echo none
             }
             else {
               echo "(none)";
             }

             // if half-siblings were found, inform the user what the asterisk flag
             // next to the siblings name stands for
             if( $are_half_sibs==1) {
               echo "<span class=\"formnote\">* Signifies a step or half
                        sibling</span>";
             }

                // if there were no parental ids given, explain to the user that there
                //are no records of the siblings
             }
             else {
               echo "(none known)";
             }

        // if both parents are listed, print a link for the user to
        // add a sibling (not half subling)

        if( (!empty($name_paternal_id)) && (!empty($name_maternal_id))){
            echo "<br /><br />
                    <a href=\"add.php?addwho=sibling&addto=".$_REQUEST['id']."\"
                        class=\"detailadd\"> + Add Sibling + </a>";
        }

        echo "</td>\n</tr>\n";
        echo "<tr>\n<td class=\"formtxt\" align=\"right\"><b></b></td><td
            class=\"formtxt\"></td>\n</tr>\n";
        ?>
        </table>
         <?php
         // if the security check has a problem, let the user know
         }
         else {
           echo "<p class=\"errortxt\">Sorry, that is an invalid request.</p>";
         }
}

include ("footer.php");
?>
```

You should now be able to view the details of any user IDs.

Add New Record

To keep things simple, all of the Add functionality is controlled on one page. The contents of the addto and addwho variables determine how the page and the database react.

This is where our config.php security code steps in. It stops the user in his tracks if he tries to manipulate the site content with a query string, thus preventing them from adding records into the database that could cause quite a bit of trouble, because he is not authorized to add any comments. In addition, whenever a user attempts to add a new record, he must supply a valid username and password.

Before we delve into this, we will create our dropdown.functions.php file. The functions that we'll add here create the drop-down menus that we will use in the add page. There is no real reason why these functions couldn't be included in our main functions.php file, however, they are effectively just a drop-down box toolkit, so we're keeping them separate for organizational purposes. These function will prove useful if we wanted to expand this program to allow record editing.

The drop-down menu functions stored here are for the selection of gender, states or provinces, and country. Rather than reinvent the wheel with each function, we'll use the gender drop-down as an example so you can see how they work, since all of the drop-down menu functions work the same way.

This function builds a select menu for the gender. There is one required parameter, that is, the Name parameter. This parameter is used when building the drop-down menu as the name of the drop-down in the <select name=""> code. There is also one optional parameter, the value of the option to be used as the selected option:

```
BEGIN Function GenderDropdown
function GenderDropdown($Name,$Selected="")
{
    // feed the dropdown options into the $DropMenu variable
```

Note the use of the **heredoc** syntax below, which is PHP borrowing from Perl. If you've not encountered it previously, heredoc provides an alternative means of assigning string values (especially long multiline strings) to variables. It can be useful in the following ways:

❑   We don't have to escape quote characters

❑   Variable interpolation within quotes is still carried out. In this instance, all text occurring between the first and second uses of the DropMenu delimiter is assigned to the $DropMenu variable. Any legal PHP identifier may be used for the delimiter string.

```
$DropMenu=<<<DropMenu
<select name="$Name" size="1">
  <option value="">---Select Gender---</option>
  <option value="m">Male</option>
  <option value="f">Female</option>
</select>

DropMenu;
```

The block above is equivalent to:

```php
$DropMenu = "<select name=\"$Name\" size=\"1\">
            <option value=\"\">---Select Gender---</option>
            <option value=\"m\">Male</option>
            <option value=\"f\">Female</option>
            </select>";
```

A word of warning: the second occurrence of the identifier used as the delimiter (in this case, `DropMenu`) **must** begin in the first column of the line in which it is used, and no other characters may be used in that line (with the exception of a semicolon, if required to terminate a PHP statement). For more information about heredoc, see
http://www.php.net/manual/en/language.types.string.php#language.types.string.syntax.heredoc.

```php
    // the Selected argument is passed, mark that one as selected in the dropdown
    if( $Selected ) {
        $DropMenu = preg_replace("|\"$Selected\">*|","\"$Selected\"
                selected=\"selected\">",$DropMenu);
    }
    return $DropMenu;
}
```

When this function is called in a script, it would be as follows:

```php
$GenderDropMenu = GenderDropdown("form_gender",$_POST['form_gender']);
```

These functions provide a great way to reuse the same drop-down menus across an entire program or web site. They also allow you to use them when editing or enforcing error checking on a form since they allow you to retain the selected option.

Open a new file and name it `dropdown.functions.php`:

```php
<?php
// file: dropdown.functions.php

// Function CountryDropMenu
function CountryDropdown($Name,$Selected="")
{

    $CountryDropMenu=<<<DropMenu
    <select name="$Name" size="1">
     <option value="">Select Country</option>
     <option value="AF">Afghanistan </option>
     <option value="AL">Albania </option>
     <option value="DZ">Algeria </option>
     // List edited for space... complete list in download file

     <option value="ZM">Zambia</option>
     <option value="ZW">Zimbabwe</option>
    </select>
    DropMenu;
```

```
    if( $Selected) {
    $CountryDropMenu = preg_replace("|\"$Selected\">*|","\"$Selected\"
                        selected=\"selected\">",$CountryDropMenu);
    }
    return $CountryDropMenu;

}  //End of function CountryDropMenu

// Function StateDropdown
function StateDropdown($Name,$Selected="")
{

    $DropMenu=<<<DropMenu
    <select name="$Name" size="1">
     <option value="">---US States---</option>
     <option value="AL">Alabama</option>
     <option value="AK">Alaska</option>
     <option value="AZ">Arizona</option>

     // Edited for space...

     <option value="">--- Canadian Provinces --- </option>
     <option value="AB">Alberta</option>
     <option value="BC">British Columbia</option>
     // Edited for space...


     <option value="YT">Yukon Territory</option>
    </select>

    DropMenu;
    if( $Selected) {
    $DropMenu = preg_replace("|\"$Selected\">*|","\"$Selected\"
               selected>",$DropMenu);
    }  if( $Selected)
    return $DropMenu;
} //end of function StateDropdown
?>
```

add.php

Our drop-down functions are all done, so we can move on to creating the "add" form. Open a new file and name it add.php. Include the following code in it:

```php
<?php include ("session.php"); ?>
<!DOCTYPE html PUBLIC "-//W3C//DTD XHTML 1.0 Transitional//EN"
"http://www.w3.org/TR/xhtml1/DTD/xhtml1-transitional.dtd">

<html xmlns="http://www.w3.org/1999/xhtml" xml:lang="en" lang="en">
  <head>
    <title>Snipe Genealogy</title>
    <?php
    $nav_section = "add";
    include ("header.php");

    //be sure to include the dropdown.functions.php file
    include ("dropdown.functions.php");
```

```
if( $is_valid==1) {
    // if this is accessed by way of a link on the details page, we
    // need to get the info to apply to the new entry  - we'll be using
    // these results further down
    if( (!empty($_REQUEST['addwho'])) && (!empty($_REQUEST['addto']))) {
        if( !empty($_REQUEST['addto'])) {
            $sql = "SELECT record_id, record_firstname,  record_middlename,
                record_lastname, record_gender, record_birthyear,
                record_deathyear, record_maternal_id, record_paternal_id FROM
                genealogy_records WHERE record_id='".$_REQUEST['addto']."'";
            $get_join_to = mysql_query($sql);
            $num_join_to = mysql_num_rows($get_join_to);
            if( $num_join_to > 0) {
                list($join_to_id, $join_to_firstname, $join_to_middlename,
                    $join_to_lastname, $join_to_gender, $join_to_birth_year,
                    $join_to_death_year, $join_to_maternal_id,
                    $join_to_paternal_id) =
                mysql_fetch_row($get_join_to);
            }
        }
    }
```

If the user tries to add a sibling to a record that does not have values for the `record_maternal_id` and `record_paternal_id` values, we display an error. Without at least one parental ID number in common, the database would never know that they are related.

```
if( ($join_to_maternal_id==0) && ($join_to_paternal_id==0)
    && ($_REQUEST['addwho']=="sibling")) {

    echo "<h3>Add Sibling to $join_to_firstname $join_to_lastname </h3>";
    echo "<p class=\"errortxt\">Sorry - you must have at least one parent
        specified in order to add a sibling. Please
        <a href=\"add.php?addwho=mom&addto=".$_REQUEST['addto']."\">
        add a maternal</a> or
        <a href=\"add.php?addwho=dad&addto=".$_REQUEST['addto']."\">
        paternal record</a>
        for $join_to_firstname $join_to_lastname first.</p>";
}
else {
```

If the `$addwho` value is "dad", we will set the `$GenderDropMenu` variable as a hidden field to make sure the new record is created for a male, otherwise we assign the `$GenderDropMenu` variable to call our handy drop-down function to create the menu for us:

```
if( $_REQUEST['addwho']=="dad") {
    $GenderDropMenu = "Male<input type=\"hidden\" name=\"form_gender\"
                            value=\"m\">";
    echo "<h3>Add Paternal Record to $join_to_firstname
            join_to_lastname</h3>";
```

If the value of $addwho is "mom", we do the same, using female as the hidden value:

```
    }
    elseif ( $_REQUEST['addwho']=="mom") {
        $GenderDropMenu = "Female<input type=\"hidden\" name=\"form_gender\"
                                value=\"f\">";
        echo "<h3>Add Maternal Record to ";
        echo "$join_to_firstname $join_to_lastname</h3>";
```

And if it's neither "dad" nor "mom" (which would be the case if they are adding an unrelated record, or if they are adding a child or sibling), we assign $GenderDropMenu as the drop-down menu function:

```
    }
    else {
        $GenderDropMenu = GenderDropdown("form_gender",$_POST['form_gender']);
        // if the addwho is a sibling, print out the sibling header info to the
        // user
        if( ($_REQUEST['addwho']=="sibling") && ($_POST['action']!="add")) {
            echo "<h3>Add Sibling to ";
            echo "$join_to_firstname $join_to_lastname</h3>\n\n";
            // If either of the parents are not present in the database
            // make sure you warn the user that they will appear as
            // half-siblings, and give them the opportunity to go back
            // and add the missing parent first
            if( ($join_to_maternal_id!=0) || ($join_to_paternal_id!=0)) {
                echo "<p>If both the sibling you wish to add and
                        $join_to_firstname $join_to_lastname have the same set of
                        parents, please <b>
                        <a href=\"details.php?id=".$_REQUEST['addto']."\">
                        go back</a></b> and make sure both parents are listed. ";
            }

            // Otherwise if the value of $addwho is a child, tell the user who
            // they are adding a child to
        }
        elseif( $_REQUEST['addwho']=="child") {
            echo "<h3>Add Child to ";
            echo "$join_to_firstname $join_to_lastname</h3>";
        }
    }
```

Error Handling

The error handling in the add form is quite extensive, and aims to prevent bogus data from being entered into the database record. Although it does not have to be quite as complex as we show here, putting in the extra time and energy to make very specific error messages will make the user's experience much better. If the error handling trips an error, the $are_errors variable is set to 1. When the user submits the form, the problem fields are flagged with our error icon and a detailed explanation of the problem.

First we check to see if the user has supplied a username and password. We then see if they are valid by querying the `genealogy_users` table:

```php
// If the form is being submitted
if( $_POST['action']=="add") {
    $thisyear = date("Y");
        // BEGIN ERROR CHECKING
    if( empty($_POST['form_username']) || empty($_POST['form_password']) )
    {
        $login_err = "User name and password required for adding a record";
        $are_errors = 1;
    }
    else
    {
        $username = $_POST['form_username'];
        $password = $_POST['form_password'];
        $sql = "SELECT user_id FROM genealogy_users WHERE user_name='$username'
                AND user_password='$password'";
        $result = mysql_query( $sql )
            or die($cfg_sql_errortxt . mysql_error());
        $userid = mysql_result($result,0);
        if( is_null($userid) )
        {
            $login_err = "Invalid user name or password -- please try again";
            $are_errors = 1;
        }
```

Now we check to make sure that all of the form's required fields have been filled in. We could improve our error checking by testing all entered values to ensure that they're of the correct type and format using string functions, regular expressions and the `ctype_*()` functions (see http://www.php.net/manual/en/ref.ctype.php). In addition, you may find the PHP form validation libraries developed in *Professional PHP 4 Programming* from *Wrox Press Ltd (ISBN 1-861002-96-3)* and *Usable Forms for the Web* from *glasshaus (ISBN 1-904151-09-4)* useful in this regard.

```php
        if( empty($_POST['form_firstname'])) {
            $firstname_err="You must enter a first name";
            $are_errors=1;
        }
        if( empty($_POST['form_lastname'])) {
            $lastname_err="You must enter a last name";
            $are_errors=1;
        }
        if( empty($_POST['form_gender'])) {
            $gender_err="Please specify a gender";
            $are_errors=1;
        }
```

We'll check to make sure that the birth year is an actual number, and that it is not a year in the future:

```php
        if( !empty($_POST['form_birth_year'])) {
            if( (!checkdate("1","1",$_POST['form_birth_year']))
                || ($_POST['form_birth_year'] > $thisyear )) {
                $death_year_err="Invalid year/range";
                $birth_year_err="Invalid year/range";
                $are_errors=1;
                $invalid_birthyear = 1;
```

Now let's make sure the date range is reasonable. If a birth year was given, make sure the difference between death year and birth year is not greater than 120 years:

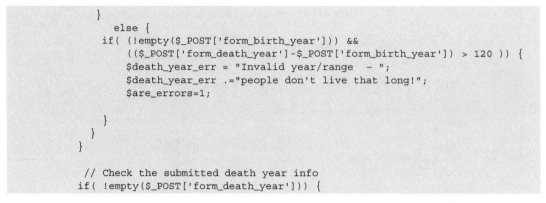

```
        }
          else {
        if( (!empty($_POST['form_birth_year'])) &&
             (($_POST['form_death_year']-$_POST['form_birth_year']) > 120 )) {
              $death_year_err = "Invalid year/range  - ";
              $death_year_err .="people don't live that long!";
              $are_errors=1;


          }
        }
      }

      // Check the submitted death year info
      if( !empty($_POST['form_death_year'])) {
```

Next we check the death year information to see that the death year is a valid year number and is not before the birth year, if a birth year, was given:

```
      if( (!checkdate("1","1",$_POST['form_death_year']))
          || ((!empty($_POST['form_birth_year']))
          && ($_POST['form_birth_year'] > $_POST['form_death_year']))) {

          $death_year_err="Invalid year/range";
          $birth_year_err=$death_year_err;
          $are_errors=1;
          $invalid_deathyear = 1;
      }
        else {
        // lets make sure the death year is not a year in the future
        if( $_POST['form_death_year'] > $thisyear) {
            $death_year_err="Invalid year/range  - ";
            $death_year_err .="death year is in the future!";
            $are_errors=1;
        }

      }

    }
```

If the user tries to add a child, make sure she doesn't enter dates that conflict; for instance, a child who was born after a parent has died, or one that was born or died before the parent was even born. These errors are very unlikely to occur, but we have to safeguard ourselves in the event of mistakes made by the user, or even malicious users of the site.

When comparing the new record's birth year and the parent record's death year, we add one year to the parent's death year; this is taken into consideration only in the case of the father. If they died towards the end of the calendar year when the child had not yet been born, the child's birth year could be in the beginning of the next year:

```
if( ($_REQUEST['addwho']=="child")
    && ($invalid_birthyear!=1)
    && ($invalid_deathyear!=1)) {
    // If the parent's death year was given in their record,
    // and the user has entered a birth year for the child ...
    if( (!empty($join_to_death_year))
        && (!empty($_POST['form_birth_year'])) ) {
        if( ($join_to_gender=="m") || (empty($join_to_gender))) {
            $possible_dod = ($join_to_death_year + 1);
        }
            else {
            $possible_dod = $join_to_death_year;
        }


            // check if the child's birth year is after the parent died
        if( $_POST['form_birth_year'] > $possible_dod) {
            $birth_year_err="Invalid year/range  - ";
            $birth_year_err .="submitted birth year is after ";
            $birth_year_err .="parent's death ($join_to_death_year)";
            $are_errors=1;
        }
    }

    // Check that the child's death year is not before
    // the parent died
    if( (!empty($join_to_death_year))
        && ((!empty($_POST['form_death_year']))
        && ($_POST['form_death_year'] < $join_to_birth_year)))) {
        $death_year_err ="Invalid year/range  - ":
        $death_year_err .="child cannot have died before parent ";
        $death_year_err ="was born ($join_to_death_year)";
        $are_errors=1;
    }
    if( (!empty($join_to_birth_year))
        && ((!empty($_POST['form_birth_year']))
        && ($_POST['form_birth_year'] <= $join_to_birth_year)))) {
        $birth_year_err ="Invalid year/range  - ";
        $birth_year_err .="child cannot be born before or in ";
        $birth_year_err .="the same year parent was born ";
        $birth_year_err .=" ($join_to_birth_year)";
        $are_errors=1;
    }

}
```

Finally, if no other errors are encountered, we check to see if there is an existing record duplicating the record we're trying to add. For our example, we check only the first and last names, gender, the year, city, state, and country of birth, but in practice you may wish to look for more or less exact matches than this:

```
if( are_errors==0 )
{
  foreach( $_POST as $form_key => $value )
  {
    $name = substr($form_key,5);
  }
  $sql = "SELECT record_id FROM genealogy_records
```

```
                    WHERE record_firstname='$firstname'
                    AND record_lastname='$lastname'
                    AND record_gender='$gender'
                    AND record_birthyear='$birth_year'
                    AND record_birthcity='$birth_city'
                    AND record_birthstate='$birth_state'
                    AND record_birthcountry='$birth_country'";
        $result = mysql_query( $sql )
          or die($cfg_sql_errortxt . mysql_error());
        $record_id = mysql_result($result,0);
```

If we do find a duplicate, we provide a link to the duplicate record:

```
    if( !is_null($record_id) )
    {
        $dup_err = "Record already exists.
                    View the complete record
                    <a href=\"details.php?id=$record_id\">here</a>,
                    or revise the data before submitting it again.";
        $are_errors=1;
    }
  }
  } // END ERROR CHECKING
```

If the form submission passed through the error checking without a hitch, the $are_errors variable will not be set to 1. On the other hand, if an error did occur, the next segment will stop the form from being submitted, and will tell the user about the error:

```
    // set the variables for the country and state dropdown menu thanks to
    // our dropdown.functions.php file

    $CountryDropMenu =
        CountryDropdown("form_birth_country",$_POST['form_birth_country']);
    $StateDropMenu =
        StateDropdown("form_birth_state",$_POST['form_birth_state']);


    if( ($are_errors==1) || ($_POST['action']!="add")) {
        // if there were errors…
        if( $are_errors==1) {
        echo "<p class=\"errortxt\">";
        if( $dup_err )
        {
            echo "<img src=\"error-alert-sm.gif\" /><br />$dup_err";
        }
            else
            {
            echo "Oops! There was a problem with your record.
                Please review the form below and complete
                the fields that are marked with a warning icon.";
        }
    echo "</p>\n";


        // Otherwise the form is not being submitted, but rather just being
        // printed out for the first time
```

```
      }
      else {
        echo "\n\n<p>Enter your new record below. Required fields ";
        echo "are marked with an asterisk. Remember that the more ";
        echo "information you can provide, the better.</p> ";
      }
  ?>
```

Now we work out the code that will display the form. This same code will be used for both a new record and the error page re displaying the form fields. Each form field will be checked to see if an error has been found in any of the fields. If it does find an error, it will display the warning icon next to the field:

```
<form method="post" action="add.php">
<table width="600" align="center">

  <tr>
    <td class="formtxt" align="right"><b>*Last Name:</b></td>
    <td class="formtxt" align="left">
    <input type="text" name="form_lastname" value="<?php echo
          $_POST['form_lastname']; ?>" maxlength="60" />

    <?php
     // if there is an error message set, print it out
     if( isset($lastname_err)) {
       echo "<img src=\"error-alert-sm.gif\" /><br />
             <span  class=\"formerror\">$lastname_err</span>";
     }
     ?>
      </td>
   </tr>

   <tr>
     <td class="formtxt" align="right">
       <b>*First Name:</b></td>
     <td class="formtxt" align="left">
      <input type="text" name="form_firstname"
          value="<?php echo $_POST['form_firstname']; ?>" maxlength="60" />
       <?php
         if( isset($firstname_err)) {
           echo "<img src=\"error-alert-sm.gif\" /><br />
                 <span class=\"formerror\">$firstname_err</span>";
       }
      ?>
     </td>
   </tr>

   <tr>
     <td class="formtxt" align="right">Middle Name:</td>
     <td class="formtxt" align="left">
     <input type="text" name="form_middlename" value="<?php echo
           $_POST['form_middlename']; ?>" maxlength="60" />
     </td>
   </tr>
```

```
<tr>
  <td class="formtxt" align="right">Birth Surname:</td>
  <td class="formtxt" align="left">
     <input type="text" name="form_given_name" value="<?php echo
        $_POST['form_given_name']; ?>" maxlength="60" /><br />
     <span class="formnote">(If different than last name)</span></td>
</tr>

<tr>
  <td class="formtxt" align="right"><b>*Gender:</b></td>
  <td class="formtxt" align="left"><?php echo $GenderDropMenu;?>
  <?php
  if( isset($gender_err)) {
      echo "<img src=\"error-alert-sm.gif\" /><br />
              <span class=\"formerror\">$gender_err</span>";
  }
  ?>
  </td>
</tr>

<tr>
  <td class="formtxt" align="right">Birth City:</td>
  <td class="formtxt" align="left">
     <input type="text" name="form_birth_city" value="<?php echo
        $_POST['form_birth_city']; ?>" maxlength="60" />
     </td>
</tr>

<tr>
  <td class="formtxt" align="right">Birth State:</td>
  <td class="formtxt" align="left"><?php echo $StateDropMenu ;?></td>
</tr>

<tr>
  <td class="formtxt" align="right">Birth Country:</td>
  <td class="formtxt" align="left"><?php echo $CountryDropMenu ;?></td>
</tr>

<tr>
  <td class="formtxt" align="right">Year of Birth:</td>
  <td class="formtxt" align="left"><input type="text"
        name="form_birth_year" size="4" maxlength="4" value="<?php echo
        $_POST['form_birth_year']; ?>" /> 
     <span class="formnote">(yyyy)</span>
        <?php
          if( isset($birth_year_err)) {
             echo "<img src=\"error-alert-sm.gif\" /><br /><span
             class=\"formerror\">$birth_year_err</span>";
          }
        ?>
   </td>
</tr>
```

```
<tr>
  <td class="formtxt" align="right">Year of Death:</td>
  <td class="formtxt" align="left">
      <input type="text" name="form_death_year" size="4" maxlength="4"
      value="<?php echo $_POST['form_death_year']; ?>" /> 
      <span class="formnote">(yyyy)</span>
        <?php
          if( isset($death_year_err)) {
              echo "<img src=\"error-alert-sm.gif\" /><br />
              <span class=\"formerror\">$death_year_err</span>";
          }
        ?>
  </td>
</tr>
<tr>
  <td class="formtxt" align="right"><b>*Login: </b></td>
  <td class="formtxt" align="left"><input type="text"
      name="form_username" size="15" /></td>
</tr>
<tr>
  <td class="formtxt" align="right"><b>*Password: </b></td>
  <td class="formtxt" align="left"><input type="password"
      name="form_password" size="15" /></td>
</tr>
```

Now that we've finished with all the form's visible fields, we use some hidden fields to preserve the ID and action values:

```
<tr>
  <td> </td>
  <td class="formtxt" align="left">
      <input type="hidden" name="action" value="add" />
      <input type="hidden" name="addwho"
              value="<?php echo $_REQUEST['addwho']; ?>" />
      <input type="hidden" name="addto"
              value="<?php echo $_REQUEST['addto']; ?>" />
```

As a matter of course, we supply submit and reset buttons.

```
      <input type="submit" value="Add Record" />  
      <input type="reset" value="Clear Form" />
  </td>
</tr>
</table>
</form>
```

If the error checking goes through with no reported errors, we add the new record to the database. First, we build the INSERT query:

```
<?php
}
else {

$sql = "insert INTO genealogy_records (record_firstname, record_middlename, ";
$sql .="record_lastname, record_maiden_surname, record_gender,
```

```
                record_birthyear, record_deathyear, ";
$sql .= "record_birthcity, record_birthstate, record_birthcountry,
            record_maternal_id, ";
$sql .= "record_paternal_id, record_created, record_created_by_user_id) values
            (";
$sql .= "'".addslashes(htmlspecialchars($_POST['form_firstname']))."',";
$sql .= "'".addslashes(htmlspecialchars($_POST['form_middlename']))."',";
$sql .=   "'".addslashes(htmlspecialchars($_POST['form_lastname']))."',";
$sql .=   "'".addslashes(htmlspecialchars($_POST['form_given_name']))."',";
$sql .=   "'".$_POST['form_gender']."',";
$sql .=   "'".$_POST['form_birth_year']."',";
$sql .=   "'".$_POST['form_death_year']."',";
$sql .=   "'".addslashes(htmlspecialchars($_POST['form_birth_city']))."',";
$sql .=   "'".addslashes(htmlspecialchars($_POST['form_birth_state']))."',";
$sql .=   "'".addslashes(htmlspecialchars($_POST['form_birth_country']))."',";
```

That takes care of the first part of the query, however we have a little more dynamic query building left:

```
    // If this is a sibling addition, keep the same mother and father
    if( $_REQUEST['addwho']=="sibling") {
        $sql .=   "'$join_to_maternal_id',";
        $sql .=   "'$join_to_paternal_id',";

        // If they are adding a child, figure out if its being added to a male
        // or female, and set that id as the appropriate parent id
    }
    elseif( $_REQUEST['addwho']=="child") {
        if( $join_to_gender=="m") {
            $sql .="'$join_to_maternal_id',";
            $sql .="'".$_REQUEST['addto']."',";
        }
        elseif( $join_to_gender=="f") {
            $sql .="'".$_REQUEST['addto']."',";
            $sql .="'',";
        }

    // If they are adding a dad or a mom, leave the parent fields
    // empty, since we don't know whom the parents are
}
else {
    $sql .=     "'',";
    $sql .=     "'',";
}
$sql .= "NOW(),$userid)";
```

Now we just need to verify that the new record was created successfully, and then determine what to do next:

```
// if the addition went through okay
if( $insert_user_data = mysql_query($sql)) {
    $new_record_id = mysql_insert_id();
    // update the main record to show the new mother

    if( $_REQUEST['addwho']=="mom") {
        $sql = "UPDATE genealogy_records set record_maternal_id='$new_record_id' ";
        $sql .="WHERE record_id='".$_REQUEST['addto']."'";
```

```php
            // if the query goes through okay, print out a
         // success message

       if( $add_mom = mysql_query($sql)) {
          echo "<p>You have successfully updated the record to
               include a maternal record. You may now
             <b><a href=\"details.php?id=$new_record_id\">view
             the new record</a></b> in our database.</p>";
       }
         // update the main record to show the new father
    }

    elseif( $_REQUEST['addwho']=="dad") {
          $sql = "UPDATE genealogy_records set
                   record_paternal_id='$new_record_id' ";
          $sql .="WHERE record_id='".$_REQUEST['addto']."'";
          // if the query goes through okay, print out a
          // success message

          if( $add_dad = mysql_query($sql)) {
           echo "<p>You have successfully updated the record to
                   include a paternal record. You may now
             <b><a href=\"details.php?id=$new_record_id\">view
             the new record</a></b> in our database.</p>";
           }

          // if the user has added a child
    }

    elseif( $_REQUEST['addwho']=="child") {
          // if it was added to a female, prompt the user to add paternal
          // information

          if( $join_to_gender=="m") {
           echo "<p>You have successfully added a child!  You may
                   wish to <b><a href=\"add.php?
                           addwho=mom&addto=$new_record_id\">add
                 a maternal record</a></b> for this child now. You may now
                 <b><a href=\"details.php?id=$new_record_id\">view
                 the new record</a></b> in our database.</p>";
             // otherwise if they added the child to a male, prompt them for
             // maternal information
           }

            elseif( $join_to_gender=="f") {
             echo "<p>You have successfully added a child!  You may wish to
                   <b><a href=\"add.php?addwho=dad&addto=$new_record_id\">add a
                 paternal record</a></b> for this child now. You may now
                 <b><a href=\"details.php?id=$new_record_id\">view the new
                 record</a></b> in our database.</p>";
           }
    }
```

```
        else {
           echo "<h3>Success!</h3>\n\n";
           echo "<p>Your entry has been successfully added!  You may now
           <b><a href=\"details.php?id=$new_record_id\">view the new record</a></b>
           in our database.</p>";
        }

    // ERROR MESSAGE
    }
    else {
        echo $cfg_sql_errortxt ;
    }

    }
}
```

Then we finish off the `$is_valid` security check, displaying an error if necessary:

```
}
else {
    echo "<p class=\"errortxt\">Sorry, that is an invalid request.</p>";
}
include ("footer.php");
?>
```

And that's it, the only thing left to do now is make a small change to the `header.php` file to utilize the information stored in `session.php`. Open your `header.php` file and change:

```
<input type="text" name="lname" />
```

to:

```
<input type="text" name="lname" value="<?php if(
!empty($_SESSION['search_lastname'])) { echo $_SESSION['search_lastname']; } ?>"
size="10" /> <input type="submit" value="go" />
```

This will keep the last name the user searched for in the upper right search box on every page.

Improvements

As was mentioned in the very beginning of this chapter, this is a case study that will get you started. Due to the complexity of human relationships, many more enhancements can be made in this application to expand its scope.

Additionally, many features that we haven't covered here would be interesting to incorporate. Below are a few suggestions:

- ❑   Authentication wrapper to allow members to edit their own entries

- ❑   Built-in messaging system to connect relatives with each other without divulging e-mail addresses

- ❑   Ability to associate marriages that bore no children and track marital name changes

- ❑   Functionality for same sex marriages and transgender individuals

- ❑   Ability to track legal non-marital name changes

- ❑   Ability to join two siblings with no known parents

- ❑   Image upload feature for individual records

- ❑   Graphical or JavaScript/CSS expanding tree menu style lineage display

- ❑   Improved server-side form validation and the addition of client-side validation for enhanced usability

- ❑   Additional fields of interest such as name suffixes (Jr., Sr., and so on) and individual occupation

- ❑   Incorporate improved matching techniques for names, making use of PHP's `metaphone()` and `levenshtein()` functions, discussed in brief earlier.

- ❑   Output related records from the database as XML for use in other applications, or to exchange with other sites, using PHP functions, one of the many custom classes available for the purpose, or a conversion tool such as that provided by phpMyAdmin (version 2.3.0 and above), For applicable techniques, see *Professional PHP4 XML* from *Wrox Press (ISBN 1-8610-0721-3)*.

In addition, there are several instances where it's quite possible to modularize and optimize further the code we've presented once you have a firm understanding of what it accomplishes, and how. Some of the application-layer functionality can be moved to the database layer. Repetitive code blocks can be rewritten as functions and function calls; many of these functions could then be encapsulated as methods of a `Record` class. We leave the creation of such a class as an exercise for the reader.

Summary

In this case study, we went through the process of creating a user-input-based genealogy server. We discussed the problems inherent in searching for records where crucial pieces of related data don't always exactly match. We also addressed some of the issues that arise when we're confronted with the uncertainties of human language in general and English phonetics (or lack thereof) in particular. Fortunately, PHP has some built-in functions that can help to compensate for variations in both names and orthography. We also showed how some of these could be used for this purpose.

Human family relationships can be quite complex, and while the data store that we created didn't cover all the possibilities in these, we were able to model the basics successfully in a straightforward manner. We discussed and implemented different levels of error handling. These included some fundamental security measures to prevent a user from being able to load potentially harmful database records, by accident or by design. These included form and query validation, as well as basic user authentication to guarantee a minimum level of data integrity and some accountability for entered data. We developed a user interface that lends itself well to entering and updating records in terms of family relationships. Finally, we looked at numerous extensions and improvements in design and implementation that could be made to the basic system for working with genealogical data that we've presented here.

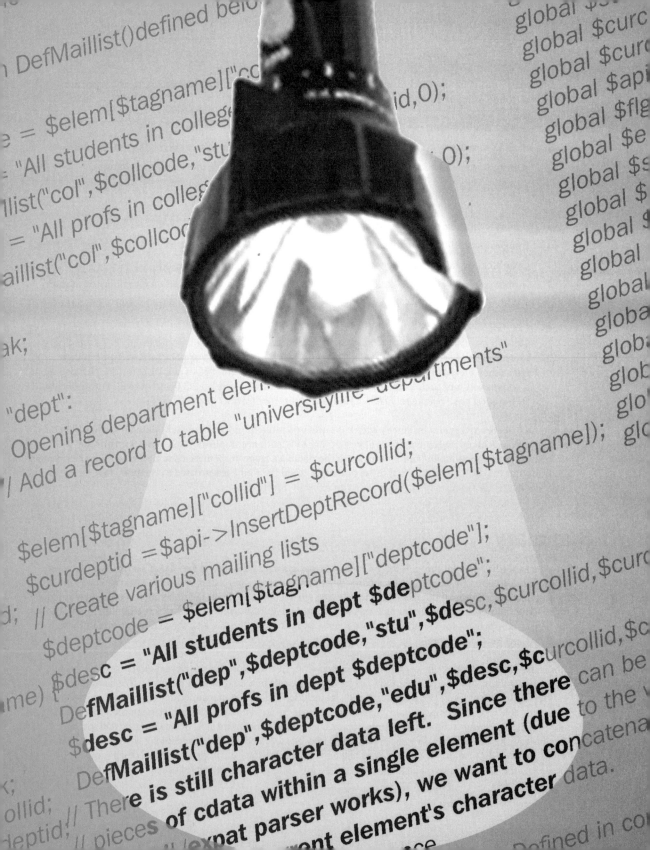

Building Portal Sites

What is a portal? Ask ten people that question and you will likely receive ten different answers. It's one of those things that you take for granted, assume you know what it is, and that you can explain it. For the last couple of years, the latest entry into this arena has been a wireless portal. Everyday a new press release appears announcing the latest wireless portal. They all do different things, however. So what made them portals?

Webopedia (http://www.webopedia.com) defines a web portal as follows:

A web site or service that offers a broad array of resources and services, such as e-mail, forums, search engines, and online shopping malls. The first web portals were online services, such as AOL, that provided access to the web, but by now most of the traditional search engines have been transformed themselves into web portals to attract and keep a larger audience.

Whatis.com (http://www.whatis.com) defines portals in this way:

Portal is a term, generally synonymous with gateway, for a World Wide Web site that is or proposes to be a major starting site for users when they get connected to the web or that users tend to visit as an anchor site.

A portal then, is exactly what the name says it is: a **doorway** or an entry point or starting point for something. Portals can be general in nature, such as the major portals like Yahoo, Excite, MSN, and AOL, or they can be very specific and interest–focused, for example, a portal for collectors of comic books, or for PHP programmers.

The web is divided into two major types of web sites: **Content Sites** and **Portal Sites**. A Content Site is a site with information, products, or services that you visit for a purpose. A portal is a site visited to locate content sites. As the Webopedia definition points out, a lot of portals have features like forums, e-mail, shopping services, and more. For our purposes, we will accept the mixed definition of portal as a starting point for a particular topic of interest with local content and services, as well as links to other sites that have relevant content.

Also, as many taxonomies for the Web already exist that may support or conflict with this one, the division of web sites into these two categories should be considered a convenient and arbitrary classification, and not the final authoritative answer to the structure of the World Wide Web.

PostNuke

Like Linux, Apache, PHP, and other major Open Source efforts, PostNuke is one of those Open Source success stories where significant and extremely useful software has been developed by the Internet Community. It is a Content Management System that provides for the easy implementation of very sophisticated and complicated sites. PostNuke is easy to extend, extremely customizable, and allows the site designer to build a content site or a portal site.

The main PostNuke site is located at http://www.postnuke.com/. The creators of PostNuke have an open contribution policy where anyone can become a PostNuke developer allowing for rich and rapid feature growth. Also, unlike a lot of Open Source projects, PostNuke has a strong focus on documentation for both site designers and project developers. You can see documentation at http://www.docs.postnuke.com/.

PostNuke is flexible enough that it can be used to generate a content site as well as a portal site. For the sake of demonstrating the features of PostNuke, we are going to generate a new site called My Wrox. The goal of this site will be to provide a portal and information on PHP books.

The rest of this chapter will proceed step-by-step through an installation of PostNuke.

PostNuke Features

To start with, let's look at some of the features of PostNuke. The version at the time of writing is 0.721. While the product is fairly stable and well featured, the authors have obviously not achieved their vision of the intended product.

A summary of the current feature set is listed below:

❑ **Automated Content Management System**
The built-in content management system provides a well controlled environment for content authors to post news articles and other types of content. There is also an approval system that allows an administrator to preview and approve the content prior to publishing on the site. PostNuke provides a content categorization system that dramatically simplifies the organization of content posted on the site.

❑ **Fully Integrated Banner Advertising System with Client Management and Statistics**
PostNuke's integrated advertising system allows a webmaster to create accounts for clients who want to post ads and to track the statistics for each banner for the client. The advertising system also provides a client login for the retrieval of these statistics. The built-in advertising system is powerful enough to be the center-piece and allows a webmaster to sell and track advertising space with little manual effort.

❑ **User Registration and Management with Personalization Features**
Personalization is a big part of a lot of portal sites and PostNuke is not lacking in this area. Users can sign up for an account on a PostNuke site and can set various personal settings including their site's theme.

❑ **User Comments for Articles, Polls, and so on**
PostNuke provides a system for allowing users to comment on a specific article. This gives users a way to express their opinions and to add their content to the site.

❑ **Online Poll/Voting System**
The ever popular web-poll is alive and well in PostNuke. By creating polls related to the site's content, you can allow users to express their opinions and track the results.

❑ **Categorized Links Directory (Similar to Yahoo)**
The links module in PostNuke allows the webmaster and the site's users to post links in a categorized directory. A built-in approval system allows the webmaster to review links before they are published on the site.

❑ **Site Visit Statistics Page**
PostNuke automatically tracks visitor statistics with breakdowns by browser, operating system, hour, week, and month.

❑ **Top 10 Lists for Articles**
As your users access the articles on your site, PostNuke maintains a Top 10 list for the most accessed articles as an indication of popularity.

❑ **Built-in Site Search Feature**
Along with its other content management features, PostNuke has a robust search engine that allows users to find specific content just by specifying the desired search terms.

❑ **Graphic Themes per Site and per User**
PostNuke's appearance and some aspects of its navigational structure can be changed by picking from one of thousands of themes that are included with PostNuke. Alternatively, these can be downloaded separately. Additionally, you can select the default theme to use for the site and each of your user's can pick their own personal theme after creating a personal account.

❑ **Support for Internationalization**
PostNuke was designed to support multiple languages as a core design goal. The current version of PostNuke has been translated into many languages such as Chinese, French, Spanish, Catalan, Portuguese, Romanian, and many more. Language packs for a specific language can be downloaded and installed as desired.

Now let's begin installing our PostNuke site.

Installation

There are two ways to install PostNuke. The first is using the automated setup scripts, which will work for most PostNuke installations. The second method is to install PostNuke manually, which involves hand-editing the configuration files and creating the MySQL database and tables using a provided SQL script. There may be other reasons why you might want to manually set up and configure PostNuke but the most common reason is to restrict security access to the Apache installation or the MySQL server. For this chapter, we'll walk through a typical installation of PostNuke using the setup scripts.

For the purpose of this setup, we are using the domain http://www.mywrox.com/ and the user account directory /home/mywrox. Apache is configured to use the /home/mywrox/html directory as the root of the web site. An example of a common configuration in the Apache httpd.conf configuration file follows:

```
<VirtualHost>
ServerName www.mywrox.com
DocumentRoot /home/mywrox/html
</VirtualHost>
```

Once you have verified that your web server is properly configured and you are running the correct versions of PHP and MySQL, download the latest PostNuke tarball from http://www.postnuke.com/. They usually have a link to this on the front page so it shouldn't be hard to find. For our example, we are using PostNuke 0.721 which is code-named Phoenix. This version requires PHP v4 (at least 4.0.1 pl2) and MySQL 3.23.

First, extract PostNuke in a convenient location, for example:

```
$ tar xvzf pn-0.7.2.1_Phoenix.tar.gz
```

This will create a directory named pn-0.7.2.1_Phoenix. If you are using a later version, the name will be different. This directory contains a collection of README files in several languages along with the phoenix-sql/ and html/ directories. Copy the html/ directory and its subdirectories to the root of your web site:

```
$ cp -R ./pn_0.7.2.1_Phoenix/html/* /home/mywrox/html
```

We then have one more step to make before we run the setup scripts. The config.php and config-old.php files must be writeable by the user account under which the web server runs. Set the permissions on these two files using the following commands:

```
$ chmod 666 $SITE_HOME/html/config.php
$ chmod 666 $SITE_HOME/html/config-old.php
```

Now, run the setup script using a browser and the following URL:

http://www.mywrox.com/install.php

This URL is specific to our installation. For it to work, you must already have a domain name configured for your web site or at least an IP address that you can use to reference the script. If you don't have a DNS server setup, you could simply add an entry to your host's file. On Unix/Linux machines, this is located in the /etc directory. On Windows machines, this is located in the C:\WINNT\System32\drivers\etc directory.

As an example, if you wanted to add a temporary entry for your local machine, a line similar to the following would work:

```
127.0.0.1    www.mywrox.com
```

The first screen will allow you to set the language used during the installation process:

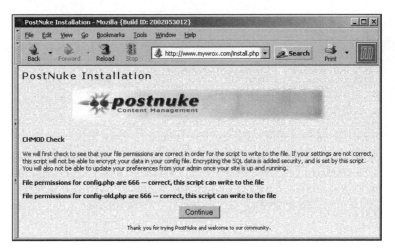

The next screen is simply an acknowledgement of the GPL license that covers PostNuke usage and distribution.

> Note that you need to turn on the `register_globals` option in your `php.ini` file if you are using PHP 4.2 or above. If this option is not turned on, the installation will not continue and you'll be presented with the same page.

The screen after that is a validation of the permissions on the configuration files, `config.php` and `config-old.php`. If the permissions on these files were set correctly, the setup script will display a screen acknowledging that fact as follows:

If the permissions are not set correctly then simply use chmod to fix them and refresh the browser to continue from this point in the setup:

```
$ chmod 666 config.php
$ chmod 666 config-old.php
```

The next screen shows the beginning of the database configuration:

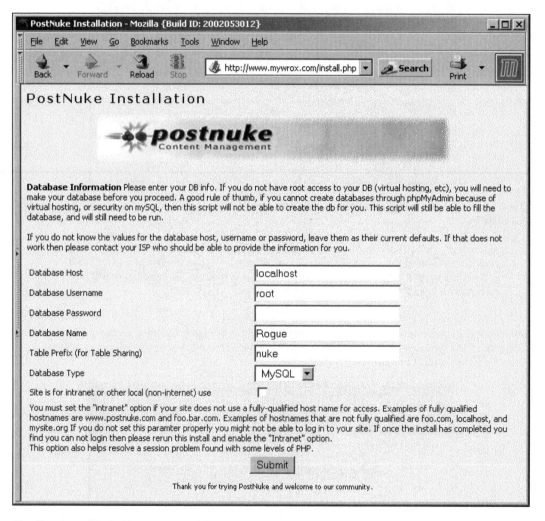

The Database Host, Username, and Password fields should be set to the host and access information for your MySQL server. It is not necessary to have root access to the server if the database being used has already been created. If the database has not yet been created, then you must have root access to the database server and the setup scripts will simply create the database for you.

The Database Name field contains the name of the MySQL database used for the setup. The Table Prefix field is used to avoid conflicts with other tables that might already exist in the database; it also provides a consistent naming convention to the PostNuke database tables. This is useful since dozens of tables are created and the prefix ensures that you won't have conflicting table names with other tables in your database.

The last option allows you to use the PostNuke installation on the Internet or an intranet. This option changes the configuration parameter that affects the way PostNuke creates URLs. If your domain name is properly configured for your site, then you do not need to check this box. If you are using PostNuke without a properly configured DNS system and a fully qualified domain name, then make sure this box is checked before continuing.

The next screen simply allows you to confirm your entries and choose between a new installation or an upgrade:

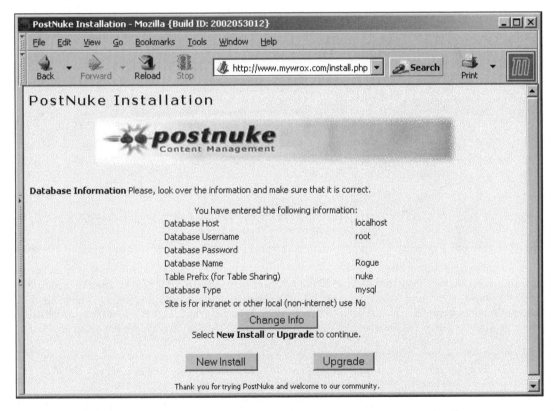

Since this is a new installation, select the New Install button. The next screen simply allows you to create the database; it is necessary to have root access to the MySQL server. To do this Press Start and, if configured properly, you will see a screen that contains a list of all 64 tables created by PostNuke. Click the Continue button to confirm that your tables were created.

The next screen allows you to set up the admin access to your PostNuke site.

This screen sets the Admin Login (the name used to login to the admin account), Admin Name (the accounts display name), Admin Password, Admin Email Address (to be used for this admin account), and Admin URL (for the administrator). PostNuke provides a full registration system allowing users to login and personalize their accounts, so the Admin URL is provided as a place to put a URL personally associated with the user. It is recommended that the administrator should use the main URL for the site being installed.

> It would be good to use a different username than Admin, since this is a very popular username. This will increase the site's security by avoiding common usernames and passwords.

Upon completing this step, you will receive one more confirmation screen. Click the Finish button and you will be presented with a PostNuke credits screen. At the bottom of this screen is a link labelled Go to your PostNuke site. Click this link to see your new site in its default state:

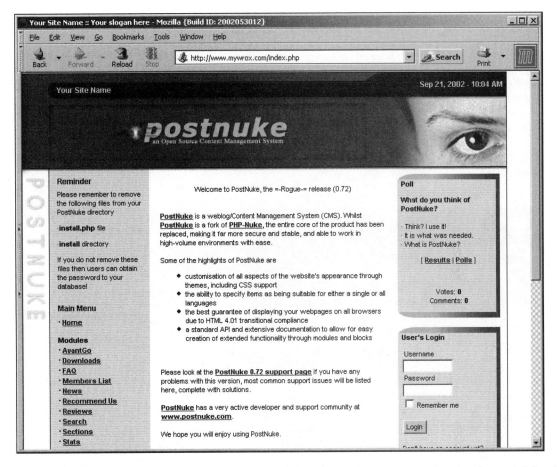

There is one more important step before starting to change the site settings, as prompted in the top left-hand column on the first page.

To protect your installation, you must remove the `install.php` file and the entire install directory. The following two commands will take care of this:

```
$ rm -f $SITE_HOME/html/install.php
$ rm -fR $SITE_HOME/html/install
```

If the above step, is not completed these files can be used to access the password to your MySQL database. It is therefore advisable to remove these files as soon as possible. Since we have the source code at our disposal, we can easily solve this issue without the need of a reminder.

Configuring Your PostNuke Site

Now that your PostNuke site is up and running, the features and configuration of the site can be explored. First, login as the administrator by entering the admin username and password in the login block at the bottom righthand side of the web page. Upon successful login, you will have several new options under the Main Menu block on the left. These include a My Account link, from which all users can configure their own account preferences for complete personalization of the site. The Administration link is only available to the administrator. As expected, with PostNuke you can have more than one administrator:

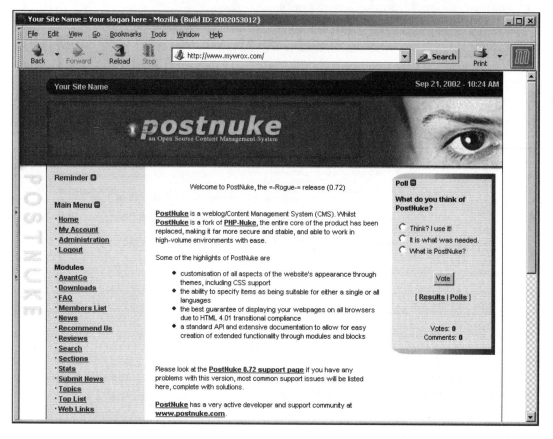

Click on the Administration link to personalize this site. The Administration Menu contains a large number of options for configuring the various parts of the site. Click on the Blocks admin link. Blocks are small content areas that can be inserted into the left or right menus depending on your preferences. Nearly anything can be a block, for example, the main menu and reminder on the left and the poll on the right are all blocks.

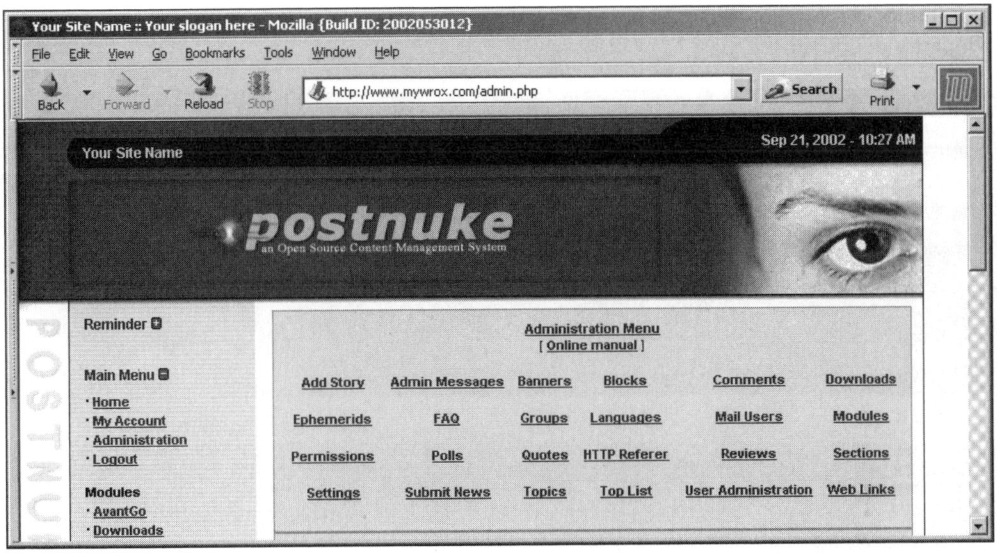

Remove the Reminder block on the left by clicking on the Delete link in the Reminder row (as shown in the screenshot below). Since installation script and directory have already been removed, we don't need this reminder anymore. On the next screen click the Show Active Blocks link to see the list of all the active blocks in the site. Each block has three options, Deactivate, Edit, and Delete. Edit allows you to change any block specific parameters and as we have just seen the Delete option removes the block permanently. Deactivate allows you to temporarily disable a block. Deactivated blocks will offer you the option to activate them again as desired:

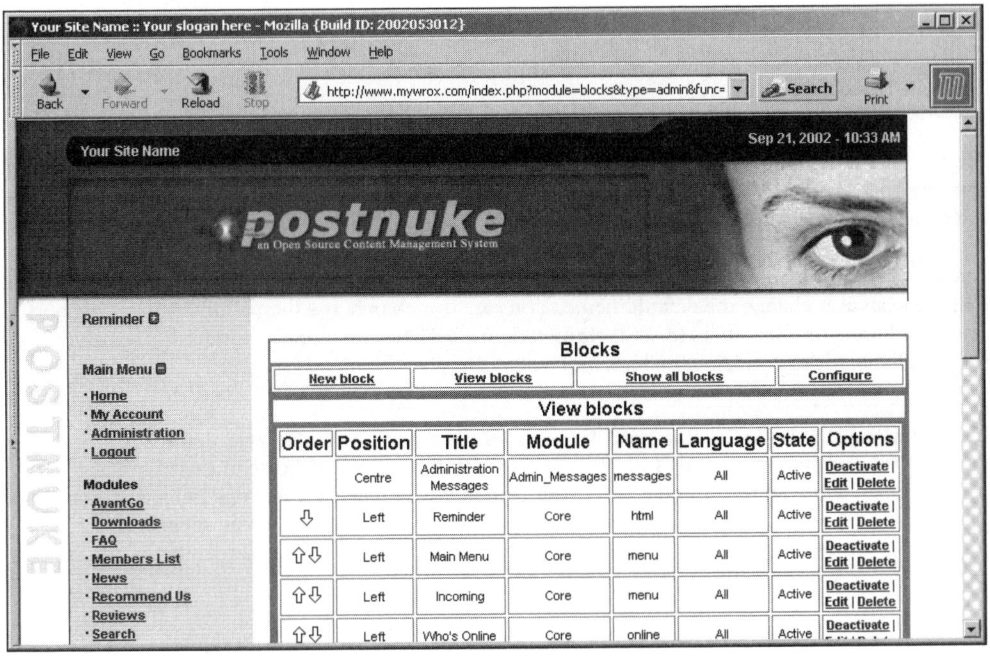

Now, return to the Administration Menu by clicking the **Administration** link on the left. This time click the **Settings** menu option:

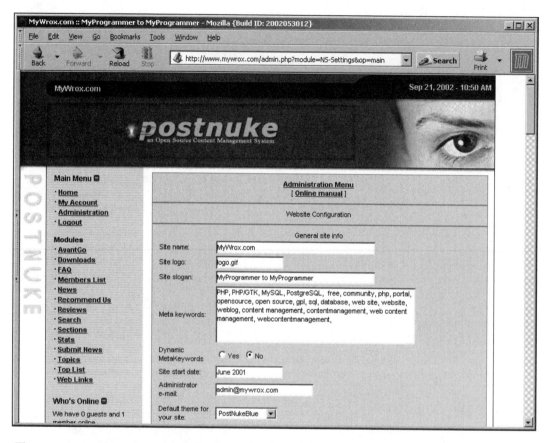

There are too many options to describe them all in detail here, but as shown above, this screen is where you set the site's name, logo, slogan, metatags, and quite a few more options that affect the various parts of your site. You are encouraged to experiment with these settings and find out how the system functions.

For now, we are just going to change a few options. You can change the site name, slogan, and administrator e-mail; you can also change the default theme. You can also change the theme for the main site and lock the theme for all users or allow them to set their own themes. There are literally hundreds of extremely good themes available for customizing the look and feel of the site.

> At this point, it is pertinent to note that some of the themes available over the web for PostNuke are not necessarily fully compatible with the version of PostNuke used in these examples. This can result in the server not responding and other abnormal behavior. You are advised to test a theme on a test installation before installing it on a development or production server.

Uploading a Logo

To upload a logo, all you need to do is to upload the file (logo.gif in this case) to both the $SITE_HOME/html/images/ directory as well as the theme specific directories in $SITE_HOME/html/themes/. For reasons that will make more sense later on, we will discuss modifying the logo for the theme in a later section.

After uploading our new logo to both places, our new site looks like this. In the example shown below, we've changed the theme to PostNuke Silver:

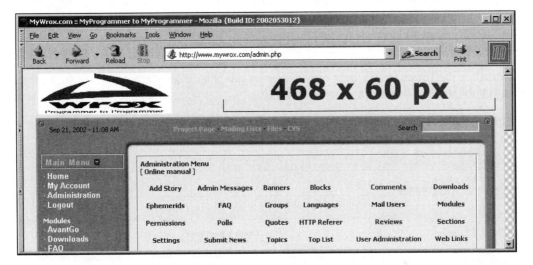

It is important to note that some themes allow easy customization and substitution of a new logo such as PostNuke Silver while others make it very difficult to customize the look and feel of the logo or other visual aspects of the theme. This will become obvious once you start playing with the different themes and installing your own themes. Also, while it might seem like a good idea, there is no simple way to customize all themes at once. Each theme installed with your PostNuke installation will have to be customized separately.

Configuring Content Submission

As demonstrated, PostNuke is a fully automated Content Management System. Due to the strong community emphasis in PostNuke, it is assumed that the users and members of your site will be submitting content.

The first thing that is critical to content submission in PostNuke is the creation of Topics. Topics are the major subsections of your site. They allow you to organize and manage all news articles, stories, and other types of information.

For our sample site, we've decided to create four topics. The information for our sample topics is as follows:

Topic Name	Topic Description	Topic Image
Beg PHP 4	Beginning PHP 4	3730.gif
Pro PHP4	Professional PHP4	6918.gif
Pro PHP 4 MM	Professional PHP4 Multimedia	7647.gif
Pro PHP4 XML	Professional PHP4 XML	7213.gif

First, we will upload the images to the `$SITE_HOME/html/images/topics` subdirectory. Next, under the Administration Menu, select the Topics link and fill in the fields for each of the four topics listed above.

Now click on the Topics section in the menu on the left side of the page. If everything was done correctly, then you will see the following topics in the list.

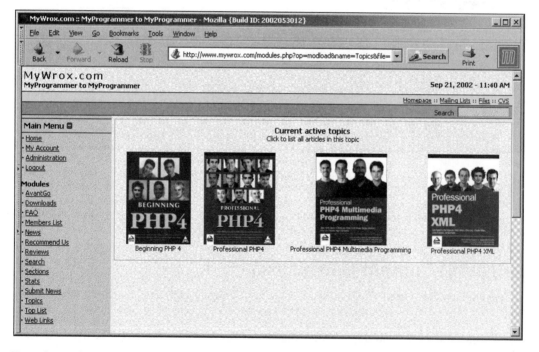

Note that we've changed the theme again here. We've used the PostNuke theme here for a better look for the site.

Submitting and Approving a Test Article

Now, just to get a feel for how content submission works, the Submit News link has been used from the menu on the left to submit an article. The news submission screen has five fields:

- ❏ **Title**
  This is the title of the story which shows up in the article listings and at the head of the article in a bold font

- ❏ **Topic**
  This is the topic used to organize the story

- ❏ **Language**
  Since PostNuke allows multiple languages; you can truly create an international site by enabling multiple languages. This is beyond the scope of this case study but feel free to experiment.

- ❏ **Article Text**
  This is the summary text for the article. It should be the first paragraph of the article or an opening summary.

- ❏ **Extended Text**
  Extended text makes up the main body of the article. As part of the administrative options in PostNuke, articles can have embedded HTML. You can configure exactly what HTML tags are allowed or prohibited. Articles cannot have multiple pages but you can post an article in multiple parts as a workaround for this limitation.

After filling in these fields with a sample article, click the Preview button to see how your article will look. If you want to make any changes, you can do so before final approval, otherwise, click OK and your article will be submitted for approval.

Now, to see how the approval process works, you must be logged in as an administrator. Once you have logged in as administrator, you will see a new block on the left side of the web page titled Waiting Content with a sub-entry labelled Submissions: 1 to indicate that we have one new article submitted and waiting for approval. Click on this link to be taken to an approval page where you can select and preview the article with an option to post the story or delete it if desired. You will also find an option to create a Programmed article, which is a story that doesn't appear on the site until a certain date and time.

After approving the article, it will appear on the front page of the site along with the topic image to give a little life to the posting. The following image shows what our site looks like now:

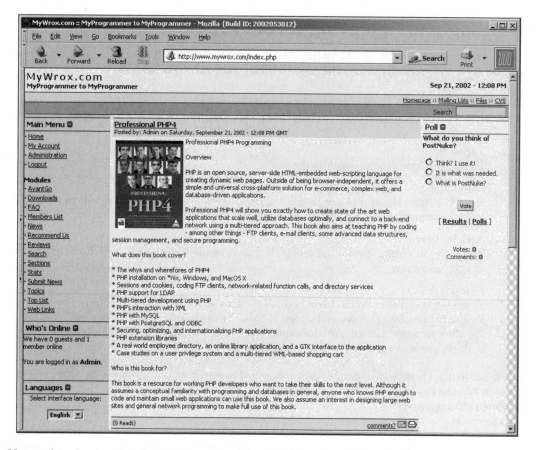

Now make a few more customizations and our site will be complete. Before finishing this section, add a poll and an admin message to the users of the site.

Creating Online Polls

To add or modify an existing poll, go to the Administration Menu and select the Polls menu item. You might want to delete the default poll before doing anything else. Just select Modify Polls and click the Delete link next to the default poll.

To add a new poll, enter the poll title and the choices for the poll. There can be as many as 12 choices for each poll. Keeping with our book focus, let's enter the following poll:

What do you think of Wrox PHP books?

- ❏ Excellent
- ❏ Good
- ❏ Average
- ❏ Poor

After entering the text, press the Create Poll button. To see the new poll, simply go to the Home page and you should see your poll on the right-hand side.

Adding an Admin Message

The Home page is the central point of the site. It is dynamically generated with a listing of the most recent news articles, and polls. In addition to these items, the administrator can add messages to this page. Admin Messages appear at the top before all other Home page content. Let's add a welcome message to the site.

Again, let's go to the Administration Menu and select the Admin Messages option. Add the following title and body text:

❑ **Title**: Welcome to MyWrox.com

❑ **Body**: If you want information on the latest and greatest books for the hottest technologies, then you have come to the right place.

Leave the default language setting, select Yes for the Active? option, and set the Who can view this? option to All visitors. Click the Add Message button and you are done with this. Now look at our Home page with the admin message and the new poll that has been added:

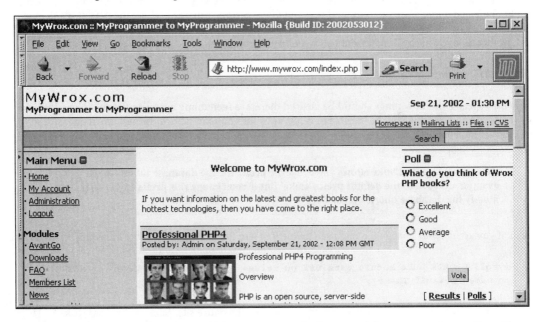

The banners at the top of the page and the page footer at the bottom of the page are also configurable; we are not, however, demonstrating these features here.

PostNuke features a full-featured banner advertisement system that can be accessed through the Banners option from the Administration Menu. The information at the bottom of the page is simply part of the page footer text. This can be configured from the Settings option in the Administration Menu.

Installing New Themes

We mentioned before that we would come back to the topic of the logo. This is possibly one of the real weaknesses of PostNuke. The authors built the system to be highly configurable and adaptable to make it easy to create a site. Unfortunately the themes tend to be a real hindrance to customizing sites since they all have built-in branding or logos. Each theme has its own logo and some have detailed branding throughout their theme graphics. To substitute our own logo for the default, the new logo must be copied to the following location: `$Site_HOME/html/themes/PostNuke/images/logo.gif`.

Also, the logo will have to be changed for each theme. For some themes, it is as simple as replacing the `logo.gif` file, for others it is not so simple. It depends on the theme designer. Fortunately, the default themes are not the only ones out there; there are many more themes available at sites such as http://www.themecentral.com/.

Most themes can be installed by copying the new theme directory into `$SITE_HOME/html/themes`. PostNuke will generate the theme drop-down list from the directory names so it will be displayed the next time you change the theme.

As mentioned before, many of the themes available for download contain bugs. If your selected theme crashes your site, it may not be possible to remove it through the web interface. To avoid serious problems, themes should be tested under a user account and changed to the account's theme and not the default site theme. If a bad theme has been installed and as a result the site will not function, the theme can be reset directly into the database. The following SQL statement will reset them for all users:

```
mysql> UPDATE nuke_users SET pn_theme='' ;
```

Any user specific theme settings should be cleared therefore reenabling access to the site. Note, this is only guaranteed to work on PostNuke 0.721. For other versions you may have to browse the database and figure out the setting yourself.

> Remember that PostNuke allows you to set the prefix for the database tables. In our example we've used the default prefix 'nuke' but if you change this prefix then you should modify the database queries accordingly.

Also, if you accidentally change the main site theme to a non-functioning theme, the following SQL will reset it.

```
mysql> UPDATE nuke_module_vars SET pn_value='s:14:"PostNukeSilver";' WHERE
pn_name='Default_Theme';
```

This query changes the value of the `Default_Theme` for the entire site, back to the `PostNukeSilver` theme, which is known to be safe. The `nuke_module_vars` table contains the site-wide preferences in a simple table designed to store name value pairs for PostNuke and its modules. The format of the field `pn_value` as shown above is a simple three part format:

```
data_type:data_length:"value" ;
```

We won't go into the details of the other types since that is only relevant if you decide to author your own PostNuke modules. If you decide to set `Default_Theme` to theme other than `PostNukeSilver`, you will have to update the data length to reflect the length of the value you are using. Also, if you do decide you want to author your own modules, please refer to the PostNuke site for more information.

A theme called PixelTwo from http://www.vipixel.com has been used for the sake of our demo PostNuke site. This is because some of the best and undoubtedly most stable themes have been made by Brumie (a graphic artist and PostNuke theme developer) of http://www.vipixel.com.

To install this theme, it is only necessary to copy the theme directory into the `$SITE_HOME/html/themes` folder as mentioned in the section. Also, while uploading a logo we need to make a few modifications to the theme header graphics to add our site name, being careful to leave the copyright notice for the graphics in place. After installing the theme and modifying the header graphics, remember to go to the preferences to change the site's default theme.

Our site now looks like this:

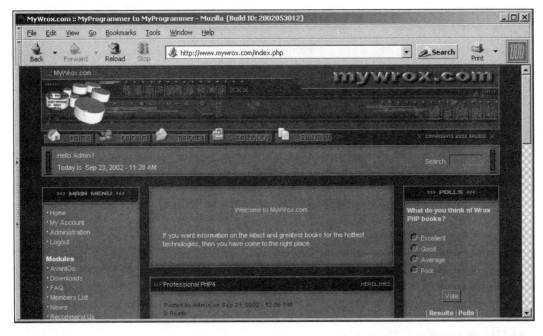

Notice, that there are two buttons at the top of the page titled Forum and Gallery. Both of these are part of the theme but they link to modules that we have not yet installed on this site.

Installing PostNuke Modules

Nearly all functionality in PostNuke is available through a structure called a PostNuke module. Since PostNuke is still under development and architectural changes are still being made, the installation of modules is likely to vary from module to module until version 1.0 has been completed. The examples below show how to install two modules that go well with this theme. The first is a chat forum called XForum, and the second is a photo gallery called My eGallery.

Both can be downloaded from the modules section of http://www.postnuke.com/. The two files are `XForumPostNuked1.81.zip` and `Meg3.0.2_postnuke.zip`. If you have trouble finding these files on PostNuke.com then you can find the latest version of XForum at the developer's site http://www.trollix.com/ and the latest version of My eGallery can be found at the http://www.marsishere.net/ site. Be sure to verify the version of PostNuke for which the module was intended to work. If the version numbers are the same, or only differ by the minor version, then the installation of the modules should work. If it doesn't, refer to the forums on http://www.postnuke.com/ for help. Also, remember that PHP-Nuke is not the same thing as PostNuke. If you find modules that were built for PHP-Nuke don't try to install them on a PostNuke site, it will not work and might even damage your site.

Both of these modules implement their own install process, which does not use the newly designed PostNuke module installation process. Also, if you use a different version of either of these modules, then you should consult the `INSTALL.txt` or `README.txt` included with the module, to insure that you are following the proper installation procedures. The installation process may change dramatically from version to version of the various modules.

Installing XForum

After unzipping XForum, copy the XForum directory into the `$SITE_HOME/html/modules` directory. Most of PostNuke is designed to keep add-ons like themes and modules, self-contained to make installation and removal easy. After copying the folder, make sure that the `settings.php` and `jumper.php` files are writeable by the web server. The following commands take care of this:

```
$ chmod 666 $SITE_HOME/html/modules/XForum/settings.php
$ chmod 666 $SITE_HOME/html/modules/XForum/jumper.php
```

The installation process modifies both of these files so do not skip this step. Next, login as the administrator (using a web browser) before running the installation script for XForum. Once you have logged in, run a simple installation script and follow the directions, to complete the task.

Installing Image Gallery

After unzipping the files and copying the module into the `$SITE_HOME/html/modules` directory, several of the directories need to be set as writeable to allow for image uploading:

```
$ chmod 777 $SITE_HOME/html/modules/My_eGallery/cache
$ chmod 777 $SITE_HOME/html/modules/My_eGallery/gallery
$ chmod 777 $SITE_HOME/html/modules/My_eGallery/temp
```

The install script for this module works similarly to the install script for XForum. Login as the administrator and run the installation script.

http://www.mywrox.com/admin.php?module=My_eGallery&op=main&type=admin&do=install

Depending on the security settings for your MySQL server, the install script may have problems creating the required tables. If this happens, the SQL script supplied with the module can be manually loaded in a file called `install.sql`. After this step, simply re-run the install script and the module should work just fine. After completing the installation, it is extremely easy to configure the module using the Administration Menu.

Upgrading an Existing PostNuke Installation

PostNuke is constantly being enhanced with new and exciting features. This unfortunately means that you will most probably need to upgrade your PostNuke site. The developers of PostNuke have spent a lot of effort insuring that sites can be upgraded to the latest PostNuke version even from PHP-Nuke and other variants. This section provides a description of the general steps required to upgrade your old site to the latest and greatest.

First, back up everything! Back up your MySQL database, your entire HTML directory, and for easy access, make a separate copy of the `config.php` and `config-old.php` files. The config files are the most important files for upgrading a PostNuke installation.

Now, delete all the files related to the previous PostNuke installation. Remove them completely. Any files left might conflict with the newer installation and cause problems. Once this has been done, copy the files for your new PostNuke installation into the HTML directory as described earlier in this chapter. Remember to make `config.php` and `config-old.php` writeable under the web server's security context for the upgrade to work.

Next, rename a copy of your old `config.php` file to `pn7config.php` and copy it into the `html` directory with the new PostNuke installation. Be careful not to overwrite the new `config.php` file. By providing your old `config.php` in this renamed condition, you are informing PostNuke that the system is being upgraded as well as all necessary information to handle the upgrade automatically.

Now it's time to actually run the upgrade process. After completing all of the above steps, all that is needed is to use a browser to run `install.php`. If you have followed the above steps correctly, the upgrade process will be handled automatically. If not, you should have your back up files.

As usual, please refer to the `INSTALL.txt` file for information specific to the version of PostNuke being installed.

Developing and Customizing PostNuke

PostNuke is written in 100% pure PHP. Due to the richness of the architecture including the security system, personalization, and support for themes, PostNuke will take a little research before you can jump in and start adding your own features and extensions. To make it easier to jump in, the PostNuke developers thoughtfully provided a Template module. You will find this in the `$SITE_HOME/html/modules/template` directory. To start writing your own module, it is best to make a copy of the template directory in a new directory, using your module name.

Modules are built with a set of pre-specified files and functions necessary for PostNuke to recognize the module and allow for its proper integration. Also, the module must make extensive use of what is referred to as the PostNuke core API or pnAPI. This API handles things like getting system settings, user settings, and module settings. It has a permissions API for authorizing different user actions and even allows module developers and system administrators to extend the authorization scheme to support module-specific actions.

Since PostNuke is still in a relatively early version, the structure of modules is likely to change often as the developers work towards the version 1.0 release. The core concepts and overall PostNuke architecture, however, are likely to stay the same. You will find that PostNuke has a rich developer community and plenty of support is available, should you decide to write your own extensions.

Useful resources for developing and extending PostNuke:

❑　Source Forge PostNuke Project Page at http://sourceforge.net/projects/post-nuke

❑　Support Forums at http://www.postnuke.com/

❑　PostNuke Documentation Central at http://centre.ics.uci.edu/~grape/index.php

List of Other Open Source Portals

This chapter has focused on PostNuke due to my preference. A number of other Portal/Content Management Systems that are available to the PHP community. Below are some of the popular choices.

PHP-Nuke

This is the one that started it all. PHP-Nuke is a closely held development effort that has spawned a number of spin-off projects. PostNuke is just one of many. There is a huge PHP-Nuke community and plenty of modules and themes to build a site that can do anything you might imagine. You can find information on PHP-Nuke at http://www.phpnuke.org/. The fundamental difference between PHP-Nuke and PostNuke is that PHP-Nuke uses a monolithic approach in its development effort while PostNuke uses a small core and several add-on modules.

Dark Portal

Dark Portal is another system often mentioned. Distinctively, it is one of the few systems that is not an off-shoot of PHP-Nuke. A sample of the Dark Portal installation can be seen at http://darkportal.sourceforge.net/index.php and the development project can be found at http://sourceforge.net/projects/darkportal/.

OpenPHPNuke

This site also seems to be an offshoot of PHP-Nuke. It seems to be fairly robust but lacks any significant information on the project, leaving the Source Forge project as the only recourse for the brave and adventurous. The Source Forge project is located at http://sourceforge.net/projects/openphpnuke/ and a sample site can be found at http://openphpnuke.com/.

xoops.org

Xoops claims to be the object-oriented portal system. It was also originally based on PHP-Nuke but now has its own development path. It is a system with a large support community and is worth considering, especially if you prefer object-oriented development. You can find more information at http://www.xoops.org/.

MyPHPNuke

This is yet another PHP-Nuke-based portal script and also has a large following. More information on MyPHPNuke can be found at http://www.myphpnuke.com/.

Summary

In this chapter we looked at the PostNuke Open Source Portal/Content Management System. We used it to build a fairly robust site architecture in a fairly short period. We installed a custom theme and extended the functionality by adding a Forum and a Gallery module. Additionally, we showed how easy it is to get involved with the development and customization of PostNuke for your own benefit or for the benefit of the Open Source community.

```
n DefMaillist()defined bef
e = $elem[$tagname]["co
= "All students in college                    id,0);
llist("col",$collcode,"stu              0);
= "All profs in colleg
aillist("col",$collco

ak;
"dept":
Opening department elem
// Add a record to table "universitylife_departments"

$elem[$tagname]["collid"] = $curcollid;
$curdeptid =$api->InsertDeptRecord($elem[$tagname]
d;  // Create various mailing lists
$deptcode = $elem[$tagname]["deptcode"];

ame) $desc = "All students in dept $deptcode";
DefMaillist("dep",$deptcode,"stu",$desc,$curcollid,$cu
desc = "All profs in dept $deptcode";
DefMaillist("dep",$deptcode,"edu",$desc,$curcollid,$c
// There is still character data left. Since there can be
// pieces of cdata within a single element (due to the
XML expat parser works), we want to concatena
current element's character data.
Defined in co
```

```
global $
global $cur
global $cur
global $ap
global $fl
global $e
global $
global $
global
global
global
glob
glob
glo
glo
gl
```

Index

A Guide to the Index

The index is arranged hierarchically, in alphabetical order. Names starting with a non-alphabetical sign are listed under the first letter following the sign. Second- and third-level entries that also occur as first-level entries exclude files, classes, methods/functions, elements etc. created locally for use in a particular example/case study. This is to avoid user confusion in finding the information they require.

C

D

E

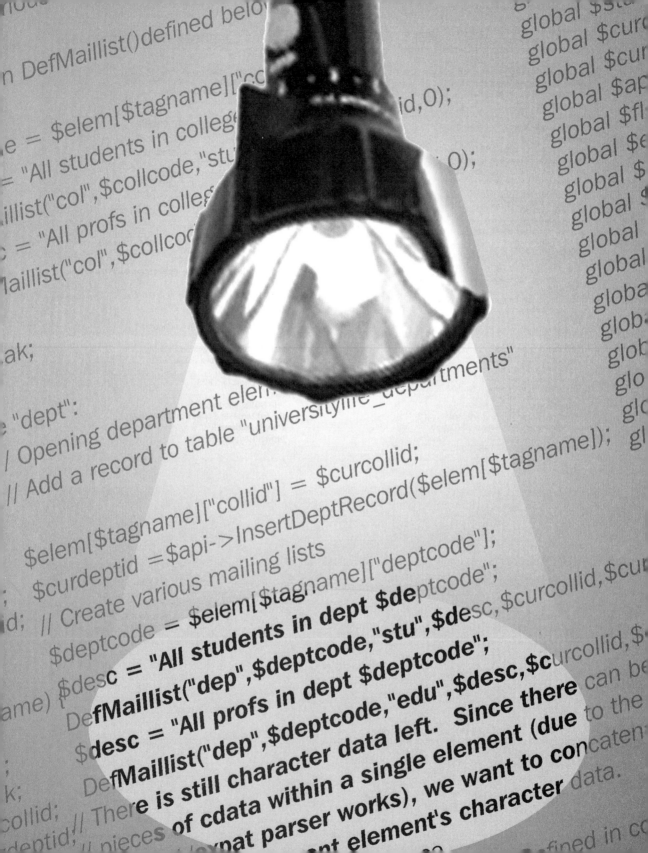

Got more Wrox books than you can carry around?

Wroxbase is the new online service from Wrox Press. Dedicated to providing online access to books published by Wrox Press, helping you and your team find solutions and guidance for all your programming needs.

The key features of this service will be:

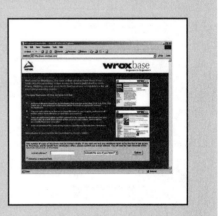

- Different libraries based on technologies that you use everyday (ASP 3.0, XML, SQL 2000, etc.). The initial set of libraries will be focused on Microsoft-related technologies.
- You can subscribe to as few or as many libraries as you require, and access all books within those libraries as and when you need to.
- You can add notes (either just for yourself or for anyone to view) and your own bookmarks that will all be stored within your account online, and so will be accessible from any computer.
- You can download the code of any book in your library directly from Wroxbase

Visit the site at: www.wroxbase.com

wrox
Programmer to Programmer™

p2p.wrox.com
The programmer's resource centre

A unique free service from Wrox Press
With the aim of helping programmers to help each other

Wrox Press aims to provide timely and practical information to today's programmer. P2P
is a list server offering a host of targeted mailing lists where you can share knowledge
with four fellow programmers and find solutions to your problems. Whatever the level of
your programming knowledge, and whatever technology you use P2P can provide you with
the information you need.

ASP Support for beginners and professionals, including a resource page with hundreds of links,
and a popular ASP.NET mailing list.

DATABASES For database programmers, offering support on SQL Server, mySQL, and Oracle.

MOBILE Software development for the mobile market is growing rapidly. We provide lists for
the several current standards, including WAP, Windows CE, and Symbian.

JAVA A complete set of Java lists, covering beginners, professionals, and server-side programmers
(including JSP, servlets and EJBs)

.NET Microsoft's new OS platform, covering topics such as ASP.NET, C#, and general
.NET discussion.

VISUAL BASIC Covers all aspects of VB programming, from programming Office macros to creating
components for the .NET platform.

WEB DESIGN As web page requirements become more complex, programmer's are taking a more important
role in creating web sites. For these programmers, we offer lists covering technologies such as
Flash, Coldfusion, and JavaScript.

XML Covering all aspects of XML, including XSLT and schemas.

OPEN SOURCE Many Open Source topics covered including PHP, Apache, Perl, Linux, Python and more.

FOREIGN LANGUAGE Several lists dedicated to Spanish and German speaking programmers, categories include.
NET, Java, XML, PHP and XML

How to subscribe
Simply visit the P2P site, at http://p2p.wrox.com/